AGRICULTURAL TRADE REFORM AND THE DOHA DEVELOPMENT AGENDA

AGRICULTURAL TRADE REFORM AND THE DOHA DEVELOPMENT AGENDA

*Edited by Kym Anderson
and Will Martin*

A copublication of Palgrave Macmillan
and the World Bank

©2006 The International Bank for Reconstruction and Development / The World Bank
1818 H Street NW
Washington DC 20433
Telephone: 202-473-1000
Internet: www.worldbank.org
E-mail: feedback@worldbank.org

All rights reserved.

1 2 3 4 09 08 07 06

A copublication of The World Bank and Palgrave Macmillan.

Palgrave Macmillan
Houndmills, Basingstoke, Hampshire RG21 6XS and
175 Fifth Avenue, New York, NY 10010
Companies and representatives throughout the world

Palgrave Macmillan is the global academic imprint of the Palgrave Macmillan division of St. Martin's Press, LLC and of Palgrave Macmillan Ltd.

Macmillan® is a registered trademark in the United States, United Kingdom and other countries. Palgrave is a registered trademark in the European Union and other countries.

This volume is a product of the staff of the International Bank for Reconstruction and Development/ The World Bank. The findings, interpretations, and conclusions expressed in this volume do not necessarily reflect the views of the Executive Directors of The World Bank or the governments they represent.

The World Bank does not guarantee the accuracy of the data included in this work. The boundaries, colors, denominations, and other information shown on any map in this work do not imply any judgement on the part of The World Bank concerning the legal status of any territory or the endorsement or acceptance of such boundaries.

Rights and Permissions

The material in this publication is copyrighted. Copying and/or transmitting portions or all of this work without permission may be a violation of applicable law. The International Bank for Reconstruction and Development/The World Bank encourages dissemination of its work and will normally grant permission to reproduce portions of the work promptly.

For permission to photocopy or reprint any part of this work, please send a request with complete information to the Copyright Clearance Center Inc., 222 Rosewood Drive, Danvers, MA 01923, USA; telephone: 978-750-8400; fax: 978-750-4470; Internet: www.copyright.com.

All other queries on rights and licenses, including subsidiary rights, should be addressed to the Office of the Publisher, The World Bank, 1818 H Street NW, Washington, DC 20433, USA; fax: 202-522-2422; e-mail: pubrights@worldbank.org.

ISBN-10: 0-8213-6239-9 (softcover)
ISBN-10: 0-8213-6369-7 (hardcover)
ISBN-13: 978-8-2136-2399-5
eISBN: 0-8213-6240-2
DOI: 10.1596 / 978-8-2136-2399-5

Library of Congress Cataloging-in-Publication Data

Agricultural trade reform and the Doha development agenda/editors. Kym Anderson and Will Martin.
      p. cm.
  Includes bibliographical references and index.
  ISBN-13: 978-8-2136-2399-5
  ISBN-10: 0-8213-6239-9
     1. World Trade Organization. 2. Agriculture and state. 3. International trade.
    I. Anderson, Kym, 1950– II. Martin, Will, 1953–
HG3881.5.W57A345 2005
382'.41—dc22
                                                                      2005050742

Cover photos: Mark Henley/Panos; Ray Witlin/The World Bank.

CONTENTS

	Acknowledgments	xiii
	Contributors	xv
	Abbreviations and Acronyms	xvii
Part I	**SETTING THE SCENE**	
1	Agriculture, Trade Reform, and the Doha Agenda *Kym Anderson and Will Martin*	3
2	What Is at Stake: The Relative Importance of Import Barriers, Export Subsidies, and Domestic Support *Thomas W. Hertel and Roman Keeney*	37
3	Special and Differential Treatment for Developing Countries *Tim Josling*	63
Part II	**AGRICULTURAL MARKET ACCESS**	
4	Consequences of Alternative Formulas for Agricultural Tariff Cuts *Sébastien Jean, David Laborde, and Will Martin*	81
5	Reducing Tariffs Versus Expanding Tariff Rate Quotas *Harry de Gorter and Erika Kliauga*	117
6	Is Erosion of Tariff Preferences a Serious Concern? *Antoine Bouët, Lionel Fontagné, and Sébastien Jean*	161

Part III EXPORT SUBSIDIES AND DOMESTIC SUPPORT

7 Removing the Exception
of Agricultural Export Subsidies   195
Bernard Hoekman and Patrick Messerlin

8 Rethinking Agricultural Domestic Support
under the World Trade Organization   221
Chad E. Hart and John C. Beghin

9 Consequences of Reducing Limits on Aggregate
Measurements of Support   245
Hans G. Jensen and Henrik Zobbe

10 Reducing Cotton Subsidies:
The DDA Cotton Initiative   271
Daniel A. Sumner

Part IV DOHA REFORM SCENARIOS

11 Holograms and Ghosts:
New and Old Ideas for Agricultural Policies   295
David Orden and Eugenio Díaz-Bonilla

12 Market and Welfare Implications
of Doha Reform Scenarios   333
*Kym Anderson, Will Martin,
and Dominique van der Mensbrugghe*

Index   401

Figures

1.1	The Declining Share of Agriculture and Food in Merchandise Exports for World and Developing Countries, 1970–2003	4
1.2	Agricultural Producer Support in High-Income Economies, by Value, Percent, and Type of Support, 1986–2003	7
1.3	Agricultural Producer Support in High-Income Economies, by Country, 1986–2003	8
2.1	Welfare Gains for Developing Countries from Freeing Trade in Services and from Trade Facilitation Compared with the Standard Removal of Merchandise Tariffs and Subsidies	55
4.1	Converting the Harbinson Formula into a Tiered Formula	85
4.2	A Tiered Tariff-Cutting Formula without Discontinuities	86
5.1	In-Quota Imports with and without Quota Fill	124
5.2	Imports with Quota Full or Underfilled	125
5.3	Out-of-Quota Imports with and without Quota Fill	126

5.4	Overquota Imports	127
6.1	European Union Trade Policy, 2004	166
6.2	U.S. Trade Policy, 2004	167
7.1	The Incidence of All Notified Export Subsidies	202
7.2	The Incidence of Quad Export Subsidy Commitments	203

Tables

1.1	Import-Weighted Average Applied Import Tariffs, by Sector and Region, 2001	5
1.2	Import-Weighted Average Agricultural Import Tariffs, by Region, 2001	6
1.3	Effects on Economic Welfare of Full Trade Liberalization by Economy and Products, 2015	12
1.4	Distribution of Global Welfare Impacts from Removing All Agricultural Tariffs and Subsidies, 2001	13
1.5	Welfare Effect of Alternative Doha Reform Scenarios, 2015	14
1.6	Effects on Bilateral Merchandise Trade Flows of Adding Nonagricultural Tariff Cuts to Agricultural Reform under Doha, 2015	16
1.7	Annual Average Growth in Output and Employment from a Comprehensive Doha Reform as Compared with the Baseline Rate, by Region, 2005–15	18
1.8	Decreases in the Number of Impoverished under Full Trade Liberalization and Alternative Doha Scenarios, 2015	19
2.1	Modeled Regions by Type of Economy	41
2.2	Agricultural Domestic Support in Selected High-Income Economies	42
2.3	Average Applied Import Tariffs, by Sector and Region, 2001	43
2.4	Average Import Tariffs in Developing Countries	45
2.5	Percentage Change in Developing-Country Imports from Removing All Tariffs and Agricultural Subsidies	46
2.6	Percentage (and Volume) Change in Developing-Country Exports from Removing All Tariffs and Agricultural Subsidies	48
2.7	Regional Welfare Effects of Removing All Agricultural Tariffs and Subsidies	49
2.8	Developing Countries' Welfare Gains from Removing All Agricultural Tariffs and Subsidies	52
2.9	Developing Countries' Welfare Gains from Removing All Nonagricultural Tariffs, Agricultural Assistance, and Merchandise Trade Distortions	54
2.10	Welfare Effects of Liberalizing All Merchandise Trade	56
2.11	Welfare Decomposition from Merchandise Trade Liberalization for Developing Countries	58

3.1	Flexibility for Developing Countries in the URAA	69
3.2	Categories of Special and Differential Treatment in Agriculture in the July Framework Agreement	71
4.1	Key Features of Applied Agricultural Tariffs, by Selected Countries and Regions, 2001	89
4.2	Bound and Applied Agricultural Tariff Rates, by Selected Countries and Regions, 2001	91
4.3	Summary Description of the Agricultural Reform Scenarios	93
4.4	Base Level and Reductions in Average Bound Duties, by Agricultural Reform Scenario	96
4.5	Reductions in Base Tariffs for Average Applied Tariffs, by Agricultural Reform Scenario	98
4.6	Cross-Product Coefficient of Variation of the Power of MFN Tariffs: Base and Reduction by Agricultural Reform Scenario	100
4.7	Implications of Alternative Formulas for Market Access, Base Tariffs, and Reductions by Agricultural Reform Scenario	106
4.8	Implications of Alternative Scenarios for Protection by Commodity: Reductions in Global Average Tariff	110
5.1	Value of Production for TRQ versus Non-TRQ Commodities in OECD Countries, 2000	120
5.2	Value of Trade for TRQ versus Non-TRQ Commodities in OECD Countries, 2000	122
5.3	Value of Trade by Regime	128
5.4	Effects of Trade Liberalization on Value of Trade	130
5.5	Estimates of Water in the Tariff for Selected TRQs	132
5.6	Value of In-Quota Trade and Fill Rates by TRQ Admnistration Method	138
5.7	Value of In-Quota Trade and Fill Rates by TRQ Additional Regulation	140
5.8	Fill Rate by Administration Method and Additional Regulation	142
5.9	Value of TRQ Trade by Economy	144
5.10	Value of Trade by Commodity	148
5.11	Changes in Admnistration Methods	153
5.12	STE, Domestic Policy Responses, and Rice Tariff Quota in Japan	156
6.1	Decomposition of the Average Duty Faced by Each Exporting Country, 2001	168
6.2	Average World Applied and MFN Tariff Protection Rates, 2001	171
6.3	Average True Preferential Margin by Country, by Sector and Commodity	173

6.4	Simulation of the Impact of a Proportional Cut in Bound Duties under Scenarios 1 and 2	175
6.5	TRQ Rents Received by Developing Country, in 2001 and after Scenarios 1 and 2	177
6.6	Sectoral and Geographical Breakdown in the Simulation Exercise	180
6.7	Simulated Impact of Two Alternative Agricultural Tariff Cut Scenarios on World Trade and Welfare	182
6.8	Simulated Impact of Two Alternative Agricultural Tariff Cut Scenarios on International Prices of Developing-Country Exports	183
6.9	Simulated Impact of Scenario 1 on Welfare, Terms of Trade, and Returns to Land, by Region	184
6.10	Detailed Impact of Two Tariff-Cutting Scenarios on Selected Sub-Saharan Countries	185
7.1	WTO Commitments and Notifications of Used Export Subsidies, 1995–2000	198
7.2	WTO Commitments and Notifications of the EU, by Product, 1995–2000	204
7.3	Export Subsidy Rates for Selected WTO Members, by Commodity	206
7.4	EU Export Subsidies and OECD PSEs, 1996–2002	208
7.5	EAGGF Subsidies by Commodity, 1995–2002	210
7.6	EAGGF Export Subsidies as a Share of All Subsidies, 1995–2002	213
7.7	EU Subsidization Rates (Relative to Value of Production), 1995–2002	214
7.8	EAGGF Refunds as a Percentage of EU Farm Exports, 1995–2002	216
7.9	Export Subsidy Equivalents for Major Users	217
8.1	Reported Domestic Support from the United States, 1995–2001	226
8.2	Reported Domestic Support from the European Union, 1995–2000	227
8.3	Reported Domestic Support from Japan, 1995–2000	228
8.4	Reported Domestic Support from Brazil, 1995–98	228
8.5	Market Price Support as a Percentage of Reported AMS, 1995–2001	231
8.6	U.S. Sugar Program AMS Calculations with External Reference Prices, 1995–2001	232
8.7	U.S. Sugar Program AMS Calculations with Actual World Prices, 1995–2001	233
8.8	U.S. Sugar Program AMS Calculations with Actual Domestic and World Prices, 1995–2001	233

9.1	Current Total AMS, 1999, by Country and Commodity	248
9.2	Payments Not Included in Current Total AMS Due to de Minimis, 1999, by Country and Commodity	250
9.3	EU15 AMS Notifications, by Commodity, 2000/01	252
9.4	United States AMS Notifications, by Commodity, 2001	253
9.5	Domestic Support Base Levels, New Commitments, and Latest WTO Notifications	254
9.6	Domestic Support Reductions Needed	260
9.7	Agenda 2000 and MTR Intervention Price Reduction	261
9.8	EU15 AMS Adjusted for Intervention Price Changes	262
9.9	U.S. AMS Adjusted for Administered Dairy Price and Market Loss Assistance Payments	263
9A.1	Domestic Support Reductions for Selected Countries	265
11.1	Alternative Reform Strategies	299
11.2	Value of the U.S. Peanut and Tobacco Buyouts	303
11.3	Cost of Possible Buyouts of the Main U.S. 2002 Farm Bill Support Payments	308
11.4	Average Tariff Protection Applied, by Economy or Region, Early 2000s	320
12.1	Effects of a Tiered Formula Cut in Agricultural Domestic Support, 2001	339
12.2	Import-Weighted Average Applied Tariffs, by Sector and Region, 2001	343
12.3	Import-Weighted Average Applied Tariffs, by Sector and Country, 2005	345
12.4	Impacts on Real Income from Full Liberalization of Global Merchandise Trade, by Country or Region, 2015	346
12.5	Impacts on Selected Trade Indicators from Full Liberalization of Global Merchandise Trade, 2015	347
12.6	Regional and Sectoral Sources of Gains from Full Liberalization of Global Merchandise Trade, 2015	349
12.7	Change in Developing Countries' Shares of Global Output and Exports under Full Global Merchandise Trade Liberalization, by Sector, 2015	349
12.8	Impacts of Full Global Trade Liberalization on Agricultural and Food Output and Trade, by Country/Region, 2015	351
12.9	Impact of Full Liberalization of Global Merchandise Trade on Self-Sufficiency in Food and Agricultural Products, Selected Regions, 2015	354
12.10	Impacts of Full Global Merchandise Trade Liberalization on Real Factor Prices, 2015	356
12.11	Impact of Full and Partial Liberalization on Agricultural Value Added, 2015	358

12.12	Summary of Doha Partial Liberalization Scenarios Considered	360
12.13	Average Applied Tariffs for All Goods by Country/Region, for 2001 and 2015 Baselines and Doha Scenarios by 2015	362
12.14	Change from Baseline in Real Income under Alternative Doha Scenarios, 2015	370
12.15	Welfare Effect of Retaining Agricultural Export and Domestic Subsidies, 2015	374
12.16	Changes from Baseline in Bilateral Trade Flows from Full Global Liberalization and from Doha Scenario 7, 2015	377
12.17	Average Annual Agricultural Output and Employment Growth under Alternative Scenarios, 2005–15	378
12.18	Share of Agricultural and Food Production Exported, by Country or Region under Alternative Scenarios, 2001 and 2015	380
12.19	Changes in Poverty under Alternative Scenarios, 2015	382
12.20	Impacts on Real Income from Full Liberalization of Global Merchandise Trade with and without Endogenous Productivity Growth, 2015	384
12A.1	Applied Tariffs by Sector for Selected Importing Regions, GTAP 6.05 (2001) Compared with GTAP5 (1997)	388
12A.2	Global Average Top-Level Armington Elasticities in the GTAP-AGR and LINKAGE Models, by Product	392
12A.3	Comparison of Base Case in 2015 versus Comparative Static Cases in 2001 for the Effects on Real Incomes of Full Liberalization of Global Merchandise Trade, by Country or Region	393

ACKNOWLEDGMENTS

The editors are extremely grateful to all the contributors to this volume for the collegiate way in which they worked so effectively as a team to produce a unified analysis of this important issue. Our thanks also extend to the Opening Discussants who participated in the workshop in The Hague, 1–2 December 2004, where first drafts were examined. In addition to the authors of the chapters, they include Nicolas Imboden, Sam Laird, John Nash, Carlos Primo Braga, Wyatt Thomson, Rod Tyers, and Frank van Tongeren. Three referees also provided useful comments on the entire manuscript.

We are grateful also to the major funder of this research project, namely the United Kingdom's Department for International Development. As well, the Dutch agricultural economics research institute, Landbouw Economisch Instituut (LEI), is to be thanked for superb local organizing of the December 2004 workshop in The Hague; and the authors of chapters 4 and 6 are thankful to the European Commission for supplementary financial support provided to the Centre d'Etudes Prospectives et Informations Internationales (CEPII).

The usual disclaimer applies, that is, the material in this volume represents the authors' own views and not necessarily those of their employers or of the World Bank Group, its Board of Executive Directors, or the governments those Directors represent.

CONTRIBUTORS

Kym Anderson, Lead Economist (Trade Policy), Development Research Group, World Bank, on extended leave from his position as Professor of Economics and Executive Director, Centre for International Economic Studies (CIES), University of Adelaide, Adelaide, Australia

John C. Beghin, Professor of Economics, Head of Trade and Agricultural Policy Division in the Center for Agricultural and Rural Development (CARD), and Director, Food and Agricultural Policy Research Institute (FAPRI), Iowa State University, Ames, Iowa

Antoine Bouët, Former Economist, Centre d'Etudes Prospectives et d'Informations Internationales (CEPII), Paris, France, but since finishing this project he has joined the International Food Policy Research Institute, Washington, DC

Eugenio Díaz-Bonilla, Executive Director for Argentina and Haiti, Inter-American Development Bank, Washington, DC

Lionel Fontagné, Director, Centre d'Etudes Prospectives et d'Informations Internationales (CEPII), Paris, France

Harry de Gorter, Professor, Department of Agricultural Economics, Cornell University, Ithaca, New York

Chad E. Hart, Research Scientist, Center for Agricultural and Rural Development (CARD), and U.S. Policy and Insurance Analyst, Food and Agricultural Policy Research Institute (FAPRI), Iowa State University, Ames, Iowa

Thomas W. Hertel, Distinguished Professor, Department of Agricultural Economics, and Research Director, Center for Global Trade Analysis, Purdue University, West Lafayette, Indiana

Bernard Hoekman, Senior Advisor, Development Research Group, World Bank, Washington, DC

Sébastien Jean, Economist, Centre d'Etudes Prospectives et d'Informations Internationales (CEPII), and Organisation for Economic Co–operation and Development (OECD), Paris, France

Hans G. Jensen, Research Fellow, Danish Research Institute of Food Economics, Royal Veterinary and Agricultural University, Copenhagen, Denmark

Tim Josling, Senior Fellow, Stanford Institute for International Studies and Professor Emeritus, Stanford University, Stanford, California

Roman Keeney, Assistant Professor, Department of Agricultural Economics, Purdue University, West Lafayette, Indiana

Erika Kliauga, Graduate Research Assistant and Ph.D. student, Department of Agricultural Economics, Cornell University, Ithaca, New York

David Laborde Debucquet, Economist, Centre d'Etudes Prospectives et d'Informations Internationales (CEPII), Paris, France

Will Martin, Lead Economist, Trade Unit, Development Research Group, World Bank, Washington, DC

Dominique van der Mensbrugghe, Lead Economist, Development Prospects Group, World Bank, Washington, DC

Patrick Messerlin, Professor, Institut d'Etudes Politiques de Paris, and Director, Groupe d'Economie Mondiale, Paris, France

David Orden, Senior Research Fellow, International Food Policy Research Institute, Washington, DC, and Applied Professor of Agricultural Economics, Virginia Polytechnic Institute and State University, Blacksburg, Virginia

Daniel A. Sumner, Frank H. Buck, Jr. Professor, Department of Agricultural and Resource Economics, and Director of the Agricultural Issues Center, University of California, Davis, California

Henrik Zobbe, Associate Professor, Danish Research Institute of Food Economics, Royal Veterinary and Agricultural University, Copenhagen, Denmark

ABBREVIATIONS AND ACRONYMS

ACP	African, Caribbean, and Pacific Group of States
AGOA	African Growth and Opportunity Act (of the United States)
AMS	Aggregate measure of support
ANZ	Australia and New Zealand
ANZCERTA	ANZ Closer Economic Relations Trade Agreement
ASEAN	Association of South East Asian Nations
AVE	Ad valorem equivalent
CAP	Common Agricultural Policy (of the EU)
CBI	Caribbean Basin Initiative
CEPII	Centre d'Etudes Prospectives et d'Informations Internationales
CES	Constant elasticity of substitution
CGE	Computable general equilibrium
CGIAR	Consultative Group on International Agricultural Research
CPI	Consumer price index
CRP	Conservation reserve program
CSE	Consumer subsidy equivalent
DDA	Doha Development Agenda
EAGGF	European Agricultural Guidance and Guarantee Fund (of the EU)
EBA	Everything But Arms (agreement of the EU)
EC	European Community
EFTA	European Free Trade Agreement
EPA	European Partnership Agreement
EU	European Union
GATS	General Agreement on Trade in Services
GATT	General Agreement on Tariffs and Trade

GEP	Global Economic Prospects (World Bank annual publication)
GSP	Generalized System of Preferences
GTAP	Global Trade Analysis Project
HS6	Harmonized System version 6 (trade classification)
IMF	International Monetary Fund
ISI	Import substitution industrialization
ITC	International Trade Centre (in Geneva)
LAC	Latin American and the Caribbean
LDC	Least developed countries
MAcMap	Trade and protection database from CEPII and ITC
MFA	Multifibre Arrangement
MFN	Most favored nation
MPS	Market price support
MTN	Multilateral trade negotiations
NAFTA	North American Free Trade Agreement
OECD	Organisation for Economic Co-operation and Development
PSE	Producer subsidy equivalent, or producer support estimate
PTA	Preferential trade agreement
Quad	Canada, European Union, Japan, and the United States
R&D	Research and development
RER	Real exchange rate
REER	Real effective exchange rate
ROO	Rules of origin
SACU	South African Customs Union
SADC	Southern African Development Community
SDT	Special and differential treatment
SSA	Sub-Saharan Africa
SSM	Special safeguards mechanism
STE	State trading enterprise
TIM	Trade Implementation Mechanism (of the IMF)
TRQ	Tariff rate quota
UNCTAD	United Nations Conference on Trade and Development
UR	Uruguay Round
URAA	Uruguay Round Agreement on Agriculture
WTO	World Trade Organization

PART I

SETTING THE SCENE

AGRICULTURE, TRADE REFORM, AND THE DOHA AGENDA

Kym Anderson and Will Martin

Agriculture is yet again causing contention in international trade negotiations. It caused long delays to the Uruguay Round in the late 1980s and 1990s, and it is again proving to be the major stumbling block in the World Trade Organization's (WTO) Doha Round of multilateral trade negotiations (formally known as the Doha Development Agenda, or DDA). For example, it contributed substantially to the failure of the September 2003 Trade Ministerial Meeting in Cancún to reach agreement on how to proceed with the DDA, after which another nine months passed before a consensus was reached on a Doha work program, in the July Framework Agreement (WTO 2004).

It is ironic that agricultural policy is so contentious, given its small and declining importance in the global economy. The sector's share of global gross domestic product (GDP) has fallen from around one-tenth in the 1960s to little more than one-thirtieth today. In developed countries the sector accounts for only 1.8 percent of GDP and only a little more of full-time equivalent employment. Mirroring that decline, agriculture's share of global merchandise trade has fallen by more than half since 1970, dropping from 22 percent to 9 percent. For developing countries, agriculture's importance in exports has fallen even more rapidly, from 42 to 11 percent (figure 1.1).

So Why All the Fuss over Agriculture?

Because policies affecting this declining sector are so politically sensitive, there are always self-interested groups suggesting it be sidelined in trade negotiations—as indeed it has been in numerous subglobal preferential trading agreements, and

FIGURE 1.1 The Declining Share of Agriculture and Food in Merchandise Exports for World and Developing Countries, 1970–2003

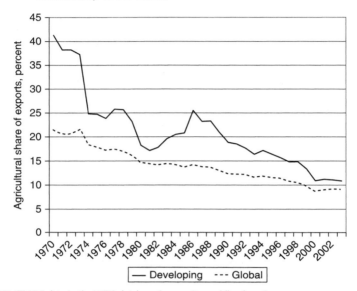

Source: COMTRADE data in the WITS database (www.wits.worldbank.org).
Note: Developing countries here do not include East Asia's newly industrialized economies of Hong Kong (China), Republic of Korea, Singapore, and Taiwan (China).

was in the General Agreement on Tariffs and Trade (GATT) prior to the Uruguay Round.[1] To do so, however, would be a major disservice to many of the world's poorest people, namely, those in farm households in developing countries. It is precisely *because* agricultural earnings are so important to a large number of developing countries that they are targeting the highly protective farm policies of a few wealthy countries in the WTO negotiations: Better access to rich countries' markets for their farm produce is a high priority for these developing countries.[2]

Some developing countries have been granted greater access to developed-country markets for a selection of products under various preferential agreements. Examples are European Union (EU) provisions for former colonies in the Africa, Caribbean, and Pacific (ACP) program and more recently for least developed countries under the Everything But Arms (EBA) agreement. Likewise, the United States has its Africa Growth and Opportunity Act (AGOA) and Caribbean Basin Initiative (CBI). These schemes reduce demands from preference-receiving countries for farm policy reform in developed countries, but they exacerbate the concerns of countries excluded from such programs and thereby made worse off through worsened terms of trade. Such schemes may even be harmful, reducing, rather than improving, aggregate global and even developing-country welfare.

Apart from that, many in developing countries say they did not get a good deal out of the Uruguay Round. From a mercantilistic view, the evidence seems to support that claim: Finger and Winters (2002) report that the average depth of tariff cut by developing countries was substantially greater than that agreed to by high-income countries.[3] As well, developing countries had to take on costly commitments such as those embodied in the SPS (Sanitary and Phytosanitary) and TRIPS (Trade-Related Aspects of Intellectual Property Rights) agreements (Finger and Schuler 2001). These countries therefore have been insisting in the Doha Round on significantly more market access commitments from developed countries before they contemplate opening their own markets further.

Market access opportunities for developing-countries exporters, and especially for poor producers in those countries, are to be found much more in agriculture (and to a lesser extent in textiles and clothing) than in other sectors. A glance at table 1.1

TABLE 1.1 Import-Weighted Average Applied Import Tariffs, by Sector and Region, 2001 (percent, ad valorem equivalent)

Exporting economies	Importing economies		
	High-income	Developing	World
Agriculture and food			
High-income	18	18	17.8
Developing	14	18	15.6
Textiles and wearing apparel			
High-income	8	15	12.0
Developing	7	20	9.3
Other manufactures			
High-income	2	9	4.1
Developing	1	7	2.5
All merchandise			
High-income	3	10	5.4
Developing	3	10	4.9

Source: GTAP Database Version 6.05 (www.gtap.org).
Note: High-income countries include the newly industrialized East Asian economies of Hong Kong (China), Republic of Korea, Singapore, and Taiwan (China) as well as Europe's transition economies that joined the EU in May 2004. The import-weighted averages for developing countries incorporate tariff preferences provided to developing countries, unlike earlier versions of the GTAP database.

shows that even after taking preferences into account, developing-country exporters face an average tariff of 15.6 percent for agriculture and food, and 9.3 percent for textiles and clothing, compared with just 2.5 percent for other manufactures. The average tariff on agricultural goods imported by developing countries themselves is high too, suggesting even more reason why attention should focus on that sector (along with textiles) in the multilateral reform process embodied in the DDA.

If agriculture were to be ignored in the Doha negotiations, there is the risk that agricultural protection would start rising again. That is what happened throughout the course of industrial development in Europe and Northeast Asia (Anderson and others 1986; Lindert 1991). It was only with the establishment of the WTO in 1995 that agricultural trade was brought under multilateral disciplines through the Uruguay Round Agreement on Agriculture (URAA).

The URAA was ambitious in scope, converting all agricultural protection to tariffs, and limiting increases in virtually all tariffs through tariff bindings. Unfortunately, the process of converting nontariff barriers into tariffs (inelegantly termed "tariffication") provided numerous opportunities for backsliding that greatly reduced the effectiveness of the agreed disciplines (Hathaway and Ingco 1996). In developing countries, the option for "ceiling bindings" allowed countries to set their bindings at high levels, frequently unrelated to the previously prevailing levels of protection. Hence agricultural import tariffs are still very high in both rich and poor countries, with bound rates half again as high as most-favored-nation (MFN) applied rates (table 1.2).

TABLE 1.2 Import-weighted Average Agricultural Import Tariffs, by Region, 2001 (percent, ad valorem equivalent)

Economies	Bound tariff	MFN applied tariff	Actual applied tariff[a]
Developed	27	22	14
Developing	48	27	21
Least developed[b]	78	14	13
World	37	24	17

Source: Jean, Laborde, and Martin (2006).
Note: Weights are based on imports.
a. Tariffs include preferences and in-quota TRQ rates where relevant, as well as the ad valorem equivalent of specific tariffs. Developed countries include the transition economies of Eastern Europe and the former Soviet Union. The *developing economies* definition used here is that adopted by the WTO and so includes East Asia's four newly industrialized economies, which accounts for the differences in the percentages for applied tariffs given in this table and table 1.1.
b. Least developed is a subset of developing.

FIGURE 1.2 Agricultural Producer Support in High-Income Economies, by Value, Percent, and Type of Support, 1986–2003

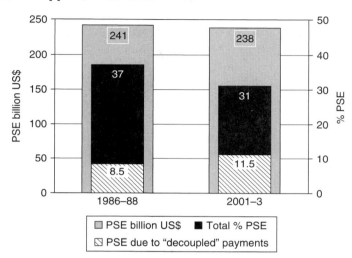

Source: OECD database (see www.oecd.org).

As well, agricultural producers in some countries are supported by export subsidies (still tolerated within the WTO only for agriculture) and by domestic support measures. Together with tariffs and other barriers to agricultural imports, these measures support farm incomes and encourage agricultural output to varying extents. The market price support component also typically raises domestic consumer prices of farm products. Figure 1.2 shows the value and the percentage of total farm receipts from these support policy measures, called the producer support estimate, or PSE, by the secretariat of the Organisation for Economic Co-operation and Development (OECD).[4] For OECD members as a group, the PSE was almost the same in 2001–3 as in 1986–88, at about $240 billion a year. But because of growth in the sector, the value of the PSE as a percentage of total farm receipts (inclusive of support) fell from 37 to 31 percent. Figure 1.2 also shows a significant increase in the proportion of that support coming from programs that are somewhat "decoupled" from current output, such as payments based on area cropped, number of livestock, or some historical reference period; these decoupled programs have less effect on current production than do measures that raise product prices.

Agricultural protection levels remain very high in these OECD countries, especially considering that the 1986–88 period had historically low international food prices and hence above-trend PSEs. And, as figure 1.3 shows, the PSEs have fallen

FIGURE 1.3 Agricultural Producer Support in High-Income Economies, by Country, 1986–2003

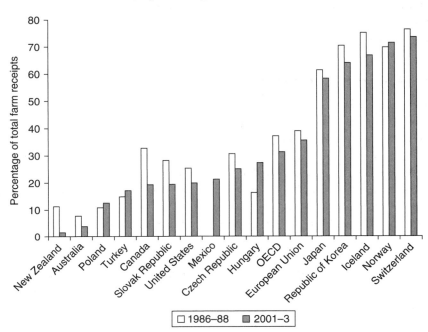

Source: OECD database (see www.oecd.org).
Note: In the 1986–88 period, data for the Czech Republic, Hungary, Poland, and the Slovak Republic are for 1991–93. Austria, Finland, and Sweden are included in the average for both periods and also in the EU average for the 2001–3 period.

least in the most-protective OECD countries. By contrast, tariff protection for OECD manufacturing has fallen over the past 60 years from above 30 percent nominal rate of protection (a level similar to that for OECD agriculure today) to only about 3 percent now. This gap in tariff protection means far more resources have been retained in agricultural production in developed countries—and hence fewer in developing countries—than would have been the case if protection had been phased down in both sectors simultaneously.

Nonetheless, the achievements of the Uruguay Round Agreement on Agriculture provide some scope for optimism about what might be achieved through the WTO as part of the Doha Development Agenda and beyond. The current Doha Round has the advantage over the Uruguay Round of beginning from a framework of rules and disciplines already agreed to in the Uruguay Round. In particular, that framework has the three clearly identified "pillars" of market access, export subsidies, and domestic support on which to focus. True, it took more than three years to agree on a framework for the current negotiations, reached at the end of July 2004 (WTO 2004), but that July Framework Agreement is likely to guide the negotiations for some time. It therefore provides a strong basis for undertaking ex ante analysis of various options potentially available to WTO members during the Doha negotiations.

What Differentiates This Book from Others?

This study builds on numerous recent analyses of the Doha Development Agenda and agricultural trade, including five very helpful books that appeared in 2004. One, edited by Aksoy and Beghin (2004), provides details of trends in global agricultural markets and policies, especially as they affect nine commodities of interest to developing countries. Another, edited by Ingco and Winters (2004), includes a wide range of analyses based on papers revised following a conference held just before the aborted WTO Trade Ministerial Meeting in Seattle in 1999. The third, edited by Ingco and Nash (2004), provides a follow-up to the broad global perspective of the Ingco and Winters volume: it explores a wide range of key issues and options in agricultural trade reform from a developing-country perspective. The fourth, edited by Anania, Bowman, Carter, and McCalla (2004), is a comprehensive, tenth-anniversary retrospective on the Uruguay Round Agreement on Agriculture and numerous unilateral trade and subsidy reforms in developed, transition, and developing economies. And the fifth, edited by Jank (2004), focuses on implications for Latin America.

All of those studies were completed well before Doha Round negotiators reached the July Framework Agreement in the early hours of August 1, 2004. The studies also preceded the public release in December 2004 of a new version of Purdue University's Global Trade Analysis Project (GTAP) database. That Version 6.05 database is a major improvement over the previous version for several reasons. One is that it includes global trade and protection data as of 2001, whereas the previous database had data for 1997. Another is that the new protection data include, for the first time, nonreciprocal as well as reciprocal tariff preferences, the ad valorem equivalents of specific tariffs (which are plentiful in the agricultural tariff schedules of many high-income, high-protection countries), and the effects of tariff rate quotas. In addition, WTO-bound tariffs and key trade policy reforms occurring irrespective of the outcome of the Doha negotiations have been added, namely, the commitments associated with accession to WTO by such economies as China and Taiwan (China), the implementation of the last of the Uruguay Round commitments (including the abolition of quotas on trade in textiles and clothing at the end of 2004, and final agricultural tariff reductions in developing countries), and the enlargement of the European Union from 15 to 25 members in May 2004.

Hence what distinguishes the current volume from others is that its ex ante analysis focuses on the core aspects of the July Framework Agreement from the viewpoint of agriculture and developing countries but also takes account of what might happen to nonagricultural market access and the other negotiating areas. Furthermore, the analysis does so in an integrated way by using the new GTAP Version 6.05 database, which we have amended to include bound tariffs and to account for key protection changes agreed to before 2005 and related global economywide models.[5]

What Questions Are Addressed in This Study?

This volume is the result of an intense program of integrated research undertaken during the latter half of 2004 and early 2005 by a complementary set of well-informed scholars from four continents. Among the core questions this volume addresses are the following:

- What is at stake in this Doha Round, in terms of efficiency gains forgone by the various regions of the world because of current tariffs and agricultural subsidies?
- How much are each of the three pillars of agricultural distortion (market access, export subsidies, and domestic support) contributing to those welfare losses, compared with nonagricultural trade barriers?
- How might the demands for special and differential treatment (SDT) for developing and least developed countries be met without compromising the potential gains from trade expansion for those economies?
- What are the consequences of alternative formulas for cutting bound agricultural tariffs for applied tariffs, trade, national income, and income distribution?
- In the case of products whose imports are subject to tariff rate quotas, what are the tradeoffs between reducing out-of-quota tariffs and expanding the quota volumes or the in-quota tariffs?
- Since MFN trade liberalization by developed countries erodes the value of tariff preferences, to what extent would this erosion reduce the developing countries' interest in agricultural and other trade reform?
- What should be done about agricultural export subsidies, including those implicit in export credits, food aid, and arrangements for state trading enterprises?
- Based on recent policy changes in key countries, how might domestic farm support measures be better disciplined in the WTO?
- If domestic support commitments made in the Uruguay Round were reduced, what would be the effects on the actual domestic support levels currently provided to farmers?
- In particular, how might reductions in cotton subsidies help developing-country farmers in West Africa and elsewhere?

- What are the effects of expanding market access for nonagricultural products at the same time as access is expanded for farm goods under a Doha agreement?
- For which developing countries would farm output and employment fall as a result of such a Doha agreement?
- Taking a broad brush, and in the light of past experience and our understanding of the political economy of agricultural policies in rich and poor countries, how might reform of those policies best be advanced during the Doha negotiations?
- What would be the overall market and welfare consequences by 2015, for various countries and regions as well as globally, of the alternative Doha reform commitments considered in addressing each of the above questions?

What Have We Learned?

In answering these questions, the following are among the key messages that emerge.

The potential gains from further global trade reform are huge. Global gains from trade reforms implemented after 2004 are estimated to be large even if dynamic gains and gains from economies of scale and increased competition are ignored.[6] Freeing all merchandise trade and eliminating agricultural subsidies are estimated to boost global welfare by nearly $300 billion a year by 2015. Additional gains would come from whatever productivity effects that reform would generate.

Developing countries could gain disproportionately from further global trade reform. The developing countries would enjoy 45 percent of the global gain from completely freeing all merchandise trade (table 1.3a), well above their current share of one-fifth of global GDP. Their welfare would increase by 1.2 percent, compared with an increase of just 0.6 percent for developed countries. The developing countries gain a higher share than developed countries partly because they have relatively high tariffs themselves (so they would reap substantial efficiency gains from reforming their own protection) and partly because their exporters face much higher farm and textile tariffs in developed-country markets than do exporters from developed countries themselves (see table 1.1)—notwithstanding nonreciprocal tariff preferences for many developing countries.

Benefits could be as much from South-South as from South-North trade reform. Trade reform by developing countries is as important economically to those countries as is reform by developed countries, including from agricultural liberalization (see table 1.3b). Hence choosing to delay their own reforms, or reforming less than developed countries and thereby holding back South-South trade growth, could substantially reduce the potential gains to developing countries.

TABLE 1.3 Effects on Economic Welfare of Full Trade Liberalization by Economy and Products, 2015 (percent)

a. Distribution of effects on global welfare				
	Full liberalization of:			
Economy	Agriculture and food	Textiles and clothing	Other merchandise	All goods
High-income	46	6	3	55
Developing	17	8	20	45
All	63	14	23	100
b. Distribution of effects on developing economies' welfare				
	Full liberalization of:			
Economy	Agriculture and food	Textiles and clothing	Other merchandise	All goods
High-income	30	17	3	50
Developing	33	10	7	50
All	63	27	10	100

Source: Anderson, Martin, and van der Mensbrugghe (2006, table 12.6).
Note: High-income economies include Europe's transition economies that joined the EU in April 2004 as well as the four newly industrialized economies in Asia.

Agriculture is where cuts are needed most. To realize the potential gain from opening up goods markets, by far the greatest cuts in bound tariffs and subsidies are required in agriculture. That is because of the very high rates of assistance in the agricultural sector relative to other sectors. Food and agricultural policies are responsible for more than three-fifths of the global gain forgone because of merchandise trade distortions (first column of table 1.3a) even though agriculture and food processing account for less than 10 percent of world trade and less than 4 percent of global GDP. Agriculture is just as important for the welfare of developing countries as it is for the world as a whole: their gains from global agricultural liberalization represent almost two-thirds of their total potential gains, which compares with gains of one-quarter from textiles and clothing and one-tenth from other merchandise liberalization (table 1.3b).

Subsidy disciplines are important, but increased market access in agriculture is crucial. Much of the attention in the negotiations has focused on the abolition of export subsidies. The framework agreement envisages their complete abolition and only partial reform of agricultural tariffs. However, extremely high applied tariffs on farm products relative to nonfarm products are the major reason that

TABLE 1.4 Distribution of Global Welfare Impacts from Removing All Agricultural Tariffs and Subsidies, 2001 (percent)

Agricultural liberalization component	Benefiting economy		
	High-income	Developing	World
Import market access	66	27	93
Export subsidies	5	−3	2
Domestic support	4	1	5
All measures	75	25	100

Source: Summarized from Hertel and Keeney (2006, table 2.7).
Note: High-income economies include the newly industrialized East Asian economies of Hong Kong (China), Republic of Korea, Singapore, and Taiwan (China) as well as Europe's transition economies that joined the EU in April 2004.

food and agricultural policies contribute 63 percent of the welfare cost of current merchandise trade distortions. Subsidies to farm production and exports are only minor additional contributors: 4 and 1 percentage points respectively, compared with 58 points attributable to agricultural tariffs.[7] This is even truer for developing countries than for developed ones (compare first two columns of table 1.4), where Panagariya (2004) has pointed to the risk of some developing countries losing from abolition of export subsidies. Disciplining those domestic subsidies and phasing out export subsidies is nonetheless very important.

Large cuts in domestic support commitments are needed to erase binding overhang. Commitments on domestic support for farmers are currently so much higher than actual support levels that the 20 percent cut in the total bound aggregate measure of support (AMS) promised in the July Framework Agreement as an early installment would require almost no actual support reductions. Indeed, a cut as large as 75 percent for those with the most domestic support is needed to get some action, and even then only four industrial countries would be required to make significant cuts from 2001 actual levels of domestic support: the United States (by 28 percent), the European Union (by 16 percent), Norway (by 18 percent), and Australia (by 10 percent). Reforms by the EU and Australia since 2001 have already delivered cuts that would satisfy those requirements, so only the United States and Norway would need to make further adjustments.

Large cuts in bound rates also are needed to erase binding overhang in agricultural tariffs. In turning from potential gains to what might be achievable under a partial reform package, it is clear the devil is going to be in the details. Table 1.2 shows a substantial binding overhang in agricultural tariffs: the average bound rate in developed countries is almost twice as high as the average applied rate; in developing countries, the ratio is even greater. Thus large reductions in bound rates are needed before *any* improvement is made in market access. To bring the global average actual agricultural tariff down by one-third, bound rates would have to be reduced for developed countries by at least 45 percent, and by as much as 75 percent for the highest tariffs, under a tiered formula.

A complex tiered formula may be little better than a proportional tariff cut. Because of the large binding overhang, a tiered formula for cutting agricultural tariffs would not generate much more global welfare—and no more welfare for developing countries as a group—than a proportional cut of the same average size (scenarios 1 and 4 of table 1.5).[8] This suggests there may be little value in arguing over the finer details of a complex tiered formula just for the sake of reducing tariff escalation. Instead, a simple tariff cap of, say, 100, or even 200, percent could achieve many of the same objectives.

TABLE 1.5   Welfare Effect of Alternative Doha Reform Scenarios, 2015 (percent difference from baseline)

Economy	Scenario 1	Scenario 4	Scenario 5	Scenario 6	Scenario 7	Scenario 8
High-income	0.20	0.18	0.05	0.13	0.25	0.30
Middle-income	0.10	0.10	0.00	0.01	0.15	0.21
of which: China	−0.02	−0.01	−0.05	−0.04	0.07	0.06
Low-income	0.05	0.04	0.01	0.00	0.18	0.30
World total	0.18	0.16	0.04	0.10	0.23	0.28
2001 US$ billions	*74.5*	*66.3*	*17.9*	*44.3*	*96.1*	*119.3*

Source: Anderson, Martin, and van der Mensbrugghe (2006, table 12.14).
Note: All six scenarios assume elimination of agricultural export subsidies and cuts in actual domestic support as of 2001 of 28 percent in the United States, 18 percent in the EU, 16 percent in Norway, and 10 percent in Australia. In scenarios 1 and 4, the applied global average tariff on agricultural products is cut by roughly one-third, with larger cuts in developed economies, smaller cuts in developing economies, and zero in least developed economies. In scenario 1 there are three tiers for developed economies and four for developing countries, following Harbinson (WTO 2003) but each tier is 10 percentage points higher. Scenario 5 is the same as scenario 4 except that it allows an exemption from the tariff cuts for sensitive and special products. Scenario 6 is the same as scenario 5 but also includes a 200 percent cap on tariffs. Scenario 7 is the same as scenario 1 except it also expands market access for nonagricultural goods, cutting tariffs by 50 percent for developed economies, 33 percent for developing economies, and zero in least developed economies. Scenario 8 is the same as scenario 7 except that developing (including least developed) economies cut all their tariffs as much as developed economies. Scenarios 2 and 3 described in Anderson, Martin, and van der Mensbrugghe (2005) are not shown here. High-income countries include the newly industrialized East Asian economies of Hong Kong (China), Republic of Korea, Singapore, and Taiwan (China) as well as Europe's transition economies that joined the EU in April 2004.

Even large cuts in bound tariffs will accomplish little if exceptions are allowed for sensitive products. If members succumb to the political temptation to put limits on tariff cuts for the most sensitive farm products, most of the prospective gains from Doha could evaporate. Allowing for just 2 percent of agricultural tariff lines to be designated as sensitive products (4 percent in developing countries, to incorporate their demand for exceptional treatment also for special products), and subjecting them to just a 15 percent cut, would shrink welfare gains from agricultural reform by three-quarters. Allowing those exceptions but capping bound tariff rates at 200 percent would offset some of the losses from the exemptions, shrinking the welfare gain by only one-third (scenarios 5 and 6 in table 1.5).

TRQ expansion could provide additional market access. Only a small number of farm products are subject to tariff rate quotas, but they protect more than half of all production in developed countries and 44 percent of their agricultural imports (de Gorter and Kliauga 2005). Bringing down (out-of-quota) MFN bound tariffs for those products could be supplemented by lowering their in-quota tariff or expanding the size of the quota itself. While doing so might increase the aggregate rent attached to those quotas and hence resistance to eventually removing them, the binding overhang is so large that quota expansion may be the only way to increase market access for some TRQ products in the Doha Round—especially for products designated as sensitive and hence subject to smaller cuts in their bound tariffs.

High binding overhang in developing countries means they would have to make few cuts. Given the high binding overhang of developing countries, even with their high tariffs and even if tiered formulas are used to cut highest bindings the most—relatively few of them would have to cut their actual tariffs and subsidies at all. That is even more the case if some special products are subjected to smaller cuts, and if developing countries exercise their right, as laid out in the July Framework Agreement, to undertake smaller cuts (zero in the case of least developed countries) than developed countries. Politically, high binding overhang makes it easier for developing and least developed countries to offer big cuts on bound rates, but it also means the benefits to them are smaller than if they had a smaller binding overhang.

Cuts in cotton subsidies would help cotton-exporting developing countries. The removal of cotton subsidies (which have raised producer prices by well over 50 percent in the United States and the EU) would raise the export price of cotton (although not equally across all exporters because of product differentiation). If those subsidies were removed as part of freeing all merchandise trade, that export price is estimated to rise 8 percent for Brazil and less for Sub-Saharan Africa on average. However, the value of cotton exports from Sub-Saharan Africa would be

75 percent greater than it is now, and the share of all developing countries in global cotton exports would be 85 percent instead of 56 percent in 2015, vindicating those countries' efforts to ensure cotton subsidies receive specific attention in the Doha negotiations.

Expanding nonagricultural market access would add substantially to the gains from agricultural reform. A 50 percent cut in nonagricultural tariffs by developed countries (33 percent by developing countries and zero by least-developed countries) added to the tiered formula or proportional cut to agricultural tariffs would double the gains from Doha for developing countries. It would also account for about one-third of the nearly $300 billion potential welfare gain from full liberalization.

Adding services reform would of course boost that welfare gain even more. Adding nonagricultural tariff reform to agricultural reform helps to balance the exchange of "concessions." A reduction of nonagricultural tariffs also would help balance the exchange of concessions between developed and developing countries: developing-country exports to high-income countries would then be $62 billion greater, compared with the estimated $55 billion increase in high-income-country exports to developing countries. With only agricultural reform, high-income country bilateral export growth to developing countries would be little more than half the export growth in the opposite direction (table 1.6).

TABLE 1.6 Effects on Bilateral Merchandise Trade Flows of Adding Nonagricultural Tariff Cuts to Agricultural Reform under Doha, 2015 (US$ billion increase over the baseline in 2015)

	Imports			
	Agriculture reform only[a]		Agriculture and nonagriculture reform[b]	
Exports	High-income economies	Developing economies	High-income economies	Developing economies
High-income economies	20	11	80	55
Developing economies	18	5	62	16
World total	38	16	142	71

Source: Anderson, Martin, and van der Mensbrugghe (2006, table 12.16).
Note: High-income economies include the newly industrialized East Asian economies of Hong Kong (China), Republic of Korea, Singapore, and Taiwan (China) as well as Europe's transition economies that joined the EU in May 2004.
a. Scenario 1 in table 1.5.
b. Scenario 7 in table 1.5.

Most developing countries gain in our Doha scenarios, and all would if they participated more fully in the reforms. Our simulations of alternative scenarios for possible outcomes of the Doha negotiations show that middle-income countries certainly stand to gain, but so too would poorer developing countries so long as they do not exercise their claims to special and differential treatment in the form of lesser requirements to reform. An important part of this result comes from the increases in market access on a nondiscriminatory basis by other developing countries.

Preference erosion may be less of an issue than commonly assumed. Some least developed countries in Sub-Saharan Africa and elsewhere appear to be slight losers in our Doha simulations when developed countries cut their tariffs and these poor countries choose not to reform at all. Our simulations overstate the benefits of tariff preferences for least developed countries, however, since they ignore the trade-dampening effect of complex rules of origin and the grabbing of much of the rents by developed-country importers. Even if least developed countries were to be losers after correcting for those realities, it remains true that preference-receiving countries could always be compensated for preference erosion through increased aid at relatively small cost to current preference providers, and in the process, other developing countries currently hurt by preferences for least developed countries would enjoy greater access to the markets of reforming developed countries.

Farm output and employment would grow in developing countries under Doha. Although a few low-income countries lose slightly under our Doha scenarios, in all the developing countries and regions shown, the levels of output and employment on farms expand. It is only in the most protected developed countries of Western Europe, Northeast Asia, and the United States that output and employment levels would fall, and then only by small amounts, contrary to the predictions of scaremongers who claim agriculture would be decimated in reforming countries (table 1.7). Even if merchandise trade were completely liberalized, the developed countries' share of the world's primary agricultural GDP by 2015 would be only slightly lower, at 25 percent instead of 30 percent. (Their share of global agricultural exports would be diminished considerably more, however: from 53 to 38 percent.)

Poverty could be reduced under Doha. Under the full merchandise trade liberalization scenario, extreme poverty—those earning no more than $1 a day—would drop by 32 million in developing countries in 2015 relative to the baseline level of 622 million, a reduction of 5 percent. The majority of the poor by 2015 are projected to be in Sub-Saharan Africa, where the reduction would be 6 percent.[9]

TABLE 1.7 Annual Average Growth in Output and Employment from a Comprehensive Doha Reform as Compared with the Baseline Rate, by Region, 2005–2015 (percent)

Region	Output		Employment	
	Baseline	Scenario 7	Baseline	Scenario 7
Australia and New Zealand	3.5	4.3	0.4	1.0
Canada	3.5	4.0	0.2	0.6
United States	2.2	1.9	−0.8	−1.4
EU25 plus EFTA	1.0	−0.3	−1.8	−2.8
Japan	0.5	−1.4	−2.7	−4.1
Korea, Republic of, and Taiwan (China)	2.2	1.5	−1.3	−2.1
Argentina	2.9	3.5	0.9	1.5
Bangladesh	4.2	4.2	1.1	1.2
Brazil	3.3	4.4	1.1	2.2
China	4.3	4.3	0.8	0.8
India	4.3	4.4	1.0	1.0
Indonesia	3.0	3.0	−0.7	−0.6
Thailand	−0.1	0.4	−4.6	−4.3
Vietnam	5.8	5.9	3.9	4.0
Russian Federation	1.5	1.4	−2.3	−2.4
Mexico	3.9	4.0	2.0	2.3
South Africa	2.5	2.6	0.0	0.1
Turkey	3.0	3.0	−0.5	−0.5
Rest of South Asia	4.8	4.9	2.0	2.1
Rest of East Asia and Pacific	3.7	3.8	0.2	0.3
Rest of Latin America and the Caribbean	4.4	5.3	1.9	2.6
Rest of Europe and Central Asia	3.3	3.3	0.0	0.0
Middle East and North Africa	4.0	4.0	1.5	1.5
Selected Sub-Saharan African countries	5.3	5.4	3.0	3.0
Rest of Sub-Saharan Africa	4.6	4.8	2.2	2.3
Rest of world	5.0	5.5	2.4	2.7

Source: Anderson, Martin, and van der Mensbrugghe (2006, table 12.17).
Note: See table 1.5 for a description of scenario 7.

TABLE 1.8 Decreases in the Number of Impoverished under Full Trade Liberalization and Alternative Doha Scenarios, 2015 (millions of people)

Region	Baseline 2015	Full liberalization	Decrease from baseline under		
			Scenario 1	Scenario 7	Scenario 8
East Asia and Pacific	19	2.2	0.1	0.3	0.5
Latin America and the Caribbean	43	2.1	0.3	0.4	0.5
South Asia	216	5.6	0.2	1.4	3.0
Sub-Saharan Africa	340	21.1	−0.1	0.5	2.2
All developing countries	622	31.9	0.5	2.5	6.3

Source: Anderson, Martin, and van der Mensbrugghe (2006, table 12.19).
Note: Poverty is defined as earnings of less than $1 a day. For description of scenarios, see table 1.5.

Under the Doha scenarios reported in table 1.8, the poverty impacts are far more modest. The number of poor living on $1 a day or less would fall by 2.5 million in the case of the core Doha scenario 7 (of which 0.5 million are in Sub-Saharan Africa) and by 6.3 million in the case of Doha scenario 8 (of which 2.2 million are in Sub-Saharan Africa). This corresponds to the relatively modest ambitions of the merchandise trade reforms as captured in these Doha scenarios. If only agriculture was reformed (Doha scenario 1), there would be much less poverty alleviation globally and none at all in Sub-Saharan Africa. This shows the importance for poverty of including manufactured products in the Doha negotiations.

Key Policy Implications

Among the numerous policy implications that are drawn out by the various chapter authors, the following are worth highlighting.

Prospective gains are too large not to find the political will needed to negotiate agricultural trade reform under Doha. With gains on the order of $300 billion a year at stake from implementing the July Framework Agreement, even if no reforms are forthcoming in services, and even if the counterfactual would be the status quo rather than protectionist backsliding, the political will needs to be found to bring the round to a successful conclusion, and the sooner the better. Multilateral cuts in MFN bindings are also helpful because they can lock in previous unilateral trade liberalizations that otherwise would remain unbound and hence vulnerable to backsliding. Implementation of the framework agreement can be used as an opportunity to multilateralize previously agreed preferential trade agreements and thereby reduce the risk of trade diversion from those bilateral or regional arrangements.

Because developed countries have the most dollars to gain, as well as the most capacity and influence, they need to show leadership at the WTO. The large developed countries cannot generate a successful agreement on their own, nor can the Doha Round succeed without a major push by the key traders. Their capacity to assist poorer economies could hardly manifest itself more clearly than in encouraging global economic integration through trade reform, and in particular by opening their markets to the items of greatest importance to poorer countries, namely, farm (and textile) products. The more that is done, the more developing countries will be encouraged to reciprocate by opening their own markets—accelerating South-South trade in addition to South-North trade.

Abolishing agricultural export subsidies is the obvious first step. That would bring agriculture into line with the basic GATT rule against such measures, and in the process help to limit the extent to which governments encourage agricultural production by other means (since a ban on export subsidies would raise the cost of surplus disposal). China has already committed not to use export subsidies, and other developing countries can also find more efficient ways of stabilizing their domestic food markets than by dumping surpluses abroad.

Domestic support bindings must be cut substantially to remove binding overhang. In so doing, the highest-subsidizing countries, namely, the EU, the United States, and Norway, need to reduce their support, not just for the sake of their own economies but also to encourage developing countries to reciprocate by opening their markets as a quid pro quo. An initial installment of a 20 percent cut is a good start, but nothing more than a start, toward eliminating that overhang.[10]

Even more important, agricultural tariff bindings must be cut deeply to remove binding overhang and provide some genuine market opening. Getting rid of the tariff binding overhang that resulted from the "dirty tariffication" of the Uruguay Round should be the first priority, but more than that is needed if market access is to expand. If a choice has to be made, reducing MFN bound tariffs in general would be preferable to raising tariff rate quotas, because the latter help only those lucky enough to obtain quotas and crowd out nonquota holders. (Because they run counter to the nondiscrimination spirit of the GATT, tariff rate quotas deserve the same fate as textile quotas, which were abolished at the end of 2004.) Exemptions for even just a few sensitive and special products would be undesirable because they would greatly reduce the gains from reform and would tend to divert resources into, instead of away from, enterprises in which countries have their least comparative advantage. If it turns out to be politically impossible not to allow some exemptions, it would be crucial to impose a cap so that any sensitive or special product with a bound tariff in excess of, say, 100 percent had to reduce it to that cap rate.

The tiered formula for cutting farm tariffs could be traded for a proportional cut with a cap. Should it prove to be too difficult or time-consuming to negotiate a complex, tiered tariff-reduction formula, our simulation results suggest that a proportional cut of nearly the same average magnitude plus a cap to bring down the very highest bound tariffs would be just as effective in raising welfare.

Expanding nonagricultural market access at the same time that agricultural trade is reformed is essential. A balanced exchange of concessions is impossible without adding other sectors, and those sectors need to include more than textiles and clothing (which also benefit developing countries disproportionately), even though textiles and clothing are the other highly distorted sector. With other merchandise included, the trade expansion would be four times greater for both rich and poor countries and poverty in low-income countries would be reduced considerably more.

South-South concessions also are needed, especially for developing countries, which means reconsidering the opportunity for developing countries to liberalize less. Because developing countries are trading so much more with each other than they once did, they are the major beneficiaries of reforms within their own regions. Upper-middle-income countries might consider giving least developed countries duty-free access to their markets (mirroring the recent initiatives of developed countries) but, rather than take such discriminatory action, it would be better for them to reduce their MFN tariffs. Even least developed countries should consider reducing their tariff binding overhang, since doing so in the context of Doha gives them more scope to demand "concessions" (or compensation for preference erosion or other contributors to terms of trade deterioration) from richer countries without requiring them to cut their own *applied* tariffs very much.

What the Subsequent Chapters Contribute

These findings and policy implications are described more fully in the following chapters. A brief description of key aspects of each chapter's analysis is given here.

What Is at Stake

In chapter 2, Tom Hertel and Roman Keeney examine the potential implications of trade reform. They estimate that eliminating all agricultural subsidies and moving to complete free trade in goods and services would boost global welfare by $151 billion a year.[11] Developing countries would enjoy a disproportionately large share of those gains at 23 percent, well above their current share of 16 percent of global GDP. The reason is twofold: they have relatively high tariffs themselves and, more importantly, their exporters face much higher tariffs in high-income markets than do exporters from the high-income countries themselves.

What are the policy measures contributing most to those potential gains from full trade liberalization? First, although agriculture contributes only 4 percent to global GDP, policies for that sector are responsible for two-thirds of the global cost of merchandise protection. Almost four-fifths of that cost is attributable to high-income country policies, with only one-fifth due to farm policies of developing countries. Not surprisingly, therefore, it is high-income countries that gain the most from reform of farm programs, but developing countries also gain a sizable portion—removing restrictions on agricultural trade accounts for more than half the total gains to developing countries from removing all merchandise trade restrictions globally.

Second, textiles and clothing liberalization would contribute only one-fifth as much to global welfare as agricultural reform. Their contribution to welfare in developing countries would be considerably greater though, equal to nearly three-quarters that from farm trade reform and accounting for most of developing-country gain from nonfarm merchandise reform.

What happens when services trade reform is included? Estimates are much more difficult to obtain for this category, especially when foreign direct investment (commercial presence) and temporary labor migration (movement of natural persons) is potentially involved. Two important points about services can be drawn from Hertel and Keeney's results. One is that even with just a small subset of services included, the potential gains from trade reform are enhanced considerably, accounting for 44 percent of the total gains from goods and services reforms. That exceeds agriculture's 37 percent share of the total (with other merchandise accounting for just 19 percent). Second, reform of developing-country services policies contributes more than one-fifth of the gain from reform of services trade, again well above their 16 percent share of global GDP. So even though the bulk of the gain from services trade reform goes to high-income countries, developing countries would do well to embrace, rather than oppose, their inclusion in the Doha round.

Chapter 2 also exposes the relative importance of the three separate pillars of agricultural support programs: import market access inhibited by tariffs and tariff rate quotas, domestic support measures, and export subsidies. According to Hertel and Keeney's results, it is market access measures that deliver by far the greatest prospects for gains from agricultural reform—ten times the combined contribution of domestic support and export subsidies. Farm export subsidies are now of relatively minor importance globally, thanks to reductions following the Uruguay Round. But developing countries as a group would lose a little from the total elimination of export subsidies because some are net food importing countries. Agricultural exporting developing countries, in contrast, would gain from the removal of developed-country subsidies.

Special and Differential Treatment for Developing Countries

In chapter 3, Tim Josling first considers the institutional arrangements for special and differential treatment in the GATT/WTO. He points out that the concept of SDT is well-established, and that the July Framework Agreement refers to it in several situations, including provisions for longer implementation periods, lower reduction commitments, consistency with the provisions of the Ministerial Decision on Least Developed and Net Food Importing Countries, and the provisions on food and livelihood security in the agricultural annex to the framework.

The key question for developing countries, however, is how they should seek to use these opportunities for SDT. Because the framework does not give quantitative magnitudes, these must be negotiated, and the results will depend on where, and to what extent, developing countries use their negotiating capital to achieve their objectives. Josling's key recommendation is that developing countries use an economic approach to evaluate where it is in their interests to push hard to avoid making commitments, and where they should use their negotiating capital to seek broader liberalization commitments from their trading partners. In particular, he suggests that developing countries "sell off" assets that are of declining value such as preferential access to markets where protection is falling—and seek greater liberalization in areas, such as agriculture, textiles, and the movement of labor, that promise longer-term gains.

Josling asks whether SDT can be meaningful when developing countries are self-designated and whether self-designation should continue. He concludes that there is little likelihood of changing this criterion, but considers the potential feasibility of Hoekman's (2005a, 2005b) suggestion that countries might be allowed to opt out of some provisions based on objective development-oriented criteria.

In market access, the framework envisages developing countries having to make smaller tariff reductions. Josling notes that developing countries tend to have much higher binding overhang than the industrial countries in agriculture and asks whether developing countries might offer to reduce this overhang as a way to ensure larger reductions in applied tariffs in the industrial countries. The framework also envisages that developing countries will have more flexible treatment on special products. Here, Josling argues that developing countries will face some major choices. Attempts to seek greater coverage of these products are likely to intensify industrial country demands for greater flexibility for their own sensitive products.

Under domestic support, Josling argues that developing countries should avoid spending negotiating capital on longer implementation periods and lower reduction commitments, since virtually no developing countries will need to undertake reduction commitments. Inclusion of some specific measures, such as some credit subsidies, in the so-called Green Box (measures not subject to discipline) might be worthwhile. He questions, however, whether establishing a new specific Development Box would be worth a substantial amount of negotiating capital given that most such measures are already in the set of allowed measures in the Green Box.

Agricultural Market Access Formulas

In chapter 4, Sébastien Jean, David Laborde, and Will Martin examine the potential impact of the framework's tiered formula approach to increasing market access. They note that this approach is more ambitious in a critical way than the preceding reform proposals in that it requires proportionately greater reductions in higher tariffs. The formula set out in the framework is very general, however, and so considerable effort is likely to be needed to convert it into specific proposals.

The fundamental notion of a tiered formula with higher cuts in higher tariffs raises important questions. Simply having higher proportional cuts in higher tiers would create discontinuities, with some tariffs being reduced by more than slightly lower tariffs. Such an effect could potentially create sharp political resistance from affected groups. Jean, Laborde, and Martin highlight this problem and point to a potential solution, which involves increasing the marginal tariff-cutting rate.

Any meaningful analysis of a nonlinear tiered formula requires detailed information on tariffs, including the effects of specific and other non-ad-valorem tariffs; information on applied tariff rates and on the levels of the bindings; the effects of tariff preferences; and the use of tariff rate quotas. Fortunately, the authors of this paper were able to base their analysis on detailed tariff databases that capture these critical features.

An important feature of the framework is greater flexibility for sensitive products in all countries and for special products in developing countries. Negotiators must choose how many such tariff lines are to be allowed, the extent of flexibility permitted, and the extent of liberalization of these products to be undertaken. Jean, Laborde, and Martin assume that policy makers will use these flexibilities to shelter important products—in the sense that these products involve substantial amounts of trade, and that substantial reductions in applied rates would have been required by application of the formula and that flexibilities will allow for only modest (15 percent) cuts in these tariffs. They then consider the implications of allowing 2 percent and 5 percent of tariff lines to be sheltered as sensitive products in the industrial countries, with twice these percentages in developing countries to allow for special products. In the baseline simulations, SDT is incorporated by allowing developing countries to make smaller tariff reductions than industrial countries.

Jean, Laborde, and Martin begin their analysis by examining a tiered formula with higher tariff cuts on higher tariff items. A tiered formula with 75 percent marginal reductions on the highest tariffs in industrial countries and 60 percent in developing countries was found to generate worthwhile increases in market access, with bound rates falling by about half on average worldwide, and applied rates by roughly one-third. The reductions in applied rates required are generally quite modest, however, with only four country groups being required to undertake a reduction in average agricultural tariffs of more than 5 percentage points.

A striking finding of this chapter is the potentially dramatic impact of incorporating flexibility for sensitive and special products. When 2 percent of tariff lines in the industrial countries are given flexibility for sensitive products, and 4 percent in developing countries for sensitive and special products, the average cut worldwide in bound duties falls from 19 percent to 6 percent. The reduction in applied rates falls by a factor of five, from 5.5 percentage points to 1.1 points. Interestingly, raising the share of sensitive products from 2 percent to 5 percent of tariff lines causes a relatively small additional diminution in market access gains—the real damage is done by the first 2 percent.

If, as experience suggests, it proves to be difficult to agree on boundaries for tiers under a tiered formula, then a proportional cut of the type used for manufactures trade in the Kennedy Round would generate large absolute—if not proportional—reductions in higher tariffs. Jean, Laborde, and Martin explore the implications of using such a formula, set to achieve the same proportional reductions in bound tariffs as the tiered formula. They find that this approach brings about rather similar tariff reduction patterns as a tiered formula, except for in the Republic of Korea, where protection is very high and which needs to make smaller reductions under the proportional-cut approach. Adding a tariff cap—even one set at a very high level such as 200 percent—is found to offset much of the lost benefit of the tiered formula of reducing the overall variability of tariffs.

The SDT provisions in the framework reduce the extent to which developing countries have to cut their bound tariff rates. With SDT, they have to cut by 21 percent; without it they would have to cut by 31 percent. The corresponding reductions in their applied rates are much smaller, however. With SDT, developing-country applied rates would have to decline on average, by 4.3 percent, while without it, the required decline would be 6.9 percent. Given the binding overhang that drives these gaps, a key question for developing-country policy makers is whether the mercantilist "benefits" of smaller tariff reductions justify the resulting loss in the negotiating capital that could be used to demand larger cuts in support in the developed countries.

The market access gains resulting from a tiered formula vary substantially across countries and commodities. The tiered formula used in this chapter would reduce the average applied tariff facing developing countries by 5.2 percent, but it reduces tariffs facing China by an extraordinary 14.8 percent. In terms of commodities, the largest gain would be in cereals, for which the average tariff worldwide would fall by more than half, from 41.2 percent to 19.2 percent. Substantial gains in market access would also be expected for sugar, meat, and dairy products.

Tariff Rate Quotas

Harry de Gorter and Erika Kliauga analyze the key issue of tariff rate quotas in chapter 5. These measures involve a lower, in-quota tariff for a limited volume of imports of a particular product, and a higher, out-of-quota tariff on additional imports of the same product. The chapter shows that TRQs have been implemented by 43 WTO members, on about 20 percent of their tariffs, for a total of 1,425 tariff lines.

However, TRQ products are subject to extraordinarily high tariffs—an average out-of-quota tariff of 115 percent. These products account for an estimated 50 percent of the agricultural production of developed countries and 43 percent of their imports, so clearly TRQs have major implications for developing-county market access. For some products, the importance of TRQs is overwhelming: 95 percent of OECD rice production is protected by TRQ regimes, and 85 percent of OECD wheat imports are regulated using TRQs.

The most effective approach to expanding market access under a TRQ regime is critically determined by whether the level of imports is being determined by the in-quota tariff, the quota, or the out-of-quota tariff. De Gorter and Kliauga show that approximately one-third of the number of quotas are filled, which translates to a trade-weighted average fill rate of 72 percent. Roughly 60 percent of TRQ imports, valued at $25 billion, are subject to a regime in which the out-of-quota tariff determines the level of imports, with a further 20 percent of imports coming under a regime where imports exceed the quota, but are not charged the out-of-quota tariff.

This chapter provides a glimpse into the complexity of the TRQ regime. The three most important means of administering TRQs are the use of applied tariffs, licenses on demand, and first-come, first-served. These forms of administration cover almost 80 percent of total TRQs, and 46 percent of TRQ imports. Yet none of these approaches to quota allocation provide a rational basis for determining who should obtain scarce and valuable rights to import. Only the less widely used forms of allocation, such as historical imports (8.2 percent of TRQs); quota auctioning (4.6 percent); and allocation to favored groups such as producers or state trading enterprises (2.1 percent) have this critical feature.

Despite the importance of out-of-quota tariffs in determining volumes of imports under TRQ regimes, a simulation exercise reported by de Gorter and Kliauga suggests that quota expansion cannot be totally dismissed as a form of market access expansion. Using an elasticity of demand similar to that used in the general equilibrium model of chapter 12, the authors found that a 50 percent increase in TRQ quota levels would generate a 14.5 percent increase in the volume of imports of these goods, while a 35 percent reduction in applied out-of-quota tariffs would result in a 52 percent increase in import volume. Given the complexity and nontransparency of the quota allocation regimes, and the fact that in-quota tariffs are not currently subject to WTO disciplines, there are grounds for concern about how effectively an agreement to expand quotas would be translated into actual import expansion.

Preference Erosion for Developing Countries

Antoine Bouët, Lionel Fontagné, and Sébastien Jean examine the implications of tariff preferences in chapter 6. Their study builds on the major data collection effort undertaken at the Centre d'Etudes Prospectives et d'Informations Internationales and the International Trade Commission. The authors note the large and rapidly growing deviations from the fundamental principle of nondiscrimination contained in Article I of the GATT—primarily as a result of preferential trade agreements, but also through expansion of nonreciprocal preferential arrangements such as Everything But Arms for least developed countries.

They examine the implications of tariff cuts for erosion of preferences. This analysis confirms the widely reported finding that the impact of liberalization on preference margins is large for only a handful of countries, including The Gambia,

Saint Lucia, Malawi, and Burkina Faso. They find that the extent of preference erosion is barely affected by whether the tariff cut is undertaken using a tiered formula or a proportional cut.

Simulation analysis concludes that the inclusion of preferences does change the estimated impact of liberalization, but only to a small extent. The chapter concludes that the current methodology for including tariff preferences in the database overstates their impact because it ignores the costs associated with using preferences—especially the costs of proving compliance and of meeting rules of origin.

Agricultural Export Subsidies

As Bernard Hoekman and Patrick Messerlin make clear in chapter 7, farm export subsidies are inconsistent with GATT rules and for that reason alone deserve to be eliminated. The empirical analysis shows that they are in any case now only a small part of agricultural support programs—even when implicit subsidies in the form of food aid and export credits are included. Their elimination would harm a few food-importing and aid-dependent developing countries, but the poor in those countries can be assisted in far more efficient ways than through these measures. A not overly optimistic scenario for the Doha Round involves a phasing out of most explicit and implicit forms of farm export subsidies over the next decade or so.

This chapter shows that the information in WTO export subsidy notifications is extremely dated and incomplete, presented on a product basis that varies between countries, and frequently inconsistent with national-level data. Clearly, the quality of these data needs to be improved if export subsidies are to be adequately monitored. This information, and national-level data, show substantial variation in export subsidy rates between countries, with the EU by far the dominant user of export subsidies. There is also a great deal of variation between commodities, with some commodities, such as dairy products, being subject to export subsidy rates of more than 100 percent in the EU, while other products, such as wine, receive extremely limited subsidies. There are substantial variations in export subsidy rates over time, highlighting the frequent use of these measures to support domestic prices that are insulated from movements in world prices.

Hoekman and Messerlin also examine estimates of export support provided through other measures subject to negotiation, such as export credits and support to state trading enterprises. While the data are weak, the authors conclude that these measures currently appear to be of little significance relative to explicit export subsidies.

Agricultural Domestic Support Disciplines

In chapter 8, Chad Hart and John Beghin discuss the structure and measurement of the domestic support limits. They point out that the market price support (MPS) element of the aggregate measure of support (AMS) is only loosely related to distorting support, being measured as the difference between an administered domestic price and an historically fixed external reference price. They also show that the importance of this form of support varies considerably from country to country, contributing only 40 percent of domestic support in the United States in recent years, compared with 70 percent in Japan and the EU.

The MPS also double-counts protection provided by administered prices because such protection must be supported by a tariff or export subsidy if it is to be sustainable. Worse, from the viewpoint of enforcing disciplines, the MPS is subject to abuse. Policies can be cosmetically reformed to eliminate the current MPS without substantively changing protection policies or reducing the limits on AMS. A country can eliminate the formal, administered price without changing the support policies used to distort it away from world prices. For countries where a large fraction of support is provided through MPS, this provides a great deal of overhang, enabling limits to be cut without requiring reductions in actual support. There has been much discussion of "box-shifting" in AMS reduction—this process allows the boxes to be vaporized.

Reducing AMS Bindings

In chapter 9, Hans Jensen and Henrik Zobbe ask what AMS reductions are likely to be required, given the current rules on domestic support and current commitments. They use data collected from country notifications to assess the implications of reform. They find that the ability to abolish notified domestic support by moving away from administered domestic support prices creates an enormous amount of "space" for cuts in domestic support in those countries where MPS makes up a large share of total support. For example, in industrial countries with substantial (more than 20 percent) domestic support, even a 75 percent cut in the AMS requires reductions in actual domestic support in only a small number of industrial countries. And because some have already reformed to more than that extent since 2001, only the United States and Norway seem likely to have to reduce their actual domestic supports.

The Cotton Initiative

In chapter 10, Dan Sumner points out that the Cotton Initiative in the Doha Agenda was placed at the center of the negotiations by four small African nations. The remarkable prominence given this initiative reflects several issues, including the increased role of developing countries in the WTO, the importance of cotton exports to a number of small African countries, and the unimportance of preferential market access for this commodity, which is supported primarily through domestic support measures. The initiative proposes gradual elimination of cotton subsidies, as well as compensation in the meantime for the damage they continue to do during the reform process. Reform of the trade-related aspects of U.S. cotton policies, in particular, is likely to be necessary, either as part of the Cotton Initiative or in response to the successful Brazilian dispute settlement challenge to these policies. The compensation elements of the Cotton Initiative could provide worthwhile benefits to the affected countries.

Holograms and Ghosts in Reforming Farm Policies

In chapter 11, David Orden and Eugenio Díaz-Bonilla explore some innovative approaches that governments might use to advance the cause of reform in the face of the powerful domestic interests likely to oppose it. They note that a major theme of recent reform in industrial countries has been the replacement of distorting support with cash-out measures that aim to reduce distortions to production and consumption decisions. They contrast this with a buyout approach that eliminates recurrent support in return for an up-front lump payment, and they examine the generally favorable experience with cash-out measures in the U.S. peanut and tobacco programs. The authors note that WTO commitments could provide a commitment mechanism to ensure that abolition of recurrent distortions is truly permanent.

For developing countries, the authors examine the changes in approaches to policy reform in the period since World War II, beginning with the initial, strong emphasis on industrialization, which frequently involved taxation of agriculture. They note that this pattern changed substantially, with a move toward technological innovation and outward orientation in the 1970s, an emphasis on structural adjustment in the 1980s, and an increased emphasis on targeted poverty alleviation in the 1990s. In the WTO, they note considerable diversity among the positions of developing countries, with some pushing for agricultural reform while others are taking a defensive stance. They conclude that the best approach for development involves a neutral trade and macroeconomic framework, backed by significant nondistortionary interventions and investments needed to overcome market failures and attack poverty problems.

Some Prospective Overall Doha Packages:
Estimating Their Consequences

In the final chapter, Kym Anderson, Will Martin, and Dominique van der Mensbrugghe bring together the evidence from earlier chapters into a synthesis designed to assess the potential impacts of a Doha Round agreement on trade, welfare, income distribution, and poverty. The analysis uses the World Bank's LINKAGE model to assess the impacts of cuts in tariffs, agricultural domestic support, agricultural export subsidies, and liberalization of manufactures, as well as potential gains from the trade facilitation elements of the Doha agreement. The study finds that gains from reform can be huge in dollar terms and that agricultural reforms can contribute more than 60 percent of the total benefits of global goods trade reforms. Various scenarios investigate the effects of different possible modalities, including allowing for exceptional treatment of some sensitive and special farm products, the use of a proportional-cut approach, and incorporation of a tariff cap.

The authors find that developing countries would gain disproportionately from global trade reform, and would also enjoy some poverty alleviation—and that the benefits would be as much from South-South trade reform as from reform in industrial countries. In terms of farm policy, a key finding is that large cuts in both agricultural tariffs and domestic support commitments are required to reduce the binding overhang and contribute to expansion of market access and trade. The authors also find that adding nonagricultural market access is vital to ensuring that a balanced package is obtained. The benefits of even a very aggressive tariff-cutting formula for agriculture would be greatly diminished, however, by an agreement allowing a small percentage of tariff lines to be given lenient treatment on the grounds of their sensitive or special product status.

What also emerges from that modeling analysis is that developing countries would not *have* to reform very much under Doha, because of the large gaps between their tariff bindings and the applied rates. That is even truer if they exercise their right (as laid out in the July Framework Agreement) to undertake smaller tariff cuts than developed countries. In that case, they would gain little in terms of improved efficiency of national resource use. Yet, as Panagariya (2004) and others have warned, reform under Doha could mean that the terms of trade deteriorate for a nontrivial number of low-income countries—some because they would lose tariff preferences on their exports, others because they are net food importers and so would face higher prices for their imports of food. To realize more of their potential gains from trade, developing and least developed countries would need to engage more fully in the Doha reform process, and perhaps also commit to additional unilateral trade (and complementary domestic) reforms as well as invest more in trade facilitation. High-income countries could encourage them to do so by being willing to open up their own markets to more developing-country exports and by providing more targeted aid.

To that end, a new proposal has been put forward to reward developing-country commitments to greater trade reform with an expansion of trade-facilitating aid. The rewards would be provided by a major expansion of the current Integrated

Framework, which is operated by a consortium of international agencies for least developed countries (Hoekman 2005a, 2005b). This may well provide an attractive path for developing countries seeking to trade their way out of poverty, not least because linking aid to greater trade reform would help offset the tendency for an expanded aid flow to cause a real exchange rate appreciation (Commission for Africa 2005, 296–97). As well, it is potentially a far more efficient way for developed countries to assist people in low-income countries than the current systems of tariff preferences.

In conclusion, the July Framework Agreement does not guarantee major gains from the Doha Development Agenda. Even if an agreement is ultimately reached, it may be very modest. How modest depends on, among other things, the nature of the agricultural tariff-cutting formula, the size of the cuts, the extent to which exceptions for sensitive and special products are allowed, whether a tariff cap is introduced, and the extent to which special and differential treatment is invoked by developing countries in terms of their market access commitments. What is clear is that major gains are possible only if the political will can be mustered to reform protectionist policies—especially in agriculture.

Notes

1. GATT rules were intended, in principle, to cover all trade in goods. In practice, however, trade in agricultural products was largely excluded from the GATT rules as a consequence of a number of exceptions. Details are to be found in Josling, Tangermann, and Warley (1996) and in Anderson and Josling (2005).

2. According to the United Nations' Food and Agriculture Organization (FAO), 54 percent of the economically active population in developing countries is engaged in agriculture, which is nearly five times larger than the sector's measured GDP share (FAO 2004, table A4). While some of that difference in shares is due to underreporting of subsistence consumption, the gap nonetheless implies that on average these people are considerably less productive and hence poorer than those employed outside agriculture.

3. Generally throughout this volume we use the term *high-income economies* to include the developed countries, the new Central European members of the EU, and the four Asian "tiger" economies of Hong Kong (China), Republic of Korea, Singapore, and Taiwan (China). The term *developing countries* generally excludes these latter four (and includes other economies in transition). However, in modeling tariff cuts in Doha scenarios, we treat these four Asian tiger economies the same as other developing economies because they have self-nominated to retain that status in the WTO (because it may bestow certain benefits including lesser obligations to cut tariffs).

4. Until recently the PSE referred to the producer subsidy equivalent. For more about the concept and its history, see Legg (2003).

5. This analysis is vastly more sophisticated than the ex ante analyses undertaken for the Uruguay Round. At that time there were very few economywide global models, so analysts relied primarily on partial equilibrium models of world food markets (see, for example, World Bank 1986, Goldin and Knudsen 1990, and Tyers and Anderson 1992). Moreover, estimates of protection rates were somewhat cruder and less complete, and analysts grossly overestimated the gains because they did not anticipate that tariffication would be so "dirty" in the sense of creating large wedges between bound tariff rates and MFN applied tariff rates, nor did they have reliable estimates of the tariff preferences enjoyed by

developing countries or the ad valorem equivalent of specific and compound tariffs. Some of these limitations also applied to ex post analyses of the Uruguay Round (see, for example, Martin and Winters 1996).

6. The evidence is that trade reform in general is also good for economic growth and, partly because of that, for poverty alleviation (Dollar and Kraay 2004; Winters 2004; Winters, McCulloch, and McKay 2004).

7. In our initial empirical analysis, we also included crude estimates of implicit forms of farm export subsidization through such venues as food aid, export credits, or state trading enterprises, but even that was not enough to raise that export subsidy share above 1 percent. The finding that tariffs distort much more than subsidies is not surprising when one recalls that subsidies involve government outlays that are scrutinized annually in the budget process, whereas import tariffs tend to *raise* government revenue.

8. Scenarios 2 and 3 of chapter 12 are not shown in this chapter.

9. The approach here has been to take the change in the average per capita consumption of the poor, apply an estimated income-to-poverty elasticity, and assess the effects on the poverty headcount index. We have done this by calculating the change in the real wage of unskilled workers and deflating it by a food/clothing consumer price index, which is more relevant for the poor than the total price index. That real wage grows, over all developing countries, by 3.6 percent, or more than four times the overall average income increase. We are assuming that the change in unskilled wages is fully passed through to households. Also, while the model closure has the loss in tariff revenues replaced by a change in direct household taxation, the poverty calculation assumes—realistically for many developing countries—that these tax increases affect only skilled workers and high-income households. While these simple calculations are not a substitute for more-detailed individual country case study analysis using detailed household surveys as in, for example, Hertel and Winters (2005), they are able to give a broad, regionwide indication of the poverty impact.

10. As Francois and Martin (2004) have shown, any binding cut is useful for the long run even if it brings no immediate cut in applied rates.

11. This is considerably below the estimate reported in Anderson and others (2001), based on the GTAP Version 5.4 database for 1997, despite the inclusion of liberalization of commercial services in the results presented here from Version 6.05 for 2001. The reasons for the differences include the reductions in global protection between 1997 and 2001, the inclusion of preferences in the latest dataset, and structural changes in the global economy.

References

Aksoy, M. A., and J. C. Beghin, eds. 2004. *Global Agricultural Trade and Developing Countries.* Washington, DC: World Bank.

Anania, G., M. Bowman, C. Carter, and A. McCalla, eds. 2004. *Agricultural Policy Reform and the WTO: Where Are We Heading?* London: Edward Elgar.

Anderson, K., B. Dimaranan, J. Francois, T. Hertel, B. Hoekman, and W. Martin. 2001. "The Burden of Rich (and Poor) Country Protectionism on Developing Countries." *Journal of African Economies* 10 (3, September): 227–57.

Anderson, K., Y. Hayami, and others. 1986. *The Political Economy of Agricultural Protection: East Asia in International Perspective.* Boston: Allen and Unwin.

Anderson, K., and T. E. Josling, eds. 2005. *The WTO and Agriculture.* London: Edward Elgar Publishers.

Anderson, K., W. Martin, and D. van der Mensbrugghe. 2006. "Market and Welfare Implications of Doha Reform Scenarios." In *Agricultural Trade Reform and the Doha Development Agenda*, ed. K. Anderson and W. Martin. Basingstoke, U.K.: Palgrave Macmillan; Washington, DC: World Bank.

Bouët, A., Y. Decreux, L. Fontagné, S. Jean, and D. Laborde. 2004. "A Consistent, ad Valorem Equivalent Measure of Applied Protection across the World: The MAcMap-HS6 Database." CEPII Working Paper, Centre d'Etudes Prospectives et d' Informations Internationales, Paris, December 20.

Bouët, A., L. Fontagné, and S. Jean. 2006. "Is Erosion of Preferences a Serious Concern?" In *Agricultural Trade Reform and the Doha Development Agenda*, ed. K. Anderson and W. Martin. Basingstoke, U.K.: Palgrave Macmillan; Washington, DC: World Bank.

Commission for Africa. 2005 . *Our Common Interest*. London: UK Department for International Development.

de Gorter, H., and E. Kliauga. 2006. "Reducing Tariffs versus Expanding Tariff Rate Quotas." In *Agricultural Trade Reform and the Doha Development Agenda*, ed. K. Anderson and W. Martin. Basingstoke, U.K.: Palgrave Macmillan; Washington, DC: World Bank.

Dollar, D., and A. Kraay. 2004. "Trade, Growth, and Poverty." *Economic Journal* 114 (February): F22–F49.

FAO (Food and Agriculture Organization). 2004. *The State of Food and Agriculture 2003–04*. Rome: FAO.

Finger, J. M., and P. Schuler. 2001. "Implementation of Uruguay Round Commitments: The Development Challenge." In *Developing Countries and the WTO: A Pro-Active Agenda*, ed. B. Hoekman and W. Martin. Oxford: Blackwell.

Finger, J. M., and L. A. Winters. 2002. "Reciprocity in the WTO." In *Development, Trade and the WTO: A Handbook*, ed. B. Hoekman, A. Mattoo, and P. English. Washington, DC: World Bank.

Francois, J. F., and W. Martin. 2004. "Commercial Policy, Bindings and Market Access." *European Economic Review* 48 (3, June): 665–79.

Goldin, I., and O. Knudsen, eds. 1990. *Agricultural Trade Liberalization: Implications for Developing Countries*. Paris: Organisation for Economic Co-operation and Development.

Hart, C. E., and J. C. Beghin. 2006. "Rethinking Agricultural Domestic Support under the World Trade Organization." In *Agricultural Trade Reform and the Doha Development Agenda*, ed. K. Anderson and W. Martin. Basingstoke, U.K.: Palgrave Macmillan; Washington, DC: World Bank.

Hathaway, D., and M. Ingco. 1996. "Agricultural Liberalization and the Uruguay Round." In *The Uruguay Round and the Developing Countries*, ed. W. Martin and L. A. Winters. New York: Cambridge University Press.

Hertel, T. W., and R. Keeney. 2006. "What Is at Stake: The Relative Importance of Import Barriers, Export Subsidies and Domestic Support." In *Agricultural Trade Reform and the Doha Development Agenda*, ed. K. Anderson and W. Martin. Basingstoke, U.K.: Palgrave Macmillan; Washington, DC: World Bank.

Hertel, T. W. and L. A. Winters, eds. 2006. *Poverty and the WTO: Impacts of the Doha Development Agenda*. Basingstoke, U.K.: Palgrave Macmillan; Washington, DC: World Bank.

Hoekman, B. 2005a. "Making the WTO More Supportive of Development." *Finance and Development* 42 (1, March): 14–18.

_____. 2005b. "Operationalizing the Concept of Policy Space in the WTO: Beyond Special and Differential Treatment." *Journal of International Economic Law* 8 (2, June): 377–404.

Hoekman, B., and P. Messerlin. 2006. "Removing the Exception of Agricultural Export Subsidies." In *Agricultural Trade Reform and the Doha Development Agenda*, ed. K. Anderson and W. Martin. Basingstoke, U.K.: Palgrave Macmillan; Washington, DC: World Bank.

Ingco, M. D., and J. D. Nash, eds. 2004. *Agriculture and the WTO: Creating a Trading System for Development*. Washington, DC: World Bank.

Ingco, M. D., and L. A. Winters, eds. 2004. *Agriculture and the New Trade Agenda: Creating a Global Trading Environment for Development*. New York: Cambridge University Press.

Jank, M. S., ed. 2004. *Agricultural Trade Liberalization: Policies and Implications for Latin America*. Washington, DC: Inter-American Development Bank.

Jean, S., D. Laborde, and W. Martin. 2006. "Consequences of Alternative Formulas for Agricultural Tariff Cuts." In *Agricultural Trade Reform and the Doha Development Agenda*, ed. K. Anderson and W. Martin. Basingstoke, U.K.: Palgrave Macmillan; Washington, DC: World Bank.

Jensen, H. G., and H. Zobbe. 2006. "Consequences of Reducing Limits on Aggregate Measures of Support." In *Agricultural Trade Reform and the Doha Development Agenda*, ed. K. Anderson and W. Martin. Basingstoke, U.K.: Palgrave Macmillan; Washington, DC: World Bank.

Josling, T. 2006. "Special and Differential Treatment for Developing Countries." In *Agricultural Trade Reform and the Doha Development Agenda*, ed. K. Anderson and W. Martin. Basingstoke, U.K.: Palgrave Macmillan; Washington, DC: World Bank.

Josling, T. E., S. Tangermann, and T. K. Warley. 1996. *Agriculture in the GATT*. London: Macmillan.

Legg, W. 2003. "Agricultural Subsidies: Measurement and Use in Policy Evaluation." *Journal of Agricultural Economics* 54 (2): 175–200.

Lindert, P. 1991. "Historical Patterns of Agricultural Protection." In *Agriculture and the State*, ed. P. Timmer. Ithaca, NY: Cornell University Press.

Martin, W., and L. A. Winters, eds. 1996. *The Uruguay Round and the Developing Countries*. New York: Cambridge University Press.

Orden, D., and E. Díaz-Bonilla. 2006. "Holograms and Ghosts: New and Old Ideas for Reforming Agricultural Policies." In *Agricultural Trade Reform and the Doha Development Agenda*, ed. K. Anderson and W. Martin. Basingstoke, U.K.: Palgrave Macmillan; Washington, DC: World Bank.

Panagariya, A. 2004. "Subsidies and Trade Barriers: Alternative Perspective 10.2." In *Global Crises, Global Solutions*, ed. B. Lomborg. New York: Cambridge University Press.

Sumner, D. A. 2006. "Reducing Cotton Subsidies: The DDA Cotton Initiative." In *Agricultural Trade Reform and the Doha Development Agenda*, ed. K. Anderson and W. Martin. Basingstoke, U.K.: Palgrave Macmillan; Washington, DC: World Bank.

Tyers, R., and K. Anderson. 1992. *Disarray in World Food Markets: A Quantitative Assessment*. New York: Cambridge University Press.

Winters, L. A. 2004. "Trade Liberalization and Economic Performance: An Overview." *Economic Journal* 114 (February): F4–F21.

Winters, L.A., N. McCulloch, and A. McKay. 2004. "Trade Liberalization and Poverty: The Empirical Evidence." *Journal of Economic Literature* 62 (1, March): 72–115.

World Bank. 1986. *World Development Report 1986*. New York: Oxford University Press.

WTO (World Trade Organization). 2004. "Doha Work Programme: Decision Adopted by the General Council on 1 August 2004." WT/L/579 (July Framework Agreement), WTO, Geneva.

2

WHAT IS AT STAKE: THE RELATIVE IMPORTANCE OF IMPORT BARRIERS, EXPORT SUBSIDIES, AND DOMESTIC SUPPORT

Thomas W. Hertel and Roman Keeney

This chapter provides an estimate of the potential welfare gains from various agricultural and trade policy reforms under the Doha Development Agenda of the World Trade Organization (WTO). Specifically, it explores the differential impacts on trade and economic welfare in developing and other countries of current restrictions on imports of agricultural and other merchandise (and services) by both rich and poor countries, as well as of agricultural export subsidies and domestic support in high-income countries.

There are two main channels through which developing countries would be affected by the removal of current trade distortions. The first is the efficiency gain achieved when a country's own trade distortions are removed, or when it interacts favorably with trade shocks abroad that increase its export prices or reduce its import prices. The efficiency effect stemming from global agricultural trade liberalization is typically positive for participating countries.

The second channel is through a change in a country's international terms of trade. Agricultural trade liberalization generally raises food prices in international markets, particularly for those temperate-zone products that are heavily protected in the high-income countries. This means that the terms of trade improve for countries that are net exporters of protected farm products (unless they are currently enjoying duty-free access to protected markets where domestic prices fall), while net food-importing countries are expected to lose (unless they become sufficient net exporters in the course of adjusting to the new conditions). Long-term subsidies for agricultural program commodities in high-income countries, coupled with agricultural disincentives in many developing countries, have left the latter increasingly dependent on imports of these subsidized products (Dimaranan, Hertel, and Keeney 2004). Thus we expect numerous developing countries would experience terms of trade losses if agricultural tariffs, domestic supports, and export subsidies were to be eliminated by high-income countries.

After examining the welfare effects on developing countries of high-income country liberalization in agriculture under the three agricultural pillars, we also examine the incidence for developing countries of increasing market access for agricultural products in other developing countries. Beyond agriculture, we then look at the additional welfare impacts of nonagricultural market access. Finally, we speculate on the relative contribution of liberalization of direct trade in services as well as trade facilitation measures in enhancing gains to developing countries from the Doha Round.

The Model Used

The predicted incidence of any economic reform depends on the relative supply and demand elasticities in the market being reformed. For example, removal of an agricultural producer subsidy in a market in which demand is elastic and supply is inelastic results in the loss being borne largely by producers of that farm product. Therefore, it is critical to use an analytical framework that pays close attention to the supply and demand characteristics in the markets to be reformed. For purposes of this study, we employed the recently developed model known as the Global Trade Analysis Project-Agriculture, or GTAP-AGR. This is a special-purpose variant of the widely used GTAP model of global trade (Hertel 1997), which has been tailored to analysis of global agricultural trade policy issues (Keeney and Hertel 2005).

As documented on the GTAP Web site, the standard GTAP model includes demand for goods for final consumption, intermediate use and government consumption; demand for factor inputs; supplies of factors and goods; and international trade in goods and services.[1] The model employs the simplistic but robust assumptions of perfect competition and constant returns to scale in production activities. Bilateral international trade flows are handled using the Armington assumption by which products are exogenously differentiated by origin.

From this standard framework, GTAP-AGR incorporates some alternative representations to bring focus on the intricacies of agricultural production and markets. Several structural features have been highlighted in the agricultural economics literature for their importance in analyzing agricultural policy changes: factor mobility and substitution in production; crop-livestock sector interactions; consumer food demand; and trade elasticities. The manner in which each of these features is introduced into the model is detailed in Keeney and Hertel (2005) and is discussed briefly below.

Recent work by the Organisation for Economic Co-operation and Development (OECD 2001) on the cost and world market impacts of agricultural support highlights the role of factor market issues in an empirical, partial equilibrium model. This work focuses on the segmentation that occurs in land, labor, and capital markets between the agricultural and nonagricultural economies, and provides the region-specific factor supply elasticities used to calibrate our model's constant elasticity-of-transformation function that allocates factors between agricultural and nonagricultural uses. We also follow the OECD's factor substitution regime for primary agriculture, focusing on substitution possibilities among farm-owned and purchased inputs, as well as between the two. We calibrate the constant elasticity-of-substitution-cost functions for farm-level sectors to the region-specific Allen elasticities of substitution provided by the OECD.

Interaction between livestock and crop sectors received considerable attention in the literature following reform of the European Common Agricultural Policy (CAP) in 1992 and has continued to be an area of concern (Peeters and Surry 1997). We follow the approach of Rae and Hertel (2000) in modeling the substitution possibilities for feedstuffs in livestock production as an additional CES (constant elasticity-of substitution) nest in the livestock sector cost function. We calibrate this region-generic parameter to an average substitution elasticity calculated from Surry's (1992) three-stage model describing the behavior of European livestock producers, composite feed mixers, and grain producers.

The importance of consumer demand for final goods is prominent in the agricultural economics literature. Estimated consumer demand systems are examined to address a variety of issues including the potential impacts from world price changes accompanying trade liberalization. The unique role of food in the consumer budget has been emphasized in much of this work, especially as it relates to the distribution of incomes (Cranfield 2002; Seale, Regmi, and Bernstein 2003). We employ a recent set of estimates from a cross-country study of demand, keying on own-price and income elasticities of demand for food. We calibrate the parameters of the constant difference elasticity demand system in GTAP to the elasticities for the eight food aggregates and an additional nonfood aggregate derived from the econometric work of Seale, Regmi, and Bernstein (2003).

International trade elasticities that describe the substitution possibilities between goods differentiated by origin have received considerable attention for the important role they play in simulation models determining the effects of liberalization on terms of trade. Hertel and others (2003) provide recent estimates of this substitution relationship at the same level of disaggregation as the sectors in the GTAP model. Those authors also show how the estimated gains from trade liberalization hinge critically on the value of these parameters. We make use of their region-generic estimates of the elasticity of substitution among imported goods from different sources, which is modeled using the Armington/CES structure.[2]

Current Patterns of Merchandise Trade Distortions

In any global economic analysis, some aggregation is required to avoid being overwhelmed by results. Therefore, for reporting summary results we group countries and regions in the GTAP 6 database into three broad sets: high-income countries, transition economies, and developing countries. Table 2.1 provides a listing of all modeled regions and the organization of these regions into the three aggregates. The high-income regions are most of the OECD countries plus the four newly industrialized East Asian "tigers." Transition economies comprise the central and eastern European nations as well as the nations of the former Soviet Union still in the process of becoming market economies and democratic. The level of disaggregation among developing countries represents a mix of focus countries in each region of the world plus composite groupings of remaining countries so that together with high-income and transition economies, they exhaust global economic activity.

The choice of base period is important. For many of the Doha negotiations, 2001 is the relevant reference period. This is convenient, as the newly available GTAP 6 database is also benchmarked to the year 2001. However, some important trade policy commitments are in place that logically precede any Doha agreement, yet were still not in place in 2001. Perhaps the most important of these is the phaseout of export quotas on textiles and apparel shipped to the United States and the European Union, as agreed to in the Uruguay Round. These quotas were abolished at the end of 2004, and their elimination has begun a substantial restructuring of the world textiles and apparel trade. Conducting an analysis of textiles and apparel trade liberalization from a 2001 base could yield very misleading results if it did not take into account the changes to take place by the end of 2004. Similarly, a number of newly acceding WTO members, most notably China, have made commitments that will be implemented only in the coming years. Thus we begin by conducting a "presimulation" that involves implementing those preexisting WTO commitments not implemented as of 2001. We then take the resulting data set from that presimulation as the base for our analysis.

Table 2.2 provides summary of the levels of domestic support for agriculture in a selection of OECD countries, as measured by the OECD's producer support estimates (PSE) database and incorporated in the GTAP database (Dimaranan and

TABLE 2.1 Modeled Regions by Type of Economy

High-income economies
European Union (EU15)
European Free Trade Area (EFTA)
Canada
United States
Mexico
Japan
Korea, Rep. of, and Taiwan (China)
Hong Kong (China) and Singapore
Australia and New Zealand (ANZ)

Transition economies
EU's 10 new entrants
Russian Federation
Other Eastern Europe and former Soviet Union

Developing economies
China
Indonesia
Philippines
Vietnam
Other East Asia (OEAsia)
India
Bangladesh
Other South Asia (OSAsia)
Argentina
Brazil
Other Latin America and Caribbean (OLAC)
Morocco
Other North Africa and Middle East (ONAM)
Southern African Customs Union (SACU)
Mozambique
Other Southern Africa (OSAfrica)
Other Sub-Saharan Africa (OSSA)

Source: Authors' classifications.

McDougall 2005).[3] The first column of Table 2.2 gives the total PSE inclusive of border measures; the second column gives the amount of that total that is explicitly attributable to domestic support. The remaining columns give the fraction of domestic support distinguished by the payment's attribution in the GTAP 6 database.

TABLE 2.2 Agricultural Domestic Support in Selected High-Income Economies

Country/region	Total PSE (2001 US$ millions)	Domestic support PSE, 2001 US$ millions (% of total PSE)	Percentage of domestic support PSE by payment basis			
			Output payments	Input payments	Land payments	Capital payments
EU15	87,734	39,585 (45)	9.2	12.3	47.9	30.6
Switzerland	4,444	1,883 (42)	18.2	4.5	47.1	30.2
Canada	3,977	2,079 (52)	11.4	12.5	72.3	3.8
United States	31,880	31,880 (62)	29.6	22.2	46.9	1.3
Mexico	7,271	2,631 (36)	17.1	19.6	49.0	14.4
Japan	45,423	4,604 (10)	37.5	21.3	20.9	25.3
Korea, Rep. of	16,680	967 (6)	0.0	18.1	51.4	30.5
ANZ	818	815 (100)	3.2	60.0	31.3	5.5

Source: OECD's PSE/CSE database (http://www.oecd.org).

For Japan and the Republic of Korea, we see that in 2001 the majority of protection was still at the border so that domestic support for these countries is minimal. In contrast, the entire PSE in Australia and New Zealand, which is very modest, is based on domestic programs. Of the remaining countries, between one- and two-thirds of assistance is domestic support. In these regions we see that the majority of payments are attached to land and capital usage, reflecting the push for decoupling in the wake of the Uruguay Round Agreement on Agriculture. Keep in mind that this aggregate measure could mask considerable domestic protection for specific products, such as sugar, that are important for developing-country welfare impacts.

Export subsidies reported to the WTO for the 2001 base period are taken from the GTAP 6 database, as assembled by Aziz Elbehri of the U.S. Department of

Agriculture's Economic Research Service. The EU is the main user of export subsidies. Indeed, among the GTAP farm and food products grouped together for this study, only cattle and vegetable oils are not supported by an export subsidy from the EU. The United States makes little use of export subsidies in trade promotion, preferring to use export credits, the impact of which is explored here as a sensitivity analysis, since the export subsidy equivalent of such credits, as well as state trading and food aid, are rather speculative and so are not included in the GTAP database.

Import tariffs for the 2001 base period in the GTAP 6 database are sourced from the MAcMap database maintained in Paris by the Centre d'Etudes Prospectives et d'Informations Internationales (CEPII). MAcMap is the most comprehensive tariff database currently available. It is maintained at the HS-6 digit level and encompasses preferential tariffs, specific tariffs, and tariff rate quotas.[4] Table 2.3 summarizes the average (trade-weighted) tariff rates applied by high-income countries, transition economies, and developing countries (the three columns of this table) on imports from one another, by four broad product categories

TABLE 2.3 Average Applied Import Tariffs, by Sector and Region, 2001 (percent, ad valorem equivalent)

	Importing region		
Exporting region	High-income economies	Transition economies	Developing economies
Agriculture			
High-income	8.4	16.8	18.8
Transition	10.3	10.3	17.4
Developing	15.9	17.2	18.3
Other primary			
High-income	0.2	0.8	4.8
Transition	0.1	0.3	1.7
Developing	0.7	0.4	3.4
Textiles and apparel			
High-income	3.4	6.4	18.2
Transition	1.8	6.5	30.9
Developing	8.4	16.2	20.5
Other manufactures			
High-income	1.0	3.7	9.9
Transition	0.8	4.0	8.7
Developing	1.3	6.0	9.2

Source: GTAP Version 6 database (http://www.gtap.org).

(table rows): agricultural and processed food products, other primary products, textiles and apparel, and other manufactured products.

The easiest way to understand the entries in table 2.3 is to walk through some specific examples. Consider the numbers in the upper left-hand cell of the table. These report that the average tariff on agricultural imports by high-income countries from other high-income countries is 8.4 percent. By contrast, the average tariff on developing-country exports to high-income markets is nearly twice as high at 15.9 percent. Since the MAcMap database includes preferences for developing countries, this result is particularly surprising. Two factors explain it, however. First, developing countries tend to export products (such as sugar) that face relatively high tariffs in high-income countries. Therefore, when we aggregate across all products within agriculture, the developing countries face higher trade-weighted average tariffs. The second reason for higher tariffs on developing-country exports is the prevalence of specific tariffs in agriculture. These tariffs are specified in dollars per unit of product rather than as a percent of the value of imports. Since developing countries tend to export lower-value products within any given tariff category, the ad valorem tariff equivalent associated with any given specific tariff tends to be a larger share of the unit value of imports from developing countries.

Moving across the top of table 2.3, we come next to the average tariffs levied on agricultural imports into the transition economies. Here, imports from high-income and developing countries face similar tariffs of about 17 percent, with a lower rate on intraregional trade within this group of countries—presumably attributable to trade agreements. The overall level of agriculture tariffs in the transition economies in 2001 is higher than that in the high-income economies, and nearly as high as that in developing countries (final column). In the developing countries the overall average tariffs are quite similar across export sources.

Other primary products face low tariffs worldwide, while textile and apparel products face high average tariffs. Once again, as for the heavily protected agricultural sector, we see the pattern of much higher average tariffs levied by the high-income countries against developing countries (8.4 percent) than they impose on other high-income countries (3.4 percent). The same applies for the transition economies' tariffs on textiles and apparel. Developing-country tariffs on these products are much higher still, reaching an average of 30 percent in the case of imports from transition economies. For other manufactures, the OECD average tariff is roughly one-third of the transition economies' tariff average, which is in turn about one-third of the tariff applied by developing countries (around 9 percent).

Table 2.4 disaggregates developing-country tariffs by individual country or region in the model we are using for this study. Note the relatively high average rate of protection for agriculture in Vietnam, India, Other South Asia, Morocco, and Other Southern Africa countries. In textiles and apparel, Vietnam, India,

TABLE 2.4 Average Import Tariffs in Developing Countries (percent, ad valorem equivalent)

Importing region	Agriculture and food	Textiles and apparel	Other merchandise
China	9.6	9.6	5.5
Indonesia	5.0	7.9	4.4
Philippines	9.5	6.5	2.2
Vietnam	36.6	28.8	12.2
OEAsia	22.6	13.5	6.2
India	50.1	26.6	25.4
Bangladesh	12.7	30.1	16.0
OSAsia	21.4	7.2	13.5
Argentina	6.9	11.1	10.1
Brazil	5.0	14.7	9.7
OLAC	10.7	12.8	8.3
Morocco	29.4	38.7	15.3
ONAM	12.8	26.4	6.8
SACU	7.8	19.6	4.9
Mozambique	13.4	21.8	8.4
OSAfrica	23.7	14.9	16.3
OSSA	20.9	27.8	13.2

Source: GTAP Version 6 database (http://www.gtap.org).

Bangladesh, Morocco, Other North Africa and Middle East (ONAM), Mozambique, and Other Sub-Saharan Africa (OSSA) all have average import barriers in excess of 20 percent. In other merchandise trade, India stands out with a 2001 average tariff rate of 25 percent, a full 10 percentage points above the other regions in this database. Removal of these import barriers would generate very substantial import flows, which in turn would require significant export increases to pay for them.

Implications of Merchandise Trade Liberalization for Developing Countries' Trade

We now combine the database discussed in the previous section with the GTAP-AGR modeling framework discussed earlier to project the impact of full merchandise trade and subsidy reform on developing-country trade flows. Table 2.5 reports the predicted percentage change in imports, by region and broad commodity category (with changes in trade volumes reported in parentheses). As expected, Vietnam, India, Other South Asia, Morocco, and Other Southern Africa

TABLE 2.5 Percentage Change in Developing Country Imports from Removing All Tariffs and Agricultural Subsidies

Importing region	Agriculture and food	Textiles and apparel	Other merchandise
China	21 (3,432)	47 (60,147)	16 (40,487)
Indonesia	13 (898)	42 (5,213)	9 (4,051)
Philippines	19 (431)	31 (1,086)	2 (619)
Vietnam	53 (1,531)	66 (3,498)	19 (849)
OEAsia	34 (6,377)	49 (7,059)	10 (14,013)
India	89 (6,035)	119 (18,046)	54 (14,008)
Bangladesh	18 (85)	80 (4,315)	22 (143)
OSAsia	42 (1,107)	24 (2,710)	21 (628)
Argentina	18 (2,365)	35 (431)	22 (2,701)
Brazil	30 (4,945)	66 (2,178)	28 (10,860)
OLAC	16 (4,114)	28 (3,218)	11 (8,344)
Morocco	50 (836)	60 (1,663)	29 (992)
ONAM	10 (847)	35 (3,070)	9 (17,548)
SACU	27 (1,279)	39 (489)	12 (4,034)
Mozambique	14 (26)	18 (1)	3 (18)
OSAfrica	27 (1,279)	39 (489)	12 (4,034)
OSSA	25 (2,199)	32 (322)	13 (3,510)
Developing countries total	(37,852)	(113,789)	(124,626)
World total	18 (88,252)	31 (150,653)	5 (232,927)

Source: Authors' simulations.
Note: Numbers in parentheses are volume changes in 2001 US$ millions.

top the list, with import increases in excess of 40 percent following full global merchandise trade reform. The percentage increases in textiles and apparel imports are even higher, reaching a maximum of 119 percent in India. This results from a higher degree of substitutability of imports sourced from different suppliers than is the case for food. Also, there is a great deal of intermediate input trade in this relatively "footloose" industry, and so when export opportunities open up elsewhere, imports must rise in order to fuel the increased production for sale overseas. Note that India also tops the list in the total rise in imports.

Table 2.6 reports the export volume changes. Unlike for imports, gross exports of some composite commodities fall. These declines include agriculture and food in Vietnam, textiles and apparel in much of Latin America as well as Other Southern Africa, and other merchandise trade in Indonesia and Brazil. China's agricultural exports rise by nearly 50 percent as trade barriers in China's trading partners in East Asia fall. However, the resulting volume change is no larger than that for other merchandise trade, which rises by only 3 percent. That is because the base level of exports is much lower for agriculture. Agriculture and food exports of South Asia rise by a similar rate as imports into that region, with the largest increase in India, followed by Other South Asia and finally Bangladesh. There are also strong export increases in Brazil and North Africa (particularly Morocco) as well as in Southern Africa.

Textiles and apparel exports rise strongly for countries in South and Southeast Asia—particularly Vietnam, the Philippines, and Bangladesh. The ONAM region and parts of Sub-Saharan Africa also experience large percentage increases, although the export base in the latter countries is quite small (for example, Mozambique, where the 80 percent rise accounts for only about one-tenth of the total export volume increase in the region following global liberalization). Outside of South Asia, the export increases for other merchandise trade are quite modest.

Trade volume changes are not a reliable indicator of the resulting changes in national welfare, which also depend on the prices at which trade is taking place (the terms of trade) and the way in which these trade flows are interacting with each countries' own policies (efficiency effects). Accordingly, we now turn to the welfare effects of global trade reform, starting with agricultural reforms and then moving on to nonagricultural trade liberalization.

Welfare Effects of Agricultural Trade Reforms

What is the distribution of gains and losses from each of the three pillars of agricultural protection in the high-income economies? The first three rows of table 2.7 report the impacts on the high-income, transition, developing-country groupings, and on the world, of full liberalization of agricultural tariffs (market access),

TABLE 2.6 Percentage (and Volume) Change in Developing Country Exports from Removing All Tariffs and Agricultural Subsidies

Exporting region	Agriculture and food	Textiles and apparel	Other merchandise
China	48 (7,669)	29 (36,733)	3 (7,883)
Indonesia	17 (1,134)	25 (3,160)	−1 (−275)
Philippines	13 (310)	47 (1,649)	0 (40)
Vietnam	−10 (−298)	70 (3,710)	7 (308)
OEAsia	35 (6,662)	24 (3,436)	4 (6,110)
India	88 (6,030)	31 (4,773)	57 (14,669)
Bangladesh	24 (116)	50 (2,697)	41 (272)
OSAsia	44 (1,170)	13 (1,465)	35 (1,040)
Argentina	11 (1,514)	−17 (−212)	12 (1,403)
Brazil	50 (8,281)	−17 (−564)	−2 (−689)
OLAC	22 (5,582)	33 (3,862)	6 (4,917)
Morocco	75 (1,235)	77 (2,136)	22 (742)
ONAM	47 (3,940)	61 (5,267)	5 (9,625)
SACU	38 (1,838)	8 (106)	0 (161)
Mozambique	13 (24)	79 (4)	5 (24)
OSAfrica	41 (1,321)	−5 (−48)	4 (331)
OSSA	21 (1,786)	53 (527)	12 (3,340)
Developing countries total	(48,314)	(68,700)	(49,884)
World total	21 (96,048)	19 (87,005)	5 (228,640)

Source: Authors' simulations.
Note: Numbers in parentheses are volume changes in 2001 US$ millions.

TABLE 2.7 Regional Welfare Effects of Removing All Agricultural Tariffs and Subsidies (2001 US$ millions equivalent variation in income)

Agricultural liberalization component	Beneficiary region			
	High-income economies	Transition economies	Developing economies	World
High-income liberalization of import market access	31,811	1,608	10,376	43,795
Export subsidies	2,554	−488	−1,023	1,043
Domestic support	2,450	76	284	2,809
Transition economies' market access liberalization	847	495	476	1,818
Developing countries' market access liberalization	3,908	468	1,817	6,193
Total agricultural liberalization	41,569	2,160	11,930	55,658

Source: Authors' simulations.

export subsidies, and domestic support by high-income countries.[5] Note from the final column that market access is the dominant source of gains for the world as a whole. Of the total $44 billion gain from freeing agricultural market access, about one-quarter accrues to the developing countries, which is well above those countries' one-sixth share of global gross domestic product (GDP) in 2001.

Not surprisingly, elimination of export subsidies in the high-income economies hurts the other regions, as numerous countries in those regions have come to depend on cheap food imports and are now net importers of the subsidized products (particularly grains and dairy). Thus, of the $2.55 billion gain to high-income economies from eliminating their export subsidies, about $1.5 billion is a transfer from transition economies and developing countries. Removal of high-income economies' domestic farm support, in contrast, benefits all regional groupings (although, as we see below, not all individual developing countries).

Agricultural trade liberalization in the transition economies and in developing countries would generate $1.8 billion and $6.2 billion, respectively, for the world as a whole. Developing countries retain about 26–30 percent of these global gains.

In sum, the aggregate distribution of global welfare gains from agricultural liberalization is roughly 75 percent for high-income economies and 21 percent for the developing countries, the rest going to transition economies.

A more disaggregated view of global agricultural reform, shown for our 17 countries or regions in table 2.8, exposes the heterogeneity of impacts. In the case of tariff removal by high-income economies (first column), the results suggest that Indonesia, Vietnam, Bangladesh, and Mozambique would lose slightly due to the dominance of preference erosion over increased export demand for their agricultural products. The only developing countries or regions to gain from elimination of farm export subsidies are Argentina, Brazil, and India, but the overall loss to developing countries is just $1 billion.[6] Numerous East and South Asian countries lose from cuts to domestic support, as does the Middle East and North Africa region, with the lion's share of the gains again accruing to Argentina and Brazil.

Columns 4 and 5 of table 2.8 report the welfare impact on developing countries of removing agricultural distortions in the transition economies and in the developing countries themselves. The developing-country impacts of transition economy reforms, including both tariff cuts and the elimination of some domestic support and export subsidies, are generally positive but modest compared with the impacts of developing countries' own reforms. While not all developing countries gain in the latter case, in all but two regions where a loss appears (Vietnam and Sub-Saharan Africa), it is offset by gains in the other columns of table 2.8.

In aggregate, six developing countries or regions experience an overall loss following agricultural liberalization: the Philippines, Vietnam, Bangladesh, ONAM, Mozambique, and OSSA. The losses to ONAM and OSSA are clearly driven by the elimination of export subsidies. In the other regions, however, the sources of loss are more varied. Because some of these economies are expected to have a comparative advantage in nonagricultural products, it is important to see whether adding nonagricultural trade reform will reverse those negative outcomes.

Welfare Impacts of Freeing Nonagricultural Market Access

Table 2.9 provides an overview of the impacts of full liberalization of nonagricultural tariffs on the three broad country groups. Because of the vastly higher average tariff levels in textiles and apparel (recall tables 2.3 and 2.4), we separate out these effects from other nonagricultural merchandise trade. As can be seen by comparing the world totals in the last three rows of table 2.9, adding nonagricultural market access boosts the comparative static global welfare gains by nearly $29 billion. Unlike the case of agricultural reform, however, the majority of the aggregate gains (nearly $15 billion) are generated as a result of reform in the developing countries themselves.

The distribution of these global welfare effects varies considerably by type of reform: nonagricultural merchandise trade liberalization by high-income economies benefits largely the developing countries, whereas developing-country cuts benefit the high-income economies. Overall, the move from agriculture-only to full merchandise trade reform nearly doubles the estimated benefits to developing countries, with most of the additional benefit coming from textiles and apparel reform.[7] By contrast, the increases in benefits accruing to the high-income and transition economies are proportionately much less.

Table 2.10 provides the 17-region breakout of the developing-country aggregate considered in table 2.9. The first column in this table reports the agricultural total from table 2.8, while the other columns show the impact of nonagricultural market access opening. In China and India, the opening of nonagricultural markets boosts gains by a factor of ten. In the case of China, most of these gains are from textiles and apparel, while for Indonesia the additional gains come from a broader range of merchandise trade. Vietnam experiences a dramatic turn of events, with its small loss becoming a large gain, illustrating the virtue of an economywide trade agreement: countries that lose in one sector may well gain in others. Countries in the Middle East and North Africa also experience a strong turnaround, with their loss becoming a gain in the wake of nonagricultural reform. However, OSSA experiences a larger loss, and Other Latin America (outside of Argentina and Brazil) sees an elimination of its agricultural gain.

Further insight into the sources of losses for the five regions that show a negative total in table 2.10 can be obtained by referring to table 2.11, which decomposes the welfare impact of each type of reform into its efficiency and terms-of-trade components. With minor exceptions, the efficiency contributions are nearly always positive. So it is the terms-of-trade component that is causing the loss of welfare for individual regions. Of course, one region's terms-of-trade loss is another's terms-of-trade gain and, as a group, the terms of trade for developing countries improve slightly as a result of merchandise trade reform. There is considerable variation across countries, however. Among the losers from merchandise trade reform, Bangladesh and OSSA lose across the board. The Philippines loses from agriculture and apparel, as does Mozambique, while Latin America's terms-of-trade loss is dominated by textiles and apparel liberalization.

The persistent losses to this group of developing countries in the face of merchandise trade reform raises the question of whether some other parts of a trade liberalization package might provide an offsetting gain. Towards this end, we now turn to the potential liberalization of services trade, as well as measures to facilitate trade flows in and out of developing countries.

TABLE 2.8 Developing Countries' Welfare Gains from Removing All Agricultural Tariffs and Subsidies (2001 US$ millions equivalent variation in income)

Benefiting region	High-income economies' agricultural liberalization		
	Market access	Export subsidies	Domestic support
China	1,141	−78	−428
Indonesia	−9	−19	−43
Philippines	11	−36	−67
Vietnam	−19	−2	51
OEAsia	807	−29	66
India	409	13	72
Bangladesh	−16	−9	−31
OSAsia	34	−9	4
Argentina	444	75	503
Brazil	4,302	24	649
OLAC	1,580	−112	−26
Morocco	232	−55	−32
ONAM	770	−547	−528
SACU	441	−17	46
Mozambique	−8	−1	1
OSAfrica	151	−33	23
OSSA	107	−189	22
Developing countries total	10,376	−1,023	284

Services Trade Liberalization and Merchandise Trade Facilitation

Thus far we have only discussed liberalization of merchandise trade. Because of the growing importance of services trade to the world economy, however, the Uruguay Round delivered the General Agreement on Trade in Services (GATS) to facilitate liberalization in this sector. Negotiations in this area have proven difficult, particularly with respect to foreign direct investment (commercial presence for the provision of services) and temporary labor migration (the "movement of natural persons" to provide services). Leaving those two areas aside, Francois, van Meijl, and van Tongeren (2003) estimate the tariff equivalent of barriers to direct trade in services (such as transportation services and business services). From these estimates it is clear that some markets are highly restrictive across the board, most notably India and South Africa, while others appear to restrict services trade

TABLE 2.8 (*Continued*)

Transition economies' agricultural liberalization (market access)	Developing countries' agricultural liberalization (market access)	Agriculture total
23	−98	560
2	155	85
1	5	−85
−5	−32	−7
39	1,252	2,135
6	774	1,275
−6	12	−50
172	30	231
42	72	1,137
109	−45	5,039
70	−432	1,079
0	−55	92
0	115	−190
8	50	529
0	3	−6
38	95	275
−22	−84	−167
476	1,817	11,930

Source: Authors' simulations.

only in selected sectors (for example, China's imports of business services or North America's imports of transport services).

Even though these estimates are highly speculative, it is worth exploring the potential impact of their removal on global trade and welfare. We find that adding services trade liberalization boosts the global gains by 80 percent, from the $84 billion shown in table 2.9 to more than $150 billion. The distribution of these gains is rather uneven, however, with the lion's share going to high-income economies. Figure 2.1 contrasts the developing-country impact of standard merchandise trade and subsidies reform with the combination of services liberalization and merchandise reform. As can be seen from this comparison, India, which currently has extremely high barriers to services trade, shows a large gain from adding services, as does the Southern African Customs Union. The gains to other regions are quite a bit smaller, but they are positive for all the developing countries or regions. And they are sufficient to reverse the aggregate losses for Latin America,

TABLE 2.9 Developing Countries' Welfare Gains from Removing All Nonagricultural Tariffs, Agricultural Assistance, and Merchandise Trade Distortions (2001 US$ millions equivalent variation in income)

Nonagricultural liberalizing region/component	Beneficiary region			
	High-income economies	Transition economies	Developing economies	World
High-income economies				
Textiles and apparel	−3,421	−338	7,783	4,024
Other merchandise	5,521	356	2,500	8,378
Transition economies				
Textiles and apparel	43	−42	480	481
Other merchandise	755	159	292	1,207
Developing countries				
Textiles and apparel	4,709	92	511	5,312
Other merchandise	10,271	420	−1,413	9,278
Nonagricultural liberalization total (sum of above rows)	17,878	647	10,153	28,680
Agricultural liberalization total (from table 2.7)	41,569	2,160	11,930	55,658
All merchandise liberalization total	59,447	2,807	22,083	84,338

Source: Authors' simulations.

but not the losses for the Philippines, Bangladesh, Mozambique, and Other Sub-Saharan Africa.

One of the main reasons for the absence of welfare gains in parts of Sub-Saharan Africa, following trade liberalization, is the region's relatively low level of current participation in the global trading system. Many of the countries in the region are landlocked, and nearly all of them have very high trade costs associated with both imports and exports. This naturally brings up the issue of trade facilitation, which is the one "Singapore issue" on the Doha agenda. Our final posed question, which we now address, is: What is the possibility of the addition of trade facilitation reversing the negative welfare outcomes for parts of Sub-Saharan Africa?

To explore this question, we draw on the recent work of Wilson, Mann, and Otsuki (2004). Hertel (2004) has incorporated their estimates into a global general equilibrium modeling framework, and it is this work that we draw on in this chapter.[8] In particular, we lower the trading costs for developing countries in line with the Wilson, Mann, and Otsuki scenario in which developing countries are brought halfway to the global average level in indexes relating to port facilities,

FIGURE 2.1 Welfare Gains for Developing Countries from Freeing Trade in Services and from Trade Facilitation Compared with the Standard Removal of Merchandise Tariffs and Subsidies

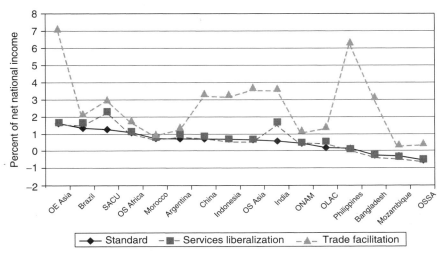

Source: Authors' calculations.

customs and regulatory procedures, and e-commerce. Based on the trade volume changes from this scenario, Hertel (2004) estimates reductions in c.i.f. (cost, insurance, and freight) prices for exports from several broad regions, which we apply as reduced trade costs for imports in these regions. The percentage cost reductions introduced to the model for this final experiment are as follows: East Asia, 9.6; South Asia, 13.2; Latin America, 3.4; Central Europe, 4.17; North Africa, 0.5; and Sub-Saharan Africa, 1.6. Wilson, Mann, and Otsuki (2004) and Hertel (2004) report estimates only for manufactures, but for purposes of this study we adopt their estimates for agricultural products as well.

The welfare impacts are displayed in figure 2.1. The combined liberalization of merchandise and services trade of $150 billion is boosted by $110 billion a year with the addition of trade facilitation. However, unlike trade policy reform, which has few direct economic costs, trade facilitation requires substantial investments in infrastructure, ports, and customs personnel. As such, that gross flow of benefits must be weighed against the potential up-front costs. But note that the distribution of benefits from trade facilitation is much more heavily skewed toward developing countries than are those from trade barrier reductions. Indeed, these gains are sufficient to reverse the losses for the Philippines, Bangladesh, Mozambique, and Other Sub-Saharan Africa.

TABLE 2.10 Welfare Effects of Liberalizing All Merchandise Trade (2001 US$ millions equivalent variation in income)

Benefiting region	Agricultural liberalization	Textiles and apparel liberalization		
		High-income	Transition	Developing
China	560 (0.05)	4,549 (0.43)	214 (0.02)	−436 (−0.04)
Indonesia	85 (0.06)	316 (0.24)	2 (0.00)	−23 (−0.02)
Philippines	−85 (−0.13)	308 (0.48)	−2 (0.00)	−38 (−0.06)
Vietnam	−7 (−0.02)	783 (2.68)	85 (0.29)	539 (1.84)
OEAsia	2,135 (0.86)	503 (0.20)	4 (0.00)	−247 (−0.10)
India	1,275 (0.29)	487 (0.11)	17 (0.00)	−321 (−0.07)
Bangladesh	−50 (−0.12)	10 (0.02)	−5 (−0.01)	−41 (−0.10)
OSAsia	231 (0.25)	209 (0.23)	−3 (0.00)	−142 (−0.16)
Argentina	1,137 (0.47)	43 (0.02)	1 (0.00)	−52 (−0.02)
Brazil	5,039 (1.13)	133 (0.03)	0 (0.00)	−181 (−0.04)
OLAC	1,079 (0.20)	770 (0.14)	−2 (0.00)	−488 (−0.09)
Morocco	92 (0.30)	−127 (−0.42)	6 (0.02)	143 (0.47)
ONAM	−190 (−0.03)	−182 (−0.02)	162 (0.02)	1,795 (0.24)
SACU	529 (0.49)	25 (0.02)	0 (0.00)	38 (0.04)
Mozambique	−6 (−0.18)	−1 (−0.03)	0 (0.00)	2 (0.06)
OSAfrica	275 (0.72)	−10 (−0.03)	0 (0.00)	−27 (−0.07)
OSSA	−167 (−0.12)	−33 (−0.02)	1 (0.00)	−10 (−0.01)
Developing countries total	11,930 (0.27)	7,783 (0.18)	480 (0.01)	511 (0.01)

TABLE 2.10 (*Continued*)

Other manufactures liberalization			
High-income	Transition	Developing	All merchandise, total
1,355 (0.13)	192 (0.02)	−1,066 (−0.10)	5,369 (0.51)
93 (0.07)	−4 (0.00)	195 (0.15)	666 (0.50)
−208 (−0.33)	0 (0.00)	−18 (−0.03)	−43 (−0.07)
56 (0.19)	−2 (−0.01)	458 (1.57)	1,911 (6.54)
18 (0.01)	24 (0.01)	1,106 (0.45)	3,543 (1.43)
48 (0.01)	26 (0.01)	142 (0.03)	1,673) (0.38)
−19 (−0.05)	−2 (0.00)	−87 (−0.21)	−194 (−0.47)
0 (0.00)	6 (0.01)	117 (0.13)	418 (0.46)
56 (0.02)	−14 (−0.01)	105 (0.04)	1,275 (0.52)
538 (0.12)	−18 (0.00)	−362 (−0.08)	5,149 (1.16)
−66 (−0.01)	12 (0.00)	−1,425 (−0.26)	−120 (−0.02)
5 (0.02)	3 (0.01)	42 (0.14)	163 (0.54)
−190 (0.08)	583 (0.01)	78 (−0.06)	−420 1,826 (0.24)
116 (0.11)	−13 (−0.01)	463 (0.43)	1,158 (1.08)
−6 (−0.18)	0 (0.00)	−6 (−0.18)	−17 (−0.52)
−22 (−0.06)	−5 (−0.01)	135 (0.35)	345 (0.90)
−47 (−0.03)	11 (0.01)	−790 (−0.58)	−1,034 (−0.76)
2,500 (0.06)	294 (0.01)	−1,411 (−0.03)	22,088 (0.50)

Source: Authors' simulations.
Note: Numbers in parentheses show welfare effects as percentages of net national income.

TABLE 2.11 Welfare Decomposition from Merchandise Trade Liberalization for Developing Countries (2001 US$ millions equivalent variation in income)

Benefiting region	Total (all products)	Total (all products) Efficiency	Total (all products) Terms of trade	Agriculture and food Efficiency	Agriculture and food Terms of trade
China	5,369 (0.51)	1,889 (0.18)	3,481 (0.33)	−138 (−0.01)	698 (0.07)
Indonesia	666 (0.50)	135 (0.10)	529 (0.40)	−1 (0.00)	86 (0.06)
Philippines	−43 (−0.07)	277 (0.43)	−320 (−0.50)	159 (0.25)	−245 (−0.38)
Vietnam	1,911 (6.54)	742 (2.54)	1,171 (4.00)	150 (0.51)	−157 (−0.54)
OEAsia	3,543 (1.43)	2,074 (0.84)	1,469 (0.59)	1,260 (0.51)	875 (0.35)
India	1,673 (0.38)	4,430 (1.01)	−2,757 (−0.63)	1,431 (0.33)	−156 (−0.04)
Bangladesh	−194 (−0.47)	361 (0.88)	−555 (−1.36)	67 (0.16)	−117 (−0.29)
OSAsia	418 (0.46)	547 (0.60)	−129 (−0.14)	188 (0.21)	43 (0.05)
Argentina	1,275 (0.52)	327 (0.13)	948 (0.39)	104 (0.04)	1,033 (0.42)
Brazil	5,149 (1.16)	1,472 (0.33)	3,678 (0.83)	497 (0.11)	4,542 (1.02)
OLAC	−120 (−0.02)	1,287 (0.24)	−1,407 (−0.26)	426 (0.08)	653 (0.12)
Morocco	163 (0.54)	612 (2.03)	−450 (−1.49)	128 (0.42)	−37 (−0.12)
ONAM	1,826 (0.24)	4,430 (0.59)	−2,605 (−0.34)	982 (0.13)	−1,172 (−0.15)
SACU	1,158 (1.08)	532 (0.50)	626 (0.58)	219 (0.20)	310 (0.29)
Mozambique	−17 (−0.52)	11 (0.34)	−28 (−0.85)	6 (0.18)	−12 (−0.37)
OSAfrica	345 (0.90)	482 (1.26)	−138 (−0.36)	167 (0.44)	108 (0.28)
OSSA	−1,034 (−0.76)	906 (0.67)	−1,941 (−1.43)	432 (0.32)	−599 (−0.44)
Developing countries total	22,088 (0.50)	20,513 (0.47)	1,569 (0.04)	6,077 (0.14)	5,852 (0.13)

TABLE 2.11 (*Continued*)

Textiles and clothing		Other merchandise	
Efficiency	Terms of trade	Efficiency	Terms of trade
872	3,456	1,155	−673
(0.08)	(0.33)	(0.11)	(−0.06)
38	257	98	186
(0.03)	(0.19)	(0.07)	(0.14)
10	258	108	−333
(0.02)	(0.40)	(0.17)	(−0.52)
285	1,123	307	205
(0.97)	(3.84)	(1.05)	(0.70)
157	103	657	491
(0.06)	(0.04)	(0.27)	(0.20)
197	−14	2,802	−2,587
(0.05)	(0.00)	(0.64)	(−0.59)
218	−254	76	−184
(0.53)	(−0.62)	(0.19)	(−0.45)
38	26	321	−198
(0.04)	(0.03)	(0.35)	(−0.22)
48	−56	175	−29
(0.02)	(−0.02)	(0.07)	(−0.01)
46	−93	929	−771
(0.01)	(−0.02)	(0.21)	(−0.17)
364	−84	497	−1,976
(0.07)	(−0.02)	(0.09)	(−0.36)
240	−219	244	−194
(0.79)	(−0.73)	(0.81)	(−0.64)
2,523	−748	925	−685
(0.33)	(−0.10)	(0.12)	(−0.09)
127	−64	186	380
(0.12)	(−0.06)	(0.17)	(0.35)
1	0	4	−16
(0.03)	(0.00)	(0.12)	(−0.49)
26	−64	289	−182
(0.07)	(−0.17)	(0.75)	(−0.47)
205	−247	269	−1095
(0.15)	(−0.18)	(1.86)	(−0.81)
5,394	3,380	9042	−7663
(0.12)	(0.08)	(0.21)	(−0.17)

Source: Authors' simulations, using the welfare decomposition technique developed by Huff and Hertel (2000).

Note: Numbers in parentheses show welfare decomposition as percentages of net national income.

Summary and Conclusions

This chapter is intended to provide an overview of the potential gains that are available from further liberalization of the multilateral trading system as we enter the next multilateral trade negotiations. It provides an upper limit on what developing (and other) countries can expect to achieve from the negotiations—leaving aside dynamic and pro-competitive gains from trade, which we do not attempt to measure.

Our results show that the effects on developing countries from multilateral trade liberalization exhibit a great deal of diversity. In terms of agricultural reforms, the vast majority of potential gains to developing countries derive from improved market access. This is reinforced by the finding that only three developing countries sustain a net loss from improved market access. The other two agricultural pillars offer much smaller prospects for gains to the developing world, and the individual country welfare changes are split between winners and losers. This is because removal of domestic support and export subsidies tend to raise world food prices and reduce domestic prices in high-income economies, thereby reducing welfare in regions that have become dependent on importing farm products or on preferential markets for their exports, while net exporters of farm products less dependent on preferences gain.

While much of the Doha debate has focused on agricultural disciplines, our full liberalization experiment indicates that other merchandise liberalization also is important, providing nearly half of the total welfare gain for the developing-country aggregate. Of equal importance is the role of merchandise liberalization in reversing or offsetting welfare losses in regions dependent on low international food prices or preferential access to protected agricultural markets. Much of the potential welfare enhancement from liberalization of nonfarm product markets comes from textiles and apparel—even after accounting for the pending removal of import quotas on these goods in the presimulation. Furthermore, services liberalization and trade facilitation appear to offer significant scope not only for improving the aggregate developing-country outcome but also for reducing the number of individual countries that may experience a welfare loss after reform.

Notes

1. http://www.gtap.agecon.purdue.edu/products/models/.
2. Unfortunately, because of a lack of data on domestic purchases and prices, those authors are unable to estimate the elasticity of substitution between domestic goods and imports. As with the standard GTAP model, these parameters are still obtained using the "rule of two" (that is, the import-import elasticities are assumed to be twice as large as the import-domestic elasticities). These model modifications are justified by evidence in the literature, but when used in combination in a CGE (computable general equilibrium) setting the question remains: how valid is the GTAP-AGR model when compared to the historical record? Hertel, Keeney, and Valenzuela (2004) address this question in a validation exercise to investigate how well it performs in reproducing price volatility in world markets for

agricultural products. The validation experiment makes use of historical output trends in wheat-producing regions to obtain a measure of the variability of output that cannot be attributed to either technical advancements or year-to-year market signals. The validation criterion is the observed variability in wheat prices for each particular region, as compared with that generated by solving the model with respect to the variability in production. These authors find that with the exception of Argentina and Brazil (where significant macroeconomic events and stabilization schemes persisted over the period evaluated), the model prediction and observed price variability are relatively close for the case of wheat. We take this as a positive indication that GTAP-AGR is a valid framework for analyzing impacts of global agricultural liberalization on world markets.

3. These estimates are different from the WTO aggregate measure of support used to measure domestic support commitments for agriculture, as discussed by Jensen and Zobbe (2006).

4. For more discussion of this database, see Bouët and others (2004) and Jean, Laborde, and Martin (2006).

5. The decomposition of individual sources of liberalization and their impacts on regional welfare is done using the technique of Harrison, Horridge, and Pearson (2000).

6. In supplementary simulations, we added speculative export subsidy equivalents for export credits, state trading, and food aid, but they did not significantly alter the impacts shown in table 2.8.

7. This may be an understatement of potential gains attributable to textiles and apparel reform, since we have assumed the nontariff trade barriers present under the Uruguay Round Agreement on Textiles and Clothing are completely eliminated before our analysis and are not replaced by an export tax in China or by safeguards.

8. These estimates are speculative, as there are significant problems in integrating the Wilson, Mann, and Otsuki econometric-based estimates into a CGE model, including inconsistency of predictions for global imports and exports, inconsistency in the responsiveness of trade volumes to prices, and incomplete coverage of merchandise trade in their 2004 study.

References

Bouët, A., Y. Decreux, L. Fontagne, S. Jean, and D. Laborde. 2004. "A Consistent, *ad valorem* Equivalent Measure of Applied Protection Across the World: The MAcMap-HS6 Database." Centre d'Etudes Prospectives et d'Informations Internationales, Paris, December 20.

Cranfield, J. A. L. 2002. "Estimating Consumer Demands across the Development Spectrum: Maximum Likelihood Estimates of an Implicit Direct Additivity Model." *Journal of Development Economics* 68 (2): 289–307.

Dimaranan, B., T. W. Hertel, and R. Keeney. 2004. "OECD Domestic Support and the Developing Countries." In *The WTO, Developing Countries and the Doha Development Agenda: Prospects and Challenges for Trade-led Growth*, ed. B. Guha-Khasnobis. London: Palgrave-Macmillan.

Dimaranan, B. V., and R. A. McDougall, eds. 2002. *Global Trade, Assistance, and Protection: The GTAP 5 Database*. West Lafayette, IN: Center for Global Trade Analysis, Purdue University.

Francois, J. F., H. van Meijl, and F. van Tongeren. 2003. "Trade Liberalization and Developing Countries under the Doha Round." CEPR Discussion Paper 4032, Centre for Economic Policy and Research, London.

Harrison, W. J., J. M. Horridge, and K. Pearson. 2000. "Decomposing Simulation Results with Respect to Exogenous Shocks." *Computational Economics* 15: 227–49.

Hertel, T. W., ed. 1997. *Global Trade Analysis: Modeling and Applications*. New York: Cambridge University Press.

———. 2004. "Assessing the Provision of International Trade as a Public Good." UN Development Programme, New York.

Hertel, T. W., D. Hummels, M. Ivanic, and R. Keeney. 2003. "How Confident Can We Be in CGE-Based Assessments of Free Trade Agreements?" GTAP Working Paper 26, Center for Global Trade Analysis, Purdue University, West Lafayette, IN. http://www.gtap.agecon.purdue.edu/resources/working_paper.asp

Hertel, T. W., R. Keeney, and E. Valenzuela. 2004. "Global Analysis of Agricultural Trade: Assessing Model Validity." Paper presented at the Global Trade Analysis Conference, June 17–19, Washington, DC.

Hertel, T. W., D. K. Lanclos, K. R. Pearson, and P. V. Swaminathan. 1997. "Aggregation and Computation of Equilibrium Elasticities." In *Global Trade Analysis: Modeling and Applications*, ed. T. W. Hertel. New York: Cambridge University Press.

Huff, K. M., and T. W. Hertel. 2000. "Decomposing Welfare Changes in the GTAP Model." GTAP Technical Paper 5, Center for Global Trade Analysis, Purdue University, West Lafayette, IN.

Jean, S., D. Laborde, and W. Martin. 2006. "Consequences of Alternative Formulas for Agricultural Tariff Cuts." In *Agricultural Trade Reform and the Doha Development Agenda*, ed. K. Anderson and W. Martin. Basingstoke, U.K.: Palgrave Macmillan; Washington, DC: World Bank.

Jensen, H. G., and H. Zobbe. 2006. "Consequences of Reducing Limits on Aggregate Measures of Support." In *Agricultural Trade Reform and the Doha Development Agenda*, ed. K. Anderson and W. Martin. Basingstoke, U.K.: Palgrave Macmillan; Washington, DC: World Bank.

Keeney, R., and T. W. Hertel. 2005. "GTAP-AGR: A Framework for Assessing the Implications of Multilateral Changes in Agricultural Policies." GTAP Technical Paper 24, Center for Global Trade Analysis, Purdue University, West Lafayette, IN.

OECD (Organisation for Economic Co-operation and Development). 2001. *Market Effects of Crop Support Measures*. Paris: OECD.

Peeters, L., and Y. Surry. 1997. "A Review of the Art of Estimating Price-Responsiveness of Feed Demand in the European Union." *Journal of Agricultural Economics* 48: 379–92.

Rae, A. R., and T. W. Hertel. 2000. "Future Developments in Global Livestock and Grains Markets: The Impacts of Livestock Productivity Convergence in Asia-Pacific." *Australian Journal of Agricultural and Resource Economics* 44: 393–422.

Seale, J., A. Regmi, and J. Bernstein. 2003. "International Evidence on Food Consumption Patterns." ERS Technical Bulletin 1904, U.S. Department of Agriculture, Washington, DC.

Surry, Y. 1992. "Econometric Modeling of the European Compound Feed Sector: An Application to France." *Journal of Agricultural Economics* 41: 404–21.

Wilson, J., C. Mann, and T. Otsuki. 2004. "Assessing the Potential Benefits of Trade Facilitation: A Global Perspective." Policy Research Working Paper 3224, World Bank, Washington, DC.

SPECIAL AND DIFFERENTIAL TREATMENT FOR DEVELOPING COUNTRIES

Tim Josling[*]

Special and differential treatment (SDT) has a long history in the General Agreement on Tariffs and Trade (GATT) and the World Trade Organization (WTO). In the GATT, developing countries were relieved of some obligations and thus were granted differential treatment in several parts of the agreement. This has influenced the role that the developing countries were able to play in the development of the trade system. Most notably, developing countries were allowed, under Article XVIII:B, to maintain quantitative import restrictions for balance of payments reasons.[1] Because developing countries commonly suffered from chronic balance of payments problems, this essentially voided any value for other countries of "concessions" that developing countries might have made in reducing tariff levels. Binding such tariffs was similarly of little meaning where trade was controlled by quantitative restrictions.

Thus developed countries expected little in the way of reciprocal tariff concessions in the periodic rounds of trade negotiations. Developed countries themselves made full use of the concept of reciprocity in successive trade rounds, particularly in the Kennedy Round (1963–68), to reduce trade barriers on manufactured goods. But agricultural and textile products, of export interest to many developing countries, were not subject to the same process of liberalization. The combination

---

[*]Comments from Bernard Hoekman and other participants are appreciated, but the author retains responsibility for the ideas herein.

of this sectoral bias, and the lack of reciprocity, reinforced the notion that the GATT was a rich-country club.

Recognition by developed countries of the problems faced by developing countries in the trade system began to emerge as early as the 1950s. But the solutions did not result in fuller inclusion in the system. The practice of nonreciprocity became elevated to the level of principle when the GATT contracting parties added Part IV in 1964, formally relieving developing countries of their obligation to offer reciprocal concessions. Part IV did include some more positive aspects of inclusion, but most were of an exhortatory nature and did not impose any obligations on developed countries.[2] In 1979, the differential rules were encompassed in the Decision on Differential and More Favorable Treatment, Reciprocity, and Fuller Participation of Developing Countries, better known as the "Enabling Clause."

In addition, SDT was built into many of the agreements that make up the WTO. In particular, it became an integral part of Uruguay Round Agreement on Agriculture (URAA) and was emphasized in the Doha Development Agenda and reinforced in the Framework Agreement of August 1, 2004, commonly known as the July Framework Agreement (WTO 2004). The task ahead is to elaborate on the details of tariff cutting, tariff caps, tariff rate quotas (TRQs), and so on, in a way that gives meaning to the commitments to developing countries.

This chapter explores, in a qualitative way, the costs and benefits to developing and developed countries of different types of SDT in the agricultural negotiations.[3] The first section addresses the strategic issues that face both sets of countries as they proceed in the negotiations cycle. The second section discusses in more detail the SDT provisions that are in the URAA and that have been incorporated in the framework for the agricultural talks. The final section discusses the economic and political merits of these provisions.

Strategic Issues for Negotiations

Given the acceptance already of some degree of SDT, the developing countries do not need to expend significant negotiating capital establishing the case for extending it. But that fact begs the question of how much SDT developing countries should demand. If too much is requested, the chance of a satisfactory outcome to the round is reduced. If too little is demanded, the developing countries may have lost an opportunity for significant "gains." But the nature of the negotiations is that political success (in terms of achieving a concession, for example) may not have much or any economic value. So one strategy would be to search for the outcome that maximizes the economic benefit for developing countries over time given their limited political clout. This strategy implies that options should be ranked by economic merit, particularly with respect to their impact on growth and development, followed by consideration of the political price to be paid as a way of gaining those benefits.[4] Because economic benefits from open trade are a positive-sum game, it should be possible to attract developed countries to such an outcome. By contrast, political benefit-seeking is often a zero-sum game and may result in overall negative economic benefits.

A developing-country strategy of gaining the most economic benefit possible for their political clout might have two key elements: selling off depreciating assets in negotiations, and use negotiating power to build market position for the future. Preferences and nonreciprocity are two examples of depreciating assets. The value of preferences has been steadily eroded with cuts in most-favored-nation (MFN) tariffs. Moreover, the removal of quotas and their replacement by tariffs tend to make preferences more difficult to administer. Reciprocity is being eroded in a different way, through the conversion of nonreciprocal preference systems operated by the European Union and the United States to fully reciprocal free trade areas. Developing countries are concluding that guaranteed market access through a free trade area is a better basis for development than unilateral preferences given at the whim of the legislature of the developed country, even if it implies opening up import markets to the free trade partner. As more countries grant reciprocal access, so the nonreciprocity enshrined in the WTO becomes less valuable.

Given these developments, developing countries might consider agreeing to an end to preferences in return for compensation in trade and aid, and to relinquish the "right" to nonreciprocity in return for specific market access benefits. Such a strategy in the multilateral negotiations would convert the stance of developing countries from a defensive use of political power (specifically, the power to slow down the talks and limit the scope of the WTO) to avoid changes that might themselves be beneficial in the longer run (such as developing agriculture and other competitive sectors) to an offensive approach focusing on speeding up the negotiations on issues of economic interest (such as agriculture and textiles, as well as services that require movement of labor) in exchange for concessions on issues such as preferences and nonreciprocity that are of dubious and declining economic value.

To be more specific, it is useful to examine the menu of SDT choices from which the developing countries can choose. Each item comes with a price tag. There are basically two types of SDT: those that directly involve developing countries, and those that are implemented by developed countries. Negotiated outcomes in turn can be expressed either in terms of schedules of tariffs and allowed subsidies or in the form of differentiation in the rules.

Concessions in the outcome of negotiations for developing countries, including the depth of cuts in tariffs and the timing of such cuts, are foreseen in the July

Framework Agreement's provisions on agriculture, which give the developing countries more time to make adjustments. The most important of these are cuts in tariffs to improve market access. However, to the extent that the protective trade policies that are subject to discipline are not in the longer-run interest of the developing countries themselves, the delaying of cuts does not satisfy the criteria for increasing economic value over time. By contrast, targeted actions by developed countries, such as larger tariff cuts on products of export interest to developing countries, or increased technical assistance for trade-related aims, do have the possibility of increasing economic value over time and so are consistent with the criteria laid out above.

One issue that could be addressed with advantage is whether some developing countries should also be required to lower tariffs further on products of interest to other developing countries. That could be done specifically, on a product-by-product basis, or it could involve a commitment from middle-income countries. The increase in South-South trade that would result would be beneficial to the countries concerned (so long as significant trade diversion was avoided) as well as contribute to the acceptability of the package as a whole to developed countries.

Special rules for developing countries, such as special safeguards, are beneficial only if they modify the general rules in a way that either assists the development process or at the least does not impede it. Special safeguards may shelter weak but potentially profitable industries from the vicissitudes of international markets. But if the special rules imply a movement away from desirable developments, then their value is much lower and may decrease further over time. For example, differential rules on implementation of quality standards could be expensive in the long run, if as a result developing countries lag even further behind international standards. In contrast, special rules for developed countries that are designed to assist developing countries, such as export credits tied to food security and ad hoc temporary finance for developing-country purchases, could have a positive impact on development and be consistent with the criteria for gaining economic advantages from political agreement.

Special and differential treatment needs to be looked at from the viewpoint of the developed countries as well as the developing world. What do developed countries "lose" from granting SDT to developing countries? In the case of smaller and more delayed tariff cuts, the losses are in potential market access. The value of these losses to developed countries depends crucially on which commodities are involved and which countries make use of such flexibility in the provisions. Against this loss of market access, developed countries have to weigh the benefits of reaching an agreement.

The question, therefore, is whether there are aspects of SDT that could be packaged as a "win-win" proposition, that is, one that might allay opposition from legislatures in developed countries that might object to conceding on points of interest for the sake of international development. One "win-win" proposition would be raising standards in developing countries, where further integration into the world economy could benefit other countries as well as those undergoing the change. In a broader perspective, helping developing countries to raise incomes through trade should have a positive payoff for all members. But the politics of employment and wages is commonly argued to be a zero- or negative-sum game, and developing-country gains may be seen as evidence of losses to the developed world.

From the point of view of the developed countries, one topic has raised more concerns that any other. Should all developing countries get the same SDT? The term *developing country* is not defined in the WTO. That designation is self-declared by countries, leading to a natural reluctance to "graduate" to developed-country status. The need to face this issue has been emphasized by the increasing success in trade of countries such as Brazil, China, and India, to whom developed countries are less than eager to give nonreciprocal benefits in trade talks. Indeed, those countries that do need extra time, or special consideration, may be disadvantaged by the spreading of such treatment to all developing countries.

The view that developing countries should not all be treated alike has considerable merit. Particular SDT elements may be inappropriate for all developing countries, and the extent of concessions to those that do need them may be limited by the number of countries that are covered. At the same time, any differentiation among developing countries threatens to open up the system to conflicting demands.

So the question remains whether self-designation should be allowed to continue. One group has argued that SDT can never be meaningful as long as near-developed countries can also be classified as developing countries (IPC 2003). Objective rules may be needed for efficient targeted assistance; monitoring by the international community may also be needed. But any differentiation leads to the problem of graduation from one category to another and raises issues of instability and adverse incentives. Political incentives would also suggest that countries are unlikely to relinquish the right to self-designate. Hoekman (2004) concludes that self-designation as developing countries is likely to survive but that specific SDT provisions could be targeted to particular circumstances that can themselves be monitored. Thus the developing-country category itself would become less important as the SDT provisions themselves cover more objective subsets of countries.

That raises the question whether it is desirable for the multilateral trade system to encourage the proliferation of groups of countries treated differently in the rules. Some differentiation of a more objective kind than exists at the moment is probably inevitable if agreement is to be reached. Targeting rules to different circumstances has advantages that are hard to ignore, even in a trade system based on nondiscrimination. But does one want a multitiered WTO? Would the "variable geometry" discussed for the expanding EU fit in a multilateral trade system? Hoekman (2004) argues for a "core" of principles that apply to everyone, with monitored opt-outs for other aspects of the agreement (in contrast to the Tokyo Round codes, which were opt-in pacts with no link to development criteria).

Even more fundamental in any consideration of differential rules is the impact that changes in them would have on the nature of the WTO as an organization (Barton and others 2005). Should the rules of the multilateral trade system be targeted to assist development? Is the WTO an appropriate place for such "results-oriented" trade rules? There may be other more appropriate ways of assisting development, and even assisting developing countries to integrate into the trade system. But whatever the merits of such a parsimonious approach, it is likely that the WTO itself would not survive in its current form if it were to ignore development issues and the demands of developing countries for differentiation in commitments and rules. So the task is to incorporate these concerns and realities in such a way that they do not offset the benefits all countries (including developing countries) gain from having a liberal, nondiscriminatory trade system. The agricultural talks are at the center of the search for such a compromise.

SDT in the Agricultural Talks

The obligation to afford developing countries SDT is mentioned in the preamble of the Uruguay Round Agreement on Agriculture and embedded in several provisions of that agreement. The preamble states that developed-country members should improve market access for agricultural products of particular interest to developing countries. There was no systematic attempt to operationalize this statement in the URAA negotiations, however, and it is not reflected in the schedules of concessions. Most of the specific manifestations of SDT came in the form of flexibility of commitments undertaken by developing countries (table 3.1), along with a provision for a longer transition period (of up to 10 years, rather than the 6 years for developed countries).

The inclusion of SDT in the agricultural talks was further emphasized in the Doha Development Agenda. Specifically, in paragraph 13 (on agriculture), the Ministerial Declaration affirmed that SDT for developing countries "shall be an integral part of all elements of the negotiations on agriculture and shall be embodied in the schedules of concessions and commitments and as appropriate in the rules and disciplines to be negotiated." It emphasizes that these aspects of SDT should be operationally effective and enable developing countries to take account of their development needs. Paragraph 44 of the declaration returns to

Special and Differential Treatment for Developing Countries 69

TABLE 3.1 Flexibility for Developing Countries in the URAA

Article	Provision
6.2	Investment subsidies generally available, input subsidies for low-income farmers, and incentives to move out of illicit narcotics exempt from reduction commitments
6.4 (b)	Higher aggregate measure of support de minimis for developing countries (5 percent)
9.2 (b)	Lower rate of reduction for export subsidy commitments
9.4	Marketing subsidies and internal transport subsidies excluded from reduction commitments
12.2	Exemption for developing-country importers from consultation obligations when using export restrictions
15.1	Special and differential treatment reflected in reduction commitments two-thirds that of developed countries
15.2	Developing countries have a 10-year transition period: least developed countries not required to undertake reductions
Annex 2	Governmental stockholding programs and domestic food aid and subsidy programs included in Green Box
Annex 5	Exemption from tariffication for some staples, subject to conditions

Source: Matthews (2003), drawing on WTO (2001).

the theme and states that "all SDT provisions shall be reviewed with a view to strengthening them and making them more precise, effective and operational" (WTO 2001).

There are compelling political reasons for taking such provisions seriously. A degree of SDT satisfactory to developing countries will be necessary for an agreement on an outcome of the talks. Both the Group of 20 and the Group of 90 developing countries are committed to meaningful SDT, although developing countries differ considerably on what that might mean.

The commitment to meaningful SDT is specifically included in the July Framework Agreement (WTO 2004). Paragraph 1 of the framework reaffirms that provisions for SDT are an integral part of the WTO agreements, and it calls on the WTO Committee on Trade and Development to complete the review of agreement-specific proposals and give recommendations to the General Council by July 2005. Other WTO bodies are instructed to give recommendations to the council by the same date, although it is not clear how well coordinated such recommendations are likely to be.[5]

In the section of the framework dealing with the task of establishing modalities for agriculture (Annex A), the need to incorporate "operationally effective and meaningful provisions" for SDT is emphasized in the second paragraph as a way of achieving a balanced outcome. Such provisions are detailed in each of the substantive parts of the framework. Paragraph 6 of the annex states that SDT remains an integral component of domestic support and includes longer implementation periods and lower reduction coefficients, as well as continued access to the Article 6.2 allowance for developing countries to exclude certain domestic support policies from the aggregate measure of support for the purposes of reductions. Paragraph 22 of the annex provides for longer implementation periods for the phasing out of export subsidies (of all forms) and allows the provisions of Article 9.4 (the use of export-related subsidies for such purposes as transportation and marketing) to be continued "for a reasonable period" after the phasing out of developed-country subsidies on exports. In addition, paragraph 24 of the framework agreement obliges countries to ensure that disciplines on food aid and export credit programs do not interfere with the actions necessary under the Decision on Measures Concerning the Possible Negative Effects of the Reform Program on Least-Developed and Net Food-Importing Developing Countries (The Decision). This is reinforced in paragraph 26 by a provision that in special circumstances "ad hoc temporary financing arrangements" can be established based on criteria to be negotiated.[6]

The most significant aspects of SDT in the framework are those related to market access. Paragraph 39 ties SDT to the issues of food security and "livelihood security," declaring that SDT will be integral to commitments on tariff reductions, the number and treatment of sensitive products, the expansion of TRQs, and the implementation period. In addition, developing countries will be able to designate a number of products as special products, based on criteria of food security, livelihood security, and rural development needs. These products would be subject to "more flexible" treatment (presumably lower tariff reductions or TRQ expansions). The establishment of a special safeguard mechanism (SSM) has been agreed for use by developing countries, although whether developed countries can maintain the SSG remains to be negotiated. Both expedited liberalization of trade in tropical products and a need to take into account existing preferences are mentioned (paragraphs 43 and 44), but no specifics are given.

These agreed elements of SDT are grouped in table 3.2 under the categories mentioned above: rules and commitments undertaken by developed and developing countries. The potential value of the most significant of these elements to developing countries is discussed below. But in general, commitments made by developed countries in the direction of greater market access and lower subsidies are likely to be the most valuable type of SDT but will require more political capital to achieve in negotiation. Agreement that developing countries give less in the way of concessions is perhaps the easiest route, but such an agreement is also less likely to be useful. Rules are likely to be more difficult to negotiate than concessions and be more divisive of the trade system.

TABLE 3.2 Categories of Special and Differential Treatment in Agriculture in the July Framework Agreement

Category	Developing country	Developed country
Concessions in tariff schedules	Smaller tariff reductions over a longer period	Take into account erosion of preferences
	Designation of special products	Reduce tariff escalation
	Longer implementation period for elimination of export subsidies	Liberalization of tropical products markets
		Market access for "alternative" products
	Smaller cuts in domestic support over a longer period	Increased technical assistance for trade capacity
	Higher de minimis for domestic support	Duty- and quota-free access for least developed countries, where possible
	No reduction commitments for least developed countries	
Differentiation in rules	Special safeguard mechanism	Decision on low-income food-deficit countries
	Article 9.4 exemption stays	Export credits allowed as appropriate to the Decision
	Article 6.2 stays	
	Special consideration in talks on state trading enterprises	Ad hoc temporary finance for developing country imports

Source: Author.

Lower Reduction Commitments for Tariffs

It is generally agreed, and explicit in the framework agreement, that developing countries should cut tariffs using a formula similar to that used by developed countries. The framework agreement mandates a tiered formula for both groups of countries but allows smaller cuts and a longer time period for developing countries. So the issues remaining to be negotiated are the size of the target cuts for developing countries, and the length of the transition period.

The size of the target cuts raises an interesting possibility for developing countries. Currently, most developing countries have considerable gaps between bound and applied tariffs, as a result of ceiling bindings in the Uruguay Round. For many countries the applied tariff is (or is scheduled to be) zero for some trade partners as the result of a preferential trade agreement, giving an even greater gap. This gap is obviously worth something at the bargaining table, but it falls into the category of a diminishing asset. So, on the principle suggested earlier, it provides a useful bargaining chip for use during this round. Specifically, the developing countries could leverage their willingness to give up the gap between applied and bound rates, and even the difference between MFN and preferential rates, in exchange for real market access in developed countries (where the gap between applied and bound rates is less). If developing countries emerge at the end of the round with considerable "gaps" intact then they will not have obtained as much market access as they might have done.

One should also consider whether a longer transition period for developing countries is a significant advantage. Clearly, when the transition period involves difficult administrative changes (what Hoekman calls resource-intensive rules), then more time is useful. And if painful domestic adjustments have to be made, involving new investments, retraining, and adjustment assistance, then there is also an argument for more time, although not quite so compelling. But if the domestic cost is minimal and the benefits from greater market access are palpable, then a slow transition may not be particularly valuable as a negotiating prize. So it may be that the bound-applied gap could be traded off for greater market access in developed countries if developing countries were not also trying to slow the transition down.

In addition to the tariff reduction schedules, the negotiators will have to deal with the question of special products, linked to commodities significant for rural development and food security. As that criterion could possibly be stretched to include most import items in developing countries (except high-value processed or exotic foods), then the issue of how widely to cast the net is important. Much of the discussion so far has been about whether there should be a formula to define what products are special or whether individual countries can nominate such commodities. But ultimately the important tradeoff is likely to be between the number (and hence coverage) of the special products and the number of sensitive products that developed countries (and developing countries) will be able to nominate. If developed countries choose to make extensive use of the sensitive product category to shelter products of interest to developing-country exporters, then the likelihood of widely drawn criteria for special products increases. Or to put it the other way, the developing countries have an opportunity to limit the scope of sensitive products by using the special product category sparingly.

Other aspects of market access also give developing countries an opportunity to influence the degree of market opening that they achieve in the round. The issue of the tariff cap is still to be negotiated, and developing countries must decide whether to accept such a discipline on their tariffs. Given the great distortions that high tariffs create, if indeed they allow any trade at all, it is not clear why developing countries should not accept such a tariff cap, knowing that to do so would increase their influence over the height of the cap set for developed countries.

Better Access for Developing Countries

The negotiating text presented at the end of the Cancún Ministerial, known as the Derbez text (WTO 2003a), suggests that developed countries "seek to provide" duty-free access for a portion of their imports from developing countries. This provision is not in the framework agreement and would not have had much impact in any case. Negotiations over the share of imports so covered would have been difficult and not necessarily have led to much market opening. The concept would certainly have favored the EU, because so many countries in its African, Caribbean, and Pacific group already have duty-free access.

The framework takes up the suggestion, contained in the Derbez text and championed by the EU, that developed countries (and developing countries in a position to do so) should grant least developed countries access that is both duty free and quota free. But this part of the framework suffers from the "best efforts" syndrome (that is, developed countries have made no commitment) that has rendered much of SDT ineffective on previous occasions (Michalopoulos 1999). If made effective, however, this provision would set a useful precedent that could be built upon to help developing countries as a whole.

Are preferences worth preserving? The framework agreement states that participants would "take into account" the importance of preferences (as in the Harbinson draft modalities paper, WTO 2003b) in their tariff schedule reductions. But that approach may run counter to the overall desire to improve market access for developing countries. Preferences are one of the declining assets mentioned above, and negotiating compensation for the reduction of preferences may be better than attempting to maintain them.

The framework agreement endorses the Harbinson solution to tariff escalation problems, which suggested that tariffs on raw and processed goods be reduced in such a way as to lessen the impact of tariff escalation. This provision is of considerable interest to developing countries. It would be constructive if developing countries were to formulate a strategy in this area based on the perceived impact of tariff escalation on their economies. This could be useful to developed countries who have less incentive to do such calculations themselves.

New Special Safeguard Mechanism

The framework agreement endorses the creation of a special safeguard mechanism for developing countries (as suggested in the Harbinson draft, incorporated in the EU-U.S. proposal of August 2003, and included in the Derbez text that survived the Cancún Ministerial). This safeguard mechanism had been accepted by the Group of 20 and other developing countries, although the technical details will not necessarily be easy to negotiate. An SSM is both politically necessary and of potential economic benefit. Small, open economies are particularly vulnerable to changes in world market prices. A simple, transparent mechanism for temporary levies triggered by both price drops and import surges could give countries the security they need to stabilize domestic markets without creating too much temptation to protect inefficient sectors in the longer run.

Several issues are still under discussion regarding the operation of the SSM. One is how wide the commodity coverage should be. From the developing-country perspective there would seem to be a benefit from a wide coverage, but that could have a cost in negotiating terms. Developed countries would see too wide a range of commodities covered by the SSM as a way for developing countries to limit market penetration, particularly if the trigger price is set high and the trigger quantity set low. Developing countries should make sure that they know what coverage and trigger conditions are essential to them and make this known.

One benefit of an SSM is that it could take the place of the "price band" systems in place in several South and Central American countries. Such bands, which trigger additional tariffs, have been ruled contrary to the GATT (at least as they were implemented in Chile). A WTO-consistent and reasonably uniform agricultural safeguard would simplify trade decisions and lower costs. The main issue is whether to have a parallel safeguard for developed countries through a continuation of the special safeguard that accompanied tariffication. This safeguard has been used by the EU and Japan, and less often by the United States. But it has aroused opposition from exporters. If this particular safeguard were to continue, its procedures, and in particular the selection of world prices, should be made more predictable and less prone to use for protection.

Domestic Support

The framework agreement provides developing countries with lower reductions in the aggregate measure of support and longer implementation periods. They would also be exempt from the requirement to reduce de minimis. These provisions are of minimal value to most developing countries, as they have not notified any Amber Box policies. So not much capital should be expended on lengthening the time and weakening the terms of the disciplines on domestic support. In fact, as the developing countries have made reducing the level of support in the developed countries a major plank in their proposals, this item would be a good candidate for showing that they do not want different rules for the sake of political victories if the economic advantage is small. Instead, maximum pressure can be brought by developing countries to persuade developed countries to remove their supports.

Two provisions in the framework may be somewhat more useful. Enhanced provisions under Article 6.2 (see table 3.1)—perhaps including credit subsidies—are worth pursuing if they would make it less likely that developed countries would challenge such policies in the dispute settlement process. Enhanced provisions under the Green Box (such as allowing more policies that stimulate output expansion) would also be useful, along with some further degree of assurance that developing-country policies that conform to the Green Box would be granted some shelter. The Peace Clause, if the issue is raised again, could usefully be limited to cover developing countries. The broader concept of a Development Box may be a useful label but not worth much at the negotiating table: most development policies are already in the Green Box.

Export Provisions

Discussion on the export competition pillar of the agricultural negotiations in the Doha Round is focused on the elimination of export subsidies, both those that are explicit and those that are embedded in other programs such as food aid, export credits, and the activities of state trading enterprises. The schedule for the elimination of export subsidies is extended for developing countries as part of SDT. Moreover, the special provisions already in the URAA are to be preserved.

Removing export subsidies in developed countries has become a major goal of developing countries. It would not be fruitful in negotiating terms to argue strongly for SDT in this area, where few policies are employed. To do so would risk weakening the pressure on the developed economies to remove their own subsidies quickly. This seems to be one area where the developing countries could offer a concession in order to achieve a more valuable overall result.

So What Makes (Economic) Sense?

Bearing all these factors in mind, what are the elements that should be included in an agreement that makes economic sense for both developing and developed countries?

First, safeguards have economic rationale and should be made a centerpiece of the specific rules applying to developing countries. The cost may be that the SSM for developed countries may have to be prolonged as well, but that could be done with some tightening of the conditions. In addition, a broader Green Box could be (marginally) helpful. Protecting development policies from WTO challenge may help acceptance of reform.

It also makes sense, at least from an economic viewpoint, to focus SDT on those countries that are not in a position to undertake the full set of WTO obligations or accept commitments. This means that there would have to be some distinctions made among developing countries. Differentiation by type of problem would help targeting of SDT. SDT would also have to be built into development plans and coordinated with regional and multilateral development agencies.

How much negotiating capital would be expended to get these advantages? And what would the cost be in terms of other objectives of developing countries? Presumably developing countries would get less access to developed country markets than otherwise, and less reduction in trade-distorting support. But these costs could be offset by other concessions. Why not "sell" parts of SDT that are not so economically beneficial while they still have value at the bargaining table?

By the same token, developing countries can make the deal more attractive to developed countries by showing a willingness to open up markets. Tariff reduction commitments by developing countries that are too modest will reduce pressure for domestic reform: the economic case is weak for blanket exemptions even for the least developed countries. The widespread use of the special products category risks distorting the domestic economy and encouraging the use of sensitive products by developed countries, so it should be used sparingly if at all.

Any package that emerges is going to have to appeal to interests in developed countries that support trade expansion. Selling the round on its development components alone will be difficult. But ignoring developing countries' requests is also not a recipe for progress. So the task is to craft a package that has economic benefits for both developed and developing countries and does not exceed the political limits of support for liberalization. A package with deep cuts in domestic support, the elimination of export subsidies, and ambitious tariff cuts combined with strong safeguards and adequate policy space for developing countries could be possible.

Conclusions

Certain structural problems exist in developing countries that make them particularly vulnerable to rapid liberalization, and it has long been recognized that not all countries have the capacity to take advantage of export possibilities. But if open economies grow faster (an underlying premise of the trade system), then encouraging countries to delay opening may be perpetuating asymmetries rather than reducing them. Permissive SDT needs to be matched with positive policies to encourage participation of developing countries, including policies for developing supply capacity and transferring technology. Trade and aid policies must be more coordinated. In addition, regulatory systems differ among countries, and the capacity to implement agreed regulatory frameworks can be lacking in developing countries. Again the approach to this problem could combine some temporary relief from obligations (so long as this relief does not exclude goods from export markets) with assistance to develop the necessary regulatory capacity.

Developing countries are faced with the potential conflict between concessions to domestic interests and economic benefits from trade. If SDT is purely a reaction to domestic pressure, then the cost is delayed reform at home and less market access in the developed countries. Such an outcome is not in the interests of any group of countries. But the negotiation of a package that includes constructive SDT that addresses real problems and yields economic benefits to developing countries is in the interests of all. Developed countries should be willing to "pay" for more market access in developing countries by agreeing to safeguards and trade assistance. This way they can help to integrate these countries into the trade system to the mutual benefit of all countries. Middle-income countries should consider what they can contribute as well as what benefits they can derive: opening up their markets in products of interest to other developing countries could stimulate South-South trade.

Developing countries should focus on what is most useful to them in the way of derogations from general rules and be prepared to forgo other rule-based aspects of SDT, including aspects that have been accepted in the past. By forgoing some of the elements of SDT that are of little long-run economic value to them, developing countries are more likely to be able to secure those rules that are most beneficial. Developed countries must accept that some derogations will be needed to get an agreement and attempt to inform domestic constituencies of the longer-run benefits of fuller integration of developing countries in the trade system.

Notes

1. The original balance of payments provision was contained in Article XII, but in the Review of the GATT in 1954–55, an explicit provision for developing countries was included in Article XVIII. This article also allowed developing countries to impose quantitative restrictions on infant industry grounds, but the balance of payments clause was by far the most used.

2. Part IV comprises three articles: Article XXXVI expresses the principle that development should be an objective of the trade system and includes nonreciprocity as a step toward that goal; Article XXXVII lays out some ways in which developed countries can assist developing countries; and Article XXXVIII provides for "joint action" to deal with development issues. Despite its symbolic significance, Part IV did not change the legal obligations of either developed or developing countries in the GATT. One institutional development survives from Part IV: the contracting parties agreed to set up a Trade and Development Committee to consider the implementation of the exhortations. However, the United Nations Conference on Trade and Development (UNCTAD) was convened in 1964 and became the preferred focus for developing-country issues. See Hudec (1987) and Finger and Winters (1998) for fuller discussions of Part IV of the GATT.

3. The more general issue of special treatment under the rule of the WTO is discussed in Hoekman (2004). Josling (2004) discusses the question of the negotiating value of some of these broader developing country provisions, such as Part IV and the Enabling Clause.

4. Notice that this approach is likely to result in a different outcome from the alternative strategy of maximizing political advantage by giving economic concessions. Only a few large developing countries (Brazil, China, and India) can offer significant economic concessions to "win" political goals.

5. One can, for instance, envisage the Committee on Trade and Development arriving at somewhat different recommendations from those agreed in the Agriculture Committee. If that is to be avoided, one of the committees would need to take the leading role in the talks.

6. The framework also promises that developing countries that have state trading enterprises to preserve price stability and ensure food security will receive special consideration with respect to their monopoly status.

References

Barton, J., J. Goldstein, T. Josling, and R. Steinberg. 2005. *The Evolution of the Trade Regime: Politics, Law, and Economics of the GATT and WTO.* Princeton, NJ: Princeton University Press.

Finger, J. M., and L. A. Winters. 1998. "What Can the WTO Do for Developing Countries?" In *The WTO as an International Organization,* ed. A. O. Krueger. Chicago: University of Chicago Press.

_____. 2005. "Operationalizing the Concept of Policy Space in the WTO: Beyond Special and Differential Treatment." *Journal of International Economic Law* 8 (2): 377–404.

Hoekman, B. 2002. "Strengthening the Global Trade Architecture for Development: The Post-Doha Agenda." *World Trade Review* 1 (1): 23–45.

_____. 2004. "Operationalizing the Concept of Policy Space in the WTO: Beyond Special and Differential Treatment." Paper presented at the conference, "Preparing the Doha Round—WTO Negotiators Meet the Academics," July 2–3, European University Institute, Florence.

Hudec, R. E. 1987. *Developing Countries in the GATT Legal System.* Thames Essay 50. London: Trade Policy Research Centre.

IPC (International Food and Agricultural Trade Policy Council). 2003. "Beyond Special and Differential Treatment." IPC Issue Brief 2, IPC, Washington, DC, August 15.

Josling, T. 2004. "Asymmetries in International Trade: In Search of Institutional Innovation." Paper presented at the European Agricultural Economics Association Conference, "Agricultural Development and Rural Poverty under Globalization: Asymmetric Processes and Outcomes," September 8–11, University of Florence, Italy.

Matthews, A. 2003. "A Review of Special and Differential Treatment Proposals in the WTO Agricultural Negotiations." Trinity College, Dublin.

Michalopoulos, C. 1999. "The Developing Countries in the WTO." *The World Economy* 22 (1): 117–43.

WTO (World Trade Organization). 2001. "Ministerial Declaration: Adopted on 14 November 2001." WT/MIN(01)/DEC/1, Ministerial Conference, Fourth Session, November 9–14, Doha.

_____. 2003a. "Draft Cancún Ministerial Text." JOB(03)/150/Rev.2 (Derbez Draft), WTO, Geneva.

_____. 2003b. "Negotiations on Agriculture: First Draft of Modalities for the Further Commitments." TN/AG/W/1/Rev.1 (Harbinson Draft), WTO, Geneva, March 19.

_____. 2004. "Doha Work Programme: Decision Adopted by the General Council on 1 August 2004." WT/L/579 (July Framework Agreement), WTO, Geneva, August 2.

PART II

AGRICULTURAL MARKET ACCESS

CONSEQUENCES OF ALTERNATIVE FORMULAS FOR AGRICULTURAL TARIFF CUTS

Sébastien Jean, David Laborde, and Will Martin

The Framework Agreement for the Doha Development Agenda (WTO 2004b) provides new and important guidelines for negotiations on agricultural market access. It adds some key objectives that were missing from the original Doha Declaration (WTO 2001). In particular, it includes an important goal that was absent from the agricultural section of the original Doha Declaration—progressivity in tariff reduction through larger cuts in higher tariffs.

The new framework for WTO agricultural negotiations is, at the same time, much less specific on market access than some of the preceding documents, particularly the Harbinson Draft (WTO 2003b). Where, for instance, the Harbinson formula proposed specific approaches for reductions in tariffs, and even offered tentative numbers, the framework speaks much more generally of a tiered formula. This alone would seem to rule out deceptive practices such as the average-cut approach, which gives members strong incentives to reduce higher tariffs by less than lower tariffs, thereby reducing gains in market access and increasing the variability of tariffs around their averages (World Bank 2003, 92; Martin 2004).

The greater generality of the framework allows for exploration of alternatives that might better achieve the objectives of countries participating in the Doha Round. The purpose of this chapter is to assess the impacts of alternative approaches to liberalizing market access within the broad guidelines provided by the framework. We consider several alternative formulas, all of which follow the framework goal of cutting higher tariffs by more than lower tariffs but do so to different degrees. We also consider the implications of different ways of designating products as sensitive or special; such products are subject to smaller reductions in protection.

Analysis of approaches to market access expansion must confront some key methodological challenges. One of these is inherent in the nonlinear nature of a tiered formula. Analysis must be undertaken using information on tariffs at a disaggregated level. Applying a tiered formula to tariff averages will not yield correct results. For this reason, we have based our analysis on applied and bound tariffs at the finest level available on an internationally comparable basis: the six-digit level of the Harmonized System.[1]

Another important condition for well-founded analysis is that it includes the effects of tariffs that are not ad valorem. Conventional tariff data sets that include only ad valorem tariffs are quite inadequate for analysis of agricultural protection in the industrial countries (World Bank 2003). The most restrictive tariffs in developed countries are typically nontransparent specific, compound, or mixed tariffs. Tariff data sets based only on the conventional ad valorem elements of tariffs lead to misleading estimates, such as a weighted-average, most-favored-nation (MFN) tariff of 6.2 percent for Japanese agriculture reported in Francois and Martin (2003). We estimate that the average MFN tariff on agricultural imports to Japan was actually 51.3 percent in 2001, with the vast majority of this attributable to non–ad valorem tariffs.

Another key issue that needs to be addressed is the implications of tariff preferences. The effects of tariff cuts on market access may be quite different for countries receiving effective tariff preferences than for countries subject to MFN status. For a country receiving MFN status, tariff cuts generally increase market access and raise the prices its producers receive for their exports. For countries receiving preferential status, the result may be an erosion in preference margins and a reduction in prices received for exports.

Tariff rate quotas (TRQs) raise some similar issues. A substantial share of developed-country imports, and a much larger share of production, is subject to TRQs. Under these, imports up to a quota limit are permitted at an in-quota tariff, which is unbound and lower than the MFN (out-of-quota) rate. If imports are occurring at the in-quota rather than the out-of-quota rate, then reductions in bound, out-of-quota tariffs may not liberalize imports until the bound tariffs fall below the in-quota tariffs. Cuts in bound tariffs may thus be less effective in reducing applied rates than they would be in a situation where imports are restricted by MFN tariffs.

An important complication for the evaluation of agricultural tariff reform is the frequent, wide divergence between the bound tariff and the tariff rate actually applied. This binding overhang means that reductions in bound tariffs will not always bring about corresponding reductions in applied rates and hence increases in market access. The phenomenon of binding overhang is widely associated with developing-country agricultural tariffs, but it is prevalent in developed countries as well (Martin and Wang 2004). The binding overhang can change radically the outcome of a given tariff-cutting formula. To the extent that the gap between MFN and bound tariffs is far from uniform across products (especially in developed countries), it is difficult to gauge a priori how much it would interfere with the application of a given formula.

Once these problems are overcome, however, quantitative analysis can play a much larger role than it has in previous negotiations. Traps and deceptions such as the use of the average-cut routine can be revealed at a much earlier stage than was the case in earlier rounds.[2] In this situation, analysis provides a basis for allowing policy makers to size up the effects of proposed agreements, taking into account the direct effects not only on their own tariff schedules but also on their potential gains in market access. In previous negotiating rounds, including the Uruguay Round, most such evaluations were undertaken only after completion of the agreement (see, for example, Martin and Winters 1996).

This chapter draws on the most detailed available data on applied tariffs, the MAcMap data set, prepared by the Centre d'Etudes Prospectives et d'Informations Internationales (CEPII) and the International Trade Centre (ITC), combined with an equally detailed data set on bound duties, using a methodology consistent with MAcMap (Bchir, Jean, and Laborde forthcoming). These data are used to examine the implications of various liberalization options for the level and dispersion of tariffs, both bound and applied. It also examines the consequences of these formulas for the market access facing countries and groups of countries. The resulting data are presented at a level of aggregation suitable both for making direct assessments of the impact of formulas on tariffs and for use as inputs into model-based analyses of the impacts of the negotiations on output, employment, trade, and welfare (as in Anderson, Martin, and van der Mensbrugghe 2006).

The first section of this chapter focuses on key design features of the proposal for market access expansion contained in the framework. Because the effects of any proposal for reform depend on the initial market access situation, the second section surveys the broad features of the initial tariff situation. Then we examine the consequences of applying particular tiered formulas to particular import markets, before examining the implications of these formulas for the market access opportunities facing countries and regions. The final section offers some conclusions.

Features of the Framework's Market Access Proposal

The four key elements of the framework agreement on market access are the application of a tiered formula that will make deeper cuts in higher tariffs; self-selection of sensitive products for which "substantial improvements" are to be made in market access through combinations of tariff reductions and TRQ expansion; smaller tariff reduction commitments in developing countries; and self-designation of special products by developing countries. Consider the issues involved in each of these areas.

The Tiered Formula

Economic theory supports the use of a formula like that proposed in the framework, in which higher tariff rates are cut more than lower tariff rates (Vousden 1990). Proportional tariff cuts potentially meet the framework requirement of "deeper cuts in higher tariffs" since higher tariffs are cut by larger absolute amounts, although the proportion cut in all tariffs is the same. A rather extreme top-down approach is the so-called Swiss formula, in which all tariffs are reduced below a coefficient that becomes the new maximum tariff, and the proportional cut in tariffs rises as the tariff rises. Francois and Martin (2003) show that the family of flexible Swiss formulas can provide a wide range of alternatives between the Swiss formula and a straight proportional reduction. The family of progressive "tiered" formulas, in which tariffs in higher bands are subject to higher proportional cuts, provides another family of formulas between the proportional cut and the Swiss formula.

The Harbinson proposal contains some elements of a tiered formula in that it involves higher cuts in higher tariffs. Unfortunately, this proposal involves the use of the average-cut routine within each group, encouraging countries to minimize disciplines by imposing larger percentage cuts on lower tariffs within each group (Martin 2004). The average-cut approach is clearly not consistent with the goal in the framework of making deeper cuts in higher tariffs nor with the ambitions of the Doha agenda to reduce tariff escalation. It is also likely inconsistent with the goal of achieving substantial gains in market access (Martin 2004).

For developed countries, the Harbinson proposal involves reductions of 40 percent in tariffs under 15 percent, 50 percent in tariffs between 15 and 90 percent, and 60 percent for tariffs above 90 percent (WTO 2003b). In developing countries, there are four tiers, with reductions of 25 percent for tariffs below 20 percent, 30 percent for tariffs between 20 and 60 percent, 35 percent for tariffs

FIGURE 4.1 Converting the Harbinson Formula into a Tiered Formula (percent)

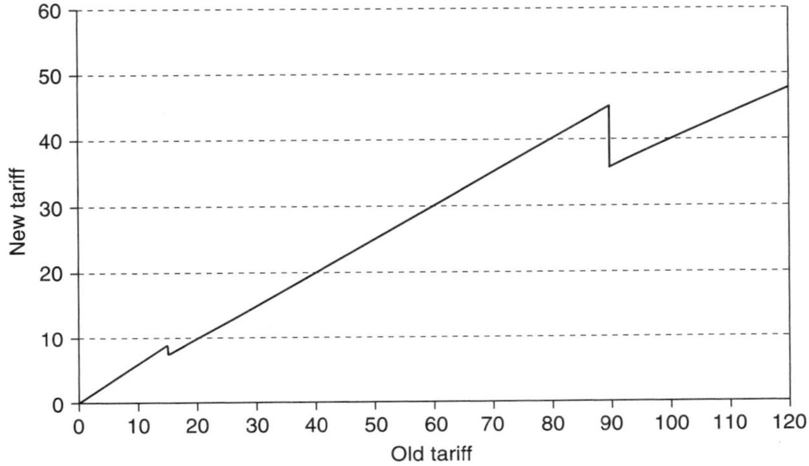

[Figure: graph plotting New tariff (y-axis, 0–60) against Old tariff (x-axis, 0–120), showing discontinuities near transition points.]

Source: Authors' calculations.

between 60 percent and 120 percent, and 40 percent in tariffs above 120 percent. Although this proposal was not adopted, its transition points clearly reflect a great deal of consultation and thought and may provide a useful indication of widely accepted transition points under a tiered-formula approach.

Attempts to convert these different rates of tariff reduction into a tiered formula confront a problem of discontinuities. This is evident in figure 4.1, which maps tariffs before application of the formula to postformula tariffs using the developed-country transition points of 15 and 90 percent. The discontinuity problem is most evident around the 90 percent transition point, where a tariff of 90 percent becomes a tariff of 45 percent, while a tariff just over 90 percent becomes a tariff of 36 percent. This discontinuity would not only result in a change in the ordering of tariffs but could potentially raise the costly variability of tariffs. Most important from a political-economy perspective, such discontinuities would likely create major political resistance from firms just above each of the transition points.

This problem of discontinuities and nonmonotonicity is inherent in any formula that attempts to apply different proportional cuts in different tariff bands.

FIGURE 4.2 A Tiered Tariff-Cutting Formula without Discontinuities (percent)

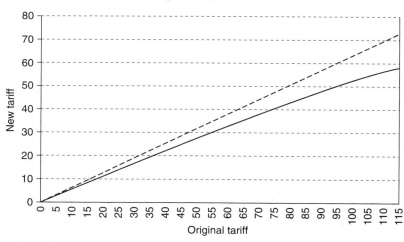

Source: Authors' calculations.
Note: Upper line shows the 40 percent reduction. Lower line shows the 40:50:60 percent progressive tiered formula.

One way to deal with it is to follow the approach of the progressive income tax, where the higher proportional rate is applied to the part of the tariff that lies above the limit of the lower band. This approach has the disadvantage of cutting high tariffs by less in absolute terms than a proportional cut (because the lower portion of the tariff is cut at a lower rate), but it does impose the higher cut on higher tariffs required by the framework. Further, it provides a continuous mapping from the old tariffs to the new, as depicted in figure 4.2.

Sensitive and Special Products

Two other key issues in assessing the implications of the framework agreement are those products to be designated as sensitive by developed countries and those products to be designated as special by developing countries. The designation of exceptions such as these is typically a key element of any formula-based negotiation (Baldwin 1986). While some such exceptions are likely to be necessary for political reasons, excessive use of exceptions can easily undermine the fundamental goal of expanding market access, contradicting the requirement in the framework that sensitive products should be allowed "without undermining the overall objective of the tiered approach" (WTO 2004b, para 31).

Since the framework allows countries to choose the products they will designate as sensitive, there is considerable uncertainty about which products will be designated and what the effects of this designation will be. In the framework, the number of tariff lines to be allowed as sensitive products is explicitly to be negotiated.[3] WTO members can readily see the politically beneficial (but economically damaging) impacts of allowing particular numbers of tariff lines on reducing the disciplines they must impose on their own politically sensitive commodities. But it is more difficult for them to assess the adverse impacts of other countries' sensitive and special products on their market access opportunities. A key goal of this chapter is to provide some of the information relevant to decisions about this tradeoff.

The approach to dealing with this problem adopted by Martin and Wang (2004) is to assume that the products treated as sensitive are those with the highest tariffs. If the number of tariff lines that can be treated as sensitive is constrained, however, it is unlikely that countries would choose to use their limited number of sensitive tariff lines on products that have high tariffs but play only a small role in trade and production. Accordingly, in this analysis, the tariff lines to be treated as sensitive were selected by ranking products by the tariff revenue that would be forgone through implementation of the formula.[4] This approach takes into account the importance of the commodity, the height of the existing applied tariff, and the gap between the tariff binding and the applied rate. The broad results of this analysis appear to be supported by an analysis in which the selection of products is based on a Grossman-Helpman political support function (Jean, Laborde, and Martin 2005).

The framework indicates that special products in developing countries are to be distinct from sensitive products available to both developed and developing countries. It nonetheless seems likely that policy makers would use similar criteria in deciding which products to designate as special. The stated criteria in the framework, such as food security, provide little guidance. In fact, tariffs are more likely to reduce than to improve food security. As Sen (1981) demonstrated, food security is not an issue of national self-sufficiency but rather one of ensuring that individuals—particularly the poor—have access to food. Raising national food self-sufficiency by raising agricultural prices through protection may well reduce the access of poor people to food. Given the lack of a convincing rationale in the framework for special products, the analysis here effectively treats this group as an increase in the number of tariff lines allowed "flexibility" of the type permitted by the sensitive products category.

We assume that tariff lines in the sensitive or special product categories would experience liberalization equivalent to a 15 percent reduction from their initial tariff levels. The framework provides for expansion of MFN tariff rate quotas, possibly together with tariff reductions, to bring about substantial improvements in market access for these products. Unless the rules for this improvement in market access for these products are extremely demanding, it seems difficult to be optimistic about the possibility of substantial market access expansion through TRQ expansion. As de Gorter and Kliauga (2005) point out, the in-quota tariffs are not bound, and TRQs are frequently not filled because of administrative devices, sometimes even when there are substantial out-of-quota imports. Quotas are frequently allocated on the basis of licenses on demand, which is not an efficient or equitable method of allocating scarce and valuable quotas. In this respect, agriculture's TRQ regime seems an even less promising vehicle for liberalization than was the labyrinthine system of textile quotas erected under the textile industry's Multifibre Arrangement. Clearly, a great deal needs to be done if any faith is to be placed in TRQ expansion as a means of improving market access.

Market Access Geography

This analysis uses the latest version of the MAcMap database, which covers tariffs for 2001 and takes into account ad valorem tariffs, specific tariffs, and tariff preferences (Bouët and others 2004). This data set underlies the Global Trade Analysis Project (GTAP) database used in global economic models for analyzing trade policy reform. CEPII has developed software allowing easy aggregation up to the GTAP level for analysis with computable general equilibrium models. Some changes in the data were required for the analysis at hand, including corrections to problems resulting from tariff rate quotas, corrections to protection estimates distorted by idiosyncrasies of the TRQ system; modification of China's tariffs to take account of WTO accession commitments; the phase-in of remaining commitments from the Uruguay Round; and changes caused by the accession in May 2004 of 10 new members to the European Union.

The tariffs applied on TRQ commodities in the MAcMap database depend on whether the quota is filled. If the quota is less than 90 percent filled, the in-quota tariff is assumed to apply to these commodities. If the quota is between 90 and 99 percent filled, the effective tariff is assumed to be the average of the in- and out-of-quota tariff. If the quota is more than 99 percent filled, then the out-of-quota tariff is applied.

Several key features of global agricultural tariffs are shown in table 4.1. The global average tariff of 17 percent includes 11 percent from ad valorem tariffs and 6 percent from the ad valorem equivalents of non–ad valorem measures. There are extraordinary variations between countries and country groups around these levels. In developed countries as a group, the average tariff is 14 percent, only 4 percentage points of which are contributed by ad valorem tariffs; the remaining

TABLE 4.1 Key Features of Applied Agricultural Tariffs, by Selected Countries and Regions, 2001 (percent, trade-weighted average)

Country/region	Overall average	Ad valorem tariffs	Specific tariffs	Tariff for TRQs	TRQ Share
Australia	3.0	2.1	0.9	1.0	5.6
Bangladesh	14.4	14.4	0.0	0.0	0.0
Canada	9.7	8.3	1.3	30.7	21.0
China	38.9	38.9	0.0	5.7	22.0
Japan	35.5	9.9	25.6	103.4	8.8
Korea, Rep. of	93.9	93.9	0.0	226.3	38.5
Mexico	10.7	10.6	0.1	33.8	23.6
Pakistan	30.4	9.7	20.7	0.0	0.0
India	55.1	54.3	0.9	0.0	0.0
Turkey	14.0	13.9	0.1	0.0	0.0
United States	2.7	0.9	1.7	11.2	17.1
Mercosur	12.9	12.9	0.0	6.9	3.3
European Free Trade Area (EFTA)	28.6	2.0	26.6	58.2	33.6
ASEAN	11.2	7.5	3.7	32.0	8.4
Sub-Saharan LDCs	13.1	13.1	0.0	0.0	0.0
Other Sub-Saharan Africa (SSA)	25.6	25.5	0.0	0.0	0.0
Maghreb	17.6	16.2	1.5	39.4	14.3
South African Customs Union (SACU)	13.0	4.4	8.6	16.3	55.9
EU	11.8	3.1	8.8	35.5	21.5
Developed	14.3	4.3	10.0	36.9	17.3
Developing	20.9	18.5	2.4	63.7	11.6
LDCs	13.4	13.0	0.3	0.0	0.0
World	17.2	10.8	6.4	46.5	14.4

Source: MAcMap-HS6 Database, Centre d'Etudes Prospectives et d'Informations Internationales (CEPIIs), Paris (see Bouët and others 2004).

Note: The Maghreb region consists of Algeria, Libya, Mauritania, Morocco, and Tunisia. Figures for regions are computed as import-weighted averages across countries.

10 percent comes from the ad valorem equivalents of specific, mixed, or compound duties. These latter duties are a particular concern to developing countries, since specific tariffs tend to impose greater burdens on developing-country exports (these exports frequently have lower per unit prices, making the tariff a

higher percentage of the export value for developing countries). Within the developed-country group, average tariffs vary considerably, with Japan having an average agricultural tariff of 36 percent, mostly derived from non–ad valorem tariffs, and the European Free Trade Area (EFTA) having a tariff of 29 percent. The average agricultural tariff in the EU is considerably lower, at 12 percent, and those in the United States and Australia, lower still, at 3 percent.

Developing countries have higher average tariffs, at 20 percent, than developed countries, but only 2 percentage points of this protection is provided by specific tariffs. Average tariffs are extremely high in the Republic of Korea, at 94 percent, and also high in China, India, Pakistan, and Sub-Saharan Africa.[5] The net agricultural exporting Mercosur region of South America has quite low tariffs, at an average of 5 percent. Interestingly, least developed countries (LDCs) as a group, and the LDCs of Sub-Saharan Africa, have quite low tariffs; that is consistent with the tendency noted in the political economy literature for poor countries to have low agricultural protection (see, for example, Anderson, Hayami, and George 1986).

Another feature of agricultural protection evident in table 4.1 is the height of the barriers on the TRQ commodities. The analysis by de Gorter and Kliauga (2005) indicates that these products cover 20 percent of agricultural tariff lines, and 52 percent of the value of production, in the countries using TRQs.[6] The fact that average applied tariffs on these commodities are so high, even though some imports are permitted at lower in-quota tariffs, is striking testimony to the importance of protection on these commodities both in developed countries and in those developing countries using these measures. Had all TRQ goods been automatically treated as sensitive products, as was proposed in WTO (2004a), a very large share of total agricultural protection would have been shielded from liberalization.

Another key element of the geography of market access is the relationship between applied and bound tariffs. The higher bindings are relative to applied rates, the larger the reductions in bound rates that must be made before applied rates must change and market access improvements are realized. The gap between applied and bound duties has two origins: the binding overhang, that is, the gap between bound and MFN tariffs, and preferential arrangements, which create a gap between the MFN and applied rates.[7]

There was substantial binding overhang in many developing countries after the Uruguay Round. Developing countries had the right to set their tariff bindings without reference to previous levels of protection, under the so-called ceiling binding option. Many developing countries used this right to set their bindings at high, and frequently uniform, levels such as 150 or 250 percent. The effects are illustrated in table 4.2, which shows that the bound tariff in developing countries is 2.4 times the average applied rate.

TABLE 4.2 Bound and Applied Agricultural Tariff Rates, by Selected Countries and Regions, 2001 (percent, trade-weighted average)

Country/region	Bound tariff	MFN tariff	Applied tariff	CV bound	CV MFN applied
Australia	5.9	3.6	3.0	1.9	1.6
Bangladesh	156.7	14.4	14.4	8.8	3.4
Canada	19.6	19.3	9.7	23.6	23.7
China[a]	16.2	51.3	38.9	11.0	18.7
Japan	62.1	52.1	34.6	81.1	90.1
Korea, Rep. of	103.5	119.8	93.9	43.3	57.5
Mexico	49.4	31.9	10.7	17.7	25.0
Pakistan	107.7	30.0	30.4	3.3	5.2
India	153.4	55.4	55.1	23.3	12.9
Turkey	50.1	16.1	14.0	12.5	7.1
United States	6.2	6.0	2.7	14.0	14.0
Mercosur	34.0	12.9	12.9	1.8	1.2
EFTA	70.8	48.2	28.6	21.7	23.6
ASEAN	59.7	12.1	11.2	25.2	10.1
Sub-Saharan LDCs	62.8	14.8	13.1	1.8	1.3
Other SSA	104.4	26.5	25.6	1.0	6.7
Maghreb	38.0	18.9	17.6	10.9	5.2
SACU	51.5	13.8	13.0	11.7	4.7
EU	20.5	17.2	11.8	40.6	36.4
Developed	27.0	22.1	14.2	37.3	37.7
Developing	48.1	26.7	20.6	13.9	15.1
LDCs	77.6	14.3	13.4	3.7	1.8
World	37.4	24.0	17.0	26.2	26.9

Source: MAcMap-HS6 Database, CEPII, Paris (see Bouët and others 2004).
Note: CV is the weighted coefficient of variation for the power of the tariff (1 + t).
a. The bound average duty reported for China takes into account commitments not in effect in 2001, hence its lower level in comparison with the MFN rate. Figures for regions are computed as import-weighted averages across countries.

Although developed countries did not have the right to use ceiling bindings, negotiators used a highly protected base period (1986–88)—and many members used so-called dirty tariffication—to set tariff rates for industrial countries well above the previously prevailing average applied tariffs (Hathaway and Ingco 1996). Table 4.2 indicates that binding overhang is substantial in developing countries and smaller, but by no means nonexistent, in developed countries.[8] These results are broadly consistent with the findings of Martin and Wang (2004), which were based on an entirely different data set.

For developed countries, the average bound rate was almost twice as high as the applied rate. This difference mainly comes from the large gap between MFN and applied rates, reflecting the importance of preferential agreements and tariff rate quotas in reducing average applied rates below their MFN levels. The difference is large in relative terms for all developed countries, highlighting the issue of preference erosion analyzed by Bouët, Fontagné, and Jean (2006). A key feature of table 4.2 is the sharp difference among countries. Low-income countries tend to have a large binding overhang, with bindings for the LDC group six times their applied rates. For Bangladesh, the average difference between bound and applied rates is more than 150 percentage points. In the European Union, Japan, and the United States, average bound rates are more than 50 percent above the applied rates, suggesting that relatively large cuts in bound rates would be needed to bring about sizeable reductions in applied rates.

Simulation Experiments

For this analysis, we assume that a reduction in a tariff binding causes a reduction in applied tariffs whenever the new binding is below the initial applied rate. This assumption is widely used, but the initial applied rate is by no means the only possible counterfactual. If, in the absence of a WTO agreement, tariffs would have increased, the effect of the WTO commitment might be greater than is implied under our assumption. If applied rates would otherwise have declined, the gain from the agreement might be less than we estimate. Even in the random-walk case, when the initial tariff rate is the best indicator of future tariff rates, our assumption that a unit reduction in the binding below the applied rate will cause a one-for-one reduction in expected applied rates is not necessarily true given the stochastic nature of unbound tariffs (Francois and Martin 2004). However, our simplified approach provides a useful, and widely adopted, rule of thumb.

Results are presented for 14 simulations designed to evaluate the consequences of different approaches to liberalization, particularly different degrees of top-down progressivity in the tariff cuts and different degrees of special and differential treatment (SDT) for developing and least developed countries. As specified in the framework, all of these cuts are made in tariff bindings, and we examine the consequences for applied rates.

The analysis begins with the 2001 tariffs that are the basis for the GTAP-6 database. Before we performed the main simulations, however, we undertook an experiment to introduce a number of developments that occurred before any tariff reductions arising from the Doha Agenda. These included the expansion of the EU to 25 members, the phase-in of remaining commitments by developing countries under the URAA, and the tariff reforms agreed by WTO accession countries, China in particular.[9]

The simulations, descriptions of which are summarized in table 4.3, begin with a tiered formula consistent with the framework (scenario 1). The effects of adding different levels of sensitive and special products were then considered. Any top-down formula is likely to involve intense negotiating difficulties, since the extent to which higher tariffs are to be cut by more must be negotiated, and non–ad valorem tariffs must be converted to ad valorem form.[10] We therefore thought it worthwhile to compare the results of the tiered formula with those from a much simpler, proportional cut approach. Next, we examine the consequences of fuller

TABLE 4.3 Summary Description of the Agricultural Reform Scenarios

Base	2001 applied protection
Agric 0	Pre-experiment (EU enlargement + WTO commitments)
Agric 1	Tiered formula for agriculture, 45, 70, and 75% cuts
Agric 2	Tiered formula + sensitive products (2% of tariff lines)
Agric 3	Tiered formula + sensitive products (5% of tariff lines)
Agric 4	Proportional cut
Agric 5	Proportional cut + sensitive products (2% of tariff lines)
Agric 6	Tiered formula + sensitive products (2% of tariff lines) + 200% tariff cap
Agric 7	"Light" tiered formula, 35, 50, and 65% cuts
Agric 8	Tiered formula with developed-country coefficients in both developed and developing countries, no reduction for LDCs
Agric 9	Tiered formula with developing countries and LDCs treated as developed countries
Agric 10	Swiss formula
Agric 11	Swiss formula + sensitive products (2% of tariff lines)
Agric 12	Tiered formula with sensitive products not exceeding 2% of import value
Agric 13	Tiered formula with sensitive products not exceeding 5% of import value
Agric 14	Tiered formula with 2% of tariff lines sensitive products (excluding alcohol and tobacco products)

Source: Authors.
Note: In developing countries, the percentage of products subject to sensitive product treatment was doubled to allow for "special" products.

participation by developing countries. Then, we consider the strongly top-down Swiss formula. Finally, we examine two important issues involving sensitive products: whether the choice of trade value, rather than number of tariff lines, greatly affects the impact of including sensitive products; and whether the impact of sensitive products is greatly influenced by the inclusion of alcohol and tobacco products.

As an initial attempt to capture the key elements of likely liberalization proposals, we first examine in scenario 1 a tiered formula with transition points at 15 and 90 percent and marginal tariff cuts of 45, 70, and 75 percent.[11] The transition points for developing countries were placed at 20, 60, and 120 percent, and the marginal cuts at 35, 40, 50, and 60 percent. Consistent with the framework, least developed countries were not required to undertake any reduction commitments.

Scenarios 2 and 3 examine the consequences of including sensitive and special products. We assume that WTO members would take into account the importance of the commodity, the height of the existing tariff, and the gap between the tariff binding and the applied rate in deciding which products to designate as special or sensitive. We consider situations in which developed countries are allowed to treat 2 percent (scenario 2) and 5 percent (scenario 3) of tariff lines as sensitive. Developing countries are allowed, in addition, to classify the same number of tariff lines as special products.

Scenario 4 considers the impact of a proportional cut formula that brings about the same reduction in average bound tariffs in developed countries as a group, and developing countries as a group, as the tiered formulas used in scenario 1. Scenario 5 uses the same proportional cut formula and allows 2 percent of tariff lines to be treated as sensitive products; developing countries are also allowed to treat an additional 2 percent of tariff lines as special products. Scenario 6 considers the effects of adding a tariff cap of 200 percent, consistent with the suggestion in the framework that the role of a tariff cap be explored. Scenario 7 considers the "light" tiered formula proposed in the Harbinson draft, with tariffs cut by 10 percentage points less than in scenario 1. Scenarios 8 and 9 examine two aspects of special and differential treatment. Scenario 8 treats developing countries the same as developed countries, but continues to exclude least developed countries from liberalization. Scenario 9 uses the tiered formula of scenario 1, but treats LDCs the same as other developing countries.

Scenario 10 examines the implications of moving to a Swiss formula approach to tariff reduction. For this scenario, the Swiss formula parameter is calibrated to bring about the same reduction in average tariffs as would have occurred using the tiered formula in scenario 1. While the reduction in the average tariff is the same, the more sharply concave nature of the Swiss formula means that higher tariffs are reduced more, and lower tariffs correspondingly less, than under the tiered or proportional cut formulas. Under scenario 11, we consider the impact of allowing developed countries to designate 2 percent of tariff lines as sensitive and developing countries to classify 2 percent as sensitive and another 2 percent as special products while using the Swiss formula approach to liberalization.

In scenarios 12 and 13, we return to the tiered formula used in scenarios 2 and 3, with exceptions for sensitive and special products. In scenarios 12 and 13, however, we specify the proportion of sensitive products to be allowed using the value of trade in those products, rather than the number of tariff lines. Finally, in scenario 14, we examine the sensitivity of our results to the exclusion of alcohol and tobacco products from the list of products that can be treated as sensitive. While the production of alcohol and tobacco is clearly protected in some cases, in other cases tariffs on these products may be intended either to raise revenue or discourage their consumption for social purposes. In these cases, governments might choose not to designate them as sensitive products, using their limited number of sensitive products for goods where the motivation for tariffs is purely protection.

The Consequences of Tiered Formulas

What happens to bound and applied rates under the scenarios outlined above? Under scenario 1, world average bound duties would fall by half, from the initial level of 37 percent down to 19 percent (table 4.4). Logically, given the special and differential treatment granted to developing countries, the reductions in average tariffs, as well as the harmonizing effects across countries, are stronger among developed countries: their average bound tariff is cut from 27 percent to 9.5 percent, with a final level lower than 10 percent for each country, except EFTA (23 percent) and Japan (20 percent). Given the progressive nature of the formula, however, the cut is also substantial for developing countries (except the least developed). The average bound tariff for developing countries is cut almost in half, from 48 percent down to 27 percent. The reductions are quite large in percentage points for India (76 points), Korea (54 points), Pakistan (47 points), and all Sub-Saharan Africa except for its LDCs (47 points).

As already emphasized, these cuts in bound duties lead to cuts in applied rates only when the new bound duty is lower than the initial applied duty. Accordingly, it is no surprise that the cuts in applied duties are not as great as the cuts in bound duties. But the extent to which the binding overhang dampens the impact on applied duties is surprisingly large: while bound duties are approximately cut in half worldwide, applied duties are cut only by one-third, that is, by 5.5 percentage points on average (table 4.5). This liberalization appears rather limited, even though the formula used is considerably more rigorous than that proposed in the Harbinson draft.

TABLE 4.4 Base Level and Reductions in Average Bound Duties, by Agricultural Reform Scenario (percentage points)

Country	Base (%)	Scenario (1)	(2)	(3)	(4)	(5)	(6)
Australia	5.9	2.8	1.0	1.0	3.9	3.2	2.2
Bangladesh	156.7	0.0	0.0	0.0	0.0	0.0	0.0
Canada	19.6	12.4	3.0	3.0	12.8	7.1	6.7
China	16.2	4.1	1.6	1.6	4.8	3.5	3.0
Japan	62.1	42.4	9.8	9.6	40.0	20.2	28.9
Korea, Rep. of	103.5	53.7	16.4	16.2	45.9	21.5	52.6
Mexico	49.4	19.9	7.5	7.5	21.9	19.2	17.6
Pakistan	107.7	47.4	16.3	16.2	47.8	21.7	27.6
India	153.4	76.1	23.2	23.2	68.0	64.5	73.3
Turkey	50.1	21.6	11.3	11.3	22.2	20.6	20.1
United States	6.2	3.3	1.4	1.4	4.0	3.1	2.4
Mercosur	34.0	12.6	6.2	5.7	15.1	13.6	12.0
EFTA	70.8	48.2	11.0	10.9	46.0	35.4	40.1
ASEAN	59.7	26.4	11.5	11.4	24.2	16.5	25.3
Sub-Saharan LDCs	62.8	0.0	0.0	0.0	0.0	0.0	0.0
Other SSA	104.4	47.4	16.7	16.3	46.3	37.0	38.1
Maghreb	38.0	15.1	5.7	5.7	16.3	11.8	12.3
SACU	51.5	21.5	11.4	11.3	22.7	20.4	21.3
EU	20.5	12.7	3.4	3.2	13.3	8.9	8.1
Developed	27.0	17.6	4.5	4.3	17.5	10.5	12.0
Developing	48.1	21.3	8.1	8.0	20.9	15.2	18.8
LDCs	77.6	0.0	0.0	0.0	0.0	0.0	0.0
World	37.4	18.9	6.0	5.9	18.7	12.4	14.8

Among the main countries listed in table 4.5, only EFTA, the EU, Japan, and Korea show reductions in applied duties of more than 5 percentage points. Indeed, liberalization appears to be overwhelmingly concentrated in Japan and Korea. In many countries, applied duties hardly change—they drop less than 1 percentage point in 8 of the 19 countries and groups shown in the table. For Pakistan, for instance, the 47 percentage point cut in the average bound duty translates into a 0.5 point cut in the average applied duty. In sum, for developing countries the formula considered in scenario 1 narrows the binding overhang in many cases without substantially changing applied duties. For developed

TABLE 4.4 (*Continued*)

Scenario							
(7)	(8)	(9)	(10)	(11)	(12)	(13)	(14)
2.2	2.8	2.8	1.2	1.1	2.6	2.4	2.5
0.0	0.0	78.2	0.0	0.0	0.0	0.0	0.0
10.5	12.4	12.4	11.6	5.5	9.7	7.4	6.4
3.0	6.1	4.1	2.2	2.0	3.5	3.0	3.0
36.1	42.4	42.4	46.7	21.7	34.3	28.0	20.9
43.3	72.7	53.7	66.6	20.1	46.0	38.5	21.7
15.0	31.1	19.9	15.1	11.7	17.2	15.9	16.9
36.7	72.6	47.4	46.5	26.6	45.7	42.6	21.3
60.8	107.4	76.1	87.5	40.2	71.5	67.5	73.6
16.6	32.4	21.6	18.9	17.7	19.1	15.8	20.1
2.6	3.3	3.3	1.9	1.5	2.7	2.1	2.4
9.2	20.1	12.6	6.9	6.0	12.2	11.5	12.1
41.1	48.2	48.2	51.5	39.2	41.8	36.4	37.6
20.6	37.5	27.5	30.1	10.0	20.2	16.6	23.0
0.0	0.0	26.0	0.0	0.0	0.0	0.0	0.0
36.9	70.9	47.4	47.9	36.9	46.0	44.1	38.6
11.4	23.4	15.1	13.0	11.0	13.9	12.5	11.9
16.4	33.2	21.6	18.9	17.3	18.1	16.8	20.9
10.7	12.7	12.7	11.1	6.7	10.6	8.5	8.1
14.9	17.6	17.6	17.6	9.6	14.5	11.9	10.5
16.6	31.1	21.3	21.3	11.5	18.9	17.1	16.7
0.0	0.0	35.3	0.0	0.0	0.0	0.0	0.0
15.3	23.3	19.6	18.9	10.3	16.2	13.9	13.1

Source: Authors' calculations, based on the MAcMap-HS6 database, CEPII, Paris.
Note: For descriptions of scenarios, see table 4.3. Figures for regions are computed as import-weighted averages across countries.

countries, the cuts in applied duties are less than on bound duties in absolute terms, but they are comparable in most cases, when expressed in relative terms.

The tiered formula does, however, have a significant harmonizing effect on applied rates across products, as illustrated by the reduction in the coefficient of variation of the power of the MFN tariff (table 4.6). On average, the coefficient of variation decreases from 36 percent to 14 percent for developed countries and from 10 percent to 7 percent for developing countries. The world average coefficient of variation decreases from 31 percent to 14 percent. The decline is sharper

TABLE 4.5 Reductions in Base Tariffs for Average Applied Tariffs, by Agricultural Reform Scenario (percentage points)

Country	Base (%)	Scenario (1)	(2)	(3)	(4)	(5)	(6)
Australia	3.0	0.9	0.3	0.2	1.5	0.9	0.4
Bangladesh	14.4	0.0	0.0	0.0	0.0	0.0	0.0
Canada	9.7	4.4	0.1	0.1	4.1	1.1	1.0
China	10.0	2.3	0.9	0.9	2.7	1.4	1.3
Japan	34.5	16.6	2.1	2.0	15.0	5.1	8.5
Korea, Rep. of	90.1	44.5	12.2	12.2	36.8	13.4	43.0
Mexico	9.5	1.5	0.2	0.2	1.8	0.3	0.2
Pakistan	30.4	0.5	0.0	0.0	0.9	0.0	0.0
India	54.5	4.4	1.7	1.6	5.1	1.8	1.7
Turkey	13.9	1.5	0.2	0.2	1.6	0.5	0.4
United States	2.7	0.9	0.1	0.1	1.2	0.6	0.3
Mercosur	12.8	0.4	0.0	0.0	0.8	0.1	0.0
EFTA	28.6	11.5	0.8	0.7	10.1	6.0	7.1
ASEAN	10.9	0.9	0.3	0.3	1.0	0.4	1.2
Sub-Saharan LDCs	13.1	0.0	0.0	0.0	0.0	0.0	0.0
Other SSA	25.4	2.8	0.6	0.6	2.7	0.8	0.8
Maghreb	16.9	2.6	0.8	0.8	2.9	1.0	1.0
SACU	12.6	0.7	0.2	0.2	1.0	0.2	0.2
EU	11.8	6.1	1.3	1.1	6.5	2.9	2.5
Developed	14.1	6.6	0.9	0.9	6.5	2.6	3.1
Developing	17.9	4.3	1.3	1.3	4.1	1.6	3.5
LDCs	13.3	0.0	0.0	0.0	0.0	0.0	0.0
World	15.8	5.5	1.1	1.0	5.3	2.1	3.2

for countries with very uneven initial bound duties, especially Japan, Korea, and to a lesser extent India, the ASEAN (Association of Southeast Asian Nations) countries, and Canada.

When 2 percent of sensitive products are exempted from the tiered formula and instead subjected only to a 15 percent cut in the bound rate (scenario 2), the cut in the average bound duty worldwide narrows from 19 to 6 percentage points. Excluding 2 percent of products is thus enough to reduce the extent of delivered liberalization of bound duties by more than two-thirds, and even more than this in countries such as Canada, Japan, and Korea. This outcome results from the

Consequences of Alternative Formulas for Agricultural Tariff Cuts

TABLE 4.5 (*Continued*)

			Scenario				
(7)	(8)	(9)	(10)	(11)	(12)	(13)	(14)
0.7	0.9	0.9	0.3	0.2	0.8	0.7	0.7
0.0	0.0	0.3	0.0	0.0	0.0	0.0	0.0
3.0	4.4	4.4	4.7	1.1	3.3	1.7	0.9
1.7	3.2	2.3	1.0	0.8	1.8	1.7	1.3
11.8	16.6	16.6	20.4	5.1	13.1	10.6	4.6
36.0	60.5	44.5	58.0	12.6	39.2	32.0	13.4
0.8	3.4	1.5	1.0	0.2	1.5	1.3	0.3
0.1	8.6	0.5	0.1	0.0	0.5	0.5	0.0
3.2	12.9	4.4	3.7	1.7	4.4	4.2	2.0
0.9	3.9	1.5	1.1	0.2	1.3	0.7	0.4
0.6	0.9	0.9	0.4	0.1	0.8	0.6	0.3
0.1	2.1	0.4	0.0	0.0	0.4	0.4	0.1
7.3	11.5	11.5	14.0	7.6	9.4	7.8	6.1
0.6	2.1	0.9	1.9	0.3	0.7	0.7	0.7
0.0	0.0	0.2	0.0	0.0	0.0	0.0	0.0
1.7	7.6	2.8	2.8	0.8	2.7	2.7	1.8
1.8	4.6	2.6	2.0	0.8	2.1	1.9	1.4
0.5	3.3	0.7	0.5	0.2	0.7	0.4	0.3
4.9	6.1	6.1	5.3	1.8	4.9	4.0	2.4
4.8	6.6	6.6	7.1	2.1	5.3	4.2	2.3
3.3	6.9	4.3	4.7	1.3	3.8	3.3	1.7
0.0	0.0	0.2	0.0	0.0	0.0	0.0	0.0
4.1	6.6	5.5	5.9	1.7	4.5	3.7	2.0

Source: Authors' calculations, based on the MAcMap-HS6 database, CEPII, Paris.
Note: For descriptions of scenarios, see table 4.3. Figures for regions are computed as import-weighted averages across countries.

strong unevenness of protection across products in most countries, with a few tariff peaks accounting for a substantial part of total average protection. But the consequences of excluding 2 percent of sensitive products are even more spectacular when it comes to applied duties. Under scenario 2, average applied duties worldwide fall a mere 1.1 points—that is just one-fifth the size of the cut delivered under the tiered formula in scenario 1.

Allowing sensitive and special products to be subject to much less rigorous tariff-cutting treatment also strongly undercuts the reductions in peak tariffs and in

TABLE 4.6 Cross-Product Coefficient of Variation of the Power of MFN Tariffs: Base and Reduction by Agricultural Reform Scenario (percentage points)

Country	Base (%)	Scenario					
		(1)	(2)	(3)	(4)	(5)	(6)
Australia	1.6	0.7	0.2	0.2	0.9	0.4	0.4
Bangladesh	3.4	0.0	0.0	0.0	0.0	0.0	0.0
Canada	23.7	15.9	3.1	3.1	14.5	3.7	5.5
China	11.0	2.7	1.0	1.0	2.9	1.9	1.8
Japan	83.2	51.8	7.9	8.0	42.4	11.6	45.2
Korea, Rep. of	45.7	19.5	4.1	4.1	13.9	4.2	21.1
Mexico	22.8	10.7	3.2	3.2	9.7	7.4	8.2
Pakistan	5.2	0.1	0.0	0.0	0.2	0.0	0.0
India	12.3	−0.6	−0.1	−0.1	−0.8	−0.1	−0.1
Turkey	7.1	1.2	0.1	0.1	1.1	0.2	0.2
United States	14.0	8.5	4.0	3.8	8.9	4.8	4.8
Mercosur	1.2	0.1	0.0	0.0	0.1	0.0	0.0
EFTA	22.1	13.9	2.2	2.2	11.8	2.2	10.8
ASEAN	9.6	0.8	0.2	0.2	0.7	0.3	2.1
Sub-Saharan LDCs	1.3	0.0	0.0	0.0	0.0	0.0	0.0
Other SSA	6.7	1.5	0.4	0.4	1.4	0.4	0.4
Maghreb	4.9	1.4	0.4	0.4	1.4	0.5	0.6
SACU	4.4	0.4	0.1	0.1	0.4	0.1	0.1
EU	36.4	23.2	4.6	4.7	22.0	5.4	5.9
Developed	36.2	22.7	4.7	4.7	20.3	5.9	13.4
Developing	10.3	3.0	0.8	0.8	2.5	1.2	2.7
LDCs	1.8	0.0	0.0	0.0	0.0	0.0	0.0
World	24.0	13.5	2.9	2.8	12.0	3.7	8.4

the variability of applied duties. Instead of 14 percent under scenario 1, the world average of the cross-product coefficient of variation of MFN tariffs falls only 3 percentage points, to 21 percent, when countries are allowed to designate 2 percent of their tariff lines as sensitive products (see table 4.6). The harmonizing impact of the formula is clearly much reduced by allowing for exceptions.

Raising the share of sensitive products to 5 percent (scenario 3) does not change the broad picture a great deal. The extent of delivered liberalization is

TABLE 4.6 (*Continued*)

			Scenario				
(7)	(8)	(9)	(10)	(11)	(12)	(13)	(14)
0.5	0.7	0.7	0.4	0.2	0.4	0.3	0.6
0.0	0.0	0.1	0.0	0.0	0.0	0.0	0.0
13.4	15.9	15.9	17.5	5.9	6.1	3.6	4.7
2.0	4.5	2.7	2.3	1.4	1.5	1.0	1.8
42.1	51.8	51.8	70.6	16.8	10.6	5.0	15.4
15.4	27.8	19.5	30.8	4.5	10.8	7.5	4.3
8.4	15.7	10.7	11.7	5.0	4.2	4.0	6.1
0.0	2.3	0.1	0.0	0.0	0.1	0.1	0.0
−0.3	0.8	−0.6	0.1	−0.1	−0.6	−0.7	0.0
0.8	2.4	1.2	1.3	0.1	1.0	0.2	0.2
7.1	8.5	8.5	7.0	4.9	4.3	2.4	4.8
0.0	0.4	0.1	0.0	0.0	0.1	0.1	0.0
11.5	13.9	13.9	17.8	6.5	3.1	1.3	3.7
0.5	2.3	0.8	3.9	0.2	0.5	0.5	0.6
0.0	0.0	0.0	0.0	0.0	0.0	0.0	0.0
1.0	3.4	1.5	1.6	0.4	1.5	1.4	1.0
1.0	2.5	1.4	1.4	0.4	0.6	0.5	1.0
0.3	1.2	0.4	0.4	0.1	0.3	0.1	0.1
19.5	23.2	23.2	23.4	6.4	11.2	6.5	5.8
18.7	22.7	22.7	26.4	7.7	7.9	4.3	7.1
2.2	5.1	3.0	4.5	1.1	1.6	1.3	1.4
0.0	0.0	0.0	0.0	0.0	0.0	0.0	0.0
11.0	14.4	13.5	16.2	4.6	4.9	2.9	4.4

Source: Authors' calculations, based on MAcMap-HS6 database, CEPII, Paris.
Note: For descriptions of scenarios, see table 4.3. Figures for regions are computed as import-weighted averages across countries.

somewhat lower, but the qualitative assessment and the general conclusion do not change: the pass-through from liberalization of bound duties to liberalization of applied duties is weak under a tiered formula such as the one studied here. Moreover, the little action that takes place is concentrated on a very small number of products, so that excluding 2 percent of tariff lines as sensitive products is enough to empty the agreement of any substantive liberalization.

Tiered Formula Versus a Proportional Cut

Scenario 4 presents results for a proportional cut delivering the same cut in average tariffs—for industrial countries and for developing countries—as the tiered formula. On an economy-by-economy basis, the cut in tariffs is not substantially different from the tiered formula, with the exception of Korea, where the cut in applied duties is significantly lower (37 points, compared with 45 points). Even in terms of cross-product variability of MFN duties, the difference is not generally large, although the decline is less pronounced for developed countries. Nor is there much change when 2 percent of sensitive product tariff lines are excluded (scenario 5) either in the country-by-country average tariffs or in the coefficient of variation of tariffs. This result raises questions about the importance of a tiered formula relative to a proportional cut. While a tiered formula is generally more ambitious in reducing peak tariffs, it is likely to present more difficulties in achieving a consensus. If the differences between tiered formulas and proportional cuts are as small as our simulations indicate—even given the aggressive nature of our tiered formula—then the loss from moving to a proportional approach may not be large.

Another topic these scenarios aim to address is the potential importance of setting a cap for bound duties. Scenario 6 introduces such a cap (at a level of 200 percent), in addition to the application of the tiered formula with 2 percent of sensitive product lines excluded (scenario 2). Although excluded from the full application of the formula, sensitive products are subject to the cap in this scenario. The results show that setting such a cap can matter a great deal: the cut in the worldwide average of applied duties is three times as large in scenario 6 as in scenario 2. Setting a cap thus appears to be a potential way to limit the loss of market access opportunities that result from excluding sensitive products from tariff reductions. For most countries and regions, the cap has a relatively small impact on the resulting tariff cut. But for EFTA, the EU, Japan, and Korea, the cap increased the cut in average applied rates considerably.

Scenario 8 illustrates the implications of special and differential treatment for tariffs. In this scenario, developing countries other than LDCs are subjected to the same formula as developed countries. Under this scenario, the absolute cut in developing countries' applied tariffs rises to 6.9 percentage points, from 4.3 percentage points registered in scenario 1. This reduction is larger in absolute value than the 6.6 percentage points in developed countries, but it is smaller proportionately (a 38 percent reduction, compared with 47 percent in developed countries). The smaller percentage cut results from the higher binding overhang in developing countries. There are, of course, considerable differences among developing countries in the extent to which the assumption of full disciplines would require larger tariff cuts. For many, such as Mexico and Turkey, the resulting tariff cuts would be proportionally larger but would remain small in absolute terms. For a few, such as India and Korea, eliminating special and differential treatment would require cuts that are larger both in absolute and proportional terms.

For developing countries, these results suggest that, because of their binding overhang, the mercantilist "cost" of full participation in the Doha Round might be considerably lower than it would at first appear. That raises an important question for developing countries: what additional gains could they obtain by offering fuller participation? This question arises even more strongly in scenario 9, which shows the effect of a potential agreement for LDCs to participate in line with other developing countries. The results show that the effect on their cuts to applied rates would be extremely modest. The average applied agricultural tariff in LDCs would decline by only 0.2 percent, because the large binding overhang in LDCs reduces the requirement to reduce tariffs to an extremely low level.

Scenarios 10 and 11 examine the effect of the Swiss formula calibrated to produce the same reductions in average bound rates for developed and developing countries as the tiered formula applied in scenarios 1, 2, and 3. A key effect of this formula is to reduce applied protection in higher-tariff economies such as EFTA, Japan, and Korea by more than they are reduced in lower-protection countries. Another key effect is to bring about a larger reduction in the coefficient of variation of tariffs than either the tiered formula or proportional cuts. The reduction in applied tariffs is larger for both developed and developing countries, however, reflecting a tendency for the Swiss formula to be more effective in reducing binding overhang. However, there are important differences in the impact of the formula between countries. In countries and groups with relatively modest agricultural protection, such as Australia, China, Mercosur, SACU, and the United States, where both the mean and the coefficient of variation are low, the strongly top-down Swiss formula would require smaller tariff reductions in applied rates than the tiered formula. By contrast, in countries with high or variable tariffs such as Japan, Korea, and EFTA, the Swiss formula would require significantly larger reductions in average applied tariffs.

Scenarios 12 and 13 shed light on the importance of the way in which the share of products to be accorded sensitive product treatment is specified. Under scenarios 2 and 3, special products could be designated for a maximum of 2 percent and 5 percent of tariff lines, respectively. Under scenarios 12 and 13, the criterion is shifted to 2 percent and 5 percent of imports, rather than tariff lines. Under scenario 12, the global reduction in average applied tariffs is 4.5 percent, compared with 1.1 percent under scenario 2. The size of the resulting cut in tariffs is reduced by 10–20 percent in most cases, in contrast with the dramatic and unpredictable reductions in disciplines associated with basing sensitive products on tariff lines.

Scenario 13 shows that expanding the volume of sensitive products to 5 percent diminishes the resulting disciplines on market access: the world average agricultural tariff falls by 3.7 percent, rather than 5.5 percent, as in scenario 1. However, even when sensitive products are allowed to make up 5 percent of imports, the negative effect on tariff reductions is nowhere near what it is when just 2 percent of tariff lines can be designated as sensitive products.

Although trade volume is also an imperfect criterion (because highly restricted products are likely to have small imports), its deficiencies as a basis for allowing sensitive products clearly appear to be less serious than those associated with using a percentage of tariff lines as a criterion. When tariff lines are used, a large and variable amount of trade can be sheltered from disciplines. Given the results in scenario 2, it seems doubtful whether a pure tariff-line criterion for allowing sensitive products could be compatible with the expansion of market access required in both the initial Doha Agenda (WTO 2001) or the framework agreement (WTO 2004b). Use of a fraction of trade volume could potentially be made consistent with the focus on number of tariff lines in the framework agreement. It would simply require defining the number of tariff lines to be permitted sensitive treatment as the number accounting for a specified volume of trade.

Scenario 14 examines the implications of excluding "sin" commodities such as alcohol and tobacco from the sensitive product category. These goods are frequently high-volume trade products, and there is some doubt about whether countries would use their scarce sensitive products allocation to shelter them. A key question is whether the dramatic reduction in the market access gains observed in scenario 2 is robust if these high-tariff goods are excluded. The results of scenario 14 should be compared with those for scenario 2, since both involve allowing 2 percent of tariff lines to be treated as sensitive. The comparison, shown in table 4.5, finds that excluding these commodities from the sensitive product category does increase the size of the cut in applied tariffs. Even with this adjustment, however, the resulting reductions in tariffs are still extremely small (2 percent, rather than 1 percent), so the exclusion still does not create the "substantial increases in market access" required in the Doha Agenda.

Implications for Market Access

What are the implications of these different tariff-cutting formulas for the market access opportunities of particular countries and regions? First, we consider the implications of different tariff-cutting formulas for the average tariffs applied on countries' agricultural exports. Table 4.7 shows that developing-country exporters of agricultural products faced an average tariff of 16 percent in 2001, a rate that is expected to fall to 15 percent once current commitments, particularly by China and other developing countries, are phased in. The average tariff facing agricultural exports from developed countries was 17 percent in 2001 and will fall to 16 percent with full implementation of current commitments. The LDCs as a group face lower but still significant barriers, with an average tariff of 12 percent even after preferences are taken into account.

The tariffs faced by different countries will differ substantially in the absence of a substantial Doha outcome. China will face the highest tariff barriers, at an average of 32 percent. Australia, the United States, and the ASEAN group will also face very high average tariffs of 18–20 percent. Korea will face an average tariff of 17 percent, while Europe will face an average tariff of 16 percent, essentially the world average. Mercosur will face average agricultural tariffs of 15 percent (down from 18 percent in 2001, prior to new WTO accessions).

The tiered formula used in scenario 1 results in a substantial reduction in the tariffs facing most countries. The worldwide average tariff falls from 16 percent in the baseline to just over 10 percent. The average tariff facing developed countries falls by almost 6 percentage points to 10.6 percent; that facing the developing countries falls from 15 to 10 percent; and that facing the LDCs from 12 to 10 percent. The fall in barriers facing developing countries and the LDCs occurs despite a lack of reduction in tariffs on exports to those countries granting full preferences; the decline reflects reductions in tariffs in those countries not giving preferences or reductions in bindings that require liberalization below initial preferential rates.

Market access gains are much lower when the tiered formula is combined with flexibility on sensitive and special products (scenario 2). With 2 percent of tariff lines subject to flexibility in developed countries, and 4 percent in developing countries (to allow for special products), the average agricultural tariff facing developing countries falls by 1 percentage point, instead of 5 points in the absence of "flexibility." For developed countries, gains in market access are reduced even more: instead of dropping 6 percentage points, tariffs drop only 1 point. For some individual countries, the loss is even greater. For China, the cut in market access barriers is only 3 percentage points instead of the 15 point decline expected when the tiered formula is used; the tariffs facing Australia drop by 2 percentage points rather than 8 points. LDCs also suffer a loss in market access opportunities; tariffs drop only one-third of a point instead of 1.5 points.

Allowing sensitive product flexibility for 5 percent of tariff lines causes a further deterioration in market access, although this is barely visible in the rounded tariff numbers presented in table 4.7. The additional loss from increasing the share of tariff lines treated as sensitive is much smaller than reported by Martin and Wang (2004), however. That is because, in this analysis, we have taken into account the importance of binding overhang, as well as the value of the import tariffs when identifying sensitive products. It seems likely that policy makers

TABLE 4.7 Implications of Alternative Formulas for Market Access, Base Tariffs, and Reductions by Agricultural Reform Scenario (percentage points)

Country	Base (%)	Scenario (1)	(2)	(3)	(4)	(5)	(6)
Australia	18.3	8.2	1.6	1.6	7.8	2.6	4.0
Bangladesh	5.7	0.2	0.0	0.0	0.2	0.1	0.1
Canada	9.3	3.3	0.3	0.3	2.9	0.9	0.8
China	31.6	14.8	3.4	3.4	12.8	5.5	14.5
Japan	10.4	2.7	1.0	0.9	3.4	1.9	1.6
Korea, Rep. of	17.0	5.0	1.6	1.2	5.7	4.1	3.4
Mexico	4.3	1.2	0.3	0.2	1.2	0.5	0.5
Pakistan	12.6	4.1	1.1	0.9	4.0	1.7	2.7
India	10.0	2.6	0.6	0.6	2.6	1.1	1.3
Turkey	10.2	2.3	0.5	0.4	2.5	1.3	1.6
United States	19.8	7.9	1.5	1.4	7.4	2.5	4.9
Mercosur	14.6	5.3	1.3	1.2	5.3	2.2	3.0
EFTA	13.8	5.1	1.1	1.0	5.8	3.4	2.5
ASEAN	19.3	3.9	0.7	0.7	4.0	1.9	2.9
Sub-Saharan LDCs	9.5	1.3	0.3	0.3	1.3	0.3	0.4
Other SSA	10.3	4.5	0.8	0.8	4.2	0.9	0.9
Maghreb	12.9	4.2	0.8	0.8	4.6	1.9	3.4
SACU	17.4	5.6	0.9	0.8	5.8	2.6	2.5
EU	15.8	4.2	0.8	0.8	4.3	2.2	2.0
Developed	16.4	5.8	1.1	1.0	5.6	2.2	3.1
Developing	15.3	5.2	1.1	1.1	5.1	2.0	3.3
LDCs	11.8	1.5	0.3	0.3	1.4	0.4	0.5
World	15.8	5.5	1.1	1.0	5.3	2.1	3.2

would base their designation of sensitive products in part on the degree of binding overhang. Even the approach used here, however, may not fully capture the adverse impacts for market access of allowing a small number of sensitive products. Many of the products identified as sensitive in our analysis were items such as tobacco products, for which tariffs are frequently used in conjunction with domestic taxes of the same magnitude to raise revenues. If this is the case, and the tariffs are replaced by pure domestic taxes, or both the tariff and the domestic tax are lowered together, there may be less trade creation than the tariff analysis would suggest.

TABLE 4.7 (*Continued*)

\multicolumn{8}{c}{Scenario}							
(7)	(8)	(9)	(10)	(11)	(12)	(13)	(14)
6.3	9.0	8.2	9.2	2.4	6.5	5.3	2.3
0.1	1.2	0.2	0.1	0.1	0.2	0.1	0.1
2.0	3.6	3.3	4.2	1.0	3.1	1.9	0.7
11.7	18.8	14.8	19.3	4.6	11.2	10.9	5.1
1.9	4.2	2.7	1.4	0.9	2.5	2.3	2.0
3.4	5.8	5.0	4.5	2.6	4.6	4.6	4.2
0.8	1.3	1.2	1.2	0.3	1.0	1.0	0.5
3.3	4.9	4.1	4.3	1.4	3.3	2.8	1.6
2.0	3.3	2.6	2.6	0.7	2.0	1.4	1.1
1.6	3.0	2.3	2.3	0.9	2.2	2.1	1.6
5.9	9.3	7.9	9.0	2.2	6.8	4.9	2.4
4.1	6.4	5.3	5.1	1.7	4.9	3.6	2.0
3.8	6.1	5.1	3.9	2.1	4.3	4.0	3.5
2.9	5.7	3.9	4.3	1.3	3.0	2.7	1.7
1.0	1.7	1.3	1.4	0.3	0.5	0.5	0.4
3.5	4.8	4.5	4.8	0.8	1.7	1.3	1.2
3.2	4.5	4.2	3.4	2.6	3.9	3.7	1.5
4.1	6.4	5.6	5.6	1.9	5.1	3.4	2.4
2.8	5.3	4.2	4.0	1.8	3.7	3.3	2.3
4.2	6.9	5.8	6.3	1.9	5.0	3.9	2.1
4.0	6.4	5.2	5.6	1.5	4.1	3.6	1.9
1.1	2.0	1.5	1.6	0.5	0.7	0.6	0.5
4.1	6.6	5.5	5.9	1.7	4.5	3.7	2.0

Source: Authors' calculations, based on MAcMap-HS6 database, CEPII, Paris.
Note: For descriptions of scenarios, see table 4.3. Figures for regions are computed as import-weighted averages across countries.

The proportional cut experiment in scenario 4 yields, by design, the same average cut in tariffs at the global level. However, the distribution varies somewhat from country to country. China, in particular, receives less of a boost to market access because it faces very high rates of protection in some key markets and so does not benefit to the same extent from reductions in peak tariffs. Interestingly, the Mercosur region benefits more from the proportional cuts than from the tiered formula because it exports relatively more products that face moderate or low tariffs. Scenario 5 shows that a proportional cut approach is just as vulnerable to erosion from sensitive products as the tiered formula. Average tariffs facing both developed and developing countries are 3 percent higher when sensitive products are allowed as when a "clean" proportional cut is applied. A key question for negotiators is whether the chances of a "clean" tariff cut would be higher with a proportional cut than with a more progressive tiered formula.

Comparison of scenario 2 with scenario 6 shows the potentially important role of a tariff cap in reducing barriers to market access. A tariff cap is particularly important to countries supplying highly protected East Asian markets, and it reduces the overall average tariff facing developing countries by 2 more percentage points.

Scenario 7, the original, weaker liberalization tiered formula, reduces market access barriers by noticeably less than scenario 1. As previously noted, this formula resulted in no reduction in applied tariffs in a number of regions.

Comparison of scenarios 1 and 8 shows the implications when developing and developed countries participate under the same rules. The average tariff facing both sets of countries falls by an additional percentage point as a consequence. As previously noted, the proportional cut in applied tariffs for developing countries remains lower than for developed countries, but both developed and developing countries gain considerably more market access.

Scenario 9 is to be compared with scenario 1. Under scenario 9, the LDCs participate on the same basis as developing countries. Not surprisingly, given the small trade and economic weight of the least developed countries, the implications for market access are too small to register on the scale used in this table. For LDCs, the case for fuller participation hinges on issues such as whether economic gains from their own liberalization are sufficiently large, whether MFN liberalization is a better option or a precursor to preferential liberalization, and whether they could negotiate some additional benefits from fuller participation.

Scenario 10 shows that the sharply top-down Swiss formula would bring about larger cuts in market access barriers than the tiered formula. The average tariff facing agricultural exporters worldwide would fall by 5.9 percentage points, compared with 5.5 points under the tiered formula in scenario 1. The gains would be particularly large for China, which would experience a 19 percentage point reduction in the average tariff against its exports. Australia and the United States would also benefit substantially. Scenario 11 shows that the Swiss formula also would be vulnerable to allowances for sensitive and special products. If countries could designate just 2 percent of their tariff lines as sensitive, the average reduction in global tariffs would be 1.7 percentage points, rather than 5.9 points when no product flexibility is allowed.

Scenarios 12 and 13 show that basing the exceptions for sensitive and special products on the value of imports, rather than on the number of tariff lines, greatly reduces the damage of this flexibility to market access opportunities. Under scenario 12, with 2 percent of trade allowed sensitive product treatment, the cut in average tariffs worldwide is 4.5 points—that is more than four times larger than the cut in scenario 2, where sensitive products were limited to 2 percent of tariff lines. The impact on the tariffs facing some countries is particularly marked. For China, for instance, the cut in tariff is only 3 points under scenario 2, but 11 points under scenario 12. For SACU, the tariff cut goes from 1 percentage point to 5 points. Increasing the share of imports allowed sensitive treatment to 5 percent (scenario 13) erodes the gains, with the global average tariff cut falling from 4.5 to 3.7 points. However, allowing sensitive product treatment on 5 percent of import value does not completely remove all discipline in the way that 2 percent of tariff lines does under scenario 2.

A comparison of scenarios 2 and 14 shows the extent to which the results in scenario 2 arise from allowing commodities such as alcohol and tobacco to be designated as sensitive products. As observed earlier, flexibility for these "sin" commodities is associated with reductions in the gains on market access. The cut in overall tariffs doubles from 1 to 2 percentage points when alcohol and tobacco products are excluded from the sensitive and special product lists and importers are therefore forced to select sensitive products that do less damage to market access opportunities. Nonetheless, the results of scenario 14 provide support for our original interpretation of scenario 2: allowing sensitive products based on even 2 percent of tariff lines would greatly diminish the discipline associated with the tiered formula.

Implications for Commodities

A key feature of agricultural protection is sharp differences in tariff rates between commodities. That difference has important implications for the effects of liberalization on different countries. Table 4.8 shows the base tariff rates for selected commodities at the worldwide average level, and the changes in rates under different agricultural scenarios. The highest base tariff rates are on cereals, sugar, tobacco, meat, and dairy products. Under the tiered formula (scenario 1), the largest cut in tariffs is on cereals, for which the worldwide average falls by more than 19 percentage points, or close to half its initial level. Sugar and meat also experience large reductions relative to their initial tariff levels. For dairy products, the cut is substantial, at 6 points, but that is less than one-third of the initial tariff rate. It appears that the tiered formula generates larger cuts on those commodities, such as cereals, where a large share of global protection is provided by very

TABLE 4.8 Implications of Alternative Scenarios for Protection by Commodity: Reductions in Global Average Tariff (percentage points)

Commodity	Base (%)	Scenario (1)	(2)	(3)	(4)	(5)	(6)
Meat	26.1	11.4	1.7	1.7	10.7	3.1	3.4
Dairy products	20.3	6.4	0.9	0.9	6.4	3.0	3.3
Vegetables	11.2	3.4	0.6	0.6	3.5	2.1	2.3
Fruit and nuts	11.7	4.3	0.7	0.7	4.8	1.8	1.4
Coffee and tea	3.4	0.5	0.2	0.2	0.6	0.4	0.3
Cereals	41.2	19.2	3.3	3.3	16.0	3.6	13.9
Oil seeds	12.3	5.5	1.4	1.4	4.6	1.6	5.4
Animal or vegetable fats	17.9	2.0	0.6	0.6	2.4	1.3	1.4
Meat preparations	12.5	4.3	0.6	0.6	4.8	3.5	3.0
Sugars	29.5	13.7	3.0	3.0	13.3	3.7	4.8
Preparations of cereals	10.4	1.6	0.3	0.3	1.9	1.7	1.4
Processed vegetables	12.0	3.5	0.7	0.7	4.4	3.9	3.2
Beverages and spirits	9.4	2.4	1.1	0.8	2.9	2.1	1.1
Tobacco	26.3	4.1	1.7	1.2	4.6	2.7	2.9
Wool	1.7	0.2	0.0	0.0	0.3	0.1	0.1
Cotton	1.4	0.1	0.0	0.0	0.1	0.1	0.0

large tariffs in a few countries than on products, such as dairy, where tariffs are high (but not stratospheric) in many countries.

Allowing flexibility for sensitive products on 2 and 5 percent of tariff lines under scenarios 2 and 3 dramatically reduces the degree of liberalization for all of the high-protection commodities. The largest tariff reduction is for cereals—3.3 percentage points instead of 19 points under scenario 1. Not only would an allowance for sensitive products cut the reduction in base tariffs and the expansion of market access, it also would sharply increase the variation across commodities around the mean.

The proportional cut approach presented in scenario 4 would reduce the tariffs on all commodities. Although protection on high-tariff commodities such as cereals and meat would not decline as much as it would under the tiered formula, it would still decline quite sharply. The tariff on cereals, for example, would fall by 16 percentage points, as against 19 percentage points under the tiered formula. For meat, the difference is less than a full percentage point. Scenario 5 shows that the market access gains under a proportional cut rule would be just as vulnerable

TABLE 4.8 (*Continued*)

			Scenario				
(7)	(8)	(9)	(10)	(11)	(12)	(13)	(14)
8.0	12.1	11.4	11.9	3.3	10.6	8.5	3.0
4.4	7.4	6.4	6.4	4.1	5.0	4.3	2.9
2.4	4.1	3.4	3.8	2.2	2.3	2.0	1.9
3.2	4.8	4.3	3.2	0.8	4.3	4.2	1.3
0.4	0.8	0.5	0.3	0.2	0.5	0.4	0.3
14.7	23.2	19.2	25.3	3.7	14.6	11.2	3.6
4.5	7.2	5.5	7.1	1.5	5.0	1.9	1.6
1.4	4.5	2.0	1.3	1.1	1.9	1.9	1.1
3.0	4.7	4.3	4.2	3.0	4.0	3.9	3.0
11.2	15.0	13.7	14.1	3.5	8.4	7.6	3.6
1.0	2.0	1.6	1.7	1.7	1.6	1.5	1.3
2.5	4.2	3.5	2.0	1.6	3.4	3.3	3.0
1.7	3.2	2.4	1.5	0.8	2.3	2.1	2.2
2.9	6.4	4.1	5.3	1.4	3.7	3.4	4.1
0.1	0.5	0.2	0.1	0.0	0.2	0.2	0.1
0.1	0.1	0.1	0.0	0.0	0.1	0.1	0.0

Source: Authors' calculations, based on MAcMap-HS6 database, CEPII, Paris.
Note: For descriptions of scenarios, see table 4.3. Commodities defined at 2-digit level of the Harmonized System.

to diminution through allowing sensitive and special products based on 2 percent of tariff lines. The tariff reduction on cereals, for instance, falls from 16 to 4 percentage points.

Scenario 6 shows that the introduction of a tariff cap is important only for cereals. For these, it dramatically increases the size of the tariff cut, from 4 percentage points under scenario 5 to 14 percentage points. Scenario 7 shows that smaller cuts in tariff rates would considerably reduce the potential market access gains from liberalization, even before allowing for any sensitive and special products.

Scenario 8 shows that special and differential treatment substantially reduces the overall gains in market access obtainable from the negotiations for several commodities. For cereals this effect is relatively large. Special and differential treatment of the type we have analyzed reduces the fall in average tariffs from 32 to 19 percentage points.

Scenario 10 shows that the sharply top-down Swiss formula would result in substantially higher cuts in protection on the most highly protected commodities. The reduction in the tariff on cereals would be 25 percentage points, compared with 19 points under the tiered formula in scenario 1. This formula, however, would be just as subject to erosion by allowing sensitive and special products as the other formulas. Designating just 2 percent of tariff lines as sensitive and special products would cause this market access gain to collapse to less than 4 percentage points.

Scenarios 11 and 12 show that the diminution in market access gains on the highest-protected products can be reduced significantly by changing the basis on which sensitive products are allowed to a percentage of trade value, rather than a percentage of tariff lines. With these products restricted to 2 percent of imports, the reduction in tariffs on cereals would fall from 19 percentage points under scenario 1 to 15 points under scenario 11. The reduction in protection to meat would be much smaller, with a decline from 11.4 percentage points to 10.6 percentage points. These results reinforce the conclusion from evaluation of the average tariffs in the previous section. If sensitive and special products are to be introduced into the negotiations, considerable attention must be paid to the manner in which this is done lest all semblance of liberalization be lost.

Conclusions

The July Framework Agreement has advanced the state of the art in the agricultural market access negotiations in a number of respects. By moving from the flawed and fundamentally deceptive average cut methodology embedded in some earlier proposals, the framework provides scope for an agreement that would not only increase market access but also lower the highest and most distorting tariffs. Further, it avoids the commitment to essentially unlimited flexibility inherent in the preceding proposal (WTO 2004a) for all of the tariff rate quota commodities, which constitute roughly 20 percent of high-income countries' agricultural tariffs and more than 50 percent of their value of output on some measures. It specifies that tariffs are to be cut in an economically desirable top-down manner, with larger cuts in higher tariff rates, and it provides scope for negotiations on the extent to which flexibility will be included in the negotiations.

This chapter points to a critical design issue in the tiered formula, namely, the discontinuities involved in a simple tiered formula with higher rates for higher tariff reductions. The principle of higher cuts in higher tariffs has strong support in economics, in equity, and in the practice of multilateral negotiations. However, literal application of a formula with higher proportional cuts in higher tariffs would lead to discontinuities in the tariff schedule with, for instance, tariffs just over 90 percent ending up close to 10 percentage points below tariffs of

90 percent. One possible solution to this problem is examined: implementation of a tiered formula that works like a progressive income tax schedule, with higher marginal rates of reduction on tariffs in higher tariff bands.

Scenarios analyzed in the chapter include tiered formulas, a tiered formula with exceptions for sensitive and special products, a proportional cut approach, and varying extents of special and differential treatment. Examination of the tiered formulas shows that only formulas that bring about very deep cuts in bound rates will have a substantial impact on applied tariffs and hence on market access, particularly when allowance is made for slippage due to smaller cuts on sensitive and special products. A progressive tariff reduction formula with cuts of 45, 70, and 75 percent in bound tariffs in developed countries would, for instance, reduce the average tariffs facing developing countries from 15 percent to 10 percent—an important gain in market access, but only one-third of the way to complete liberalization. Large cuts such as this would be required for there to be a major impact on market access.

Another key finding from the scenarios is the extraordinary sensitivity of the results to self-selected sensitive and special products. We made the assumption that countries would put into these categories products that are important in trade, subject to high tariffs, and have relatively little binding overhang. Under this assumption, we found that even allowing 2 percent of products in developed countries to have this treatment (and 4 percent in developing countries) would dramatically reduce the effectiveness of tariff reductions as a means of increasing market access. The reduction in the tariff barriers facing developing countries fell from 5 percentage points without sensitive products to 2 percentage points when such flexibilities were included. A tariff cap of 200 percent helped reduce the losses resulting from inclusion of sensitive and special products, particularly by bringing about substantial reductions on cereals. Clearly, if the Doha Round is to be successful in increasing market access, these results suggest that great care will need to be taken to ensure that the share of products allowed special treatment is extremely limited, or that substantial reductions in protection occur even on these products, or that the number of products to be included is restricted in a more meaningful way than by the number of tariff lines.

Comparison of the tiered formula with a regime of proportional cuts confirmed that either approach could bring about a substantial increase in market access. A proportional cut regime reduces high tariffs by larger absolute numbers of percentage points, although not by a larger proportion, as under the tiered formula. The key difference with the proportional cut approach is that some of the countries with the highest tariffs are required to make smaller reductions. This, in turn, reduces the market access gains to countries such as China that face particularly high agricultural tariff barriers.

Examination of the impact of special and differential treatment shows that the developing countries can expand each other's market access opportunities substantially by participating fully in the negotiations. While developing countries' tariffs would fall by more in absolute terms than tariffs in developed countries, the proportional fall would still be smaller because of the bigger tariff binding overhang in developing countries. A factor not considered in this analysis is the potential further gains in market access if developing countries were able to trade fuller participation for deeper cuts in protection in developed countries or for reductions in the use of sensitive products of particular interest to developing countries.

Notes

1. Martin and Wang (2004) experiment with using tariff-line level data instead of 6-digit data, but find that the broad results are not greatly affected.

2. In the Uruguay Round, it was only after the negotiations were completed that the full extent of the slippage associated with the use of "dirty tariffication" and the average cut routine was revealed (see Hathaway and Ingco 1996).

3. This was an important advance from the preceding draft text (WTO 2004a), which would have treated all TRQ commodities, roughly 20 percent of high-income country agricultural tariff lines and a staggering 52 percent of high-income economy agricultural production, as "sensitive" (de Gorter and Kliauga 2005).

4. Note that for the sake of simplicity, the corresponding calculation is carried out assuming the value of imports (net of taxes) to be unchanged.

5. Korea is a self-declared developing country in the WTO, but a high-income country by World Bank standards and a member of the OECD.

6. This percentage corresponds to products that are at least partly protected by a TRQ (see de Gorter and Kliauga 2005 for details). It should therefore be considered as an upper bound.

7. Note, however, that given the methodology used here, TRQs are also a source of difference between MFN and applied rates, since the MFN duty is always assumed to be equal to the out-of-quota tariff rate, while that is not the case for the applied duty as soon as the quota is not filled by more than 99 percent.

8. Computing perfectly comparable information on MFN and bound ad valorem equivalent tariffs is a complex task. Because treating the information concerning MFN tariffs sometimes involves specific difficulties, such as incomplete raw information, we suspect that the extent of the binding overhang found here for developed countries, although already small, is still overstated (because the level of MFN duties might have been slightly understated in some cases). This is likely to be the case in particular for the EU and for Japan.

9. Developing countries had 10 years from 1994 to implement their Uruguay Round commitments.

10. Very extensive negotiations in the first part of 2005 were required to reach agreement on the technical issue of converting non–ad valorem tariffs into ad valorem equivalents, and the chairman's summary of June 2005 (WTO 2005) makes clear the difficulties remaining ahead.

11. An initial simulation was undertaken with cuts of 35, 60, and 65 percent and is reported in scenario 7. It was not chosen as the base for further simulations because it created insufficient liberalization to allow evaluation of the effects of liberalization erosion through the addition of sensitive and special products.

References

Anderson, K., Y. Hayami, and others. 1986. *The Political Economy of Agricultural Protection: East Asia in International Perspective.* Boston: Allen and Unwin.

Anderson, K., W. Martin, and D. van der Mensbrugglie. 2006 "Market and Welfare Implications of Doha Reform Scenarios." In *Agricultural Trade Reform and the Doha Development Agenda,* ed. K. Anderson and W. Martin. Basingstoke, U.K.: Palgrave Macmillan; Washington, DC : World Bank.

Baldwin, R. E. 1986. "Toward More Efficient Procedures for Multilateral Tariff Negotiations." *Aussenwirtschaft* 41 (2/3): 379–94.

Bchir, M., S. Jean, and D. Laborde. Forthcoming. "Binding Overhang and Tariff-Cutting Formulas: A Systematic, Worldwide Quantitative Assessment." Working Paper, Centre d'Etudes Prospectives et d'Informations Internationales, Paris.

Bouët, A., Y. Decreux, L. Fontagné, S. Jean, and D. Laborde. 2004. "A Consistent, ad Valorem Equivalent Measure of Applied Protection across the World: The MAcMap-HS6 Database." Centre d'Etudes Prospectives et d'Informations Internationales, Paris.

Bouët, A., L. Fontagné, and S. Jean. 2006. "Is Erosion of Tariff Preferences a Serious Concern?" In *Agricultural Trade Reform and the Doha Development Agenda,* ed. K. Anderson and W. Martin. Basingstoke, U.K.: Palgrave Macmillan; Washington, DC: World Bank.

de Gorter, H., and E. Kliauga. 2005. "Reducing Tariffs Versus Expanding Tariff Rate Quotas." In *Agricultural Trade Reform and the Doha Development Agenda,* ed. K. Anderson and W. Martin. Basingstoke, U.K.: Palgrave Macmillan; Washington, DC: World Bank.

Francois, J., and W. Martin. 2003. "Formula Approaches for Market Access Negotiations." *World Economy* 26 (1): 1–28.

———. 2004. "Commercial Policy, Bindings, and Market Access." *European Economic Review* 48 (2, June): 665–79.

Hathaway, D., and M. Ingco. 1996. "Agricultural Liberalization and the Uruguay Round." In *The Uruguay Round and the Developing Countries,* ed. W. Martin and L. A. Winters. New York: Cambridge University Press.

Jean, S., D. Laborde, and W. Martin. 2005. "Sensitive Products: Selection and Implications for Agricultural Trade Negotiations." Paper presented to the Conference on Global Economic Analysis, June, Lubeck. http://www.gtap.agecon.purdue.edu/resources/res_display.asp?RecordID=1850.

Martin, W. 2004. "Market Access in Agriculture—Beyond the Blender." Trade Note 16, World Bank, Washington, DC.

Martin, W., and Z. Wang. 2004. "Improving Market Access in Agriculture." World Bank, Washington, DC.

Martin, W., and L. A. Winters, eds. 1996. *The Uruguay Round and the Developing Countries.* New York: Cambridge University Press.

Sen, A. 1981. *Poverty and Famines: An Essay on Entitlement and Deprivation.* Oxford, UK.: Clarendon Press.

Vousden, N. 1990. *The Economics of Trade Protection.* New York: Cambridge University Press.

World Bank. 2003. *Global Economic Prospects 2004.* Washington DC: World Bank.

World Customs Organization. 1996. *Harmonized Commodity Description and Coding System.* 2d ed. World Customs Organization, Brussels.

WTO (World Trade Organization). 2001. "Ministerial Declaration: Adopted on 14 November, 2001, Ministerial Conference, Fourth Session, Doha, 9–14 November." WT/MIN(01)/DEC/1. WTO, Geneva.

———. 2003a. "Draft Cancun Ministerial Text." JOB(03)/150/Rev.2 (Derbez Draft), WTO, Geneva.

———. 2003b. "Negotiations on Agriculture: First Draft of Modalities for the Further Commitments." TN/AG/W/1/Rev.1, 19 March (Harbinson Draft), WTO, Geneva.

———. 2004a. "Doha Development Agenda: Draft General Council Decision of July 2004." JOB(04)/96 (Groser Draft), WTO, Geneva.

———. 2004b. "Doha Work Programme: Decision Adopted by the General Council on 1 August 2004." WT/L/579 (July Framework Agreement), WTO, Geneva.

———. 2005. "Agricultural Negotiations—Status Report: Key Issues to be Addressed by 31 July 2005." JOB(05)/126, WTO, Geneva.

5

REDUCING TARIFFS VERSUS EXPANDING TARIFF RATE QUOTAS

Harry de Gorter and Erika Kliauga

Tariff rate quotas (TRQs) are two-level tariffs, with a limited volume of imports permitted at the lower "in-quota" tariff and all subsequent imports charged the (often much) higher "out-of-quota" tariff (Ingco 1996; OECD 2001). In lieu of high bound tariffs resulting from tariffication in the Uruguay Round Agreement on Agriculture (URAA), TRQs were adopted for commodities previously subject to nontariff protection. They were meant to guarantee minimum levels of market access (initially 3 percent of domestic consumption, gradually expanded to 5 percent by the end of the implementation period) through "minimum access quotas" and to safeguard current levels of access through "current access quotas" (IATRC 2001a). Hence TRQs may have expanded imports during the URAA implementation period. A total of 1,425 TRQs have been notified to the World Trade Organization (WTO) by 43 countries (WTO 2002c). The implementation was envisioned to maintain or improve preferential market access for developing countries, while often continuing to maintain a managed trade regime (Abbott 2002). Since a substantial proportion of agricultural production in developed countries is protected by TRQs, there is an interest in determining the potential effects of the different ways of liberalizing TRQs.

When demand for imports at the low, in-quota tariff is greater than the level of imports allowed by the quota, imports must be rationed, and so the method by which the rights to the quotas are allocated also becomes important. The rights to the quota are allocated by one of several methods, each with numerous conditions that affect "fill" rates and efficiency. Although TRQs may have provided for more trade, a majority of the TRQs are not being filled (WTO 2002a, 2002b, 2002c).

While market forces may be a factor, there is widespread agreement that quota under-fill is in part attributable to the administration methods employed to implement TRQs.[1]

The purpose of this chapter is to evaluate the relative importance of tariff reductions versus quota expansion in liberalizing agricultural trade. In doing so, the extent of quota underfill and the potential influence of quota administration methods on imports is explored. The effects of expanding TRQs or reducing tariffs in the WTO negotiations on agriculture depend on several key factors: which instrument is binding (the quota itself, or the in-quota or out-of-quota tariff), whether there are imports above the quota at in-quota tariff rates ("overquota imports"), the extent if any of quota underfill, the levels of in-quota and out-of-quota tariffs, the level of water in the tariffs and tariff binding overhang, the methods of administering the rights to the quotas (with or without licenses), and any government responses in changing domestic policy instruments.[2]

The rest of this chapter is organized as follows. The next section presents data showing the importance of TRQs in protecting domestic agricultural production and trade in developed countries. We then explain the economics of liberalizing TRQs by identifying four basic regimes: the first three are where the in-quota tariff, the quota, and the out-of-quota tariff, respectively, determine imports, while the fourth regime is where the government allows for overquota imports at the in-quota tariff (where no trade liberalization occurs initially with either an out-of-quota tariff reduction or an increase in the quota). Data are presented on the value of trade, quota under- or overfill, and tariff levels for each of these regimes. We then evaluate the trade liberalizing effects of a 35 percent reduction in tariffs compared with a 50 percent increase in quotas to obtain a glimpse of the situation regarding TRQs and the relative importance of each initial regime. Data are then presented along with an analysis of the administration methods and additional regulations for the TRQs notified to the WTO. Summary data by country and commodity are presented on tariff levels, import values, and quota underfill. We touch on some important issues that may affect the efficacy of TRQs, including minimum versus current access quotas, changes in TRQ administration methods over time, dynamic rent-seeking activities, and domestic policy responses. The chapter ends with some concluding comments and identifies priorities for further research.

The Importance of TRQs

As many as 43 of the nearly 150 members of the WTO employ TRQs in agriculture, and 20 percent of their agricultural tariff lines involve TRQs (Gibson and others 2001; Wainio 2001). Table 5.1 summarizes the value of production protected by TRQs for the countries and commodities monitored by the Secretariat of the OECD (Organisation for Economic Co-operation and Development). It shows that 51 percent of the total is protected by tariff quotas. This number understates the true magnitude because it omits the lightly shaded cells in table 5.1, which indicate commodity groups that have at least some tariff quota lines and situations that are not officially tariff quotas but act like them (sugar import barriers in Japan, for example).[3] Milk, maize, eggs, and other grains account for a substantially larger proportion of the total value of production protected by tariff quotas than their share of the total value of production, while the opposite is true for beef and veal, rice, oilseeds, and sugar. The Quad countries (Canada, European Union, Japan, and the United States) have well over half of their total production in tariff quota commodities, while the Republic of Korea, Norway, and Poland have close to 90 percent.

Using the same assumptions as in table 5.1 on OECD commodity coverage, we estimate that imports under tariff quotas represent 43 percent of total agricultural imports, valued at world prices, in developed countries (table 5.2). Hence, commodities facing tariff quotas have import values disproportionately lower than their share of total value of agricultural production, perhaps reflecting the higher protection tariff quotas afford. Beef, oilseeds, wheat, dairy, and maize have the highest value of trade in agriculture covered by TRQs. The share of total trade in tariff quota commodities mimics the share of total trade, except for TRQ trade in wheat, maize, rice, and sheep meat, where the shares are substantially higher (whereas those of other grains and pig meat are substantially lower). The EU, Japan, Korea, and the United States have by far the largest share of the total value of tariff quota trade.

The Economics of Trade Liberalization with TRQs

The impact of reducing tariffs versus expanding quotas depends critically on the instrument that is binding initially, how soon a regime change will occur as a result of trade liberalization, and whether underfill occurs because of the quota administration method (Skully 2001a, 2001b).[4] We can identify four basic regimes: the in-quota tariff is binding (because of market conditions or by government decree); the quota is binding (resulting in some tariff-equivalent level of protection less than the out-of-quota tariff would otherwise provide); the out-of-quota tariff is binding (out-of-quota imports occur at the high out-of-quota tariff); and the quota is filled, but by government decree, imports beyond the quota level are allowed entry at the in-quota tariff.

Figure 5.1 depicts the in-quota tariff regime. Figure 5.1a shows the case of quota overfill, where the government has decreed that the in-quota tariff remains

TABLE 5.1 Value of Production for TRQ versus Non-TRQ Commodities in OECD Countries, 2000 (US$ millions except where indicated)

Country	Milk	Beef and veal	Pig meat	Poultry meat	Rice	Wheat	Maize
United States	20,677	31,226	10,791	16,861	1,061	5,848	18,441
European Union	34,659	15,959	21,222	7,906	627	11,533	4,834
Japan	6,058	5,388	4,346	1,900	19,827	938	2
Korea, Rep. of	1,206	2,085	1,852	644	9,323	1	31
Canada	2,798	3,660	2,271	1,088	0	2,297	592
Mexico	2,715	2,061	1,462	2,098	73	531	2,840
Turkey	1,974	1,418	0	918	257	2,684	315
Australia	1,643	3,320	450	617	169	2,533	36
Poland	2,103	252	1,639	327	—	1,005	96
New Zealand	2,281	832	67	100	0	37	18
Switzerland	1,513	675	617	114	0	245	62
Hungary	523	93	679	426	3	363	448
Czech Republic	524	203	462	165	0	323	30
Norway	622	283	231	77	0	76	0
Slovak Republic	199	68	212	76	0	101	34
Total production	79,496	67,522	46,301	33,318	31,340	28,517	27,779
TRQ share (%)	40.6	80.7	58.1	38.4	95.0	59.6	29.7

operative even above the quota, while figure 5.1b depicts the case of underfill. Figure 5.2 depicts the quota binding regime (exactly 100 percent fill rate in figure 5.2a, and quota underfill in figure 5.2b). Figure 5.3 depicts the out-of-quota tariff regimes with exact, underfill, and overfill of the quota shown in figures 3a, 3b, and 3c, respectively.[5] Finally, figure 5.4 depicts the regime where the quota is binding but there is quota overfill at the in-quota tariff rate. Reducing the in-quota tariff has a direct impact on imports only in regime 1, but further reductions can become ineffective in figure 5.1b if the government then allows the quota to become binding. Expanding the quota has an immediate impact only in regime 2, while a reduction in the out-of-quota tariff has an immediate impact in regime 3 only. Under regime 4, a reduction in either tariff or an expansion of the quota has no immediate impact on trade.

These four regimes thus present eight cases. Table 5.3 presents summary data for each regime on the value of trade, under- or overfill, out-of-quota imports, tariff levels, and value of tariff revenues and quota rents.[6] The out-of-quota tariff regime has the highest value of trade ($22.7 billion, the sum of in-quota and out-of-quota imports) with regime 4 well behind at $7.5 billion, regime 1 (in-quota tariff

TABLE 5.1 (*Continued*)

Oilseeds	Eggs	Other grains	Sugar	Sheep meat	Total production	TRQ share (%)
12,549	4,347	1,557	2,129	357	125,845	42.9
2,676	3,694	6,002	4,755	3,616	117,482	60.0
173	3,589	267	126	61	42,676	63.3
251	538	172	0	—	16,103	89.2
1,642	337	798	31	31	15,546	63.3
23	1,301	773	1,283	240	15,399	43.8
269	547	952	1,414	812	11,562	0.0
352	213	899	389	703	11,325	0.0
178	477	700	307	9	7,092	90.1
0	51	29	0	798	4,213	0.0
32	89	83	98	36	3,563	43.1
83	197	89	48	24	2,975	68.4
133	156	121	70	3	2,190	47.3
1	57	181	0	82	1,611	100.0
40	54	39	21	2	847	47.1
18,403	15,648	12,660	10,671	6,774	378,429	n.a.
4.2	3.4	2.8	79.4	55.2	n.a.	51.6

Source: OECD (2003).
Note: n. a. = not applicable. The darkly shaded cells represent tariff quotas, while the lightly shaded cells have few tariff quota lines and so are not included as TRQs in this table. The commodities are those covered.

operational) at $3.06 billion, and regime 2 (quota binding) at $2.07 billion. Notice that the value of underfill in regime 3 with out-of-quota imports is almost four times that of regime 2 (where the quota is binding), while underfill is significantly lower in the other two regimes. But net quota underfill (underfill minus overquota imports at the in-quota tariff) is slightly negative in regimes 1 and 4.

Using the simple average of bound tariffs, the implied total value of tariff revenues is $26 billion (in-quota plus out-of-quota tariffs), and quota rents are $16 billion. Data using trade-weighted applied tariffs indicate that tariff revenues are significantly lower at $19.7 billion using the WTO's Integrated Database data (last column of Table 5.3). Notice that the simple average bound in-quota tariff is lowest in regime 3, where out-of-quota imports occur, and is highest where the in-quota tariff itself is binding in regime 1. Notice also that the total value of quota underfill is 48 percent of the total value of the quota, which has implications for how the quota is administered (see later).[7]

TABLE 5.2 Value of Trade for TRQ versus Non-TRQ Commodities in OECD Countries, 2000 (US$ millions except where indicated)

Country	Oilseeds	Beef and veal	Pig meat	Milk	Maize	Wheat	Poultry meat
Japan	1,993	2,667	3,502	744	1,887	1,030	1,400
European Union	4,347	1,093	172	1,217	466	634	773
United States	378	2,551	1,040	1,351	174	295	48
Mexico	1,144	783	338	630	548	340	285
Korea	410	736	263	147	933	471	80
Canada	213	524	187	261	170	13	221
Turkey	233	0.0	0.1	33	147	126	1.0
Poland	45	2.1	56	129	59	95	15
Switzerland	42	76	72	190	10	49	109
Australia	58	9	87	157	0.1	0.6	1.0
Norway	96	13	29	20	3.1	26	0.9
New Zealand	14	20	23	18	1.7	30	13
Czech Republic	24	5.8	29	60	10	3.4	24
Slovak Republic	14	10	20	26	31	6.6	12
Hungary	19	6.6	32	48	11	0.2	5.9
Total imports	9,031	8,496	5,849	5,031	4,453	3,120	2,989
TRQ share (%)	28.6	59.3	11.5	49.8	45.4	85.2	47.4

Approximately 45 percent of all tariff quotas are *minimum access* quotas, representing a lower share of total value of TRQ trade (42 percent; see the third column in table 5.3). Under the URAA, these quotas increased from 3 to 5 percent of consumption during each country's implementation period.[8] Note that the highest share of minimum access quota trade is in regimes that have lower trade liberalization effects with quota expansion, namely, regimes 1b and 2b. Quotas do not matter in regime 1, but quota underfill in 2b and overfill in regime 4 lower the impact of increases in quotas. The other 55 percent of the quotas are current access quotas, which were implemented to allow developed countries (such as the EU) to continue to extend preferential access to developing countries or to maintain historical access in cases where imports are a large proportion of domestic consumption (for example, wheat in Japan). If only minimum access quotas were to be expanded in the negotiations, as in the URAA, only 45 percent of quotas would be expanded, substantially reducing the impact of any given expansion of TRQs.

TABLE 5.2 (*Continued*)

Sugar	Other grains	Rice	Sheep meat	Eggs	Total imports	TRQ share (%)
305	556	265	68	20	14,438	27.9
863	49	419	713	6.8	10,752	47.7
552	261	210	238	2.1	7,099	62.7
11	511	101	46	1.4	4,739	25.0
293	56	46	5.1	0.8	3,441	87.0
210	5.0	113	48	3.1	1,967	51.8
0.9	8.4	108	0.003	0.3	658	0
14	61	25	0.2	0.6	502	88.0
38	17	29	61	11	704	28.0
1.7	0.1	29	0.7	0.3	346	0
47	6.9	10	6.5	0.1	259	77.6
51	10	15	4.8	0.3	201	0
14	12	16	0.6	0.7	200	41.8
15	6.8	8.2	0.0	0.5	149	37.4
2.3	9.2	12	0.4	0	146	46.7
2,419	1,569	1,408	1,193	47	45,603	43.7
59.6	4.0	58.4	60.4	1.5	n.a.	n.a.

Source: FAOSTAT (http://faostat.fao.org).
Note: n.a. = not applicable. The darkly shaded cells represent tariff quotas, while the lightly shaded cells have few tariff quota lines and so are not included as TRQs in this table. The commodities are those covered.

An Empirical Assessment of Trade Liberalization

An estimate of the effect on the total value of TRQ imports of a 35 percent reduction in tariffs and a 50 percent expansion in import quotas is presented in table 5.4. A 35 percent reduction in the out-of-quota tariffs has a larger impact, expanding trade by $18.3 billion, which is a 51.5 percent increase in the value of total TRQ trade. Most of the increase in trade with a reduction in out-of-quota tariffs comes from changes in imports under regime 3; very little comes from regime 2. The relative increase in imports from regimes 2, 3, and 4 with a decrease in the out-of-quota tariff depends on the level of trade initially in each regime and on the level of out-of-quota tariffs. The trade liberalization effects also depends critically on the amount of water in the tariff for regimes 2 and 4 (assumed here to be 50 percent of the gap between the out-of-quota and in-quota tariff levels, as assumed by Bouët, Fontagné, and Jean 2006). We also assume that the elasticity of excess demand is 4.63 and that world prices do not change.[9] These assumptions affect the results

FIGURE 5.1 In-Quota Imports with and without Quota Fill

a. Regime 1a: In-quota tariff with overquota imports

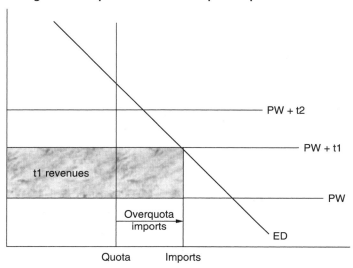

b. Regime 1b: In-quota tariff with quota underfill

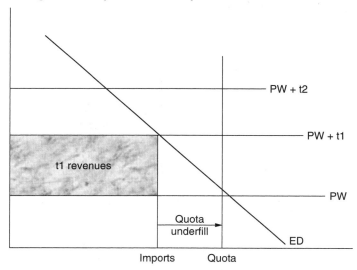

Source: Authors.
Note: PW = world price; t2 = out-of-quota tariff; t1 = in-quota tariff; ED = excess demand curve.

FIGURE 5.2 Imports with Quota Full or Underfilled

a. Regime 2a: Quota filled

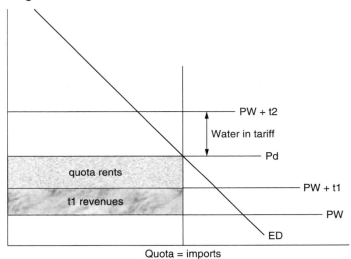

b. Regime 2b: Quota underfilled

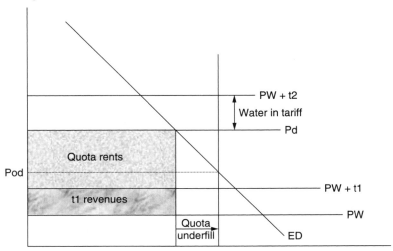

Source: Authors.

FIGURE 5.3 Out-of-Quota Imports with and without Quota Fill

a. Regime 3a: Out-of-quota imports with quota filled

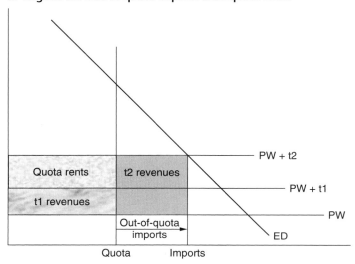

Source: Authors.

b. Regime 3b: Out-of-quota imports with quota underfill

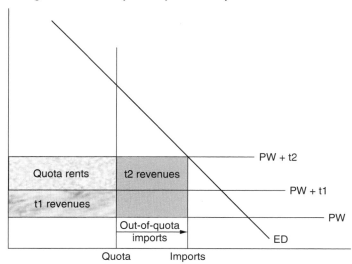

Source: Authors.

FIGURE 5.3 *(Continued)*

c. Regime 3c: Out-of-quota and overquota imports

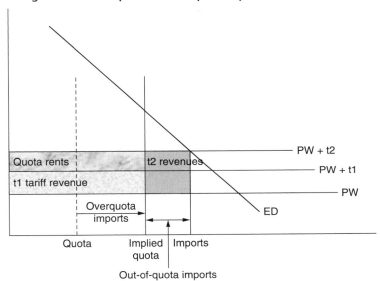

Source: Authors.

FIGURE 5.4 Overquota Imports

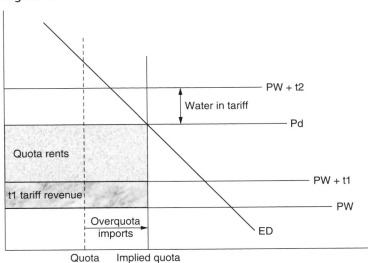

Source: Authors.

TABLE 5.3 Value of Trade by Regime (US$ millions except where indicated)

Regime	Number of TRQs	In-quota imports					Out-of-quota imports
		Total	% min access	Overquota	Underfill[a]	
In-quota tariff						
Regime 1a	216	1,953	15	1,161	0	0
Regime 1b	224	1,104	75	0	846	0
Total	440	3,057	n.c.	1,161	846	0
Quota binding						
Regime 2a	16	362	3	0	0	0
Regime 2b	86	1,706	70	0	3,064	0
Total	102	2,068	n.c.	0	3,064	0
Out-of-quota tariff						
Regime 3a	74	1,784	28	0	0	5,487
Regime 3b	386	6,029	52	0	12,014	7,515
Regime 3c	32	926	16	206	0	988
Total	492	8,739	n.c.	206	12,014	13,990
Overquota imports						
Regime 4	87	7,560	37	1,735	821	0
Total	1,121	21,424	42	3,102	16,744	13,990

(the most critical assumption relates to water in the tariff), but a sense of the relative impacts of tariff reductions versus quota expansion is nonetheless obtained.

Expanding quotas by 50 percent, in contrast, results in a 14.5 percent increase in the value of total TRQ imports ($5.1 billion). The increase in trade comes from regimes 2, 3, and 4, the latter case where the quota is not binding initially. Note that quotas up to a 105 percent fill rate were included in regime 4 (instead of assuming the out-of-quota tariff is automatically binding for fill rates between 100 and 105 percent). This means overquota imports are a lower percent of the quota in many instances in regime 4, so a quota expansion has a relatively larger impact.

Three key factors determine the relative amount of trade expansion resulting from an increase in quotas: the level of initial trade in each regime; the degree of underfill in regimes 2b and 3b, and the level of overfill in regimes 3c and 4. If quota overfill is significant, then an increase in quotas will have no effect on trade. The impact of underfill on trade liberalization with a quota increase (regimes 2b and 3b)

TABLE 5.3 (*Continued*)

Tariffs[b]		Tariff revenues			Applied tariffs	
In-quota (%)	Out-of-quota (%)	In-quota	Out-of quota	Quota rents	Trade-weighted (%)	Tariff revenue
138	177	1,146	0	0	74	2,003
193	233	587	0	0	51	842
n.c.	n.c.	1,733	0	0	n.c.	2,845
29	98	189	0	66	41	147
40	126	248	0	233	42	716
n.c.	n.c.	438	0	299	n.c.	863
24	132	82	5,622	3,827	82	5,967
27	111	773	12,999	6,873	36	4,887
41	198	194	796	810	12	233
n.c.	n.c.	1,049	19,417	11,510	n.c.	11,086
62	176	3,411	0	4,182	65	4,888
59	115	6,631	19,417	15,991	54	19,682

Source: WTO notifications and Integrated Database (http://www.wto.org/english/tratop_e/agric_e/agric_e.htm); Agricultural Market Access Database (AMAD; http://www.amad.org).

Note: n.c. = not calculated.

a. Overquota imports are defined as in-quota imports minus quota while underquota imports equal quota minus in-quota imports.

b. Overquota imports are defined as in-quota imports minus quota while underquota imports equal quota minus in-quota imports.

depends on the assumption one makes as to how the fill rate changes (de Gorter and Boughner 1999). Here we assume the fill rate remains constant, so an increase in the quota has a proportionate increase in observed imports. But one could consider two other plausible scenarios: the underfill has to disappear before trade shows a change, or the absolute level of the underfill is fixed so that the initial change in trade equals the change in the import quota. Which of the three assumptions one makes in analyzing the impact of quota expansion rests heavily on one's view as to why there is underfill in the first place, a topic we take up later with our discussion of the importance of administration methods on quota underfill.

TABLE 5.4 Effects of Trade Liberalization on Value of Trade (US$ millions except where indicated)

Regime	Number of TRQs	Value of trade	35% reduction in out-of-quota tariffs		50% increase in quota		Minimum increase in value of trade
			Δ value	%	Δ value	%	
In-quota tariff							
Regime 1a	216	1,953	493	25.2	n.a.	n.a.	493
Regime 1b	224	1,104	426	38.6	n.a.	n.a.	426
Total	440	3,057	919	30.0	n.a.	n.a.	919
Quota binding							
Regime 2a	16	362	149	41.1	680	187.9	149
Regime 2b	86	1,706	97	5.7	920	53.9	97
Total	102	2,068	246	11.9	1,600	77.4	246
Out-of-quota tariff							
Regime 3a	74	7,271	5,274	72.5	85	1.2	85
Regime 3b	386	13,543	9,128	67.4	1,115	8.2	1,115
Regime 3c	32	1,914	1,468	76.7	129	6.8	129
Total	492	22,729	15,870	69.8	1,329	5.8	1,329
Overquota imports							
Regime 4	87	7,560	1,215	16.0	2,203	29.1	1,215
Total	1,121	35,414	18,249	51.5	5,132	14.5	3,709

Source: WTO notifications and Integrated Database (http://www.wto.org/english/tratop_e/agric_e/agric_e.htm); Agricultural Market Access Database (AMAD; http://www.amad.org).
Note: Δ value = change in value of; n.a. = not applicable.

Imports can expand in regimes 2, 3, and 4 if the quota expands substantially (but this is less likely in regime 3, where imports are initially above the quota), but the in-quota tariff may put a brake on the effectiveness of the quota increase. Hence, it is important to emphasize the benefits of a simultaneous reduction in in-quota tariffs, even though these tariffs directly affect imports only in regime 1. Negotiators will have to decide whether to increase both current and minimum access quotas (by, say, 50 percent) or to increase minimum access quotas to 10 percent of consumption (current consumption or that in the base year 1986–88) and require no increases in current access quotas.[10]

Average in-quota tariffs are still very high, compared with tariffs on products not attached to TRQs, so room for either increasing imports or increasing quota rents remains substantial. However, trade-weighted tariffs are lower: 54 percent, compared with 59 and 115 percent for in-quota and out-of-quota simple average tariffs, respectively (table 5.3). Using the simple average tariff may not be so misleading because bound tariffs are to be negotiated, and if an average tariff-cut formula is used, or sensitive products are not controlled tightly, tariff peaks may remain. Average tariffs need to be interpreted with care because production-weighted tariff equivalents of import barriers as calculated by the OECD are not directly comparable with average tariffs. This is because so many tariff lines and associated imports do not directly protect domestic production. Take the U.S. dairy case as an example: because so many different cheeses and other dairy products are imported (with more than half the value of U.S. dairy imports being nonquota), the average applied tariff (whether a weighted or a simple average) is far lower than the level of protection of domestically produced dairy products.

The last column of table 5.4 gives an estimate of the minimum increase in value of trade across the two possible instruments to liberalize for each of the eight cases presented. The change in total value of trade under the minimum is $2.8 billion, significantly less than the increase with either the quota expansion or the out-of-quota tariff reduction scenarios. This finding emphasizes the importance of not allowing importing countries to choose between reducing tariffs or expanding quotas, as has been proposed.

The reduction of out-of-quota tariffs holds much promise in liberalizing trade, as the simulations earlier indicated. The outcome depends heavily on what level of tariff reduction versus quota expansion one assumes and also on the level of water in the tariffs. Table 5.5 provides some estimates of water in the tariff for selected countries and commodities. Estimates of the tariff equivalent of the binding quota are given (taken from nominal protection coefficients given in OECD 2003), alongside the implied tariff equivalent with our assumption of the water to be 50 percent of the difference between the out-of-quota and in-quota tariff levels. We present two possibilities: using the average out-of-quota tariff or the line with the highest tariff included in the quota category. The actual and assumed water in the tariff are then compared, with the last two columns of table 5.5 indicating the error in our assumption using the average and the maximum out-of-quota tariffs, respectively. We overestimate the water and hence underestimate the trade liberalizing effects of an out-of-quota tariff reduction when using average tariffs, but we underestimate water and so overestimate trade liberalization effects when we assume that a maximum tariff protects domestic production. Hence, substantial reductions in out-of-quota tariffs may be needed in regimes 2 and 4 before trade liberalization occurs, especially with the high number of tariff peaks and tariff dispersion.

TABLE 5.5 Estimates of Water in the Tariff for Selected TRQs

Country	TRQ number[a]	Product category	In-quota	Tariffs Actual (Out-of-quota)	Max. (Out-of-quota)
Canada	2	Poultry meat	4.3	246	298
Canada	3	Poultry meat	5	161	200
Canada	1	Eggs	0.3	238	283
European Union	83	Rice	31.1	73.7	73.7
European Union	84	Rice	0	123	133
European Union	38	Sugar	0	118	118
European Union	7	Beef and veal	20	153	153
European Union	11	Sheep meat	0	92.3	92.3
European Union	64	Poultry meat	0	83	83
European Union	69	Eggs	19.34	38.7	84
European Union	70	Eggs	11.6	24.1	79
Hungary	42	Rice	25	57.5	63.4
Hungary	52	Sugar	60	61.5	63.8
Hungary	7	Milk	30	51.2	51.2
Hungary	2	Beef and veal	17.5	56	71.7
Hungary	5	Poultry meat	25	35.5	39.0
Hungary	11	Eggs	35	38.3	38.3
Hungary	13	Potatoes	10	44.2	44.2
Hungary	16	Cabbage	12	32	32
Hungary	37	Red peppers	40	44.2	44.2
Hungary	14	Tomatoes	12	46.1	46.1
Hungary	30	Grapes	40	48	51.0
Hungary	32	Apples	25	49.3	49.3
Hungary	65	Coffee	60	51.2	51.2
Hungary	45	Beans	30	29.8	29.8
Iceland	80	Beef and veal	32	511	511
Iceland	82	Sheep meat	32	372	372
Iceland	83	Sheep meat	32	0	220
Iceland	81	Pig meat	32	470	470
Iceland	84	Poultry meat	32	529	529
Iceland	87	Eggs	32	406	460
Japan	14	Wheat	19	201	693
Japan	1	Milk	0	174	174
Japan	2	Milk	20	198	198
Japan	3	Milk	30	0	—
Japan	4	Milk	30	388	388

TABLE 5.5 (*Continued*)

Tariffs equivalent (%)			Water in the tariffs (%)				Error (%)	
	Assumed		Actual		Assumed			
Actual	Average	Max.	Average	Max.	Average	Max.	Average	Max.
0.01	1.25	1.51	2.45	2.97	1.21	1.47	−1.24	−1.50
0.01	0.83	1.02	1.6	1.98	0.78	0.97	−0.82	−1.01
0.2	1.19	1.42	2.18	2.63	1.19	1.42	−0.99	−1.22
0.53	0.52	0.52	0.2	0.2	0.21	0.21	0.01	0.01
0.53	0.62	0.67	0.7	0.8	0.62	0.67	−0.08	−0.13
0.87	0.59	0.59	0.32	0.32	0.59	0.59	0.28	0.28
5.45	0.86	0.86	−3.92	−3.92	0.66	0.66	4.58	4.58
1.17	0.46	0.46	−0.25	−0.25	0.46	0.46	0.71	0.71
0.84	0.42	0.42	−0.01	−0.01	0.42	0.42	0.42	0.42
0.06	0.29	0.52	0.33	0.78	0.10	0.32	−0.23	−0.46
0.06	0.18	0.45	0.18	0.73	0.06	0.34	−0.12	−0.39
0	0.41	0.44	0.58	0.63	0.16	0.19	−0.41	−0.44
0.1	0.61	0.62	0.52	0.54	0.01	0.02	−0.51	−0.52
0.26	0.41	0.41	0.25	0.25	0.11	0.11	−0.14	−0.14
0.14	0.37	0.45	0.42	0.57	0.19	0.27	−0.22	−0.30
0.12	0.30	0.32	0.24	0.27	0.05	0.07	−0.18	−0.20
1.52	0.37	0.37	−1.14	−1.14	0.02	0.02	1.16	1.16
0.2	0.27	0.27	0.24	0.24	0.17	0.17	−0.07	−0.07
0	0.22	0.22	0.32	0.32	0.10	0.10	−0.22	−0.22
0	0.42	0.42	0.44	0.44	0.02	0.02	−0.42	−0.42
0	0.29	0.29	0.46	0.46	0.17	0.17	−0.29	−0.29
0	0.44	0.46	0.48	0.51	0.04	0.06	−0.44	−0.46
0	0.37	0.37	0.49	0.49	0.12	0.12	−0.37	−0.37
0	0.56	0.6	0.5	0.5	0	0	−0.6	−0.6
0	0.3	0.3	0.3	0.3	0	0	−0.3	−0.3
0.99	2.71	2.71	4.11	4.11	2.39	2.39	−1.72	−1.72
0.13	2.02	2.02	3.59	3.59	1.70	1.70	−1.89	−1.89
0.13	0.16	1.26	−0.13	2.07	−0.16	0.94	−0.03	−1.13
0.18	2.51	2.51	4.52	4.52	2.19	2.19	−2.33	−2.33
4.36	2.81	2.81	0.94	0.94	2.49	2.49	1.55	1.55
2.14	2.19	2.46	1.92	2.46	1.87	2.14	−0.05	−0.32
2.80	1.1	3.56	−0.79	4.13	0.91	3.37	1.70	−0.76
2.75	0.87	0.87	−1.01	−1.01	0.87	0.87	1.88	1.88
2.75	1.09	1.09	−0.77	−0.77	0.89	0.89	1.66	1.66
2.75	0.15	—	−2.75	—	−0.15	—	2.60	—
2.75	2.09	2.09	1.13	1.13	1.79	1.79	0.66	0.66

TABLE 5.5 (*Continued*)

Country	TRQ number[a]	Product category	In-quota	Tariffs Out-of-quota Actual	Tariffs Out-of-quota Max.
Korea, Rep. of	42	Other grains	3	779	779
Korea, Rep. of	41	Rice	5	0	n.a.
Korea, Rep. of	63	Oil seeds	5	63	63.0
Korea, Rep. of	1	Beef and veal	0	89.1	89.1
Korea, Rep. of	10	Milk	20	49.5	176
Korea, Rep. of	12	Eggs	30	41.6	89.1
Korea, Rep. of	15	Eggs	8	18	18
Korea, Rep. of	19	Potatoes	30	304	304
Korea, Rep. of	49	Potatoes	8	325	320
Korea, Rep. of	21	Garlic	50	360	360
Norway	224	Pig meat	137	363	363
Norway	173	Poultry meat	64.5	331	331
Norway	228	Poultry meat	160	425	425
Norway	91	Apples	0.7	94.3	188
Norway	93	Apples	0.7	94.3	188
Poland	69	Sugar	67.7	148	96
Poland	27	Tomatoes	20	224	40
Slovak Republic	17	Sugar	50	28.3	60
Switzerland	9	Eggs	25.7	191	244
Switzerland	17	Apples	6.4	85.9	145
United States	21	Sugar	4	93.8	93.8
United States	2	Milk	0	0	57.6
United States	4	Milk	1.5	39.7	44.4
United States	5	Milk	4.5	71.6	71.6
United States	8	Milk	2.9	37	49
United States	35	Cotton	0	17	17
United States	37	Cotton	2.4	17	18.8
United States	38	Cotton	0.8	17	17
Average	n.a.	n.a.	n.a.	n.a.	n.a.

TABLE 5.5 (Continued)

Tariffs equivalent (%)			Water in the Tariffs (%)				Error (%)	
	Assumed		Actual		Assumed			
Actual	Average	Max.	Average	Max.	Average	Max.	Average	Max.
2.39	3.91	3.91	5.40	5.40	3.88	3.88	-1.52	-1.52
4.09	0.03	—	-4.09	—	-0.03	—	4.07	—
0.62	0.34	0.34	0.01	0.01	0.29	0.29	0.28	0.28
1.82	0.45	0.45	-0.93	-0.93	0.45	0.45	1.37	1.37
1.82	0.35	0.98	-1.33	-0.06	0.15	0.78	1.47	0.84
0.14	0.36	0.60	0.27	0.75	0.06	0.30	-0.21	-0.45
0.14	0.13	0.13	0.04	0.04	0.05	0.05	0.01	0.01
0	1.67	1.67	3.04	3.04	1.37	1.37	-1.67	-1.67
0	1.67	1.64	3.25	3.20	1.59	1.56	-1.67	-1.64
0.28	2.05	2.05	3.32	3.32	1.55	1.55	-1.77	-1.77
0.24	2.50	2.50	3.39	3.39	1.13	1.13	-2.26	-2.26
1.72	1.98	1.98	1.58	1.58	1.33	1.33	-0.25	-0.25
1.72	2.93	2.93	2.53	2.53	1.33	1.33	-1.20	-1.20
0	0.48	0.94	0.94	1.88	0.47	0.94	-0.48	-0.94
0	0.48	0.94	0.94	1.88	0.47	0.94	-0.48	-0.94
0.95	1.08	0.82	0.53	0.01	0.40	0.14	-0.13	0.13
0	1.22	0.30	2.24	0.40	1.02	0.10	-1.22	-0.30
0.39	0.39	0.55	-0.11	0.21	-0.11	0.05	0.00	-0.16
3.28	1.08	1.35	-1.37	-0.83	0.83	1.09	2.19	1.93
0.00	0.46	0.76	0.86	1.45	0.40	0.70	-0.46	-0.76
1.32	0.49	0.49	-0.38	-0.38	0.45	0.45	0.83	0.83
0.93	0.00	0.29	-0.93	-0.36	0.00	0.29	0.93	0.65
0.93	0.21	0.23	-0.54	-0.49	0.19	0.21	0.73	0.70
0.93	0.38	0.38	-0.22	-0.22	0.34	0.34	0.55	0.55
0.93	0.20	0.26	-0.56	-0.44	0.17	0.23	0.73	0.67
0	0.09	0.09	0.17	0.17	0.09	0.09	-0.09	-0.09
0	0.10	0.11	0.17	0.19	0.07	0.08	-0.10	-0.11
0	0.09	0.09	0.17	0.17	0.08	0.08	-0.09	-0.09
n.a.	n.a.	n.a.	n.a.	n.a.	n.a.	n.a.	0.05	-0.17

Source: WTO notifications and Integrated Database (http://www.wto.org/english/tratop_e/agric_e/agric_e.htm); Agricultural Market Access Database (AMAD; http://www.amad.org).

Note: — = not available; n.a. = not applicable.

a. Refers to a number that each country designates to each TRQ.

Finally, one has to allow for the possibility of tariff binding overhang for both in-quota and out-of-quota tariffs, where the applied tariff is below the bound tariff. Overhang would make tariff reductions in table 5.4 even more muted, given that bound rates are assumed to be affecting trade levels in our analysis. Jean, Laborde, and Martin (2006) present estimates of the binding overhang. They find that the average applied tariff is about half of the bound tariff in several developed countries and even less in developing countries.

Preliminary Conclusions from Empirical Evidence

Our empirical data thus indicate that reducing out-of-quota tariffs is the most effective means of liberalizing trade—the same result that the OECD (2002) found. Our conclusion, however, is heavily dependent on the level of water assumed in the tariffs. Also, we do not know what would happen if all three liberalizations occurred simultaneously. Reducing the in-quota tariff for those cases where the in-quota tariff is binding and there is no in-quota tariff binding overhang has limited effects (as shown in table 5.4), because the in-quota tariff is binding initially for so little trade in TRQ commodities. In cases where the in-quota tariff is not binding, however, an increase in quota rents will occur, perhaps spurring more political pressure from domestic firms to maintain the status quo and reducing efficiency, depending on the quota administration method (discussed later).

Reductions in out-of-quota tariffs will be more effective only if water in the tariffs can be eliminated and only where fill rates are less than 100 percent because of administration methods and additional regulations. Which approaches to reform are of greatest benefit to developing countries will depend critically on who obtains the quota rents. Reductions in out-of-quota tariffs can reduce rents while expansion of the quota can increase rents, even when the per unit rent falls.

Methods of Quota Administration and Additional Regulations

TRQ administration involves distributing the rights to import at the in-quota tariff. Whoever obtains such rights can make a risk-free profit from the difference between the domestic price and the world price inclusive of the in-quota tariff (Skully 1999, 2001a). Therefore, governments need to ration or otherwise administer the TRQ. We summarize the definitions of the alternative tariff quota administration methods in table 5.6. Applied tariffs are by far the most used method, representing 39.3 percent of the total number of TRQs (but only 14.4 percent of the total value of TRQ trade). Licenses on demand; first-come, first-served; and historical importers are the next most commonly used methods in descending order of importance, representing 28, 12, and 9 percent of total TRQs (but each having 17–19 percent of the total value of trade). Auctions are the next most commonly used method, representing only 5.4 percent of the total number of TRQs and less than 1 percent of the total value of trade. Other administration methods include state trading enterprises (STEs) (producer groups are subsumed in this category) and mixed methods (a combination of at least two administration methods), for which the share of trade was much higher than the corresponding share of TRQs. Finally, for some TRQs, no administration methods are specified, so the information on how these TRQs are administered is incomplete.

First-come, first-served is the third most widely used administration method in terms of trade value. The high use of this method has several implications, one of which is that some of the potential quota rents are likely to be appropriated by consumers or middlemen (Chau, de Gorter, and Hranaiova 2003). Furthermore, there is the likelihood of rent dissipation in rent seeking as firms try to mitigate the negative impacts of first-come, first-served on prices when imports are brought forward in order to obtain the quota rents.

Approximately 36 percent of all tariff quotas are filled (407 TRQs have a fill rate above 100 percent, divided by a total of 1,121 TRQs in table 5.6). Quota overfill occurs in the applied tariff, state trading enterprise, and mixed allocation categories. A total of 278 quotas were overfilled (at the in-quota tariff) and 129 quotas exactly filled at 100 percent fill rate (data are not reported in table). There is a bimodal distribution of fill rates, with 339 TRQs having a fill rate of less than 20 percent with a simple average fill rate of only 4 percent, but the trade-weighted fill rates are significantly higher (no average was calculated for the trade-weighted fill rates). The simple average fill rates as reported by the WTO and cited by many academic studies give the same picture as the trade-weighted fill rates developed in this paper. The average fill rate as reported in this paper is 60.6 percent excluding overquota imports, while the trade-weighted fill rate is 60.9 percent. Indeed, the quota overfill for the applied tariff, state trading enterprise, and mixed allocation categories amounted to $3.1 billion (see table 5.3). Underfill net of overquota imports, in contrast, is $13.7 billion, with license on demand; first-come, first-served; and historical importer categories having the largest underfill levels. These three administration types have the highest share of trade and so are important to analyze. As we show later, these three administration types are prone to inefficiency. Finally, the value of quota underfill is estimated to be $16.8 billion, approximately 48 percent of the value of the quota when filled (assuming world prices do not change), thereby representing a huge amount of trade and rents forgone.[11] This lost potential value of tariff revenues and quota rents may be dissipated to a large extent (or appropriated by other countries or groups), so further analysis of tariff quota administration methods and additional regulations is warranted (see later discussion).

TABLE 5.6 Value of In-quota Trade and Fill Rates by TRQ Administration Method

Administration method	Number of TRQ	Share (%)		Quota fill < 20			
		Number	Value (US$ millions)	Number	Value (US$ millions)	Fill rate (%)	
						Simple	Weighted
Applied tariff	440	39.3	14.4	104	91	5.0	12.1
Licenses on demand	310	27.7	18.1	129	94	3.8	1.3
First-come, first-served	138	12.3	16.8	56	145	3.8	3.7
Historical importers	105	9.4	18.8	18	14	4.7	1.0
Auctioning	60	5.4	0.5	24	1	4.2	5.6
State trading enterprises	29	2.6	12.2	3	0	1.1	1.1
Mixed allocation	11	1.0	4.6	0	0	0	0
Nonspecified	28	2.5	14.9	5	39	5.5	8.6
Total	1,121	100	100	339	384	4.0	n.c.

Average in-quota tariffs are highest for applied tariffs and auctions, while the average out-of-quota tariffs are also high for these same methods, as well as for the state trading enterprise method. Reducing in-quota tariffs would have an impact on trade only for cases described by regime 1. Even then, the benefits of some reductions in the in-quota tariff would end when it causes a regime change to a binding quota, thereby generating quota rents. Either way, the reduction of in-quota tariffs increases quota rents and hence political opposition to trade liberalization. As we show later, the increase in per unit rent can have very different effects on efficiency, depending on the quota administration method in place.

Several other key regulations can also affect the fill rate, such as time limits, past trading performance (applied to methods other than historical importers), license limits per firm, seasonal quotas (quarterly or semiannual), domestic purchase requirements, and taxes for licenses and nonuse. Table 5.7 summarizes the number of quotas, countries, commodities, and filled quotas for each additional type of regulation. These additional conditions imposed on firms are very significant, affecting many quotas, countries, and commodities. Time limits, for example, affect $7.7 billion of trade. Fill rates are particularly low for seasonal, export

TABLE 5.6 (*Continued*)

	Quota fill ≥ 100			Total in-quota imports			Quota	Tariffs (%)	
Number	Value (US$ millions)	Fill rate (%) weighted)	Value (US$ millions)	Fill rate (%) Truncated	Weighted		Underfill net	In-quota	Out-of-quota
230	1,982	241	3,057	68	111		-315	166	206
63	2,340	141	3,874	48	34		7,635	35	110
37	878	107	3,581	52	46		4,151	20	72
44	2,927	146	4,026	73	85		679	37	143
8	7	120	116	46	75		39	56	210
10	1,028	897	2,585	79	152		-886	31	286
8	945	114	985	91	111		-96	40	200
7	885	100	3,200	65	56		2,545	23	150
407	10,993	n.c.	21,424	61.0	61.0		13,753	59	115

Source: WTO notifications and Integrated Database (http://www.wto.org/english/tratop_e/agric_e/agric_e.htm); Agricultural Market Access Database (AMAD; http://www.amad.org).

Note: n.c. = not calculated. "Simple" is the simple average fill rate, defined as the average of the ratios of the value of in-quota imports over the value of the quota (can be greater than 100 percent if overquota imports dominate underfill). "Truncated" is the simple average fill rate except it takes a maximum value of 100 percent (ignores overquota imports). "Weighted" is the trade-weighted fill rate, defined as the sum of the value of in-quota imports divided by the sum of the value of the quota (can be greater than 100 percent). "Nonspecified" refers to TRQs whose administration method was not specified in the WTO notifications.

certificates, license fees, and provision for unused licenses. For example, less than 10 percent of the seasonal quotas are filled, while the "provision for entry" has a high proportion of filled quotas, second only to license fees; later, we show how fees can increase efficiency. Note that "use-it-or-lose-it" is one of three regulations with a trade-weighted fill rate over 100 percent, implying that firms perhaps import when it does not pay in order to hold the valuable asset for later use, thereby adding to inefficiencies.

The next step is to match each additional regulation with the principal quota administration method (table 5.8). Analysis of this table reveals a high number of additional regulations for licenses on demand; historical importers; first-come, first-served; and state trading enterprise administration methods. The implications

TABLE 5.7 Value of In-quota Trade and Fill Rates by TRQ Additional Regulation

Aditional regulation	Number of TRQ	Share (%) Number	Share (%) Value (US$ millions)	Quota fill < 20 Number	Quota fill < 20 Value (US$ millions)	Fill rate (%) Simple	Fill rate (%) Weighted
Time limit	247	17.1	25.7	76	66	5.1	1.84
Past trading performance	170	11.7	12.9	53	174	5.6	2.72
Limit per firm	133	9.2	2.4	48	30	4.5	0.92
Seasonal	101	7.0	0.5	49	39	3.7	0.99
Domestic purchase requirement	44	3.0	6.6	4	1	7.4	3.26
Provision for entry	30	2.1	4.1	5	0	0.0	0.00
Use it or lose it	35	2.4	1.6	14	2.7	2.5	6.02
Export certificate	26	1.8	12.0	6	5.2	3.5	0.45
License fee	26	1.8	2.2	8	17	10.0	1.35
Provision for unused licenses	23	1.6	0.4	10	1.4	6.2	10.87
Nonuse penalty	13	0.9	0.2	3	0	6.2	17.61
Refundable down payment	4	0.3	0.1	1	0	3.6	0.00
No descriptions were identified	422	29.2	13.3	109	131	4.7	6.37
None of above	173	12.0	17.9	46	20	2.6	2.52
Total	1,447	100	100	432	489	4.0	n.c.

of additional conditions are manifold. For example, one cannot automatically assume "applied tariffs" are represented by regime 1 (in-quota tariff binding) because one of several additional conditions associated with applied tariffs (such as domestic purchase requirements) may increase the costs of importation (or act as a nontariff barrier), thus creating rents. At the same time, methods other than applied tariffs could produce a regime 1 result, especially if there are no additional conditions and the quota is not binding. Notice that the value of trade affected by additional regulations for the license auction method is higher than the value of trade under auctions, implying that no trade may occur under a basic auction system that economists appear to favor. Additional regulations impose costs on the classic textbook case of efficiency with auctions.

TABLE 5.7 (*Continued*)

	Quota fill ≥ 100		Total in-quota imports			Quota underfill net	Tariffs ($)	
Number	Value (US$ millions)	Fill rate ($) weighted	Value (US$ millions)	Fill rate ($) Truncated	Weighted		In-quota	Out-of-quota
78	4,865	127	7,686	60.9	69.5	3,313	20.5	129.6
36	1,050	131	3,783	56.9	37.4	6,336	23.9	105.1
14	148	134	851	52.7	17.6	3,330	31.3	101.6
8	28	100	150	40.6	3.6	3,992	26.8	49.8
25	1,692	207	1,946	78.5	143.8	−593	86.6	183.9
16	942	100	1,203	75.7	92.2	102	21.8	193.0
15	468	119	479	54.3	106.5	−29	20.7	94.7
6	2,782	136	3,519	59.6	77.4	1,025	13.3	128.9
14	347	207	654	68.6	36.5	1,141	37.6	92.3
1	0	0	111	40.3	46.1	129	239.6	400.5
3	44	113	45	64.2	111.2	−5	31.1	55.8
0	0	0	25	53.9	0.0	22	30.0	49.5
205	1,349	372	3,886	64.4	54.7	3,222	169.4	212.4
63	2,643	147	5,256	63.2	93.2	380	35.0	93.3
484	16,361	n.c.	29,592	60.6	60.9	22,365	59	115

Source: WTO notifications and Integrated Database (http://www.wto.org/english/tratop_e/agric_e/agric_e.htm); Agricultural Market Access Database (AMAD; http://www.amad.org).

Note: n.c. = not calculated. "Simple" is the simple average fill rate, defined as the average of the ratios of the value of in-quota imports over the value of the quota (can be greater than 100 percent if overquota imports dominate underfill). "Truncated" is the simple average fill rate except it takes a maximum value of 100 percent (ignores overquota imports). "Weighted" is the trade-weighted fill rate, defined as the sum of the value of in-quota imports divided by the sum of the value of the quota (can be > 100 percent).

A Note on TRQ Fill Rates

Fill rates do not give a complete picture of the efficacy of a tariff quota regime. A fill rate of less than 100 percent may not imply inefficiency if demand and supply conditions are such that the in-quota tariff is binding. But a fill rate of 100 percent does not necessarily mean efficiency either, because the lowest-cost supplier may not have been used.

TABLE 5.8 Fill Rate by Administration Method and Additional Regulation

Aditional regulation	Applied tariff				Historical importer		
	Number of TRQ	Number	Value (US$ millions)	Weighted fill rate(%)	Number	Value (US$ millions)	Weighted fill rate (%)
Time limit	247	15	723	97.9	71	3,224	83.1
Past trading performance	170	11	37.6	145	32	1,022	96.5
Limit per firm	133	7	19.0	96.1	10	272.7	88.9
Seasonal	101	0	0	0	0	0	0
Domestic purchase requirement	44	1	16.9	110	0	0	0
Provision for entry	30	0	0	0	23	291.6	74.6
Use it or lose it	35	0	0	0	8	249.3	120.5
Export certificate	26	0	0	0	3	1,981	140.7
License fee	26	11	37.6	145	15	616.7	34.9
Provision for unused licenses	23	6	1.6	18.5	3	3.0	77.1
Nonuse penalty	13	1	44.0	113	11	0.4	44.0
Refundable down payment	4	0	0	0	0	0.0	0.0
No description	422	369	1,402	124	3	101.2	148.7
None of above were identified	173	41	851	108	18	435.8	102.5
Total	1,447	462	3,132	nc	197	8,198	nc

Average fill rates as reported by the WTO and academic studies can be misleading because of aggregation problems: a subset of some commodity or country groupings may have zero fill rates and others 100 percent fill rates. Trade-weighted fill rates are more indicative of import performance (OECD 2002). Data published so far do not take into account overquota imports assessed the in-quota tariff rate, biasing the fill rates downward. Furthermore, some countries only report imports up to the quota level (ignoring imports at the in-quota tariff that are over the quota), while others simply report the number of import licenses issued, which may not be fully used.

To overcome these difficulties, we present both the number and the value of trade corresponding to the simple average (truncated) fill rate reported by the

Reducing Tariffs Versus Expanding Tariff Rate Quotas

TABLE 5.8 (*Continued*)

	Licenses on demand			First-come, first-served			STEs and producer groups			Auction	
No.	Value (US$ mil.)	Weighted fill rate(%)	No.	Value (US$ mil.)	Weighted fill rate(%)	No.	value	Weighted fill rate (%)	No.	value	Weighted fill rate (%)
85	2,321	49.0	46	200	49.3	14	98.9	121.0	4	0.4	13.2
104	963	22.8	18	260	7.9	4	1,497	99.7	0	0	0
75	197.8	5.8	17	184	75.8	0	0	0	22	14.8	60.1
100	149.7	3.6	1	0.1	1.1	0	0	0	0	0.0	0.0
30	729.9	121.0	1	44	98.2	1	396.9	2,164	1	1.4	100
3	5.7	81.2	0	0	0	0	0	0	0	0	0
26	229.7	97.0	1	0.1	1.1	0	0	0	0	0	0
18	1,299	48.1	5	238	55.0	0	0	0	0	0	0
0	0.0	0	0	0	0	0	0	0	0	0	0
4	101.2	46.9	0	0	0	0	0	0	10	4.8	41.7
1	0.7	82.7	0	0	0	0	0	0	0	0.0	0.0
4	24.8	0	0	0	0	0	0	0	0	0.0	0.0
22	150.7	13.1	1	1	0	0	0	0	11	6.5	0.0
22	217.8	44.4	59	2,830	81.1	10	592.0	607.8	22	93.1	82.0
494	6,392	nc	149	3,758	nc	29	2,585	nc	70	121	nc

Source: WTO notifications and Integrated Database (http://www.wto.org/english/tratop_e/agric_e/agric_e.htm); Agricultural Market Access Database (AMAD; http://www.amad.org).

Note: nc = not calculated. Weighted fill rate is the sum of the value of in-quota imports divided by the sum of the value of the quota (can be greater than 100 percent). Data are for most recent year reported.

WTO as well as the trade-weighted fill rates. Fill rates weighted by value take into account overquota imports at the in-quota tariff.

TRQs by Country and Commodity Group

The number of tariff quotas by country and commodity group is given in tables 5.9 and 5.10, respectively. The total value of in-quota plus out-of-quota trade is $35.4 billion, while net quota underfill (subtracting overquota imports) is $13.7 billion, or 39 percent of the total TRQ trade. Countries with the highest levels of

TABLE 5.9 Value of TRQ Trade by Economy (US$ millions unless otherwise indicated)

Economy	Number of TRQ	Fill rate (%) Truncated	Fill rate (%) Weighted
Australia	2	90	100
Barbados	5	80	69
Brazil	1	100	2,825
Bulgaria	62	40	37
Canada	20	85	106
Chile	0	0	0
China	10	30	30
Colombia	56	75	187
Costa Rica	10	29	185
Croatia	0	0	0
Czech Republic	24	55	49
Dominican Republic	7	74	140
European Union	72	56	72
El Salvador	11	67	44
Ecuador	8	53	15
Guatemala	22	82	149
Hungary	65	48	2
Iceland	49	83	66
Indonesia	2	100	584
Israel	0	0	0
Japan	18	70	89
Korea, Rep. of	67	68	79
Latvia	3	33	8
Lithuania	0	0	0
Malaysia	16	40	53
Mexico	11	87	122
Morocco	3	100	100
New Zealand	3	34	2
Nicaragua	8	92	0
Norway	219	64	96
Panama	19	49	88
Philippines	13	66	46
Poland	36	26	5
Romania	7	10	4
Slovak Republic	24	33	29
Slovenia	20	38	112
South Africa	42	67	85

TABLE 5.9 (*Continued*)

Imports		Quota underfill (net)	Tariffs (%)	
In-quota	Out-of-quota		In-quota	Out-of-quota
66	86	0[b]	9	25
1	0	0[b]	125	125
177	0	−170	14	29
115	46	196	26	71
703	183	−43	4	179
0	0	0	0	0
2,338	214	5,533	0	0
952	40	−444	133	135
15	2	−7	48	111
0	0	0	0	0
72	94	75	28	49
65	0	−19	0	0
4,500	7,710	1,759	15	67
52	4	66	34	68
10	52	58	29	42
146	15	−48	31	121
81	391	3,619	25	40
21	4	11	32	187
659	0	−546	65	185
0	0	0	0	0
1,851	415	218	20	536
1,807	1,746	488	20	277
0[a]	1	2	25	47
0	0	0	0	0
107	16	93	103	233
887	0	−158	45	152
185	1	0	115	115
1	0	66	0	6
52	0	−51	43	67
194	111	8	296	319
29	4	4	15	84
0	296	0[c]	35	35
61	267	1,244	37	81
2	1	42	97	249
19	131	47	28	42
46	38	−5	18	67
217	77	37	20	60

TABLE 5.9 (*Continued*)

Economy	Number of TRQ	Fill rate (%) Truncated	Fill rate (%) Weighted
Switzerland	27	89	106
Taiwan (China)	22	61	72
Thailand	23	40	166
Tunisia	13	59	82
United States	41	70	80
Venezuela, R.B. de	60	59	41
Total	1,121	61	61

in-quota trade are Canada, China, Colombia, the EU, Indonesia, Japan, Korea, Mexico, Thailand, Switzerland, the United States, and República Bolivariana de Venezuela. Notice countries with high levels of overquota imports (in absolute terms and even more so in relative terms) are predominantly developing countries. Countries with high levels of out-of-quota imports are China, the EU, Hungary, Japan, Korea, the Philippines, Poland, República Bolivariana de Venezuela, and the United States. Quota underfill is dominated by six economies: China, the EU, Hungary, Poland, República Bolivariana de Venezuela, and the United States. The simple average in-quota and out-of-quota bound tariffs are also presented in table 5.9. The simple average fill rates and trade-weighted fill rates for each country also are presented in table 5.9.

Corresponding data by commodity in table 5.10 show that the value of in-quota trade and the quota are evenly distributed by level of trade. The highly traded group of commodities includes cereals, dairy, fruit and vegetables, meat, oilseeds, and sugar. Overquota imports are highest for cereals and oilseeds. Out-of-quota imports are high for cereals, fruit and vegetables, meat, and sugar. Net quota underfill is highest for beverages, cereals, fibers, fruit and vegetables, and meat. Trade-weighted fill rates are below average for beverages, cereals, eggs, fibers, fruit and vegetables, and other. Notice that the trade-weighted fill rate is substantially higher than that of the simple average for coffee and tea, dairy, meat, and sugar.

In-quota tariffs are above average for beverages, cereals, eggs, fruit and vegetables, meat, other products, and tobacco. Except for beverages, the same commodities have an above-average out-of-quota tariff. Average tariffs for quotas with several tariff lines that differ may be misleading because of aggregation problems. A simple or trade-weighted average does not overcome the impact of a few high tariffs protecting most of domestic production.

TABLE 5.9 (*Continued*)

Imports		Quota underfill (net)	Tariffs (%)	
In-quota	Out-of-quota		In-quota	Out-of-quota
1,581	10	−83	41	205
98	57	38	0	0
688	69	−273	28	98
186	106	41	26	100
2,508	1,075	613	7	64
929	727	1,345	37	101
21,424	13,990	13,752	59	115

Source: WTO notifications and Integrated Database (http://www.wto.org/english/tratop_e/agric_e/agric_e.htm); Agricultural Market Access Database (AMAD; http://www.amad.org).
Note: "Truncated" is the simple average fill rate as defined in table 5.6 except it takes a maximum value of 100 percent (ignores overquota imports). "Weighted" is the trade-weighted fill rate, defined as the sum of the value of in-quota imports divided by the sum of the value of the quota (can be >100 percent).
a. $200,000
b. $300,000
c. $400,000

Can TRQ Administration Methods and Regulations Affect Trade?

Earlier we discussed five major quota administration methods (or combinations thereof) and a host of additional conditions that have the potential to affect not only efficiency but also quota fill rates (Mönnich 2003; Skully 2001a). At first glance, one would expect that applied tariffs would allow for unrestricted levels of imports at the in-quota tariff. But several applied tariff quotas are restricted by time limits, past trading performance, volume limits per firm, domestic purchase requirements, and license fees. These regulations are in the notifications (several may be unreported) and can all reduce fill rates. The number and significance of these regulations are shown in table 5.8.

License allocation on the basis of historical imports is the second most commonly used method of quota administration. This trade liberalization has the opposite effect on efficiency from licenses on demand. For example, a decrease in the in-quota tariff decreases efficiency under licenses on demand, but increases efficiency under historical shares unless high-cost firms hold a disproportionate share of the quota licenses according to historical performance. Meanwhile, an increase in the quota, holding per unit rents constant, increases efficiency with licenses on demand because high-cost firms are already at their desired level of

TABLE 5.10 Value of Trade by Commodity (US$ millions unless otherwise indicated)

Commodity	Number of TRQ	Fill rate (%)		In-quota	Quota
		Truncated	Weighted		
Beverages	27	43	16	536	3,283
Cereals	185	58	53	5,420	10,197
Coffee and tea	44	62	92	128	138
Dairy products	144	63	78	2,402	3,048
Eggs and egg products	19	34	21	77	359
Agricultural fibers	12	41	48	932	1,950
Fruits and vegetables	281	66	64	3,160	4,937
Meat products	205	52	76	3,900	5,099
Other agricultural products	45	55	55	70	128
Oilseeds products	106	67	75	2,775	3,689
Sugar and sugar products	42	67	89	1,574	1,771
Tobacco	11	76	78	451	579
Total	1,121	60.6	60.9	21,424	35,178

licenses and additional imports are allocated to lower-cost firms only. The decline in per unit rent resulting from a quota increase reinforces this increase in efficiency effect with high-cost firms exiting (unless no high-cost firms exist and the most efficient allocation is achieved). With historical shares, however, an increase in the quota unambiguously reduces efficiency (and potentially reduces fill rates), except in the unlikely event that the historical share to each firm corresponds exactly to optimal shares with an auction. This example emphasizes the potential importance of quota administration methods on trade patterns and how trade-liberalizing effects can have opposite effects, depending on the method used.

Licenses on demand are the third most commonly used administration method in terms of the value of trade. Licenses are allocated on a prorated basis, whereby the amount that can be imported is reduced proportionately if total requests exceed the quota. Inefficiency is incurred because licenses tend to be allocated to high-cost firms away from low-cost firms (Hranaiova, de Gorter, and Falk 2003). The higher the firm's costs, the closer the allocated quantity to its desired allocation and the higher the probability that it will receive its desired

TABLE 5.10 (*Continued*)

Overquota	Out-of-quota	Underfill		Tariffs (%)	
		Total	Net	In-quota	Out-of-quota
0.5	90	2,747	2,746.8	66	114
1,027	4,372	5,804	4,777	91	155
31	101	41.2	10.1	48	121
318	715	964	646	57	152
10	8	293	283	75	126
78	246	1,096	1,018	17	101
309	2,903	2,086	1,777	110	170
270	4,153	1,469	1,199	105	174
21	79.7	78	57	145	255
882	288	1,796	915	46	115
72	961	269	197	55	104
84	72	212	128	110	337
3,103	13,990	16,856	13,753	59	115

Source: WTO notifications and Integrated Database (http://www.wto.org/english/tratop_e/agric_e/agric_e.htm); Agricultural Market Access Database (AMAD; http://www.amad.org).
Note: "Truncated" is the simple average fill rate as defined in table 5.6 except it takes a maximum value of 100 percent (ignores overquota imports). "Weighted" is the trade-weighted fill rate, defined as the sum of the value of in-quota imports divided by the sum of the value of the quota (can be greater than 100 percent).

allocation. Quota expansion causes high-cost firms to decrease their bids and so reduces inefficiency. The entry of a new firm causes all incumbent firms to increase bids or bid the quota. How that affects efficiency depends on whether high-cost or low-cost firms enter. Failure to penalize firms for not using their licenses almost guarantees quota underfill, which also increases with the heterogeneity of cost structures across firms. In-quota tariff reductions cause per unit rents to increase and so provide incentives for high-cost firms not to exit (or to enter), thereby increasing inefficiency.[12] When a limit is imposed on the licenses received by each firm, inefficiency increases because the limit is more binding on low-cost firms.

First-come, first-served is the next most commonly used method. It can generate inefficiencies due to hurrying up imports and waiting in line (Chau, de Gorter, and Hranaiova 2003). Time limits are very common under this method (see table 5.8).

Countries that are close to the exporting country and so easier to reach will benefit, and uncertainty as to whether the quota will be filled upon arrival at the border is increased with the time limits. Commodities that are more perishable reduce rents, to the disadvantage of importing firms, exporting countries, and producers in the importing region. The degree of "rent appropriation" (rather than "rent dissipation") depends critically on, among other things, the ratio of the import quota volume to free trade levels. Given that first-come, first-served represents 16.8 percent of the total value of TRQ commodities traded, the scope for rent appropriation is very large indeed. Licenses allocated on a first-come, first-served basis reduce the effectiveness of quotas in protecting domestic producers in the importing country but aid domestic consumers. Furthermore, some of the rents may be dissipated in rent seeking where firms try to avoid the consequences of hurried-up imports and reduced domestic prices by changing the timing of domestic production or storing the domestically grown product. Although these latter practices increase profits for the firms involved, they also increase social costs relative to what they would be if property rights to the import licenses were clearly defined.

State trading enterprises can also have significant impacts on efficiency and fill rates, because such enterprises are immune to some degree from market forces and so may not have the incentive to fill the quota. If the STE represents producers' interests, it may choose to limit the quota to lower-valued imports within the category or to pay exporters lower prices for the goods in question. STEs also have been alleged to price discriminate and to allocate export quotas to higher-cost exporters for political reasons. If the quota rents are blended with revenues from domestic production, domestic production expands beyond efficient levels for a given domestic price determined by the import quota.

The impact of the STE on efficiency and fill rates depends on its objective function (maximizing producer profits, for example, or stabilizing prices) and on the degree of control it has over imports and the domestic market. In many countries with STEs, some of the import quotas are given directly to private traders. STE influence on domestic market prices and production varies by country and over time. The outcome also depends on whether the STE feels obligated to fill the quota or, when it does, whether it sells the product on the domestic market or uses it in noncompetitive markets (livestock feed, for example). The effect of the STE also depends on what the initial regime of the tariff quota would be under perfect competition (quota binding, in-quota tariffs, or out-of-quota tariffs), while the effects of trade liberalization through tariff reductions and quota expansion depend on which instrument is binding under the initial STE equilibrium.

Imperfect competition can result in higher quota fill rates. It can also alter the effects of liberalization because of monopoly or monopsony water in the tariff and the interaction effects between the two tariffs and the quota (Hranaiova and de Gorter 2002; de Gorter and Hranaiova 2004). The effectiveness of market power increases with the tariff, but trade liberalization may not increase social welfare. Regime switches may occur, with the possibility of losses in efficiency and social welfare. Trade liberalization outcomes depend on the initial optimal solution for the imperfect competitor (that is, which tariff quota instrument is binding), the level of the binding instrument, and the type and degree of trade liberalization (McCorriston and Sheldon 1994).

The import quota fill rate is not necessarily an indicator of economic efficiency. A quota may be underfilled under perfect competition, yet can be fully filled under a monopoly solution. For a monopsonist, there is no partial underfill of the quota. A decrease in the in-quota tariff may induce a switch in regimes from a price taker to a monopsonist.

Import quotas may be superior to tariffs in achieving the same level of protection in the case of monopsony. This is because the domestic buyer can exercise full monopsony power at low levels of tariffs, while the introduction of a quota increases welfare. The decrease in economic efficiency due to a switch to a monopsonistic solution when sufficiently high tariffs are introduced may offset any efficiency advantages of tariffs over quotas. For a monopolist-monopsonist, the outcome is further complicated by the possibility of two discrete changes in the optimal solution and two supply curves to choose from.

The Role of Dynamic Rent Seeking

The widespread use of additional regulations in combination with each other and with major quota administration methods can also potentially affect trade in a dynamic rent-seeking context. For example, rules governing entry of new firms can either increase or decrease efficiency, depending on the administration method, the level of out-of-quota tariffs, and the regulations determining entry. Some firms, either high- or low-cost, may import at a loss to build up a historical import level so that they can then receive licenses under the historical share allocation method or qualify to be either a bona fide importing firm (potentially relevant to all administration methods) or fulfill the "past trading performance" additional condition for nonhistorical administration methods. Use-it-or-lose-it rules imply access to the quota in the following year, so firms may import—even at a loss—in order to have access to excess rents in the future.

A firm may engage in rent-seeking activities to mitigate the costs (in forgoing economies of scale) of a limit on the number of licenses it can receive. For example, firms try to obtain more licenses by splitting up into smaller entities, yet incur extra costs in so doing. Seasonal licenses (quarterly or semiannual) are very common and do not allow for the exploitation of seasonality in the gap between world and domestic prices. Not taking advantage of seasonal high prices may be particularly important for developing countries where harvest seasons are often different from those of countries in the North.

Once a license is allocated, time limits on its use introduce uncertainty and transactions costs. The resulting inefficiency also depends on whether other conditions are required (such as losing the right to the license).

Domestic purchase requirements may result in consolidation of the importing and domestic production sectors, which can dissipate rents and perhaps spark an increase in the domestic price.

The notifications do not indicate whether licenses are permanent or must be renewed annually, or whether licenses can be traded to other firms within a year. These two features can have significant impacts on the efficiency of quota administration methods. Undocumented regulations also may have a significant impact on efficiency and fill rates. Mexico, for example, has issued quarterly import permits (*cupos*) for imports into specific regions of the domestic market.

Changes in Administration Methods

There have been significant increases in the level of the quotas for each administration method category since 1995, especially for applied tariffs and licenses on demand. This increase probably reflects relatively more minimum, versus current access, quotas designated in these administration categories (WTO 2002a). Table 5.11 provides summary data on the number of tariff quotas that changed from one administration method to another. A total of 64 applied tariffs were switched to other methods, with most becoming historical importers or licenses on demand.

Potential Domestic Policy Responses to TRQ Liberalization

Import quotas give domestic firms, STEs, or domestic governments more latitude in fixing domestic prices and hence reducing their volatility. This means world prices are more volatile except in some circumstances (Tyers and Anderson 1992). Imperfect competitors can charge higher prices under a quota than under tariffs; STEs and producer groups that control import licenses can also charge higher prices under a quota than under a tariff. At the same time, governments often try

TABLE 5.11 Changes in Administration Methods

Away from (1995)	To (most recent)	Number of TRQs
Applied tariffs	Historical importers	36
	Licenses on demand	20
	Mixed allocation	7
	Auctioning	1
	Total	64
Licenses on demand	Applied tariff	10
	Historical importers	3
	Auctioning	2
	Mixed allocation	2
	Other	2
	Producer groups	2
	Total	21
Historical importers	Applied tariff	3
	Producer groups	1
	Mixed allocation	1
	Licenses on demand	1
	Total	6
Other	Historical importers	5
	Total	5
Mixed	Applied tariff	1
	Licenses on demand	3
	Total	4
State trading	Licenses on demand	3
	Total	3
Auction	Licenses on demand	2
	Total	2
Producer group	Licenses on demand	1
	State trading enterprises	1
	Total	2
Not specificed	Applied tariff	1
	Licenses on demand	1
	Total	2
First-come, first-served	Applied tariff	1
	Total	1
Total number of changes		110

TABLE 5.11 Changes in Administration Methods (*Continued*)

Increases in administration methods

Method	Number of increases
Historical importers	44
Licenses on demand	31
Applied tariff	16
Mixed allocation	10
Producer groups	3
Auctioning	3
Other	2
State trading enterprises	1
Not specified	0
First-come, first-served	0
Total	110

Source: WTO notifications and Integrated Database (http://www.wto.org/english/tratop_e/agric_e/agric_e.htm); Agricultural Market Access Database (AMAD; http://www.amad.org).

to stabilize domestic prices (albeit at levels sometimes much higher than world prices) through several mechanisms, depending on the country and commodity. Both an expansion of the quota and reductions in out-of-quota tariffs increase efficiency and decrease international price volatility.

It is also possible that inefficiency increases with domestic policy responses to trade liberalization (Schmitz, de Gorter, and Schmitz 1995). In almost all cases, government employs domestic policy price supports and other instruments in tandem with a TRQ. Canada, for example, has supply management schemes, whereas the European Union employs acreage restrictions, production quotas, stockpiling, and export subsidies. The U.S. sugar program uses the loan rate as the target farm price and allocates "flexible marketing allotments" to farmers who accept bids from processors to obtain defaulted loans in exchange for reducing sugar production. So the benefits of liberalizing TRQs can be at least partially offset by adjusting domestic policy parameters.

To illustrate, consider Asian rice markets with TRQs that employ several domestic policy instruments simultaneously to stabilize domestic prices. Mandatory acreage set-asides, purchase limits by the STEs (or marketing controls), the importation of low-quality rice (sometimes fed to livestock and even destroyed in one country; see Choi and Sumner 2000) by that proportion of the TRQ controlled by the STE, an increase in stocks year to year, and the use of exports as food aid represent the portfolio of policy instruments typically used to stabilize prices.

An example of how this works in Japan is given in table 5.12. Although Japan's rice imports increased substantially (from zero before the URAA), the increase in supply to domestic markets has often been less than half the increase in imports. Exports as food aid have increased over the years, and stocks have always been increasing. Acreage reduction requirements have been ratcheted upward as well. Imports by private traders represent a growing share of the import quota, but rents remain high for the STE. All of these actions illustrate the potential for government policy responses to mitigate the positive liberalization effects of TRQs.

Concluding Comments

This chapter shows that TRQs protect more than 50 percent of agricultural production and approximately 43 percent of agricultural trade of developed countries, even though the total number of tariff lines under TRQs is relatively low. Using applied tariffs, annual total tariff revenues and quota rents are estimated to be on the order of $19.6 billion. We identify four key TRQ regimes associated with the in-quota tariff, quota, out-of-quota tariff, and overquota imports that determine the market equilibrium. There are a total of eight cases under these four regimes, depending on whether there is exact fill, underfill, or overfill of the TRQ. Data show that the out-of-quota regime has the largest value of trade at $22.7 billion, followed by the overquota import regime at $7.5 billion and the quota binding regimes at $2 billion. The value of trade for the in-quota tariff regime is $3 billion.

A reduction in out-of quota tariffs has the largest impact on trade liberalization. Our analysis shows that out-of quota reductions increase the value of trade by $18.2 billion, while a quota expansion increases trade by $5.1 billion. But the outcome also depends critically on the level of water assumed to be in the tariff, the relative values of tariff reduction versus quota expansion (assumed to be 35 percent and 50 percent, respectively) and the level of under- and overfill in each case. We also assume simple average bound tariffs are reduced (rather than trade-weighted applied tariffs). The analysis shows that in-quota tariffs may stifle trade liberalization in the quota expansion and out-of-quota tariff reduction scenarios, the extent to which was not analyzed empirically. Nevertheless, this finding highlights the importance of including in-quota tariff reductions in the WTO negotiations, even though they are not officially bound and no in-quota tariff reductions were required in the URAA. Furthermore, if countries are allowed to choose the least liberalizing of the two trade liberalization options, we show empirically that it is possible that the increase in the total value of trade would only be 40 percent of that under the quota expansion case for all countries and 25 percent of the trade expansion if all countries followed the out-of-quota tariff reduction case only.

TABLE 5.12 STE, Domestic Policy Responses, and Rice Tariff Quota in Japan (metric tons unless otherwise specified)

Year	Minimum access imports			Supply to domestic markets			
	Quantity	Rate[a] (%)	Rate[b] (%)	Total	Total (% of quota)	Private	STE
1995–96	43	4.0	4.2	12	27.9	1	11
1996–97	51	4.8	5.0	31	60.8	1	30
1997–98	60	5.6	5.9	23	38.3	5	18
1998–99	68	6.4	6.9	38	55.9	12	26
1999–2000	72	6.8	7.3	34	47.2	12	22
2000–1	77	7.2	7.9	37	48.1	12	25
2001–2	77	7.2	8.0	34	44.2	10	24
2002–3	77	7.2	8.1	25	32.5	10	15

The trade-weighted fill rates were calculated by administration method and additional regulation. Although applied tariffs are used in 39 percent of the cases, they represent only 14 percent of trade. Auctions, in contrast, are used about 5 percent of the time but account for only 0.5 percent of the total value of trade. The importance of licenses on demand; historical importers; first-come, first-served; and state trading enterprises were also analyzed. Fill rates for quotas are sharply split, with many falling below 20 percent, many at 100 percent or above, and comparatively few in the middle ranges. The average fill rate is 60.5 percent, similar to the percentage reported by the WTO (2002b, 2002c), and our calculated trade-weighted fill rate is almost identical at 61.1 percent. We discuss how licenses on demand and historical importer methods allow high-cost importers to operate; and how the first-come, first-served method results in lower prices earlier in the season; that in turn results in rent appropriation by consumers and middlemen or in rent dissipation as producers trying to circumvent the price declines. State trading enterprises can negatively affect efficiency as well, depending on their objective function, constraints such as international obligations, and their control of domestic market parameters such as marketings, stocks, or prices.

The interaction of additional regulations with each of these major administration methods is also shown to be important for fill rates and efficiency. Fully $7.6 billion worth of trade is subject to time limits on quotas, $3.7 billion to past importing performance, $3.5 billion to export certificates, and $1.9 billion to domestic purchase requirements. Each of these regulations and others (including seasonal licenses and limits per firm) increase the costs of importing and so inevitably affect fill rates.

TABLE 5.12 *(Continued)*

| Exports as food aid | Stock flow | Ending-period stocks | Quota rents[c] | | Acreage control (%) |
			Total US$ millions	Private[d] (%)	
0	31	31	33.7	8.4	24.3
12	8	39	27.9	9.7	28.5
34	3	42	47.2	28.8	28.7
28	2	44	60.8	74.8	34.8
26	12	56	70.8	56.3	35.0
21	19	75	78.7	47.6	35.2
23	20	95	77.5	37.9	37.2
20	32	127	75.8	36.3	37.4

Source: Kimura (2004).
a. Rate of base period consumption.
b. Rate of current period consumption.
c. In-quota and out-of-quota tariffs are zero.
d. Rents to private traders are higher than share of import quota because of higher quality imports that have higher margins.

Even applied tariffs have significant regulations associated with them; pure tariff regimes do not exist in many cases. More analysis is required on the extent to which additional regulations are pervasive in either out-of-quota or in-quota tariff regimes before definitive conclusions can be made about how much they limit the effects of trade liberalization.

We also present summary data on the levels of out-of-quota and overquota imports and quota underfill by commodity and country. These data can be cross-referenced to administration type, additional regulation, minimum or current access, and other relevant indicators in analyzing various factors that may influence TRQ fill rates. The total value of TRQ trade is $35.4 billion, with net quota underfill (after adjusting for overquota imports) at $13.7 billion, or about 39 percent of total TRQ trade. Quota underfill by itself totals $16.8 billion, amounting to 48 percent of the value of the total quotas. The average applied tariff is 53.5 percent, considerably lower than the average bound in-quota tariff of 59 percent and out-of-quota tariff of 115 percent. But this trade-weighted applied average tariff for TRQ commodities is much higher than the average applied tariff for all of agriculture (World Bank 2003, ch. 3).

We also determined that 42 percent of TRQ trade is under minimum access quotas, which were required to expand during the URAA implementation time period. But the majority of minimum access quotas are in regimes where a quota increase has no immediate impact on imports. We also found that a significant numbers of TRQs once administered as applied tariffs had been shifted to the license-on-demand and historical importer categories, both methods that are deemed fraught with inefficiencies (along with first-come, first-served and state trading enterprises). Consideration was also given to the ways in which some administration methods can lead to dynamic rent seeking and further inefficiencies in the quota administration system. Finally, we consider potential domestic policy responses to TRQ liberalization that mitigate the effects of trade liberalization.

The data and analysis in this chapter cannot come to any definitive conclusion as to how well the TRQs liberalized trade in agriculture, not least because of the assumptions that had to be made and the further work required in analyzing the extensive database that has been developed. In particular, analysis of a combination of tariff reductions and quota expansion is warranted, along with an analysis of how in-quota tariffs stifle quota expansion. To obtain a better understanding of TRQs, even more data and information are required, especially on the exact levels of water in the tariffs and tariff binding overhang. The impact of preferential tariffs also requires investigation, as does the distribution of rents between importers and exporters. The analysis here also does not analyze TRQs that are not administered under the WTO, nor does it compare our results to non-TRQ imports and tariffs.

Notes

1. This and various other problems identified in the implementation of TRQs have been analyzed by, for example, Skully (1999, 2001a, 2001b); Abbott and Paarlberg (1998); and de Gorter and Sheldon (2000, 2001).

2. *Water in the tariff* and *tariff binding* overhang refer to situations where a reduction in out-of-quota tariffs has no initial impact on trade. Water refers to situations where there are no out-of-quota imports and the domestic price is below the out-of-quota tariff-inclusive world price. Binding overhang refers to the gap between bound tariffs (to be reduced in the negotiations) and applied tariffs.

3. At the same time, the data overestimates the level of coverage in that it includes commodities that are heavily exported (such as wheat for Canada).

4. See Moschini (1991), Boughner, de Gorter, and Sheldon (2000), and IATRC (2001b) for more detail on the economics of TRQs.

5. Figure 5.3b shows that there can be quota underfill and out-of-quota imports at the same time. This necessarily implies inefficiency in the quota administration method because traders are forgoing potential quota rents that, if available, they would gladly have taken.

6. Although the total number of TRQs notified to the WTO is 1,425, totals for the data presented in the tables are often less than that because of missing data.

7. Calculated as quota underfill of 16,744 as a percentage of quota calculated as in-quota imports of 21,424 less overquota imports of 3,102 plus quota underfill of 16,744.

8. Six years from 1995 for developed countries and ten years for developing countries.

9. For consistency with other estimates in this volume, the import elasticity used is the average of the elasticities of substitution used in the LINKAGE model for agriculture discussed in chapter 12 of this volume.

10. For example, a minimum access quota of 5 percent of baseline consumption is equivalent to 8 percent of current rice consumption in Japan today.

11. This ignores the fact that in many cases, out-of-quota imports replace the quota underfill so the actual value of trade at observed prices attributed to quota underfill is even lower.

12. A tariff reduction has the opposite effect of introducing a license fee.

References

Abbott, P. 2002. "Tariff Rate Quotas: Failed Market Access Instruments." *European Review of Agricultural Economics* 29 (1): 109–30.

Abbott, P., and P. Paarlberg. 1998. "Tariff Rate Quotas: Structural and Stability Impacts in Growing Markets." *Agricultural Economics* 19: 257–67.

Bouët, A., L. Fontagné, and S. Jean. 2006. "Is Erosion of Tariff Preferences a Serious Concern?" *Agricultural Trade Reform and the Doha Development Agenda,* ed. K. Anderson and W. Martin. Basingstoke, U.K.: Palgrave Macmillan; Washington, DC: World Bank.

Boughner, D., H. de Gorter, and I. Sheldon. 2000. "The Economics of Tariff-Rate Quotas in the Agricultural Agreement in the WTO." *Agricultural and Resource Economics Review* 20: 58–69.

Chau, N., H. de Gorter, and J. Hranaiova. 2003. "Rent Dissipation versus Consumer Appropriation of Rents with First-Come, First-Served Import Quotas in Agriculture." Paper presented at International Agricultural Trade Research Consortium Summer Symposium on Agricultural Policy Reform and the WTO, Capri, Italy, June 23–26.

Choi, J. S., and D. A. Sumner. 2000. "Opening Markets while Maintaining Protection: Tariff Rate Quotas in Korea and Japan." *Agricultural and Resource Economics Review* 29 (1): 91–102.

de Gorter, H., and D. Boughner. 1999. "U.S. Dairy Policy and the Agreement on Agriculture in the WTO." *Canadian Journal of Agricultural Economics* 47 (5): 31–42.

de Gorter, H., and J. Hranaiova. 2004. "Quota Administration Methods: Economics and Effects with Trade Liberalization." In *Agriculture and the WTO: Creating a Trading System for Development,* ed. M. Ingco and J. Nash. New York: Oxford University Press.

de Gorter, H., and I. Sheldon. 2000. "Issues in the Administration of Tariff-Rate Import Quotas in the Agreement on Agriculture in the WTO: An Introduction." *Agricultural and Resource Economic Review* 20: 52–57.

de Gorter, H., and I. Sheldon, eds. 2001. "Issues in Reforming Tariff-Rate Import Quotas in the Agreement on Agriculture in the WTO." International Agricultural Trade Research Consortium Commissioned Paper 13, University of Minnesota, St. Paul.

Gibson, P., J. Wainio, D. Whitley, and M. Bohman. 2001. "Profiles of Tariffs in Global Agricultural Markets." Agricultural Economic Report 796, Economic Research Service, U.S. Department of Agriculture, Washington DC, January.

Hranaiova, J., and H. de Gorter. 2002. "The Economics of Tariff Quotas with Imperfect Competition." Department of Applied Economics and Management, Cornell University, Ithaca, NY.

Hranaiova, J., H. de Gorter, and J. Falk. 2003. "The Economics of Administering Import Quotas with Licenses on Demand." Paper presented at International Agricultural Trade Research Consortium Summer Symposium on Agricultural Policy Reform and the WTO, Capri Italy, June 23–26.

IATRC (International Agricultural Trade Research Consortium). 2001a. "The Current WTO Agricultural Negotiations: Options for Progress." IATRC Commissioned Paper 18, University of Minnesota, St. Paul, May.

———. 2001b. "Market Access: Issues and Options in the Agricultural Negotiations." IATRC Commissioned Paper 14, University of Minnesota, St. Paul, May.

Ingco, M. 1996. "Tariffication in the Uruguay Round: How Much Liberalization?" *World Economy* 19 (4, July): 425–47.

Jean, S., D. Laborde, and W. Martin. 2006. "Consequences of Alternative Formulas for Agricultural Tariff Cuts." *Agricultural Trade Reform and the Doha Development Agenda*, ed. K. Anderson and W. Martin. Basingstoke, U.K.: Palgrave Macmillan; Washington, DC: World Bank.

Kee, H. L., A. Nicita, and M. Olarreaga. 2004. "Import Demand Elasticities and Trade Distortions." World Bank working paper, Washington, DC, December. http://siteresources.worldbank.org/INTRANETTRADE/Resources/239054-1101918045494/KNO-elasticity.pdf

Kimura, T. 2004. "An Economic Analysis of Post–Uruguay Round Reforms of Rice Policies in Japan." MSc thesis, Cornell University, Ithaca, NY.

McCorriston, S., and I. M. Sheldon. 1994. "Selling Import Quota Licenses: The U.S. Cheese Case." *American Journal of Agricultural Economics* 76 (4, November): 818–28.

Mönnich, C. 2003. "Tariff Rate Quotas: Does Administration Matter?" Paper presented at International Agricultural Trade Research Consortium Summer Symposium on Agricultural Policy Reform and the WTO, Capri, Italy, June 23–26.

Moschini, G. 1991. "Economic Issues in Tariffication: An Overview." *Agricultural Economics* 5: 101–20.

OECD (Organisation for Economic Co-operation and Development). 2001. *The Uruguay Round Agreement on Agriculture: An Evaluation of Its Implementation in OECD Countries.* Paris: OECD.

———. 2002. "Tariff-Rate Quotas and Tariffs in OECD Agricultural Markets: A Forward Looking Analysis."*Agriculture and Trade Liberalization: Extending the Uruguay Round Agreement*, Part 1. Paris: OECD.

———. 2003. *Agricultural Policies in OECD Countries: Monitoring and Evaluation.* Paris: OECD. http://www1.oecd.org/publications/e-book/5103081E.PDF

Schmitz, A., H. de Gorter, and T. Schmitz. 1995. "Consequences of Tariffication." In *Regulation and Protectionism under GATT*, ed A. Schmitz, G. Coffin, and K. Rosaasen. Boulder CO: Westview Publishing Co.

Skully, D. 1999. "Economics of TRQ Administration." International Agricultural Trade Research Consortium Working Paper 99–6, University of Minnesota, St. Paul.

———. 2001a. "Economics of Tariff Rate Quota Administration." ERS Technical Bulletin 1893, Economic Research Service, U.S. Department of Agriculture, Washington, DC.

———. 2001b. "Liberalizing Tariff Rate Quotas, Background for Agricultural Policy Reform in the WTO: The Road Ahead." ERS-E01-001, Economic Research Service, U.S. Department of Agriculture, Washington, DC.

Tyers, R., and K. Anderson. 1992. *Disarray in World Food Markets : A Quantitative Assessment.* New York: Cambridge University Press.

Wainio, J. 2001. "Market Access: Tariffication and Tariff Reduction." ERS Issues Series, Economic Research Service, U.S. Department of Agriculture, Washington, DC.

Wainio, J., P. Gibson, and D. Whitley. 2001. "Options for Reducing Agricultural Tariffs. Background for Agricultural Policy Reform in the WTO: The Road Ahead." ERS-E01-001, Economic Research Service, U.S. Department of Agriculture, Washington, DC.

World Bank. 2003. *Global Economic Prospects 2004: Realizing the Development Promise of the Doha Agenda.* Washington, DC: World Bank.

WTO (World Trade Organization). 2002a. "Changes in Tariff Quota Administration and Fill Rates." G/AG/NG/S/20, WYO, Geneva, November 8.

———. 2002b. "Tariff Quota Administration Methods and Tariff Quota Fill." Background paper TN/AG/S/6, WTO, Geneva, March 22.

———. 2002c. "Tariff Quota and Other Quotas." Background paper TN/AG/S/5, WTO, Geneva, March 21.

6

IS EROSION OF TARIFF PREFERENCES A SERIOUS CONCERN?

Antoine Bouët, Lionel Fontagné, and Sébastien Jean

Preferential trade arrangements (PTAs) have become a key feature of the world trading system, with their number rising dramatically since the early 1990s. More than 200 have been notified to the WTO (World Trade Organization). Their objectives have also widened in scope. In particular, trade preferences are being used increasingly as a substitute for more ambitious development policies, especially since the Singapore WTO Ministerial Conference in 1996. Granting developing countries nonreciprocal preferential access to markets is not new. However, the long-standing importance to developing countries of schemes such as European Union's Cotonou Agreement (formerly Lomé Convention) or the United States' Caribbean Basin Initiative (CBI), as well as the use of new schemes targeted on least developed countries (LDCs) or on Sub-Saharan Africa (SSA), have changed the nature of this issue. Preferences in general, and nonreciprocal preferences in particular, are among the important issues to be addressed during the Doha Round. A major concern of the G-90 member countries, in particular those in SSA, is that multilateral trade liberalization will erode these preferences.[1] This concern contributed to its inclusion as an issue in the July 2004 Framework Agreement (WTO 2004).

This chapter aims to clarify the specific issues raised by trade preferences, in particular nonreciprocal ones, as they pertain to the Doha Round. How important are trade preferences for developing countries, and for which developing countries are such preferences of special importance? What issues arise from the perspective of multilateral liberalization for preference-receiving countries? In particular, is the erosion of preferences a legitimate concern? If so, for which countries? And what are the possible policy implications?

The importance of preferences for numerous developing countries is well recognized and has been widely documented and discussed. Preferences have not interfered much with multilateral trade liberalization in the past, however, for at least two reasons. First, the impact of preferences was most substantial in agriculture and textiles and clothing, sectors where previous trade rounds failed to expand market access, at least until the recent phaseout of the Multifibre Arrangement (MFA). Second, until recently, the quantitative economic analysis of multilateral liberalization failed to deal satisfactorily with trade preferences.

No comprehensive global database describing the levels of protection adequately took into account preferences until 2004. Since the Uruguay Round, most worldwide empirical studies of multilateral liberalization have been based on computable general equilibrium (CGE) models that drew on Purdue University's Global Trade Analysis Project (GTAP) database. But until GTAP Version 6, released in late 2004, this database did not take into account PTAs, except five among the most important reciprocal agreements: the European Union, EU–European Free Trade Association (EU-EFTA), North American Free Trade Agreement (NAFTA), Australia–New Zealand Closer Economic Relations Agreement (ANZCERTA), and SACU (South African Customs Union). Until now virtually all global quantitative assessments of the impact of multilateral liberalization have been unable to address the issue of nonreciprocal trade preferences.

That lacuna has now been filled by the MAcMap database, jointly developed by the Centre d'Etudes Prospectives et d'Informations Internationales (CEPII) in Paris and the International Trade Commission (ITC, a joint agency of WTO and the UN Conference on Trade and Development, or UNCTAD, in Geneva). That database now offers a consistent and near-complete set of ad valorem protection rates across the world for 2001, taking account of all preferential agreements enforced at that date (Bouët and others 2005b).

In this chapter we take advantage of this new protection database, as well as of a series of studies recently carried out by CEPII (Bouët and others 2005a; Bchir, Jean, and Laborde forthcoming; Candau, Fontagné, and Jean 2004), to determine whether the erosion of trade preferences is a serious concern. The scenarios considered are a subset of those described in Jean, Laborde, and Martin in chapter 4, but the information is used directly at the HS6 level of product disaggregation.

The "mechanics" of the erosion of preferences are simple. Following multilateral trade negotiations, cuts are applied to bound import duties, not directly to applied tariffs. A most-favored-nation (MFN) applied duty is reduced only if the liberalized bound duty for this product is lower than the initial applied duty, and then only to the extent of that difference. In turn, preferential rates (which are applied duties that had been set lower than the MFN rate) typically are cut by less than the

MFN applied rates because they are not affected until the bound rate comes below the preferential rate. This means preferential margins are eroded when tariffs are cut, other things equal. Also important is the fact that preferential tariff rate quotas (TRQs) are fairly common among agricultural products. Many of them give rise to substantial rents for some developing countries, and those rents are reduced if multilateral trade negotiations result in cuts in the out-of-quota tariff rate.

This chapter begins by reviewing the historical context of preferences and by exploring their effect on market access for developing-country exporters. It then assesses how multilateral liberalization following the Doha Round could erode preferences. This assessment clarifies the mechanics of preference erosion and evaluates the corresponding implications for preference margins. CGE simulations are then conducted to gauge the impact of preference erosion on trade, output, and welfare. Policy implications are discussed in the final section.

An Overview of Preferences

The current situation is the result of a gradual piling up of numerous individual preference schemes. The situation is particularly complicated for farm products, not only because of the nature of the instruments used (specific tariffs and TRQs) but also because these instruments are frequently managed in a nontransparent manner.

The Starting Point

WTO members are generally constrained to offer all other members nondiscriminatory access to their markets. A core rule of the multilateral trade system holds that a member should not discriminate between its trading partners or between its domestic products and imports. This rule is manifested in the MFN clause, which requires MFN tariffs to be applied equally to all WTO members. Accordingly, Article I (paragraph 1) of GATT (WTO's predecessor, the General Agreement on Tariffs and Trade) states that "any advantage, favor, privilege or immunity granted by any contracting party to any product originating in or destined for any other country shall be accorded immediately and unconditionally to the like product originating in or destined for the territories of all other contracting parties." Despite this very clear statement, substantial amounts of goods shipped around the world do not face an MFN tariff when entering the destination market.[2] The reason for this is the existence of preferences, introduced in Paragraph 2 of that same Article I: "The provisions of paragraph 1 of this Article shall not require the elimination of any preferences."

Generally speaking, two kinds of preferential schemes operate: symmetric schemes, under which two countries mutually offer preferential access to their market; and asymmetric ones in which one country unilaterally concedes preferential access to a well-defined (but not necessarily stable) list of exporting countries. The former includes the treatment of regional agreements by the GATT, while the latter is associated with the Generalized System of Preferences (GSP) and its extensions. These include the EU's recent Everything But Arms (EBA) Initiative, which offers duty- and quota-free market access for LDCs; the United States' African Growth and Opportunity Act (AGOA); and development-targeted agreements introduced earlier (such as Cotonou and the CBI).

Article XXIV of the GATT, which allows the formation of customs unions and free trade areas, has also translated into myriad preferential agreements.[3] Many of these trade agreements are regional; examples are the Common Market in the late 1950s, NAFTA, and Mercosur.[4] But plenty of bilateral agreements involve noncontiguous countries (United States–Morocco or Mexico-Israel, for instance). According to notifications to the WTO, the number of such agreements in force by the end of 2005 might approach 300. Many of the 148 WTO members participate in various trade agreements. Accordingly, their tariff schedules involve many different levels of treatment, often defined at the product level, and frequently embodying numerous exceptions to the MFN principle. The official and optimistic view that regionalism is a building block toward multilateral trade liberalization leaves unexplained the desire by WTO members to use these efforts to escape from complying with the nondiscrimination clause in Article 1 of the GATT.

For nonreciprocal trade agreements, the picture is even more complicated. The Millennium Development Goals aim, among other things, at developing a global partnership for development through more aid, better market access, and debt sustainability. This target is an extension of the decision taken in 1968 under the auspices of UNCTAD to grant developing countries nonreciprocal preferential access to developed-country markets under the GSP scheme.[5] Under GSP, rich countries offer nonreciprocal preferential access to products originating in a list of developing countries, with preference-giving countries unilaterally choosing countries and products to be included in their GSP schemes. The lists are revised on a regular basis, leading to "entries" and "exits." In addition, the preferences conceded can include products subject to quotas or considered politically "sensitive."

Not surprisingly, preferences generally aim at preserving the vested interests of domestic producers. For instance, until 1994, the EU's GSP scheme applied quantitative limits on GSP imports.[6] This system has been replaced by "tariff modulation" in which reduced rates of duty are classified into four categories: very sensitive products (preferential margin equal to 15 percent of the MFN tariff), sensitive products (30 percent), semisensitive (65 percent), nonsensitive products (duty free). There are also special incentive schemes, offering additional tariff preferences for specific development purposes (such as the protection of labor rights or efforts to combat drug production and trafficking).

The general goal of such asymmetric, or nonreciprocal, preferences is to make it possible for countries with limited export potential to more easily reap the benefits of globalization. The multilateral trading system also provides "special and differential treatment" (SDT) to developing countries according to the so-called "Enabling Clause."[7] Besides longer implementation periods or smoother commitments, SDT offers asymmetric market access. A recent extension of such agreements involves specific concessions granted to LDCs by the EU, Japan, Norway, and the United States. The European initiative is the previously mentioned Everything But Arms deal, which offers duty-free and quota-free access to all products originating in LDCs except for weapons and three agricultural products for which liberalization has been delayed (banana, rice, and sugar).

The EU and U.S Preferential Schemes at a Glance

Figure 6.1 illustrates the intricacy of the European Union's trade policy in 2004.[8] The EU has negotiated several regional (European Free Trade Association/European Economic Area) and bilateral (including with Chile, Mexico, and Turkey) free trade agreements. It has also entered into a trading framework with a number of Mediterranean countries, known as the Euromed Initiative. The structure of European preferences has reached great complexity. Since 1995, the European GSP has been divided into five regimes: the standard GSP, the GSP granted to countries fighting against drug production and trafficking, the one granted to countries enforcing labor rights, the scheme for environmental protection (which has not been granted so far), and the EBA Initiative for LDCs.

A preferential regime has long been established with developing countries of Africa, the Caribbean, and the Pacific (ACP), with which the EU has historical links. This scheme, which is not WTO-compatible but has survived under a GATT waiver, expires on January 1, 2008, and must be replaced if preferential treatment is to continue. The Cotonou Agreement, signed in 2000, renewed the nonreciprocal ACP preferential arrangements formerly offered under the Lomé Convention, but it also foreshadowed the negotiation of Economic Partnerships Agreements (EPAs) with six groups of countries, later defined as countries from Central Africa, Eastern and Southern Africa, the Southern African Development Community (SADC), the Pacific, the Caribbean Islands, and Western Africa. The EPAs are currently scheduled to come into force by the end of 2007, but that may change if the GATT waiver is extended.

These myriad trade preference regimes mean that EU trade policy is highly fragmented. Today for Europe as an importing zone, the WTO multilateral regime

FIGURE 6.1 European Union Trade Policy, 2004

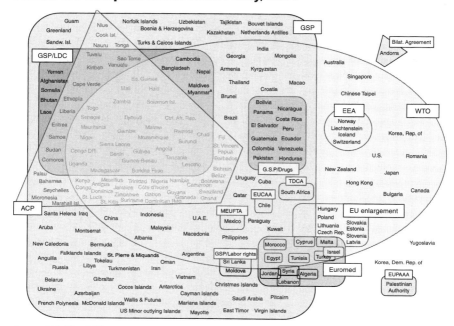

Source: MAcMap-HS6.

Note: ACP = African, Caribbean and Pacific Group of States; EEA = European Economic Area; EUCAA = European Union-Chile Association Agreement; EUPAAA = European Union-Palestinian Authority Association Agreement; Euromed = Euro-Mediterranean Partnership; GSP = Generalized System of Preferences; LDC = least developed countries; MEUFTA = Mexico-European Union Free Trade Agreement; TDCA = Trade Development Cooperation Agreement; WTO = World Trade Organization.
a. Tariff preferences temporarily withdrawn.

applies to only 11 countries among the 208 potential exporting countries. Under the GSP scheme as it was originally negotiated in 1971, tariff preferences had to be nondiscriminatory with deeper preferences applying only to the LDCs. Figure 6.1 reveals how much the current scheme has departed from that initial principle. In part the multiple trade preferences reflect the fact that trade policy has been the European Community's only foreign policy instrument.

U.S. trade policy is also fragmented, although not as much as the EU's; under U.S. trade policy, the WTO regime applies to 25 partners (figure 6.2). Recently the United States has been pursuing a bilateral path, negotiating free trade agreements with single trade partners including Australia, Bahrain, Jordan, Morocco, Panama, and Singapore. Trade preferences granted to developing countries are also less fragmented than the EU's, with just four preferential regimes being defined (the

FIGURE 6.2 U.S. Trade Policy, 2004

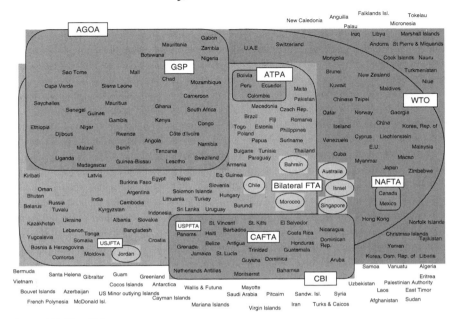

Source: MAcMap-HS6.
Note: AGOA = African Growth and Opportunity Act; ATPA = Andean Trade Preference Act; CAFTA = Central American Free Trade Agreement; NAFTA = North American Free Trade Agreement; CBI = Caribbean Basin Initiative; GSP = Generalized System of Preferences; USJFTA = United States-Jordan Free Trade Agreement; USPFTA = United States-Panama Free Trade Agreement; WTO = World Trade Organization.

GSP, CBI, Andean Trade Pact Agreement, and AGOA). Another noteworthy difference is that, unlike the EU, the United States has designated a set of sensitive products that are excluded from all preferential schemes (although the United States' GSP scheme generally offers duty-free access to all products that benefit, in contrast with only partial reductions in tariffs from MFN levels applied by the EU).

Implications of Preferences on Market Access

What are the implications of these intricate preference schemes for the exports of both developed and developing countries? The MAcMap HS6 database allows for an aggregation of applied duties across all products and all reporters (importers), for each partner (exporter), to obtain the average duty faced by each country on its exports to the rest of the world. The first and fifth columns in table 6.1 report this average for agricultural and industrial products, respectively, using the MAcMap's reference-group based weighting scheme (see Bouët and others 2005b).

TABLE 6.1 Decomposition of the Average Duty Faced by Each Exporting Country, 2001 (percent, ad valorem equivalent duty)

	Agriculture			
	Applied duty	Apparent margin	Composition effect	True margin
Lesotho	18.4	0.8	−24.1	24.9
Aruba	26.7	−7.6	−32.2	24.6
Gambia, The	16.6	2.6	−13.3	15.9
St. Vincent	22.3	−3.2	−13.4	10.2
Uruguay	25.4	−6.3	−16.0	9.7
Yugoslavia, former	15.9	3.3	−5.2	8.5
St. Lucia	18.6	0.6	−7.5	8.0
Guyana	87.1	−67.9	−75.6	7.6
Suriname	38.8	−19.6	−27.3	7.6
Turkmenistan	3.3	15.8	8.4	7.5
Virgin Islands	12.0	7.1	0.4	6.8
Mali	2.9	16.3	9.9	6.4
Burkina Faso	9.2	9.9	4.0	5.9
Benin	8.2	10.9	5.6	5.3
Dominica	17.1	2.1	−3.0	5.1
Malawi	21.6	−2.5	−7.3	4.9
Kiribati	10.3	8.9	4.0	4.8
Kazakhstan	21.4	−2.3	−6.3	4.0
Vanuatu	4.1	15.1	11.2	3.9
Argentina	18.7	0.5	−3.4	3.8
Belize	42.8	−23.6	−27.4	3.8
Sudan	10.1	9.0	5.7	3.3
Iraq	30.5	−11.4	−14.4	3.0
Saudi Arabia	29.0	−9.8	−12.7	2.9
Togo	8.6	10.5	7.8	2.7
Andorra	12.1	7.1	4.6	2.4
Turks and Caicos	17.5	1.7	−0.7	2.3
Croatia	22.0	−2.9	−5.0	2.0
Dominican Rep.	21.2	−2.0	−4.0	2.0
Eritrea	8.8	10.3	8.5	1.9
Zimbabwe	23.5	−4.4	−6.2	1.8
Botswana	35.9	−16.8	−18.5	1.7
Bolivia	13.7	5.4	3.9	1.5
Egypt, Arab Rep. of	14.0	5.2	3.9	1.3
Jamaica	33.2	−14.1	−15.3	1.2

TABLE 6.1 (*Continued*)

Industry	Applied duty	Apparent margin	Composition effect	True margin
Seychelles	3.8	0.7	−7.2	8.6
Lesotho	5.4	−0.8	−7.0	6.9
Haiti	5.3	−0.7	−6.5	6.5
Madagascar	4.1	0.5	−5.0	6.2
Bangladesh	5.3	−0.7	−6.2	6.2
Cambodia	6.0	−1.5	−6.7	6.0
Mauritius	7.3	−2.7	−7.3	5.3
Maldives	9.2	−4.6	−9.2	5.3
Nicaragua	5.7	−1.2	−5.4	4.9
Honduras	5.9	−1.4	−5.5	4.8
Fiji	4.8	−0.2	−4.3	4.8
Palau	5.1	−0.5	−4.6	4.7
Djibouti	12.0	−7.4	−11.3	4.7
Nepal	10.1	−5.5	−9.3	4.5
Greenland	4.1	0.5	−3.1	4.3
Dominican Republic	4.3	0.3	−3.2	4.2
El Salvador	9.6	−5.0	−8.3	4.0
St. Pierre and Miquelon	2.8	1.8	−1.4	3.9
Tonga	3.3	1.3	−1.8	3.8
Belize	3.9	0.7	−2.2	3.7
Guatemala	9.6	−5.0	−7.8	3.6
Pakistan	6.2	−1.6	−4.3	3.4
Tunisia	4.8	−0.2	−2.9	3.4
Morocco	4.7	−0.2	−2.7	3.3
Cape Verde	3.6	1.0	−1.5	3.2
Turkey	6.5	−1.9	−4.3	3.1
Falkland Islands	2.8	1.8	−0.6	3.1
Turks and Caicos	3.9	0.7	−1.6	3.0
Malawi	15.3	−10.7	−13.0	3.0
Sierra Leone	2.9	1.7	−0.5	2.9
Mozambique	2.4	2.2	0.0	2.9
Albania	4.9	−0.3	−2.4	2.8
Uganda	6.1	−1.5	−3.5	2.7
Senegal	10.4	−5.8	−7.7	2.7
Micronesia	9.6	−5.0	−6.9	2.6

Source: Authors' calculations, based on MAcMap-HS6 Version 1.

Note: Countries are ranked by decreasing true preference margin, and the table is limited to the first 35 countries.

In agriculture, the average duty faced on exports ranges from 0.6 percent (Equatorial Guinea) to 87 percent (Guyana). For member countries of the Organisation for Economic Co-operation and Development (OECD), the average duty faced is regularly below 20 percent (except for Australia and New Zealand), whereas products originating from numerous small developing countries (such as Barbados, Belize, Botswana, Gabon, Guyana, and Mauritius) are highly taxed. These huge differences result from a combination of two different effects: a composition effect and a true preferential margin. The composition effect refers to variation in exports caused by product specialization and the geographic destination of exports.[9] The true preferential margin captures the fact that each country is benefiting from an average preferential margin, thanks to the trade regimes it has been conceded. Compared with the world average preferential margin (the worldwide average difference between MFN and applied duties), a country might benefit from a higher or lower average preferential margin. We call this variation from the world average the "true" preferential margin.

To understand the implications of these different components, we derive the following equation. Let $t_{s,r}^h$ be the applied ad valorem equivalent (AVE) duty imposed by country s on product h exported by country r, let $w_{s,r}^h$ be the weight of this flow, let $MFN_{s,r}^h$ be the MFN AVE duty imposed by country s on product h.[10]

For a given country i, let us define the apparent margin, AM_i, as:

$$(6.1) \quad AM_i = \frac{\sum_r \sum_s \sum_h w_{s,r}^h t_{s,r}^h}{\sum_r \sum_s \sum_h w_{s,r}^h} - \frac{\sum_s \sum_h w_{s,i}^h t_{s,i}^h}{\sum_s \sum_h w_{s,i}^h}$$

The first term on the right-hand side of equation 6.1 is the applied duty faced by the world, the second one is the applied duty faced by country i. From equation 6.1, we derive:

$$(6.2) \quad \begin{aligned} AM_i &= \left[\frac{\sum_r \sum_s \sum_h w_{s,r}^h t_{s,r}^h}{\sum_r \sum_s \sum_h w_{s,r}^h} - \frac{\sum_r \sum_s \sum_h w_{s,r}^h MFN_{s,r}^h}{\sum_r \sum_s \sum_h w_{s,r}^h} \right] \\ &+ \left[\frac{\sum_r \sum_s \sum_h w_{s,r}^h MFN_{s,r}^h}{\sum_s \sum_h w_{s,r}^h} - \frac{\sum_s \sum_h w_{s,r}^h MFN_{s,r}^h}{\sum_s \sum_h w_{s,i}^h} \right] \\ &+ \left[\frac{\sum_s \sum_h w_{s,i}^h MFN_{s,r}^h}{\sum_s \sum_h w_{s,i}^h} - \frac{\sum_s \sum_h w_{s,i}^h t_{s,i}^h}{\sum_s \sum_h w_{s,i}^h} \right] \end{aligned}$$

The apparent preferential margin obtained by country i on its exports is thus defined by the sum of three components. The first term is the worldwide difference between the average applied duty and the MFN duty. It is the opposite of the world average preferential margin. The second term is the difference between the MFN duty faced by the world and the one faced by country i. It measures a composition effect of country i's exports. The third term is the difference between the average MFN duty and the average applied duty faced by country i; it is country i's preferential margin. What we call the true preference margin is the sum of the first and the third terms, that is, the difference between the country's and the world's average preferential margin, defined as the weighted average across products of the difference between the MFN and the applied rate.

Based on equations 6.1 and 6.2, the average applied duty faced by country i on its exports can thus be defined as the applied duty faced by the world, minus the composition effect (the second difference term in equation 6.2), minus the true preferential margin effect. A positive composition effect means that country i is specialized in products (or in geographical destinations) that are less protected all around the world. A positive true preferential margin means that, on average across its export markets, country i reaps a larger preference on its exports compared with the world average. The corresponding decomposition is reported in table 6.1. For the sake of clarity, since world average levels are taken as references in these calculations, they are reported in table 6.2.

Table 6.1 should be read as follows. The first row shows that Lesotho's agricultural exports face an average applied AVE tariff duty of 18.4 percent, 0.8 percentage points less than the world average. But this tiny apparent preference margin results from the combination of strongly negative composition effect (−24.1 percentage points), revealing specialization in highly taxed products, and of strongly positive true average preferential margin (24.9 percentage points), because of the preferential agreements from which Lesotho benefits.

In agriculture, the composition effect appears to vary strongly across countries. It is strongly negative for several countries (Guyana, −76 percent; Mauritius, −36 percent, St Kitts and Nevis, −35 percent; Barbados, −25 percent; Belize, −27 percent),

TABLE 6.2 Average World Applied and MFN Tariff Protection Rates, 2001 (percent)

Sector	Applied duty faced	MFN duty faced	MFN-applied margin
Agriculture	19.1	26.8	7.6
Industry	4.6	5.3	0.7

Source: Authors' calculations, based on MAcMap-HS6 Version 1.

as a result of their specialization in products still highly protected in most large markets.[11] These large, negative composition effects are likely to be primarily endogenous: although preferential agreements frequently exclude highly sensitive products, preferential margins, by construction, can only be large in highly protected products. As a matter of fact, preference-receiving countries thus face incentives to specialize in highly protected products, since that is where their preferential margin is higher. This is not a systematic rule, however; some developing countries tend to specialize in largely liberalized products, as reflected in a positive composition effect (Equatorial Guinea, 26 percent; Chad, 20 percent). Orders of magnitude are far lower in nonagricultural products, but it is even more striking that most countries with significant true preferential margins exhibit large, negative composition effects.

Although the true average preferential margin does not reach the extreme values seen in the composition effects, it does reach almost 25 percentage points for Lesotho and Aruba, and it is above 6 points for 10 countries. Overall, the true average preferential margin in agriculture is above 1 point for 47 developing countries, and above 2 points for 33 countries, according to our calculations. Countries with high true preferential margins are primarily Sub-Saharan and Caribbean countries. True preferential margins are less varied in nonagricultural products, with a maximum of 8.6 points for the Seychelles, but they are significant for large numbers of countries: 103 countries exhibit a true average preferential margin above 1 percentage point; 57 a true margin higher than 2 percentage points. The countries exhibiting the largest true preferential margins are those that benefit from important preferential arrangements *and* that are specialized in exporting textiles and apparel—although, as already noted, this specialization is likely to be at least partly endogenous. This important role of textiles and apparel explains why several South Asian countries are among those exhibiting the highest margin in industrial products.

Many developing countries export only a few, highly specialized products, and that lack of diversification is often interpreted as an economic weakness. During the Doha Round, LDCs voiced their concern that countries with highly concentrated exports would be especially vulnerable to preference erosion. A few products appear to be the source of this concern: bananas, sugar, meat, vegetables and fruits, and textiles and apparel. Table 6.3 reports the true average preferential margin for each of these products for those developing countries belonging to WTO that display the highest preferential margins in agriculture. Importantly, this average is calculated (as above) using trade flows from the exporter to the reference group of the importer, thus minimizing the extent of the endogeneity bias (linked to the influence of applied tariffs on the level of bilateral exports), which is likely to be sizable for such highly protected products.[12] The table shows

TABLE 6.3 Average True Preferential Margin by Country, by Sector and Commodity (percent)

Country	By sector		By commodity					
	Agriculture	Industry	Sugar	Meat	Banana	Vegetables, fruit	Textiles, apparel	Other
Lesotho	24.9	6.9	−6.0	47.4	−7.2	8.2	5.2	4.6
Aruba	24.6	1.1	52.9	−7.4	−7.2	−5.0	−1.4	1.2
Gambia, The	15.9	2.5	−11.6	−8.6	−7.2	−0.5	0.0	14.5
St. Vincent	10.2	1.5	−11.6	−9.2	13.6	−2.9	−1.6	2.6
Uruguay	9.7	2.3	−5.2	13.6	−2.5	0.3	0.8	6.1
Yugoslavia, former	8.5	1.3	78.5	−8.1	−7.1	−1.0	1.6	1.2
St. Lucia	8.0	2.2	−11.6	−1.7	13.8	6.0	3.6	0.2
Guyana	7.6	1.5	−3.1	−8.5	9.5	1.2	4.2	4.1
Suriname	7.6	2.0	16.0	−8.6	11.6	2.4	1.4	1.5
Turkmenistan	7.5	0.1	−11.4	−9.2	−7.2	−4.5	−1.5	0.1
Virgin Islands	6.8	0.4	15.7	−8.5	14.9	−1.7	0.1	−0.3
Mali	6.4	0.7	−5.3	−6.4	−7.2	1.2	0.4	9.8
Burkina Faso	5.9	0.9	12.4	−8.0	−5.4	1.3	−0.4	9.5
Benin	5.3	1.1	−8.3	8.3	−7.2	−3.6	−0.8	11.4
Dominica	5.1	0.8	−11.6	−2.0	11.8	−2.8	2.6	−0.1
Malawi	4.9	3.0	−5.1	−8.4	−7.2	11.1	1.4	11.6
Kiribati	4.8	1.7	−11.6	−9.2	−7.2	−4.6	2.2	0.7
Kazakhstan	4.0	0.2	11.3	−8.9	−6.5	−2.9	0.1	−0.0
Vanuatu	3.9	0.9	−11.6	53.1	−7.2	31.2	2.8	0.3
Argentina	3.8	0.6	−5.9	2.8	−6.4	−0.6	−1.2	4.5
Belize	3.8	3.7	−2.9	−7.6	13.9	−0.4	3.9	4.1
Sudan	3.3	0.6	−4.3	−7.8	−6.4	−2.2	−0.6	1.1
Iraq	3.0	−0.0	−0.8	−0.6	−4.9	−2.4	−0.1	−1.0
Saudi Arabia	2.9	0.1	0.5	−0.5	−7.2	−0.2	−1.0	−0.9
Togo	2.7	0.9	−9.5	−2.8	−7.2	2.8	6.2	3.0
Andorra	2.4	1.4	51.6	9.7	−7.2	3.0	1.8	0.3
Turks and Caicos	2.3	3.0	−11.6	−9.2	−7.2	−4.6	2.1	2.9
Croatia	2.0	1.8	61.3	−5.5	14.9	0.5	2.9	0.6
Dominican Republic	2.0	4.2	−4.6	−8.7	14.1	2.0	3.9	2.0
Eritrea	1.9	1.5	−11.6	9.5	−7.2	4.1	−0.2	1.2
Zimbabwe	1.8	1.8	−1.1	−3.4	1.0	0.7	1.7	4.7
Botswana	1.7	0.9	−7.1	2.0	−7.2	−2.6	1.8	−0.5
Bolivia	1.5	0.9	8.6	−8.6	−0.2	−2.7	1.8	2.3
Egypt, Arab Rep. of	1.3	2.2	−9.7	−7.2	−4.6	0.7	2.6	1.7
Jamaica	1.2	2.5	−3.4	−5.0	14.5	2.4	3.8	1.8

Source: Authors' calculations, based on MAcMap-HS6 Version 1.
Note: Countries are ranked by decreasing order of initial true preference margin in agriculture. The commodity figures are computed in the same way as indicated above for true preference margins by large sector: average preferential margin for the country (that is, the average across markets and products concerned of MFN duty minus the applied duty faced by the country), minus world average preferential margin for the products concerned.

that preferential margins are also highly concentrated, as Alexandraki and Lankes (2004), among others, have already emphasized. For most countries exhibiting a significant true preferential margin, one single (group of) products turns out to be the source of this preferential margin: meat products for Lesotho, Uruguay, and Vanuatu; sugar for Aruba, Croatia, Suriname, and the former Yugoslavia; bananas for several Caribbean countries. With exports concentrated on a small number of products, on which their preferential margin is especially high, these countries are likely to be very vulnerable to the erosion of preferences.

Assessing the Interaction of Preferences and Multilateral Liberalization

Multilateral liberalization, as it is conducted under the aegis of the WTO, can lead to an erosion of preferences. Tariff formulas are applied to cut bound tariffs, which are greater than or equal to MFN applied tariffs, which are greater than or equal to preferential tariffs. The preferential tariffs are set either as a fixed proportion of the MFN applied duty (the most frequent case) or as a lower duty independent of the MFN rate. When bound duties are reduced, several implications for developing countries benefiting from trade preferences may arise:

- The MFN applied duty may not be changed, in which case market access and preferential margins are not affected;
- The MFN tariff may be reduced, so if the preferential tariff is a fixed proportion of the MFN duty, then market access is improved for developing countries, but their preferential margin is reduced, leading to more competition from MFN duty-paying countries; or
- The preferential tariff is independent of the MFN duty (it might be zero), in which case market access is not improved for preference-receiving developing countries and their preferential margin is eroded.

The magnitude of the erosion may depend on the tariff-cutting formula adopted. Following the approach taken by Jean, Laborde, and Martin (2006), we simulate the impacts on preference margins of two liberalizing scenarios. Scenario 1 is a tiered tariff-cutting formula in agriculture and a 50 percent cut in industrial tariffs.[13] Scenario 2 adds a sensitive products clause, which allows 2 percent of tariff lines to be reduced by only 15 percent.

In most cases, the impact of scenario 1 on the true preferential margin is spectacular in agriculture: among the 12 countries with an initial preference margin higher than 6 points, only 4 end up with a margin higher than 3 points after the tariff-cutting formula is applied (table 6.4). The results are varied across countries,

TABLE 6.4 Simulation of the Impact of a Proportional Cut in Bound Duties under Scenarios 1 and 2

Country	Initial true margin		Scenario 1		Scenario 2	
	Farm	Nonfarm	Farm	Nonfarm	Farm	Nonfarm
Lesotho	24.9	6.9	3.2	5.3	7.7	6.3
Aruba	24.6	1.1	−3.3	−0.5	21.2	0.5
Gambia, The	15.9	2.5	2.1	1.0	2.1	2.0
St. Vincent	10.2	1.5	1.8	−0.1	8.1	0.9
Uruguay	9.7	2.3	2.6	0.7	6.4	1.7
Yugoslavia, former	8.5	1.3	−3.3	−1.2	2.0	−0.2
St. Lucia	8.0	2.2	−1.1	0.6	6.8	1.6
Guyana	7.6	1.5	−0.7	−0.1	1.3	1.0
Suriname	7.6	2.0	3.9	0.5	13.3	1.6
Turkmenistan	7.5	0.1	3.1	−3.2	2.5	−2.1
Virgin Islands	6.8	0.4	1.5	−1.8	3.1	−0.8
Mali	6.4	0.7	3.1	−0.9	2.4	0.1
Burkina Faso	5.9	0.9	2.6	−0.8	1.9	0.3
Benin	5.3	1.1	2.6	−0.5	2.0	0.5
Dominica	5.1	0.8	−0.9	−0.8	5.1	0.2
Malawi	4.9	3.0	3.6	1.3	2.6	2.4
Kiribati	4.8	1.6	0.5	−0.8	1.0	0.2
Kazakhstan	4.0	0.2	−3.3	−1.5	−1.1	−0.5
Vanuatu	3.9	0.9	0.6	−1.1	3.8	0.0
Argentina	3.8	0.6	1.7	−1.1	1.4	0.0
Belize	3.8	3.7	0.3	2.3	2.6	3.3
Sudan	3.3	0.6	−2.7	−1.4	−2.1	−0.3
Iraq	3.0	−0.1	−6.1	−1.7	−3.2	−0.7
Saudi Arabia	2.9	0.1	−12.8	−1.6	−12.5	−0.6
Togo	2.7	0.9	2.0	−0.7	1.3	0.3
Andorra	2.4	1.4	−0.6	−0.1	3.5	0.9
Turks and Caicos	2.3	3.0	−6.1	1.4	5.0	2.5
Croatia	2.0	1.8	1.5	0.1	3.2	1.1
Dominican Republic	2.0	4.2	1.5	2.6	2.1	3.7
Eritrea	1.9	1.5	−3.1	−0.1	0.5	0.9
Zimbabwe	1.8	1.8	2.2	0.2	1.6	1.2
Botswana	1.7	0.9	1.0	−0.7	2.1	0.3
Bolivia	1.5	0.9	−0.5	−0.7	−1.2	0.3
Egypt, Arab Rep. of	1.3	2.2	1.2	0.6	0.5	1.6
Jamaica	1.2	2.5	0.1	1.0	0.6	2.0

Source: Authors' calculations based on MAcMap-HS6 Version 1.

Note: Countries are ranked by decreasing true preference margin. Only countries with a true preference margin higher than 1 percent are shown in agriculture (1.5 percent for industry). See text for explanation of scenarios.

but in most cases, the preferential margin is largely swept out in this scenario. Scenario 2 leads to very different results in some cases, with preference margins essentially preserved (see, for example, Aruba, St. Vincent and the Grenadines, or St. Lucia). In other cases, the results are broadly comparable to those under scenario 1. This suggests that products identified as sensitive are the main source of the preference margin for a number of countries, but not for all. That is because sensitive products are frequently excluded from preferential agreements and because preferences for such products are frequently tied to quantitative limitations.

TRQ Rents and Their Erosion

Lower tariff duties are not the only type of trade preferences. In many instances (particularly for the most sensitive products), they are granted through preferential tariff rate quotas. In such cases, the benefit of a reduced (frequently to zero) tariff within a quota is limited either to a given country or to a set of preference-receiving countries. As soon as such preferential TRQs are filled, they give rise to rents, since the quantitative limitation on sales at the in-quota tariff is binding. These rents are not necessarily wholly captured by the exporter (see de Gorter and Kliauga 2006 for a detailed discussion). Still, exporters generally earn a substantial part of these rents, and this benefit often represents an important share of the benefit countries are able to reap from their preferential access.

Table 6.5, based on Bouët and others (2005b), displays the magnitude of these rents, for those developing countries for which they represented more than 0.15 percent of gross domestic product (GDP) in 2001. The methodology used to assess TRQ rents can be summarized as follows (for details, see Bouët and others 2005b). The rent is assumed to be zero when the fill rate of the TRQ (restricted to the partners the quota is allocated to, if applicable) is below 90 percent.[14] The calculation is based on the shadow tariff, defined as the ad valorem tariff that would lead to the same level of imports as is observed under the tariff rate quota. This shadow tariff is computed as a simple arithmetic average of the in-quota and the out-of-quota tariff rates when the fill rate lies between 90 and 99 percent, based on the assumption that the quota is binding, but that the out-of-quota tariff rate is prohibitive. As soon as the fill rate is higher than 99 percent, the shadow tariff is assumed to be equal to the out-of-quota tariff rate.

For each HS-6 product concerned, the quota rent is then computed as follows:

$$\text{rent} = \text{Min}\left(uv \times q \times \frac{SR - IQTR}{1 + IQTR}, \text{tradev} \times \frac{SR - IQTR}{1 + SR} \right)$$

where uv refers to the unit value, q to the quota allocated to the line, *tradev* to the trade value, SR to the shadow tariff rate, and $IQTR$ to the in-quota tariff rate.

TABLE 6.5 TRQ Rents Received by Developing Country, in 2001 and after Scenarios 1 and 2

Country	2001 (US$ millions)	TRQ rents received (as % of GDP)		
		2001	Scenario 1	Scenario 2
Guyana	59.8	8.28	3.28	7.89
Fiji	51.4	3.26	1.27	3.09
Mauritius	125.8	2.89	1.37	2.68
Belize	20.5	2.40	1.09	2.32
Ecuador	267.3	1.60	0.72	1.55
Panama	143.1	1.44	0.67	1.40
Costa Rica	228.2	1.37	0.63	1.33
St. Kitts and Nevis	4.1	1.26	0.59	1.16
Malawi	17.3	0.99	0.62	0.92
Jamaica	51.3	0.68	0.29	0.65
St. Vincent	2.3	0.67	0.48	0.67
Swaziland	6.0	0.52	0.21	0.49
Barbados	13.5	0.52	0.19	0.49
Honduras	31.7	0.50	0.26	0.48
Dominica	1.3	0.47	0.34	0.47
St. Lucia	3.3	0.46	0.33	0.46
Nicaragua	8.3	0.33	0.21	0.32
Zimbabwe	30.6	0.33	0.22	0.32
Suriname	2.3	0.26	0.21	0.26
Colombia	199.0	0.25	0.12	0.24
Côte d'Ivoire	23.3	0.25	0.16	0.24
Zambia	7.6	0.24	0.18	0.23
Dominican Republic	50.4	0.22	0.17	0.22
Cameroon	17.4	0.20	0.15	0.20
Trinidad and Tobago	14.5	0.18	0.09	0.16
Guatemala	30.0	0.15	0.08	0.14

Source: Authors' calculations, based on MAcMap-HS6 Version 1.
Note: Developing countries only, ranked by decreasing order of rents received in 2001 as a percentage of gross domestic product (GDP), and limited to countries for which this value is higher than 0.15 percent. See text for explanation of scenarios.

Assessed rents are as high as 8.3 percent of GDP in Guyana, 3.3 percent in Fiji, 2.9 percent in Mauritius, and 2.4 percent in Belize, suggesting that quota rents are important for these countries. Several other countries were earning rents in 2001 amounting to more than 1 percent of GDP, and another six countries were earning rents higher than 0.5 percent of GDP. Countries earning substantial rents as a share of GDP are mainly Sub-Saharan and Caribbean countries, but Central American countries are also strongly represented in table 6.5.

To assess how multilateral liberalization is likely to change the magnitude of these rents, the same calculations were carried out for scenarios 1 and 2, described earlier. For this exercise, we assumed that in-quota tariff rates and fill rates remained unchanged. This is a crude proxy, but because it is unclear how in-quota tariff rates will be liberalized, it is difficult to evaluate how liberalization will change fill rates.[15] These calculations suggest that applying scenario 1 would strongly erode the value of TRQ rents; in most cases the rents are more than halved. Such a reduction would represent a sizable shock, even at a macroeconomic level, especially for those countries with the highest rents. Although it is questionable whether TRQ rents are effectively used in many cases, such a sudden fall would certainly involve significant adjustment cost for the economies concerned. Scenario 2 presents a striking contrast: as soon as sensitive products are granted flexible treatment, multilateral liberalization does not entail such strong drops in TRQ rents. This result illustrates the well-known fact that TRQs generally apply to highly sensitive products. Exempting such products from substantial liberalization would thus largely maintain these rents.

Assumptions of CGE Simulations

The purpose of this section is to see how taking preferences into account modifies our conclusions regarding the expected benefits of trade liberalization, and how countries are affected differently as a result of the inclusion of preferences and their erosion. We draw on Bouët and others (2005a) and make use of the same model, which is an adapted version of the MIRAGE CGE model, to include more explicit modeling of agricultural policies. A number of liberalization scenarios, which correspond to plausible outcomes of the negotiations on market access in agriculture, are considered by simulating their consequences with and without preferences taken into account. Liberalization is limited to the agricultural sector in this exercise. Accordingly, tariffs on nonagricultural merchandise are not liberalized, nor is trade in services. Distortions such as export subsidies or domestic support also are not reduced. TRQs are explicitly modeled (and we assume that their rents accrue entirely to the exporters). The assessed impact of eroded preferences thus takes into account both the decrease in the tariff preference margin and the fall in TRQ rents.

Our baseline incorporates the most recent developments in the agricultural sector: the implementation of the EU's 2000 Agenda, the recent (partial) decoupling introduced into European policy, and the 2002 U.S. farm bill. The 2001 protection data were also amended to take into account the addition of 10 members to the EU (by freeing trade between the old and new members and replacing the new members' external tariff structure with the existing EU structure) and the accession of China to the WTO.

To assess the specific impact of preferences on multilateral liberalization, scenarios 1 and 2 are each modeled twice: with preferences and without preferences, meaning that preferential agreements are ignored when measuring initial protection in the model (except for a handful of large free trade agreements between developed countries), such that applied rates are assumed to be equal to MFN rates. This alternative dataset is introduced as a change in the initial dataset, not as a shock.[16] The liberalization is modeled with the MIRAGE-AG model (see Bchir and others 2002 for the base model and Bouët and others 2004a for the model devoted to the analysis of agricultural liberalization). The regional and sectoral breakdowns are reported in table 6.6.

Results of CGE Simulations

Do preferences matter? The simulation results in table 6.7, where overall results at the world level are considered for our two scenarios, show that the answer is definitively yes. The simulated increase in world agricultural exports associated with the tiered formula (scenario 1) is 14 percent when preferences are taken into account, but 21 percent when neglecting preferences. The difference in the effect on world welfare is not quite as large but still sizable.

Not surprisingly (given the results reported in Jean, Laborde, and Martin 2006), exempting sensitive products from tariff cuts (scenario 2) has a much more limited impact on world agricultural exports and welfare. But the impact of including preferences is even higher in scenario 2 than in scenario 1: if preferences were neglected, the estimated increase in exports would be twice as large and the impact on welfare three times as large.

Overvaluation of the impact of trade liberalization when preferences are not taken into account translates into larger estimated impacts of liberalization on world prices. Since we are mostly interested in developing countries, we show only the expected changes in international prices faced by these countries. They are much lower than those generally reported using models that do not account for preferences, averaging no more than 2 percent in scenario 1 and even less in scenario 2 (table 6.8). The impact under scenario 1 is most pronounced for sugar, meat, oilseeds, and cereals. When sensitive products are excluded from the tariff cuts (scenario 2), the effect is greatest on wheat, while rice is one of the less-affected products.

Results also vary across regions. For the first, more ambitious, trade liberalization scenario, table 6.9 shows that Argentina, Brazil, CairnsAsia, SADC (Southern

TABLE 6.6 Sectoral and Geographical Breakdown in the Simulation Exercise

Sector	Counterparts in GTAP
Rice	Paddy rice, processed rice
Wheat	Wheat
Cereals	Cereal grains nec
VegFruits	Vegetables, fruit, nuts
Oilseeds	Oilseeds
Sugar	Sugar cane, sugar beet, sugar
Fibers	Plant-based fibers
OthAgr	Crops nec, animal products nec; wool, silk-worm cocoons
Meat	Cattle, sheep, goat, horses; meat: cattle, sheep, goat, horse; meat products nec
Milk	Raw milk, dairy products
Fats	Vegetable oils and fats
Food	Food products nec, beverages and tobacco products
Clothing	Wearing apparel, leather products
AgrInputs	Chemical, rubber, plastic products; machinery and equipment nec
Other	Forestry; fishing; coal; oil; gas; minerals nec; textiles; wood products; paper products, publishing; petroleum, coal products; mineral products nec; ferrous metals; metals nec; metal products; motor vehicles and parts; transport equipment nec; electronic equipment; manufactures nec
TrT	Trade; transport nec; sea transport; air transport
OthSer	Electricity; gas manufacture, distribution; water; construction; communication; financial services nec; insurance; business services nec; recreation and other services; public administration/defense/health/education; dwellings

Note: nec = not elsewhere classified.

African Development Community), and South Africa would enjoy significant welfare gains and positive changes in the returns to land. (In contrast, the factor price change is negative in Canada, European Free Trade Agreement [EFTA], the EU, Japan, and the Republic of Korea.) Including preferences in the exercise reduces the positive impacts of agricultural trade liberalization for most regions, but especially for CairnsAsia and SADC.

Sub-Saharan African (SSA) countries excluding SADC, however, sustain losses when preferences are taken into account, but not when they are assumed not to exist. Table 6.10 provides more detailed results for SSA countries excluding SADC. In scenario 1, their export volume increases by 0.5 percent when preferences are not taken into account, but decreases by 3.9 percent when preferences are included.

Geographical Breakdown

1. ANZCERTA: Australia, New Zealand
2. Bangladesh
3. BraArg: Brazil, Argentina
4. CairnsAsia: Indonesia, Malaysia, Philippines, Thailand
5. Canada
6. CentrAmCar: Central America, Rest of FTAA, rest of Caribbean
7. China
8. DdAsia: Rest of developed Asia—Hong Kong (China), Singapore, Taiwan (China)
9. EU25: European Union—25 countries
10. EFTA: Iceland, Norway, Switzerland
11. India
12. Japan
13. Korea, Rep. of
14. MorTun: Morocco, Tunisia
15. OthLatAm: Other Latin America (Chile, Colombia, Mexico, Peru, Uruguay, R.B. Venezuela, rest of Andean Pact, rest of South America)
16. Row: Rest of the world (Albania, Bulgaria, Croatia, Romania, Russian Federation, Sri Lanka, Vietnam, rest of former Soviet Union, rest of East Asia, rest of Oceania, rest of Southeast Asia, rest of South Asia, rest of Middle East, rest of North Africa, rest of North America)
17. SADCxSA: South African Development Community except South Africa
18. SouthAf: South Africa
19. SSAxSADC: Sub-Saharan Africa except SADC
20. Turkey
21. US: United States

Source: Authors.

Agricultural imports are boosted in both scenarios, however, leading to an overall reduction in agrofood production in these countries. The magnitude of these effects is large enough to lead to a depreciation of the real exchange rate and a decline in unskilled wages when preferences are included. The returns to land are depressed too, but less in scenario 1 than in scenario 2. Overall welfare changes very little in both scenarios but is slightly positive if preferences are ignored and slightly negative when they are taken into account.

Utilization of Preferences

So far, we have taken for granted that exporters fully used statutory trade preferences without restriction or any cost. In reality, however, that may not be the case, since benefiting from a preferential scheme requires complying with several

TABLE 6.7 Simulated Impact of Two Alternative Agricultural Tariff Cut Scenarios on World Trade and Welfare (percent change)

Scenario	Including preferences (a)	Excluding preferences (b)	Ratio (a)/(b)
Scenario 1			
World trade	0.80	1.22	1.5
World agricultural exports	13.59	21.08	1.6
World welfare	0.14	0.18	1.3
Scenario 2			
World trade	0.25	0.49	2.0
World agricultural exports	4.21	8.72	2.1
World welfare	0.02	0.06	3.0
Ratio (2)/(1)			
World trade	0.30	0.40	
World agricultural exports	0.30	0.40	
World welfare	0.10	0.30	

Source: Authors' MIRAGE-Agr model simulation results.
Note: See text for explanation of scenarios.

requirements: purely administrative issues, technical requirements that may be attached to the benefit of the scheme, other specific conditions, and most of all rules of origin (ROOs). A priori, there is no reason to contest the legitimacy of these conditions attached to the benefit of preferential schemes.

ROOs are of special importance. They are justified by the need to avoid trade deflection, that is, reexports through the preference-receiving country of goods essentially produced in a third country. ROOs prevent misuses of preference schemes, arguably reinforcing the benefit of the scheme for the preference-receiving country to the extent that they create an incentive for third countries to invest in the preference-receiving country in order to benefit from preferential market access. There can be a direct cost associated with meeting the ROOs, however. Required administrative paperwork is potentially cumbersome and costly if it requires operating a parallel accounting system differing in definition, scope, and concept from the system imposed by domestic legal requirements.[17] ROOs also constrain the sourcing of intermediate inputs. These costs have been the subject of close scrutiny, because of the widespread suspicion that requirements associated with preferential agreements, and especially ROOs, are used as protective measures that undermine the benefit of preferential access (Krishna and Krueger 1995;

TABLE 6.8 Simulated Impact of Two Alternative Agricultural Tariff Cut Scenarios on International Prices of Developing-Country Exports (percent change)

Export	Scenario 1		Scenario 2	
	Including preferences	Excluding preferences	Including preferences	Excluding preferences
Cereals	1.1	1.85	0.31	0.75
Fats	0.77	1.14	0.21	0.44
Fibers	0.38	0.79	0.08	0.29
Food	0.54	0.9	0.13	0.36
Meat	1.39	2.07	0.33	0.61
Milk	0.63	1.18	0.19	0.68
Oilseeds	1.31	2	0.32	0.56
OthAgr	0.67	1.34	0.2	0.52
Other	0.42	0.67	0.1	0.28
Rice	0.99	1.33	0.19	0.51
Sugar	1.5	2.12	0.36	0.72
VegFruits	0.89	1.46	0.19	0.57
Wheat	0.79	1.27	0.51	1.99
Clothing	0.41	0.68	0.09	0.3
AgrInputs	0.43	0.69	0.11	0.29
OthSer	0.48	0.76	0.12	0.31
TrT	0.45	0.73	0.11	0.32

Source: Authors' MIRAGE-Agr model simulation results.
Note: See text for explanation of scenarios.

Falvey and Reed 1998, 2002). It has also been argued that ROOs are sometimes used as export subsidies, insofar as restrictive rules can create an incentive for the preference-receiving country to buy its inputs from the preference-granting country (Cadot, Estevadeordal, and Suwa-Eisenmann 2004).

In practice, the magnitude of these costs is difficult to assess. Based on indirect evidence, several studies estimate the administrative compliance costs of preferential schemes to be between 1 and 5 percent of the value of exports (Herin 1986; Anson and others 2004), depending on the precise nature of the requirements and on the technical capacity of exporters to comply with them. Nonadministrative costs, linked in particular to the constraint on sourcing imposed by ROOs, vary even more across products and countries. They depend in particular on the possibilities for splitting the value-added chain for the product among countries and on whether the agreement includes low-cost input suppliers. In addition, several different types of ROOs are used (Estevadeordal and Suominen 2003),

TABLE 6.9 Simulated Impact of Scenario 1 on Welfare, Terms of Trade, and Returns to Land, by Region (percent change)

Region	Welfare		Terms of trade		Returns to land	
	Including preferences	Excluding preferences	Including preferences	Excluding preferences	Including preferences	Excluding preferences
ANZCERTA	0.06	0.23	1.04	2.28	9.25	8.83
Bangladesh	−0.04	−0.05	−0.02	0.01	0.04	0.04
BraArg	0.10	0.16	1.22	1.75	0.20	0.32
CairnsAsia	0.29	0.48	0.18	0.28	0.67	1.01
Canada	0.19	0.74	−0.07	−0.22	−0.23	−1.75
CentrAmCar	−0.09	−0.05	0.39	0.65	1.13	1.30
China	0.06	0.09	0.12	0.24	0.03	0.47
DdAsia	−0.01	0.01	−0.03	−0.02	−1.06	2.45
EFTA	0.50	2.07	−0.06	−0.23	−2.30	−3.37
EU25	0.16	0.21	−0.20	−0.33	−0.65	−0.92
India	0.09	0.10	0.34	0.39	1.49	1.26
Japan	1.08	1.37	−0.34	−0.50	−13.67	−19.19
Korea, Rep. of	1.95	2.13	−0.22	−0.31	−5.64	−4.23
MorTun	1.20	1.59	−0.14	0.04	−0.13	−1.28
OthLatAm	0.04	0.08	0.14	0.33	−0.12	0.07
RoW	0.09	0.11	0.09	0.18	−0.67	−0.71
SADCxSA	0.13	0.42	0.86	1.67	1.49	1.71
SouthAf	0.12	0.20	0.15	0.34	1.00	5.50
SSAxSADC	−0.02	0.00	−0.03	0.17	−0.16	−0.37
Turkey	0.10	0.15	0.15	0.40	−0.13	0.37
United States	−0.02	−0.02	0.05	−0.02	2.22	1.86

Source: Authors' MIRAGE-Agr model simulation results.
Note: See text for explanation of scenario 1. See table 6.6 for geographical breakdown.

the restrictiveness of which differs widely. Based on the detailed work undertaken by Estevadeordal (2000), several studies have focused on the North American Free Trade Agreement and have found that ROOs hamper Mexican exports to the United States, particularly in the automotive and textile-clothing sector (Cadot and others 2002; Anson and others 2004). Their cost varies with the nature of the rule, but the whole cost seems to be close to the preferential margin itself, suggesting that the value of the agreement would be very low for Mexican exporters. Studying free trade agreements between the EU and Central European partners, Brenton and Manchin (2003) conclude that the rules associated with the agreements preclude

TABLE 6.10 Detailed Impact of Two Tariff-Cutting Scenarios on Selected Sub-Saharan Countries (percent change)

Indicator affected	Scenario 1		Scenario 2	
	Including preferences	Excluding preferences	Including preferences	Excluding preferences
Agricultural exports (volume)	−3.90	0.58	−1.36	0.16
Agricultural imports (volume)	2.01	3.17	0.26	0.53
Agricultural real wages	−0.35	0.19	−0.09	0.06
Agro-food production	−0.57	−0.29	−0.16	0.00
Agro-food production price	0.05	0.57	0.01	0.24
Exports (volume)	0.08	0.61	−0.02	0.16
GDP (volume)	0.01	0.01	0.00	0.00
Imports (volume)	−0.05	0.29	−0.04	0.06
Nonagricultural unskilled real wages	−0.04	0.09	−0.02	0.04
Real effective exchange rate	−0.03	0.21	−0.01	0.09
Real return to capital	0.14	0.09	0.03	0.05
Real return to land	−0.16	−0.37	−0.07	−0.15
Real return to natural resources	0.64	0.34	0.16	0.10
Skilled real wages	0.05	−0.01	0.00	0.03
Terms of trade	−0.03	0.17	−0.02	0.07
Unskilled real wages	−0.24	0.15	−0.07	0.05
Welfare	−0.02	0.00	−0.01	0.01

Source: Authors' MIRAGE-Agr model simulation results.
Note: See text for explanation of scenarios.

exporters from reaping any substantial benefit, as evidenced by the very low use of these agreements.[18]

Nonreciprocal preferences face the same kind of issues, but not necessarily the same results because of differences in rules applied, in product specialization, and in income levels of the exporters. Reporting that the EBA initiative was very underused by LDC exporters to the EU in 2001, Brenton (2003) casts doubts on the actual benefit of this preferential scheme and points to the stringency of rules of origin as the main culprit. Subramanian, Mattoo, and Roy (2002) make a similar point about AGOA, showing that rules of origin, in particular, strongly undermine the "generosity" of this agreement. These findings of a poor utilization rate, not only for both EBA and AGOA but also for the GSP scheme, have been confirmed and qualified by Inama (2003).

However, studying the utilization of various preferential schemes individually may be misleading. Candau, Fontagné, and Jean (2004) and OECD (2004) emphasize the problem of "competing preferences": when a country is eligible for several preferential schemes (and this is the case with numerous developing countries, with preferential access to the EU or the U.S. market), underuse of a given scheme can merely mean that another scheme is judged more interesting by the exporter. In this case, underutilization may not be a problem, since the exporter still enjoys the benefit of preferential market, although the preference margin available under the chosen scheme may be lower than under the one with more restrictive rules. Typically, the very low utilization rate of EBA among ACP LDCs (3 percent on average for all products in 2001, according to Candau, Fontagné, and Jean 2004) simply means that exporters prefer to use the preferential access offered through the Cotonou Agreement, which has existed for a long time and has less-restrictive rules.[19]

When due account is taken of these overlapping preference schemes, preferences appear to have been well utilized in agricultural products, at around 90 percent. Wainio and Gibson's (2004) analysis of U.S. nonreciprocal preferential regimes for agricultural products confirms this finding. In summarizing four case studies carried out in Botswana, Kenya, Lesotho, and Mauritius, Stevens and Kennan (2004) also report that very few exports from these countries to the EU (1–6 percent) do not benefit from any preference (or from zero MFN duty). As they conclude, it is "inherently implausible that for the countries and products studied, preferences have not been well utilized," given the magnitude of preferential margins, and the place they take in the long-standing export structure of these countries. In addition, Stevens and Kennan report that their detailed analysis does not show product coverage significantly limiting the benefit of the Cotonou Agreement (except for quantitative limitations linked to preferential tariff quotas). Indeed, no significant exports are made to the EU, nor to markets in Canada, Japan, or the United States, for products for which preferences were not available (Stevens and Kennan 2004, 8).

The average figures given by Candau, Fontagné, and Jean (2004) summarize the resulting effects on market access barriers: for raw agricultural products in 2001, the lowest duty available to Sub-Saharan countries (assuming perfect utilization of preferences) was zero for LDCs and 0.4 percent for non-LDCs and the average duty actually faced was 0.8 percent in both cases; for food products, the lowest duty available averaged 4.9 percent for LDCs and 12.6 percent for non-LDCs, while the average duty faced was respectively 5.4 percent for LDCs and 13.8 percent for non-LDCs.[20]

Introducing preferences more explicitly in the CGE simulations allows a quantitative assessment of the impact concerning the erosion of preferences. Although existing data do not raise any particular technical problem, we feel that they fall short of paving the way for a complete and detailed analysis, mainly because of incomplete geographical coverage. More important, the results show that taking underutilization of preferences into account changes only marginally the broader effect caused by the erosion of preferences in agricultural products.

Nevertheless, it is worth emphasizing that this conclusion is not true outside agriculture. Here the main concern is textiles and clothing, both because a deep international division of labor takes place in this industry and because it is the main industrial sector for which poor countries have a significant export potential. It is also an industry where lobbies have played a significant role in recent decades. As a result, the arguments about the use of ROOs as protective instruments are fully applicable. The use of preferences in textiles and clothing is as low as 35 percent under AGOA (Inama 2003), and Brenton (2003) and Inama (2003) point to the low utilization rate of the EU's EBA preferences in textiles and clothing, even by non-ACP countries. (In particular, Bangladesh uses this scheme for only about half its exports in the sector, and Cambodia hardly makes any use of it). Candau, Fontagné, and Jean (2004) confirm this finding but also show that the problem of underusage of preferences in textiles and clothing is limited to the GSP scheme and does not, for instance, extend to the Cotonou Agreement, although this agreement fully covers the sector. Still, the problem is important, especially for the EBA Initiative, where preferential margins are rather large. According to calculations by Candau, Fontagné, and Jean (2004), the average duty rate faced by non-ACP LDCs exporters in textiles and clothing is 5.2 percent, even thought they are eligible for duty-free access. As far as textiles and clothing are concerned, underuse of preferential schemes is thus widespread. All authors agree in pointing out the prominent role of stringent ROOs as the overwhelming cause for this underusage, thus suggesting that even exports benefiting from preferential access might suffer from the additional costs imposed by these rules. ROOs thus seem to seriously undermine the benefit that poor countries can reap from most nonreciprocal preferential agreements.

Conclusions and Policy Implications

It is clear that the threat of preference erosion following the Doha Round is real, insofar as trade preferences are now playing a key role in the world trading system, and in particular in the pro-poor policies undertaken by rich countries. But it is equally clear that these concerns are likely to be used by vested interests to lobby against multilateral liberalization as they try to take advantage of the convergence of interests between poor countries' producers benefiting from rents created by preferential access to rich markets and rich countries' protected producers.

The conventional response to these concerns is to assume that the erosion of preferences is a problem of limited magnitude, focused on a handful of products and on a limited number of countries (Subramanian 2003; Alexandraki and Lankes 2004). Our analysis is consistent with this view, but it suggests that the magnitude of forthcoming difficulties for poor countries has perhaps been understated. Preferences can have perverse consequences, they suffer from several drawbacks, and they can be underutilized. Still, preferential schemes such as the Cotonou Agreement or the CBI are of particular importance for benefiting countries. In other words, the erosion of preferences is most of all a problem for a limited number of African and Caribbean countries, whose export specialization is largely a function of preferences. Sugar, bananas, textiles and clothing, and meat products play a central role. In addition, poor countries generally have a very low adjustment capacity because of a combination of deficient capital markets, obstacles to labor mobility, the absence of safety nets, and the lack of training capacities. The adjustment costs for poor countries faced with eroded preferences may therefore be fairly high.

Thus we believe the erosion of preferences to be a serious concern for poor countries (although further research is needed to determine to what extent the benefits of preferences within those countries accrue to poor households). What are the possible policy responses to this issue? The alternative should not be the status quo, not least because EU-ACP nonreciprocal preferences have been ruled incompatible with WTO rules and a WTO waiver protecting them is scheduled to expire in 2008. At that time, this nonreciprocal scheme could be replaced by reciprocal Economic Partnership Agreements (EPAs), negotiated between the EU and regional groupings of ACP countries, as planned in the Cotonou Agreement. The perspective of eroded preferences must therefore be gauged against this background, although the precise shape of EPAs is difficult to foresee.[21]

The possibility of granting preference-dependent countries an adjustment package has been repeatedly mentioned, including during the Cancún Ministerial Conference. The basis for such an approach was set up with the launch in April 2004 of the International Monetary Fund's Trade Integration Mechanism, designed to "assist member countries to meet balance of payments shortfalls that might result from multilateral trade liberalization."[22] This new instrument is explicitly motivated by adjustments required as a result of "measures implemented by other countries that lead to more open market access for goods and services," which clearly includes preference erosion.[23] It creates a new framework within which future adjustment packages could be managed, and it could be helpful to the extent that adjustment costs are likely to be substantial in several poor countries. It remains doubtful, however, whether such a temporary adjustment facility is a suitable answer to the permanent shock resulting from the erosion of preferences. If preferences have been of some interest to recipient countries—and, notwithstanding their drawbacks, we believe they have—then an adjustment package would not be a satisfactory answer. The record of technical assistance so far has not proven to be very convincing, so other possibilities should be considered to make trade liberalization "work for the poor." In the current case, that means making sure that vulnerable countries gain elsewhere from the Doha Round. Improving market access conditions for poor countries can contribute, particularly by allowing the poorest countries duty-free, quota-free access to rich countries' markets. Easing restrictive ROOs in textile and clothing can also be of interest in this perspective, as can giving preferential schemes more predictability and stability across time.[24] The benefits poor countries could reap from such measures are not clear, however. Targeted offensive initiatives are thus also of interest. These could include the cotton initiative discussed in Sumner (2006), or a more proactive stance on Mode IV trade in services (trade where the service provider moves to the consuming region) (Winters and others 2003). The difficulties of standards and technical barriers to trade, particularly those linked to the Sanitary and Phytosanitary Agreement, also need to be acknowledged for poor countries trying to access rich-country markets. Here, a balance is very difficult to strike between legitimate collective choices and preserved opportunities for poor countries to integrate into world markets.

Perhaps consideration needs to be given to a new proposal, mentioned in Anderson, Martin, and van der Mensbrugghe (2006), to reward developing-country commitments to greater trade reform with an expansion of trade-facilitating aid, to be provided by a major expansion of the current Integrated Framework, which is operated by a consortium of international agencies for least developed countries (Hoekman forthcoming). This approach may well provide an attractive path for developing countries seeking to trade their way out of poverty, as well as a potentially more efficient way for developed countries to assist people in low-income countries than the current systems of tariff preferences (provided of course that governments spend that additional aid on initiatives that benefit the poor).

Notes

1. The G-90 is an umbrella body of the African Group, which is composed of the least developed countries, and the African, Caribbean, and Pacific (ACP) Group. It is the largest grouping of members in the WTO.

2. According to World Bank (2004), regional trade agreements cover more than 20 percent of world trade when imports subject to zero MFN tariffs are excluded.

3. Article XXIV states, "the provisions of this Agreement shall not prevent, as between the territories of contracting parties, the formation of a customs union or of a free-trade area."

4. Mercosur includes Argentina, Brazil, Paraguay, and Uruguay.

5. Resolution 21(ii), taken at the UNCTAD II conference in New Delhi in 1968, states that "the objectives of the generalised, non-reciprocal, non-discriminatory system of preferences in favour of the developing countries, including special measures in favour of the least advanced among the developing countries, should be: to increase their export earnings; to promote their industrialisation; and to accelerate their rates of economic growth." The resolution was a follow-up to a proposal made in 1964 by Raúl Prebisch, the first secretary-general of UNCTAD.

6. See UNCTAD (2003) for an overview.

7. This Enabling Clause is the translation into GATT law of the GSP scheme, formally undertaken in 1979; it states that "notwithstanding the provisions of Article I of the General Agreement, contracting parties may accord differential and more favourable treatment to developing countries, without according such treatment to other contracting parties." For more on SDT as it relates to Doha, see Josling (2005).

8. The complexity also concerns exporting countries: for example, products shipped by 28 countries, including Angola, Burundi, Chad, Malawi, Sierra Leone, and Solomon Islands, might be taxed under any of four alternative tariff regimes and administrative rules. This creates sizeable information costs for small exporters.

9. The unit value used in computing the ad valorem equivalent of specific tariffs also varies across reference groups.

10. The MFN AVE duty is defined as a three-dimensional variable (reporter, product, and partner) due to the calculation of the ad valorem equivalent of specific duties based on a bilateral unit value.

11. Some of the examples cited here are not reported in the table, since it includes only countries with the highest true preferential margin, in order to save space.

12. When aggregating tariffs across products, exporters, and importers, MAcMap-HS6 uses a weighting scheme based on trade flows between the exporter and the reference group to which the importer belongs. Reference groups gather similar countries and are determined by use of a clustering analysis. This method tends to limit the extent of the well-known endogeneity bias arising when bilateral trade flows are used as weighting schemes. For a more detailed explanation, see Bouët and others 2004b.

13. The tiered formula is directly inspired by the Harbinson proposal, but it is corrected to avoid discontinuities (see Jean, Laborde, and Martin 2006).

14. Note, however, that this is a crude approximation. In many cases, the quota is not filled because of limitations imposed by the administrative regime, not by the level of the in-quota tariff rate (see de Gorter and Kliauga 2006). Because of data limitations, we do not take this into account.

15. A priori, however, should in-quota tariff rates remain unchanged, multilateral liberalization should decrease fill rates of TRQs, since competition from out-of-quota exports would be tougher.

16. The algorithm used to make this change is intended to distort the initial dataset as little as possible; in particular, we leave unchanged the international trade flows. The welfare results would not differ widely if we had used an initial shock.

17. See, for example, UNCTAD (2003, 54) and Inama (2003).

18. They found that only 35 percent of Central and Eastern European countries' exports enter the EU using the lowest tariff for which they would be eligible.

19. The EBA initiative is embedded in the GSP scheme, the rules of origin of which are far more stringent than under the Cotonou Agreement. In particular, no diagonal cumulation is allowed among beneficiaries of the GSP schemes, except under a few regional agreements, while such cumulation is possible across Cotonou Agreement's beneficiaries.

20. The statistics refer only to the import regime requested by the importer; it does not make clear how customs officers treat these requests. Differentiating raw agricultural products and food products makes sense as rules of origin are supposed to have different impact on preference utilization according to the level of product transformation (UNCTAD 2003).

21. In principle, countries signing an EPA with the EU should benefit from the same access as they do under the EBA Initiative, although the detailed conditions remain to be defined. EPAs may not be fully reciprocal, however, and market access offered by signing countries to EU's exporters has not been clearly defined so far.

22. See http://www.imf.org/external/np/exr/facts/tim.htm.
23. The Trade Integration Mechanism explicitly "does not cover the implications of 'own liberalization' measures" (www.imf.org).
24. The GSP schemes and AGOA, in particular, do not offer long-term stability.

References

Alexandraki, K., and H. P. Lankes. 2004. "The Impact of Preference Erosion on Middle-Income Developing Countries." IMF Working Paper 04/169, International Monetary Fund, Washington DC, September.

Anderson, K, W. Martin, and D. van der Mensbrugghe. 2006. "Market and Welfare Implications of Doha Reform Scenarios." In *Agricultural Trade Reform and the Doha Development Agenda*, ed. K. Anderson and W. Martin. Basingstoke, U.K.: Palgrave Macmillan; Washington, DC: World Bank.

Anson, J., O. Cadot, A. Estevadeordal, J. de Melo, A. Suwa-Eisenmann, and B. Tumurchudur. 2004. "Rules of Origin in North-South Preferential Trading Arrangements, with an Application to NAFTA." CEPR Discussion Paper 4166. Centre for Economic Policy Research, London.

Bchir, M. H., Y. Decreux, J.-L Guérin, and S. Jean. 2002. "MIRAGE: a General Equilibrium Model for Trade Policy Analysis." *CEPII Working Paper* 2002–17, Centre d'Etudes Prospectives et d'Informations Internationales, Paris.

Bchir, M., S. Jean, and D. Laborde. Forthcoming. "Binding Overhang and Tariff-cutting Formulas: A Systematic, Worldwide Quantitative Assessment." Working Paper, Centre d'Etudes Prospectives et d'Informations Internationales, Paris.

Bouët, A., J.-C Bureau, Y. Decreux, and S. Jean 2005a. "Multilateral Agricultural Trade Liberalization: The Contrasting Fortunes of Developing Countries in the Doha Round." *The World Economy*.

Bouët A., Y. Decreux., L. Fontagné, S. Jean, and D. Laborde. 2005b. "Tariff Duties in GTAP6: The MAcMap-HS6 Database, Sources and Methodology." In *Global Trade, Assistance, and Production: The GTAP6 Database*, ed. B. Damaranon and R. McDougall. West Lafayette, IN: Purdue University.

Brenton, P. 2003. "The Value of Trade Preferences: The Economic Impact of Everything but Arms." World Bank, International Trade Department, Washington, DC.

Brenton, P., and M. Manchin. 2003. "Making EU Trade Agreements Work: The Role of Rules of Origin." *World Economy* 26 (5): 755–69.

Cadot, O., A. Estevadeordal, J. de Melo, A. Suwa-Eisenmann, and B. Tumurchudur. 2002. "Assessing the Effect of NAFTA's Rules of Origin." University of Lausanne, Lausanne.

Cadot, O., A. Estevadeordal, and A. Suwa-Eisenmann. 2004. "Rules of Origin as Export Subsidies." CEPR Discussion Paper 4999. Centre for Economic Policy Research, London.

Candau, F., L. Fontagné, and S. Jean. 2004. "The Utilisation Rate of Preferences in the EU." Paper presented at 7th Global Economic Analysis Conference, CEPII working paper (in progress), June 17–19, Washington, DC.

de Gorter, H., and E. Kliauga. 2006. "Reducing Tariffs Versus Expanding Tariff Rate Quotas." In *Agricultural Trade Reform and the Doha Development Agenda*, ed. K. Anderson and W. Martin. Basingstoke, U.K.: Palgrave Macmillan; Washington, DC: World Bank.

Estevadeordal, A. 2000. "Negotiating Preferential Market Access: The Case of the North American Free Trade Agreement." *Journal of World Trade* 34: 141–66.

Estevadeordal, A., and K. Suominen. 2003. "Rules of Origin: A World Map." Inter-American Development Bank, Integration and Regional Programs Department, Washington, DC.

Falvey, R., and G. Reed. 1998. "Economic Effects of Rules of Origin." *Weltwirtschifliches Archiv* 134: 209–29.

―――. 2002. "Rules of Origin as Commercial Policy Instruments." *International Economic Review* 43 (2, May): 393–408.

Herin, J. 1986. "Rules of Origin and Differences between Tariff Levels in EFTA and in the EC." *EFTA Occasional Paper* 13, European Free Trade Association, Geneva, February.

Hoekman, B. Forthcoming. "Operationalizing the Concept of Policy Space in the WTO: Beyond Special and Differential Treatment." *Journal of International Economic Law* 8.

Inama, S. 2003. "Trade Preferences for LDCs: An Early Assessment of Benefits and Possible Improvements." ITCD/TSB/2003, United Nations Conference on Trade and Development, Geneva.

Jean, S., D. Laborde, and W. Martin. 2006. "Consequences of Alternative Formulas for Agricultural Tariff Cuts." In *Agricultural Trade Reform and the Doha Development Agenda*, ed. K. Anderson and W. Martin. Basingstoke, U.K.: Palgrave Macmillan; Washington, DC: World Bank.

Krishna, K., and A. O. Krueger. 1995. "Implementing Free Trade Areas: Rules of Origin and Hidden Protection." In *New Directions in Trade Theory*, ed. A. Deardorff, J. Levinsohn, and R. Stern. East Lansing: University of Michigan Press.

OECD (Organisation for Economic Co-operation and Development). 2004. *The Utilisation of Trade Preferences by OECD Countries: The Case of Agricultural and Food Products Entering the European Union and United States*, Paris: OECD.

Stevens, C., and J. Kennan. 2004. "The Utilisation of EU Preferences to the ACP." Paper presented to the technical seminar on tariff preferences and their utilization, WTO Secretariat, Geneva, March 31.

Subramanian, A. 2003. "Financing of Losses from Preference Erosion." WT/TF/COH/14, International Monetary Fund, Washington, DC, January.

Subramanian, A., A. Mattoo, and D. Roy. 2002. "The Africa Growth and Opportunity Act and Its Rules of Origin: Generosity Undermined?" Working Paper 2908, World Bank, Washington DC, October.

Sumner, D. 2006. "Reducing Cotton Subsidies: The DDA Cotton Initiative." In *Agricultural Trade Reform and the Doha Development Agenda*, ed. K. Anderson and W. Martin. Basingstoke, U.K.: Palgrave Macmillan; Washington, DC: World Bank.

UNCTAD (United Nations Conference on Trade and Development). 2003. "Trade Preferences for the LDCs: An Early Assessment of Benefits and Possible Improvements." UNCTAD/ITCD/TSB/2003/8, UNCTAD, Geneva.

Wainio, J., and J. Gibson. 2004. "The Significance of Nonreciprocal Trade Preferences for Developing Countries." In *Agricultural Reform and the WTO: Where Are We Heading?* ed. G. Anania, M. E. Bowman, C. A. Carter, and A. F. McCalla. London: Edward Elgar.

Winters, L. A., T. Walmsley, Z. K. Wang, and R. Grynberg. 2003. "Liberalizing Temporary Movement of Natural Persons: An Agenda for the Development Round." *World Economy* 26 (8, August): 1137–61.

World Bank. 2004. *Global Economic Prospects 2005*, Washington, DC: World Bank.

WTO (World Trade Organization). 2004. "Decision Adopted by the General Council on 1 August 2004" (July Framework Agreement). WT/L/579, WTO, Geneva.

PART III

EXPORT SUBSIDIES AND DOMESTIC SUPPORT

7

REMOVING THE EXCEPTION OF AGRICULTURAL EXPORT SUBSIDIES

Bernard Hoekman and Patrick Messerlin

Agricultural support policies pursued by high-income countries—domestic production and export subsidies, as well as trade barriers—hurt developing-country exporters of the affected commodities. They do so by boosting domestic production of the supported products, depressing international prices, exacerbating the volatility of world prices by insulating domestic markets, and reducing the scope for contesting markets. These policies may, however, benefit net importers of the products concerned by providing access to the subsidized commodities at lower prices. Thus, national interests regarding reform of agricultural trade and support policies may differ substantially, both across countries and within countries, depending on the pattern of production and consumption of the commodities involved.

To date, the Doha Round has been similar to the Uruguay Round in placing heavy emphasis on strengthening disciplines on a specific subset of the agricultural policy mix, namely, export subsidies. Much effort has focused on obtaining agreement to ban export subsidies in this sector, bringing it into line with other sectors. Elimination of export subsidies was finally accepted by those World Trade Organization (WTO) members that are the most intensive users of such subsidies—most notably, the European Union (EU)—in the July 2004 Framework Agreement (WTO 2004). That agreement spells out in some detail how liberalization is to occur: export subsidies are to be eliminated by a "credible" date, decreases are to be implemented in annual installments during the transition period, and an explicit link is to be made between the abolition of export subsidies and the negotiation of equivalent disciplines on other forms of export support, in particular the subsidy component of export credits, subsidies granted by state trading enterprises (STEs), and food aid. Special and differential treatment for export support granted by developing countries is to be limited to a longer transition period and "special consideration" for poorer countries' state trading enterprises.

In contrast to the specificity with which export subsidies are treated, the Framework Agreement is much vaguer when it comes to other dimensions of agricultural support policies such as market access and nonexport subsidies. It merely notes the need for "substantial improvements in market access for all products," it does not specify the formula to be used for cutting tariffs, and opens the door to many exceptions to tariff cuts by, among other things, accepting the possibility for countries to define sensitive and special products and by allowing for safeguard measures (Jean, Laborde, and Martin 2006). From an economic perspective, the emphasis on export subsidies is somewhat puzzling in that the available evidence and analysis suggests that domestic market price supports, especially through trade restrictions (tariffs, tariff rate quotas) can be expected to have the greatest impact on world prices (Hertel and Keeney 2006).

The magnitude of export subsidies is determined by the gap between domestic and world prices. Export subsidies are used when high tariffs raise the domestic price of commodities as a result of which domestic output expands. If there are also domestic production support programs, this output expansion will be greater, potentially affecting world prices through an artificially increased global supply. In principle it would be much more logical to see the elimination of export subsidies as a key *consequence* of reducing the gap between domestic and world prices created by border barriers and domestic support programs. Eliminating export support without reducing tariffs and domestic support would simply result in putting world agriculture in the situation faced by manufacturing at the dawn of the General Agreement on Tariffs and Trade (GATT) in the late 1940s—no export subsidies but high tariffs and domestic support. The abolition of export subsidies would be an achievement in itself, but from an economic perspective, it is likely to have a limited impact. How large the impact would be is of course an empirical matter, as is the incidence of the associated benefits and costs.

In this chapter we do not undertake a quantitative assessment but instead review the available information on the magnitude of export subsidies, the products that are subsidized, and the countries that are affected. The first section documents the trend in export subsidies in the world since the end of the Uruguay Round. The available information provides some evidence of a noticeable decline of export subsidies since 2000, as well as an interest on the part of middle-income and emerging market economies to be able to use export subsidies as well. The second section focuses on the use of export subsidies by the EU, given that the EU is the WTO member that dominates in this area. The data reveal that the use of export subsidies has declined significantly since 2000, suggesting that the EU may be selling a rapidly depreciating "asset." The third section summarizes the available evidence on the other forms of export support (export credits, STEs, and food aid) before some conclusions are presented.

Export Subsidies: On a Declining Path?

The Uruguay Round Agreement on Agriculture (URAA) allows 25 WTO members to subsidize exports, but only for products for which they have made URAA "commitments" (in WTO parlance) regarding the maximum value and quantities of farm exports that can be subsidized. In other words, commitments establish the limits on members' capacity to subsidize their farm exports. Other WTO members may not subsidize agriculture (or any other) exports at all. In the case of developing countries, subsidies are, however, allowed for certain inputs. Article 9.4 of the URAA permits developing countries to pay subsidies for internal transport and for marketing during the Uruguay Round implementation period. The July Framework envisages continuation of Article 9.4 "for a reasonable period." Indirectly, therefore, developing countries will continue to be allowed to support exports insofar as the commodities involved are exported.

An Aggregate, Country-Based Perspective

The total amount of export subsidy commitments across WTO members amounted to $96 billion in the 1995–2000 period. High-income countries accounted for some 85 percent of the total commitments; middle-income economies accounted for the remainder. Least developed countries (LDCs) do not report any export subsidies. Table 7.1 lists the 25 countries, ranked by decreasing magnitude of their commitments in value terms (aggregated over the period 1995–2000).[1] Eight of the 25 are developing countries—two of them (Brazil and South Africa) being leaders of the G-20 coalition that plays a key role in the Doha Round. The URAA requires these 25 countries to notify the extent to which they actually use subsidies. Table 7.1 also reports notified use (in value terms) of these subsidies. The data suggest four observations.

First, the WTO notification procedure does not work well. There is no consolidated information on the actual use of subsidies after 2000, and almost none for 2002 and after. For 2000 there is no information on some $1.7 billion of commitments—an amount equivalent to one-fourth of total EU commitments, or two-thirds of the amount notified as actually used by the EU in 2000. In several years members did not notify the use of their commitments for all their products. This is a poor record from a transparency perspective and somewhat surprising given the high profile and contested nature of export subsidies. The lack of data may imply that

TABLE 7.1 WTO Commitments and Notifications of Used Export Subsidies, 1995–2000

WTO member	Number of products	Commitments (US$ millions)							
		1995	1996	1997	1998	1999	2000	All	Average[a]
European Union	20	15,371	13,809	11,374	10,269	8,848	6,859	66,530	3,327
United States	13	1,168	1,053	939	824	709	594	5,288	407
Mexico	5	728	708	689	670	650	631	4,076	815
Turkey	44	872	787	702	617	532	446	3,956	90
Poland	17	737	690	643	596	549	500	3,713	218
Canada	11	502	466	420	356	320	284	2,348	213
Colombia	18	367	367	357	347	337	327	2,101	117
Switzerland	5	547	490	399	361	—	—	1,798	360
Czech Republic	16	240	220	175	160	137	112	1,045	65
South Africa	62	232	183	159	123	103	83	883	14
Bulgaria	44	195	175	146	133	118	94	657	15
Norway	11	151	134	109	90	75	56	614	56
Hungary	16	167	129	98	79	66	51	591	37
New Zealand	1	140	138	123	92	84	0	577	577
Brazil	16	94	92	89	87	85	82	529	33
Australia	5	101	99	87	67	63	51	468	94
Slovak Republic	17	82	74	63	56	44	36	355	21
Israel	6	55	53	52	51	49	48	308	51
Venezuela, R. B. de	72	34	33	33	32	31	30	193	3
Indonesia	1	28	27	26	26	25	24	156	156
Iceland	2	26	24	21	19	18	16	124	62
Uruguay	3	2	2	2	2	2	2	10	3
Panama	1	—	—	—	—	—	—	—	—
Cyprus	9	—	—	—	—	—	—	—	—
Romania	13	—	—	—	—	—	—	—	—
Total		21,839	19,754	16,707	15,056	12,843	10,325	96,254	—

TABLE 7.1 (Continued)

Used subsidies (US$ millions)							Utilization rates (%)						
1995	1996	1997	1998	1999	2000	All	1995	1996	1997	1998	1999	2000	All
6,390	7,057	4,946	5,976	5,978	2,544	32,891	41.6	51.1	43.5	58.2	67.6	37.1	49.4
26	121	112	147	80	—	486	2.2	11.5	12.0	17.8	11.3	—	9.2
0	0	14	2	—	—	15	0.0	0.0	2.0	0.2	—	—	0.4
30	17	39	29	28	27	170	3.4	2.2	5.5	4.7	5.3	6.1	4.3
0	16	9	14	55	37	130	0.0	2.3	1.4	2.3	10.0	7.4	3.5
37	4	0	0	0	—	42	7.5	0.9	0.0	0.0	0.0	—	1.8
15	19	23	20	0	0	77	4.0	5.2	6.4	5.8	0.0	0.0	3.6
447	369	296	292	—	—	1,403	81.7	75.2	74.1	80.8	—	—	78.0
40	42	40	42	35	24	223	16.7	19.0	22.9	26.2	25.2	21.6	21.3
40	42	18	3	5	3	111	17.3	22.7	11.4	2.7	4.8	3.8	12.6
0	0	0	0	0	—	0	—	—	0.0	0.0	0.0	—	0.0
83	78	102	77	128	—	470	55.3	58.6	94.0	86.0	171.2	—	76.5
41	18	10	12	13	—	94	24.6	14.0	9.9	14.8	20.0	—	15.9
0	0	0	0	0	0	0	0.0	0.0	0.0	0.0	0.0	0.0	0.0
0	0	0	0	—	—	0	0.0	0.0	0.0	0.0	—	—	0.0
0	0	0	1	2	0	4	0.0	0.0	0.0	1.9	3.8	0.0	0.8
8	8	13	12	12	12	65	10.2	11.0	19.9	22.0	27.1	32.3	18.3
19	13	6	1	1	0	40	34.4	23.7	11.3	1.9	2.9	0.0	12.9
3	20	2	6	—	—	31	9.4	60.0	7.3	17.3	—	—	16.2
0	0	0	0	0	0	0	0.0	0.0	0.0	0.0	0.0	0.0	0.0
5	1	0	0	0	—	6	20.7	3.1	0.7	0.0	0.0	—	5.1
0	0	0	0	0	—	0	0.0	0.0	0.0	0.0	0.0	—	0.0
—	—	—	—	—	—	—	—	—	—	—	—	—	—
—	—	—	—	—	—	—	—	—	—	—	—	—	—
—	—	0	0	—	—	—	—	—	—	—	—	—	—
7,185	7,829	5,629	6,634	6,338	2,648	36,258	29.5	35.8	32.0	41.8	49.4	25.6	37.6

Source: WTO (2002).
Note: — = not available.
a. Average commitment value per product.

WTO members do not regard the issue of monitoring use of export subsidies as being very important, or that key players obtain the information through other channels. In any event, it is clear that the notification process is not working well. An implication of the data gap is that inferences from what is reported should be drawn with some caution.

Second, table 7.1 does not suggest a clear trend on the use of export subsidies: they increased up to 1999 but declined substantially in 2000. Although the aggregate decline for 2000 largely reflects the evolution of the EU export subsidies (the next section confirms this observation), it is interesting to note that a similar decline with respect to the level of subsidies actually used in 1999 is observed for all other members for which data are reported.

Even if this decline is confirmed, it should be kept in mind that governments do not define or apply export subsidies on an ad valorem or percentage basis (say, as a percentage of world prices), but rather as an amount of money that is necessary to offset the gap between domestic and world prices. The low level of export subsidies in 1995–96 reflects high world prices (relative to domestic prices) in key farm products such as cereals. Indeed, during a few months of this period, world prices were so high (relative to domestic prices) that the EU imposed export *taxes* on products traditionally benefiting from export subsidies. Declining world prices after 1996 automatically generated increasing export subsidies because domestic prices were held constant—as a result of insulation of markets through trade barriers and other forms of market price support. Between 2000 and 2004, world prices increased significantly for commodities such as wheat and maize. The world price of wheat rose 40 percent from a cyclical low in 1999, whereas the world price for maize increased 30 percent relative to a cyclical low in 2000.[2]

The third observation concerns utilization rates, defined as actually used subsidies as a percentage of the maximum permitted, that is, the commitments. Until 1999, utilization rates increased under the combined evolution of declining commitments and increasing use of permitted subsidies. These utilization ratios deserve two comments. First, there is only one instance where the ratio exceeds 100 percent at the aggregate country level. This finding can be regarded as reassuring because it shows that WTO members appear to be abiding by their commitments. There are caveats, however: it remains to be seen whether the existing commitments impose effective disciplines (the next section suggests doubts are in order); and it is also not evident that at the product level "utilization ratios" are below 100 percent (the discussion in the next section reveals that they are not). Second, utilization rates vary greatly by country, but there is no clear correlation between the level of commitments and the level of subsidies granted.

Last, WTO notifications reveal that middle-income countries perceive an interest in having the ability to use export subsidies. The absence of information on actual use of subsidies again poses a problem: it is not known to what extent notifications lead to actual subsidies being applied. Even if in practice the countries concerned have not implemented much in the way of export subsidization, the fact that commitments were made suggests that an additional rationale for seeking to discipline the use of export subsidies is to prevent the gradual expansion of the use of these instruments. As discussed later, the poorest countries in particular appear to have a strong incentive to seek such disciplines, as the notified subsidy commitments from middle-income countries pertain much more to products that LDC countries also export than is the case for high-income countries.

The Incidence of Notified Export Subsidy Commitments

The global pattern of protection and support to agriculture has different impacts on countries depending on whether they are net producers or consumers of the commodities affected. A first cut at identifying the likely implications of protectionist policies for individual countries is to calculate the relative importance of the products for which export subsidies have been notified to the WTO in terms of a country's exports and imports. Because farm export subsidies depress the prices of the targeted agricultural products, eliminating the subsidies reduces the welfare of net importers and increases that of net exporters. It should be underlined, however, that the net trade status of countries is not necessarily very indicative of the longer-run impacts. Even in the short run, negative impacts will be attenuated or reversed if market access is (seriously) improved (Anderson 2005).

A more precise assessment of the effects of agricultural support policy reforms requires formal modeling, but as we show later, the (short-run) effect that emerges from model-based analyses is quite consistent with the conclusions that emerge from a simple analysis based on trade shares. At the same time, analysis of "affected" trade on a country-by-country basis has the advantage of showing which export subsidies have the greatest affect on and thus relevance for specific low-income economies.

The WTO notifications have a noteworthy feature: the products notified by middle-income countries are much more heavily concentrated in commodities that LDCs either export or import. Indeed, on average, the pattern of trade of developing countries is such that subsidies in the Quad (Canada, EU, Japan, and the United States) appear to have a smaller net negative impact on LDCs than do the agricultural support policies of middle-income countries. Around 17 percent of the value of LDC exports comprise products that are subject to an export subsidy in one or more WTO members (Hoekman, Olarreaga, and Ng 2004). The numbers for developed and developing countries are 5 and 4 percent, respectively. More than half of the exports from Benin, Burkina Faso, Burundi, Chad, Côte d'Ivoire, Malawi,

Mali, Rwanda, Tanzania, and Uganda are affected by export subsidies in some WTO member country. Most of these export subsidies are actually notified by other developing countries, however, rather than developed countries. Indeed, the share of the exports from these 10 countries that are potentially affected by an export subsidy in the Quad is below 1 percent. Overall, 6 percent of imports of LDCs are subject to export subsidies in the OECD (5 percent by export subsidies in the Quad), and 2 percent of imports from all developing countries are potentially affected by export subsidies in the Quad. More than 10 percent of the import bundle from Algeria, Cuba, the Arab Republic of Egypt, the Islamic Republic of Iran, Jordan, and Mauritania is subject to an export subsidy in at least one developed country.

Figures 7.1 and 7.2 plot the relationship between the indicator $I = s^x - s^m$ and the log of GDP (gross domestic product) per capita across countries, where s^x is the share of exports that is affected by an export subsidy and s^m is the share of imports that is affected by an export subsidy in each country (a large value for I suggests that the country is likely to benefit from the removal of export subsidies). Figure 7.1 plots these relationships for export subsidy notifications (commitments) across all WTO members, while figure 7.2 plots a similar relationship for export subsidies of Quad members only.

FIGURE 7.1 Incidence of All Notified Export Subsidies

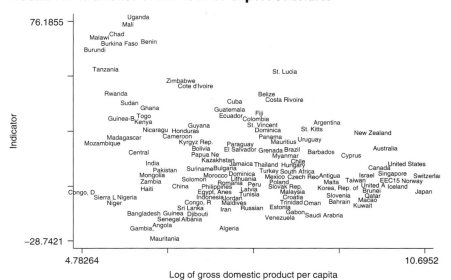

Source: WTO (2002).

FIGURE 7.2 Incidence of Quad Export Subsidy Commitments

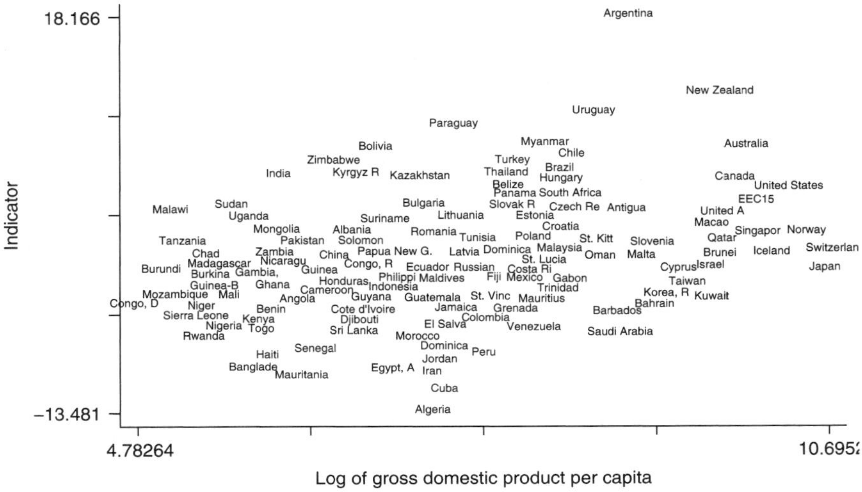

[Scatter plot: y-axis "Indicator" ranging from −13.481 to 18.166; x-axis "Log of gross domestic product per capita" ranging from 4.78264 to 10.6952. Countries plotted include Argentina (highest), New Zealand, Uruguay, Paraguay, Bolivia, Myanmar, Chile, Australia, Zimbabwe, Turkey, Brazil, India, Kyrgyz R, Kazakhstan, Thailand, Hungary, Canada, United States, Belize, Panama, South Africa, EEC15, Malawi, Sudan, Bulgaria, Slovak R, Czech Re, Antigua, United A, Uganda, Suriname, Lithuania, Estonia, Macao, Singapore, Norway, Tanzania, Mongolia, Albania, Romania, Croatia, Pakistan, Solomon, Tunisia, Poland, St. Kitt, Slovenia, Qatar, Chad, Zambia, Papua New G., Latvia, Dominica, Malaysia, Oman, Malta, Brunei, Iceland, Switzerlan, Burundi, Madagascar, Nicaragua, China, Congo R, Ecuador, Russian, St. Lucia, Cyprus, Israel, Japan, Burkina, Gambia, Guinea, Costa Ri, Guinea-B, Ghana, Honduras, Philippi, Maldives, Fiji, Mexico, Gabon, Taiwan, Mozambique, Mali, Cameroon, Indonesia, Trinidad, Korea R, Kuwait, Congo D, Niger, Angola, Guyana, Guatemala, St. Vinc, Mauritius, Bahrain, Sierra Leone, Kenya, Cote d'Ivoire, Jamaica, Grenada, Barbados, Nigeria, Togo, Benin, Djibouti, Colombia, Rwanda, Sri Lanka, El Salva, Venezuela, Saudi Arabia, Haiti, Senegal, Morocco, Bangladesh, Mauritania, Egypt A, Dominica, Peru, Jordan, Iran, Cuba, Algeria (lowest)]

Source: WTO (2002).

As illustrated in figure 7.1, the share of exports, relative to imports, that is affected by an export subsidy in at least one WTO member decreases with GDP per capita, suggesting that poorer countries tend to be disproportionately hurt by export subsidies. As noted earlier, this effect is driven primarily by export subsidy notifications of other developing countries. Indeed, figure 7.2 shows that the share of exports relative to imports that is affected by an export subsidy in one or more Quad members is increasing with GDP per capita. Thus, Quad export subsidies tend to hurt poorer countries less than richer ones. Not surprisingly, the indicator *I* is very high for the Cairns Group, at around 15.[3] That suggests that the Cairns Group as a whole is likely to experience large gains from the elimination of export subsidies. However, there is diversity within this group. Indonesia, Malaysia, and the Philippines all have a negative value of *I*.[4]

Export Subsidies by Product

Unfortunately, the information reported to the WTO on export subsidies by product is also problematic. Some WTO members have defined their commitments by broad product categories, whereas others use narrowly specified product groups. For instance, the EU uses 2 broad categories of fruits and vegetables (fresh

TABLE 7.2 WTO Commitments and Notifications of the EU, by Product, 1995–2000

Product categories	Commitments (% of total commitment)						
	1995	1996	1997	1998	1999	2000	All
Alcohol	1.20	1.21	1.23	1.25	1.27	1.29	1.24
Processed products	6.11	6.03	5.95	5.84	5.72	5.57	5.88
Sugar	6.24	6.30	6.38	6.46	6.57	6.70	6.43
Other milk products	8.72	8.81	8.91	9.04	9.18	9.37	8.99
Rice	0.46	0.47	0.47	0.48	0.49	0.49	0.48
Wine	0.49	0.49	0.50	0.51	0.52	0.53	0.50
Poultry meat	1.16	1.17	1.18	1.19	1.20	1.22	1.18
Fruits and vegetables, processed	0.10	0.10	0.11	0.11	0.11	0.11	0.11
Pig meat	2.46	2.47	2.49	2.51	2.54	2.57	2.50
Fruit and vegetables, fresh	0.66	0.67	0.67	0.68	0.70	0.71	0.68
Beef meat	16.36	16.43	16.50	16.59	16.70	16.83	16.56
Cheese	5.06	4.99	4.92	4.83	4.72	4.59	4.86
Skim milk powder	3.46	3.49	3.53	3.58	3.63	3.70	3.56
Coarse grains	13.66	13.72	13.78	13.86	13.95	14.06	13.83
Butter and butter oil	11.85	11.97	12.11	12.28	12.48	12.72	12.21
Olive oil	0.68	0.69	0.69	0.70	0.71	0.73	0.70
Eggs	0.52	0.53	0.54	0.55	0.57	0.59	0.55
Wheat and wheat flour	19.65	19.33	18.96	18.51	17.97	17.32	18.68
Raw tobacco	0.82	0.78	0.74	0.68	0.62	0.54	0.70
Rapeseed	0.35	0.35	0.35	0.36	0.36	0.37	0.36

and processed), while Bulgaria distinguishes no fewer than 28 types of fruits and vegetables (from cherries to cucumbers). This variation in reporting further reduces the transparency and surveillance value of the WTO in this area. Assessing the effects of export support on world markets requires information on the level of subsidies for a given product category, as the overall or aggregate amount of subsidies by country is not very informative. Reporting by broad category, as is done by the EU, allows for potentially substantial discretion in reallocating subsidies across products within an aggregate category. This permits the continued insulation of domestic markets (rigid domestic prices) from fluctuating world prices as long as the fluctuations are dispersed among specific products within a product category.

Table 7.2 reports a breakdown of the subsidies by product category reported by the EU. Table 7.2 is based on the same WTO data as is table 7.1 (maximum commitments and actually used subsidies). It reports the shares of each product

TABLE 7.2 (Continued)

Used subsidies (% of total used subsidies)							Utilization rates (%)						
1995	1996	1997	1998	1999	2000	All	1995	1996	1997	1998	1999	2000	All
1.05	2.13	2.42	2.27	3.89	3.46	2.59	36.3	89.6	85.6	106.1	208.0	99.5	104.9
10.05	10.17	12.68	10.75	12.82	14.98	11.75	68.5	86.2	92.7	107.0	151.3	99.8	100.2
7.76	9.43	17.86	14.89	8.37	13.49	11.65	51.7	76.5	121.8	134.1	86.1	74.7	90.9
14.89	13.15	17.34	14.22	16.13	14.84	15.12	71.0	76.3	84.6	91.6	118.6	58.8	84.4
0.62	1.30	0.75	0.48	0.47	1.17	0.75	55.5	141.3	68.6	58.3	65.3	87.8	79.1
1.05	1.07	0.85	0.55	0.47	0.86	0.77	88.9	110.6	74.1	63.0	61.2	60.5	76.8
2.37	1.31	1.74	1.68	1.34	2.06	1.69	85.0	57.4	64.5	82.4	75.3	62.6	71.5
0.23	0.18	0.13	0.08	0.10	0.14	0.14	92.6	89.5	53.3	45.5	60.4	47.0	65.3
2.06	1.28	1.71	6.67	4.33	1.22	3.18	34.8	26.4	29.8	154.6	115.3	17.7	63.8
1.44	1.11	0.60	0.59	0.66	0.98	0.87	90.7	85.1	38.4	50.4	64.4	51.1	63.8
30.84	27.43	19.28	12.05	12.93	13.87	19.04	78.4	85.4	50.8	42.3	52.3	30.6	57.7
8.96	4.88	4.04	2.79	4.20	8.61	5.18	73.7	49.9	35.7	33.7	60.1	69.7	53.5
2.88	3.06	2.67	3.59	6.02	0.95	3.56	34.7	44.8	32.9	58.4	111.9	9.5	50.2
6.21	6.99	6.26	14.32	13.01	6.93	9.55	18.9	26.0	19.8	60.1	63.0	18.3	34.7
5.24	9.92	7.12	5.35	5.94	12.23	7.23	18.4	42.3	25.6	25.4	32.2	35.7	29.7
1.27	0.70	0.18	0.00	0.00	0.00	0.34	77.8	52.2	11.2	0.0	0.0	0.0	24.3
0.26	0.12	0.30	0.32	0.25	0.29	0.26	21.3	12.0	24.1	34.3	29.9	18.5	23.5
2.43	5.71	4.07	9.38	9.07	3.92	6.27	5.1	15.1	9.3	29.5	34.1	8.4	16.8
0.37	0.06	0.00	0.00	0.00	0.00	0.07	18.8	4.0	0.0	0.0	0.0	0.0	4.7
0.00	0.00	0.00	0.00	0.00	0.00	0.00	0.0	0.0	0.0	0.0	0.0	0.0	0.0

Source: WTO (2002).
Note: Products are ordered by decreasing utilization rate.

category in the EU's total subsidy allocation, with categories sorted in decreasing order as a share of actually used export subsidies. It reveals an interesting feature for the six product categories that account for the largest "commitment shares" (arbitrarily defined as exceeding 6 percent). The six categories can be divided in two groups: three exhibiting a much larger use than the commitment level (processed products, other milk products, and sugar, in decreasing order) and three facing the converse situation (wheat, coarse grains, and butter). Grains and butter were subjected to a substantial decrease in price support as a result of the 1992 MacSharry reform of the Common Agricultural Policy, and butter also was subject to a quota regime, which reduced the need to have recourse to export support. The fact that actual levels of intervention appear to exceed bound levels can be explained in part by the differences in time periods for reporting (the EU

TABLE 7.3 Export Subsidy Rates for Selected WTO Members, by Commodity

Commodity	Switzerland	Czech Republic	Hungary	EU15
Wheat	0.00	0.00	0.00	6.12
Other grains	0.00	0.00	0.36	10.79
Fruits and vegetables	162.44	0.00	0.00	2.73
Cattle	37.17	0.00	0.00	0.00
Other livestock	0.00	0.00	0.00	0.38
Bovine meat	0.00	0.00	0.00	39.73
Nonbovine meat	0.00	0.16	1.28	10.15
Vegetable oils	0.00	0.00	0.00	0.00
Dairy	30.19	11.63	0.22	56.52
Rice	0.00	0.00	0.00	15.05
Sugar	0.00	0.00	0.00	72.76
Beverages and tobacco	0.00	0.00	0.00	2.72
Other food	5.01	0.64	0.11	1.70

uses a different definition of the accounting year than the WTO) and/or, the differences in the commodity definitions.

Similar tables can be constructed for other countries on the basis of notifications. Table 7.3 shows a synthesis of aggregate subsidy figures across reporting WTO members for 2000–2001. However, the limited information content of the WTO commitments and notifications on the use of export subsidies prevent meaningful comparisons between countries on the basis of product categories. In our view such comparisons must be regarded as indicative only.

Export Subsidies and EU Farm Trade Policy: A Depreciating Negotiating Asset?

The severe limitations of the WTO data on export subsidies suggest that any assessment of trends in the use of these instruments should employ national data. What follows therefore focuses on national information for the EU, as the EU is by far the largest provider of export subsidies. The primary source of information on farm support (both domestic and export subsidies) is the European Agriculture Guarantee and Guidance Fund (EAGGF), the body responsible for providing all the EU-level farm subsidies. The EAGGF provides detailed reports on its activities.[5]

In EAGGF parlance, export subsidies are recorded as "refunds." Table 7.4 reports the aggregate data on refunds as well as data from WTO and OECD

TABLE 7.3 (*Continued*)

Korea, Rep. of	Poland	Slovak Republic	Turkey	United States	Israel	Norway
0.00	0.00	0.00	0.00	0.00	0.00	0.00
0.00	0.00	0.00	0.00	0.00	0.00	0.00
7.39	0.00	0.28	0.33	0.00	1.40	0.00
0.00	0.00	0.00	0.00	0.00	0.00	0.00
0.00	0.00	0.00	0.23	0.00	0.00	2.20
0.00	0.00	0.00	0.00	0.00	0.00	10.30
0.35	3.03	0.00	0.93	0.19	0.17	7.22
0.00	0.00	0.00	2.12	0.00	0.00	0.00
0.00	1.57	14.59	0.00	1.36	0.00	39.99
0.00	0.00	0.00	0.00	0.00	0.00	0.00
0.00	18.28	0.00	1.44	0.00	0.00	0.00
0.00	0.00	0.00	0.00	0.00	0.00	0.12
0.00	0.13	0.31	0.42	0.00	0.00	0.00

Source: Elbehri (2005).
Note: Data are for 2000/1 as notified by WTO members to the WTO.

(Organisation for Economic Co-operation and Development). It reveals some serious differences between the WTO and EU data for three years (1995, 1997, and 2000), with the EAGGF subsidies being systematically (and sometimes much) larger than what is reported by (notified to) the WTO. For 1995–2000, EAGGF refunds are 25 percent higher than the sum of actual subsidization that the EU reported to the WTO. Although discrepancies might arise for any given year because of differences in the period covered, such a large difference over a five-year period cannot be explained solely by such differences. Because EAGGF reports are audited and because individual member states have an incentive to monitor the distribution and use of refunds, there is a presumption that the EAGGF data are more accurate.

Whatever source is used, however, the differences in magnitude of subsidization do not modify the conclusion that there appears to be a declining trend. The share of export subsidies in the OECD-based producer support estimates (PSE)—which is the best estimate of the aggregate level of protection of farm production, and hence the best reference basis—falls by a factor of two between 1995 and 2000 or 2001 (depending whether one uses the WTO or the EAGGF data; see table 7.4). In sharp contrast to the observed decline in export subsidies, however, the PSE estimates for the EU are very stable over the sample period as a whole. In other

TABLE 7.4 EU Export Subsidies and OECD PSEs, 1996–2002

Subsidy	1995	1996	1997
€ millions			
WTO commitments	11,751	10,890	9,605
WTO notified uses	4,885	5,565	4,361
EAGGF refunds	7,802	5,903	6,020
PSE estimates	102,728	98,463	97,313
Percent of PSE			
WTO commitments	11.4	11.1	9.9
WTO notified uses	4.8	5.7	4.5
EAGGF refunds	7.6	6.0	6.2

words, the EU farm sector is as much protected at the end of the period as at its beginning. This suggests that although export subsidies may have been falling, protection has not, and that a significant decline in world prices could well lead to a subsequent rise in export subsidies.

The EU's less aggressive use of export subsidies, despite the stability of its farm protection, can be seen as a positive development for the world trade regime, even if it has little positive effect from an economic perspective. From a negotiating perspective, the decreasing use of export subsidies raises the question whether the EU is selling its WTO partners a rapidly "depreciating" asset. Since the major WTO members are likely well aware of EU's declining use of the subsidies, the emphasis on their elimination may reflect the reluctance, by the EU as well as many of its trading partners, to address the core issue of market access (import protection and domestic support).

Export Subsidies in the EU's Overall Subsidization Scheme

Alternatively, the push to abolish all export subsidies may be explained by the fact that it is directed at specific products that are of prime importance to efficient exporters in the rest of the world and to powerful EU farm lobbies.[6] EAGGF data on subsidies by product categories, reported in table 7.5, show that export subsidies do constitute a large share of total EAGGF funds (table 7.6) and hence are important, particularly for those EU farmers who produce sugar, rice, milk and dairy products, pig meat, eggs, and poultry. (Beef was also important until 2000, when the emergence of "mad cow" disease in several EU countries triggered bans on imports of EU beef in the rest of the world.) These few sectors presumably

TABLE 7.4 (*Continued*)

1998	1999	2000	2001	2002	1995–2000
9,169	8,848	6,859	—	—	57,122
5,336	5,978	2,544	2,297	—	30,966
5,070	5,572	5,646	3,401	3,432	36,013
105,869	108,103	97,092	99,295	100,577	609,568
8.7	8.2	7.1	—	—	9.4
5.0	5.5	2.6	2.3	—	4.7
4.8	5.2	5.8	3.4	3.4	5.9

Source: WTO (2002); EAGGF (various years); OECD (Database 1998–2003).
Note: — = not available.

represent the core of the lobbies interested in keeping export subsidies, or, at least, in looking for compensation if the subsidies are eliminated.[7]

Another way to assess the importance of export subsidies is to relate them to the corresponding EU farm production to see whether they represent a significant share of production values. Although there are some difficulties and limits in matching the EAGGF product categories with the EU production classification, table 7.7 offers a reasonably accurate picture of subsidization rates based on production for the period 1995–2002. It suggests two conclusions. First, consistent with the OECD PSE numbers (see table 7.4), the total level of subsidization of EU farm production (that is, including all EAGGF funds) has declined only marginally since 1995. It varies between 15 and 18 percent, with a peak in the late 1990s. However, this stability hides substantial changes at the product category level: a strong decline in overall subsidization rates is observed for cereals, tobacco, ovine (sheep) meat, and milk and dairy products. In sharp contrast, some product categories have enjoyed an increasing level of subsidization, including fiber plants, wine, rice, and bovine meat. These four products are all of prime interest for many developing countries.

If one focuses on export subsidization rates only (instead of total subsidies), the picture changes dramatically. The ratio of export subsidies to EU production has been declining to the point of becoming negligible (1 percent or less). There is one exception: sugar. This exception is clearly one of the key reasons for the continuing emphasis on export subsidies in the WTO negotiations.

From the perspective of typical individual farmers, the size of the total transfer from subsidies and border protection relative to production is probably the important

TABLE 7.5 EAGGF Subsidies by Commodity, 1995–2002 (€ millions)

Commodity	All subsidies (intervention and refunds)						
	1995	1996	1997	1998	1999	2000	2001
Cereals	15,018.3	16,372.3	17,414.1	17,945.3	17,865.9	16,663.1	17,466.2
Wheat	—	—	—	—	—	—	—
Barley	—	—	—	—	—	—	—
Durum wheat	—	—	—	—	—	—	—
Other cereals	—	—	—	—	—	—	—
Sugar	1,831.0	1,711.3	1,607.8	1,776.6	2,112.8	1,910.2	1,497.1
Olive oil	807.1	1,988.1	2,196.0	2,266.7	2,091.8	2,210.1	2,523.8
Dried fodder	342.0	365.2	367.4	377.5	376.4	381.3	374.8
Fiber plants	887.7	851.7	906.9	869.8	1,027.1	991.4	826.3
Cotton	846.5	762.7	800.0	761.0	903.2	854.7	733.0
Fruits and vegetables	1,826.2	1,589.3	1,555.3	1,509.5	1,454.1	1,551.3	1,558.0
Fresh	891.3	678.3	655.5	840.7	682.1	832.9	965.5
Processed	934.9	902.8	902.2	670.0	774.7	720.5	597.8
Wine	850.1	776.9	1,030.1	700.0	614.6	765.5	1,196.7
Tobacco	993.0	1,025.6	998.0	870.3	911.1	987.7	973.4
Other plants	276.9	204.5	187.4	271.9	285.3	350.0	297.3
Rice	49.6	33.3	82.2	166.1	164.8	228.4	182.3
All plant products	22,832.3	24,884.9	26,263.0	26,587.5	2,739.2	25,812.3	26,713.5
Dairy products	3,891.0	3,441.2	2,984.9	2,596.7	2,510.1	2,544.3	1,906.6
Milk	—	—	—	—	—	—	—
Butter and butter oil	—	—	—	—	—	—	—
Skimmed milk powder	—	—	—	—	—	—	—
Cheese and others	—	—	—	—	—	—	—
Bovine	4,090.8	6,797.0	6,580.4	5,160.6	4,579.0	4,539.6	6,054.0
Ovine	2,203.0	1,681.1	1,424.9	1,534.6	1,894.3	1,735.6	1,447.3
Pig, eggs, and poultry	343.8	262.9	557.5	327.9	432.8	435.2	137.1
Pig meat	143.3	124.2	479.2	238.3	320.9	354.2	69.7
Eggs	28.6	12.2	8.7	13.6	17.6	12.9	9.0
Poultry	171.9	127.0	70.8	77.1	92.9	72.8	60.5
Other animals	0.9	0.9	5.6	1.4	16.0	11.7	0.0
Fish	28.2	25.3	21.8	10.4	7.8	9.4	13.3
All animals	10,558.6	12,208.4	11,575.1	9,631.5	9,440.1	9,275.7	9,558.3
Other products	574.3	491.0	566.0	553.0	573.0	572.2	435.6
Food aid (domestic)	—	—	—	—	309.4	281.8	—
Total	34,501.7	39,107.8	40,675.1	38,748.1	39,876.3	40,466.0	42,083.0

TABLE 7.5 (Continued)

2002	Export subsidies (refunds)							
	1995	1996	1997	1998	1999	2000	2001	2002
18,590.1	1,092.7	312.8	532.3	478.9	883.1	823.6	259.8	99.3
—	—	—	—	—	376.2	409.2	106.2	18.7
—	—	—	—	—	357.9	253.2	33.3	3.3
—	—	—	—	—	2.0	2.2	0.5	0.6
—	—	—	—	—	146.9	158.9	119.3	76.8
1,395.9	1,312.1	1,230.0	1,015.7	1,370.2	1,591.1	1,438.0	1,008.2	1,151.6
2,329.3	38.2	59.3	42.7	24.9	2.5	0.0	0.2	0.1
388.3	0.0	0.0	0.0	0.0	0.0	0.0	0.0	0.0
816.4	0.0	0.0	0.0	0.0	0.0	0.0	0.0	0.0
804.0	0.0	0.0	0.0	0.0	0.0	0.0	0.0	0.0
1,551.4	239.5	98.4	84.0	58.3	40.4	46.1	50.8	46.4
804.0	203.0	73.4	67.0	40.8	23.2	32.8	36.1	29.3
757.9	36.5	25.0	17.0	17.5	17.3	13.3	14.8	17.1
1,348.7	36.7	40.8	59.7	41.2	27.4	21.0	22.5	23.8
963.2	35.1	2.4	−2.7	0.4	0.0	0.0	0.0	0.0
303.0	0.0	0.0	0.0	0.0	30.2	38.4	38.7	41.1
232.7	—	—	—	—	30.2	38.4	38.1	41.1
27,686.2	2,754.3	1,743.7	1731.7	1,973.9	2,574.7	2,368.6	1,380.2	1,362.3
2,360.0	2,267.1	1,605.2	1,753.3	1,426.7	1,439.2	1,670.9	1,106.5	1,159.6
—	—	—	—	—	788.0	831.1	452.9	498.9
—	—	—	—	—	297.8	337.8	335.6	382.0
—	—	—	—	—	196.5	275.9	81.7	57.7
—	—	—	—	—	156.9	226.1	236.2	221.1
7,071.9	1,761.0	1,559.4	1,496.9	774.5	594.9	661.0	362.6	386.7
552.4	0.0	0.0	0.0	0.0	0.0	0.0	0.0	0.0
107.2	318.7	240.1	151.7	165.2	385.5	348.0	115.7	104.4
30.0	118.2	101.4	72.2	74.5	275.0	263.0	55.2	27.3
6.0	28.6	12.2	8.7	13.6	17.6	13.0	8.6	5.9
71.0	171.9	127.0	70.8	77.1	92.9	73.0	51.9	71.1
12.0	0.0	0.0	0.0	0.0	0.0	0.0	0.0	0.0
15.3	0.0	0.0	0.0	0.0	0.0	0.0	0.0	0.0
10,118.8	4,346.8	3,404.7	3,401.9	2,366.4	2,419.9	2,680.5	1,584.8	1,650.7
409.7	574.3	491.0	566.0	553.0	573.0	572.2	435.6	409.7
242.7	—	—	—	—	—	100.8	—	5.6
43,214.3	7,675.4	5,705.0	5,883.9	4,286.3	5,572.8	5,646.2	3,401.0	3,432.3

Source: EAGGF (various years).
Note: — = not available.

factor in their decision making. But from a negotiating point of view, it is necessary to look at export subsidization rates as a share of actual exports. This indicator can be constructed by using the EAGGF export subsidy data, with no serious problems matching the data to the actual export data for cereals, sugar, wine, rice, milk and dairy products, bovine meat, and poultry, which are the major subsidized commodities. Table 7.8 reports the calculated export subsidization rates. It suggests a wide range of subsidization rates, with the highest numbers for sugar, bovine meat, and dairy products.

Should Efforts in the Doha Round Go Beyond Export Subsidies?

As part of the Doha Round discussions on export subsidies, the EU, supported by Brazil and some other members of the Cairns Group and the G-20, has extended the principle of the elimination of export subsidies to all key existing "equivalent" forms of export subsidization: specifically to the subsidy component of official export credits, the activities of state trading enterprises (STEs), and food aid.[8] One interpretation of this LINKAGE is that it is largely tactical. While the EU is by far the largest user of export subsidies, a number of traditional export-oriented and pro-liberalization countries make use of these alternative instruments. For example, the United States grants both export credits and food aid, and Canada has made long-standing use of STEs for specific commodities.[9] Alternatively, the focus on equivalent forms of export subsidies can be perceived as a necessary step to ensure that governments do not engage in "reinstrumentation" following a full-fledged WTO ban on explicit export subsidies on farm products.

Whatever the motivation, a pertinent question is how much importance the Doha negotiations should give to extending a ban on export subsidies to all forms of export support. Given the myriad problems that will need to be addressed—defining what is permissible when it comes to the financing of food aid or agricultural export credits, or determining what constitutes an implicit or explicit subsidy, for example—a case can be made from an economic perspective that going down this path only makes sense in the short run if the distortions associated with these activities are significant. If so, a second question is whether the WTO is the appropriate forum for international cooperation in these areas. Export credits have already been subjected to disciplines and surveillance in the OECD. An obvious question is why these disciplines cannot be extended to agriculture, and indeed, whether there is anything special about agriculture in terms of the allocation of official export credits.

How large is the subsidization component of these instruments? Unfortunately, very little good information exists that can be used to provide an answer. For instance, calculating the subsidy component of an export credit requires

TABLE 7.6 EAGGF Export Subsidies as a Share of All Subsidies, 1995–2002 (percent)

Commodity	1995	1996	1997	1998	1999	2000	2001	2002
Cereals	7.3	1.9	3.1	2.7	4.9	4.9	1.5	0.5
Wheat	—	—	—	—	—	—	—	—
Barley	—	—	—	—	—	—	—	—
Durum wheat	—	—	—	—	—	—	—	—
Other cereals	—	—	—	—	—	—	—	—
Sugar	71.7	71.9	63.2	77.1	75.3	75.3	67.3	82.5
Olive oil	4.7	3.0	1.9	1.1	0.1	0.0	0.0	0.0
Dried fodder	0.0	0.0	0.0	0.0	0.0	0.0	0.0	0.0
Fiber plants	0.0	0.0	0.0	0.0	0.0	0.0	0.0	0.0
Cotton	0.0	0.0	0.0	0.0	0.0	0.0	0.0	0.0
Fruits and vegetables	13.1	6.2	5.4	3.9	2.8	3.0	3.3	3.0
Fresh	22.8	10.8	10.2	4.9	3.4	3.9	3.7	3.6
Processed	3.9	2.8	1.9	2.6	2.2	1.8	2.5	2.3
Wine	4.3	5.3	5.8	5.9	4.5	2.7	1.9	1.8
Tobacco	3.5	0.2	−0.3	0.0	0.0	0.0	0.0	0.0
Other plants	0.0	0.0	0.0	0.0	10.6	11.0	13.0	13.6
Rice	0.0	0.0	0.0	0.0	18.3	16.8	20.9	17.7
All plant products	12.1	7.0	6.6	7.4	9.6	9.2	5.2	4.9
Dairy products	58.3	46.6	58.7	54.9	57.3	65.7	58.0	49.1
Milk	—	—	—	—	—	—	—	—
Butter and butter oil	—	—	—	—	—	—	—	—
Skimmed milk powder	—	—	—	—	—	—	—	—
Cheese and others	—	—	—	—	—	—	—	—
Bovine	43.0	22.9	22.7	15.0	13.0	14.6	6.0	5.5
Ovine	0.0	0.0	0.0	0.0	0.0	0.0	0.0	0.0
Pig, eggs, and poultry	92.7	91.3	27.2	50.4	89.1	80.0	84.4	97.4
Pig meat	82.5	81.6	15.1	31.3	85.7	74.3	79.2	91.0
Eggs	100.0	100.0	100.0	100.0	100.0	100.8	95.6	98.3
Poultry	100.0	100.0	100.0	100.0	100.0	100.3	85.8	100.1
Other animals	0.0	0.0	0.0	0.0	0.0	0.0	0.0	0.0
Fish	.0	0.0	0.0	0.0	0.0	0.0	0.0	0.0
All animals	41.2	27.9	29.4	24.6	25.6	28.9	16.6	16.3
Other products	100.0	100.0	100.0	100.0	100.0	100.0	100.0	100.0
Food aid (domestic)	—	—	—	—	—	—	—	—
Total	22.2	14.6	14.5	11.1	14.0	14.0	8.1	7.9

Source: EAGGF (various years).

Note: — = not available.

TABLE 7.7 EU Subsidization Rates (Relative to Value of Production), 1995–2002

Commodity	All subsidies				
	1995	1996	1998	2000	2001
Cereals	82.3	76.0	93.4	48.1	52.4
Wheat	—	—	—	—	—
Barley	—	—	—	—	—
Durum wheat	—	—	—	—	—
Other cereals	—	—	—	—	—
Sugar	35.3	32.5	33.3	40.9	33.1
Olive oil	32.4	53.2	59.0	44.7	49.6
Dried fodder	13.7	13.9	11.8	7.3	7.4
Fiber plants	71.3	64.6	67.9	90.2	73.1
Cotton	—	—	—	—	—
Fruits and vegetables	5.9	4.6	4.5	3.6	4.0
Fresh	2.9	2.0	2.5	2.0	2.5
Processed	—	—	—	—	—
Wine	6.9	5.4	4.9	5.0	8.3
Tobacco	159.6	155.6	101.9	89.9	86.2
Other plants	1.5	1.4	1.6	1.3	0.9
Rice	6.0	3.0	19.4	27.7	21.5
All plant products	25.0	25.2	26.9	18.8	19.7
Milk and dairy products	10.1	9.0	6.8	6.7	4.7
Milk	—	—	—	—	—
Butter and butter oil	—	—	—	—	—
Skimmed milk powder	—	—	—	—	—
Cheese and others	—	—	—	—	—
Bovine	17.8	31.6	24.2	16.5	23.6
Ovine	62.5	38.3	35.9	28.7	25.6
Pig, eggs, and poultry	0.9	0.6	0.9	1.1	0.3
Pig meat	0.6	0.5	1.1	1.5	0.2
Eggs	0.6	0.2	0.3	0.3	0.2
Poultry	1.9	1.1	0.7	0.6	0.5
Other animals	0.0	0.0	0.0	0.1	0.0
Fish	0.7	0.8	0.3	0.2	0.2
All animals	9.0	10.1	8.5	6.8	6.5
Other products	—	—	—	—	—
Food aid	—	—	—	—	—
Total	16.6	17.8	18.2	14.8	14.9

TABLE 7.7 (*Continued*)

	Export subsidies						
2002	1995	1996	1998	1999	2000	2001	2002
53.9	6.0	1.5	2.5	2.7	2.4	0.8	0.3
—	—	—	—	2.3	2.3	0.6	0.1
—	—	—	—	4.4	3.0	0.4	0.0
—	—	—	—	0.2	0.3	0.0	0.1
—	—	—	—	2.0	2.1	1.6	0.9
29.3	25.3	23.3	25.7	32.9	30.8	22.3	24.2
37.8	1.5	1.6	0.6	0.0	0.0	0.0	0.0
8.7	0.0	0.0	0.0	0.0	0.0	0.0	0.0
—	0.0	0.0	0.0	0.0	0.0	0.0	0.0
—	—	—	—	—	—	—	—
3.8	0.8	0.3	0.2	0.1	0.1	0.1	0.1
2.0	0.7	0.2	0.1	0.1	0.1	0.1	0.1
—	—	—	—	—	—	—	—
9.4	0.3	0.3	0.3	0.2	0.1	0.2	0.2
85.9	5.6	0.4	0.0	0.0	0.0	0.0	0.0
0.9	0.0	0.0	0.0	0.1	0.1	0.1	0.1
27.7	0.0	0.0	0.0	3.7	4.7	4.5	4.9
19.9	3.0	1.8	2.0	1.9	1.7	1.0	1.0
6.0	5.9	4.2	3.7	3.8	4.4	2.7	3.0
—	—	—	—	—	—	—	—
—	—	—	—	—	—	—	—
—	—	—	—	—	—	—	—
—	—	—	—	—	—	—	—
25.5	7.6	7.2	3.6	2.2	2.4	1.4	1.4
8.2	0.0	0.0	0.0	0.0	0.0	0.0	0.0
0.3	0.9	0.5	0.4	1.1	0.9	0.3	0.3
0.1	0.5	0.4	0.3	1.4	1.1	0.2	0.1
0.1	0.6	0.2	0.3	0.4	0.3	0.2	0.1
0.6	1.9	1.1	0.7	0.9	0.6	0.4	0.7
0.1	0.0	0.0	0.0	0.0	0.0	0.0	0.0
0.2	0.0	0.0	0.0	0.0	0.0	0.0	0.0
7.1	3.7	2.8	2.1	1.9	2.0	1.1	1.2
—	—	—	—	—	—	—	—
—	—	—	—	—	—	—	—
15.4	3.7	2.6	2.0	2.1	2.1	1.2	1.2

Sources: Authors' calculations based on EC (various years) and EAGGF (various years).

Note: — = not available.

TABLE 7.8 EAGGF Refunds As a Percentage of EU Farm Exports, 1995–2002

	1995	1996	1997	1998	1999	2000	2001	2002
Cereals	57.5	14.5	25.8	28.3	37.9	27.1	11.6	4.7
Sugar	82.6	97.6	69.0	86.9	155.3	105.2	62.1	106.4
Olive oil	7.8	8.0	5.7	4.0	0.4	0.0	0.0	0.0
Dried fodder	0.0	0.0	0.0	0.0	0.0	0.0	0.0	0.0
Fruit vegetables	6.2	2.5	1.9	1.2	0.9	0.9	0.9	0.7
Fresh	9.2	3.2	2.5	1.5	0.9	1.1	1.0	0.7
Processed	2.2	1.5	0.9	0.9	0.9	0.6	0.6	0.7
Wine	0.5	0.5	0.6	0.5	0.3	0.2	0.2	0.2
Tobacco	10.6	0.6	−0.7	0.1	0.0	0.0	0.0	0.0
All plant products	15.8	9.6	8.4	9.9	12.6	10.0	5.6	5.2
Milk	55.1	40.0	38.3	33.8	36.0	34.8	22.9	25.9
Bovine	188.5	184.1	153.8	99.8	62.3	103.9	63.5	76.2
Pig, eggs, poultry	16.3	12.0	6.5	7.4	15.0	11.6	4.0	3.7
Pig meat	10.5	8.9	5.4	6.1	16.5	13.1	3.0	1.5
Eggs	23.4	10.2	6.4	8.7	11.1	8.6	5.0	3.1
Poultry	24.2	17.1	8.0	8.9	12.3	8.6	5.8	8.0
All animals	62.1	49.7	43.1	32.7	32.2	31.8	19.1	21.0
Total	31.3	22.8	20.6	15.7	20.0	17.5	10.3	10.1

Sources: Authors' calculations based on EAGGF (various years) and Comtrade.

knowing not only the amount of the credit but also its terms—maturity, interest rate structure—as well as having information on the creditworthiness of the borrower-recipient. The counterfactual is difficult to determine—would a bank or other financial services provider have lent at all? If so, what would be the difference in basis points? Can one use a "market reference interest rate"?

Inherently there will be a subjective element to any assessment of the export subsidy equivalent associated with export credits, the operation of STEs, and food aid. In sum, one needs very detailed information on existing transactions and on the hypothetical market-based transaction. Another important issue concerns the ability of importers to borrow from intermediaries to finance their purchases. If they confront liquidity constraints, there may be a welfare-based argument for export credits. Rude and Gervais (2004) argue that in a world where poor countries confront liquidity constraints and demand is very elastic, a ban on export credit interest rate

TABLE 7.9 Export Subsidy Equivalents for Major Users (percent)

Equivalent	United States	EU	Canada	Australia
Export credits (all destinations)	6.6[a]	2.0[b]	1.2	0.3
STEs (all destinations)			4.6	
Food aid (developing country destinations)	1.0	0.5	0.2	0.1
Total				
To nondeveloping countries	6.6	2.5	5.8	0.3
To developing countries	7.6	2.5	6.0	0.4
Share of exports benefiting from export credits	5.2	1.9	5.4	15.1

Source: OECD (2001).
a. U.S. dairy exports to all destinations also totaled 6.6 percent.
b. Estimates range from 0.6–1 percent for Austria, Belgium, Finland, Germany, and the Netherlands; for France the estimate is 3.8 percent.

subsidies may raise import prices (see also Hyberg and others 1998). However, because most credits are extended to other OECD countries, and because available estimates of subsidy equivalents suggest that they are quite low (see below), any such effects are likely to be small.

Table 7.9 reports the results of an attempt by the OECD to calculate the export subsidy equivalent of these other instruments for affected products in Australia, Canada, the EU, and the United States during 1995–98 (OECD 2001). The United States provides the most export credits—data on U.S. allocations by product and recipient are available from FAS (2004). For the four countries mentioned, ad valorem subsidy equivalents do not exceed 7 percent for any of the instruments considered. Overall, the share of total agricultural exports to which these instruments apply is small, ranging from less than 2 percent for the EU to around 5 percent for Canada and the United States. It is highest for Australia (15 percent). Bulk cereals were found to account for almost half of the total subsidy element of export credits granted. When used in a simulation model to assess the impact of these programs on prices, it was found that U.S. export and domestic prices would be only 2 and 1 percent lower, respectively, if export credits were banned. Moreover, the bulk of export credits apply to intra-OECD trade. In the case of the United States, for example, the Republic of Korea and Mexico are the major recipients. It would appear therefore that these export subsidy equivalents are of second-order importance compared with explicit export subsidies (which in turn are second order compared with market price support).

Policy Recommendations

The foregoing has sought to provide an overview of the available information on export subsidies. Rather than summarize the findings here, we conclude with some policy recommendations.

First, the WTO "machinery" for compiling and reporting data on the use of export subsidies should be strengthened. In all instances where "commitment notifications" are made, they should be accompanied by information on the actual use of subsidies.

Second, effective monitoring and surveillance (and analysis of the impacts) of export subsidies require that WTO members all use the same product classification. That classification should be as disaggregated as possible, both to constrain the capacity to continue to subsidize exports and to allow more effective analysis of their impacts.

Last but not least, the evidence suggests that the subsidy element of export credits is much less of a problem in terms of distorting world markets than are direct export subsidies. Assessing the magnitude of the associated distortions and determining the subsidy equivalent is difficult, however, and much more work is required to understand better the prevailing situation and the possible benefits and costs of alternative types of multilateral disciplines. One way forward would be to delegate a program of technical work to, for example, the OECD's Agricultural Directorate or the Food and Agriculture Organization to provide a better monitoring of the effects of the programs concerned.

Notes

1. After this paper was completed, the WTO released two new documents that update information to 2002 for 11 members. See WTO document TN/AG/S/13.

2. World Bank Global Prospects, http://econ.worldbank.org/.

3. Members of the Cairns Group are Argentina, Australia, Bolivia, Brazil, Canada, Chile, Colombia, Costa Rica, Guatemala, Indonesia, Malaysia, New Zealand, Paraguay, the Philippines, South Africa, Thailand, and Uruguay.

4. This finding is consistent with the evidence in Hertel and Keeney (2006, table 2.8). From a normative perspective, the ability of a country to incur a possible negative terms-of-trade shock is important. Many of the countries that might incur a loss as a result of export subsidy elimination are middle-income and have greater capacity to address the shocks than the poorest ones, located in the bottom left corner of the figures.

5. Individual EU member states also provide subsidies, but these are either production- or consumption-related, or horizontal in nature (such as broad infrastructure funding, or assistance to young farmers).

6. EAGGF provides a relatively disaggregated breakdown of subsidies by product except for two large groups of products—cereals and dairy. A breakdown was not given for cereals because, during the period examined, production subsidies (a substantial portion of the EAGGF funds) were granted on the basis of hectares grown rather than the type of cereal. (Some production subsidies were strictly related to a specific kind of cereal, such as durum wheat or rye, but these were relatively limited.) In other

words, the lack of disaggregated data in cereals indicates that a limited decoupling regime was implemented for cereals as part of the 2003 CAP reform and hence that the reform is much more limited than it appears. In the case of dairy, the technical relations between milk and its derived products, such as cheese or milk powder, explain the difficulty in decomposing milk subsidies among dairy products.

7. The two bottom rows of Table 7.6 suggest it is important to take into consideration additional farm products, such as those used as inputs for beverages, as well as in food aid (although this item includes food aid to European consumers). However, these types of aid cannot be mapped to products in a precise way. As a result, this analysis ignores the figures reported in these rows, notwithstanding their relative importance.

8. Note that this was also an objective during the Uruguay Round; Article 10 of the WTO Agreement on Subsidies and Countervailing Measures foreshadows the extension of export subsidy disciplines to similar instruments such as export credits.

9. STEs and food aid programs generally do not have the objective of subsidizing exports, but they may have that effect.

References

Anderson, K. 2005. "Agricultural Trade Reform and Poverty Reduction in Developing Countries." In *Trade Policy Reforms and Development: Essays in Honour of Peter Lloyd, Volume II*, ed. S. Jayasuriya. London: Edward Elgar.

EAGGF (European Agriculture Guarantee and Guidance Fund). Various years. "Annual Report." Commission of the European Communities, Brussels.

EC (European Commission). Various years. "The Agricultural Situation in the EC." EC, Brussels.

Elbehri, A. 2005. "Agricultural Export Subsidies." GTAP database documentation 16.E, March 30. http://www.gtap.agecon.purdue.edu/resources/download/2228.pdf.

FAS (Foreign Agriculture Service). 2004. "Summary of Export Credit Guarantee Program Activity (Country Allocations)." FAS, U.S. Department of Agriculture, Washington, DC. www.fas.usda.gov/excredits/Monthly/ecg.html.

Hertel, T. W., and R. Keeney. 2006. "What Is at Stake: The Relative Importance of Import Barriers, Export Subsidies, and Domestic Support." In *Agricultural Trade Reform and the Doha Development Round*, ed. K. Anderson and W. Martin. Washington, DC: World Bank.

Hoekman, B., M. Olarreaga, and F. Ng. 2004. "Reducing Agricultural Tariffs versus Domestic Support: What Is More Important for Developing Countries?" *World Bank Economic Review* 18 (2): 175–204.

Hyberg, B., M. Smith, D. Skully, and C. Davison. 1998. "Export Credit Guarantees: The Commodity Credit Corporation and U.S. Agricultural Export Policy." *Food Policy* 20: 27–39.

Jean, S., D. Laborde, and W. Martin. 2006. "Consequences of Alternative Formulas for Agricultural Tariff Cuts." In *Agricultural Trade Reform and the Doha Development Round*, ed. K. Anderson and W. Martin. Washington, DC: World Bank.

OECD (Organisation for Economic Co-operation and Development). 2001. *An Analysis of Officially Supported Export Credits in Agriculture*. Paris: OECD.

_____. "Producer and Consumer Support Estimates, OECD Database 1998–2003." http://www.oecd.org/document/58/0,2340,en_2649_37401_32264698_1_1_1_37401,00.html.

Rude, J., and J.-P. Gervais. 2004. "An Analysis of a Rules-based Approach to Disciplining Export Credits in Agriculture." Department of Agribusiness and Agricultural Economics, University of Manitoba.

WTO (World Trade Organization). 2002. "Export Subsidies: Background Paper by the Secretariat." WTO TN/AG/S/8/, WTO, Geneva.

_____. 2004. "Doha Work Programme: Decision Adopted by the General Council on 1 August 2004." WT/L/579 (July Framework Agreement). WTO, Geneva.

8

RETHINKING AGRICULTURAL DOMESTIC SUPPORT UNDER THE WORLD TRADE ORGANIZATION

Chad E. Hart and John C. Beghin

Reforms in agricultural trade essentially began with the Uruguay Round and lag behind reforms in manufacturing sectors, which have gone through eight GATT (General Agreement on Tariffs and Trade) rounds of reductions. Under the previous GATT rounds, agriculture had remained on the sidelines. The Uruguay Round negotiations established the "three pillars" of agricultural support: market access, export subsidies, and domestic support. The market access provisions required, among other things, tariffication; that is, all nontariff trade barriers had to be replaced by tariffs, and bounds were set on those tariffs. The export subsidy provisions established maximum ceilings on the trade quantity and budgetary expenditures for export subsidies and implemented reductions in those ceilings over time. The domestic support provisions outlined various types of support, classified them by their apparent trade effects, and limited those programs deemed the most trade distorting. In this chapter, we concentrate our efforts on third-pillar issues.

The WTO negotiations under the Doha Round are slowly progressing toward an eventual new agreement on agriculture. A new framework for the agriculture agreement was approved by the WTO membership at the end of July 2004 (WTO 2004a). The pace of the agricultural negotiations has offered an opportunity to do some fundamental rethinking of the current definition of domestic support. The agreed-upon July framework outlines reforms in all three agriculture pillars. The changes in the guidelines for domestic support could have effects on many countries and many types of support. Many of the details on the specific regulations of the framework agreement are yet to be determined, however. There is potential for dramatic reforms in agriculture under the framework, but the decisions made in filling it out will determine if that potential is realized.

Governments provide domestic support to agriculture in myriad ways: direct payments, research grants, loan programs, storage programs, and so forth. Under the current Uruguay Round Agreement on Agriculture (URAA), domestic support programs are divided into three "boxes" that indicate the trade effects of the programs. Green Box programs are programs that are considered minimally trade distorting. The URAA sets out specific guidelines for the structure of such programs but does not set any limits on program expenditures by member countries. Blue Box programs are those that are considered more trade distorting, but the programs have production limits embedded in them. These programs also are not limited currently. All other programs are Amber Box programs. Amber Box programs are considered the most trade distorting and are limited under the URAA. Within the Amber Box, programs are classified as either product- or non-product-specific. These classifications also affect the so-called de minimis rules by which certain Amber Box programs may be exempt from domestic support calculations.

WTO member states have had a decade to examine their domestic support guidelines and restructure their agricultural support to fit under these guidelines. For example, the 1996 and 2002 farm bills in the United States and the Agenda 2000 and 2003 Common Agricultural Policy (CAP) reforms in the European Union were all designed after the acceptance of the URAA. But has this restructuring led to more open agricultural markets, or has support just shifted to programs that were deemed minimally trade distorting even when they actually have significant trade effects? With negotiations for a new agriculture agreement under way, we use this opportune time to examine the rules governing domestic support, explore how well those rules have performed, and outline possible changes that would lead to more substantial trade reform.

The Rules as They Now Stand

The URAA is quite specific about the programs that can be classified as Green or Blue Box. Blue Box policies are production-limiting policies that base payments on fixed yields and acreage. Payments must be limited to 85 percent of a base level of production.[1] The old target price deficiency payment program that existed before 1996 in the United States was a Blue Box program, as are the compensatory payments in the European Union and the rice farming income stabilization program in Japan. Green Box policies are policies that are seen to have minimal trade impacts. Payments from

Green Box policies cannot be linked to current production or prices. The URAA lists several types of Green Box policies and the guidelines that they must follow:

- General services, public stockholding for food security purposes, domestic food aid, direct payments to producers, decoupled income support
- Government financial participation in income insurance and income safety net programs
- Payments for relief from natural disasters, adjustment assistance provided through producer or resource retirement programs, adjustment assistance provided through investment aids
- Payments under environmental programs
- Payments under regional assistance programs

Each of these program types has guidelines that define the eligibility of the program for the Green Box. Any direct payments to producers provided by a government program cannot involve transfers from consumers (only from taxpayers). Thus Green Box programs cannot support domestic prices. The guidelines for decoupled income support are as follows: eligibility for the program must be based on clearly defined criteria over a fixed base period; payment amounts cannot be related to production, prices, or input usage after the base period; and no production can be required to receive payments.

For government-provided income insurance or safety net programs to be eligible for the Green Box, income and income loss can only be from agricultural sources; the loss must exceed 30 percent of average gross income (or an equivalent amount of net income) where average income is determined by a three-year average income (from the previous three years) or a five-year "olympic" average income (removing the high and low years before averaging). If payments are provided by this program and a natural disaster relief program, the total amount of payments cannot exceed 100 percent of the producer's total loss.

The requirements for natural disaster relief follow a similar logic: eligibility is determined by a formal disaster announcement from the government with at least a 30 percent production loss based on average production (the previous three-year average or the five-year olympic average); payments may only be made on losses attributable to the disaster; payments cannot be for more than the amount of loss and requirements on future production; and if payments are provided by this program and a government-provided income insurance or safety net program, the total amount of payments cannot exceed 100 percent of the producer's total loss.

Producer retirement programs qualify for exemption if eligibility for the program is clearly defined on criteria to transition the producer out of agricultural production and if the payments are conditional on complete retirement from agricultural production. Resource retirement programs qualify under the following stipulations: payments are conditional on the resource staying out of agricultural production for at least three years; requirements cannot be placed on alternative use of the resource or other resources employed in agricultural production; and payments cannot be related to any remaining agricultural production in which the producer is involved.

Environmental program payments qualify for the Green Box exemption if eligibility requirements are clearly defined and dependent on specific conditions, possibly involving production inputs or practices, and if the payment is limited to the extra cost or income loss the producer faces to be in compliance. Programs that fit these general types but fail to meet the exemption conditions (such as programs where payments exceed the cost of compliance) and all other domestic support programs would fall into the Amber Box and would possibly be limited under the URAA.

The Aggregate Measure of Support

The aggregate measure of support (AMS) is a measure, expressed in monetary terms, of the annual level of domestic support—other than Green Box support—provided to producers of agricultural products. The AMS limit is based on the member state's agricultural support over a base period, usually 1986–88. The countries that signed the URAA agreed to limit Amber Box spending to a level at or below their AMS for their base period. Implementation of the reforms began in 1995. Developed countries were given 6 years to meet the commitments, while developing countries had 10 years. Developed countries were to reduce their AMS by 20 percent, and developing countries by 13 percent, during the implementation period (WTO 2000).

Amber Box policies can be exempted from the AMS counted against a country's limit if the policy is termed de minimis. Within the Amber Box, support is divided into product-specific and non-product-specific groups. The non-product-specific support (the definition of which is still contentious) is not specifically tied to a certain product, and the AMS is assigned to all agricultural production. Once the AMS is classified, the values are compared against minimum values, called de minimis values. The de minimis rule states that, for developed (developing) countries, AMS values below 5 (10) percent of the product's value of production for product-specific support and AMS values below 5 (10) percent of the country's overall value of agricultural production for non-product-specific support are exempted from the URAA's domestic support limits. When countries design their policies accordingly, and most would, they effectively treat these two constraints additively to 10 (20) percent. The United States arguably used such an approach with market loss assistance payments in 1999–2001, stating that the payments were non-product-specific and qualified as nonspecific de minimis. Also, several commodity associations in the United States have reported to their members that the base for U.S. domestic support under the new framework would be roughly $49 billion (American Farm Bureau 2004; National Cotton Council of America 2004; American Soybean Association 2004). To have a domestic support base this large, the United States must treat the product- and non-product-specific de minimis as separate rules, obtaining $19 billion from the existing limit on AMS and $10 billion each from product-specific de minimis, non-product-specific de minimis, and the Blue Box.

Thirty-four WTO member states had base-period AMS values exceeding their de minimis levels (WTO 2004b). Thus, only these 34 members (out of the entire membership of the WTO) faced the prospect of cutting domestic support programs. There have been five reported cases (Argentina in 1995, Hungary in 1998, and Iceland in 1998, 1999, and 2000) where countries have exceeded their commitment levels; however, these countries had not exceeded the levels if inflation is factored in. An aspect of more concern relates to attempts to water down the AMS ceilings by either crediting negative and positive commodity supports or "carrying over" unused AMS limits from year to year to meet the AMS ceiling on average (Shetkari Sanghatana 2001). For example, India proposed that negative AMS values from product-specific support be allowed to offset positive non-product-specific support (WTO 2001). Nevertheless, these attempts have been limited and unsuccessful and are clearly not allowed by Article 6 of the URAA (WTO 1995). The consensus view is that a new agreement on agriculture should not allow such dilution of the original intent of the URAA.

The use of WTO-limited domestic support programs varies by member states. Over the reporting periods, New Zealand has not used any of its domestic support limits. Canada has restructured programs so that its AMS has fallen to 15 percent, on average, of the country's allowable amount. The average AMS level for Australia is 27 percent of the limit. The United States utilized 54 percent of its limit. The average AMS levels for Japan, the European Union, and the Republic of Korea were 45, 67, and 90 percent of their respective limits. As these numbers show, the participating countries have reduced their spending on programs that are classified as trade distorting, and these reductions have met or exceeded the requirements of the URAA.

AMS calculations are meant to estimate the amount of support provided to the commodity as close as possible to the point of the commodity's first sale. AMS can be calculated in two ways. For most types of support, the direct measure of the budgetary outlays and forgone revenue to the government for the program is used as the AMS figure. National and subnational support is to be included in the figure, while any fees or levies paid by producers are to be deducted. For market price support (MPS) programs, the AMS for particular products is based on the price gap between a fixed external reference price and the applied administered price from the program and the quantity of production eligible under the program. Hence, the MPS component of the AMS is not based on actual expenditures or current price gap information.

This is a fundamental difference between the AMS and the market price support component of the producer support estimate (PSE) prepared by the Organisation for Economic Co-operation and Development (OECD). The OECD relies on actual market data to compute a price gap leading to the MPS component of the PSE.

The fixed external reference prices were set based on prices during the base period. They represent the average free-on-board price for the commodity in a net-exporting country and the average cost, insurance, and freight price for the commodity in a net-importing country. Adjustments to the fixed external reference prices are allowed for differences in commodity quality.

Total AMS is the sum of all AMS figures (both product-specific and non-product-specific). Current total AMS is the sum of all AMS figures after accounting for exemptions for Blue Box programs and the de minimis rules. To examine the issues outlined in the introduction, we have chosen four member states to highlight: the United States, the European Union, Japan, and Brazil. Tables 8.1 to 8.4 show the domestic support for agriculture that these member states have reported to the WTO as of the end of 2004. For Green Box support, we report the total amount of support, decoupled income support, marketing support, and transportation and infrastructure support. Total Blue Box support is also listed, along with figures for the Amber Box, or AMS limits, total AMS, and current total AMS (the support actually counted against the limits after de minimis exemption).

In the United States, Green Box support represents most of the support to agriculture, as illustrated in table 8.1. Roughly 60 percent of this support is in domestic food aid. Decoupled income support is roughly 10 percent of all Green Box

TABLE 8.1 Reported Domestic Support from the United States, 1995–2001 (US$ billions)

Category	1995	1996	1997	1998	1999	2000	2001
Green							
Total	46.0	51.8	51.2	49.8	49.7	50.1	50.7
Decoupled income support	0.0	5.2	6.3	5.7	5.5	5.1	4.1
Marketing[a]	0.7	0.7	0.8	0.8	0.8	0.8	1.0
Blue	7.0	0.0	0.0	0.0	0.0	0.0	0.0
Amber							
Limit	23.1	22.3	21.5	20.7	19.9	19.1	19.1
Total	7.9	7.0	7.0	15.1	24.3	24.1	21.5
Current total	6.2	5.9	6.2	10.4	16.9	16.8	14.4

Source: See data sources for tables at end of chapter.
a. Transportation and infrastructure support is included in marketing category; data could not be separated.

support in the United States. Subsidies that are directly targeted at marketing, transportation, and infrastructure are about 2 percent of Green Box support. The United States eliminated its Blue Box support with the 1996 farm bill. In the late 1990s the United States expanded its Amber Box support, as some existing and some new programs provided support to counter the low prices experienced during the time. The latest U.S. farm legislation maintains most of the existing programs, including decoupled income support payments, and incorporates a new Amber Box program that provides support in low-price scenarios. The United States has used the de minimis rules very effectively to meet its limits and would be seriously constrained by a phaseout of the exemptions.

The European Union has reported significant support in all three boxes. However, the reports show a trend toward an increase in Green Box support and a decrease in Amber Box support. Decoupled income support and subsidies tied to marketing, transportation, and infrastructure account for less than 20 percent of all Green Box support. The Blue Box support consists of compensatory payments for grains, oilseeds, and livestock—programs that have production limits embedded in them. Recent changes in the European Union's CAP are structured to transfer much of the EU's Blue and Amber Box support to the Green Box and are not fully reflected in the recent history shown in table 8.2. The incorporation of many of the EU commodity-specific compensatory payments into a single farm payment that is tied to a payment entitlement will transfer a great deal of EU agricultural support to the Green Box as decoupled income support payments.

TABLE 8.2 Reported Domestic Support from the European Union, 1995–2000 (€ billions)

Category	1995	1996	1997	1998	1999	2000
Green						
Total	18.8	22.1	18.2	19.2	19.9	21.8
Decoupled income support	0.2	0.2	0.2	0.1	1.0	0.5
Marketing	0.5	0.6	0.8	1.1	1.1	1.0
Transportation, infrastructure	0.8	1.3	0.6	0.6	2.4	1.0
Blue	20.8	21.5	20.4	20.5	19.8	22.2
Amber						
Limit	78.7	76.4	74.1	71.8	69.5	67.2
Total	52.4	51.5	50.5	46.8	47.9	43.9
Current total	50.0	51.0	50.2	46.7	47.9	43.6

Source: See data sources for tables at end of chapter.

TABLE 8.3 Reported Domestic Support from Japan, 1995–2000 (¥ billions)

Category	1995	1996	1997	1998	1999	2000
Green						
Total	3,169	2,818	2,652	3,002	2,686	2,595
Decoupled income support	0	0	0	0	0	0
Marketing	21	17	17	20	20	20
Transportation, infrastructure	1,908	1,681	1,488	1,801	1,552	1,621
Blue	0	0	0	50	93	93
Amber						
Limit	4,801	4,635	4,469	4,304	4,138	3,973
Total	3,625	3,434	3,282	922	851	719
Current total	3,508	3,330	3,171	767	748	709

Source: See data sources for tables at end of chapter.

Japan also utilizes support in all three boxes (table 8.3). More than half of its Green Box support is targeted at agricultural transportation and infrastructure. A shift in the Japanese rice program moved some agricultural support from the Amber Box to the Blue Box. The shift resulted in a significant decrease in AMS figures: current total AMS fell by more than 75 percent. The shift also moved Japanese AMS levels well below the targeted limits.

TABLE 8.4 Reported Domestic Support from Brazil, 1995–98 (US$ millions)

Category	1995	1996	1997	1998
Green				
Total	4,883	2,600	3,458	2,420
Decoupled income support	0	0	0	0
Marketing	56	26	21	34
Transportation, infrastructure	597	436	716	617
Blue	0	0	0	0
Amber				
Limit	1,039	1,025	1,011	997
Total	432	376	310	578
Current total	0	0	0	83

Source: See data sources for tables at end of chapter.

Brazil, like the United States, has provided most of its agricultural support through the Green Box (table 8.4). While the total amount of Green Box support has varied considerably over the reported years, support targeted at marketing, transportation, and infrastructure has held between $450 million and $750 million. The first year that Brazil reported any support that counted against the AMS limits was in 1998—before that all Amber Box support was below the de minimis levels.

The July Framework, Recent Policy Changes, and WTO Rulings

The July 2004 framework for agricultural domestic support is targeted at achieving substantial reductions in trade-distorting domestic support. Harmonization of permitted support levels is approached by requiring larger cuts in higher bound levels of permitted support. The framework proposes new limits be put in place on de minimis support, Blue Box support, and product-specific AMS. Total support, as measured by the sum of permitted AMS, de minimis, and Blue Box support, is also to be limited. This limit on total support is to be reduced during the implementation period. All member states would face a 20 percent reduction in the total support limit in the first year of implementation. Additional reductions in the total support limit are to be based on a tiered formula that is yet to be determined. However, the formula will result in larger reductions for member states that have higher levels of permitted support.

Permitted total AMS and de minimis levels will also be lowered throughout implementation. Product-specific AMS and Blue Box support are only capped. Article 9 of the framework states, however, that the required reductions in total support and total AMS will force reductions in product-specific support as well. The Blue Box is redefined to include direct payment schemes that either limit production or do not require production at all. A member state's limit for Blue Box support will be based on 5 percent of its average total value of agricultural production over a historical period or the amount of existing Blue Box payments over a historical period, whichever is higher. Green Box guidelines are to be reviewed to ensure that all Green Box programs are only minimally trade or production distorting. Monitoring of compliance with the new agreement, through "timely and complete notifications with respect to the commitments in market access, domestic support and export competition," is to be enhanced (WTO 2004a, A-7).

Both the United States and the European Union have significantly altered their agricultural support in the last few years. These changes have moved a great deal of their agricultural support to direct payments to agricultural entities. The direct and countercyclical payments in the United States and the Single Farm Payments in the European Union all fit the description of direct payments. Given the current structure of the Green Box and the new definition of the Blue Box, the U.S. direct payments and the EU Single Farm Payments would be filed in the Green Box, and the U.S. countercyclical payments would go in the Blue Box. These moves would seem to give the United States and the European Union a great deal of flexibility in dealing with the proposed reductions.

However, the WTO panel ruling on the Brazil-U.S. cotton dispute has questioned whether the U.S. direct payments belong in the Green Box. The panel concluded that the U.S. direct payments "do not fully conform" to the guidelines for Green Box direct payments. The major reason for this conclusion is the restriction on the production of fruits and vegetables on the payment base acreage (WTO 2004b). By the same argument, the EU Single Farm Payments would not conform to the Green Box requirements. It would be relatively easy to fix both issues.

Article 9 of the framework explicitly states that the reductions in total AMS permitted levels "will result in reductions of some product-specific support" (WTO 2004a, A-2). But given the loopholes with MPS, discussed in the next section of this chapter, and the flexibility of member states to channel support through other mechanisms, true reductions may not be achieved or the results may not be as dramatic as hoped. For example, the United States could utilize the MPS loopholes and make cosmetic changes to the dairy and sugar programs to fulfill a target in product-specific support reductions without truly affecting actual support. Another example would be if the United States moved to lower loan rates in the marketing loan program (reducing product-specific AMS) and augmented the countercyclical program to make up the support difference (by changing the target price). Aggregate support would remain the same, but support would shift from the Amber Box to the Blue Box. The ability of reductions in total permitted AMS levels to force reductions in product-specific support will also hinge on the product-specific AMS limits. These limits have yet to be determined, although the framework does state that the limits will be based on "respective average levels" (WTO 2004a, A-2). To guarantee product-specific support reductions, the final level of total permitted AMS must be less than the sum of the product-specific AMS limits.

Should AMS Be Redefined?

AMS is calculated in two ways. For support financed from the budget, the actual government expenditures on the program are used. However, for MPS programs, the AMS calculations depend on fixed external reference prices that are derived from import and export prices during the 1986–88 base period. The calculations also depend on the administered or policy prices set by the member state during the given marketing year. AMS is computed as the product of the difference between the administered price and the external reference price and the amount of eligible production, less any fees or levies associated with the program.

Having the calculations based on fixed prices simplifies them, as the only random parts of the AMS calculation are then the eligible production and program fees. But does this definition of AMS truly capture the amount of support from these programs? The use of the administered price does not necessarily reflect the market situation in the member state for the given year, just as the external reference price does not reflect the world market situation. If domestic market prices are lower than the administered price or the actual world price is above the external reference price, or both, then the amount of support, as computed under current AMS guidelines, is overestimated. If these price relationships are reversed (the domestic market price exceeds the administered price or the actual world price is below the reference price), then the amount of support is underestimated.

Many of the agricultural programs in the four member states we consider here are considered market price support programs. In the United States, the dairy, sugar, and pre-2002 farm bill peanut programs fell into this category. The European Union has market price support programs for beef, butter, corn, rice, sugar, wheat, and several other commodities. Japan supports barley, beef, milk, pork, potatoes, sugar, and wheat. Brazil has price support programs for corn, cotton, edible beans, rice, sisal, soybeans, and wheat.

Table 8.5 shows the proportion of reported AMS that comes from MPS programs for these four member states. The table shows that the United States, European Union, and Japan have all relied on price support programs for a majority of their reported agricultural support. The U.S. proportion has sizably dropped over the period, as other support programs have grown. The EU proportion has remained steady over the period. The Japanese proportion has fallen, mainly because of the shift in support for rice. Almost all of Brazil's support comes from other types of programs.

TABLE 8.5 Market Price Support as a Percentage of Reported AMS, 1995–2001

Country/Region	1995	1996	1997	1998	1999	2000	2001	Average
United States	100	100	93	56	35	35	40	66
European Union	64	68	69	73	71	70	—	69
Japan	93	94	94	84	83	71	—	87
Brazil	0	0	0	1	—	—	—	0

Source: See data sources for tables at end of chapter.
Note: — = not available.

TABLE 8.6 U.S. Sugar Program AMS Calculations with External Reference Prices, 1995–2001

Year	Administered price (US$/metric ton)	External reference price (million metric tons)	Eligible production (million metric tons)	AMS (US$ millions)
1995	396.8	230.8	6.7	1,107.8
1996	374.8	230.8	6.5	937.2
1997	374.8	230.8	7.3	1,045.4
1998	374.8	230.8	7.6	1,093.2
1999	374.8	230.8	8.2	1,180.2
2000	374.8	230.8	7.9	1,132.8
2001	374.8	230.8	7.2	1,031.8

Source: See data sources for tables at end of chapter.

As an example, consider the U.S. sugar program. It is a price support program in which the support originates in the form of commodity-backed loans. The administered price is the loan rate for the program less a forfeiture penalty. The external reference price is the 1986–88 average Caribbean price for sugar plus transportation costs to the United States. No fees or levies are associated with the program. Table 8.6 displays the reported AMS figures for the U.S. sugar program from 1995 to 2001. The administered price changes only with a change in the loan rate for the program, as happened with the passage of the 1996 farm bill. The external reference price is a constant (the 1986–88 average Caribbean price of $202.16 per metric ton plus $28.66 per metric ton transportation charge). Thus, the AMS for the program varies only with the eligible production. The average level of AMS was $1.075 billion and the range between high and low years was roughly $250 million.

To show the effects of moving to different prices in the AMS calculation, we have calculated the AMS for the U.S. sugar program using the actual Caribbean sugar prices for the given years. These prices and the resulting AMS figures are given in table 8.7. On average, the change has a minor effect, as the average AMS would have been $1.034 billion annually over the period. Thus, on average, the amount of calculated support from the program fell when actual world prices were used. But the variability of the AMS figures dramatically increased with the inclusion of actual world prices. The range between high and low years increased to nearly $900 million.

A similar exercise for the EU sugar program shows parallel results. On average, annual AMS levels for the program would fall modestly over the reported period if actual world prices were used in the calculation, but the variability of the AMS

TABLE 8.7 U.S. Sugar Program AMS Calculations with Actual World Prices, 1995–2001 (US$ per metric ton except where indicated)

Year	Administered price	Freight on board Caribbean price	Transportation adjustment	Eligible production (million metric tons)	AMS (US$ millions)
1995	396.8	273.0	28.6	6.7	635.1
1996	374.8	257.0	28.6	6.5	580.2
1997	374.8	238.0	28.6	7.3	785.2
1998	374.8	155.0	28.6	7.6	1,451.4
1999	374.8	166.0	28.6	8.2	1,476.7
2000	374.8	216.0	28.6	7.9	1,024.0
2001	374.8	167.0	28.6	7.2	1,283.8

Source: See data sources for tables at end of chapter.

levels would increase. Reported AMS for the EU sugar program ranged from €5.72 billion in 1999 to €5.8 billion in 2000. Calculated AMS with actual world prices ranged from €4.5 to €6.5 billion.

If actual domestic prices were used in the AMS calculation, then additional shifts would be expected. In table 8.8, we have calculated AMS for the U.S. sugar program using the actual Caribbean sugar prices and estimates for the U.S. domestic prices for the given years. The estimated domestic prices are based on

TABLE 8.8 U.S. Sugar Program AMS Calculations with Actual Domestic and World Prices, 1995–2001 (US$ per metric ton except where indicated)

Year	Market price	Freight on board caribbean price	Transportation adjustment	Eligible production (million metric tons)	AMS (US$ millions)
1995	501.6	273.0	28.7	6.7	1,333.7
1996	496.0	257.0	28.7	6.5	1,369.1
1997	485.0	238.0	28.7	7.3	1,584.9
1998	486.9	155.0	28.7	7.6	2,301.8
1999	486.4	166.0	28.7	8.2	2,392.0
2000	405.6	216.0	28.7	7.9	1,266.2
2001	464.4	167.0	28.7	7.2	1,926.7

Source: See data sources for tables at end of chapter.

U.S. raw sugar prices that are reported with duty fees paid in New York on a fiscal year basis. This change has a major impact on AMS figures. The average annual AMS level over the reported period would have been $1.74 billion, a jump of nearly $700 million in estimated support. In some of the years, the estimated AMS levels in table 8.8 are double the actual reported values from table 8.6.

Whether such changes to the definition of AMS would increase or decrease a WTO member's chances of violating WTO commitments depends on the relative relationships among the administered program price, the domestic market price, the external reference price, and the actual world price. As the U.S. sugar example shows, any new definition of AMS may lead to decreased chances of violations in some years but increased chances in others. The current definition has the relative benefit to member states of being fairly stable (only varying with production and policy changes), while new definitions of AMS would likely be more variable, at least based on this example. However, if domestic and world prices move together (as they would with more open trade), then the variability of the AMS calculations using actual prices would be lower than was previously demonstrated. An increase in AMS variability would also contribute to a higher chance of violations, especially given the lower levels of AMS commitments put forth under the July Framework. Also, the change from the administered price to an actual domestic market price changes the meaning of the support estimate. One argument for staying with the administered price is that it represents the price supported by the domestic support program in question. By moving to an actual domestic price, the support estimate is picking up the effects of other policies (such as tariffs) and market events not embodied in the domestic support program. With an eye toward the goal of the negotiations, the potential variability from these changes to AMS calculations could bring more policy discipline and decrease the reliance on anticyclical support. But the panel ruling on the Brazil-U.S. cotton dispute also gives some insight on the framing of the URAA. In the ruling, the panel discussed MPS calculations for AMS. They stated that "a prime consideration of the drafters was to ensure that Members had some means of ensuring compliance with their commitments despite factors beyond their control" (WTO 2004b, 134). Thus, the framers of the URAA chose to provide member states a greater degree of control over their MPS measurement at the expense of an updated representation of the effective support from the programs.

Another question related to AMS is the "double coverage" of such programs under the URAA. MPS programs essentially fall under two of the three pillars, market access and domestic support. Does it make sense to cover these programs twice? It does not in terms of the accounting of agricultural support, but in political economy terms, this was not an innocuous oversight. Indeed, it would be relatively simple to remove MPS programs from both the base and annual AMS calculations and allow the market access commitments to govern their behavior. This change would make clear how the programs are treated.

The removal of the MPS programs from both reported and base AMS would also remove the possibility of another policy change like the one in Japanese rice policy. The Japanese government abolished its official price for rice. This move dramatically reduced Japan's reported AMS (shown in table 8.3) without any reduction in permitted support. But the level of protection for rice was maintained. Events such as this highlight the loopholes in the MPS approach. It is likely that new approaches will bring new loopholes or new policies circumventing the new rules, especially as long as market access limits allow high protection paid by consumers. The Japanese rice example also shows the importance of the administered price in MPS and the possible moves a member state can make to remove an MPS program from its notifications. One tactic WTO negotiators could use to tighten controls on MPS programs would be to define more clearly what constitutes an administered price and how an MPS program must be changed before it can be removed from notifications.

Another example of double coverage is U.S. dairy policy before the 2002 farm bill. This program consisted of border protection measures and a domestic support price. Thus, the policies were covered by both the market access and domestic support pillars. But as Sumner (2003, 104) points out, the domestic support price "provides almost no support in addition to that provided by the dairy trade barriers." Under the current structure of domestic support reporting, though, the United States reports $4.5 billion in dairy AMS for domestic support. U.S. sugar policy could also be amended in a way that would make the sugar MPS ($1.1 billion) vanish without significant changes in the actual support received by U.S. sugar growers.

However, the current double coverage does have the trade benefit of allowing either the market access or domestic support commitments to be binding. Thus, while an MPS program may be acceptable under the market access commitments, its domestic support commitments may not be met (or vice versa) and support reductions would be warranted. In different states of the world, different pillars may become binding. Also, many governments use trade restrictions to decrease the expected treasury cost of their farm support. A fundamental issue is whether the domestic program would indeed become fiscally unsustainable with open borders. The answer is a qualified yes. It is clear that the foreseeable reduction in border protection is driving many of the EU's CAP reforms, the recent reform of the U.S. peanut program, and other reforms. Yet there are a few powerful counterexamples such as U.S. and EU cotton subsidies, which appear sustainable despite open borders. A government's largesse is also conditioned on fiscal surpluses or deficits. The budgetary situation has been deteriorating for the largest providers of farm support in OECD countries.

Is the Domestic Support Pillar Worth the Trouble?

With market price support programs covered by market access commitments, and most member states moving to Green Box support for most agricultural support, does it make sense to continue to discipline domestic support in the WTO? Only 20 percent of the WTO membership currently has explicit domestic support commitments. Many of the domestic support programs can be or are covered by the other pillars. Works such as that by Hoekman, Ng, and Olarreaga (2004) have shown that tariff reductions generate much larger welfare gains than similarly sized reductions in agricultural subsidies. However, Hoekman, Ng, and Olarreaga still conclude that it is important to focus on both tariffs and subsidies.

With some caveats on dirty tariffication and tariff rate quota administration, the two trade pillars have fairly clear measures of their effectiveness, whereas the domestic support pillar is much less transparent. The rules of the domestic support pillar are structured to separate those programs that have minimal or no trade effects from those that are trade distorting. But a program's ability to distort trade is in the eye of the beholder. Earlier in this chapter, we outlined the list of program descriptors that define minimal- to non-trade-distorting programs (the Green Box guidelines). Recent disputes within the WTO (such as the U.S.-Brazil cotton dispute) have questioned the trade impacts of some of these Green Box programs, however. The goal of the domestic support commitments is to allow member states to direct support to the agricultural sector while limiting the trade effects from such support. The ability of the commitments to do this is strictly dependent on the precision of the domestic support guidelines in categorizing programs in their trade impacts. Judging from recent trade disputes, precision is somewhat lacking.

This lack of precision was recognized in the URAA, as Blue and Amber Box programs were not completely restricted. If only non-trade-distorting programs had been allowed, the ability of member states to reach consensus on the guidelines for such programs would have been severely tested. The Uruguay Round lasted eight years and the current agricultural negotiations are already in their sixth year. If the negotiations included strict guidelines on non-trade-distorting domestic support, we can imagine that the negotiations might take considerably longer and be even more contentious. One potential way to avoid this situation is to provide a temporarily generous definition of the Green Box, which would allow buyout or phaseout of Amber and Blue Box forms of support. Then a progressive phasedown of the Green Box would discipline remaining farm support over time. It took eight GATT rounds to get rid of industrial protection. It is foolish to hope that vested agricultural interests in some of the high- and middle-income countries would give up huge and concentrated rents without virulent and long fights. Part of the solution is also demographic in the European Union and North America, where farming populations and farm political representation are aging rapidly and not being replaced.[2] This withering process is happening in a new political economy context for farm subsidies. The general public now perceives OECD subsidies as exacerbating development and environment problems thanks to greater transparency induced by nongovernmental organizations such as Oxfam and the Environment Working Group.

Another approach to defining the degree of trade distortion from agricultural support is through litigation. The U.S.-Brazil cotton dispute is but one example of this approach. The litigation approach would allow for an examination of specific aspects of the programs in question and provide a finer breakdown of the trade impacts. However, the possible costs of such an approach could be prohibitive.

Looking at the approved July Framework, negotiators are exploring extensions of current guidelines on domestic support, with the possible redefinition of what may be considered minimal- to-non-trade-distorting policy. As the possibility of changing domestic support guidelines is discussed, it is important to try to balance the many issues linked with the support. Agricultural research, marketing, transportation, infrastructure, and inspection services are all covered by the Green Box. Programs with links to conservation, agricultural retirement, and disaster assistance efforts are also included. Many of these programs have multiple targets, and some of these targets are nonagricultural in nature. Part of the issue of tightening Green Box rules will be the tradeoff between limiting the possible trade-distorting effects of current Green Box programs and limiting a country's ability to fund multipurpose projects.

Transportation and infrastructure support can illustrate this point. A seemingly farfetched example is the U.S. interstate highway system. The system was envisioned as part of a strategic plan for the defense of the nation. The system now serves more in an economic capacity than in a defense capacity (Weingroff 1996) and has become a nontrivial factor of production, especially for agriculture and food processing. Any infrastructure investment that decreases transaction costs of production and trade will potentially distort trade in agriculture (Anderson and van Wincoop 2004).

There are two main areas of concern in the Green Box: the trade impacts from decoupled income support; and marketing, transportation, and infrastructure subsidies. The current guidelines indicate these programs are minimally trade distorting, but on the basis of the Brazil-U.S. cotton dispute ruling and other comments by WTO member state delegations, those assumptions are being questioned. Proposals, such as those from Pakistan and India, have called for an investigation of Green Box policies in combination with a reshaping of the Green Box guidelines (Ingco and Kandiero 2003). The framework explicitly calls for a review of Green Box criteria. Decoupled income support has become a favored way to support agriculture in the United States and European Union. The United States shifted to decoupled income support with the 1996 farm bill and continued this type of support through the 2002 farm bill. The European Union, in its latest agricultural policy change, moved to combine many individual commodity payments into decoupled income support, known as the Single Farm Payment.[3]

The G-20 developing countries have questioned whether this income support is truly decoupled. The payment bases for the U.S. and EU income support programs are set on historical, but recent, production decisions. In the case of the United States, the 2002 farm bill allowed producers to update their payment base to reflect recent shifts in production patterns and to allow the incorporation of a new commodity in the program.

The decoupled income support used by the United States and European Union is being criticized on a number of other grounds as well. Many argue that the sheer size of the payments may affect producer decisions. As an example, for the 2001 marketing year, the decoupled income support received by U.S. rice producers equaled 38 percent of the total value of the U.S. rice crop. Second, the payments may reduce the risk of producing payment crops and the associated income stream, possibly creating incentives to increase output. These wealth and input effects have been examined and found to be small (Hennessy 1998; Young and Westcott 2000). Third, as was the case for the U.S. program, the possibility of updating payment bases may induce links between current production and the payments. Fourth, these programs often require that the land remain in agricultural use and the program may restrict the ways in which the land can be used. For example, producers receiving decoupled income support in the United States cannot shift the payment acreage to the production of certain fruits and vegetables. In a recent study, de Gorter, Ingco, and Ignacio (2004) explore in depth the factors that could link income support payments to production decisions. As was noted earlier in this chapter, a WTO dispute panel found that U.S. direct payments fail to meet Green Box guidelines. Ongoing negotiations should further strengthen and clarify the Green Box guidelines for direct support.

Marketing, transportation, and infrastructure subsidies have also received scrutiny from member states, often for mercantilist reasons. As exemplified by a letter from U.S. Senator Charles Grassley to the U.S. Department of Agriculture and the Office of the United States Trade Representative (Grassley 2003), this concern is targeted mostly at specific developing countries and comes from developed countries. Protectionist interests in developed countries, such as the U.S. sugar lobby, regularly complain about unfair infrastructure subsidies in competing developing countries (Roney 2004). The situation in Brazil is probably at the forefront of this discussion. As indicated in table 8.4, Brazil has spent more than $500 million annually on marketing, transportation, and infrastructure support. Most of this support has been targeted at improvements in the Center-West region, where there has been tremendous growth in agricultural production.[4]

In a study of Brazilian and Argentine agricultural development, Schnepf, Dohlman, and Bolling (2001) refer to "the Brazil Cost," the additional costs and distortions that affect Brazil's ability to market agricultural commodities effectively. One of the major components of the Brazil Cost is the country's inefficient infrastructure and transportation system. In their analysis, Schnepf, Dohlman, and Bolling find that Brazil and Argentina have production cost advantages in comparison with the United States, but these advantages are largely eliminated by the difference in internal transportation and marketing costs.

Fuller and others (2000) examine five potential transportation improvements that could be made in Brazil and find that these improvements could lead to significant increases in producer prices for soybeans, in the range of $0.30 to $0.60 a bushel. Such changes in producer prices are likely to have major implications for the continued expansion of agriculture in the Brazilian Center-West, for the trading capacity of Brazil, and for the world agricultural trade outlook. Thus, it would be hard to argue that these expenditures will have minimal trade effects. But just as in the example of the U.S. interstate highway system, there will likely be other beneficiaries from the transportation and infrastructure expenditures, as reductions in transaction costs are often nontrivial. These beneficiaries will mostly be from nonagricultural sectors, giving the expenditures a public-good aspect. As a developing member, Brazil could also use Article 6.2, which explicitly allows for infrastructure subsidies and exempts them from domestic support commitment. Article 6.2 is seldom used and it has been extended in the July Framework. In the long run, it will represent some option value for developing members whenever infrastructure subsidies under the Green Box may be capped or cut. Subsidies under Article 6.2 will then become another potential loophole to scrutinize.

Blue Box supports have been significantly affected under the July Framework. The changes include an expansion of the box by adding an additional category of payments, namely direct payments with a fixed payment base and no production requirement. Also, limits have been placed on the amount of support that can come from Blue Box programs, whereas the URAA placed no such limits. The vast majority of WTO member states do not use Blue Box programs. Only seven (the European Union, Iceland, Japan, Norway, the Slovak Republic, Slovenia, and the United States) have reported Blue Box support, and the United States eliminated its Blue Box programs with the passage of the 1996 farm bill. However, the new definition of the Blue Box opens its usage to all member states. The U.S. countercyclical program would seem to be a candidate for the new Blue Box. If U.S. direct payments and EU Single Farm Payments fail to meet Green Box guidelines, then those payments may find a home in the Blue Box.

Ways to Improve Domestic Support Guidelines

This discussion has highlighted some of the issues embedded in the current WTO domestic support negotiations. The issues are many because of the myriad agricultural programs used by WTO members throughout the world. But the July Framework for categorizing all of the programs has allowed us to condense this support into manageable points in which further clarifications can be made.

Given the possible effects of decoupled income support and marketing, transportation, and infrastructure support on world trade, these programs may not truly fit the Green Box target of minimally trade-distorting policies. However, these programs are not directly linked to current production or prices and may have other nonagricultural benefits. Therefore, leaving them in the Green Box but tightening the rules for them may make the most sense. The new rules might include expenditure limits patterned after the de minimis rules and stricter guidelines on the definition of base periods and production for decoupled income support. Such changes would address the concerns raised about these programs while allowing members to continue to employ them. As we explained previously, there is a political economy tradeoff in disciplining the Green Box too much. An initially generous Green Box definition may facilitate negotiation of a phaseout of the Amber Box policies, which are the most damaging distortions.

The current AMS framework for market price support, while providing a stable estimate of support, cannot adequately reflect actual support levels. Moving to an AMS based on current world and domestic prices would better capture the actual level of support and align market price support programs with other Amber Box programs in which actual expenditures are used in the calculations. An alternative change would be to remove the market price support programs from both the AMS limits and the current AMS calculations. As shown by Japan, the URAA market price support AMS structure has a significant loophole, allowing the possibility that countries can make small changes in official policy (resulting in minimal changes in agricultural trade protection) and provide themselves large cushions from agricultural support reductions. Either of the proposals suggested here would close this loophole. Resistance to closing the loophole is likely to be strong, given the vested interest of some OECD countries in the loophole.

The July Framework has provided the *possibility* for significant agricultural trade reform in domestic support. New limits, such as those for Blue Box support and product-specific AMS, encompass more support programs than before and provide additional rules for programs already covered by existing limits. Unfortunately, the Blue Box cap proposed in the framework is so generous that many programs could be folded into the Blue Box with no effective change in policy.

Actually the MPS loopholes, initial AMS bindings, and Blue Box caps are so generous that no actual change in aggregate support would occur. As the framework stands now, actual cuts in support would have to wait for a third round of agricultural negotiations.

Further steps could be taken to convert the possibility of reform into genuine reductions in agricultural support. Changes such as the ones we have outlined address many of the concerns various member states have expressed during the negotiations while still allowing flexibility in domestic support. Additional changes, such as explicit language on the role of inflation in support limits, scheduled reductions in Blue Box and product-specific AMS limits, a cap on and eventually future cuts in Green Box payments, and rules evaluating the effects of different policies on domestic versus export markets, may also be beneficial to agricultural trade reform. A more radical approach, but an unlikely one because of its political economy, may be to require drastic cuts (75 percent or more) in bound AMS (Jensen and Zobbe 2006). This would bring cuts in actual supports, not just in bindings, and would somewhat compromise the ability of a country to play the color box game, although the Green Box would remain uncapped. As the negotiations continue, these issues will have to be addressed by member states as they strive for a new agreement.

Notes

1. The limit on base-level production is somewhat arbitrary but has become almost irrelevant given the new cap on Blue Box payments at a maximum of 5 percent of production value agreed upon in the July Framework document (WTO 2004a).
2. A similar observation can be made of the agricultural economics profession!
3. See Messerlin (2003) for a discussion of the political economy associated with these changes.
4. This region consists of the states of Goiás, Mato Grosso, and Mato Grosso do Sul, along with the Federal District, which includes Brasilia.

References

American Farm Bureau. 2004. "Framework Gets WTO Talks Moving Again." *Farm Bureau News*, August 23. http://www.fb.org/news/fbn/04/08_23/html/framework.html (accessed November 17, 2004).

American Soybean Association. 2004. "WTO Trade Negotiations (Doha Round)." http://www.soygrowers.com/policy/backgrounders/wto.htm (accessed November 17, 2004).

Anderson, J., and E. van Wincoop. 2004. "Trade Costs." *Journal of Economic Literature* 42: 691–751.

de Gorter, H., M. D. Ingco, and L. Ignacio. 2004. "Domestic Support: Economics and Policy Instruments," In *Agriculture and the WTO: Creating a Trading System for Development*, ed. M. D. Ingco and J. D. Nash. Washington DC: World Bank.

Fuller, S., L. Fellin, A. Lawlor, and K. Klindworth. 2000. "Agricultural Transportation Challenges for the 21st Century: Effect of Improving South American Transportation Systems on U.S. and South American Corn and Soybean Economies." Agricultural Marketing Service, U.S. Department of Agriculture, Washington DC, October.

Grassley, C. 2003. "Grassley Seeks More Answers on Brazil Soybean Production." Press release containing Grassley's letter of September 3, 2003, to Ellen Terpstra, administrator for the Foreign Agricultural Service, U.S. Department of Agriculture. http://grassley.senate.gov/releases/2003/p03r09-03a.htm (accessed June 14, 2004).

Hennessy, D. A. 1998. "Production Effects of Income Support under Uncertainty." *American Journal of Agricultural Economics* 80: 46–57.

Hoekman, B., F. Ng, and M. Olarreaga. 2004. "Agricultural Tariffs Versus Subsidies: What's More Important for Developing Countries?" *World Bank Economic Review* 18 (2): 175–204.

Ingco, M. D., and T. Kandiero. 2003. "Introduction." In *Directions in Development: Agriculture, Trade, and the WTO in South Asia*, ed. M. D. Ingco. Washington DC: World Bank.

Jensen, H. G., and H. Zobbe. 2006. "Consequences of Reducing Limits on Aggregate Measures of Support." In *Agricultural Trade Reform and the Doha Development Agenda*, ed. K. Anderson and W. Martin. Washington, DC: World Bank.

Messerlin, P. 2003. "Agriculture in the Doha Agenda." World Bank Policy Research Working Paper 3009, World Bank, Washington DC, April.

National Cotton Council of America. 2004. "Domestic Support Provisions of WTO Framework Agreement Clarified." http://www.cotton.org/news/2004/WTO-clarify.cfm (accessed November 17, 2004).

Roney, J. 2004. "United States Sugar Program 101." Presentation at the American Farm Bureau Federation Task Group Meeting 6, "Making American Agriculture Productive and Profitable," Fargo, ND, September 27.

Schnepf, R. D., E. Dohlman, and C. Bolling. 2001. "Agriculture in Brazil and Argentina: Developments and Prospects for Major Field Crops." Agriculture and Trade Report WRS-01-3, ERS Market and Trade Economics Division, U.S. Department of Agriculture, Washington DC, November.

Shetkari Sanghatana. 2001. "Package of Fiscal and Economic Policies." In *Report on Task Force on Agriculture*. Maharashtra: Shetkari Sanghatana (an Indian farmers' organization).

Sumner, D. A. 2003. "Implications of the US Farm Bill of 2002 for Agricultural Trade and Trade Negotiations." *Australian Journal of Agricultural and Resource Economics* 46: 99–122.

Weingroff, R. F. 1996. "Federal-Aid Highway Act of 1956: Creating the Interstate System." *Public Roads* 60 (1), Federal Highway Administration, U.S. Department of Transportation, Washington DC. http://www.tfhrc.gov/pubrds/summer96/p96su10.htm (accessed June 13, 2004).

WTO (World Trade Organization). 1995. "Agreement on Agriculture." Final Act of the 1986–94 Uruguay Round Agreements. WTO, Geneva. http://www.wto.org/english/docs_e/legal_e/14-ag.pdf (accessed October 2004).

_____. 2000. "Domestic Support, Background Paper by the Secretariat." Report of the Committee on Agriculture, Special Session, G/AG/NG/S/1, WTO, Geneva, April 13. http://docsonline.wto.org/DDFDocuments/t/G/AG/ngs1.doc (accessed October 2004).

_____. 2001. "Negotiations on WTO Agreement on Agriculture: Proposals by India in the Areas of: (i) Food Security, (ii) Market Access, (iii) Domestic Support, and (iv) Export Competition." Report of the Committee on Agriculture, Special Session, G/AG/NG/W/102, WTO, Geneva, January 15. http://docsonline.wto.org/DDFDocuments/t/G/AG/NGW102.doc (accessed October 2004).

_____. 2004a. "Doha Work Programme, Decision Adopted by the General Council on 1 August 2004." Report of the General Council, WT/L/579, WTO, Geneva, August 2. http://www.wto.org/english/tratop_e/dda_e/ddadraft_31jul04_e.pdf (accessed October 2004).

_____. 2004b. "United States: Subsidies on Upland Cotton, Report of the Panel." Panel of the Dispute Settlement Body, WT/DS267/R, WTO, Geneva, September 8. http://docsonline.wto.org/DDFDocuments/t/WT/DS/267R.doc (accessed October 2004).

_____. 2004c. "WTO Agricultural Negotiations: The Issues, and Where We Are Now." Committee on Agriculture Briefing Document, WTO, Geneva, April 20, updated October 25. http://www.wto.org/english/tratop_e/agric_e/agnegs_bkgrnd_e.pdf (accessed October 2004).

Young, C. E., and P. C. Westcott. 2000. "How Decoupled Is U.S. Agricultural Support for Major Crops?" *American Journal of Agricultural Economics* 82: 762–67.

Data Sources for Tables

Economic Research Service (various issues), *Sugar and Sweeteners Outlook*, U.S. Department of Agriculture, Washington DC.

World Trade Organization, Committee on Agriculture. "Notification, Brazil, Domestic Support." G/AG/N/BRA/18, Geneva, January 19, 2001. http://docsonline.wto.org/DDFDocuments/t/G/AG/NBRA18.doc.

———. "Notification, Brazil, Domestic Support." G/AG/N/BRA/13, Geneva, March 24, 1999. http://docsonline.wto.org/DDFDocuments/t/G/AG/NBRA13.doc.

———. "Notification, Brazil, Domestic Support." G/AG/N/BRA/10, Geneva, March 9, 1998. http://docsonline.wto.org/DDFDocuments/t/G/AG/NBRA10.wpf.

———. "Notification, Brazil, Domestic Support." G/AG/N/BRA/6/Rev.1, Geneva, October 21, 1997. http://docsonline.wto.org/DDFDocuments/t/G/AG/NBRA6R1.wpf.

———. "Notification, Brazil, Domestic Support." G/AG/N/BRA/6, Geneva, September 23, 1996. http://docsonline.wto.org/DDFDocuments/t/G/AG/NBRA6.wpf.

———. "Notification, European Communities, Domestic Support." G/AG/N/EEC/41, Geneva, December 20, 2002. http://docsonline.wto.org/DDFDocuments/t/G/AG/NEEC41.doc.

———. "Notification, European Communities, Domestic Support." G/AG/N/EEC/38, Geneva, June 27, 2002. http://docsonline.wto.org/DDFDocuments/t/G/AG/NEEC38.doc.

———. "Notification, European Communities, Domestic Support." G/AG/N/EEC/39, Geneva, June 27, 2002. http://docsonline.wto.org/DDFDocuments/t/G/AG/NEEC39.doc.

———. "Notification, European Communities, Domestic Support." G/AG/N/EEC/30/Corr.1., Geneva, July 25, 2001. http://docsonline.wto.org/DDFDocuments/t/G/AG/NEEC30C1.doc.

———. "Notification, European Communities, Domestic Support." G/AG/N/EEC/30, Geneva, March 22, 2001. http://docsonline.wto.org/DDFDocuments/t/G/AG/NEEC30.doc.

———. "Notification, European Communities, Domestic Support." G/AG/N/EEC/26/Corr.1, Geneva, October 30, 2000. http://docsonline.wto.org/DDFDocuments/t/G/AG/NEEC26C1.doc.

———. "Notification, European Communities, Domestic Support." G/AG/N/EEC/26, Geneva, June 21, 2000. http://docsonline.wto.org/DDFDocuments/t/G/AG/NEEC26.doc.

———. "Notification, European Communities, Domestic Support." G/AG/N/EEC/12/Rev.1/Corr.1, Geneva, May 12, 2000. http://docsonline.wto.org/DDFDocuments/t/G/AG/NEEC12R1C1.doc

———. "Notification, European Communities, Domestic Support." G/AG/N/EEC/12/Rev.1, Geneva, September 21, 1999. http://docsonline.wto.org/DDFDocuments/t/G/AG/NEEC12R1.doc.

———. "Notification, European Communities, Domestic Support." G/AG/N/EEC/16/Rev.1, Geneva, September 21, 1999. http://docsonline.wto.org/DDFDocuments/t/G/AG/NEEC16R1.doc.

———. "Notification, European Communities, Domestic Support." G/AG/N/EEC/17, Geneva, September 17, 1999. http://docsonline.wto.org/DDFDocuments/t/G/AG/NEEC17.doc.

———. "Notification, European Communities, Domestic Support." G/AG/N/EEC/16, Geneva, March 22, 1999. http://docsonline.wto.org/DDFDocuments/t/G/AG/NEEC16.doc.

———. "Notification, European Communities, Domestic Support." G/AG/N/EEC/12/Corr.2., Geneva, August 14, 1998. http://docsonline.wto.org/DDFDocuments/t/G/AG/NEEC12C2.doc.

———. "Notification, European Communities, Domestic Support." G/AG/N/EEC/12/Corr.1, Geneva, May 25, 1998. http://docsonline.wto.org/DDFDocuments/t/G/AG/NEEC12C1.wpf.

———. "Notification, European Communities, Domestic Support." G/AG/N/EEC/12, Geneva, May 8, 1998. http://docsonline.wto.org/DDFDocuments/t/G/AG/NEEC12.doc.

———. "Notification, Japan, Domestic Support." G/AG/N/JPN/98, Geneva, May 19, 2004. http://docsonline.wto.org/DDFDocuments/t/G/AG/NJPN98.doc.

———. "Notification, Japan, Domestic Support." G/AG/N/JPN/72, Geneva, February 19, 2002. http://docsonline.wto.org/DDFDocuments/t/G/AG/NJPN72.doc.

———. "Notification, Japan, Domestic Support." G/AG/N/JPN/62, Geneva, March 1, 2001. http://docsonline.wto.org/DDFDocuments/t/G/AG/NJPN62.doc.

———. "Notification, Japan, Domestic Support." G/AG/N/JPN/61, Geneva, February 28, 2001. http://docsonline.wto.org/DDFDocuments/t/G/AG/NJPN61.doc.

———. "Notification, Japan, Domestic Support." G/AG/N/JPN/47, Geneva, February 21, 2000. http://docsonline.wto.org/DDFDocuments/t/G/AG/NJPN47.doc.

———. "Notification, Japan, Domestic Support." G/AG/N/JPN/34, Geneva, March 2, 1999. http://docsonline.wto.org/DDFDocuments/t/G/AG/NJPN34.doc.

———. "Notification, Japan, Domestic Support." G/AG/N/JPN/21/Corr.1, Geneva, September 25, 1997. http://docsonline.wto.org/DDFDocuments/t/G/AG/NJPN21C1.wpf.

———. "Notification, Japan, Domestic Support." G/AG/N/JPN/21, Geneva, June 12, 1997. http://docsonline.wto.org/DDFDocuments/t/G/AG/NJPN21.wpf.

———. "Notification, United States, Domestic Support." G/AG/N/USA/51, Geneva, March 17, 2004. http://docsonline.wto.org/DDFDocuments/t/G/AG/NUSA51.doc.

———. "Notification, United States, Domestic Support." G/AG/N/USA/43, Geneva, February 5, 2003. http://docsonline.wto.org/DDFDocuments/t/G/AG/NUSA43.doc.

———. "Notification, United States, Domestic Support." G/AG/N/USA/37, Geneva, October 5, 2001. http://docsonline.wto.org/DDFDocuments/t/G/AG/NUSA37.doc.

———. "Notification, United States, Domestic Support." G/AG/N/USA/36, Geneva, June 26, 2001. http://docsonline.wto.org/DDFDocuments/t/G/AG/NUSA36.doc.

———. "Notification, United States, Domestic Support." G/AG/N/USA/28, Geneva, November 16, 1999. http://docsonline.wto.org/DDFDocuments/t/G/AG/NUSA28.doc.

———. "Notification, United States, Domestic Support." G/AG/N/USA/27, Geneva, June 28, 1999. http://docsonline.wto.org/DDFDocuments/t/G/AG/NUSA27.doc.

———. "Notification, United States, Domestic Support." G/AG/N/USA/25, Geneva, March 11, 1999. http://docsonline.wto.org/DDFDocuments/t/G/AG/NUSA25.doc.

———. "Notification, United States, Domestic Support." G/AG/N/USA/17, Geneva, June 15, 1998. http://docsonline.wto.org/DDFDocuments/t/G/AG/NUSA17.doc.

———. "Notification, United States, Domestic Support." G/AG/N/USA/10, Geneva, June 12, 1997. http://docsonline.wto.org/DDFDocuments/t/G/AG/NUSA10.wpf.

———. "Notification, United States, Domestic Support." G/AG/N/USA/5, Geneva, September 16, 1996. http://docsonline.wto.org/DDFDocuments/t/G/AG/NUSA5.wpf.

9

CONSEQUENCES OF REDUCING LIMITS ON AGGREGATE MEASUREMENTS OF SUPPORT

Hans G. Jensen and Henrik Zobbe[*]

Throughout the history of the General Agreement on Tariffs and Trade (GATT), agriculture has been a major issue of conflict. That has been especially obvious since the full inclusion of the sector in the Uruguay Round negotiations (1986–93). For many developed countries, agricultural policies are sensitive. These domestic policies are deeply founded in a long list of historical events and conditional economic and political structures and institutions (Zobbe 2003). Further domestic reforms are complicated and are slowing the multilateral process under the World Trade Organization's (WTO) current Doha Round. The overall aim of this round is to discipline agricultural protection and ensure serious reductions in support programs that distort agricultural production and trade.

The Uruguay Round Agreement on Agriculture (URAA) established the disciplinary framework for domestic agricultural support in WTO member countries by categorizing support into three boxes: an Amber Box, with support coupled with production, a Blue Box, with production-coupled support combined with production reduction programs, and a Green Box, with decoupled support programs (see chapter 8 for details). The URAA introduced commitments on reductions in the amount of domestic support allowed in the Amber Box, while subsidies paid under the Blue and Green Boxes were exempt from reduction commitments.

---

[*]The authors thank Soren Frandsen, Will Martin, Kym Anderson, John Nash, Harry de Gorter, and other workshop participants for their comments and discussions.

In the Amber Box, an aggregate measure of support (AMS) was defined, after long and tough negotiations, as an indicator of the amount of support found in this box category. Initial levels of AMS were determined, and developed countries agreed to cut these initial levels by 20 percent (13 percent in developing countries) in the URAA. In principle, all production-coupled support should have been cut. But because of the exemption of the Blue Box, a historical base period reflecting very high initial support levels, and de minimis exemptions, domestic support cuts following the URAA have been rather disappointing (OECD 2001).[1]

The objective of this chapter is to analyze prospects for significant reductions in AMS, de minimis, and Blue Box domestic support commitments across WTO member countries, and to compare those prospective reductions in commitments with recent policy reforms in the European Union and the United States. The next section introduces the concept of AMS more formally and presents current AMS values distributed both by products and by countries. A scenario of possible AMS, de minimis, and Blue Box reductions is then presented. The third section compares that scenario with post-2001 policy changes in the European Union and the United States, before conclusions are drawn in the final section.

Domestic Support Levels

As a basis for projecting the effects of commitments that might be undertaken following the current negotiations, table 9.1 presents a snapshot of notified current total AMS levels in 1999 (the most recent year with a full data set) by country for 18 aggregated products and for non-product-specific support. The European Union, the United States, and Japan account for more than 90 percent of the $81 billion notified AMS in 1999. The European Union alone accounts for more than 60 percent ($50 billion). This snapshot also gives some information about politically sensitive products, which include beef, fruits and vegetables, grains, milk, and sugar. Table 9.2 presents notified data for domestic support under the de minimis rule for 1999, by country and products. The United States accounts for more than 80 percent ($7 billion) of total de minimis, and just about all of it is non-product-specific. Only a few other countries have some de minimis payments.

For both the European Union and the United States, which are critically important providers of domestic support, AMS notifications are also available for 2001. These are presented in tables 9.3 and 9.4. Total AMS in the EU equaled €44 billion, and the most supported products were beef, fruits and vegetables, grains, milk, and sugar. Market price support was the most important support element. For the United States, total AMS was $14 billion, and the most supported products were milk, oilseeds, and non-product-specific support. But because of the de minimis rule, the $6.8 billion in non-product-specific support is not included in total AMS. Direct payments not eligible for exemption from the reduction commitments were the most important support element in the United States, in contrast with the EU where market price support was the dominant form.

Possible Reduction Scenarios

Since the conclusion of the URAA in 1994, the agenda for the current round of negotiations on domestic support has been more or less clear. The negotiating framework decided upon by the WTO General Council on August 1, 2004, is the most specific document available that sketches some possible outcomes (WTO 2004a). Overall, the so-called July Framework Agreement calls for "substantial reductions in trade-distorting domestic support" and specifies that special and differential treatment remain an integrated part of domestic support. It also calls for strong harmonization in the reductions made by developed countries. To secure substantial reductions, both the de minimis level and the allowed amount of Blue Box support are to be capped. More specifically, overall trade-distorting domestic support, as measured by the final bound total AMS plus the permitted de minimis level plus the highest level of Blue Box payments (or 5 percent of the value of output as a ceiling on Blue Box payments) during a recent representative period, is to be reduced according to a tiered formula. In the first year of implementation, countries are to reduce total trade-distorting support by 20 percent relative to this overall base. Total AMS is also to be reduced according to a tiered formula. Reductions in de minimis are to be negotiated during this Doha Round; Blue Box support in the future is not to exceed 5 percent of a WTO member's average total value of production during a historical period to be agreed upon; and direct payments that do not require production can be placed in the Blue Box under certain conditions.

Following these guidelines, table 9.5 was constructed to analyze the outcome of a possible future agreement. For all countries, the overall base value of all trade-distorting domestic support (column 4) is presented in the first row (base commitments) for each country listed. This level was calculated by adding total AMS base levels from the URAA final bound AMS levels (column 1) to the permitted de minimis payments in a given reference period (column 2) plus the highest of existing Blue Box payments during the 1995–2002 period or 5 percent of the total value of agricultural production, whichever was highest (column 3). The reduction modeled in this chapter uses a tiered formula reducing base AMS commitments and total trade-distorting domestic support by 75 or 60 percent in developed countries and by 40 percent in all developing countries.[2]

The second row presents for each country the new commitments: 75, 60, or 40 percent reductions are made in both total AMS and the overall base level of

TABLE 9.1 Current Total AMS, 1999, by Country and Commodity (US$ millions)

Country	Rice	Wheat	Grains	Fruits & vegetables	Oil-seeds	Sugar	Fibers	Wine
Developed								
Iceland	0	0	0	0	0	0	3	0
Norway	0	42	144	18	0	0	0	0
Switzerland[a]	0	163	158	75	30	0	0	0
Japan	0	617	197	0	89	492	9	0
EU15	410	3,048	4,593	9,933	2,273	6,004	794	2,140
Israel	0	0	0	0	0	0	0	0
Canada	0	0	136	0	29	0	0	0
United States	435	974	2,779	119	3,400	1,207	2,364	0
New Zealand	0	0	0	0	0	0	0	0
Australia	0	0	0	0	0	0	0	0
Developing								
Argentina	0	0	0	0	0	0	0	0
Brazil[a]	0	27	0	0	0	0	55	0
Bulgaria	0	0	0	0	0	0	0	0
Colombia	4	0	0	0	0	0	0	0
Costa Rica	0	0	0	0	0	0	0	0
Jordan[a]	0	1	0	0	0	0	0	0
Korea, Rep. of	1,278	0	42	0	0	0	0	0
Mexico[a]	2	26	307	67	0	0	0	0
Morocco	0	18	0	0	0	0	0	0
South Africa	0	0	0	0	0	128	0	0
Thailand[a]	428	0	0	0	0	0	3	0
Tunisia	0	9	0	0	0	0	0	0
Venezuela, R. B. de[a]	0	0	146	0	0	0	0	0
Total	2,556	4,927	8,501	10,212	5,821	7,831	3,231	2,140

trade-distorting domestic support. The percentage reduction for each country is shown in Column 7. The de minimis is reduced from 5(10) percent of the value of production to 2.5(5) percent of the value of production in developed (developing) countries. This second row can be compared to the third row, which for each country presents the latest notification to the WTO for each element of support.

That set of domestic support commitments would be binding for just ten countries or regions, namely Iceland, Norway, Switzerland, EU, Canada, the

TABLE 9.1 (Continued)

Tobacco	Live-stock	Beef	Pork	Poultry	Other meat	Milk	Non-product-specific	Others	Total
0	0	14	15	20	29	103	0	0	185
0	0	259	195	130	113	467	−9	0	1,359
5	0	383	458	187	0	651	0	0	2,110
0	0	1,503	2,370	0	0	1,270	0	143	6,690
1,027	0	13,649	0	0	0	6,064	0	0	49,934
0	0	0	0	52	0	205	0	0	257
0	5	0	109	0	0	361	0	0	639
924	0	0	0	0	0	4,660	0	0	16,862
0	0	0	0	0	0	0	0	0	0
0	0	0	0	0	0	40	0	0	40
80	0	0	0	0	0	0	0	0	80
0	0	0	0	0	0	0	0	0	83
10	0	0	0	0	0	0	0	0	10
0	0	0	0	0	0	0	0	0	7
0	0	0	0	0	0	0	2	0	2
0	0	0	0	0	0	0	0	0	1
0	0	0	0	0	0	0	0	0	1,319
0	0	0	0	0	0	0	0	0	401
0	0	0	0	0	0	0	0	0	18
0	0	0	0	0	0	0	0	0	128
0	0	0	0	0	0	0	0	0	431
0	0	0	0	0	0	15	0	0	24
0	0	0	0	0	0	0	65	0	211
2,047	5	15,807	3,147	389	143	13,836	57	143	80,792

Source: WTO 2004b; USDA 2004.
a. Switzerland's reported AMS is for the year 1998; Brazil's for 1997/8; Jordan's, 2002; Mexico's, 1998; Thailand's, 1998; and Venezuela's, 1998.

United States, Australia, Argentina, Republic of Korea, and Thailand (see table 9.5). Consider the examples of the United States and the European Union (table 9.6). In the United States, the new commitments for total AMS, non-product-specific de minimis, and total domestic support are binding, compared with the latest notification from the United States to the WTO. Of the notified total AMS to the

TABLE 9.2 Payments Not Included in Current Total AMS Due to de Minimis, 1999, by Country and Commodity (US$ millions)

Country	Rice	Wheat	Grains	Fruits & vegetables	Oil-seeds	Sugar	Fibers	Wine
Developed								
Iceland	0	0	0	0	0	0	0	0
Norway	0	0	0	0	0	0	0	0
Switzerland[a]	0	0	0	0	0	0	0	0
Japan	0	0	0	80	0	0	0	0
EU15	0	16	0	2	0	0	0	0
Israel	0	3	0	9	0	0	0	0
Canada	0	42	0	11	14	0	0	0
United States	0	0	0	14	2	0	0	0
New Zealand	0	0	0	0	0	0	0	0
Australia	0	1	0	0	0	0	0	0
Developing								
Argentina	0	0	0	0	0	0	0	0
Brazil	26	0	51	15	89	89	0	0
Bulgaria	0	7	0	1	1	0	0	0
Colombia	0	0	0	0	0	0	0	0
Costa Rica	0	0	0	0	0	0	0	0
Jordan[a]	0	0	0	0	0	0	0	0
Korea, Rep. of	0	0	5	46	5	0	0	0
Mexico[a]	0	0	0	0	0	0	0	0
Morocco	0	0	0	0	0	0	0	0
South Africa	0	0	0	0	0	0	0	0
Thailand[a]	0	0	0	0	0	0	0	0
Tunisia	0	0	0	0	0	0	0	0
Venezuela, R. B. de[a]	0	0	0	0	0	0	0	0
Total	26	69	56	177	111	89	0	0

WTO of $14.4 billion, $5.8 billion stems from market price support (MPS) through official administered prices. In the modeled domestic support reduction scenarios outlined in this chapter, we allow for the possibility of removing (vaporizing) the MPS from the current total AMS notification by simply abolishing the "official administered prices," without necessarily changing the trade policies

TABLE 9.2 (*Continued*)

Tobacco	Live stock	Beef	Pork	Poultry	Meat	Other Milk	Non-product-specific	Others	Total
0	0	0	0	0	0	0	0	0	0
0	0	0	0	0	0	0	0	0	0
0	0	0	0	0	0	0	0	0	0
0	0	0	0	13	0	0	199	0	292
0	0	0	0	0	0	0	303	0	322
0	0	1	0	7	0	0	60	7	88
0	0	45	0	0	0	0	0	2	115
0	13	0	0	0	0	0	7,406	0	7,435
0	0	0	0	0	0	0	0	0	0
0	0	0	7	0	4	0	3	0	14
0	0	0	0	0	0	0	0	0	0
0	0	0	0	0	0	0	105	34	409
0	0	0	0	0	0	0	18	0	27
0	0	0	0	0	0	0	0	0	0
0	0	0	0	0	0	0	0	0	0
0	28	0	0	0	0	0	5	0	34
0	0	2	9	0	0	0	344	2	414
0	0	0	0	0	0	0	0	0	0
0	0	0	0	0	0	0	0	0	0
0	0	0	0	0	0	0	1	0	1
0	0	0	0	0	0	0	0	0	0
0	0	0	0	0	0	0	7	0	7
0	0	0	0	0	0	0	0	0	0
0	41	49	15	21	4	0	8,451	45	9,156

Source: WTO 2004b; USDA 2004.

a. Switzerland's reported AMS is for the year 1998; Brazil's for 1997/8; Jordan's, 2002; Mexico's, 1998; Thailand's, 1998; and Venezuela's, 1998.

needed to maintain an administered price out of line with world market prices. But the measured MPS in the base period remains in the commitment limits, so that current AMS falls relative to the commitment level, without any reduction in actual protection.

TABLE 9.3 EU15 AMS Notifications, by Commodity, 2000/01 (€ millions)

Commodity	MPS	Non exempt direct payments	Other product specific Support	Equivalent measure of support	Non-product-specific	AMS	Commitment
Rice	393	0	0	0	0	393	
Wheat	1,932	8	0	0	0	2,271	
Grains	3,350	306	0	0	0	3,672	
Fruits & vegetables	0	746	0	8,796	0	9,537	
Oilseeds	2,070	0	0	103	0	2,173	
Sugar	5,797	12	0	0	0	5,809	
Fibers	0	0	0	888	0	888	
Wine	0	0	0	807	0	807	
Tobacco	0	964	0	0	0	964	
Livestock	0	0	0	0	0	0	
Beef	11,190	0	0	0	0	11,190	
Pork	0	10	0	0	0	0	
Poultry	0	0	0	0	0	0	
Other meat	0	0	0	0	0	0	
Milk	5,951	0	0	0	0	5,951	
Non-product-specific	0	0	0	0	538	0	
Total	30,684	2,047	0	10,593	538	43,654	67,159

Source: EU notifications to the WTO.

We also assume that all MPS ($5.8 billion) is abolished, which, together with reductions in non-MPS schemes, makes the United States able to meet its new commitments. The non-MPS payments are actual cash payments (subsidies) supporting farming, which amounted to $15.6 billion in the U.S. notification to the WTO for the year 2001. These payments would have to be reduced by $6.0 billion. Once this has been done, the United States would be within its new total domestic support limit of $9.6 billion when no support is given in the Blue Box. Overall, the United States would have to reduce its notified domestic support in the year 2001 by 55 percent, with MPS accounting for 27 percentage points of the reduction and a cut in cash payments (non-MPS) accounting for 28 points.

In table 9.6b, a similar story is shown for the European Union. The same method of reducing domestic support is implemented.[3] As can be seen, the EU

TABLE 9.4 United States AMS Notifications, by Commodity, 2001 (US$ millions)

Commodity	MPS	Non-exempt direct payments	Other product specific support	Equivalent measure of support	NPS	AMS	Commitment
Rice	0	728	35	0	0	763	
Wheat	0	177	13	0	0	0	
Grains	0	1,219	77	0	0	1,270	
Fruits & vegetables	0	0	0	0	0	0	
Oilseeds	311	3,533	160	0	0	4,004	
Sugar	1,032	27	2	0	0	1,061	
Fibers	0	2,723	87	0	0	2,810	
Wine	0	0	0	0	0	0	
Tobacco	0	6	−7	0	0	0	
Livestock	0	22	0	0	0	22	
Beef	0	0	0	0	0	0	
Pork	0	0	0	0	0	0	
Poultry	0	0	0	0	0	0	
Other meat	0	0	0	0	0	0	
Milk	4,483	0	0	0	0	4,483	
Non-product-specific	0	0	0	0	6,828	0	
Total	5,826	8,435	367	0	6,828	14,413	19,103

Source: U.S. notifications to the WTO.

has to reduce its reported total domestic support in the year 2001 by 62 percent, where 46 percentage points, or about three-fourths, of the reduction is accounted for by the abolition of MPS and 16 percentage points by reduced cash payments (Blue Box subsidies) to farming.[4]

Recent Policy Reforms and Implications for Domestic Support

Since the mid-1980s, most Organisation for Economic Co-operation and Development (OECD) countries have made some reforms to their agricultural policies. Many economists argue that the OECD Trade Mandate of 1982 and the launch of the Uruguay Round negotiations in 1986 triggered this reform process.

TABLE 9.5 Domestic Support Base Levels, New Commitments, and Latest WTO Notifications

Country		Currency	Total AMS (1)	de minimis (2)
Developed				
Iceland	Base commitment	ISK millions	130	6
	New commitment		33	2.5%
	Notif. 2000		117	0
Norway	Base commitment	NKr millions	11,449	884
	New commitment		2,862	2.5%
	Notif. 2001		10,700	0
Switzerland & Liechtenstein	Base commitment	Sw F millions	4,257	365
	New commitment		1,064	2.5%
	Notif. 1998		3,273	0
Japan	Base commitment	€ billions	3,973	452
	New commitment		993	2.5%
	Notif. 2000		709	32
EU15	Base commitment	€ millions	67,159	12,097
	New commitment		16,790	2.5%
	Notif. 2000/01		43,654	561
Canada	Base commitment	Can$ millions	4,301	1,537
	New commitment		1,075	2.5%
	Notif. 1999		939	1,102
United States	Base commitment	US$ millions	19,103	9,656
	New commitment		4,776	2.5%
	Notif. 2001		14,413	7,045
New Zealand	Base Commitment	$NZ millions	288	669
	New Commitment		115	2.5%
	Notif. 2001		0	0
Australia	Base commitment	$A millions	472	1,747
	New commitment		189	2.5%
	Notif. 2002/03		213	20

TABLE 9.5 *(Continued)*

Blue Box (3)	Total (4) = (1 + 2 + 3)	Production value (5)	Total as % of product value (6) = (4/5)	% Total reduction (7)
15	150	114	132	75
6	38			
0	117			
7,880	20,213	17,682	114	75
884	5,053			
7,240	17,940			
365	4,987	7,304	68	75
365	1,247			
0	3,273			
452	4,878	9,047	54	75
452	1,219			
93	833			
21,521	100,777	241,943	42	75
12,097	25,194			
22,223	66,438			
1,537	7,375	30,737	24	75
1,537	1,844			
0	2,041			
9,656	38,416	193,129	20	75
9,656	9,604			
0	21,458			
669	1,626	13,385	12	60
669	651			
0	0			
1,747	3,965	34,934	11	60
1,747	1,586			
0	233			

TABLE 9.5 Domestic Support Base Levels, New Commitments, and Latest WTO Notifications (*Continued*)

Country		Currency	Total AMS (1)	de minimis (2)
Developing				
Argentina	Base commitment	US$ thousands	75,021	n.a.
	New commitment		45,013	
	Notif. 2000/01		79,600	0
Brazil	Base commitment	US$ thousands	912,105	n.a.
	New commitment		547,263	
	Notif. 1997/98		82,820	408,714
Bulgaria	Base commitment	€ millions	520	359
	New commitment		312	5%
	Notif. 2001		26	9
Colombia	Base commitment	US$ thousands	344,733	n.a.
	New commitment		206,840	
	Notif. 1999		6,805	0
Costa Rica	Base commitment	US$ thousands	15,945	n.a.
	New commitment		9,567	
	Notif. 1999		1,595	0
Israel	Base commitment	US$ thousands	568,980	327,239
	New commitment		341,388	5.0%
	Notif. 2002		248,155	27,131
Jordan	Base commitment	JD thousands	1,334	55,533
	New commitment		800,	5.0%
	Notif. 2002		743	10,775
Korea, Rep. of	Base commitment	W billions	1,490	3,214
	New commitment	894	5.0%	
	Notif. 2000	1,691	526	
Mexico	Base commitment	1991 Mex$ millions	25,161	29,582
	New commitment		15,097	5.0%
	Notif. 1998		3,799	0
Morocco	Base commitment	DH millions	685	n.a.
	New commitment		411	
	Notif. 2001		300	0

Consequences of Reducing Limits on AMS

TABLE 9.5 (*Continued*)

Blue Box (3)	Total (4) = (1 + 2 + 3)	Production value (5)	Total as % of product value (6) = (4/5)	% Total reduction (7)
n.a.	n.a.	n.a.	n.a.	40
0	79,600			
n.a.	n.a.	n.a.	n.a.	40
	491,534			
180	1,059	3,594	29	40
180	635			
0	35			
n.a.	n.a.	n.a.	n.a.	40
0	6,805			
n.a.	n.a.	n.a.	n.a.	40
0	1,595			
163,620	1,059,839	3,272,391	32	40
163,620	635,903			
0	275,286			
27,767	84,634	555,333	15	40
27,767	50,780			
	11,518			
1,607	6,311	32,137	20	40
1,607	3,786			
0	2,217			
14,791	69,534	295,821	24	40
14,791	41,721			
0	3,799			
n.a.	n.a.	n.a.	n.a.	40
0		300		

TABLE 9.5 Domestic Support Base Levels, New Commitments, and Latest WTO Notifications (*Continued*)

Country		Currency	Total AMS (1)	de minimis (2)
Papua New Guinea	Base commitment New commitment Notif. not available	US$ millions	33 20	n.a.
South Africa	Base commitment New commitment Notif. 2002	R millions	2,015 1,209 0	4,665 5% 0
Taiwan (China)	Base commitment New commitment Notif. not available	NT$ millions	14,165 8,499	n.a.
Thailand	Base commitment New commitment Notif. 1998	B millions	19,028 11,417 16,402	n.a. 0
Tunisia	Base commitment New commitment Notif. 2000	TD millions	59 35 0	374 5% 26
Venezuela, R.B. de	Base commitment New commitment Notif. 1998	US$ thousands	1,130,667 678,400 210,578	n.a. 0

Others argue that the reform process in the European Union and the United States has been driven mainly by domestic rather than international politics (Paarlberg 1996). During the Uruguay Round negotiations, the EU implemented the MacSharry Reform of the Common Agricultural Policy (CAP) and the United States implemented new agricultural policies enacted in 1990. Both sets of legislation introduced more market-oriented policies and helped the multilateral agreement on its way and, in turn, the URAA helped reinforce the market policies. Since the conclusion of the URAA in late 1993 and the official launch of the Doha Round, both the EU and the United States have enacted further agricultural policy legislation.

In the case of the EU, the Agenda 2000 reform was adopted in 2000 and a more far-reaching Midterm Review (MTR) reform will be implemented across Europe in 2005 (Jensen and Frandsen 2003). The Agenda 2000 reform made further

TABLE 9.5 (*Continued*)

Blue Box (3)	Total (4) = (1 + 2 + 3)	Production value (5)	Total as % of product value (6) = (4/5)	% Total reduction (7)
n.a.	n.a.	n.a.	n.a.	40
2,333	9,013	46,655	19	40
2,333	5,408			
0	0			
n.a.	n.a.	n.a.	n.a.	40
n.a.	n.a.	n.a.	n.a.	40
0		16,402		
187	620	3,738	17	40
187	372			
0	26			
n.a.	n.a.	n.a.	n.a.	40
0	210,578			

Source: WTO (2004b); OECD (2003); authors' assumptions.

Note: n. a. = not applicable. For the base commitment, the total AMS (1) base level values are taken from the Uruguay Round's final bound AMS levels. The permitted de minimis (2) payments included in the overall base level of trade-distorting domestic support are calculated as 5/10 percent of the total value of agricultural production as defined by an average production value in a given reference period (column 5). Blue Box (3) payments included in the total base level of all trade-distorting support is the higher of existing Blue Box payments during the 1995–2000 period or 5 percent of the value of agricultural production (column 5). The total value (column 4) of overall base level of support is column (1) + (2) + (3). The reference value of agricultural production (5) in OECD countries is calculated as the average production value in the period 1999–2002 using values found in the PSE tables. For other countries, an average of the reported total value of agricultural production found in the WTO notifications has been used where available. In column 6, the total value of the overall base level of all trade-distorting domestic support is calculated as a percentage of the value of agricultural production with Iceland having the largest percentage value and Australia the lowest among developed countries. In column 7, the assumed reduction commitments for the overall base level of domestic support is specified, where developing countries with the highest level of possible trade-distorting domestic support as defined in column 6 making the largest reductions.

For new commitments, the total AMS is reduced by the same reduction commitment as used to reduce the overall base level of domestic support. The permitted de minimis value of domestic support is reduced from 5/10 percent of agricultural production value, to 2.5/5 percent. Blue Box payments are limited to 5 percent of the agricultural production value found in column (5). The total overall base level of domestic support is reduced by the percentage found in column (7).

The notification date is the latest notification to the WTO.

TABLE 9.6 Domestic Support Reductions Needed

(a) In the United States (US$ millions)

	AMS	de minimis Non-product-specific	de minimis Product specific	Blue Box	Total domestic support	Percent reduction in support
Base commitment	19,103	9,656	0	9,656	38,415	
New commitment	4,776	4,828	0	9,656	9,604	
Notif. 2001	14,413	6,828	217	0	21,458	
of which MPS	5,826					
Reductions						
MPS	−5,826	0	0	0	−5,826	−27.2
Non-MPS	−3,822	−2,000	−206	0	−6,028	−28.1
New domestic support	4,765	4,828	11	0	9,604	−55.2

(b) In the European Union (€ millions)

	AMS	de minimis Non-product-specific	de minimis Product specific	Blue Box	Total domestic support	Percent reduction in support
Base commitment	67,159	12,097	0	21,521	100,777	
New commitment	16,790	6,049	0	12,097	25,194	
Notif. 2000/01	43,654	538	40	22,223	66,455	
of which MPS	30,684					
Reductions						
MPS	−30,684	0	0	0	−30,684	−46.2
Non-MPS	0	0	−17	−10,560	−10,577	−15.9
New domestic support	12,970	538	23	11,663	25,194	−62.1

Source: WTO notifications and authors' assumptions.

reductions in some of the administrative prices in key market organizations under the CAP. In contrast with the MacSharry Reform, these price cuts were only partly replaced by compensatory payments based on areas planted or numbers of livestock. The price support element of the CAP is part of the Amber Box and hence of AMS.

TABLE 9.7 Agenda 2000 and MTR Intervention Price Reduction (€ per metric ton)

Commodity	Notification 2000/01 administered price	New administered price
Cereals	110.25	101.3
Rice	298.40	150.0
Skimmed milk powder	2,055.20	1,747.0
Butter	3,282.00	2,464.0
Beef	3,242.00	2,224.0[a]
Sugar	631.90	385.5[a]

Source: European Commission 2005, 2003a, 2003b, 2003c, 1999.

a. The Agenda 2000 reform of the CAP and the proposed sugar reform abolish the intervention prices for beef and sugar, respectively. Until now, those prices had been used in the calculation of MPS in the EU's notifications to the WTO. Instead the EU introduces a basic price of 2,224 € per metric ton of beef and a reference price for sugar of 385.5 € per metric ton. The new basic and reference prices act as trigger level for private storage as well as setting the level of border protection in the EU. In the calculation made in this chapter, it is assumed that the EU will notify these prices as new administered prices and use them in the calculation of the MPS component of the AMS.

The compensatory payments are paid to farmers in combination with set-aside programs and are therefore allocated to the Blue Box. The MTR reform introduces decoupled payments. The idea is to change both the hectare and animal premiums into payments based on historical criteria. EU member countries can choose to keep a small amount of the production-coupled premiums, and the European Commission expects about 10 percent of payments to remain coupled to production. This policy change will probably mean that most of the support now placed in the Blue Box will be moved to the Green Box. Nevertheless, the EU will still need the Blue Box for future reform scenarios. The MTR reform introduces only minor changes in the market price support regimes.

The EU sugar regime has not yet been reformed, but the European Commission has put forward a rather serious reform plan. The administrative sugar price would be reduced by 39 percent over a few years. Sugar beet growers would be partly compensated by decoupled payments. Table 9.7 sums up the reductions in administrative prices included in Agenda 2000, the MTR reform, and the commission proposal. Table 9.8 shows what the total AMS would be if the commission's price reductions are implemented, and compares that AMS with the new possible commitment presented in table 9.5a. The bottom line is that the EU's total AMS is reduced from €44 billion to €29 billion, €11.9 billion above the calculated new commitment of €16.8 billion.

TABLE 9.8 EU15 AMS Adjusted for Intervention Price Changes (€ millions)

Commodity	MPS	Non-exempt direct payments	Other product specific support	Equivalent measure of support	Non-product-specific	AMS	New commitment
Rice	17	0	0	0	0	17	
Wheat	997	8	0	0	0	1,415	
Grains	2,388	306	0	0	0	2,771	
Fruits & vegetables	0	746	0	8,796	0	9,537	
Oilseeds	2,070	0	0	103	0	2,173	
Sugar	2,372	12	0	0	0	2,372	
Fibers	0	0	0	888	0	888	
Wine	0	0	0	807	0	807	
Tobacco	0	964	0	0	0	964	
Livestock	0	0	0	0	0	0	
Beef	3,657	0	0	0	0	3,657	
Pork	0	10	0	0	0	0	
Poultry	0	0	0	0	0	0	
Other meat	0	0	0	0	0	0	
Milk	4,058	0	0	0	0	4,058	
Non-product-specific	0	0	0	0	538	0	
Total	15,559	2,047	0	10,593	538	28,659	16,790

Source: EU WTO notification and authors' assumptions.
Note: Intervention price changes are a result of the Agenda 2000, the MTR reform, and the proposed sugar reform of the Common Agricultural Policy in the EU.

In the United States, the 1996 farm bill fundamentally changed the traditional approach to agricultural policy to one of market reliance. Supply management in most areas was abolished, and deficiency payment programs were converted to decoupled payments based on historical production data. The income security net also was lowered. The loan rate and hence loan deficiency payments were reduced. The consequences for the commitments under the WTO were lower Amber Box support and a move of all Blue Box support to the Green Box. For political reasons the United States then argued for complete abolition of the Blue Box, but soon thereafter things changed for the worse: market prices fell, and bad weather across the country squeezed farm incomes. The political response was to provide ad hoc

TABLE 9.9 U.S. AMS Adjusted for Administered Dairy Price and Market Loss Assistance Payments (US$ millions)

Commodity	MPS	Non-exempt direct payments	Other product specific support	Equivalent measure of support	Non-product-specific	AMS	New commitment
Rice	0	728	35	0	0	763	
Wheat	0	177	13	0	0	189	
Grains	0	1,219	77	0	0	1,286	
Fruits & vegetables	0	0	0	0	0	0	
Oilseeds	311	3,533	160	0	0	4,004	
Sugar	1,032	27	2	0	0	1,061	
Fibers	0	2,723	87	0	0	2,810	
Wine	0	0	0	0	0	0	
Tobacco	0	6	−7	0	0	0	
Livestock	0	22	0	0	0	22	
Beef	0	0	0	0	0	0	
Pork	0	0	0	0	0	0	
Poultry	0	0	0	0	0	0	
Other meat	0	0	0	0	0	0	
Milk	0	0	0	0	0	0	
Non-product-specific	0	0	0	0	2,188	0	
Total	1,342	8,435	367	0	2,188	10,136	4,776

Source: U.S. WTO notification and authors' assumptions.

payments year after year, which brought the total AMS back up to its former levels. The 2002 farm bill introduced a new policy instrument, which institutionalized the former ad hoc arrangements as countercyclical payments that are non-product-specific and partly decoupled.

Table 9.9 incorporates legislation already implemented and possible future policy changes together with the new commitments from table 9.5a. The new commitment equals a total AMS binding of $4.8 billion. The most likely result in the Doha negotiations will be that the ad hoc payments, notified in 2001 as $4.0 billion, will be moved to the Blue Box. Another issue, touched on by Sumner (2003), relates to dairy policy. His argument is that the notified MPS amounting to $4.4 billion could be removed from AMS without affecting U.S. farmers. The high domestic milk price is supported by border measures, with the administered market price playing little independent role. The current small support element could then be changed to a more or less decoupled direct payment (Sumner 2003). After these changes, the new total AMS is $10.1 billion—$5.3 billion short of the calculated new commitments.

Conclusions

The most important messages from this chapter are that serious reductions are needed in both the bound AMS and de minimis support, tiered reductions are needed to level the playing field, and future commitments need to be placed not only in the Amber Box but also in the Blue Box. The July Framework Agreement provides a basis to develop a reduction scenario for countries that hold commitments, and that scenario suggests that Australia, Argentina, Canada, the EU, Iceland, Korea, Norway, Switzerland, Thailand, and the United States are the members most likely to need to reduce support. More specifically, the scenario indicates that the EU15 (not counting its 10 new members) needs to make serious reductions in both Amber and Blue Box support. The United States needs to make serious reductions in its Amber Box and de minimis support.

A country's position in the Doha negotiations necessarily reflects domestic politics, both current and prospective. As under the Uruguay Round negotiations, the direction of causality is not obvious: domestic politics influence the negotiations and the negotiations influence domestic politics. A comparison of recent agricultural policy reforms in the EU and the United States gives some insight. In the case of the EU, we looked at the effects of Agenda 2000, the Midterm Review reform and the proposed sugar reform; in the United States, we looked at the farm bills of 1996 and 2002 and a possible milk policy reform.

Finally, two important assumptions behind this analysis need some discussion. First, further negotiations may alter the details of the framework agreement on which this analysis is based. For example, the potential loopholes regarding base periods, reference periods, and specific percentages of reduction will be decided later. Second, AMS is not the complete story on domestic support. AMS is politically defined, and it excludes some important current support measures because it uses historical prices fixed by the URAA and because it uses administrative prices as the indicator of whether the particular support policy will be included in the measure at all. A discussion to broaden the concept of AMS is thus needed.

TABLE 9A.1 Domestic Support Reductions for Selected Countries

(a) Australia ($A millions)

	AMS	de minimis Non-product-specific	de minimis Product specific	Blue Box	Total domestic support	Percent reduction in support
Base commitment	472	1,747	0	1,747	3,965	
New commitment	189	874	0	1,747	1,586	
Notif. 2002/3	213	1	19	0	233	
of which MPS	0					
Reductions						
MPS	0				0	0.0
Non-MPS[a]	−24	0	0	0	−24	
New domestic support	189	1	19	0	209	−10.4

(b) Canada (Can$ millions)

	AMS	de minimis Non-product-specific	de minimis Product specific	Blue Box	Total domestic support	Percent reduction in support
Base commitment	4,301	1,537	0	1,537	7,375	
New commitment	1,075	769	0	1,537	1,844	
Notif. 1999	939	1,102	0	0	2,041	
of which MPS	440					
Reductions						
MPS	−197				−197	−9.7
Non-MPS[b]	334	−334	0	0	0	0.0
New domestic support	1,075	769	0	0	1,844	−9.7

a. In Australia $A203 million is given as dairy structural adjustment programs in the 2002 (notification by Australia to the WTO), which would have to be reduced to meet the new AMS commitment by $A24 million.

b. Reducing non-product-specific de minimis from 5 percent to 2.5 percent of the value of agricultural production moves Can$334 million back into the AMS calculation. To keep Canada's domestic support below its new commitments, MPS is reduced by Can$197 million.

TABLE 9A.1 Domestic Support Reductions for Selected Countries (Continued)

(c) Norway (NKr millions)						
		de minimis				
	AMS	Non-product-specific	Product specific	Blue Box[c]	Total domestic support	Percent reduction in support
Base commitment	11,449	884	0	7,880	20,213	
New commitment	2,862	442	0	3,940	5,053	
Notif. 2002/3	10,700	0	0	7,240	17,940	
of which MPS	10,866					
Reductions						
MPS	−9,587				−9,587	−53.4
Non-MPS	0	0	0	−3,300	−3,300	−18.4
New domestic support	2,862	0	0	3,940	5,053	71.8
(d) Iceland (ISK millions)						
		de minimis				
	AMS	Non-product-specific	Product specific	Blue Box	Total domestic support	Percent reduction in support
Base commitment	130	6	0	15	150	
New commitment	33	3	0	6	38	
Notif. 2000	117	0	0	0	117	
of which MPS	83					
Reductions						
MPS	−83				−83	−70.9
Non-MPS	−1	0	0	0	−1	−0.9
New domestic support	33	0	0	0	33	−71.8

c. Because Norway has a high proportion of its support in the Blue Box, its reduction commitment is reduced to a 50 percent reduction of its base commitment of NKr 7,880 million compared with the 5 percent rule, where Norway would have to reduce its Blue Box payments to NKr 884 million.

TABLE 9A.1 (*Continued*)

(e) Switzerland (Sw F millions)

		de minimis				
	AMS	Non-product-specific	Product specific	Blue Box	Total domestic support	Percent reduction in support
Base commitment	4,257	365	0	365	4,987	
New commitment	1,064	183	0	365	1,247	
Notif. 1998	3,273	0	0	0	3,273	
of which MPS	3,138					
Reductions						
MPS	−2,209				−2,209	−67.5
Non-MPS	0	0	0	0	0	0.0
New domestic support	1,064	0	0	0	1,064	−67.5

(f) Argentina (US$ millions)

		de minimis				
	AMS	Non-product-specific	Product specific	Blue Box	Total domestic support	Percent reduction in support
Base commitment	75,021	—	0	—	—	
New commitment	45,013	—	0	—	—	
Notif. 1998	79.600	0	0	0	79.600	
of which applied administered price support	79,600					
Reductions						
MPS	−34,587				−34,587	−43.5
Non-MPS[d]	0	0	0	0	0	0.0
New domestic support	45,013	0	0	0	45,013	−43.5

d. The reported domestic support in Argentina is support to tobacco, through an applied administered price, which would have to be reduced by 43.5 percent.

TABLE 9A.1 Domestic Support Reductions for Selected Countries (*Continued*)

(g) Republic of Korea (W billions)

	AMS	de minimis Non-product-specific	de minimis Product specific	Blue Box	Total domestic support	Percent reduction in support
Base commitment	1,490	3,214	0	1,607	6,311	
New commitment	894	1,607	0	1,607	3,786	
Notif. 1998[e]	1,691	413	113	0	2,217	
of which MPS	1,691					
Reductions						
MPS	−809		−35		−844	−38.0
Non-MPS[e]	+12	0	−12	0	0	0.0
New domestic support	894	413	66	0	1,373	−38.0

(h) Thailand (B millions)

	AMS	de minimis Non-product-specific	de minimis Product specific	Blue Box	Total domestic support	Percent reduction in support
Base commitment	19,028	—	0	—	—	
New commitment	11,417	—	0	—	—	
Notif. 1998[f]	16,402	0	0	0	16,402	
of which MPS	0					
Reductions						
MPS	0					0.0
Non-MPS[f]	−4,985	0	0	0	−4,985	30.4
New domestic support	11,417	0	0	0	11,417	30.4

Source: WTO notifications and authors' assumptions.

Note: — = not available.

e. The reported domestic support in the Republic of Korea is mainly for rice (W 1,647 billion), through an applied administered price (MPS).

f. The reported domestic support in Thailand is mainly for rice (B 16,282 million). The support is mainly a paddy pledging scheme and soft loan measure.

Notes

1. See chapter 8 for a discussion of de minimis measures.
2. In developed countries, the 75 percent reduction in total AMS and total trade-distorting support is implemented in countries where the total value of possible trade-distorting support as a percent of the value of agricultural production is equal to or greater than 20 percent.
3. Appendix table 9.A1 shows the reductions in domestic support in Iceland, Norway, Switzerland, Canada, Australia, Argentina, Korea, and Thailand.
4. It is very doubtful that official administrative prices would be abolished in the EU. Since the establishment of the Common Agricultural Policy in 1960, the backbone of the system has been various market organizations. The core of this market price support has always been an administrative price, and this is still true for the CAP today. The Midterm Review reform barely touched on the level of market price support.

References

Anderson, K., W. Martin, and D. van der Mensbrugghe. 2006. "Market and Welfare Implications of Doha Reform Scenarios." In *Agricultural Trade Reform and the Doha Development Agenda*, ed. K. Anderson and W. Martin. Basingstoke, U. K.: Palgrave Macmillan; Washington, DC: World Bank.

European Commission. 1999. Council Regulation (EC) No. 1254/1999 of 17 May, on the Common Organization of the Market in Beef and Veal. European Commission, Brussels.

———. 2003a. Council Regulation (EC) No. 1787/2003 of 29 September, on the Common Organization of the Market in Milk and Milk products. European Commission, Brussels.

———. 2003b. Council Regulation (EC) No. 1785/2003 of 29 September, on the Common Organization of the Market of Rice. European Commission, Brussels.

———. 2003c. Council Regulation (EC) No. 1784/2003 of 29 September, on the Common Organization of the Market in Cereal. European Commission, Brussels.

———. 2005. "Proposal for a Council Regulation on the Common Organization of the Market in the Sugar Sector." COM (2005) 263 final. European Commission, Brussels.

Jensen, H. G., and S. E. Frandsen. 2003. "Impacts of the Eastern European Accession and the 2003 Reform of the CAP: Consequences for Individual Member Countries." Working Paper 11, Danish Institute of Food Economics, Copenhagen.

OECD (Organisation for Economic Co-operation and Development). 2001. *The Uruguay Round Agreement on Agriculture: An Evaluation of its Implementation in OECD Countries*. Paris: OECD.

OECD. 2003. *OECD Agricultural Databases*, 2003 ed. Paris: OECD.

Paarlberg, R. L. 1996. "The Uruguay Round and Agriculture: International Path to Domestic Policy Reform?" Paper 96-1, Weatherhead Center for International Affairs, Harvard University, Cambridge, MA. January 30.

Sumner, D. A. 2003. "Implications of the US Farm Bill of 2002 for Agricultural Trade and Trade Negotiations." *Australian Journal of Agricultural and Resource Economics* 46(3): 99–122.

USDA (United States Department of Agriculture), Economic Research Service. 2004. Data on WTO Domestic Support Notifications. http://www.ers.usda.gov/db/Wto/AMS_database/ Default.asp?ERSTab=3&view=DS6 (accessed June 2005).

WTO (World Trade Organization). 2004a. "Doha Work Programme, Decision Adopted by the General Council on 1 August 2004." Report of the General Council, WT/L/579, August 2. http://www.wto.org/english/tratop_e/dda_e/ddadraft_31jul04_e.pdf (accessed October 2004).

———. 2004b. WTO Notifications. http://docsonline.wto.org/gen_home.asp?language=1&_=1 (accessed August 2004).

Zobbe, H. 2003. "The Economic and Historical Foundation of Agricultural Policy in Europe and the United States." Ph.D. thesis, Royal Veterinary and Agricultural University, Copenhagen.

10

REDUCING COTTON SUBSIDIES: THE DDA COTTON INITIATIVE

Daniel A. Sumner[*]

The current round of World Trade Organization (WTO) negotiations differs in several ways from the previous half-century of multilateral negotiations under the General Agreement on Tariffs and Trade (GATT). It is not just that there is now a formal organization to convene the talks, or that the talks are not called a "round" (as in "Uruguay Round" or "Kennedy Round") but the Doha Development Agenda (DDA). The most important differences in the current set of negotiations are the shifts in attention toward developing countries and even some of the least developed countries (LDCs). Cotton subsidy issues have been near the center of both these changes.

That the DDA was delayed and that one significant source of the roadblock was agriculture was not surprising. The same delays plagued the GATT Uruguay Round negotiations that dragged on for seven years. This time, however, the important division is not mainly between Japan and the European Union on one side and the United States and its Cairns Group allies on the other. In the DDA, the split has been between the rich agricultural subsidizers, especially the United States and the European Union, and large developing countries, led by Brazil. Part of Brazil's influence and leadership has resulted from its successful WTO challenges of cotton policies in the United States and sugar export subsidies in the European Union. Furthermore, LDCs, led by four West and Central African cotton exporters with

---

[*]The author was a consultant to the Brazilian government in the WTO dispute settlement case against the U.S. cotton subsidy regime. He is grateful for comments and suggestions from Henrich Brunke, Christian Lau, Kym Anderson, John Baffes, Will Martin, Nicolas Imboden, and Tim Josling.

271

their "cotton initiative," have also garnered much attention and caused the Doha negotiations to focus on links between farm subsidies in rich countries and economic development of agriculture in poor countries.

Benin, Burkina Faso, Chad, and Mali, the countries that proposed the cotton initiative, have tiny economies and no particular clout in international relations or in the international economy. Nonetheless, their proposal for accelerated elimination of trade-distorting cotton subsidies and financial compensation for losses while subsidies are being eliminated has been included as a central issue in the WTO negotiations. (The WTO summarizes the issue and provides access to documents at its Web site; WTO 2005a.)

Why Cotton?

Many countries have specific products, services, or issues that are of particular concern in their trade relationships. These seldom are proposed as separate initiatives in trade negotiations. When they are proposed, such initiatives seldom get much attention. The experience of the cotton initiative in the DDA has been different. It has been embraced at the highest levels of the WTO and has been accorded unprecedented global attention. All this for a farm commodity with total global export value of less than $10 billion, only a small percentage of the value of world agricultural exports, and a truly tiny fraction of the value of global trade in goods.

The cotton issue caught the attention of world leaders and WTO negotiators for several reasons. First, heads of state of several very poor nations have championed the issue. They flagged the issue as vital to their overall national interests and the very survival of large segments of their populations.

Second, their arguments were more than political rhetoric. Cotton is a very important tradable commodity for the countries that have sponsored the initiative. Cotton comprises approximately 30 percent of total exports of the four West African nations that proposed the initiative and accounts for a significant share of rural incomes of millions of poor farmers in that region (Minot and Daniels 2001).

Third, cotton subsidy policy is concentrated in a few rich countries. Developing countries provide little domestic support, but they do apply agricultural border barriers. Therefore, a sector initiative that focuses on subsidies may garner broad support among developing countries. The EU provides the highest per unit support, but cotton is a minor crop even in the two EU countries, Greece and Spain, that produce cotton. The United States is the only WTO member that highly subsidizes cotton and that plays a significant role in the global cotton market.

Fourth, cotton subsidies have little second-round benefit for poor countries. Sugar and rice are also heavily subsidized and protected and contribute to the incomes of many of the world's poor. Widespread import barriers restrict sugar and rice trade, however. Unlike rice, where poor nonfarm consumers likely gain from lower world prices, the rich-country cotton subsidies likely have little benefit for any of the poor in poor countries. And, unlike sugar, for which some poor countries get valuable preferential access to rich-country markets, there are no poor-country cotton producers that gain from the rich-country cotton subsidies.

Finally, the cotton cause was adopted as the lead issue by global nongovernmental organizations, especially IDEAS in Switzerland, which helped develop the initiative (Baffes 2005), and Oxfam, which developed some of the most dramatic evidence and publicized the issue effectively in Europe and North America (Oxfam 2002, 2004).

These reasons may help explain why the cotton initiative got as much attention as it did. However, none of this discussion suggests that removing cotton subsidies alone, while leaving other subsidies and trade barriers in place, would improve substantially the lot of the world's poor overall, or that it is an optimal negotiating strategy for LDCs.

The DDA Cotton Initiative: Original Content and Negotiating Developments

Suggestions for separate negotiating initiatives for specific products or services sometimes have been raised in the GATT/WTO. Historically, broad areas such as textiles and agriculture have been separated because of special rules and exceptions and, typically, a *reduced* pace of liberalization. Those wishing faster or more complete liberalization for some product groupings have sometimes suggested that accelerated tariff cuts be agreed on a sectorwide basis. These suggestions have not survived to the final agreements, however. For example, in the Uruguay Round negotiations, suggestions for zero-for-zero tariffs for oilseeds were discussed but not implemented. Currently U.S. industry interests are urging elimination of market access restrictions for all fruits and vegetables. This sectorwide initiative has received little attention.

The proposed cotton sector initiative for the Doha negotiations is unique in its combination of elements. It was proposed at the highest political level mainly to deal with domestic support policies of one major export competitor. The proposing nations also suggested compensation for commercial losses caused by lowered prices resulting from the offending subsidies. In the DDA negotiations in Cancún, the proposed initiative was the subject of extensive media coverage, and the WTO director general led the discussions (WTO 2003a).

The four African cotton-exporting nations initially submitted their cotton initiative in a letter to the director general on April 30, 2003, and presented the initiative to the WTO Trade Negotiating Committee on June 10, 2003 (WT0 2003b). President Blaise Compaore of Burkina Faso stated the objectives and motivation of the four countries in a speech to that committee on the same day (WTO 2003c). He urged that "a mechanism be set up to progressively reduce support to cotton production and export, with a view to fully suppressing all cotton subsidies at a defined deadline." Moreover, he asked that "as an immediate and transitory measure in favor of least developed countries, a mechanism be adopted to compensate their farmers for the revenue losses incurred because of cotton subsidies." And to emphasize the importance of the initiative, he further stated, "African countries share the opinion that a satisfactory settlement for the cotton subsidy issue is both a must for the current negotiation round and a test that will allow member States to prove their sincerity behind the commitments taken at Doha."

Under the proposal, compensation is to be paid to cotton growers or their local organizations. The specific compensation proposal has four elements. First, it asks that the amount of the proposed compensation be calculated on the basis of cotton subsidies and market conditions during the period 1999 though 2002. The amount of $250 million a year is highlighted in the proposal, based on data from the International Cotton Advisory Committee (ICAC 2002) and the work of Goreux (2003). Second, compensation would be reduced proportionately as subsidies are phased down on the path toward elimination. Third, responsibility for compensation payments would be allocated on the basis of each member's share of total cotton subsidies, and fourth, payments would be allocated to beneficiary LDC countries based on their share of cotton production.

The cotton initiative began receiving serious consideration as soon as it was proposed. The failure of the Cancún ministerial to reach a framework agreement was attributed in part to the failure to address the cotton initiative adequately. For that reason, the December 2003 meeting of the General Council of the WTO devoted considerable attention to the cotton initiative and reported enough progress to allow the general Doha negotiation to proceed.

The August 2004 WTO decision of the General Council that set the framework for the final stage of negotiations (known as the July Framework Agreement) dealt with the cotton initiative in the main text in paragraph 1(b) (WTO 2004a). It states that the trade-related aspects of the initiative will be dealt with in the context of the agricultural negotiations. The development (or compensation) aspects of the initiative are being dealt with by a separate WTO committee in a process that includes the World Bank and the Food and Agriculture Organization of the United Nations (FAO), among other institutions. Thus, while they continue to be linked in the rhetoric, the proposed subsidy reductions and the proposed development aid that now encompass the "compensation" part of the cotton initiative are being pursued separately.

In Annex 1 of WTO (2004a), where the framework for the agricultural negotiations is laid out, the cotton initiative is given considerable additional discussion beginning in paragraph 4, which is worth listing in full:

> The General Council recognizes the importance of cotton for a certain number of countries and its vital importance for developing countries, especially LDCs. It will be addressed ambitiously, expeditiously, and specifically, within the agriculture negotiations. The provisions of this framework provide a basis for this approach, as does the sectoral initiative on cotton. The Special Session of the Committee on Agriculture shall ensure appropriate prioritization of the cotton issue independently from other sectoral initiatives. A subcommittee on cotton will meet periodically and report to the Special Session of the Committee on Agriculture to review progress. Work shall encompass all trade-distorting policies affecting the sector in all three pillars of market access, domestic support, and export competition, as specified in the Doha text and this Framework text.

Surrounded by nice rhetoric, two key points are contained in this statement. First, the reduction of cotton subsidies will not be negotiated on a fast track separate from the rest of the Doha negotiations. Instead cotton subsidy reductions will be negotiated as a part of the overall agriculture agreement. Second, negotiating the reduction of cotton subsidy rates as a part of the agricultural agreement does not preclude applying higher reduction rates or other special provisions to cotton. This point is made implicitly by noting that the "Special Session of the Committee on Agriculture shall ensure appropriate prioritization of the cotton issue independently from other sectoral initiatives."

Cotton Production and Trade

To appreciate the economic context of the cotton initiative, it is important to have some background on global cotton production, consumption, and trade. Baffes (2005) provides a very useful interpretive summary of the global cotton situation and outlook. For most of the past 15 years, China has produced about 25 percent of the world total. Currently, the United States accounts for another 20 percent of world production, as do India and Pakistan together. China, India, and Pakistan are such major cotton textile-processing centers that all are net importers of cotton. The United States and the countries of West and Central Africa (taken together) are the major exporters, along with Uzbekistan and to a lesser degree Australia. Europe is a minor cotton producer (represented mainly by Greece and Turkey) and a large net importer.

Cotton textile manufacturing has shifted increasingly to developing countries as the textile trade has been liberalized. About two-thirds of cotton produced in the United States is now exported and U.S. exports account for about 40 percent of world exports. The United States cotton-milling industry continues to shrink. This means an increasing share of cotton production in the United States is exported and re-imported as textile products. The baselines by the Food and Agricultural Policy Research Institute (FAPRI 2004) and U.S. Agriculture Department's Economic Research Service (ERS 2004) provide much more detail on the outlook for global cotton production and trade if no change is made in the current policy path.

Global Cotton Subsidies and Protection

Cotton import tariffs are applied mainly in cotton-exporting countries and are typically in the range of 10 percent. Some countries also impose import tariff rate quotas, with very high tariffs for above-quota quantities, but these quotas are not filled and the prohibitive tariffs are not applied. For example, in the United States in 2002, the cotton quota was about 73,000 metric tons, but imports totaled 6 metric tons. In China the in-quota quantity has been unilaterally increased to assure that the official tariff rate quota does not restrict imports (Baffes 2003).

There are no WTO-notified export subsidies for cotton such as those the European Union continues to use for many other commodities. The United States, however, applies programs that the recent WTO cotton panel ruled were unlisted export subsidies (Schnepf 2004; WTO 2004c). These include both the Step 2 export program and the export credit guarantee programs operated by the general sales manager of the U.S. Department of Agriculture (USDA). The International Cotton Advisory Committee also classifies the U.S. Step 2 export program as an export subsidy; in addition it has calculated what it considers to be export subsidies for China, based on information about differences between internal and border prices (ICAC 2004).

The Chinese cotton subsidy situation is complex and unsettled with conflicting information and a lack of transparency. Baffes has summarized data from the ICAC and other sources (Baffes 2004, 2005; ICAC 2002, 2004). Shui (2004) also provides recent information. The general consensus is that China provided a major subsidy to the industry in managing liquidation of its cotton stocks from the late 1990s through 2001. The government registered financial losses during that period because it sold cotton, which it bought at higher prices in the 1990s, at the bottom of the market—even though that further depressed prices. Thus it is not clear that growers benefited much from the government's mishandling of an attempted stabilization policy that actually caused more market price variability and accentuated market price declines in the later period. The FAO and others have investigated the current Chinese cotton policy situation, but those results have not yet been published. As Baffes (2005) notes, "the fact that China subsidizes its cotton, however, is not uniformly accepted. Fang and Beghin (2003), for example, estimate that between 1997 and 2000, the nominal protection coefficient for cotton averaged 0.80, implying that China taxes its cotton sector. The different views on the nature and degree of intervention reflect the complexities of China's agricultural policies as well as the unreliability of the data." Current policy changes in China suggest that production or export subsidies are now quite small (Goreux 2004).

According to ICAC, Brazil, the Arab Republic of Egypt, Mexico, and Turkey have also provided domestic support for cotton. Support has tended to be small and intermittent and has been zero in Brazil in more recent years (ICAC 2002, 2004). In Uzbekistan, the world's fourth-largest producer of cotton, the sector is largely controlled by the government with a net tax applied on cotton production rather than a subsidy. Furthermore, it appears that price transmission to that market from world market conditions is quite limited (Baffes 2004).

Because other programs are small, or not well understood and expected to be small, the cotton initiative in the Doha negotiations targeted domestic support programs in the United States and the European Union and not other barriers and subsidies. In addition, of course, developing-country cotton producers would be unlikely to provide significant compensation, even if their subsidies were to continue.

European Union cotton production is concentrated in Spain and Greece. Production grew rapidly after these countries entered the EU and became eligible for Common Agricultural Policy subsidies (Karagiannis 2004, Baffes 2004). ICAC data show that average assistance in the European Union has been in the range of $1.00 a pound in 2002 and 2003, whereas the world price has been in the range of $0.50 to $0.60 a pound. ICAC lists a total EU subsidy of slightly less than $1 billion in recent years, with production in the range of 425,000 metric tons. Hence, the benefits from the subsidy have been about double the potential revenue from market sales at world prices. Substantial subsidies also appear in EU notifications to the WTO (Poonyth and others 2004). The form of subsidy to cotton in the EU is complex and includes various output-related programs and some input subsidies. The EU also applies limits on production eligible for subsidy, but these do not apply to individual farms and thus it is not clear that they are binding on farmer production behavior (Baffes 2004). It is not correct to consider the EU programs as a pure per unit or ad valorem production subsidy. Furthermore, in 2005 the EU is scheduled to change the program to a partially decoupled area payment together with a direct payment tied to cotton production for the 2005 season (Karagiannis 2004).

The United States also applies a wide range of complex programs that subsidize cotton production and trade, and, because the United States is a large cotton producer and exporter, the effects of these subsidies are larger than the higher per unit subsidies applied in the European Union. The U.S. programs apply primarily to upland cotton, which is the most common type in world markets. Major subsidy programs that apply to cotton include crop insurance subsidies, export credit guarantees, direct payments, countercyclical payments, marketing loan benefits, Step 2 payments to domestic users, and Step 2 payments to exporters. This list alone suggests the complexity of cotton subsidy programs, but each of the individual programs also has an array of provisions (WTO 2004c; Sumner 2003).[1]

The overall budget outlay for these programs varies inversely with various market prices and, in the case of crop insurance subsidy, with the weather and crop conditions. Recent total annual subsidies have ranged between $1.5 billion and nearly $4.0 billion (Baffes 2004; ICAC 2004). The totals do not include outlays or budget commitments for crop insurance and export credit guarantee programs.

Measures such as budget costs or contributions to the aggregate measure of support are interesting summaries but are not sufficient for analysis of impacts. For example, the direct payment program and the countercyclical payment program each pay recipients per unit of land on which cotton was historically grown, not per unit of current cotton output. Nonetheless, most land receiving these payments continues to be used for cotton, and subsidy rules limit what can be grown on the base. These and other features suggest that these payment programs likely affect production, but to a smaller degree than would per-unit production subsidies tied to current output. The marketing loan program offers payments per unit of upland cotton production whenever the specified market price is below the "loan rate" or government-set trigger price for payments. The marketing loan program therefore has direct and significant production effects.

The Step 2 program pays exporters and domestic users of U.S. cotton the difference between the internal U.S. market price and an average of selected low-end prices in international markets. Hence, eligible buyers are assured that the net price for U.S. cotton will remain competitive. This program stimulates demand for U.S. cotton. The export credit guarantee program promises banks financing exports of U.S. cotton that the U.S government will repay loans should the buyer fail to repay them. This allows buyers to acquire lower-cost credit to make purchases of U.S. cotton. Finally, the crop insurance program provides premium subsidies of more than 50 percent and covers excess losses of insurance companies should they occur. The result is availability of crop insurance coverage that would not otherwise be found and at a far lower cost than would be charged in a purely commercial insurance market.

Effects of Cotton Subsidies on Markets

The effects of these EU and U.S. subsidies on global markets for cotton have been the subject of intense analysis and attention for several years, in large part because of the high profile of both the WTO dispute on U.S. cotton subsidies brought by Brazil and the DDA cotton initiative. This section examines the likely effects of removing the subsidy and looks at the magnitude of appropriate compensation.

Various studies differ in their coverage of subsidy policies, time horizons, and base periods, that is, they ask different specific questions about the effects of cotton subsidies. The studies also differ in parameter choices and thus would arrive at different results even if they focused on the same questions. Many of the relevant studies have been helpfully reviewed by the FAO (2004) and by other recent reports, including Goreux (2004), Poonyth and others (2004), Gillson and others (2004), Oxfam (2004), and Baffes (2005). Earlier studies include Goreux (2003), Sumner (2003), ICAC (2002), Oxfam (2002), Tokarick (2003), and Reeves and others (2001). Additional studies include Shepherd (2004), Pan and others (2004), Fadiga, Mohanty, and Pan (2004), and Karagiannis (2004). The last of those was the only study to concentrate on the effects of removing EU subsidy programs.

The basic approach of all the studies, except Shepherd's, has been to develop simulation models specified with a set of supply and demand parameters. The models are used to pose counterfactual questions of the following form: what would the market prices, quantities, and other aggregates be (or have been) in the absence of the subsidy programs considered? Karagiannis (2004) not only considered past program effects in Greece and Spain, he also analyzed the likely effects of the EU reform scheduled for 2005. The reform reduces the subsidy effects, but the new regime continues to have a substantial subsidy tied to the production of cotton. Given high costs of cotton production in Europe and the very high base-subsidy levels, complete removal of the production subsidy element would further reduce EU cotton output.

Several studies examined how past market conditions would have been affected if subsidies had not been in place during the periods considered. That was the main relevant question posed in the WTO dispute concerning U.S. cotton subsidies, for which the Sumner (2003) analysis was developed. Some recent work motivated in part by the WTO dispute misses that important point (Pan and others 2004). For the cotton initiative (and for the "threat" issues posed in the WTO cotton dispute), the more relevant issue is how removal of cotton subsidies now would affect the future path of cotton prices, quantities, and other aggregates. For example, simulations by Sumner (2003); Pan and others (2004); and Fadiga, Mohanty, and Pan (2004) explicitly project how removing U.S. subsidies would affect future market conditions under assumptions of baseline projections.

The recent FAO review lists estimated price declines from removing subsidies that range from about 30 percent (ICAC 2002) to a low of about 3 percent (Tokarick 2003). The closely related studies by Pan and others (2004) and Fadiga, Mohanty, and Pan (2004) find estimates at the low end of the range, as does the study by Poonyth and others (2004). Studies at the upper end of the range include those by Gillson and others (2004) for some of their scenarios. The studies by Sumner (2003), Reeves and others (2001), and Goreux (2003) (for some of his scenarios) are in the middle of the range for price effects, although they are quite different in parameters and some findings. The studies at the high end of the range tend to treat all subsidy outlays as fully tied to production. They also begin with low-priced base years and use relatively inelastic demand elasticities and relatively low supply elasticities. In addition, ICAC considers relatively high subsidies on Chinese production in the base case. The studies at the low end of the range leave out some subsidy programs (such as partially decoupled payments, crop insurance, Step 2 programs, and export credit programs in the United States). These studies, especially the ones by Pan and others (2004) and Fadiga, Mohanty, and Pan (2004), also use high demand and supply elasticities or begin with high-priced baselines.

The projected baseline matters significantly, in part because the degree of subsidy in the United States depends on the baseline prices for cotton and on commodities that compete for the same land and other resources. If cotton prices are expected to be high, then the marketing loan benefits and countercyclical payments would be low as a consequence. In a high-priced baseline, these two important subsidy programs would have relatively small effects on the expected revenue from cotton compared with other crops, and therefore they would have relatively small effects on area planted and quantity produced. Cotton prices have moved up and down dramatically in recent years. Baseline (especially short-term) projections have also moved up and down. Expectations about prices over a longer horizon determine the expected impact of the subsidy programs in the future, and these projections are more stable.

A more inelastic demand function for cotton reduces price impacts from subsidy reductions. Econometric estimates typically find an inelastic demand for cotton, often in the minus range of −0.1 to −0.5. Cotton comprises a relatively small share of the total retail cost of textile products, and these products comprise a relatively small share of consumer expenditures. Thus, income effects are likely to be small, and substitution away from cotton textiles by final consumers is unlikely to be significant. The significant issue for the elasticity of demand for cotton is the substitution between cotton and other fibers, especially synthetics, by textile manufacturers. The overall share of the fiber market taken by synthetics has grown slowly over time even as the real price of cotton has declined (Baffes 2004).

Focusing on long-run effects of the cotton initiative, a demand elasticity nearing −1.0 might be expected. Such a demand elasticity may be appropriate for questions about the long-term price gains to be expected from removal of subsidies. For shorter-term effects, such as the immediate price impacts of subsidy reductions, a demand elasticity below −0.5 is more consistent with the econometric evidence as well as with evidence of large short-run price swings.

Three supply response parameters are important in considering the impacts of the cotton initiative on prices and welfare of LDC cotton producers. First, the supply responses to subsidy reduction (as well as to market price increases) in the EU and the United States will determine the reductions in cotton production from removal of program benefits. Second, the supply response to higher market prices in the rest of the world will determine (along with the demand elasticity) how much the price can rise before market-clearing equilibrium is restored. Finally, the supply response in the LDCs indicates how much they will increase output in response to higher global prices. Given that these countries make up only a small share of the world cotton supply, their gain in total revenue and producer surplus (or net revenue) is greater the more elastic their supply.

Econometric estimates suggest quite inelastic values for all three sets of supply elasticities, but again there are reasons to believe that these estimates apply to relatively short-run analysis. Farmers adjust slowly to changes in relative net revenue and, given adjustment costs, they shift only partially unless relative price changes are expected to be permanent. The more the reductions in program benefits are expected to be permanent, and the more time that farmers, input suppliers, and marketers have to make adjustments, the larger the expected acreage shifts.

Estimated supply elasticities are small for the United States, but given that alternative crops are available in most cotton-growing regions, a substantial drop in cotton area would be expected in response to a permanent and expected reduction in subsidies. McDonald and Sumner (2003) also show how the estimated supply response elasticities, which apply to policy-constrained responses, are smaller than those applicable to the question of policy reform. In the European Union, the response may be even larger given the very high subsidy rates and the fact that cotton production initially expanded in response to the subsidies. In both cases, it may take a few years before the full adjustment is completed.

In other countries, supply responses to higher prices are likely more muted. First, land and other resource restraints often limit cotton expansion in well-established growing areas. For example, water concerns may limit cotton expansion in Australia and China. Second, some major growing areas are insulated from world price movements by domestic policy (for example, China, Uzbekistan, and countries in Africa), or infrastructure problems (for example, China, India, and especially countries in Africa). Overall, supply elasticities averaging 1.0 in the medium term may be reasonable in the United States, the EU, and Brazil, with elasticities more nearly in the range of 0.5 in poorer countries.

The effects of removing a given subsidy also depend on whether other farm programs are maintained or eliminated simultaneously with cotton subsidies. Given that the DDA cotton initiative has now been wrapped into the overall negotiations on agriculture, it is important to recognize that the supply response to reductions in cotton subsidies will be smaller when other subsidies are also reduced than if cotton subsidies alone were removed. Farmers compare expected net revenue from using land for the relevant competing crops. If program benefits from other crops are reduced at the same time cotton subsidies are reduced, relative impacts on net revenue are smaller than if cotton subsidies alone are removed. Recent research examining cotton liberalization has considered impacts of removing cotton subsidies alone, which was the relevant question in the WTO cotton case.

Sumner (2003) estimated that eliminating all U.S. cotton programs, while other farm programs remained in place, would reduce U.S. production by 25–30 percent, reduce U.S. exports by about 40 percent, and raise world prices by about 10 percent. These are averages of estimates that apply over a range of base periods and initial price assumptions. Under a longer-run scenario, with other program subsidies reduced at the same time as cotton subsidies are eliminated, then the effects on U.S. supply would likely be smaller, as would the resulting effects on world prices. However, adding the removal of EU programs would likely add another 2–3 percent to the overall world price effect of cotton subsidy removal. Weighing all the evidence from a variety of sources, a 10 percent increase in the world price of cotton is a reasonable estimate if the cotton subsidy programs were removed under the cotton initiative while other farm production subsidies were also reduced substantially.[2]

Benefits of the Initiative for LDC Cotton Producers

The DDA cotton initiative includes proposals for elimination of subsidies and for compensation for losses incurred before their elimination. Given the background developed on the impacts of subsidies, consider now the potential benefits for least developed countries of this compensation as well as the elimination of the subsidies.

Compensation

Clearly, benefits of higher world prices that would follow from subsidy reductions benefit all cotton producers (and taxpayers in the EU and the United States). They also cost cotton users globally. Compensation is designed to offer LDC cotton producers and their rural economies benefits commensurate with what they would have received if subsidy reductions had proceeded more rapidly.

Direct financial contributions are not the way that the GATT or WTO normally deals with compensation for noncompliance. Traditionally, if a WTO member does not choose to implement a ruling, the offended member is allowed to "withdraw trade concessions" from the member that is out of compliance. There are instances of more direct compensation, and the concept is not inconsistent with WTO principles, but it simply has not been applied in a context similar to the cotton initiative. A recent report by International Lawyers and Economists Against Poverty (ILEAP 2004) provides detailed legal analysis of the prospects of direct financial compensation and finds that such a proposal, while unusual, is within the legal boundaries of WTO principles.

As the membership of the WTO has expanded, the use of the odd mechanism of withdrawing concessions is not only in conflict with the basic principles of the WTO, it is also simply not practical for many members. Exports from LDCs generally already face very low import duties in rich countries, and LDCs buy very little on a commercial basis. For an LDC such as Benin, for example, to raise its tariffs on imports from the United States would not only be self-defeating for Benin, it would also cause little or no notice in the United States and hence negligible pressure for the United States to come into compliance. In the absence of another feasible compensation mechanism, a direct financial transfer may be the only approach that actually provides some relief. It is also an approach that economists support on efficiency grounds.

The total amount of loss from the continuation of subsidies depends on the size of the estimated world price effects and the size of the estimated LDC supply response to these effects. These, in turn, depend on the length of run considered appropriate for the analysis. The argument for a short-run scenario is that these payments are meant to compensate for the failure to remove subsidies now, rather than for what world prices would be now if subsidies had been removed many years ago and full adjustment had already taken place. A second issue is the revenue basis for the compensation criteria. The natural approach is to use estimates of forgone producer surplus or net revenue. But, since the subsidy effects reach beyond the farm to local input suppliers, forgone producer surplus would include local suppliers of farm inputs and marketing services (including local laborers). This concept of producer surplus would leave out suppliers of imported inputs and marketing services, because while these suppliers would benefit from subsidy reduction, they are likely to be associated with rich rather than poor countries. Goreux (2004) finds that the losses in poor countries from rich-country cotton subsidies are substantial, amounting to more than 10 percent of all the official development assistance to the four African countries that proposed the initiative.

A focus on LDC cotton producers suggests that production, not exports, should be the basis for compensation under the initiative. While producers in net importing nations would gain from higher prices, the textile industries in those countries, and presumably their workers, would lose. Thus the initiative has focused on exports or on production in countries that are net exporters. Goreux (2004) lists 22 LDCs that would be eligible for compensation based on their per capita incomes and their status as net cotton exporters. This later criterion leaves out Bangladesh, which is a significant cotton user in its textile industry and thus a net cotton importer. Based on 2001 and 2002 data, Goreux (2004) finds about 1.1 million metric tons of production in eligible countries and exports from these countries of about 0.8 million metric tons. It would be more now, as production has grown since 2002 in many LDCs.

For some sample calculations of the potential losses and compensation, let us use a world price increase of 10 percent and a supply elasticity of 0.5 for the relevant LDC recipient countries. Assuming a subsidy-suppressed base production of 1.2 million metric tons (continuing to leave aside production in Bangladesh) and applying an additional price of 10 percent on top of a subsidy-suppressed base price of $1,100 a metric ton ($0.50 a pound), the removal of subsidies adds $132 million in revenue for the original production. In addition, production would expand by 5 percent (with an elasticity of supply of 0.5), and producers would gain one-half of this revenue, $33 million, in surplus. The total annual gain from removing rich-country cotton subsidies is therefore approximately $165 million, based on the price effect and supply elasticity chosen for illustration. This amount would provide the basis for compensation. Goreux (2004) arrived at a figure of $250 million, mainly because he assumed larger price increases as a result of the subsidy reduction.

Two points are striking about these figures. First, they are quite modest compared with the budget outlays of $2.5 billion–$5 billion that the United States and the European Union typically spend on cotton subsidies every year. Second, compensation is modest compared with the global effects of the subsidies. This latter result is a simple reflection of the facts that about half the production outside the United States and the European Union is in China and India, and that cotton production in LDC exporters is only about one-fourth of total production outside of the subsidizing countries. Thus many developing-country cotton farms who currently lose from rich-country subsidies would not receive compensation from the initiative and would therefore much prefer subsidy elimination.

The criteria for distributing the compensation are closely related to the criteria for determining its magnitude. Goreux (2004) considers distributing the compensation among countries on the basis of either cotton production or cotton exports. The distributions are very similar. In both cases Benin, Burkina Faso, and Mali would each receive between 15 and 20 percent of the compensation. Chad,

Togo, and Sudan would each receive 7–8 percent, with the final 22 percent divided among the other 16 LDCs of Africa and Asia that export cotton.

The amount and national distribution of benefits is only part of the compensation story. The other issue is how poor farmers and other target groups actually benefit. Goreux (2003, 2004) and Baffes (2005) discuss how to ensure that compensation actually reaches intended recipients. The simplest way is to allow compensation to flow to the same beneficiaries as would higher cotton prices. Another approach would use the compensation fund to supplement the market price for cotton with payments on a per unit basis made through the normal marketing channels. Such an approach would mimic the impact of the price gains from subsidy removal around which the compensation idea was developed. This "second-best" offset would correct the original policy-induced price distortion and hence give LDC cotton farmers cotton price incentives that approximate those that would be achieved under full reform. The effective cotton price they faced would, in fact, be higher than if subsidies were removed, because other cotton-producing countries, such as China and Brazil, would not face the higher effective prices and so would not increase production as they would if rich-country subsidies were removed.

It is important to remember that the Doha negotiations refer to the compensation issue as the "development" discussions. In this context, the emphasis seems to be on using compensation funds not to compensate cotton producers for their losses but to make investments in public goods, such as roads or other infrastructure developments, that benefit cotton farmers and their local communities. Such ideas have merit where investment funds or incentives for such projects are lacking. Such indirect compensation for growers means that those who have suffered direct losses will be less likely to see direct benefits. Such indirect compensation also suffers from the concern that development aid in general has not been effective in lifting the rural poor from poverty in these countries and that the new source of funds may contribute relatively little to the well-being of the cotton farmers in whose name the initiative is being pursued.

Trade Benefits

As noted above, the global trade benefits exceed the gains to the LDC farmers by a substantial margin. But consider the trade benefits just to these same LDC farmers that are the focus of the cotton initiative, leaving aside the trade benefits to farmers in Brazil, China, and other major producing regions (and the benefits to taxpayers in rich countries).

Based on the discussion outlined above, the key determinants of trade benefits are the various supply and demand elasticities and the production-distorting degree of the policies being reformed. Benefits to LDC cotton producers from removing rich-country subsidies are larger the more inelastic is the demand for cotton; the larger is the rich-country supply response to subsidy reduction, which is composed of the supply elasticity and the degree of subsidy in the programs; the smaller is the supply elasticity in the nonsubsidized countries; and the larger is the supply elasticity in the LDC countries.

There are several issues to consider in negotiating cotton subsidy reforms. Given that the cotton initiative is now a part of the Doha agricultural negotiations, the achievements of the larger negotiations may be of vital importance, but this is not a necessary condition. If the cotton negotiations are conducted (in the recently organized subcommittee) separately from the rest of the agricultural negotiations, then cotton subsidies could be eliminated even if relatively little else is achieved in the broader agricultural negotiations. But such an outcome seems unlikely. Much more likely is that the two negotiations will be closely linked, with the cotton agreement supplemental to whatever is achieved in the overall agricultural talks (which in turn depend on what is agreed in nonagricultural negotiations).

With the cotton initiative tied to the rest of the deal, cotton may be used as a leading edge that stimulates deeper subsidy cuts for other commodities than would otherwise occur. In that case, an adequate outcome for cotton would be achieved only if the subsidy reductions across all commodities were based on a solid starting point. Therefore, those urging cotton subsidy reductions have an incentive to achieve subsidy reductions across all commodities and then to push for additional or accelerated cotton subsidy reduction as a supplement to those established for other commodities.

The DDA agricultural negotiations are unlikely to eliminate trade-distorting agricultural subsidies, and some remaining support for cotton is also likely to continue at least for several years into the future. That means the cotton initiative proponents must consider what subsidy programs cause the most harm to the interests of LDC farmers per unit of political resistance in the United States and European Union.[3]

A focus on the most "coupled" subsidies is likely to get the most response in world markets and be resisted least by the U.S. and EU negotiators. However, the complexities of domestic farm programs for cotton illustrate a serious concern in using WTO negotiations to define reduction commitments for these programs. Several of the U.S. programs have been notified to the WTO as "minimally distorting" Green Box programs, while others have been notified as non-product-specific support. U.S. notifications of these programs were not challenged at the time they were submitted, and the mechanism for timely challenges does not seem to be well developed. (These notifications were implicitly challenged in the context of the WTO cotton dispute brought by Brazil, as discussed below.)

For the 2005 EU cotton policy, a focus on the most distorting programs suggests spending less effort to remove area payments but carefully monitoring the definitions so that area payments are truly neutral across crops (Karagiannis 2004). For the U.S. programs, simulations reported in Sumner (2003) and summarized by Goreux (2004) can provide guidance. Sumner's table 1.4 shows that the Step 2 program, which is unique to cotton, has the largest projected impact on world price in the years 2004–7, closely followed by the marketing loan program. The countercyclical payment program also has significant price impacts, as do crop insurance subsidies. The least impact on world prices, at about 1 percent, is from the direct payment program. A reasonable objective for a partial reform of U.S. cotton program might therefore be to press first for immediate elimination of the Step 2 program. A second objective is a rapid and substantial reduction in the marketing loan subsidies by lowering the loan rate and changing the formula to raise the effective loan repayment rate. This is a natural agenda item for the overall DDA agricultural negotiations because the marketing loan program is also important for the other major supported crops. A third objective would be the reform of the countercyclical program to reduce the size of the payments by reducing the target price and removing remaining restrictions on land use. Even better would be a shift of the countercyclical program funds to the direct payment program and elimination of the payments tied to the price of the specific commodity. Finally, crop insurance subsidies could be reduced by reducing premium subsidies and shifting to whole farm insurance with area-wide triggers and reduced repayment of program losses.

Any reasonable negotiation strategy must take into consideration the results achieved under the cotton dispute brought by Brazil against U.S. upland cotton programs. The WTO cotton panel ruled largely in favor of Brazil's position, and this ruling was upheld by the appellate body (WTO 2004c; WTO 2005b; Baffes 2005; Schnepf 2004). The final WTO ruling is available to provide context for the DDA negotiations and especially the cotton initiative subcommittee negotiations, allowing it to be used as a starting point for further efforts. Implementation of the cotton policy adjustments under the ruling is a much larger concern, however. It is unlikely to begin before late 2005, and full implementation that satisfies Brazil and other cotton producers is uncertain and is likely to entail additional negotiations.

The WTO ruled that the Step 2 export program and the export credit guarantees for cotton (and some other commodities) were prohibited export subsidies, and that the Step 2 domestic program was a prohibited domestic-content subsidy. These cotton programs were then listed for early elimination—within months of the final ruling. Clearly, if the United States indicates that it will comply with the ruling and eliminate the prohibited subsidies, there is no reason to target the Step 2 program or export credit guarantees for vigorous negotiation in the DDA cotton initiative. The United States has already signaled a willingness to negotiate removal of the subsidy elements of the export credit guarantee program in the DDA, so this program, in particular, seems likely to be reformed. The cotton initiative could aid in the rapid reform of these "prohibited" programs by reinforcing the extreme pressure the United States would face if it fails to comply fully with the dispute resolution results.

A second major set of findings of the cotton dispute is that none of the U.S. domestic support programs for cotton properly belonged in the Green Box of minimally trade-distorting programs. In particular, the direct payment program, by prohibiting production of fruits and vegetables on base land eligible for payments, more than minimally restricted the use of the cotton base area and thereby likely stimulated cotton production, the WTO panel ruled. This ruling suggests that the WTO interpreted the Green Box more narrowly than the United States in its notifications under the Uruguay Round. This ruling has implications for compliance with constraints on aggregate measures of support, even without tightening the definitions that have been proposed for the DDA. Thus the DDA and the cotton initiative could take this ruling as a starting point for tightening definitions and categories surrounding classification of subsidy programs.

Third, the WTO cotton panel found the Step 2 programs, the marketing loan program, and the countercyclical program all caused serious prejudice to Brazil's interests by depressing and suppressing the world price of cotton. The WTO panel did not specify a quantitative threshold that the effects of these programs exceeded. However, the panel did find, and the appellate body confirmed, that the United States was required to withdraw the programs or at least remove the significant price suppression that they cause. This finding not only reinforces the claims that motivated the cotton initiative but also makes it more difficult for the United States to argue, for example, that the countercyclical program should be placed in an enhanced Blue Box and secured from meaningful DDA disciplines.

Overall, if the United States implements the ruling in a timely and forthright manner, the WTO cotton dispute will have achieved much of what the cotton initiative is seeking from the United States, except compensation during the implementation process. The other value of the WTO cotton dispute is to place additional pressure on the EU to commit to adjustments to its cotton program.

The separation of the compensation or development aid and subsidy reduction elements of the initiative during the negotiation process does not preclude linkage in the final stages of a deal. This is clearly defined in the original proposal. The danger is that compensation does not provide significant incentives for large and rapid subsidy reductions. Under any reasonable estimate, the amount of compensation is small relative to the outlays that the European Union and the United States are already spending for cotton subsidy programs. It may be more feasible politically to reduce subsidies by less and compensate more. For example, in the United States, where the cotton subsidy program has routinely cost $2 billion and more a year, the farm lobby may consider adding another $100 million or $200 million to maintain the subsidy as simply a cost of doing business. Then, with LDCs legitimately satisfied by compensation, the cotton programs would be free of that additional pressure to reform. This would leave other developing-country cotton producers, including Brazil, China, and India, with no benefit from the initiative and a smaller coalition to press for real reforms.

Final Words

The DDA cotton initiative has the potential to put additional pressure on the United States and the European Union to reduce cotton subsidy programs further and more rapidly than they reduce subsidies for other commodities. Most of that incentive derives from unwelcome global attention and scrutiny from other WTO members. The most important leverage is the link between the cotton initiative and success of the DDA as a whole as well as the willingness of members to offer trade liberalization measures that are high on the agendas of the EU and the United States. If the United States complies expeditiously with the WTO cotton dispute, many of the trade objectives of the cotton initiative will be satisfied. The two approaches to trade policy reform (complying with the panel ruling or multilateral negotiation) are partial substitutes. Nonetheless, given the uncertainty associated with the U.S. response to the dispute settlement case, continuing a vigorous pursuit of the cotton initiative makes sense for developing countries.

The DDA cotton initiative is likely to result in compensation that can provide significant benefits to LDC cotton producers, if handled carefully. The appropriate amount of compensation is likely in the range of $120 to $240 million a year based on the world price–suppressing effects of U.S. and EU subsidies. As the subsidies are partially reformed, the compensation rate would decline. The form of the compensation affects the within-country distributions as well as the effects on cotton markets. The most natural compensation scheme would be to distribute funds in a way that mimics the effects of higher prices. This could be done with a direct payment per unit of production at the same rate as the estimated price suppression caused by the subsidies. The benefits would flow through the system precisely as would the benefits of higher market prices, and producers would not see any difference. The alternative of broad development assistance may be appropriate on its own merits. However, development project funding, even for projects tied to cotton productivity, cannot mimic the effects of higher prices in the way that adding the compensation to the market returns would.

As with the WTO cotton dispute, the cotton initiative may also be used to stimulate more, rather than less, policy reform in the DDA for the rest of the farm commodities. For this to occur, it is important that cotton not drain negotiating resources and incentives from the rest of the negotiations. Less than complete elimination of cotton subsides or a slower path of cotton policy reform might be exchanged for substantially more in the rest of the negotiations. Such a deal could improve LDC welfare more than demanding complete acquiescence to the goals of the cotton initiative.

Finally, even if the cotton initiative achieves significant success, the result will not be the end of rural poverty even in cotton-producing regions. An extra $110 per metric ton of cotton, or $200 million a year is important, but many more investments and institutional changes will be required for rural economic development to be successful.

Notes

1. Other policies also affect cotton, such as irrigation water subsidies in Arizona and California. These policies are less important to stimulating cotton production nationwide, and they apply not only to cotton but to all crops and to pasture grown in the affected regions.

2. For an estimate of the impact on cotton if all merchandise trade distortions were removed, and of the impact of cotton subsidy removal on agricultural value added in Sub-Saharan Africa, see Anderson, Martin, and van der Mensbrugghe (2006, p. 350).

3. For a discussion of negotiating efforts on domestic support in this spirit, see Sumner (2000).

References

Anderson, K., W. Martin, and D. van der Mensbrugghe. 2006. "Market and Welfare Implications of the Doha Agenda." In *Agricultural Trade Reform and the Doha Development Agenda*, ed. K. Anderson and W. Martin. Washington, DC: World Bank.

Baffes, J. 2003. "Cotton and Developing Countries: A Case Study in Policy Incoherence." Trade Note 10, World Bank, Washington, DC, September 10. http://siteresources.worldbank.org/ INTRANET-TRADE/Resources/TradeNote10.pdf.

———. 2004. "Cotton: Market Setting, Trade Policies, and Issues." Policy Research Working Paper 3218, World Bank, Washington, DC, February.

———. 2005. "The 'Cotton Problem.'" *World Bank Research Observer* 20 (1, Spring): 109–43.

ERS (Economic Research Service). 2004. *USDA Agricultural Baseline Projections to 2013,* WAOB-2004-1, ERS, U.S. Department of Agriculture, Washington, DC, February. http://www.ers.usda.gov/publications/waob041/.

Fadiga, M., L. S. Mohanty, and S. Pan. 2004. "The Impacts of U.S. and European Union Cotton Programs on the West and Central African Countries Cotton Export Earnings." Paper presented at the American Agricultural Economics Association Annual Meeting, Denver, August 1–3. http://agecon.lib.umn.edu/cgi-bin/pdf_view.pl?paperid=14572.

Fang, C., and J. C. Beghin. 2003. "Protection and Comparative Advantage of Chinese Agriculture: Implications for Regional and National Specialization." In *Agricultural Trade and Policy in China: Issues, Analysis, and Implications*, ed. S. Rozelle and D. Sumner. London: Ashgate Press.

FAO (Food and Agriculture Organization). 2004. "The Impact of Cotton Sector Support on Developing Countries: A Guide to Contemporary Analyses." FAO, Rome, September.
FAPRI (Food and Agricultural Policy Research Institute). 2004. "U.S. and World Agricultural Outlook, 2004." Center for Agricultural and Rural Development, FAPRI, Iowa State University, Ames, Iowa. http://www.fapri.iastate.edu/Outlook2004/.
Gillson, I., C. Poulton, K. Balcombe, and S. Page. 2004. "Understanding the Impact of Cotton Subsidies on Developing Countries." ODI Background Report, Overseas Development Institute, London, May. http://www.odi.org.uk/publications/cotton_report/cotton_report.pdf.
Goreux, L. 2003. "Prejudice Caused by Industrialised Countries Subsidies to Cotton Sectors in Western and Central Africa: Background Document to the Submission Made by Benin, Burkina Faso, Chad and Mali to the WTO." TN/AG/GEN/4, World Trade Organization, Geneva, June.
———. 2004. "Cotton after Cancun." Organization for Economic Co-operation and Development, Paris, March. http://www.oecd.org/dataoecd/38/48/30751318.pdf.
ICAC (International Cotton Advisory Committee). 2002. "Production and Trade Policies Affecting the Cotton Industry." ICAC, Washington, DC. http://www.icac.org/icac/Meetings/cgtn_conf/documents/icac_ccgtn_report.pdf.
———. 2004. "Production and Trade Policies Affecting the Cotton Industry." ICAC Standing Committee, Attachment 1 to SC-N-473, Washington, DC. May 18.
ILEAP (International Lawyers and Economists Against Poverty). 2004. "Legal Issues in Relation to Financial Compensation under the Cotton Initiative." ILEAP, Rome. http://www.fao.org/es/ESC/en/20953/22215/highlight_47647en.html.
Karagiannis, G. 2004. "The EU Cotton Policy Regime and the Implications of the Proposed Changes for Producer Welfare." FAO Commodity and Trade Policy Research Working Paper 9, Food and Agriculture Organization, Rome, April. www.fao.org/documents/show_cdr.asp?url_file=/docrep/007/j2732e/j2732e00.htm.
McDonald, J. D., and D. A. Sumner. 2003. "The Influence of Commodity Programs on Acreage Response to Market Price: With an Illustration Concerning Rice Policy in the United States." *American Journal of Agricultural Economics* 85 (4): 857–71, November.
Minot, N., and L. Daniels. 2001. "Impact of Global Cotton Markets on Rural Poverty in Benin." MSSD Discussion Paper 48, International Food Policy Research Institute, Washington, DC.
Oxfam. 2002. "Cultivating Poverty: The Impact of US Cotton Subsidies on Africa." Briefing Paper 30, Oxfam, London.
———. 2004. "Finding the Moral Fiber." Oxfam Briefing Paper, London, October.
Pan, S., S. Mohanty, D. Ethridge, and M. Fadiga. 2004. "The Impacts of U.S. Cotton Programs on the World Market: An Analysis of Brazilian and West African WTO Petitions." Department of Agricultural and Applied Economics, Texas Tech University, Lubbock.
Poonyth, D., A. Sarris, R. Sharma, and S. Shui. 2004. "The Impact of Domestic and Trade Policies on the World Cotton Market." Commodity and Trade Policy Research Working Paper, Food and Agriculture Organization, Rome.
Reeves, G., D. Vincent, D. Quirke, and S. Wyatt. 2001. "Trade Distortions and Cotton Markets: Implications for Australian Cotton Producers." Centre for International Economics for Australia's Cotton Research and Development Corporation, Canberra. http://www.crdc.com.au/documents/Tradereport_april2001.pdf.
Schnepf, R. 2004. "U.S.-Brazil WTO Cotton Subsidy Dispute." CRS Report for Congress, Order Code RL32571, Congressional Research Service, Washington, DC, September 10.
Shepherd, B. 2004. "The Impact of US Subsidies on the World Cotton Market: A Reassessment." Groupe d'Economie Mondiale, Institut d'Etudes Politiques de Paris. http://www.oecd.org/dataoecd/0/9/31592808.pdf.
Shui, S. 2004. "Measuring the Impact of Domestic Support on the World Cotton Market: An Overview of Existing Research and Research Issues." Background paper presented at the FAO Informal Expert Consultation on Cotton, Rome, May 31–June 1.

Sumner, D. A. 2000. "Domestic Support and the WTO Negotiations." *Australian Journal of Agricultural and Resource Economics* 44 (3, September): 457–74.

———. 2003. "A Quantitative Simulation Analysis of the Impacts of U.S. Cotton Subsidies on Cotton Prices and Quantities." Paper presented to the WTO Cotton Panel, October. http://www.fao.org/es/ESC/en/20953/22215/highlight_47647en_sumner.pdf.

Tokarick, S. 2003. "Measuring the Impact of Distortions in Agricultural Trade in Partial and General Equilibrium." IMF Working Paper WP/03/110, International Monetary Fund, Washington, DC. http://www.imf.org/external/pubs/ft/wp/2003/wp03110.pdf.

WTO (World Trade Organization). 1994. "WTO Legal Texts: Subsidies and Countervailing Measures." WTO, Geneva. http://www.wto.org/english/docs_e/legal_e/legal_e.htm.

———. 2002. "United States: Subsidies on Upland Cotton: Request for Consultations by Brazil." WT/DS267/1, WTO, Geneva, October 3.

———. 2003a. "Fifth Ministerial Conference: Day 1: Conference Kicks off with 'Facilitators' Named and Cotton Debated." WTO, Geneva. http://www.wto.org/english/thewto_e/minist_e/min03_e/min03_e.htm.

———. 2003b. "Poverty Reduction: Sectoral Initiative in Favour of Cotton: A Joint Proposal by Benin, Burkina Faso, Chad, and Mali." TN/AG/GEN/4, WTO, Geneva, May 16. Revised, WT/MIN(03)/W/2, August 15. http://docsonline.wto.org/DDFDocuments/t/WT/Min03/W2.doc.

———. 2003c. "Trade Negotiations Committee: Address by President Blaise Compaore of Burkina Faso on the Cotton Submission by West and Central African Countries to the Trade Negotiations Committee of the World Trade Organization." WTO, Geneva, June 10. http://www.wto.org/english/thewto_e/minist_e/min03_e/min03_e.htm.

———. 2004a. "Decision Adopted by the General Council on 1 August 2004." WT/L/579 (July Framework Agreement), WTO, Geneva, August 2. http://www.wto.org/english/tratop_e/dda_e/draft_text_gc_dg_31july04_e.htm#par1b.

———. 2004b. "Sub-committee Set up on Cotton." WTO, Geneva, 19 November. http://www.wto.org/english/news_e/news04_e/sub_committee_19nov04_e.htm.

———. 2004c. "United States—Subsidies on Upland Cotton: Report of the Panel." WT/DS267/R, WTO, Geneva, September 8.

———. 2005a. "Agriculture: The Cotton Sub-Committee." WTO, Geneva. http://www.wto.org/english/tratop_e/agric_e/cotton_subcommittee_e.htm.

———. 2005b. "United States—Subsidies on Upland Cotton: Report of the Appellate Body." WT/DS267/AB/R, WTO, Geneva, March 3.

PART IV

DOHA REFORM SCENARIOS

11

HOLOGRAMS AND GHOSTS: NEW AND OLD IDEAS FOR AGRICULTURAL POLICY

David Orden and Eugenio Díaz-Bonilla[*]

As the Doha Round of the World Trade Organization (WTO) negotiations progresses, achieving substantial liberalization of agricultural trade looks as problematic as always. One reason is that just a few years after the Uruguay Round agreements put the first full set of multilateral trade and subsidy rules in place for agriculture, world prices of agricultural commodities plummeted. Despite the new rules, the levels of subsidies rose sharply among developed countries and, simultaneously, some countries with fewer fiscal resources responded by increasing border protection to shield their domestic farmers from the price decline. Continuation of a prisoner's dilemma—with high subsidies in developed countries matched by high bindings on tariffs in developing countries—remains a possible Doha result. If so, the Doha Round may be lauded for what it accomplishes, but it will not have accomplished very much in agriculture. A more desirable outcome would be the globally efficient and welfare-enhancing one of low subsidies and low protection. The negotiations as of mid-2005 have demonstrated the difficulty of achieving this goal in this round. They have demonstrated equally that an unbalanced outcome of high subsidies in developed countries but low protection in developing countries, or of low developed-country subsidies with high developing-country protection, will not happen either.

---

[*]The authors thank Fuzhi Cheng for assistance, and John Nash, other participants at the project's December 2004 workshop in The Hague, Ed Young, and Paul Westcott for helpful comments. Financial support was provided by the World Bank and the Economic Research Service, U.S. Department of Agriculture. Opinions expressed are those of the authors and should not be attributed to the institutions with which they are affiliated.

One problem that has made progress difficult is "dirty decoupling," which has discredited the constructive reform strategy of reducing the production- and trade-distorting effects of farm support programs, just as "dirty tariffication" marred the Uruguay Round elimination of quantitative trade restrictions and left high levels of protection in place. Decoupling of payments is supposed to eliminate distorting policy effects. But governments of developing countries, and others that provide few subsidies, are skeptical that the payments implemented as "decoupled" are isolated from production decisions. In any case, when prices are low, these payments extend help from governments to farm producers. The countries with less budgetary latitude are loath to give up their tools to extend such aid, even tools that are economically inefficient, as long as the subsidizers keep subsidizing.

In this chapter we explore the policy instruments that developed and developing countries might adopt to facilitate a substantial liberalization of agricultural trade. The various rules and derogations in place and being negotiated under different colored boxes or pillars inherited from the Uruguay Round Agreement on Agriculture (URAA) are far from being a template for optimal agricultural policies worldwide or a road map for how to get there.[1] We keep these pillars and assessments in mind but step back from the negotiation specifics to look at the broad outlines of policy.

For the developed countries, we focus first on whether decoupling can be made more convincing. One approach would be a commitment to end farm programs by buying out program beneficiaries so that subsidies are terminated. In the past, bringing an end to farm support programs has proven to be a hologram: the image sometimes appears but can never be grasped and made real. We also consider a very different way to end current subsidy payments through strengthened supply management to prop up farm commodity prices. This is a ghost of farm policies past, being revived in the guise of such programs as bioenergy production. By restricting output in the implementing country, such programs are trade distorting, but they are unlikely to draw objections from competitors in world markets.

For developing countries, the agrarian problem involving both rural growth and poverty issues has been the subject of many grand strategies, while the nuts-and-bolts policies have usually consisted of a complex mix of price interventions with public enterprises and parastatals operating in output and input markets and high protection. The ghosts of complex distorting interventions and of increased protection haunt the policy landscape. For developing countries, an integrated, efficient, and equitable set of macro, meso, and micro policies and investments, backed by sufficient resources, has been the intangible hologram that always seems to fade away.

Reforming Agricultural Policies in Developed Countries

Several types of policy measures have been used over time to reform support for developed-country farmers to lessen their reliance on trade measures affecting prices. The most common policy has been a "cash-out" but "buyouts," or an uncompensated "squeeze-out" or "cutout" are alternatives. Each is discussed in turn, then buyouts are examined in depth.

The Cash-Out Shift away from Market Interventions

Farm policies within the developed countries have undergone substantial reform since price supports and supply control measures were introduced in the United States during the 1930s New Deal and since the Common Agricultural Policy (CAP) was inaugurated in Europe in the 1950s to provide a unified price support regime there. Orden, Paarlberg, and Roe (1999) call the U.S. farm policy reforms that have proven feasible over the past half century largely a cash-out, in which direct payments to farmers from taxpayers have replaced the support programs that earlier propped up commodity market prices. The price support programs required various interventions in markets to be operational, including tariff or quota protection, government stock accumulations, domestic supply controls, use of export subsidies, or some combination of these interventions. As the cash-out reforms have proceeded, the New Deal programs have remained in effect only for a group of specialty crops, particularly peanuts, tobacco, and sugar—and they too are now coming under reform.

The cash-out reform of U.S. farm policy, which began in the 1960s, took a substantial step forward in the 1985 farm bill, which lowered minimum price support guarantees (loan rates) while providing cash ("deficiency") payments for a large portion (fixed yields on 85 percent of "base" acreage) of the output of supported crops whenever market prices fell below legislated "target price" levels. Eligibility for the cash payments required production of specific crops. To control fiscal costs, a voluntary conservation reserve program (CRP) was initiated and annual land idling was required. The cashed-out support program of payments on limited output combined with annual land-idling authority was exempted from WTO expenditure disciplines under the Uruguay Round's Blue Box; the CRP is a Green Box policy.

The 1996 U.S. farm bill went further in the cash-out direction. Key new reforms suspended the authority for annual land set-asides and production of specific crops as conditions for payment eligibility and replaced the deficiency payments, at a time of high market prices, with fixed annual payments based on past production. Even the minimum loan rate prices were guaranteed with payments ("loan deficiency payments") instead of by government stock-holding interventions. Thus, the 1996 policies were more decoupled from production and caused less market distortion than previously. The 1996 regime ostensibly paved the way for the United States to abandon the Blue Box in the WTO. But when market prices of farm commodities fell after 1996, support to farmers was supplemented with additional payments. Initially these "emergency" payments were reported to the WTO as non-product-specific de minimis. The 2002 farm bill then legislated new countercyclical payments tied directly to the levels of market prices but again not to current crop production.[2] With this added support enacted, the United States began to argue in the Doha Round for relaxation of the Blue Box criteria to include the countercyclical payments instead of seeking its elimination.[3]

In the European Union, a similar cash-out of price support interventions has occurred, from higher initial levels and starting later chronologically than in the United States.[4] Through the 1980s, intervention prices above world market levels made the EU dependent on direct export subsidies. The 1991 MacSharry reforms began a cash-out, with direct payments offered as compensation for lower intervention prices and acreage idling required to limit costs. It was this reform, followed by the Agenda 2000 and 2003 CAP reforms, that allowed the EU to reduce sharply its use of export subsidies and paved the way for the Doha Round framework agreement calling for their elimination by a certain date. The 2003 reforms took the decoupling step of introducing whole-farm payments for which production of specific crops would not be required. Although there are messy implementation rules allowing some support payments still tied to production, to an extent the EU with its whole-farm payments has moved decoupling beyond the U.S. policy, which retains its price-linked countercyclical payments.

Alternatives to Cash-Out Programs

A cash-out is a gradual and partial reform process that reduces the market intrusiveness of farm programs over the long run by offering their beneficiaries a continuous stream of cash compensation payments. The gains for those countries pursuing a cash-out are fewer market distortions, fewer production restraints, and more competitive export pricing. The extent to which cash-out measures have decoupled farm support from production decisions and trade effects remains under scrutiny. Even when decoupled, a cash-out entails an open-ended commitment to support payments. Thus, cash-outs have drawbacks. Dirty decoupling under a cash-out and the ongoing character of the subsidization remain obstacles to trade liberalization.

Alternatives to the cash-out approach for ending intrusive farm program interventions, or even for ending a cash-out itself, can be distinguished based on the

TABLE 11.1 Alternative Reform Strategies

Compensation	Speed of implementation	
	Slow	Fast
Yes	Cash-out	Buyout
No	Squeeze-out	Cutout

Source: Orden, Paarlberg, and Roe (1999).

speed of reform implementation and whether compensation is provided to beneficiaries of the programs (table 11.1). A buyout is a quick termination of support entitlements, made politically palatable through significant but temporary compensation up-front, in the form of a large cash windfall. A squeeze-out is an incremental reduction in the market intrusiveness and generosity of farm programs, managed slowly enough to avoid triggering a defensive backlash from lobby groups representing subsidy-dependent farmers, yet significant enough over time to reduce distortions and costs, and to inspire voluntary nonparticipation by market-oriented commercial farmers. A cutout is a quick termination of all program support entitlements without compensation. None of these alternatives to a slow compensated cash-out has proven feasible on a large scale in the United States or Europe. But could a buyout bring an end to domestic farm support programs in developed countries, thus advancing the prospects for a liberalized agricultural trade regime?

Recent Small-Scale Buyouts: Divergence among U.S. Peanut, Tobacco, and Sugar Reforms

A number of recent policy reforms have been cited as buyouts. Interestingly, in the United States these have occurred around the specialty crops that had until recently avoided cash-out reforms. Here, we briefly examine the recent and divergent policy outcomes for peanuts, tobacco, and sugar.

2002 U.S. Peanut Reform. Under the traditional peanut program, holders of location-specific domestic quotas received preferential prices for peanuts supplied to the domestic market for edible uses compared with prices received for peanuts (known as "additionals") that went into processing (crushing into oil and meal) or were exported.[5] Access to the domestic edible market by foreign competitors has been restricted by import quotas.

The 2002 farm bill made fundamental changes to the U.S. peanut program. The quota-based dual market structure was replaced with direct payments similar to most other supported crops: loan rates and related payments, fixed direct payments, and countercyclical payments. The 2002 reform was a substantial cash-out but in most respects not a buyout. The only buyout dimension was that for a limited time peanut quota holders were compensated for their loss of quota rights.

The 2002 peanut program is quite lucrative for both former quota holders and for producers of peanuts once sold as additionals. The cash-out had an initial estimated cost of $4 billion over 10 years, essentially equal to the expected value of peanut production at world prices. Under the 2002 bill, any producer of peanuts is eligible for a loan rate of $355 a short ton on all current production. Those who qualify as "historical producers" of quota or additional peanuts are also guaranteed a direct fixed payment ($36 a short ton) and a target price ($495 a short ton) with countercyclical payments for the output from 85 percent of historical peanut acres and recent yields. The traditional producers also gain planting flexibility—they can receive the fixed and countercyclical payments without growing peanuts. If peanuts are grown, the new guaranteed revenue is higher than received in the past by producers of additionals, who had been eligible only for a loan rate of less than $200 a short ton. The quota owners receive a buyout payment of $220 a short ton for five years, which can also be taken as a one-time lump sum. Thus, for the next five years the total guaranteed revenue is essentially $694 a short ton for a quota owner, compared with a domestic price of $610 under the traditional program in the 1996 farm bill.[6] After five years, guaranteed revenue for a quota holder falls below the previous level. But the quota buyout of $220 a short ton for five years compared favorably with market prices for sales of quota rights before the 2002 farm bill was passed.[7]

There are several other political economy aspects to the reforms adopted for peanuts in 2002. The price support had been lowered by 10 percent in the 1996 farm bill and the annual quota had fallen to an average of 1.24 million short tons during 1996–2000, only 82 percent of its average in the preceding three years. Despite the reduced quota, domestic peanut production remained nearly constant, so domestic peanut producers were selling a relatively smaller proportion of their output at a lower quota support price than earlier and a relatively higher proportion of their peanuts at much lower prices in the additionals market.

One reason for the declining quota for the domestic edible market was the international trade agreements to which the United States committed in the 1990s. Foreign producer access to the U.S. domestic market for peanuts increased from less than 1 percent of consumption before the 1993/4 marketing year to nearly 10 percent by the 1999/2000 marketing year due to market-access provisions of the WTO's URAA and of NAFTA (North American Free Trade Agreement). The increased imports and potential future trade liberalization that would expand foreign access to the domestic edible market were used as arguments to motivate the 2002 peanut policy change as necessary to "preserve the domestic industry." Foreign producers who had attained market access under the tariff rate quota (TRQ) for peanuts were disadvantaged by the change. Unlike domestic producers, the foreign producers did not receive any payments as compensation for the lower U.S. peanut prices. With the new program in place, U.S. peanut imports dropped from an average of 105,000 short tons in 2000 and 2001 to 32,500 short tons in 2002 and 2003.[8]

2004 U.S. Tobacco Reform. Like peanuts, tobacco has been subject to location-specific production quotas to support market prices. Tobacco production is concentrated in the southern states (with Kentucky and North Carolina accounting for two-thirds of the output). Domestic tobaccos are imperfect substitutes for foreign tobaccos and historically have commanded higher prices for higher quality. The United States both imports and exports leaf tobacco and primarily exports tobacco in the form of cigarettes. Domestic cigarette consumption in the United States has declined by one-third since the early 1980s, including by 18 percent since 1996. Tobacco imports have not been nearly as restricted as imports of peanuts, allowing domestic cigarette producers to blend tobaccos from different sources. Foreign tobacco had comprised 45 percent of the content of U.S. manufactured cigarettes by 1994, when domestic content legislation was passed to restrict the imported share to 25 percent. A less restrictive TRQ was adopted in 1995, and by 2002 imported tobacco accounted for 55 percent of the content of U.S. cigarettes (Womach 2004b).

In addition to quota restrictions, tobacco has been subject to loan rates that set annual price floors, with cooperatives holding stock when necessary to maintain the floor price. The tobacco program was legislated to operate at no net cost to taxpayers, with a unique industry-financed fund designed to cover any losses incurred in operation of the loan rate program.[9] With declining domestic consumption associated with the negative health effects from smoking, and growing competition both for domestic usage and in export markets, the levels of quota production and tobacco producer revenues were in decline. The value of U.S. tobacco production averaged $2.8 billion during the 1990s but fell to under $2 billion in 2003 and 2004. From 1998 to 2004, quotas declined by nearly 50 percent.

The sharp drop in quotas and revenue, along with changes in marketing channels toward increased contracting by cigarette manufacturers, consolidated support among producers for a new tobacco program. A tobacco program buyout was enacted in October 2004.[10] Earlier buyout efforts had begun in conjunction with a national tobacco settlement that emerged after numerous states sued the tobacco companies for health care cost recovery.[11] These early buyout efforts fell short, but the idea survived. Subsequent discussion of a buyout centered on four dimensions: the compensation level to be provided, the structure of tobacco support policy after the buyout, the source of funding for the buyout, and whether additional health-related regulatory authority over tobacco would be granted to the Food and Drug Administration (FDA) (Brown and Snell 2003).

The tobacco reform of October 2004 provides a clean buyout to eliminate the tobacco quotas and price support loan rates. Owners of quota for the 2004 marketing year are to receive $7 a pound in equal payments over 10 years. Growers of tobacco during 2001–3 are to receive an additional payment of $1 a pound for each year they had acreage ($3 a pound if they produced in all three years). Estimated cost of the buyout of owners and growers is $9.6 billion, more than twice the cost of the peanut reform. This cost is to be financed by tax assessments on tobacco product manufacturers and importers, not by general tax revenue. The tobacco buyout ended authority for any price support or price stabilization programs. Production can take place anywhere in the country with no limit on volume. In short, with the legislation as enacted there will cease to be a tobacco farm program, but elimination of the support program is not accompanied by authority for health-related FDA regulation.

The tobacco buyout raises questions about its effects on U.S. production and trade and how lucrative the payments are to past tobacco producers. With removal of the tobacco quotas, domestic prices can be expected to drop by somewhat less than the past quota rental rates, and total national production is likely to increase. Brown and Thurman (2004), for example, project flue-cured tobacco prices will fall by one-fifth (from $1.85 a pound to $1.46 a pound), with production rising 180–280 million pounds from its 2004 level of 520 million pounds. Shifts among regions and types of tobacco produced are also anticipated, together with consolidation of production onto larger farms (Snell 2002).

In terms of the compensation level of the buyouts, table 11.2 compares a seven-year (1995–2001) average of poundage quota rental rates for peanuts and flue-cured and burley tobacco with the quota buyout payments for peanuts and the quota and total (quota owner and operator) buyout payments for tobacco. For peanuts, the lump-sum payment of $0.55 a pound is equivalent to an infinite stream of payments of $0.026 a pound at a 5 percent discount rate. This is about 70 percent of the average of past rental rates. Alternatively, the quota buyout payment is equivalent to average rental payments discounted at 5 percent for a period of 24 years. The buyout payment per pound exceeds this potential future payment stream to the extent that domestic peanut prices might fall had the earlier program continued. Likewise, the total buyout payment would exceed the total rental revenue stream under the old program if the quantity eligible for sale in the domestic market continued to decline under its continuation. With the peanut

TABLE 11.2 Value of the U.S. Peanut and Tobacco Buyouts (US$ per pound)

Measure	Peanuts	Flue-cured tobacco	Burley tobacco
Seven-year simple average quota rent (1995–2001)	0.037	0.471	0.411
		$7.00 tobacco buyout	
Quota buyout present value	0.550	5.675	5.675
Equivalent infinite annuity	0.026	0.270	0.270
Years for average rent	24	16	21
		$10.00 tobacco buyout	
Quota buyout present value	n.a.	8.108	8.108
Equivalent infinite annuity	n.a.	0.386	0.386
Years for average rent	n.a.	34	56

Source: Womach (2003) and authors' calculations. Present value and years of average rent are based on a 5 percent discount rate.
Note: n.a. = not applicable.

program reform, producers are also expected to receive (as of July 2004) nearly $2 billion of new fixed and countercyclical support payments in just the six years of the 2002 farm bill.

For tobacco, the 10-year stream of owner buyout payments is first discounted at a 5 percent rate to an equivalent initial lump sum. This reduces the payment from the nominal $7.00 a pound to $5.68, as shown in table 11.2. The lump-sum payment is equivalent to an infinite stream of payments of $0.27 a pound, about 57 percent of the average of past quota rentals for flue-cured tobacco and about 66 percent for burley tobacco. The lump-sum payment is more than double the private market prices that had prevailed for sales of quota rights before the reform. It is equivalent to discounted average rental payments for 16 and 21 years for flue-cured and burley tobacco, respectively. Inclusion of the $3 payments to growers (also discounted to an up-front lump sum) raises the equivalent infinite payments and number of years of past rentals covered.[12] Again, the buyout is more lucrative for producers to the extent that tobacco prices or quota allocations were likely to have continued to fall under continuation of the old program.

No Reform for Sugar. In contrast to the reforms that took place for peanuts in 2002 and tobacco in 2004, there has been an absence of reform in the support program for sugar. The United States is a sugar importer, with the domestic industry protected by quantitative import restrictions (TRQs) and high overquota tariffs. Sugar demand fell markedly in the 1980s with the development of corn sweeteners, but most of the adjustment was channeled into reduced imports rather than reduced domestic production. Still, the support policies authorize domestic marketing allotments to restrict supply in order to keep prices above loan rates, and the sugar program is designed to operate at no net cost to the government. Thus the sugar program is similar in design to the traditional peanut and tobacco programs, and its support program faces similar pressures from limited demand and increased imports under the URAA, NAFTA, and other trade agreements that might require tighter domestic marketing allotments or support price reductions.

The 1996 farm bill kept sugar loan rates fixed nominally at previous rates ($0.18 a pound for raw cane sugar and $0.23 a pound for refined beet sugar). Small changes in the provisions of the program made it potentially less beneficial for producers. The requirement that the sugar program operate to the extent possible at no net cost was eliminated. This was a change in legal status that technically created room for intrusive stock-holding expenditures or even for direct cash-out payments, but neither was imminent with high agricultural prices in 1996.

A policy crunch arose for sugar in 2000 when domestic production plus minimum U.S. import commitments exceeded domestic consumption and private stock-building demand at the supported domestic prices. To sustain those prices, the U.S. Department of Agriculture (USDA) accumulated stocks and offered a "plow-down" under which it exchanged stockpiled sugar for destruction of some of the planted sugar beet crop. A similar payment-in-kind (PIK) program was initiated to reduce future beet planting and avoid having to plow down another growing crop. Supply pressure on the sugar market eased in 2001, lessening political pressure for reform.

Sugar producers failed to endorse a cash-out reform along the lines of peanuts in the 2002 farm bill. Instead, they opted to tighten restrictions under their traditional program to defend the existing support prices. The 2002 bill stipulated again that the sugar program operate at no net cost to the government. The PIK program was continued, and authority was restored to control domestic supply through marketing allotments but only when annual sugar imports remained below 1.5 million short tons. The combination of the no-net-cost provision and the constraint on the use of domestic marketing allotments was designed, in the words of the U.S. producers, to ensure that the USDA and U.S. trade representative stood "shoulder to shoulder" with the domestic industry to oppose loosening of import restrictions. Together these provisions tie the hands of trade policy negotiators. Imports above 1.5 million short tons cannot be offset by restrictive domestic marketing allotments to sustain the supported price under the 2002 farm bill, while allowing imports to exceed this level would induce violation of the no-net-cost provision if USDA stockpiling were the result. Thus, the sugar program has to continue to be administered with tight import restraints, which sets it firmly against trade liberalization and makes U.S. sugar an obstacle to a liberalizing outcome within the Doha Round.

Synopsis from the Three Recent U.S. Policies. The contrasting recent policy outcomes among the historically similar U.S. peanut, tobacco, and sugar support programs provide some evidence about the conditions conducive to a buyout and its consequences. Narrowly defined benefits, specifically quota rights, may be easier to buy out than broader support policies: binding quota rights were bought out for both peanuts and tobacco, whereas sugar marketing allotments that are only intermittently binding have not been bought out.

The onset of reform aligns closely with a sharp shrinkage of the benefits obtained by participants in the old program. The pressure from reduced quotas and revenue was most severe for tobacco, and the tobacco buyout is the most complete. Unique dimensions with respect to tobacco also explain the more complete buyout of tobacco support compared to peanuts. Domestic tobacco producers were the least successful of the three sectors in securing restrictions on imports to protect their quota rents. The emergence of substantial health-cost-related transfers financed by manufacturers, importers, and consumers is also unique to the tobacco industry and set the precedent for financing the tobacco buyout with specific assessments instead of general tax revenue.[13] Had the sectoral tax precedent not existed, the higher cost of the tobacco buyout compared with peanuts might have blocked its enactment. The health issues associated with tobacco consumption also contributed to the outcome of full elimination of the support programs for producers. In contrast, peanut producers were able to align ongoing support with the cashed-out programs for other crops.

Consumers influence the buyout outcomes to the extent that their demand behavior contributes to declining benefits under a quota program. But the political economy condition necessary for a buyout still appears to be the emergence of substantial support for a reform among producers. Emergence of such opinion is obviously related to the shrinkage of benefits. Producers excluded from the quota program also align to favor reform. That was especially evident in the case of producers of additional peanuts, who gained from becoming eligible for a stronger support program. The opinion in favor of reform among producers does not have to be unanimous. In both the peanut and tobacco cases, minorities of producers in high-cost production regions opposed elimination of the location-specific quotas.

In terms of compensation, the evidence suggests that for reform to occur, the buyout payments have to be quite lucrative, especially given the circumstances of declining benefits to quota owners that provide the reform trigger. The buyout payments for peanuts and tobacco are equivalent to continuation of total prereform quota rental revenue for a period of 15 years or more.

It is also the case that while a buyout may be conducive to liberalization of trade policy, the peanuts and tobacco buyouts were designed to benefit domestic, not foreign, producers. The United States was already a net peanut exporter of additionals—imports were artificially drawn in only because of the market discrimination under the quota program. In the case of tobacco, total U.S. output is likely to rise with the buyout, displacing imports.

The Debate over Larger Buyouts

As the cash-out of farm support policies for most crops has been pursued, buyouts have on occasion been proposed, either as a means to facilitate adjustment out of agriculture or as compensation for elimination of a support program. These buyouts have not been adopted because the main thrust of farm support programs in developed countries has been to dampen pressure for adjustment, not to facilitate it or speed it up.[14] The time has largely passed when farm poverty or large migrations out of agriculture provided a rationale for adjustment-dampening policies, and in any case the effectiveness of those policies can be questioned. Yet the argument that farm policy should facilitate adjustment out of the sector is still not widely held. Nor has reform gone so far as to eliminate the main support programs and offer buyout compensation.

Bond Schemes in the EU. A "bond scheme" for transforming EU CAP policies was proposed in 1991 by Stefan Tangermann, then of the University of Gottingen (Swinbank and Tranter 2004; Daugbjerg and Swinbank 2004). The initial bond proposal was made before the EU adopted the 1992 MacSharry reforms. As characterized recently by Swinbank and Tangermann (2004), the proposal incorporates six steps: decouple crop payments from current land use; extend this principle to livestock; decouple payments from land and attach the entitlements to individuals; limit the duration of payments to, say, 10 or 20 years, and (possibly) make payments degressive over time; definitively fix the future level of payments; and transform payment entitlements into bonds.

Swinbank and Tangermann (2004) recognized that by 2003, the EU cash-out reforms had largely accomplished their first two proposed steps. The last four steps, they argue, would add two advantages. First, these steps would facilitate structural adjustments in production by allowing land prices to fall. Second, they would create certainty about future payments, while at the same time bringing the payments to an eventual end.[15]

The Tangermann bond scheme was an innovative proposal when it was first presented. Whether the bond scheme proposal would be a buyout or a delayed cutout depends on the level of associated payments. Swinbank and Tangermann (2004) center their discussion on payments starting at the level of the existing EU farm programs, a level that they argue would avoid putting additional pressure on the EU budget. But guaranteed payments at existing levels for 10 or even 15 years is not very lucrative for producers by the standard of the quota buyouts for U.S. peanuts or tobacco. There remains ambiguity in the 2003 CAP reforms, so the benefits being bought out by the bonds are not yet narrowly defined. A sharp diminution of benefits under the existing programs is not evident. There is no groundswell of calls for a buyout from producers, although producers are not opposed to the scheme, according to survey analysis undertaken by bond researchers (Tranter and others 2004). For these reasons, the prospects may be low for adoption of a bond scheme in the near term. Yet introduction of such bonds, especially with declining annual payments over an agreed implementation period, could provide a convincing domestic subsidy counterpart to phasing in substantial tariff reductions through the WTO.

How Might a Buyout Look in the United States? There has never been a convincing buyout proposal for the main farm support programs in the United States. The fixed payments adopted in the 1996 farm bill provided a windfall to farmers in a year of high market prices, but it failed to ensure a buyout in three respects: a budget baseline remained in place for future farm program spending, the permanent farm program legislation from 1949 and related acts was retained, and the 1996 farm bill took no other steps to bind the actions of a future Congress. As discussed above, when farm prices fell, the next Congress quickly stepped in with additional payments.

A buyout of the 2002 U.S. farm programs could focus on the fixed direct payments, the countercyclical payments, or the loan rate price guarantees. The fixed payments are a narrowly defined benefit, which increases the feasibility of a buyout. Bringing about their eventual elimination might ease concerns about continued subsidization, but it would accomplish the least economically or institutionally: either the fixed payments or a buyout replacement (perhaps through a bond) are WTO Green Box measures and are relatively decoupled.

A buyout of the countercyclical payments would accomplish more, since these payments are a particularly contentious form of decoupling more likely to have production-stimulating effects. A buyout of countercyclical payments would allow the United States to abandon the Blue Box, potentially allowing simplification and improved transparency of the WTO rules. The value of countercyclical payments is not as certain as the fixed payments under the 2002 farm bill, but there is an upper bound because the payments are made on fixed quantities and at per-unit levels no greater than the difference between the target price and the sum of the loan rate and per-unit fixed payment for each commodity. The farm lobby succeeded in building the countercyclical payments into the 2002 farm bill to address what it viewed as an inadequate safety net in the 1996 legislation, so there is no clamor from producers to eliminate these payments. But government fiscal deficits that had eased as the 2002 farm bill was enacted have tightened again. So farm program spending will be under scrutiny and may require some adjustment. And the question remains: with widespread opposition among nonsubsidizing countries, is the Blue Box doomed in the future even if it survives in the Doha Round?

Table 11.3 provides some information on the potential costs of several buyout options. Results are shown separately for a buyout (for all commodities aggregated) of the annual fixed payments, the maximum possible countercyclical payments, and the expected countercyclical payments as projected in the president's 2006 budget.

TABLE 11.3 Cost of Possible Buyouts of the Main U.S. 2002 Farm Bill Support Payments (US$ billions)

Buyout cost	Fixed direct payments	Countercyclical payments	
		Maximum possible	Projected level
2002 farm bill payments (crop years 2002–2007)	5.292 (average) 28.198 (lump sum)	7.302 (average) 38.787 (lump sum)	3.505 (average) 18.303 (lump sum)
Buyout payments over 10 years equivalent to annual payments at 2002 farm bill level for 25 years	9.659 (annual) 78.311 (lump sum)	13.328 (annual) 108.065 (lump sum)	6.398 (annual) 51.870 (lump sum)
Infinite annuity equivalent of buyout payments	3.729 (annual)	5.146 (annual)	2.470 (annual)

Source: Fixed direct payments and projected countercyclical payments are based on the president's 2006 budget. Estimate of maximum countercyclical payments is from calculations provided by the U.S. Department of Agriculture's Economic Research Service. Buyout payments are assumed to be made in equal installments over 10 years. Present values and infinite annuities are based on a 5 percent discount rate.

The 2002 farm bill payments are assumed to occur for six consecutive years (crop years 2002–7). The nominal average annual payment and the present value of the payments (at a 5 percent discount rate) are shown as a benchmark in the first row of table 11.3. The buyout payments are assumed to be made in equal nominal installments over 10 years, as in the tobacco case. The costs shown in the second row are those required to compensate for discounted farm bill payments for 25 years—roughly consistent with the buyouts provided for peanuts and tobacco. The nominal value of an infinite annuity equivalent of the annual payments are shown in the third row.

A buyout of the fixed direct payments along these lines nearly doubles the annual expenditure that would have to be made for 10 years compared to expenditures each year under the 2002 farm bill, and almost triples the present value of the payments. This buyout raises short-term costs, but the value of equivalent annual payments in perpetuity is less than the 2002 farm bill delivers during crop years 2002–7. A buyout of the maximum countercyclical payments that could be made is the most costly, while a buyout of their projected value has a lower cost than for the fixed direct payments. Still, with the 2002 farm bill put into place, and these projected and potential costs of the countercyclical payments, it is not surprising that the United States has invested so much negotiating effort to ensure their inclusion in a continuation of the Blue Box, despite the merit of abandoning these payments as a step toward facilitating trade liberalization. The expected cost of the price-linked countercyclical payments underscores that use of the Blue Box for these subsidies will remain contentious.[16]

If farm subsidy payments were to be bought out, there is also a time-consistency problem of whether any buyout could be enforced. Based on the increase in support enacted after 1996, the record is not encouraging. The 1996 farm bill included "production flexibility contracts" designed to assure farmers of the stream of legislated payments regardless of future federal budget constraints. These contracts proved one-sided, as taxpayers were not assured that farmers would receive only the contracted level of support.

Several steps can be envisioned that would improve the prospects for adherence to a buyout. The first would be to eliminate the permanent legislation for farm support programs. Stronger steps could also be taken. Contracts for buyout payments could require that the acreage for which the payments were being bought out (and the output from that acreage) be ineligible for future support legislated by Congress. Such contracts could be structured similarly to those by which some farmers sell their "development rights" to state and local governments so that their land must remain in rural condition or agricultural use.[17] The state governments have devised binding legal criteria to ensure compliance from the contract beneficiaries who have sold their development rights.

A WTO agreement built around a buyout of U.S. countercyclical payments would also provide an enforcement mechanism. If the Blue Box were eliminated, and Amber Box constraints were made sufficiently tight, countercyclical payments could become infeasible. Even tighter Amber Box constraints could bind the loan rate program too. Constraints through the WTO are less likely to reinforce a buyout of fixed payments. Countercyclical and loan-rate-based payments are never going to fit into the WTO Green Box. But there are many loopholes through which farm support programs, including trade-distorting programs, can be renewed within the Green Box.

Revived Supply Management: A Ghost of Policies Past

There are other policy options that might end current subsidy programs of developed countries by moving in quite different directions from a buyout of the existing payments. One option would be to replace the commodity-based payments with expanded "green-payment" subsidies tied to environmental criteria and made in a way that keeps land in agricultural production. If the new subsidies stimulated production, this approach would constitute "dirty environmentalism" and would leave ample room for conflict in the WTO (as have dirty tariffication and dirty decoupling). Yet for the United States, for example, as domestic policy it would build upon a conservation working lands program introduced in the 2002 farm bill. Interventions along such lines fit under the broad rubric of dampening adjustment pressures, a feature that has characterized past farm support programs.

A second alternative to a buyout would be a revival of supply management. Sufficient revival of this ghost of past policies would also allow existing subsidy payments to be eliminated, but only by exacerbating the market-distorting effects that have been moderated with past cash-outs and that would be further avoided with a buyout.[18]

Control of supplies and diversion of crop outputs to shore up prices have never faded far from the policy mix under the cash-out reforms that have occurred. In the EU, acreage set-asides are still in use with the program of Single Farm Payments. One-tenth of the cropland in the United States is idled under the CRP, even though annual acreage controls have been eliminated. Ethanol production now absorbs more than 10 percent of the U.S. corn crop. This use of corn has been stimulated by tax breaks on blended fuels, but regulations that require blending could supplant the tax-break stimulus.

While there are proponents of a simple revival of annual acreage idling to push up prices, the more innovative recent supply management proposals focus on diverting additional acreage into bioenergy production, with the implicit effect that crop supplies would tighten and prices rise. A range of proponents has emerged, who tie their arguments to the conflict over subsidies in the WTO. The former CIA director James Woolsey, for example, argues that a shift from current subsidies to subsidized bioenergy crop production could "help resolve global trade deadlocks that center on whether our support for agriculture undermines the rural poor in the rest of the world" (EFC 2004). Proponents describe this as a "farmer-oriented" policy and have offered only corresponding partial assessments of its economic impacts.[19]

The point of briefly calling attention to these alternatives to a buyout of farm support programs is not to assert their merit but rather to demonstrate that the evolution of farm policies in the developed countries toward efficient and trade-facilitating outcomes is not assured. War in Iraq and high oil prices in 2004 have not yet given a noticeable boost to the bioenergy subsidy proposals. Neither has any clear momentum yet arisen for ending the current farm programs with a large buyout.

Efficient Policies toward Agriculture in Developing Countries

We turn next to the agricultural policy challenges in developing countries. These diverse countries have always confronted a double policy dichotomy. First is the issue of the balance between the agricultural sector vis-à-vis other productive sectors (especially industry) in their general economic strategies. This issue has been manifest in the dilemma of trying to maintain prices at high levels for agricultural producers while keeping them affordable for consumers, and in the debate about the balance between rural areas and urban centers (Lipton 1977). Second is the policy issue of growth versus equity. Should the agricultural sector pursue growth and production, usually concentrating support on "modern" and larger agricultural units, or emphasize poverty reduction and food security with a focus on small farmers, landless rural workers, and other vulnerable groups? This dilemma has many facets, including the possibility of complex two-way influences, such as whether more equal societies have higher and more stable rates of growth than their more unequal counterparts (Alessina and Perotti 1996; Deininger and Squire 1997). Others note the positive impacts of an agrarian structure based on family farms on the emergence of democratic governance (Moore 1967) and on the formation of larger domestic markets that allow the development of industry and other activities. The environmental sustainability of a strategy based on large commercial farms, versus another focused on small-scale agriculture, has also been amply debated.

Agricultural trade policies historically have been just a component of the broader policy debates relating to agricultural development and the "agrarian question" in general. Those trade policies (and related price schemes) often taxed export goods, while import-competing goods, mainly food products, were more likely than not supported through direct border protection and a variety of price mechanisms. The nature of such agricultural trade policies has changed over time, as has the general matrix of macroeconomic policies and trade policies for other sectors, which together determine the net effect on the agricultural sector of developing countries. The possibility of achieving welfare-enhancing results in the agricultural negotiations of the Doha Round requires placing the debate about agricultural trade policies within this broader context.

Evolution of Agricultural Policies toward Less State Intervention

Just as agricultural policy in developed countries has evolved through partial reform toward less-intrusive interventions in markets, so too policies toward agriculture in developing countries have seen a substantial evolution away from state management since the 1950s—but with significant differences that shape the approach that developing countries have taken in the WTO agricultural negotiations. In the discussion that follows, we highlight key dimensions of this reform. The review frames the policy options that could facilitate trade liberalization in the WTO while promoting, in particular, rural and agricultural development, poverty alleviation, food security, and environmental sustainability within developing countries without resorting to distorting-trade measures.

The 1950s and 1960s: Industrial Focus, Community Development, and Land Reform. According to the post–World War II development strategy, the role of agriculture was to be subordinated to the needs of industrialization, within what has been called Import Substitution Industrialization (ISI). Different arguments were used to support this view. Quantitative historical analysis (for instance, Kuznets 1966) showed that agriculture declined in importance with the advance of economic development. Also it was argued, especially in Latin America, that inelastic supply and demand for agricultural goods and deteriorating terms of trade suggested the need to diversify the economic structure out of agriculture and into industry (CEPAL 1969). Other arguments were based on the structure of national and international power. Many developing countries were economically dependent on the former colonial powers and, from this perspective, deemphasizing the role of the agricultural sector in development was part of a double process of economic independence and political sovereignty, combined with a more equitable internal distribution of income.

Therefore the prevalent approach during the 1950s and 1960s was to support the process of industrialization by making the agricultural sector perform four main functions: a transfer of labor surpluses would occur as workers supposedly underemployed in agriculture shifted to industry; agriculture would provide food ("wage goods") and raw materials to the industrial sector; savings in the agricultural sector would be taxed away to sustain the process of investment in the industrial sector and for the development of public infrastructure; and the agricultural sector had to generate surpluses of foreign currency to pay for the importation of capital goods and industrial inputs (Johnston and Mellor 1961).Within the ISI approach, the nuts and bolts of agricultural policies were based mostly on the use of administered prices at different stages of the market chain; the existence of public and parastatal enterprises operating in product and input markets, in good measure to enforce the administered prices but also with the avowed objective of ensuring the supply of some inputs; and the establishment of public agricultural banks and the supply of subsidized credit. In many cases those policies tried to help "modern," more productive units. The issue of poverty in rural areas was addressed mainly through community development and land reform.

Community development that spread during the late 1950s and 1960s was a political rather than economic approach. The idea was to stimulate the population to organize, so the people could exert initiative and improve their communities through cooperative efforts based on self-help and mutual help, leading to increases in welfare and reductions in poverty. The expectation was that a successful program would result not only in improved economic conditions but also in more stable and democratic communities (Holdcroft 1977; Uphoff and others 1979). Community development, however, was not exempt from criticisms. In particular, the focus on the use of the community's own resources was considered by some a subterfuge of the governments to avoid investing the additional resources that were required to effectively develop those communities, while at the same time concentrating resources in the urban sector.[20] Furthermore, in some cases mobilization began to exceed what some governments considered controllable limits, and many other countries had serious difficulties showing quantifiable results in aspects such as "participation," "institutional capacity," and "democratic organization."

Another important approach to agricultural development during the 1950s and 1960s was land reform. After the Second World War successful land reforms were carried out in Japan, Taiwan (China), and the Republic of Korea under U.S. influence. In Latin America and the Caribbean (LAC), there were several important land reforms before 1960 (Mexico in the 1920s, Bolivia and Guatemala in the early 1950s, and Cuba in the late 1950s), but it was the Alliance for Progress in 1961 that launched a widespread program. Africa also saw different attempts at land reform in the Arab Republic of Egypt, Ethiopia, Kenya, and several of the other countries emerging from colonial rule and acquiring their independence.

The results in many countries in Latin America (and Asian countries such as the Philippines with similar land structures) were less favorable than in Japan, Korea, and Taiwan (China), mostly because their more unequal and dualistic initial structures proved more difficult to reform (due to political resistance) than in Asia with its more equal initial distribution and a larger number of family farms. The problems in most of Sub-Saharan Africa (SSA), where land also tended to be more equally distributed than in LAC, were mainly related to the tension between traditional communal land tenure systems and the attempts at creating commercial land tenure structures. In any case, by the mid-1970s and early 1980s the priority of land reform, which, in many cases, was linked to the fear of peasant revolutions in developing countries, began to fade along with the prospects of the spread of communism in Latin America and the Caribbean or Asia.

The 1970s: New Technology and Outward-Oriented Development Strategies. Both the overall development strategy and agriculture's role within it, as well as sectoral policies, began to be reviewed in the mid-1960s and early 1970s, when different concerns arose about the adequacy of a development strategy that concentrated savings and investment in industrial development and discriminated against the agricultural sector. Schultz (1964), in an influential book, argued that the farmers in developing countries were "poor but efficient," reacting with economic rationality to changes in prices and incentives. Debates over the operation of "dual economies" (Fei and Ranis 1966 versus Jorgenson 1967), specifically on whether efficiency gains could be made by moving labor from agriculture to industry, suggested the importance of supporting agriculture through technological development and human capital formation in rural areas. The idea that there could be a technological solution to the rural problem infused the Green Revolution of the 1970s, replacing community development and land reform as the main rural development strategy.

This approach led to the creation of the system of international agricultural research centers (the Consultative Group on International Agricultural Research, or CGIAR) and of national agricultural research institutes and extension services in many developing countries during the 1970s. Complementary irrigation investments expanded in several countries, particularly in Asia. The Green Revolution was criticized for concentrating on better-off areas and farmers (which, it was argued, worsened income distribution and poverty). However, the increases in productivity since the mid-1970s, especially in food crops, allowed the world to increase the level of available calories per capita even though population doubled, using about the same land and with real prices half the levels of the 1960s, all of which helped to alleviate poverty and malnutrition.[21]

Another argument emphasizing the importance of agriculture in the development process was provided by the realization that the poor in developing countries were concentrated mainly in rural areas. If poverty alleviation was to be an important objective of economic policy, this argument went, then greater attention should be given to agricultural and rural development. Chenery and others (1974), in another influential book entitled, suggestively, *Redistribution with Growth*, presented the case for an investment program centered especially on accumulation of human and physical capital by the rural poor.[22] Under the auspices of the World Bank, international organizations began to increase investment in agriculture, mainly through integrated programs in rural areas targeted to reach low-income groups, including productive and social investments in what was called Integrated Rural Development.

While highlighting the importance of agriculture, both the Green Revolution and the Integrated Rural Development approaches were undertaken within the framework of development and macroeconomic policies still shaped by ISI. Other analyses were appraising that overall approach critically. Little, Scitovsky, and Scott (1970) and Balassa and Associates (1971) called for a modification of the import-substitution approach that protected industry and the elimination of policy biases against agriculture. They highlighted the negative impacts on growth and poverty alleviation of the structure of "macro prices" enforced through governmental policies. Poverty alleviation appeared impaired by policies that protected capital-intensive industrialization and limited the development of agriculture. The slow employment growth in industry and the stagnation of agriculture had adverse effects on income distribution, limited participation of the population in productive employment, and contributed to persistent poverty (Johnston 1977). Thus, poverty problems could not be resolved simply by restructuring micropolicies or by reallocating investments to the poor. The development strategy had to be refocused to take advantage of opportunities in international trade, eliminate distortions created by extreme government intervention, allow prices to operate more freely, and make sure that technology and investment reflected the endowment of human and other resources by positively reappraising the role of agriculture in the economy (Balassa 1984; Little, Scitovsky, and Scott 1970; Krueger 1978).

Through the 1970s, while many countries in LAC and Africa continued within the ISI approach, several countries in Asia as well as some in LAC began to move to an export-oriented strategy. In the agricultural sector, the nuts-and-bolts approach continued to be administered prices, public sector interventions and institutions, and directed credit, combined with the Green Revolution (cum irrigation) and Integrated Rural Development. A "basic-needs" approach to poverty also emerged in the late 1970s. It was argued that objectives such as growth, or even employment and income redistribution, were means to the more concrete objective of attending to the specific basic needs of the population (defined primarily by nonfinancial indicators, and including both "material" and "immaterial" components), especially for the poor and vulnerable.[23]

The 1980s: Fiscal Retrenchment and Structural Adjustment. The two oil shocks of the 1970s and the change in macroeconomic policies in developed countries in the early 1980s (with sharp increases in real interest rates and the subsequent recession) severely affected many developing countries and led to the debt crisis of the 1980s, mostly in LAC and Africa. Agricultural prices collapsed in the mid-1980s, primarily as a result of those macroeconomic changes and expanded public support of agricultural production in developed countries, particularly as the EU increased subsidization of exports and the cash-out reforms in the United States reduced price-supporting loan rates. The agricultural transformation in China, the expansion of the Green Revolution in many developing countries, and the break-up of the Soviet Union were developments that added to global agricultural supplies or weakened demand within agricultural markets, exacerbating the collapse in prices (Díaz-Bonilla 1991; Borensztein and others 1994). The possibility of financing import substitution industrialization with the rents extracted from agriculture basically disappeared, leading to the progressive reduction of taxes (and of price schemes with similar effects) on agricultural export goods.

What prompted the change in overall development strategies in the 1980s, much more than the analytical studies showing the economic limitations of ISI, was this sequence of macroeconomic shocks and the ensuing debt problem. The success of export-oriented strategies, mostly in Asia, also contributed to the reevaluation of ISI. At the agricultural level, the nuts-and-bolts approach of government intervention and Integrated Rural Development underwent a thorough revision that substantially changed them, while the technological-development approach continued as a crucial strategy (although with less funding, because of the fiscal retrenchment).

Additional analyses, mostly covering the period from the 1960s to mid-1980s and focusing on macroeconomic policies and the direct and indirect effects of trade, also argued that price incentives were tilted against agriculture and impaired growth (Krueger, Schiff, and Valdés 1988; Bautista and Valdés 1993). The price bias resulting from these factors was different from the more general urban bias discussed by Lipton (1977), which included an emphasis on urban areas in public investment and expenditures. From the perspective of the macroeconomic approach to incentives, investments in the agricultural sector were considered far less effective within a framework of distorting macroeconomic and trade policies.

At the sectoral level, one of the characteristics of the interventions of the 1960s and 1970s was the granting of preferential loans in many developing countries through sectorally specialized institutions (industrial as well as agricultural and rural banks).[24] The expansion of credit was commonly financed through rediscounts from the central bank or similar institutions, which expanded money supply, basically in the context of closed capital accounts. Different studies had warned about the inefficiencies and waste in the complex maze of price policies and market interventions by public enterprises in developing countries (see, for example, Bates 1981 for Africa). Studies of "financial repression" (McKinnon 1973) argued that administered interest rates, which tended to become negative either because of delayed adjustment to inflation or because subsidized interest rates were considered necessary to accelerate investment, ended up discouraging savings (at least in the formal financial system) and generating excess demand for credit, with negative effects on growth and efficiency. Focusing on rural financial markets, Adams, Graham, and von Pischke (1984) argued that subsidized agricultural credit generated a misallocation of resources in the rural sector (excessive capital intensity and land speculation), did not reach the poorest sectors because preferential credit was absorbed by the largest farms, and discouraged rural savings and the development of rural financial institutions and markets.

The World Bank's *World Development Report* for 1986, which focused on agriculture, codified these lines of analysis into several policy recommendations: developing countries should eliminate inefficient industrial protectionism; correct the overvaluation of the exchange rate; eliminate export taxes on agriculture; reduce the government's involvement in agricultural markets; and phase out administered prices, public sector enterprises operating in output and input markets, and state-owned agricultural banks and directed agricultural credit schemes. Budgetary savings from the elimination of public interventions, which were considered inefficient, contradictory, and open to waste and corruption, could be reassigned to investments in technology, extension and training, and infrastructure. General and sectoral "structural adjustment programs," by the World Bank and other international banks and donors, financed the implementation of those policy changes in many developing countries.

Within the new general framework, the poor, particularly in rural areas, were supposed to benefit from more sustainable growth once the capital-intensive and antiagricultural development strategy was corrected. The remaining poor could then be aided through focused policies. The basic-needs approach that had emerged in the late 1970s provided a possible rationale for this reorientation and focalization of social services in the 1980s.

International organizations and donors basically reoriented their activities to cover both the more macroeconomic level of policies for productive purposes and the more narrowly focused social interventions for poverty alleviation, mostly abandoning the midlevel of sectoral productive interventions. In particular, World Bank agricultural lending, including for Integrated Rural Development, was sharply curtailed as the decade of the 1980s progressed (Lipton and Paarlberg 1990). It declined (in constant 2001 U.S. dollars) from about $5 billion and some 30 percent of total World Bank lending in the late 1970s and the first half of the 1980s to $3 billion and 10–15 percent of total lending in the second half of the 1980s. By the early 2000s, agricultural lending had declined further to about $1.5 billion, or 7 percent, of total World Bank loans. Similar trends occurred in other multilateral institutions and individual donors.

The 1990s and Beyond: Further Adjustment and Targeted Poverty Alleviation. Changes in macroeconomic and trade policy in developing countries during the 1980s and 1990s led to depreciated real exchange rates and reduced overall trade protection. Wood (1988) calculated that the real exchange rates of most developing countries (except oil-exporters) had been declining from the 1960s to the 1980s. More recent data from Cashin, Céspedes, and Sahay (2002) on real, effective exchange rates for different countries during the period 1980 to 2002 also show further devaluations: real, effective exchange rates in LAC were on average below the early 1980s' values by 15–20 percent, in Asia by about 40 percent, and in Africa by 45–55 percent.[25]

With respect to trade policy, except for the Middle East and North Africa where the levels of protection have increased, average total tariffs in the early 2000s are 40 percent to 70 percent lower than during the 1980s. Looking at tariffs by sectors, the conventional wisdom around the mid-1980s (World Bank 1986; Krueger, Schiff, and Valdés 1988; Bautista and Valdés 1993) that industrial protection in developing countries was higher than for agricultural products, imparting an antiagricultural bias to overall incentives, can be questioned. Cernat, Laird, and Turrini (2002) suggest that tariff protection of agriculture is at least as high as for manufacturing now (table 11.4), while Jensen, Robinson, and Tarp (2002) calculate that whatever antiagriculture bias existed as a result of trade and macroeconomic policies in the 1960s and 1970s was largely eliminated during the 1990s, at least for the 15 countries they examine.

At the same time that price distortions were reduced or eliminated, other developments, however, were moving against the agricultural sector. At least in LAC and SSA, economic growth declined significantly during the 1980s and 1990s, affecting demand for agricultural goods. Overall fiscal positions of developing countries deteriorated during the 1980s (for SSA fiscal problems began in the 1970s). Deteriorating public sector finances, both in developing and developed countries, along with the decline in world agricultural prices in the mid-1980s, led to fiscal adjustments and pressures to reduce support for agriculture in many countries.[26]

Credit conditions also changed. During the 1980s, and then more markedly in the 1990s, many developing countries began to open up their capital accounts, expecting beneficial impacts on growth, efficiency, and smoothing of volatility (Prasad and others 2003). This changed the context for monetary policies. The limits of the impossible trinity began to be recognized: a country could not have a fixed exchange rate, an open capital account, and an independent monetary policy at the same time, but could pick only two out of those three policy instruments. Considering the tendency in developing countries to try to maintain stable exchange rates (what Calvo and Reinhart 2002 have called "fear of floating"), and with a capital account open, a consequence appears to have been more constrained monetary policies. At the same time the International Monetary Fund, World Bank, and other international organizations, as part of the structural adjustment and stabilization programs of the mid-1980s and 1990s, supported financial sector reforms including changes in public agricultural agencies such as agricultural banks and parastatal companies that, among other things, provided credit to farmers (FAO/GTZ 1998; Kherallah and others 2003). Some of the reforms, while eliminating many of the inefficient and contradictory public sector interventions, have at the same time dismantled the institutional infrastructure that provided technical assistance and some key inputs to agricultural production (including credit, seeds, and fertilizers) and marketing services, without ensuring the creation of private sector institutions that could provide similar services and inputs (Kherallah and others 2003).

Several developing countries, particularly in Africa but not only there, have been affected further by armed conflicts that have reduced agricultural production and increased poverty and hunger. According to FAO (2004), conflict in Africa resulted in lost agricultural production of more than US$120 billion during the last three decades of the 20th century. Conflict there has sometimes been the result of competition over scarce natural resources, including land and water.

In addition to the changes in growth, fiscal and monetary policies, institutional arrangements, and internal conflict, there were also two important changes in external conditions. First, particularly since the 1980s, the extensive support and protection of agriculture in developed countries led to surpluses that were sold with subsidies in international markets, depressing prices there. Those policies discouraged investments in the rural sector of many developing countries that came to depend on cheap and subsidized food from abroad, and contributed to turning many of them, including a number of countries in Sub-Saharan Africa, from net exporters to net importers of food. Cuts in loans to agricultural and rural development projects by the World Bank and other development banks appear to have been influenced, at least in part, by low international food prices that reduced the expected returns of future projects and depressed the ex post results of evaluated projects (Lipton and Paarlberg 1990).

TABLE 11.4 Average Tariff Protection Applied, by Economy or Region, early 2000s (percent)

Sector	Average applied MFN tariff rate			
	Asian NIEs	China	South Asia	Transition economies
Primary agriculture	38	16	21	13
Processed agriculture	20	15	29	20
Other primary sectors	2	2	14	1
Textiles and apparel	8	13	28	14
Other manufactures	5	6	24	9

Second, expanded capital flows seem to have led to a more volatile economic environment for developing countries, with the sequence of crises in Mexico in 1995, East Asia in 1997, Russia in 1998, Brazil in 1999, and Argentina in 2001. The impacts of these financial crises on world agricultural prices and markets, as well as domestic conditions in the countries affected, appear to have been substantial (IMF 1999; USDA 2000).[27]

In summary, the policy changes linked to structural adjustment during the second half of the 1980s and 1990s appear to have reduced the incentive bias against agriculture, but gaps in private sector development, tighter fiscal and monetary conditions, lower growth in some regions, and external events such as depressed agricultural prices and volatility in financial markets, have influenced negatively the performance of the agricultural sectors of developing countries.

In terms of poverty alleviation, in the second half of the 1990s a new type of program began to be implemented in some of the more advanced developing countries (such as the case of Mexico's "Progresa" and now "Oportunidades" program, Brazil's "Bolsa Scola," and Argentina's "Jefes y Jefas de Hogar"). Although the details vary, they basically consist of income transfers given mostly to female heads of households but with specific commitments required related to attendance at school and health care for their children. These programs are trying to break the intergenerational transfer of poverty across members of the family. They have been complemented by other institutional and policy changes related to education, health, and labor markets, trying to improve the existing supply of services that cover the target population. The programs appear to have positive impacts on local activity and short-term growth, and on accumulation

TABLE 11.4 (Continued)

Sub-Saharan Africa	Middle East and North Africa	Latin America	Western Europe	North America	Japan	Rest of the world
16	49	12	12	9	30	6
27	58	17	21	10	46	13
5	4	5	0	0	0	5
21	13	15	5	10	6	14
11	8	11	2	1	0	9

Source: Cernat, Laird and Turrini (2002).
Note: NIEs are the newly industrialized economies of Hong Kong (China), Republic of Korea, Singapore, and Taiwan (China).

of physical capital and formation of human capital, so as to boost long-term growth prospects.[28]

Developing Country Views of the Doha Trade Negotiations

By the time the Doha Round was launched, trade policies taxing agricultural exports had largely disappeared in developing countries, and their price supports and subsidies had been deeply curtailed by the crises (and related policy adjustments) of the 1980s and 1990s, leaving agricultural protection as the main available policy instrument to support agriculture. Those facts have shaped the views of many developing countries, which as members of the WTO have become more active participants in the negotiations. Although they have presented a large variety of proposals, developing countries can be divided into two main groups, depending on their emphasis on two different approaches. One approach is to "play offense," by trying to limit the ample legal room developed countries have under current WTO rules to protect and subsidize their own agriculture (for which they also have large financial resources). The other is to "play defense," asking for special and differential treatment (SDT) to be able to protect (and potentially subsidize) agriculture in developing countries.

Countries following a defensive approach see their agricultural sector as vulnerable and consider agriculture as special, requiring separate treatment in the WTO. Although these opinions may appear to put them close to the "multifunctional" arguments of some developed WTO members, the developing countries do not want their special problems of agriculture to be confused with the multifunctionality claims by rich countries. While they want tighter disciplines on developed countries' agricultural policies, these countries do not agree with the view that agriculture should be treated similarly to industry under WTO rules. In particular, because they believe that developed countries will not reduce their levels of protection and subsidies, or because, even if that happens, they think that their agriculture would still not be competitive, they have asked for special and differential treatment to have ways to promote their agricultural sectors.

One argument used to support this line of reasoning is that the legal exemptions allowed for developing countries under the Green Box and Article 6.2 of the Uruguay Round Agreement on Agriculture are of little use to developing countries because the financial, technical, and human resources required by the permitted policies make them very difficult to implement (UNCTAD 2000). The conclusion reached is that the developing countries need flexibility on the levels of protection allowed and possible subsidies under the label of development or food-security boxes.[29]

A subset of these developing countries, particularly in Africa, is concerned about maintaining the perceived value of their preferential access to the markets of developed countries that may decline if protection in those markets is reduced (Bouët, Fontagné, and Jean 2006). Also, those developing countries in this subset that are net food importers emphasize the problem of possible increases in the cost of food imports in a liberalized world.[30]

Another (smaller) block of developing countries is part of the Cairns Group (whose 17 members include 14 developing countries).[31] The Cairns Group's offensive approach has focused on including agriculture in the disciplines of the WTO, asking for lower levels of protection and domestic subsidies and a prohibition on export subsidies. Although Cairns Group members are often thought of as large and competitive exporters, some of the developing countries in this group (such as Bolivia, Guatemala, and the Philippines) have the profile of food-insecure countries (Díaz-Bonilla and others 2000). The Cairns Group developing countries share with many other developing countries their criticism of export subsidies as unfair and disruptive of international trade. These two groups agree on the need to drastically reduce domestic support in rich countries, including the Blue Box and several of the payments to farmers allowed in the Green Box. The main difference has been that the Cairns Group has not considered appropriate the ample SDT provisions favored by the first group of developing countries that, it is feared, would reinforce the protection of developed countries while also reducing trading opportunities in other markets.

Some developing countries have tried to apply both approaches (offense and defense), reflecting in part the nature of their agriculture. India is an interesting case. Playing offense seems reasonable for a country that in the past few years has emerged as a net exporter of agricultural products.[32] At the same time, a large share of India's poor population lives in rural areas, and concerns about possible negative impacts on that group have underpinned the strong defensive components in India's WTO proposal (embedded in the notion of a food-security box).[33]

The balance between defensive and offensive approaches in several developing countries was changed by the joint U.S.-EU framework of August 2003, which was perceived as moving the United States toward the EU's more protectionist stance in exchange for maintaining American subsidies. This perception generated a parallel realignment within developing countries leading to the creation of the G-20 that brought together many Cairns Group's members (Argentina, Brazil, Costa Rica, Indonesia, South Africa, and Thailand) and several of the development-box countries (Dominican Republic, Arab Republic of Egypt, Pakistan, and Sri Lanka) along with countries such as China, India, and Mexico. The Cairns Group's developing countries accepted a larger component of defensive policies, while other developing countries moderated somewhat their aspirations for stronger SDT.

The heterogeneity of developing-country interests nonetheless increases the risk of "lose-lose" scenarios in which developed countries retain their high levels of protection and subsidization while developing countries reinforce their levels of farm protection. This type of outcome is not at all precluded under the WTO's July 2004 Framework agreement of the Doha Development Agenda. It is basically the option offered by the EU, Japan, and countries with comparable agricultural policies. The United States, for its part, has pushed developing countries toward a similar defensive approach by asking for wide liberalization while trying to retain policy instruments (basically domestic subsidies) that enhance its competitiveness in world markets. In such a nonliberalizing bargaining equilibrium, developing countries would lose export opportunities that generate employment and incomes, while paying the cost of higher food items in their own markets, likely impairing food security. In developed countries, taxpayers and consumers would still be burdened with the costs of subsidizing inefficient producers in ways that do not necessarily protect the environment or achieve a more equitable income distribution in their societies, while agricultural development in poorer countries would continue to be stifled, leaving in place the negative effects of those policies on poverty, hunger, and malnourishment.

If developing countries want to avoid such a Doha Round outcome and benefit from the negotiations, they should maintain their focus on playing offense. Limiting the possibilities for subsidization and protection in developed countries would stimulate opportunities for production in developing countries, both for export markets and for their domestic markets, where they have to compete with subsidized products from the developed countries. The separate issue of the erosion of preferences of low-income countries with access to protected markets in developed countries must be quantified, and losses could be compensated directly to those countries through some form of buyout payments. Food-insecure and vulnerable developing countries will need some SDT, including simplified and streamlined instruments to confront unfair trade practices and import surges that may irreparably damage the livelihoods of small farmers, and longer transition times for adjustments to be undertaken. But to be constructive, SDT must avoid a strong protectionist component and instead focus on Green Box and other investment-centered approaches to agriculture, that being the best strategy for rural development and poverty alleviation.[34]

Avoiding Distortionary Protection and Agricultural Subsidies in Developing Countries

Our review has highlighted different ghosts that still haunt agricultural policies in developing countries and that could be revived. One possibility is to go back to the multiple, contradictory, and inefficient policies of public sector intervention in agricultural and related markets. Although many low-income countries lack the fiscal resources to implement those policies, this option is becoming increasingly open to middle-income countries as agriculture's share of their economies becomes smaller. Another possibility is to increase agricultural protection in developing countries. In the context of the WTO Doha Round, some negotiators and civil society groups have argued that increased agricultural trade protection in developing countries would ease poverty and promote food security. But this would be equivalent to a regressive tax on food consumption, which would harm poor consumers, and its benefit to farmers would go mostly to large producers.

A better approach than increasing distortionary farm subsidies and protection in developing countries is ensuring a neutral trade and macroeconomic framework, coupled with significant nondistortionary interventions and investments. The so-far intangible hologram for developing-country policy is precisely an integrated program, backed by enough resources, to address the multiple issues that require consideration: the macroeconomic and trade framework, specific policies and investments at the household and individual levels, and meso-level sectoral and regional policies and investments. Remaining price policy biases against agriculture, where they still exist, should be eliminated—but not by changing the sign of that policy bias in favor of agriculture. Price bias is different from the more general urban bias that still affects agriculture and rural areas in many developing countries. Increased rural investments in health, education, and human capital are needed, along with strengthening networks of small urban centers and villages; improving management of land and water resources; facilitating land ownership by small producers and landless workers; promoting improved agricultural technology; investing more in rural infrastructure (including rural roads, communications, and energy) and nonagricultural rural enterprises; encouraging organizations to expand the social capital and political participation for small producers and the poor; and providing adequate safety nets, including conditional income transfers that are now expanding in some middle-income countries.

These latter policies and interventions are basically allowed under the Green Box of the URAA and do not need special dispensations within the WTO. What developing countries require, however, are additional financial resources to support agricultural and rural development policies and investments, part of which must come from the international community. Such support is not, institutionally, within the purview of the WTO. However, a credible and binding commitment by developed countries and international organizations to provide additional funding for rural development, poverty alleviation, and food security in developing countries might well be included as a side agreement in the new WTO texts, reducing the possibility of a Doha Round outcome that allows continued subsidies and protection worldwide.

Notes

1. T. N. Srinivassan points out that were trade liberalization accepted as the goal, the agricultural agreement could simply state a future date for low tariff levels and let each country decide for itself on a path to meet the requirements. In our formulation, simple rules for subsidy elimination would also have to be included.

2. Farmers were also allowed to update their base of eligible output, and direct payments were extended to oilseeds. Westcott, Young, and Price (2002) provide a summary of the provisions of the 2002 farm bill. Orden (2003) provides a political economy assessment of its enactment.

3. The change proposed was that payments otherwise eligible for the Blue Box be extended from those made "under production limiting programs" to also include those that "do not require production."

4. Swinbank (2004) provides a concise appraisal of the EU reform process since the late 1980s.

5. From the 1930s until 1996, quota peanuts had to be grown in the county and state in which the quota had originally been assigned. Under the 1996 farm bill, up to 40 percent of quota could be transferred (leased or permanently sold) across county lines within a state. The largest shift of production occurred in Texas, where nearly all of the allowed quota transfer moved from the high-cost central production area to the lower-cost western region.

6. For a traditional producer who continues to grow peanuts, the minimum average revenue is $474 a short ton on a level of production equal to recent output $[(0.85)*(\$495) + (0.15)*(\$355) = \$474]$ plus the $220 quota buyout payment.

7. Alston and Sumner (2004) conclude that agricultural quota-right purchase prices are usually heavily discounted.

8. Potentially the exporters could pursue a dispute under the WTO for impairment and nullification of concessions, but that has not occurred. Domestic peanut production also dropped in 2003 but recovered in 2004 to a level above the prereform average. Abolishing location-specific quotas has had substantial effects on the regional distribution of domestic production, with a shift from high-cost to low-cost areas. For example, planted acreage fell more than 50 percent in Oklahoma and Virginia

between 2001 and 2003 while rising in Georgia and Florida. Quota rents were lower in the high-cost production areas, so the uniform national quota buyout payments provided somewhat more compensation in those areas.

9. Exceptions are recent tobacco quota-loss payments in fiscal years 2000, 2001, and 2003, totaling $860 million, and the Commodity Credit Corporation's takeover of 1999 loan stocks, amounting to about $625 million (Womach 2004a).

10. The buyout was added to tax legislation (the American Jobs Creation Act of 2004) prompted by the successful EU case in the WTO against export subsidies embedded in U.S. tax laws. In the indirect sense of providing this legislative vehicle, WTO disciplines (but not on agriculture) played a role in the U.S. tobacco reform.

11. Unlike other crops, tobacco is not included in the general farm bills. Senator Richard Lugar of Indiana had proposed a buyout early in the debate over a health-costs settlement. As an offshoot of the 1998 national settlement (the Master Settlement Agreement), the National Tobacco Growers Settlement Trust (or the Phase II payments) provided a distribution of $5.15 billion to tobacco quota owners and producers over a 12-year period (Womach 2004a).

12. This is not to say that either the quota owner or total payment is comparable, in terms of owner plus producer welfare, to the past rental payments. With removal of the quotas and an increase in production, the growers are better off even without any compensation since producer surplus increases (as represented in a single-region, static partial equilibrium model). The intense political battles over compensation of quota owners versus growers are a bit curious in this context. Similar debates took place over the rights to decoupled payments in the 1996 farm bill between owners and producers under various rental and share-cropping arrangements. In the quota removal case, growers capture some of the former quota rents, so quota owners could be partly compensated, in principle, directly by producers. All rents are captured by growers and consumers when the quotas are eliminated.

13. Buyout experiences in other countries provide additional insights. For example, in July 2000 Australia implemented a buyout in its dairy sector paid over eight years, financed by a consumer tax during that period. Again, shrinking quotas and other marketing restrictions led to support for reform among producers. The compensation package of Australian $1.8 billion was equivalent only to two or three years of previous transfers to farmers (Edwards 2003). The rate of exit from the sector tripled during the three subsequent years (8.2 percent of dairy farmers exited in 2000/1), but total milk production remained stable (Harris and Rae 2004).

14. Orden, Paarlberg, and Roe (1999) and de Gorter and Baffes (2004) review several past buyout proposals. Blandford and Boisvert (2004) call for a buyout of land asset values to facilitate an end to existing U.S. farm support programs, a proposal that they characterize as being to "think the unthinkable."

15. Swinbank and Tangermann (2004, 65) argue that the issuing of tradable bonds to a finite-length stream of fixed payments would create a flexible asset for the beneficiaries and "lock in" the policy reform since payments "could not be altered without impacting on the wealth of bondholders who are no longer the original farm recipients."

16. The actual and projected costs of countercyclical payments vary with commodity prices and forecasts. Relatively high prices in 2002–3 fleetingly created the prospect that market conditions would make the countercyclical payments less controversial, but they ultimately demonstrated their contentious subsidy dimension when prices were low. USDA projected in July 2004 that average costs of countercyclical payments would be only $1 billion for fiscal 2003–8. When prices dropped sharply based on good harvests later in 2004, the July projection proved too optimistic, and USDA revised its estimate of countercyclical payments upward again. For the July 2004 projected cost of countercyclical payments, annual expenditures for a buyout as described above would be just $1.83 billion.

17. The intent of a buyout of farm support payments is quite different from the rationale for purchase of development rights. The latter is to temper local adjustment pressure to exit agriculture, not facilitate it.

18. Even the well-known international economist William Cline has apparently mixed up decoupling and supply management. Cline (2004, 290) highlights the importance of agriculture in a comprehensive assessment of the effects of multilateral trade liberalization in reducing global poverty.

He recommends that developed countries "decouple forcefully any domestic subsidies from exports and production." But he then goes on to write: "The prime example of a decoupled subsidy is one that rewards the farmer for removing land from production, rather than for producing. Such 'set-aside' conservation-oriented subsidies featured prominently in earlier periods of U.S. farm support, and they could easily once again become the centerpiece of farm programs."

19. Among other prominent proponents of bioenergy, Wirth, Gray, and Podesta (2004) argue likewise that "farmers in this country [the United States] and elsewhere in the Americas could be big winners." Ugarte and Hellwinckel (2004) estimate that a subsidized price of $40 a dry ton for switchgrass would induce a shift of 12 million acres into its production and push other crop prices up 10 percent or more, reducing projected costs of loan rate and countercyclical payments. They provide no analysis of net welfare effects.

20. Related criticisms of community development were that despite an emphasis on participation, in many cases governments imposed the schemes, using them as more or less disguised mechanisms of social control. Another problematic issue was that the communities were not socially homogeneous and that the emphasis of working with the leaders of each community ended up aligning social promoters with the elite of local power, reinforcing the possibilities of elite domination over the rest. Focusing on communities also ignored the broader national and even international structures of which they were part and that defined their political, social, and economic functioning.

21. In terms of direct poverty effects in rural areas, studies of the Green Revolution also tend to paint a positive view, usually showing advances for the poor, attributable to production, employment, and food price effects, although recognizing that uniform attainment of benign outcomes is by no means guaranteed (Hazell and Ramaswamy 1991, IFAD 2001).

22. Redistributing investment was considered better than the alternatives of redistributing incomes to the poor for consumption (which was considered unsustainable fiscally) or redistributing fixed assets such as land (which faced strong political resistance).

23. The basic-needs approach implied an important role for the public sector in the provision of certain public services and required improvements in both the provision and access, so as to effectively reach the poorest sectors. It would also require promoting organization of the population that was to receive the services and their participation in the decisions and actions to be implemented (Streeten and Burki 1978).

24. For example, in Brazil during the second half of the 1970s, agricultural credit represented about 100 percent of agricultural gross domestic product (GDP), with interest subsidies that in some years amounted to some 5 percent of GDP (World Bank 1986).

25. The real exchange rate is defined as the ratio of nontraded to traded goods' prices, while the real, effective exchange rates are trade-weighted currency exchange rates adjusted for inflation measured by the Consumer Price Index. For both measures a higher value of the index indicates an appreciation of the domestic currency relative to foreign currencies.

26. For instance, at the beginning of the 1980s, several countries in South America (among them, Brazil and Chile) embarked on accelerated programs to expand wheat and other cereal production, due to concerns about shortages that were heightened by the high prices in the mid-1970s. When prices collapsed in the mid-1980s, those programs represented a high cost for the government, and support for those crops was substantially diminished (Díaz-Bonilla 1999). In Asia, estimates of public sector agricultural expenditures (measured in purchasing power parity values) by Fan and Pardey (1998) show that they grew at 9.5 percent during the 1970s, slowed down to 3.5 percent during the 1980s, and had a negligible increase of less than 0.5 percent during 1990–93.

27. Domestically, increases in capital flows may have led to positive growth and investment effects on those products such as livestock and dairy that are more closely linked to the evolution of income and demand in the domestic market, but it also led to overvaluation of domestic currencies (mostly in LAC), which hurt tradable sectors. Then a reversal of capital flows also contributed to growth declines (affecting those products that depend on domestic market incomes) and to banking and fiscal crises (negatively impacting the supply of government services for a variety of products).

28. The programs generate focused inflows of liquidity that appear to lead to local growth multiplier effects in poor communities. Those transfers have smaller or no leakages in terms of import content and savings at the more macro level.

29. The development box idea, presented by Sri Lanka, Dominican Republic, Pakistan, Cuba, and others, or the food-security box, advocated by India, for example, combines a series of existing exceptions and additional proposals for special and differential treatment for developing countries in the areas of market access, domestic support, and export subsidies.

30. Within a mostly defensive approach, the main topic on which African countries are challenging developed countries' policies (i.e. "playing offense") relates to cotton subsidies, mostly in the United States. Benin, Burkina Faso, Chad, and Mali (all of them least developed countries) are seeking compensation for past subsides and elimination of future subsidies (Sumner 2006). This is one of the few issues in which these countries can oppose developed countries' agricultural policies without fearing negative impacts on either the perceived rents gained by developing countries from protection in developed countries' markets or the price of food items in world markets.

31. The members of the Cairns Group are Argentina, Australia, Bolivia, Brazil, Canada, Chile, Colombia, Costa Rica, Guatemala, Indonesia, Malaysia, New Zealand, Paraguay, the Philippines, South Africa, Thailand, and Uruguay.

32. In the 1995–2000 period, corresponding to the implementation of the Uruguay Round, India has exported about $2 of agricultural products for every $1 of agricultural imports, a ratio comparable to that in Latin America and far higher than in South Asia as a whole.

33. In terms of external vulnerability, it is interesting to note that India has a low percentage of food imports (a mere 6 percent) compared with total exports (an indicator of how vulnerable the country is to changes in international food markets). This percentage is much lower than India's average for the four decades since the 1960s as a whole (almost 20 percent), and it is below the average for other developing regions such as Latin America (9.5 percent), the whole South Asian region (11 percent), and least developed countries (28 percent) (Díaz-Bonilla 2003).

34. For instance Díaz-Bonilla, Diao, and Robinson (2004) simulate those two alternatives in a world model. In the first scenario there is an arbitrary increase in protection on food-security crops (assumed to be grains in the simulations) only in those countries that supported the concept of a development or food-security box. In the second scenario, the governments in those countries collect, through an explicit tax, the equivalent of the implicit consumption tax privately collected through protection and invest that amount in agricultural research and development (R&D). The increase in agricultural protection results in a negative effect on GDP and employment for those countries, where there is less consumption of food products, suggesting that food-security declines with increased protection. An increase in investment in agricultural R&D financed by an equivalent tax calculated from the first scenario shows increases in GDP, employment, agricultural production, and consumption including food items. Also, in the first simulation, agricultural trade among developing countries, including those applying the higher levels of protection, also declines by about $300 million, suggesting that the development and food-security boxes hurt South-South agricultural trade.

References

Adams, D. W., D. H. Graham, and J. D. von Pischke, eds. 1984. *Undermining Rural Credit through Cheap Credit.* Boulder, CO: Westview Press.

Alessina, A., and R. Perotti. 1996. "Income Distribution, Political Instability, and Investment." *European Journal of Political Economy* 40: 1203–28.

Alston, J., and D. Sumner. 2004. "Compatibility of National Policies and Multinational Agreements: An Introductory Overview of Issues and Approaches." Paper presented at the Silverado Symposium on Agricultural Policy, January, Napa, CA.

Balassa, B. 1984. "Adjustment Policies in Developing Countries: A Reassessment." *World Development* 12 (9, September): 955–72.

Balassa, B., and Associates. 1971. *The Structure of Protection in Developing Countries.* Baltimore: Johns Hopkins University Press.

Bates, R. 1981. *Markets and States in Tropical Africa: The Political Basis of Agricultural Policies.* Berkeley, CA: University of California Press.

Bautista, R. M., and A. Valdés, eds. 1993. *The Bias against Agriculture.* San Francisco: ICS Press.

Blandford, D., and R. Boisvert. 2004. "U.S. Policies for Agricultural Adjustment." Paper presented at the IATRC (International Agricultural Trade Research Consortium) symposium on Adjusting to Domestic and International Agricultural Policy Reform in Industrial Countries, June, Philadelphia.

Borensztein, E., M. Khan, C. Reinhart, and P. Wickham. 1994. "The Behavior of Non-Oil Commodity Prices." Occasional Paper 112, International Monetary Fund, Washington, DC.

Bouët, A., L. Fontagné, and S. Jean. 2006. "Is Erosion of Tariff Preferences a Serious Concern?" In *Agricultural Trade Reform and the Doha Development Agenda,* ed. K. Anderson and W. Martin. Basingstoke, U.K.: Palgrave Macmillan; Washington, DC: World Bank.

Brown, B., and W. Snell. 2003. "Policy Issues Surrounding Tobacco Quota Buyout Legislation." University of Kentucky Cooperative Extension Service, Lexington.

Brown, B., and W. Thurman. 2004. "Impact of Elimination of the U.S. Flue-Cured Tobacco Program." Seminar paper presented in October at Virginia Polytechnic University, Blacksburg, VA.

Calvo, G., and C. Reinhart. 2002. "Fear of Floating." *Quarterly Journal of Economics* 117 (2): 379–408.

Cashin, P., L. Céspedes, and R. Sahay. 2002. "Keynes, Cocoa, and Copper: In Search of Commodity Currencies." IMF Working Paper WP/02/223, International Monetary Fund, Washington, DC.

CEPAL (Comisión Económica para America Latina). 1969. *América Latina: El Pensamiento de la CEPAL.* Santiago: Editorial Sudamericana.

Cernat, L., S. Laird, and A. Turrini. 2002. "How Important Are Market Access Issues for Developing Countries in the Doha Agenda?" CREDIT Research Paper 02/13, Centre for Research on Economic Development and International Trade, University of Nottingham, Nottingham.

Chenery, H., M. Ahluwalia, C. Bell, J. Duloy, and R. Jolly. 1974. *Redistribution with Growth.* New York: Oxford University Press.

Cline, W. 2004. *Trade Policy and Global Poverty.* Washington, DC: Institute for International Economics.

Daugbjerg, C., and A. Swinbank. 2004. "The CAP and EU Enlargement: Prospects for an Alternative Strategy to Avoid the Lock-in of CAP Support." *Journal of Common Market Studies* 42 (1): 99–119.

Deininger, K., and L. Squire. 1997. "Economic Growth and Income Inequality: Reexamining the Links." *Finance and Development* 34 (1): 38–41.

de Gorter, H., and J. Baffes. 2004. "Disciplining Agricultural Support through Decoupling." Development Prospects Group, World Bank, Washington, DC.

Díaz-Bonilla, E. 1991. "Global Grain Wars and Argentina." Paper presented at Canada Grains Council, 22nd Semiannual Meeting, October 23, Toronto.

———. 1999. "South American Wheat Markets and MERCOSUR." In *The Economics of World Wheat Markets,* ed. J. M. Antle and V. H. Smith. London: CABI.

———. 2003. "Can WTO Agricultural Negotiations Help The Poor?" and "Negotiating Strategies by Developing Countries." *SAIS Review* 23 (1, Winter/Spring).

Díaz-Bonilla, E., X. Diao, and S. Robinson. 2004. "Thinking Inside the Boxes: Alternative Policies in the Development and Food Security Boxes." In *Agricultural Policy Reform and the WTO. Where Are We Heading?* Ed. G. Anania, M. E. Bohman, C. A. Carter and A. F. McCalla. Cheltenham: Edward Elgar.

Díaz-Bonilla, E., M. Thomas, A. Cattaneo, and S. Robinson. 2000. "Food Security and Trade Negotiations in the World Trade Organization: A Cluster Analysis of Country Groups." TMD Discussion Paper 59, International Food Policy Research Institute, Washington, DC.

Edwards, G. 2003. "The Story of Deregulation in the Dairy Industry." *Australian Journal of Agricultural and Resource Economics* 47 (1): 75–98.

EFC (Energy Future Coalition). 2004. "American Farmers Can Cut U.S. Oil Dependence: Boyden Gray, James Woolsey Testify." EFC press release, May 6, Washington, DC.

Fan S., and P. G. Pardey. 1998. "Government Spending on Asian Agriculture: Trends and Production Consequences." In *Agricultural Public Finance Policy in Asia.* Tokyo: Asian Productivity Organization.
FAO (Food and Agriculture Organization). 2004. *The State of Food Insecurity in the World.* Rome: FAO.
FAO/GTZ (Gesellschaft für Technische Zusammenarbeit). 1998. "Agricultural Finance Revisited: Why?" FAO/GTZ AFR Series 1, FAO, Rome, June.
Fei J., and G. Ranis. 1966. "Agrarianism, Dualism, and Economic Development." In *Theory and Design of Economic Development,* ed. I. Adelman and E. Thorbecke. Stanford, CA: Stanford University Press.
Harris, D., and A. Rae. 2004. "Agricultural Policy Reform and Industry Adjustment in Australia and New Zealand." Paper presented at the IATRC symposium on Adjusting to Domestic and International Agricultural Policy Reform in Industrial Countries, June, Philadelphia.
Hazell, P., and C. Ramaswamy. 1991. *The Green Revolution Reconsidered: The Impact of High-Yielding Rice Varieties in South India.* Baltimore: Johns Hopkins University Press.
Holdcroft, L. 1977. "The Rise and Fall of Community Development in Developing Countries, 1950–65: A Critical Analysis and Annotated Bibliography." MSU Rural Development Papers 2, Michigan State University, East Lansing, MI.
IFAD (International Fund for Agricultural Development). 2001. *The Challenge of Ending Rural Poverty.* New York: Oxford University Press.
IMF (International Monetary Fund). 1999. *World Economic Outlook,* Washington, DC: IMF.
Jensen H., S. Robinson, and F. Tarp. 2002. "General Equilibrium Measures of Agricultural Policy Bias in Fifteen Developing Countries." TMD Discussion Paper 105, International Food Policy Research Institute, Washington, DC, October.
Johnston, B. 1977. "Food, Health, and Population in Development." *Journal of Economic Literature* 15 (3, September): 879–910.
Johnston, B., and J. Mellor. 1961. "The Role of Agriculture in Economic Development." *American Economic Review* 51 (4): 566–93.
Jorgenson D. 1967. "Surplus Agricultural Labor and the Development of a Dual Economy." *Oxford Economic Papers,* 19 (3, November): 288–312.
Kherallah, M., C. Delgado, E. Gabre-Madhin, N. Minot, and M. Johnson. 2003. *Agricultural Market Reforms in Sub-Saharan Africa: A Synthesis of Research Findings.* IFPRI Research Report, Washington, DC: International Food Policy Research Institute.
Krueger, A. 1978. *Foreign Trade Regimes and Economic Development: Liberalization Attempts and Consequences.* Cambridge, MA: Ballinger.
Krueger, A.O., M. Schiff, and A. Valdés. 1988. "Agricultural Incentives in Developing Countries: Measuring the Effects of Sectoral and Economywide Policies." *World Bank Economic Review* 2 (3, September): 255–71.
Kuznets S. 1966. *Modern Economic Growth.* New Haven, CT: Yale University Press.
Lipton, M. 1977. *Why Poor People Stay Poor: Urban Bias in World Development.* Cambridge, MA: Harvard University Press.
Lipton, M., and R. Paarlberg. 1990. "The Role of the World Bank in Agricultural Development in the 1990s." International Food Policy Research Institute, Washington, DC.
Little, I., T. Scitovsky, and M. Scott. 1970. *Industry and Trade in Some Developing Countries.* London: Oxford University Press.
McKinnon, R. 1973. *Money and Capital in Economic Development,* Washington, DC: Brookings Institution.
Moore, B., Jr. 1967. *Social Origins of Dictatorship and Democracy: Lord and Peasant in the Making of the Modern World.* London: Penguin Books.
Orden, D. 2003. "U.S. Agricultural Policy: The 2002 Farm Bill and WTO Doha Round Proposal." TMD Discussion Paper 109, International Food Policy Research Institute, Washington, DC, February.
Orden, D., R. Paarlberg, and T. Roe. 1999. *Policy Reform in American Agriculture: Analysis and Prognosis.* Chicago: University of Chicago Press.
Prasad E., K. Rogoff, S. Wei, and M. A. Kose. 2003. "Effects of Financial Globalization on Developing Countries: Some Empirical Evidence." IMF Occasional Paper 220, International Monetary Fund, Washington, DC, August.

Schultz, T. W. 1964. *Transforming Traditional Agriculture*. New Haven, CT: Yale University Press.
Snell, W. 2002. "Tobacco Quota Buyout Issues and Update." University of Kentucky Cooperative Extension Service, Lexington.
Streeten, P., and C. Burki. 1978. "Basic Needs: Some Issues." *World Development* 6 (3, March): 411–21.
Sumner, D. 2006. "Reducing Cotton Subsidies: The DDA Cotton Initiative." In *Agricultural Trade Reform and the Doha Development Agenda*, ed. K. Anderson and W. Martin. Basingstoke, U.K.: Palgrave Macmillan; Washington, DC: World Bank.
Swinbank, A. 2004. "Direct Payments in the EU and Their Treatment in the WTO." In *A Bond Scheme for Common Agricultural Policy Reform*, ed. A. Swinbank and R. Tranter. London: CABI.
Swinbank, A., and S. Tangermann. 2004. "A Bond Scheme to Facilitate CAP Reform." In a *Bond Scheme for Common Agricultural Policy Reform*, ed. A. Swinbank and R. Tranter. London: CABI.
Swinbank, A., and R. Tranter, eds. 2004. *A Bond Scheme for Common Agricultural Policy Reform*. London: CABI.
Tranter, R., L. Costa, T. Knapp, J. Little, and M. Sottomajor. 2004. "Asking Farmers about Their Responses to the Proposed Bond Scheme." In *A Bond Scheme for Common Agricultural Policy Reform*, ed. A. Swinbank and R. Tranter London: CABI.
Ugarte, D., and C. Hellwinckel. 2004. "Commodity and Energy Policies under Globalization." Agricultural Policy Analysis Center, University of Tennessee, Knoxville.
UNCTAD (United Nations Conference on Trade and Development). 2000. "Impact of the Reform Process in Agriculture on LDCs and Net Food-Importing Developing Countries and Ways to Address Their Concerns in Multilateral Trade Negotiations: Background Note by the UNCTAD Secretariat." TD/B/COM.1/EM.11/2, UNCTAD, Geneva.
Uphoff, N., and others. 1979. "Feasibility and Application of Rural Development Participation: A State-of-the-art Paper." Rural Development Committee, Cornell University, Ithaca, NY.
USDA (U.S. Department of Agriculture). 2000. "International Financial Crises and Agriculture." ERS-WRS-99-3, USDA, Washington, DC.
Westcott, P. C., C. E. Young, and J. M. Price. 2002. "The 2002 Farm Act: Provisions and Implications for Commodity Markets." Agriculture Information Bulletin 778, Economic Research Service, U.S. Department of Agriculture, Washington, DC, November. www.ers.usda.gov.
Wirth, T. E., C. B. Gray, and J. D. Podesta. 2004. "Agriculture: Let's Grow Our Own Fuel." *St. Louis Post-Dispatch*, May 12.
Womach, J. 2003. "Comparing Quota Buyout Payments for Peanuts and Tobacco." CRS Report RS2 1642, Congressional Research Service, Washington, DC, October 14.
_____. 2004a. "Tobacco Farmer Assistance." CRS Report RS20802, Congressional Research Service, Washington, DC, June 10.
_____. 2004b. "Tobacco Price Support: An Overview of the Program." CRS Report 95–129 ENR, Congressional Research Service, Washington, DC, June 10.
Wood, A. 1988. "Global Trends in Real Exchange Rates, 1960–84." World Bank Discussion Paper 35, World Bank, Washington, DC. Reprinted in 1991 in *World Development* 19 (4): 317–32.
World Bank. 1986. *World Development Report*. New York: Oxford University Press.

12

MARKET AND WELFARE IMPLICATIONS OF DOHA REFORM SCENARIOS

*Kym Anderson, Will Martin, and Dominique van der Mensbrugghe**

The aims of this chapter are threefold: to summarize, from the preceding chapters and other material, some likely and some more ambitious scenarios that might emerge as part of an eventual Doha agreement, particularly with respect to agriculture; to analyze empirically the market, trade, and welfare consequences of such scenarios relative to two benchmarks (the baseline, and a world free of distortions to goods trade); and to draw out implications of those Doha scenarios for developing countries especially.

More specifically, the chapter shows what the world economy would look like in 2015 with and without a successful conclusion to the Doha Round, how far Doha could take the world toward where it would be in the absence of all distortions to merchandise trade, and what contribution could be made by the various elements of a Doha package. For present purposes we make use of the World Bank's recursive dynamic model known as LINKAGE (van der Mensbrugghe 2004b), rather than the GTAP-AGR (Global Trade Analysis Project—Agriculture) model used by Hertel and Keeney (2006), because LINKAGE has a longer-run focus that is used for the World Bank's standard decade-long projections of the global economy and its earlier trade analysis (for example, World Bank 2002, 2004). We also use the latest version (6.05) of the GTAP database, which includes the tariff

---

*The authors are grateful for helpful comments from project participants, especially Rod Tyers, and for tariff-cutting data from CEPII staff in Paris (with special thanks to David Laborde).

preferences enjoyed by many developing countries (see www.gtap.org). The distinction is made in our results between effects on developing countries and effects on more advanced economies, but in doing so, it is necessary to take into account not only the World Bank's country classification based on income level but also the self-nominated classification practiced in the WTO, in which even economies as advanced as Hong Kong (China), Republic of Korea, Singapore, and Taiwan (China) claim developing country status and so are eligible for special and differential treatment (SDT), including smaller tariff cuts and longer phase-in periods than what is likely to be eventually agreed for developed countries under Doha.

Our analysis suggests most of the potential gains from multilateral trade reform are from agriculture. Because of huge gaps between WTO-bound and applied rates of protection, however, there would be little real agricultural reform globally as a result of the Doha Round—especially by developing countries—unless WTO members are willing to make very substantial cuts to their bound tariff rates and domestic farm subsidy commitments. Without that, the gap between agricultural and manufacturing protection is likely to widen, as is the gap between developed- and developing-country protection rates, thereby limiting the welfare gains from reform to a small number of more advanced economies. We therefore explore the effects of a more ambitious agricultural reform package and of developing countries participating more fully in the Doha Round rather than invoking SDT to avoid reform. In both cases, we show how much closer the world could come to realizing the full benefits of trade if these more ambitious reform commitments were to be made and implemented over the next decade.

The chapter begins with an overview of the key elements of a prospective Doha agreement, focusing especially on the agricultural elements discussed in preceding chapters. It then describes the model of the global economy to be used to analyze the consequences of such an agreement and of alternative, more ambitious reforms, including a move to complete free trade (which provides a helpful benchmark). The estimates of protection and subsidy rates for each region are a crucial part of the data in the global model, and so they are discussed in some detail before the key results of the simulations are presented. After discussing some qualifications, the chapter concludes by highlighting the key messages and drawing out implications for developing countries in particular.

Key Elements of a Prospective Doha Agreement

To what extent are reform commitments likely to emerge from the Doha Round? In addressing that question, one needs to remember that WTO trade negotiators are focusing on reductions not to the applied tariffs and subsidies but rather to members' legally bound import tariffs, agricultural export subsidies, and bound commitments on domestic support to farmers. These bound rates are higher than applied rates in nearly all countries, but especially so in most developing countries. Hence if cuts to bound rates are sufficiently small, or the gap between bound and applied rates is sufficiently large, an agreed set of bound rate reductions could result in no actual reform.

The Doha Round was launched in late 2001, but the following trade ministerial meeting, in Cancún in September 2003, ended with acrimony and without an agreement on how to proceed. Developing countries made it abundantly clear that further progress would not be possible without a commitment by developed countries to significantly lower their import barriers and agricultural subsidies (especially for cotton, despite its relatively minor role in developed-country agriculture, see Sumner 2006). An intense period of consultations in July 2004 ended in the early hours of August 1 with a decision on how the Doha Work Programme should proceed (WTO 2004). The decision, known as the July Framework Agreement, reiterates the importance of keeping development at the heart of the Doha agenda, and it stresses agricultural reform as key to that. In its annexes, the decision provides guidance on how a Doha agreement might be structured, with frameworks outlined for agriculture and for nonagricultural market access, and for negotiations on trade facilitation, as well recommendations for trade in services. What emerged with respect to the three agricultural pillars has been the subject of careful scrutiny in this book because—as was the case in the Uruguay Round Agreement on Agriculture—the devil will be in the details. We begin by summarizing the July Framework Agreement as it pertains to those three agricultural pillars.

Agricultural Market Access

Jean, Laborde, and Martin (2006) examine the consequences of different tariff-cutting formulas, bearing in mind the tariff rate quotas (TRQs) described by de Gorter and Kliauga (2006), the prevalence of preferences for developing countries as described in Bouët, Fontagné, and Jean (2006), the need to accommodate sensitive and special farm products, and the special and differential treatment outlined in the July Framework and discussed by Josling (2006). For our purposes, tariff cutting is implemented at the six-digit level of the Harmonized System and involves a detailed comparison of each country's bound tariff, which is the negotiators' focus, with the applied MFN (most-favored-nation) tariff on a given bilateral trade flow. The gap between bound and applied MFN tariffs is the so-called binding overhang, and it can blunt significantly the impact of any negotiated outcome—so much so that in some scenarios countries are not required to change their applied tariffs at all. Once the detailed tariff analysis was conducted, the results were aggregated up to the GTAP and LINKAGE models' regions and sector levels by the CEPII (Centre d' Etudes Prospectives et d'Informations Internationales) staff in Paris.[1] Applied tariff cuts vary not only by sector but also by trading partner—and may involve smaller cuts on imports from those developing countries currently enjoying nonreciprocal preferential access to richer countries' markets (Hoekman and Özden 2006).

Jean, Laborde, and Martin (2006) evaluate the effects of different approaches to liberalization on 2001 applied rates. They focus on different degrees of top-down progressivity in the bound tariff cuts, as well as on different degrees to which developing countries participate in reform. They look first at a proposal similar to the Harbinson progressive reduction formula (WTO 2003b), with marginal tariff rate reductions of 35 percent for tariffs below 15 percent, 65 percent for tariffs above 90 percent, and 60 percent for tariffs within the 15–90 percent bracket.[2] Harbinson's proposal for tariff cuts for developing countries also follow a progressive tiered formula, but Harbinson suggested four rather than three brackets, with inflexion points placed at tariff levels of 20, 60, and 120 percent, to maintain his criterion of cutting by an average of 25, 30, 40, and 45 percent, respectively, in those four brackets.

That set of cuts, it turns out, would lead to very little import liberalization, because bound tariffs in many countries exceed applied rates by such large margins. As a result, Jean, Laborde, and Martin focus on a set of reforms that involves cuts in applied agricultural protection rates that are at least 10 percentage points higher than Harbinson proposed, namely, 45, 70, or 75 percent bound rate cuts for developed countries and 35, 40, 50, or 60 percent cuts for developing countries. Consistent with the framework, least developed countries make no reduction commitments in either of these two cases.[3]

Jean, Laborde, and Martin then examine, and we model, the consequences of:

- Allowing smaller tariff cuts for self-nominated sensitive farm products, assuming that countries take into account the importance of the commodity, the height of the existing tariff, and the gap between the tariff binding and the applied rate in deciding which products to grant such treatment. Countries are allowed to treat 2 percent (in scenario 2) and 5 percent (in scenario 3) of tariff lines as sensitive, making those lines subject to just a 15 percent tariff cut;
- Including special agricultural products for developing countries, by adding another 2 percent (in Doha scenario 2) and 5 percent (in Doha scenario 3) of tariff lines as special and so subject to just a 15 percent tariff cut;
- Using instead a proportional cut formula that brings about the same reduction in average tariffs in industrial countries as a group, and developing countries as a group, as the tiered formulas used; and
- Adding a tariff cap of 200 percent, consistent with the suggestion in paragraph 30 of the July Framework Agreement that the role of a tariff cap be explored.

Agricultural Domestic Support

Reductions in domestic support have been a particular concern of developing countries. Developed countries are the major providers of such assistance, and many developing countries are concerned about the ability of their producers to compete with developed-country producers receiving large amounts of domestic support. While the marked asymmetry between industrial and developing countries is worrisome, evidence from Hertel and Keeney (2006) and from Hoekman, Ng, and Olarreaga (2004) suggests that the benefits to developing countries from reductions in domestic support may be substantially smaller than the potential gains from reductions in barriers to market access. Nonetheless, disciplining domestic support programs is crucial to ensure that when tariffs are lowered, import protection is not simply replaced by equally trade-distorting domestic measures.

Under the July framework, the base from which reductions in domestic support are to take place is in the commitments on the total bound aggregate measure of support (AMS) agreed under Article 6 of the Uruguay Round Agreement on Agriculture. Key elements of this framework are the distinction between nondistorting Green Box measures and trade-distorting Amber Box measures, together with a Blue Box containing measures tied to specific areas or livestock numbers.

Several features of this framework will influence the ability of negotiators to achieve substantial reductions in domestic support. One of these features is the de minimis provision that allows industrial countries to exclude from measurement up to 5 percent of the value of their agricultural output in commodity-specific support, and another 5 percent as non-commodity-specific support. Another feature is the market price support (MPS), which is based on a comparison of the official domestic price (which need not be closely related to domestic market prices) with the 1986–88 external reference price for each product. This MPS measure may not be associated with actual support and, to the extent that it is, it generally double-counts support provided by border price measures. A potentially more serious problem with the MPS is that countries can remove this element from their current AMS—without changing the amount of actual support provided—simply by abolishing the applied administered price used in calculating MPS. Because that does not alter the AMS binding commitments, it allows countries that formerly made extensive use of MPS to create substantial scope in their commitments to expand their actual support.

The July framework proposes tiered reductions in the total bound AMS, with larger reductions by members with higher initial AMS levels. In addition, it proposes capping product-specific AMS. De minimis levels are to be reduced to an extent to be negotiated. The definition of the Blue Box measures based on specific areas or livestock numbers is to be tightened by requiring these numbers to be "fixed and unchanging" and capped either at historical levels or at 5 percent of the value of production. The Green Box is to be clarified to ensure that the measures it incorporates are at most minimally trade distorting.

The MPS element of the AMS seems worthy of special attention because it does not measure trade-distorting support, and because of the scope it provides for avoiding disciplines. One option considered by Hart and Beghin (2006) is to redefine it so that it measures actual protection. Under some circumstances, this approach would impose greater discipline and would certainly encourage countries to adopt policies that reduce the damaging insulation of their domestic prices from world prices. Another alternative is to ensure that the MPS element is removed from both the current total AMS and the bound AMS. A third and potentially important reform canvassed by Hart and Beghin is to phase out the de minimis and Blue Box measures in favor of a (perhaps temporarily) expanded Green Box.

To provide negotiators with some insights into the prospective effects of these changes, we consider how various levels of cuts in the total bound AMS would affect the total distorting assistance that could be provided. How much would actual distorting support be reduced under various degrees of reduction in each country's total *bound* AMS? To answer this question, we assume that countries would take advantage of the loophole allowing them to reduce their current AMS by abolishing the administered domestic price, while retaining its effects in their bound AMS (a change already made by Japan in the case of rice).

A striking feature of the findings is that extraordinarily large reductions in bound AMS are required before any reductions in actual support would occur—an outcome required by paragraph 9 of the July Framework Agreement. Results for a tiered formula in which all countries with AMS notifications above 20 percent of the value of production cut their bound protection by 75 percent, and all others by 60 percent, are given in table 12.1. These results highlight just how deep cuts in bound levels of domestic support must be to bring about reductions in applied rates. Clearly, the offer of an initial reduction of 20 percent in bound AMS, contained in Paragraph 7 of Annex A of the July framework, is likely to have no direct impact.

The very limited actual reductions required from such a large reduction in bound rates are a consequence in part of the high level of the bindings, which in turn reflect the choice of a period of very depressed world prices—1986–88—for the base. A cynical way of thinking about this is that WTO members can avoid disciplines by exploiting the ability to "abolish" their MPS without abolishing the actual support to which it is related. This problem is serious for the AMS but should be kept in perspective if there are strong reforms of market access and export competition, since reductions in these trade measures will reduce market price support.

Finally, there is the issue of cotton subsidies, addressed by Sumner (2006). Almost no cut is likely to be required under the July Framework Agreement, but

TABLE 12.1 Effects of a Tiered Formula Cut in Agricultural Domestic Support, 2001 (percent)

Country or region	AMS	Cut in support binding	Cut in applied support
United States	20	75	−28
Norway	114	75	−18
EU15	42	75	−16
Australia	11	60	−10
Canada	24	75	0
All other countries		60	0

Source: Jensen and Zobbe (2006).
Note: All countries with aggregate measure of support (AMS) notifications of 20 percent or more of the value of production cut their bound domestic support by 75 percent. All other industrial countries cut their bound domestic support by 60 percent and developing countries by 40 percent.

the United States might agree to larger (phased) cuts of its cotton subsidies as part of complying at some future date with the WTO's dispute settlement outcome (see Sumner 2006). In that case, less could be needed in the way of U.S. cuts in its other domestic support programs.

Agricultural Export Subsidies

As Hoekman and Messerlin (2006) make clear, farm export subsidies are inconsistent with GATT (General Agreement on Tariffs and Trade) rules, so for that reason alone they deserve to be eliminated. The empirical analysis summarized in Hertel and Keeney (2006) shows that export subsidies are now only a small part of agricultural support programs—even when implicit subsidies in the form of food aid and export credits are included. A gradual phasing out over the next decade of both explicit and implicit forms of farm export subsidies should therefore be a politically feasible component of a comprehensive Doha agreement. Their elimination in isolation could harm a few food-importing and aid-dependent developing countries, but the poor net buyers of food in those countries can be assisted in far more efficient ways than through these measures.

Nonagricultural Market Access

Negotiations in the area of nonagricultural tariffs have been lagging those on farm products. Developing countries have clearly indicated that they wish to make smaller tariff cuts than developed countries do, and least developed countries expect not to have to make any cut commitments. A Doha Round is unlikely to require that all nonagricultural bound tariffs be cut by more than half, so in our analysis we assume a 50 percent cut in these tariffs by developed countries and a 33 percent cut by developing countries other than least developed ones (from whom no cuts are being demanded). Since those reductions in bound tariffs could lead to very little reform by developing countries, given their high tariff bindings relative to their applied tariffs, a more ambitious scenario may see them prepared to commit to more reform in order to entice deeper cuts in developed countries' agricultural and textile tariffs. Perhaps the most optimistic possibility is that developing countries would agree to cut nonagricultural bound tariffs as much as developed countries (that is, by the 50 percent we assume). Especially if that were coupled by more ambitious cuts in agricultural tariffs on the part of developing countries, developed countries could well respond with larger commitments themselves not only in trade but also with development aid. Indeed the experience of earlier multilateral trade negotiations showed that developing countries tended to receive only to the extent they were willing to give "concessions" themselves, such is the reciprocal nature of these negotiations.[4]

Services Trade

To date, WTO members have been slow in coming forward during the Doha negotiations with proposals to reform trade in services. At this stage it seems likely that, as with the Uruguay Round, countries will make few meaningful commitments to open up their services sectors during the Doha Round. For that reason, and because services trade is less adequately represented in trade models than is goods trade, we have chosen to assume no reductions in barriers to services trade resulting from the Doha Round, even though, as Hertel and Keeney (2006) and Winters and others (2003) indicate, gains from services reform could well be enormous, even for developing countries.

Trade Facilitation Measures

Trade facilitation is a key to enlarging the opportunities for developing countries to benefit from market opening at home and abroad. The poorest of countries in particular could well be able to turn any losses from others' trade liberalization into gains with a bit of investment in trade facilitation, as they could with some other domestic reforms that would help to make their internal factor and product markets work more efficiently. Funding agencies are showing an increasing interest in lending for such purposes, but it is impossible to know how much influence such moves would have on the outcome of the Doha negotiations.

Therefore we do not consider them further here except indirectly in the sense that the Armington trade elasticities used in the LINKAGE model are set a little above those in the GTAP model in part to capture some elements of trade facilitation, such as harmonization of standards, that tend to occur over the longer term as countries open up.

The Global LINKAGE Model for Assessing Effects of Future Trade Reform

The model used for this analysis is the World Bank's global, dynamic computable general equilibrium (CGE) model, known as LINKAGE (van der Mensbrugghe 2004b). It is a relatively straightforward CGE model but with some characteristics that distinguish it from standard comparative static models such as the GTAP model. A key difference is that it is recursive dynamic, so it begins with 2001 as its base year and can be solved annually through to 2015. The dynamics are driven by exogenous population and labor supply growth, savings-driven capital accumulation, and labor-augmenting technological progress (as assumed for the World Bank's *Global Economic Prospects* exercise in 2004).[5] In any given year, factor stocks are fixed. Producers minimize costs subject to constant returns to scale in production technology; consumers maximize utility; and all markets, including the market for labor, are cleared with flexible prices. There are three types of production structures. Crop sectors reflect the substitution possibility between extensive and intensive farming. Livestock sectors reflect the substitution possibility between pasture and intensive feeding. All other sectors reflect the standard capital-labor substitution (with two types of labor, skilled and unskilled). There is a single representative household for each modeled region, allocating income to consumption using the extended linear expenditure system. Trade is modeled using a nested Armington structure in which aggregate import demand is the outcome of allocating domestic absorption between domestic goods and aggregate imports, and then aggregate import demand is allocated across source countries to determine the bilateral trade flows.

The model covers six sources of protection. The most important involves the bilateral tariffs. There are also bilateral export subsidies. Domestically, there are subsidies only in agriculture, where they apply to intermediate goods, outputs, and payments to capital and land.

Three closure rules are used. First, government fiscal balances are fixed in any given year.[6] The fiscal objective is met by changing the level of lump-sum taxes on households. This implies that losses of tariff revenues are replaced by higher direct taxes on households. Second, the current account balance is fixed. Given that other external financial flows are fixed, this implies that ex ante changes to the trade balance are reflected in ex post changes to the real exchange rate. For example, if import tariffs are reduced, the propensity to import increases. Additional imports are financed by increasing export revenues, which is typically achieved by a real exchange rate depreciation. Finally, investment is driven by savings. With fixed public and foreign saving, investment is driven by two factors: changes in the savings behavior of households, and changes in the unit cost of investment. The latter can play an important role in a dynamic model if imported capital goods are taxed. Because the capital account is exogenous, rates of return across countries can differ over time and across simulations. The model solves only for relative prices. The numéraire, or price anchor, in the model is given by the export price index of manufactured exports from high-income countries. This price is fixed at unity in the base year and throughout the projection period to 2015.

The newest version of the LINKAGE model is based on the latest release of the GTAP database, Release 6.05. Compared with Version 5 of the GTAP database, Version 6.05 has a 2001 base year instead of 1997, updated national and trade data and, importantly, a new source for the protection data. The detailed database on bilateral protection integrates, at the HS6 tariff level, trade preferences, specific tariffs, and a partial evaluation of nontariff barriers such as tariff rate quotas. Tariffs are lower in the new GTAP database than they were in the previous version (see appendix table A12.1) because of the inclusion of bilateral trade preferences and of major trade reforms between 1997 and 2001. These included the continued implementation of the Uruguay Round Agreement, especially the elimination of quotas on textile and clothing trade, and China's progress toward WTO accession. Together, these reforms boosted trade's share of world GDP (gross domestic product) from 44 to 46 percent during those four years.

The version of the LINKAGE model used for this study is a 27-region, 25-sector aggregation of the GTAP database (see Appendix table A12.2). There is a heavy emphasis on agriculture and food, which account for 13 of the 25 sectors, and a focus on the largest commodity exporters and importers.

The Subsidies and Import Protection Database

The main source of protection resides in tariffs or border barriers, although some countries—notably, high-income countries—also have significant agricultural production and export subsidies. The average import tariff for agriculture and food is 16.0 percent for high-income countries and 17.7 percent for developing countries, while for manufactures other than textiles and clothing, it is 8.3 percent for developing countries and just 1.3 percent for high-income countries (table 12.2). The averages of course obscure large variations across countries and commodities.

TABLE 12.2 Import-Weighted Average Applied Tariffs, by Sector and Region, 2001 (percent)

Importing region	Agriculture, processed food	Textiles, clothing	Other manufacturing	All goods
High-income	16.0	7.5	1.3	2.9
Developing countries[a]	17.7	17.0	8.3	9.9
	(14.2)	(14.3)	(7.1)	(8.4)
Middle-income	16.5	16.8	7.3	8.9
Low-income	22.2	17.9	14.5	15.9
Developing countries by region				
East Asia and the Pacific	26.3	17.8	8.6	10.5
of which China	37.6	19.4	11.3	13.6
South Asia	33.9	20.1	22.2	23.5
Europe and Central Asia	14.8	10.7	4.1	6.0
Middle East and North Africa	14.1	27.1	7.2	9.8
Sub-Saharan Africa	18.2	23.7	10.5	12.6
Latin America and the Caribbean	10.3	11.3	7.1	7.7
World total	16.7	10.2	3.5	5.2

Source: Authors' compilations from the GTAP database Version 6.05.
a. Numbers in parentheses are the averages at the start of 2005 following WTO accessions including China; the completion of Uruguay Round implementation, including the end of textile quotas under the Multifibre Arrangement; and the eastward enlargement of the European Union to 25 members.

For example, if high-income countries put tariffs on temperate zone farm products at a prohibitive 100 percent but set tariffs on tropical products such as coffee at zero, the import-weighted average agricultural tariff could be quite low. Commodity averages also obscure bilateral differences. India, for example, has an average tariff on agriculture and food of 82 percent on imports from East Asia, but only 20 percent on imports from Sub-Saharan Africa. For high-income countries, agricultural tariffs on goods from low-income countries are lower than on imports from high- and middle-income countries. In other sectors, however, there is less evidence of preferences at this level of aggregation. Imports of textiles and clothing—indeed, of all merchandise—from low-income countries face a higher average tariff in high-income countries than do imports from middle- or high-income countries.

Welfare Impact of Current Protection Policies

The LINKAGE model provides a baseline projection of the world economy first from 2001 to the start of 2005, following accession to the WTO by China and Taiwan (China), the EU expansion eastward in 2004 that added 10 more countries to the EU15, and completion of Uruguay Round implementation including the phaseout of the textile and clothing quotas under the Multifibre Arrangement (MFA).[7] The model then provides a baseline projection to 2015 assuming no other policy changes. The projected tariffs as of 2005, and hence in the baseline in 2015, are summarized in table 12.3. Deviations from that baseline in 2015, attributable to phased partial or total liberalization from 2005, are examined next.

One benchmark against which to measure the results of Doha is that which would come if merchandise trade were completely freed over the 2005–10 period. That would lead to global gains by 2015 of $287 billion a year, according to the LINKAGE model. Another benchmark involves the internationally agreed reforms incorporated in the presimulation experiment for the 2001–5 period: had those reforms not been implemented, the dynamic gains in 2015 from freeing global merchandise trade would have been $341 billion instead of $287 billion, or another $54 billion (that calculation indicates the benefits of those recent reforms). The removal of the MFA quotas accounts for nearly half of that difference and thus should be considered part of the Uruguay Round's legacy (assuming safeguards by high-income countries or export taxes by China do not replace textile and clothing quotas).[8]

Table 12.4 reports the distribution of the standard economic welfare, or real income (equivalent variation) effects, of removing all merchandise trade barriers and agricultural subsidies globally. Two-thirds of the $287 billion annual gain in 2015 and after would accrue to the high-income countries. As a share of income, however, developing countries (as self-defined by WTO members) do twice as well, with an average increase of 1.2 percent compared with 0.6 percent for high-income countries. The results vary widely across developing countries, ranging from little impact in the case of Bangladesh and Mexico to increases of 4–5 percent in parts of East Asia. The second column of numbers in that table shows the amount of that welfare gain resulting from changes in the international terms of trade for each country. For developing countries as a group, the terms-of-trade effect is negative, reducing somewhat the gains from improved efficiency of domestic resource use (especially in China and India). That effect would dissipate over time, however, as developing countries diversify their exports in the course of their industrialization. Other macroeconomic effects, including on real exports, imports, exchange rates, and terms of trade, are summarized in table 12.5.

There are several ways to decompose the real income gains from global trade reform so as to better understand the sources of the gains. One way is to assess the

TABLE 12.3 Import-Weighted Average Applied Tariffs, by Sector and Country, 2005 (percent)

Importing region	Agriculture, processed food	Primary agriculture only	Processed food only	Textiles, clothing	Other manufacturing
High-income					
Australia and New Zealand	2.6	0.3	3.3	13.9	4.1
EU25 and EFTA	13.9	13.2	14.7	5.1	1.7
United States	2.4	2.3	2.5	9.6	0.9
Canada	9.0	1.2	14.1	8.7	0.5
Japan	29.3	48.0	20.8	9.0	0.4
Korea, Rep. of, and Taiwan (China)	53.0	84.5	22.4	9.2	3.6
Hong Kong (China) and Singapore	0.1	0.0	0.2	0.0	0.0
Developing countries					
Middle-income					
Argentina	7.1	5.6	7.8	11.1	10.1
Brazil	5.0	2.4	9.0	14.7	9.7
China	10.3	9.9	11.0	9.6	5.5
Mexico	10.3	10.8	9.7	7.8	4.3
Russian Federation	13.5	14.6	12.8	15.8	7.8
South Africa	8.6	5.9	10.6	21.9	5.4
Thailand	16.7	12.7	19.2	16.4	7.6
Turkey	16.6	16.4	17.0	3.8	1.2
Rest of East Asia	13.4	18.6	9.0	8.7	3.5
Rest of Latin America and the Caribbean	10.8	9.2	11.8	12.9	8.4
Rest of Europe and Central Asia	15.7	10.4	19.5	9.3	3.2
Middle East and North Africa	13.1	8.2	18.3	23.9	7.2
Low-income					
Bangladesh	12.7	7.4	21.2	29.9	16.2
India	49.9	25.7	75.6	26.5	24.2
Indonesia	5.0	4.3	6.2	8.0	4.3
Vietnam	37.1	13.1	44.8	29.1	12.3
Rest of South Asia	21.1	14.2	32.0	6.6	14.3
Selected Sub-Saharan Africa[a]	11.8	10.2	13.0	12.5	7.5
Rest of Sub-Saharan Africa	21.2	18.0	23.6	26.2	14.0
Rest of world	11.8	1.9	18.7	5.6	8.9

Source: Authors' projections from the GTAP database Version 6.05 using the World Bank's LINKAGE model.

a. The Selected Sub-Saharan African countries (for which national modules are available in the LINKAGE model) include Botswana, Madagascar, Malawi, Mozambique, Tanzania, Uganda, Zambia, and Zimbabwe.

TABLE 12.4 **Impacts on Real Income from Full Liberalization of Global Merchandise Trade, by Country or Region, 2015 (2001 US$ billions)**

Country/region	Real income gain	Change in real income due just to change in terms of trade	As % of baseline income in 2015
Australia and New Zealand	6.1	3.5	1.0
EU25 and EFTA	65.2	0.5	0.6
United States	16.2	10.7	0.1
Canada	3.8	−0.3	0.4
Japan	54.6	7.5	1.1
Korea, Rep. of, and Taiwan (China)	44.6	0.4	3.5
Hong Kong (China) and Singapore	11.2	7.9	2.6
Argentina	4.9	1.2	1.2
Bangladesh	0.1	−1.1	0.2
Brazil	9.9	4.6	1.5
China	5.6	−8.3	0.2
India	3.4	−9.4	0.4
Indonesia	1.9	0.2	0.7
Mexico	3.6	−3.6	0.4
Russian Federation	2.7	−2.7	0.6
South Africa	1.3	0.0	0.9
Thailand	7.7	0.7	3.8
Turkey	3.3	0.2	1.3
Vietnam	3.0	−0.2	5.2
Rest of South Asia	1.0	−0.8	0.5
Rest of East Asia and the Pacific	5.3	−0.9	1.9
Rest of Latin America and the Caribbean	10.3	0.0	1.2
Rest of Europe and Central Asia	1.0	−1.6	0.3
Middle East and North Africa	14.0	−6.4	1.2
Selected Sub-Saharan Africa	1.0	0.5	1.5
Rest of Sub-Saharan Africa	2.5	−2.3	1.1
Rest of world	3.4	0.1	1.5
High-income countries	201.6	30.3	0.6
Developing countries	141.5	−21.4	1.2
Developing countries—WTO definition	85.7	−29.7	0.8
Middle-income countries	69.5	−16.7	0.8
Low-income countries	16.2	−12.9	0.8
East Asia and the Pacific	23.5	−8.5	0.7
South Asia	4.5	−11.2	0.4
Europe and Central Asia	7.0	−4.0	0.7
Middle East and North Africa	14.0	−6.4	1.2
Sub-Saharan Africa	4.8	−1.8	1.1
Latin America and the Caribbean	28.7	2.2	1.0
World total	287.3	0.6	0.7

Source: Authors' World Bank LINKAGE model simulations.
Note: Data are given relative to the baseline.

TABLE 12.5 Impacts on Selected Trade Indicators from Full Liberalization of Global Merchandise Trade, 2015 (percent)

Country/region	Real exports	Real imports	Real exchange rate[a]	Terms of trade[b]
Australia and New Zealand	8.4	11.3	2.6	2.4
EU25 and EFTA	2.9	3.4	−0.8	0.5
United States	5.5	5.3	−0.3	0.9
Canada	2.5	2.8	−0.2	0.1
Japan	10.1	12.8	1.3	1.3
Korea, Rep. of, and Taiwan (China)	15.9	16.5	4.3	−0.8
Hong Kong (China) and Singapore	−3.3	−1.1	2.3	2.2
Argentina	19.8	24.5	1.6	2.5
Bangladesh	51.5	37.7	−6.3	−5.5
Brazil	28.5	31.9	4.4	4.2
China	17.2	19.4	1.6	−0.1
India	63.7	57.2	−4.2	−5.1
Indonesia	10.5	13.7	2.0	0.3
Mexico	13.3	13.0	−0.5	−1.1
Russian Federation	12.9	14.2	−0.8	−1.0
South Africa	14.3	18.0	0.8	0.4
Thailand	22.3	26.4	7.0	0.8
Turkey	11.6	13.3	0.9	1.1
Vietnam	55.5	42.4	11.3	−1.3
Rest of South Asia	30.0	28.8	−1.0	−0.8
Rest of East Asia and the Pacific	7.5	8.1	3.2	−0.6
Rest of Latin America and the Caribbean	20.5	18.0	0.7	−1.0
Rest of Europe and Central Asia	17.7	15.9	−0.4	−0.5
Middle East and North Africa	16.2	15.0	0.1	−0.9
Selected Sub-Saharan Africa	15.5	17.8	3.1	2.7
Rest of Sub-Saharan Africa	30.3	25.1	−0.1	−1.9
Rest of world	39.4	33.2	1.2	0.2

Source: Authors' World Bank LINKAGE model simulations.
Note: Data are given relative to the baseline.

impacts of developing-country liberalization versus industrial-country liberalization in different economic sectors; another is to decompose by policy instrument.[9] The latter gave results very similar to those reported in Hertel and Keeney (2006), namely, that barriers to market access explain almost all the welfare effects of agricultural policies, with removal of domestic support and export subsidy programs playing only a very minor role and in fact slightly harming developing countries as a group (since some food-importing developing countries gain from farm export subsidies in industrial countries). In our case, all but about 1 percent of the global welfare gains from full removal of all merchandise trade barriers and agricultural subsidies are accounted for by cuts in import tariffs, which is also what Hoekman, Ng, and Olarreaga (2004) estimate would result from halving all agricultural distortions (in their case using partial equilibrium analysis). Hertel and Keeney's estimate from full liberalization of all merchandise markets was only slightly higher, at 7 percent (see their table 2.7).

Our results decomposed by sector are provided in table 12.6. They suggest that global liberalization of agriculture and food yields 63 percent of the total global gains (similar to Hertel and Keeney's 66 percent). This finding is consistent with the high tariffs in agriculture and food (17 percent global average) versus other sectors, but it is nonetheless remarkable given the low shares of agriculture in global GDP (4 percent) and global merchandise trade (9 percent). The elimination of trade-distorting farm policies in high-income countries accounts for three-fourths of those gains. Notice too that as much of the gain to developing countries from farm reform results from South-South agricultural liberalization as from developing countries' unrestricted access to markets in high-income countries. That is almost equally true in manufacturing in aggregate, despite the big gains from textiles and clothing reform ($13 billion from market access in high-income countries compared with $9 billion attributable to South-South textiles trade growth). In other words, reform by developing countries is as important for economic welfare gains to the South as reform by high-income countries. It is clear that reforming agricultural policies in both sets of countries is crucial for developing countries, with reform by high-income countries in textiles only half as important as is their agricultural reform.

Politicians also have an eye on what happens to their country's volume of output and exports in sectors whose protection is cut, and on earnings of constituents. Contrary to much rhetoric from protectionist groups, the full liberalization results suggest little change in the high-income countries' shares of global output and exports of processed food, beverages and tobacco, and "other manufactures." Only for primary agriculture are the changes noticeable: the export share falls by more than one-quarter, from 53 percent to 38 percent (including trade within the EU), but the output share falls by only one-sixth, from 30 to 25 percent The converse of these share changes are shown for developing countries in table 12.7.

TABLE 12.6 Regional and Sectoral Sources of Gains from Full Liberalization of Global Merchandise Trade, 2015

Liberalizing region	Gains by region (US$ billions)			Percent of global gain		
	Developing	High-income	World	Developing	High-income	World
Developing countries						
Agriculture, food	28	19	47	33	9	17
Textiles, clothing	9	14	23	10	7	8
Other merchandise	6	52	58	7	26	20
All sectors	43	85	128	50	42	45
High-income countries						
Agriculture, food	26	109	135	30	54	46
Textiles, clothing	13	2	15	17	1	6
Other merchandise	4	5	9	3	3	3
All sectors	43	116	159	50	58	55
All countries						
Agriculture, food	54	128	182	63	63	63
Textiles, clothing	22	16	38	27	8	14
Other merchandise	10	57	67	10	29	23
All sectors	86	201	287	100	100	100

Source: Authors' World Bank LINKAGE model simulations.
Note: Data are given relative to the baseline (see text). Small interaction effects are distributed proportionately, and numbers are rounded to sum to 100 percent.

TABLE 12.7 Change in Developing Countries' Shares of Global Output and Exports under Full Global Merchandise Trade Liberalization, by Sector, 2015 (percent)

	Primary agriculture	Processed food, beverages, and tobacco	Textiles, clothing	Other manufacturing
Output				
Baseline	70	40	62	35
Free trade	75	40	65	35
Exports				
Baseline	47	34	63	30
Free trade	62	40	67	32

Source: Authors' World Bank LINKAGE model simulations.
Note: Data include intra-EU trade.

In absolute terms, agricultural and food output in high-income countries would decline but only by 0.1 percent a year over the projection period to 2015 following a move to free trade in all merchandise, instead of rising by a projected 1.6 percent a year in our baseline.

The impact of full reform on agricultural and food output and trade is shown for each country or region in table 12.8; the table also shows clearly that exports are enhanced much more than output. As a consequence, the global share of agricultural and food production exported rises from 9.5 to 13.2 percent (or from 6.6 to 11.6 percent when trade within the EU is excluded). Developing countries would earn an additional $192 billion each year from these increased exports. Latin America accounts for a large part of that increase, but exports expand in all regions, and even low-income countries would sell an additional $36 billion worth of such goods each year (an increase of 52 percent). The situation with food imports is also noteworthy. Middle-income countries as a group would see food imports grow less rapidly than farm exports, while imports and export would grow at the same pace in low-income countries, leaving their food and agricultural self-sufficiency ratio unchanged. Even for high-income countries, that ratio would fall only five percentage points, although it is concentrated in primary agricultural products (table 12.9). Self-sufficiency ratios improve for Sub-Saharan Africa and Latin America, while China and India maintain their agricultural self-sufficiency levels, despite their expansion of exports in labor-intensive manufactures.

Cotton trade distortions and subsidies raise producer prices by more than 50 percent in the United States and even more in the EU. What effect would their removal have in this context of freeing all merchandise trade and agricultural subsidies? The price of cotton in international markets is estimated to be considerably higher in 2015 than it would be without reform, including for U.S. exports because its subsidies no longer depress that price. However, the volume of U.S. cotton exports shrinks when those subsidies are removed, raising the price for other countries' exports. The price rise would not apply equally to all exporters, however, because of product differentiation as captured in the Armington elasticities. For Australia and Brazil, the rise is 8 percent, while for Sub-Saharan Africa it averages less than 2 percent (relative to the numéraire, which is the average price of exports of manufactures by developed countries). However, cotton exports from Sub-Saharan Africa would be 73 percent greater under this reform scenario. Indeed, developing country output and exports of cotton would expand by about the same amounts as the U.S. levels would shrink, with Sub-Saharan Africa enjoying more of that gain than any other region—and cotton is so important in Sub-Saharan Africa (minus South Africa) that it contributes one-quarter of that region's net gain in agricultural value

TABLE 12.8 Impacts of Full Global Trade Liberalization on Agricultural and Food Output and Trade, by Country/Region, 2015

Country/region	Value (US$ billions)			Percent change in volume		
	Exports	Imports	Output	Exports	Imports	Output
Australia and New Zealand	18.0	1.4	27.9	38.0	23.0	20.5
EU25 and EFTA	21.7	103.5	−185.8	−10.8	39.3	−12.3
United States	18.4	16.5	30.7	11.6	25.6	0.0
Canada	14.6	6.9	7.2	40.2	54.3	4.8
Japan	2.8	34.7	−91.7	60.4	169.7	−18.4
Korea, Rep. of, and Taiwan (China)	33.2	12.3	−0.4	600.2	189.8	20.2
Hong Kong (China) and Singapore	7.0	1.5	7.4	115.2	7.6	35.4
Argentina	10.4	0.7	12.2	44.2	36.9	11.5
Bangladesh	0.8	0.4	−2.5	60.9	15.6	0.8
Brazil	38.0	2.8	66.4	120.6	48.4	34.0
China	15.1	24.1	−9.9	145.6	27.3	−0.9
India	5.1	13.4	−23.8	53.2	165.4	−3.7
Indonesia	3.6	1.9	4.5	32.2	23.5	2.4
Mexico	11.9	6.7	6.2	66.0	52.9	2.2
Russian Federation	0.7	4.4	−7.8	15.4	22.3	−5.4
South Africa	2.4	1.1	1.4	55.9	40.2	4.9
Thailand	5.6	5.2	5.3	29.2	57.2	4.7
Turkey	4.3	4.3	−0.1	109.4	140.3	0.5
Vietnam	1.2	3.3	−2.1	13.9	170.4	−13.3
Rest of South Asia	2.9	3.7	−1.5	57.1	83.3	−1.8
Rest of East Asia and the Pacific	9.4	5.8	7.4	61.7	50.7	6.8
Rest of Latin America and the Caribbean	36.0	9.6	37.0	68.1	42.3	11.7
Rest of Europe and Central Asia	9.2	10.9	−22.2	106.0	90.5	−1.6
Middle East and North Africa	13.2	17.5	−7.8	64.1	43.1	−1.2
Selected Sub-Saharan Africa	4.5	1.3	5.3	50.0	74.4	9.2
Rest of Sub-Saharan Africa	9.5	8.1	−4.1	45.4	79.2	−0.6
Rest of world	8.2	5.8	2.9	168.3	123.3	4.4

Table 12.8 (*Continued*)

Country/region	Value (US$ billions)			Percent change		
	Exports	Imports	Output	Exports	Imports	Output
High-income countries	115.8	176.7	−204.7	15.7	65.5	−5.3
Developing countries	191.9	131.0	66.8	67.4	51.5	2.2
Middle-income countries	156.1	93.1	88.2	72.7	41.9	3.2
Low-income countries	35.8	37.9	−21.4	52.3	99.3	−1.0
East Asia and the Pacific	34.8	40.4	5.2	54.4	35.5	0.1
South Asia	8.9	17.5	−27.8	55.1	122.9	−3.0
Europe and Central Asia	14.2	19.6	−30.0	79.7	62.6	−1.9
Middle East and North Africa	13.2	17.5	−7.8	64.1	43.1	−1.2
Sub-Saharan Africa	16.4	10.5	2.6	47.7	71.6	2.1
Latin America and the Caribbean	96.3	19.8	121.8	75.7	46.1	13.8
World total (excluding intra-EU trade)	307.7	307.7	−137.8	36.3	59.8	−1.3

Source: Authors' World Bank LINKAGE model simulations.
Note: Data are given relative to the baseline (see text).

added from full global trade liberalization (Anderson, Martin, and van der Mensbrughe 2005, table 14). In 2015, the share of all developing countries in global cotton exports would be 85 percent instead of 56 percent, vindicating their efforts to ensure that cotton receives specific attention in the Doha negotiations (Sumner 2006; Baffes 2005).

The relatively small percentage changes in net national economic welfare hide the fact that redistributions of welfare among groups within each country following trade reform can be much larger. This is clear from the effects on real rewards to labor, capital, and land that are reported in table 12.10. The results also strongly support the expectation from trade theory that returns to unskilled labor rise substantially in developing countries, and by more than wages of skilled workers, which in turn rise more than earnings of capitalists. Trade reform therefore would be likely to improve equity and reduce poverty in those countries, given that the vast majority of the poor are unskilled laborers (and farmers). For high-income countries, again consistent with standard trade theory, skilled workers gain more than unskilled workers. Those farmers in Europe and northeast Asia who rent agricultural land would benefit from a large fall in rental costs, more or less offsetting the fall in prices for their output, while owners of land in those countries would lose if uncompensated.

Those changes in factor rewards assume labor is mobile between sectors. In the most densely populated developing countries, full liberalization would encourage more farm workers to take up now-more-rewarding work in labor-intensive manufacturing and service activities, so value-added in agriculture would fall not only in economies where it has been highly protected (Europe, northeast Asia, and the United States) but also in South Asia. All other developing-country regions would see a rise in net farm income. That is true even of China, because it has already reduced much of its agricultural protection as part of its reforms associated with its accession to WTO at the end of 2001 (table 12.11).

These results are for full trade liberalization. Smaller changes can be expected to result from partial reforms of the sort being negotiated currently under the Doha Development Agenda. It is to those that we now turn our attention.

Some Prospective Doha Scenarios: Estimating Their Consequences

What will the Doha package ultimately contain? To focus on the agricultural component in particular, we make simplifying assumptions about nonagricultural components, namely, we assume no reform in services and no new trade facilitation measures. We also assume that agricultural export subsidies are eliminated and that domestic support for agriculture is cut in just the four economies noted earlier in the discussion of table 12.1.

More difficult to determine are the likely nature and extent of reductions in market access barriers, so several scenarios are considered initially for agricultural and food products in isolation from nonagricultural tariff cuts, before incorporating some cuts in nonagricultural market access barriers. A total of eight simulations are designed to evaluate the consequences of different approaches to liberalization; the simulations focus on different degrees of top-down progressivity in the tariff cuts, and on different levels of developing-country participation in the reforms (for a summary list, see table 12.12). As suggested in the Girard text (WTO 2003a), the bound tariff on a good for which no bound tariff has been set is assumed to be double the applied MFN rate. Throughout

TABLE 12.9 Impact of Full Liberalization of Global Merchandise Trade on Self-Sufficiency in Food and Agricultural Products, Selected Regions, 2015 (percent)

Product	High-income countries		Developing countries	
	Baseline	Global lib'n	Baseline	Global lib'n
Rice	97	49	99	101
Wheat	137	118	89	91
Other grains	103	99	90	84
Oilseeds	119	55	75	90
Sugar	92	47	100	113
Plant-based fibers	117	78	95	104
Vegetables, fruits	83	72	103	105
Other crops	83	85	110	106
Livestock	103	104	98	98
Other natural resources	91	91	102	102
Fossil fuels	81	81	119	120
Processed meats	99	89	98	109
Vegetable oils, fats	96	91	98	99
Dairy products	103	100	88	92
Other food, beverages, tobacco	97	99	101	96
Textiles	91	91	99	98
Wearing apparel	63	55	153	162
Leather products	58	53	136	138
Chemicals, rubber, plastics	103	104	89	87
Iron, steel	99	100	97	96
Motor vehicles, parts	101	102	87	82
Capital goods	101	100	93	93
Other manufacturing	95	95	105	104
Agriculture and food	98	93	99	100
Agriculture	97	84	98	100
Processed foods	98	97	99	98
Textile and wearing apparel	74	70	114	116
Other manufacturing	98	98	98	97

TABLE 12.9 (Continued)

Sub-Saharan Africa		Latin America & Caribbean		South Asia		China	
Baseline	Global lib'n	Baseline	Global lib'n	Baseline	Global lib'n	Baseline	Global lib'n
91	78	97	98	102	102	100	108
53	35	90	119	98	98	90	92
101	102	104	103	99	99	76	32
158	279	184	247	100	102	1	1
109	116	126	173	99	99	45	27
385	694	94	109	87	92	93	95
137	141	146	183	95	88	97	97
167	174	140	132	104	104	11	10
103	103	103	102	99	99	94	94
125	125	128	127	95	95	92	92
147	154	116	115	66	57	85	82
96	136	105	132	98	101	89	85
85	72	111	106	65	25	96	90
74	78	92	94	97	97	60	57
100	93	106	106	111	108	97	96
75	62	85	79	130	134	99	98
78	62	92	80	513	765	225	255
85	59	107	87	170	186	156	164
70	66	79	74	91	89	92	89
94	93	100	92	95	92	93	92
58	68	101	99	94	84	88	79
45	45	81	79	79	79	104	106
115	108	98	92	97	94	111	112
108	111	111	120	99	96	91	91
118	123	121	134	99	98	88	88
98	97	105	111	98	87	96	94
77	61	92	81	149	163	125	129
92	91	93	89	88	85	101	101

Source: Authors' World Bank LINKAGE model simulations.
Note: Self-sufficiency is defined as the percentage of domestic consumption that has been produced domestically.

TABLE 12.10 Impacts of Full Global Merchandise Trade Liberalization on Real Factor Prices, 2015 (percent)

Country/region	Unskilled wages	Skilled wages	Capital[a] user cost	Land[a] user cost	CPI
Australia and New Zealand	3.1	1.1	−0.3	17.4	1.2
EU25 and EFTA	0.0	1.3	0.7	−45.4	−1.3
United States	0.1	0.3	0.0	−11.0	−0.4
Canada	0.7	0.7	0.4	22.8	−0.9
Japan	1.3	2.2	1.1	−67.4	−0.1
Korea, Rep. of, and Taiwan (China)	6.5	7.1	3.8	−45.0	−0.7
Hong Kong (China) and Singapore	3.2	1.6	0.3	4.4	1.1
Argentina	2.9	0.5	−0.7	21.3	0.3
Bangladesh	1.8	1.7	−0.2	1.8	−7.2
Brazil	2.7	1.4	1.6	32.4	2.2
China	2.2	2.2	2.8	−0.9	−0.4
India	2.8	4.6	1.8	−2.6	−6.0
Indonesia	3.3	1.5	0.9	1.0	0.5
Mexico	2.0	1.6	0.5	2.8	−1.4
Russian Federation	2.0	2.8	3.5	−2.2	−3.3
South Africa	2.8	2.5	1.8	5.7	−1.6
Thailand	13.2	6.7	4.2	11.4	−0.6
Turkey	1.3	3.4	1.1	−8.1	−0.3
Vietnam	25.3	17.6	11.0	6.8	−2.3
Rest of South Asia	3.7	3.2	0.1	0.1	−2.7
Rest of East Asia and the Pacific	5.8	4.2	5.2	−0.9	−1.6
Rest of Latin America and the Caribbean	5.7	1.4	−0.4	17.8	−1.2
Rest of Europe and Central Asia	2.3	4.2	2.1	−0.3	−2.6
Middle East and North Africa	4.1	4.1	2.6	2.4	−3.1
Selected Sub-Saharan Africa	6.0	1.6	0.0	4.6	0.4
Rest of Sub-Saharan Africa	8.2	6.5	2.2	5.2	−5.0
Rest of world	4.4	2.7	1.1	6.3	−1.4
High-income countries	0.6	1.1	0.5	−20.0	−0.6
Developing countries	3.5	3.0	1.9	0.9	−1.7
Middle-income countries	3.2	2.6	1.9	2.2	−1.1
Low-income countries	4.2	3.9	1.9	−1.0	−4.0
World total	1.2	1.5	0.8	−0.8	−0.8

Source: Authors' World Bank LINKAGE model simulations.

Note: Data are given relative to the baseline. Nominal factor prices are deflated by the consumer price index (CPI).

a. The user cost of capital and land represents the subsidy-inclusive rental cost.

this section, the WTO usage of the term *developing countries* applies when allocating special and differential treatment in the form of lesser commitments to reform. As a result Hong Kong (China), Korea, Singapore, and Taiwan (China) are all subjected to the same tariff cuts as other developing economies despite their high-income status.

The experiments begin with scenario 1, which assumes a tiered reduction formula with marginal agricultural tariff rate reductions of 45, 70, and 75 percent within each of the three bands defined by the Harbinson (WTO 2003b) inflection points of tariff rates of 15 percent and 90 percent for developed countries (that is, for low agricultural tariffs the marginal rate of reduction is 45 percent, for medium-level tariffs it is 70 percent, and for the highest tariffs it is 75 percent). For developing countries, the reductions are 35, 40, 50, and 60 percent within each of their four bands. Least developed countries are not required to undertake any reduction commitments. These cuts are greater than those proposed in the Harbinson draft because we found its cuts were too light to have much impact (providing only two-thirds of the global welfare gain of scenario 1 and leading to zero gain in scenario 2).

Scenarios 2 and 3 examine the consequences of including the sensitive farm products allowed for in the framework, with developed countries allowed to treat 2 percent (in scenario 2) and 5 percent (in scenario 3) of their HS6 agricultural tariff lines as sensitive and thereby subject to a tariff cut of only 15 percent (as a substitute for the TRQ expansion mentioned in the framework agreement); those proportions are doubled for developing and least developed countries, in part to incorporate their special farm products demand.[10]

Scenario 4 considers the impact of a proportional cut formula that brings about the same reduction in average agricultural tariffs in developed countries as a group (44 percent), and developing countries as a group (21 percent), as the tiered formulas used in scenario 1.

Scenario 5 uses the same proportional cut formula as scenario 4 but allows 2 percent of tariff lines in developed countries to be treated as sensitive products, and 4 percent in developing countries, to cover sensitive and special products. This approach reduces the average tariff cut to 16 percent for developed countries and 9 percent for developing countries.

Scenario 6 considers the effects of adding to scenario 5 a tariff cap of 200 percent so that any product with a bound tariff in excess of that limit will be reduced to that cap rate. This scenario leads to average cuts in food and agricultural tariffs of 18 percent for both developed and developing countries.

Scenario 7 adds to scenario 1 the cuts in nonagricultural tariff bindings of 50 percent in developed countries, 33 percent in developing countries, and zero in least developed countries.

TABLE 12.11 Impact of Full and Partial Liberalization on Agricultural Value Added, 2015

Country/region	Value (US$ billions)		Percent change	
	Full global liberalization	Doha scenario 7	Full global liberalization	Doha scenario 7
Australia and New Zealand	6.4	2.4	25.6	9.8
EU25 and EFTA	−39.1	−20.4	−26.4	−13.8
United States	−18.2	−6.3	−15.0	−5.2
Canada	3.4	0.9	23.3	5.8
Japan	−17.7	−7.4	−39.5	−16.6
Korea, Rep. of, and Taiwan (China)	−9.5	−3.4	−33.3	−12.1
Hong Kong (China) and Singapore	0.1	0.0	7.5	1.4
Argentina	6.1	1.7	33.8	9.4
Bangladesh	−0.5	0.0	−4.4	0.4
Brazil	15.1	5.5	46.3	16.7
China	0.3	1.8	0.1	0.4
India	−17.1	0.4	−8.1	0.2
Indonesia	0.8	0.5	2.7	1.7
Thailand	3.8	1.1	25.0	7.2
Vietnam	0.8	0.0	13.6	0.3
Russian Federation	−1.4	−0.2	−6.5	−0.8
Mexico	0.9	1.2	2.5	3.2
South Africa	0.5	0.1	9.6	1.2
Turkey	−2.0	−0.1	−7.2	−0.3
Rest of South Asia	−0.6	0.8	−1.3	1.8
Rest of East Asia and the Pacific	−0.2	0.5	−0.7	1.9
Rest of Latin America and the Caribbean	22.9	8.4	30.2	11.1
Rest of Europe and Central Asia	−1.1	−0.1	−1.8	−0.2
Middle East and North Africa	0.3	1.0	0.3	0.9
Selected Sub-Saharan Africa	1.5	0.3	9.1	1.7
Rest of Sub-Saharan Africa	2.3	0.8	5.4	1.9
Rest of world	3.1	1.0	16.4	5.4

TABLE 12.11 (*Continued*)

Country/region	Value (US$ billions)		Percent change	
	Full global liberalization	Doha scenario 7	Full global liberalization	Doha scenario 7
High-income countries	−74.6	−34.2	−19.4	−8.9
Developing countries	35.6	24.8	2.9	2.0
Middle-income countries	45.3	20.9	5.3	2.4
Low-income countries	−9.7	3.9	−2.5	1.0
East Asia and the Pacific	5.5	3.9	1.1	0.8
South Asia	−18.1	1.2	−6.8	0.5
Europe and Central Asia	−4.5	−0.3	−4.0	−0.3
Middle East and North Africa	0.3	1.0	0.3	0.9
Sub-Saharan Africa	4.3	1.1	6.7	1.8
Latin America and the Caribbean	45.0	16.7	27.4	10.2
World total	−39.0	−9.5	−2.4	−0.6

Source: Data are given relative to the baseline (see text). See table 12.12 for description of scenario 7.
Note: Authors' World Bank LINKAGE model simulations.

Finally, scenario 8 makes developing (including least developed) countries full participants in the Doha Round, undertaking the same reductions in bound (but not necessarily applied) tariffs as the developed countries in scenario 7.

The average tariffs resulting from all these scenarios are summarized for each region in table 12.13, along with the original projected baseline tariffs if there were to be no Doha reform.

Estimated Welfare and Trade Effects of Scenarios in 2015

The welfare consequences of implementing these various reforms over the 2005–10 period and allowing the global economy to adjust to 2015 are summarized in table 12.14, in dollar terms and as percentage changes in real income. The first column suggests that agricultural liberalization using the harmonizing formula (scenario 1) would generate a global gain of $75 billion even without the inclusion of nonagricultural tariff reform. But almost all those benefits accrue to the reforming high-income countries; developing countries would gain only $9 billion

TABLE 12.12 Summary of Doha Partial Liberalization Scenarios Considered

Baseline	Amends 2001 protection measures by allowing EU eastward enlargement to 25 members, implementation of WTO accession commitments by China, and implementation of Uruguay Round commitments including abolition of quotas on textiles and clothing by the end of 2004, followed by normal global growth projection for 10 more years to 2015 (baseline simulation)
Scenarios 1–8	All assume cuts in agricultural domestic support in four developed country markets and abolition of agricultural export subsidies in all countries, plus:
Scenario 1	Harmonizing formula for agricultural market access with smaller tariff cuts for developing countries and none for least developed countries
Scenario 2	Scenario 1 plus exceptions for sensitive products (2 percent of agricultural tariff lines for developed countries and 4 percent for developing countries)
Scenario 3	Scenario 1 plus exceptions for more sensitive products (5 percent for developed countries and 10 percent for developing countries)
Scenario 4	Proportional cut in agricultural tariffs of developed countries (with smaller cuts for developing countries and none for least developed countries) to achieve the same cut in the average tariff as in scenario 1
Scenario 5	Proportional cut as in scenario 4 plus exceptions for sensitive products (2 percent for developed countries and 4 percent for developing countries)
Scenario 6	Scenario 5 plus a cap on tariffs, limiting boundrates to no more than 200 percent
Scenario 7	Scenario 1 plus 50 percent cut in all tariffs on nonagricultural products for developed countries, 33 percent for developing countries, and none for least developed countries
Scenario 8	Developed countries' harmonizing formula cuts for agriculture, plus developed countries' 50 percent cut in all nonagricultural tariffs, are also each applied in developing and least developed countries

Source: Authors' assumptions (see text).

because their bound tariffs are so high as to lead to almost no reform by them.[11] Were the high-income countries allowed to exclude from cuts even just 2 percent of their sensitive farm products (and developing countries 4 percent), those global gains would shrink to just $18 billion. If that tolerance is raised to 5 percent (10 percent for developing countries), the gain would drop to $13 billion. In both cases, developing countries as a group would lose (scenarios 2 and 3).

Should the tiered formula be replaced by a straightforward proportional cut that brings about the same average agricultural tariff reduction as the tiered formulas used in scenario 1, the global gains are lower, but not by much ($66 billion, compared with scenario 1's $75 billion). And the developing countries' share of that is larger than in scenario 1. Even if sensitive and special farm products are allowed with the harmonized formula, as in scenario 5, the global gains would be no lower than under the tiered formula, and they could be raised substantially, as in scenario 6, simply by putting a cap of 200 percent on bound tariffs. Together these six scenarios suggest that the complexity of negotiating a tiered formula may simply not be worth the effort, especially if it leads high-income countries to insist on exceptional treatment for their sensitive farm products.

The final two scenarios add nonagricultural tariff cuts to the agricultural reforms in the preceding scenarios. In scenario 7, special and differential treatment is provided for developing countries' nonagricultural cuts, as is the case for all the preceding agricultural cut scenarios. Even so, the gain to developing countries by adding these nonfarm reforms doubles relative to scenario 1, where only agriculture tariffs are cut, contributing one-third of the extra boost to global welfare ($7 billion out of the $22 billion difference in global gains between scenarios 1 and 7). In scenario 8, the developing countries (including least developed) fully engage in the reform process, forgoing the special and differential treatment provided under in scenarios 1 and 7. That approach substantially boosts their welfare as well as global welfare, because it ensures that their cuts in bound tariffs lead to considerably larger cuts in applied tariffs (shown in table 12.13). Nonetheless, agricultural reform alone hardly changes the global average tariff for goods, whereas that average falls by almost one-third, or 1.5 percentage point, when manufacturing is included (see table 12.13d).

Retaining special and differential treatment as in scenario 7 would yield a global gain of $96 billion from Doha merchandise liberalization, which is one-third of the potential welfare gain from full liberalization of $287 billion. But for developing countries the gain would be only $16 billion, which is less than one-fifth of that group's potential gain shown in table 12.2 of $86 billion. Forgoing special and differential treatment (scenario 8) raises their gain by 42 percent, or an extra $7 billion. Much of those gains go to the largest developing economies, but note that in percentage terms Sub-Saharan Africa also gains substantially if it liberalizes more, contrary to the presumptions of many commentators. By contrast, under scenario 7 those Sub-Saharan African countries simply are not liberalizing enough to get sufficient efficiency gains to offset the terms-of-trade losses they suffer as net food importers, as recipients of tariff preferences that have eroded with the decline in high-income countries' MFN tariffs, or as a result of the combined export growth from reforming economies with similar export compositions.

The aggregate global welfare consequences of scenario 7 are hardly altered if agricultural domestic and export subsidies are not reduced at the same time. The welfare effects on reforming countries and their significant trading partners are altered, however, table 12.15 shows the changes to the national welfare effects for scenario 7, first

TABLE 12.13 Average Applied Tariffs for All Goods by Country/Region, for 2001 and 2015 Baselines, and for Doha Scenarios by 2015 (percent)

a. Agricultural and food tariffs

Country/region	Baseline 2001	Baseline 2015	Scen. 1 2015
Australia and New Zealand	2.6	2.6	1.7
EU25 and EFTA	13.9	13.9	7.2
United States	2.4	2.4	1.7
Canada	9.0	9.0	4.9
Japan	29.4	29.3	15.2
Korea, Rep. of, and Taiwan (China)	55.0	53.0	28.4
Hong Kong (China) and Singapore	0.1	0.1	0.1
Argentina	7.1	7.1	6.9
Bangladesh	12.7	12.7	12.7
Brazil	5.0	5.0	4.9
China	37.6	10.3	8.2
India	50.3	49.9	45.5
Indonesia	5.0	5.0	4.9
Mexico	11.6	10.3	8.6
Russian Federation	13.5	13.5	8.8
South Africa	8.8	8.6	8.1
Thailand	29.7	16.7	13.9
Turkey	16.7	16.6	13.8
Vietnam	37.1	37.1	37.1
Rest of South Asia	21.3	21.1	20.9
Rest of East Asia and the Pacific	13.7	13.4	12.7
Rest of Latin America and the Caribbean	11.0	10.8	9.8
Rest of Europe and Central Asia	16.0	15.7	14.3
Middle East and North Africa	14.1	13.1	11.6
Selected Sub-Saharan Africa	11.9	11.8	11.6
Rest of Sub-Saharan Africa	21.4	21.2	19.6
Rest of world	12.1	11.8	11.5
High-income countries	16.0	15.9	8.4
Developing countries	17.7	14.2	12.5
Developing countries (WTO definition)	20.0	16.9	13.1
Middle-income	16.5	12.1	10.4
Low-income countries	22.2	22.0	20.7
World total	16.7	15.2	10.0

TABLE 12.13 (*Continued*)

Scen. 2	Scen. 3	Scen. 4	Scen. 5	Scen. 6	Scen. 7	Scen. 8
2015							
2.3	2.3	1.3	2.1	2.3	1.7	1.7
11.2	12.0	7.0	10.8	11.1	7.0	7.0
2.2	2.3	1.4	2.1	2.2	1.7	1.7
8.1	8.8	5.2	8.1	8.1	4.9	4.9
25.5	26.6	16.7	25.4	21.7	14.7	14.7
45.3	45.8	32.4	45.1	29.8	27.9	18.7
0.1	0.1	0.1	0.1	0.1	0.1	0.1
7.1	7.1	6.7	7.0	7.1	6.9	6.1
12.7	12.7	12.7	12.7	12.7	12.7	11.9
5.0	5.0	4.9	5.0	5.0	4.9	4.4
9.1	9.3	7.9	9.0	9.1	7.9	6.9
47.9	48.3	45.0	47.9	47.9	45.5	37.4
5.0	5.0	4.8	5.0	5.0	4.9	4.5
10.0	10.0	8.3	9.9	10.0	8.6	6.5
10.9	11.2	7.8	10.6	10.9	8.7	6.5
8.5	8.5	7.9	8.4	8.5	8.1	6.6
15.1	15.4	13.2	14.8	15.1	13.5	11.0
15.8	16.0	13.8	15.7	15.8	13.8	10.6
37.1	37.1	37.1	37.1	37.1	37.1	37.1
21.1	21.1	20.7	21.1	21.1	20.9	16.5
13.2	13.3	12.8	13.2	10.3	12.7	11.2
10.3	10.4	9.5	10.3	10.3	9.8	8.9
14.9	15.1	14.0	14.8	14.9	14.3	12.9
12.6	12.7	11.6	12.6	12.6	11.5	10.4
11.8	11.8	11.6	11.7	11.8	11.5	11.0
20.8	20.8	19.7	20.8	20.8	19.6	16.1
11.7	11.8	11.6	11.7	11.5	11.5	9.4
13.5	14.1	8.9	13.3	11.5	8.2	7.5
13.4	13.5	12.3	13.4	13.3	12.4	10.6
15.5	15.7	13.3	15.4	13.9	13.0	10.7
11.4	11.5	10.1	11.3	11.2	10.3	8.9
21.5	21.6	20.7	21.5	21.5	20.7	17.5
13.5	13.9	10.3	13.3	12.2	9.9	8.8

TABLE 12.13 Average Applied Tariffs for All Goods by Country/ Region, for 2001 and 2015 Baselines, and for Doha scenarios by 2015 (percent) (*Continued*)

b. Textile and clothing tariffs

Country/region	Baseline 2001	Baseline 2015	Scen. 1 2015
Australia and New Zealand	13.9	13.9	13.9
EU25 and EFTA	5.2	5.1	5.1
United States	9.8	9.6	9.6
Canada	9.0	8.7	8.7
Japan	9.7	9.0	9.0
Korea, Rep. of, and Taiwan (China)	9.2	9.2	9.2
Hong Kong (China) and Singapore	0.0	0.0	0.0
Argentina	11.1	11.1	11.1
Bangladesh	29.9	29.9	29.9
Brazil	14.7	14.7	14.7
China	19.4	9.6	9.6
India	26.6	26.5	26.5
Indonesia	8.0	8.0	8.0
Mexico	7.8	7.8	7.8
Russian Federation	15.8	15.8	15.8
South Africa	22.3	21.9	21.9
Thailand	17.4	16.4	16.3
Turkey	3.8	3.8	3.8
Vietnam	29.1	29.1	29.1
Rest of South Asia	6.9	6.6	6.6
Rest of East Asia and the Pacific	8.7	8.7	8.7
Rest of Latin America and the Caribbean	12.9	12.9	12.9
Rest of Europe and Central Asia	9.3	9.3	9.3
Middle East and North Africa	27.1	23.9	23.9
Selected Sub-Saharan Africa	12.6	12.5	12.5
Rest of Sub-Saharan Africa	26.4	26.2	26.2
Rest of world	5.6	5.6	5.6
High-income countries	7.5	7.3	7.3
Developing countries	17.0	14.3	14.3
Developing countries (WTO definition)	13.4	11.4	11.4
Middle-income	16.8	13.6	13.6
Low-income countries	17.9	17.9	17.9
World total	10.2	9.3	9.3

TABLE 12.13 (*Continued*)

Scen. 2	Scen. 3	Scen. 4	Scen. 5	Scen. 6	Scen. 7	Scen. 8
2015							
13.9	13.9	13.9	13.9	13.9	12.9	12.9
5.1	5.1	5.1	5.1	5.1	3.0	3.0
9.6	9.6	9.6	9.6	9.6	4.9	4.9
8.7	8.7	8.7	8.7	8.7	4.9	4.9
9.0	9.0	9.0	9.0	9.0	5.2	5.2
9.2	9.2	9.2	9.2	9.2	8.1	7.0
0.0	0.0	0.0	0.0	0.0	0.0	0.0
11.1	11.1	11.1	11.1	11.1	11.1	9.7
29.9	29.9	29.9	29.9	29.9	29.9	29.9
14.7	14.7	14.7	14.7	14.7	14.7	13.3
9.6	9.6	9.6	9.6	9.6	6.5	4.9
26.5	26.5	26.5	26.5	26.5	20.4	17.0
8.0	8.0	8.0	8.0	8.0	8.0	8.0
7.8	7.8	7.8	7.8	7.8	6.4	5.2
15.8	15.8	15.8	15.8	15.8	10.6	8.0
21.9	21.9	21.9	21.9	21.9	17.4	13.2
16.3	16.3	16.3	16.3	16.3	15.2	12.3
3.8	3.8	3.8	3.8	3.8	3.8	3.8
29.1	29.1	29.1	29.1	29.1	29.1	29.1
6.6	6.6	6.6	6.6	6.6	6.2	5.5
8.7	8.7	8.7	8.7	8.7	7.9	7.0
12.9	12.9	12.9	12.9	12.9	12.5	12.0
9.3	9.3	9.3	9.3	9.3	8.8	8.3
23.9	23.9	23.9	23.9	23.9	22.2	20.0
12.5	12.5	12.5	12.5	12.5	12.4	12.2
26.2	26.2	26.2	26.2	26.2	25.9	24.6
5.6	5.6	5.6	5.6	5.6	5.2	4.7
7.3	7.3	7.3	7.3	7.3	4.1	4.1
14.3	14.3	14.3	14.3	14.3	12.7	11.3
11.4	11.4	11.4	11.4	11.4	10.1	9.0
13.6	13.6	13.6	13.6	13.6	11.7	10.3
17.9	17.9	17.9	17.9	17.9	17.2	16.5
9.3	9.3	9.3	9.3	9.3	6.6	6.2

TABLE 12.13 Average Applied Tariffs for All Goods by Country/Region, for 2001 and 2015 Baselines, and for Doha Scenarios by 2015 (percent) (*Continued*)

c. Other merchandise tariffs

Country/region	Baseline 2001	Baseline 2015	Scen. 1 2015
Australia and New Zealand	4.2	4.2	4.2
EU25 and EFTA	1.8	1.7	1.7
United States	0.9	0.9	0.9
Canada	0.5	0.5	0.5
Japan	0.4	0.4	0.3
Korea, Rep. of, and Taiwan (China)	3.8	3.6	3.6
Hong Kong (China) and Singapore	0.0	0.0	0.0
Argentina	10.2	10.1	10.1
Bangladesh	16.2	16.2	16.2
Brazil	9.7	9.7	9.7
China	11.3	5.5	5.5
India	25.6	24.2	24.2
Indonesia	4.4	4.3	4.3
Mexico	4.3	4.3	4.3
Russian Federation	7.8	7.8	7.7
South Africa	5.4	5.4	5.4
Thailand	8.3	7.6	7.6
Turkey	1.2	1.2	1.2
Vietnam	12.3	12.3	12.3
Rest of South Asia	14.3	14.3	14.3
Rest of East Asia and the Pacific	3.6	3.5	3.5
Rest of Latin America and the Caribbean	8.4	8.4	8.4
Rest of Europe and Central Asia	3.2	3.2	3.2
Middle East and North Africa	7.2	7.1	7.1
Selected Sub-Saharan Africa	7.7	7.7	7.7
Rest of Sub-Saharan Africa	13.9	13.9	13.9
Rest of world	9.1	8.8	8.8
High-income countries	1.3	1.2	1.2
Developing countries	8.3	7.1	7.1
Developing countries (WTO definition)	6.7	5.8	5.8
Middle-income countries	7.3	6.0	6.0
Low-income countries	14.5	14.1	14.1
World total	3.5	3.1	3.1

TABLE 12.13 (*Continued*)

Scen. 2	Scen. 3	Scen. 4	Scen. 5	Scen. 6	Scen. 7	Scen. 8
\multicolumn{7}{c}{2015}						
4.2	4.2	4.2	4.2	4.2	3.4	3.4
1.7	1.7	1.7	1.7	1.7	0.9	0.9
0.9	0.9	0.9	0.9	0.9	0.4	0.4
0.5	0.5	0.5	0.5	0.5	0.3	0.3
0.3	0.3	0.3	0.3	0.3	0.2	0.2
3.6	3.6	3.6	3.6	3.6	3.0	2.6
0.0	0.0	0.0	0.0	0.0	0.0	0.0
10.1	10.1	10.1	10.1	10.1	10.0	9.4
16.2	16.2	16.2	16.2	16.2	16.2	16.1
9.7	9.7	9.7	9.7	9.7	9.4	8.6
5.5	5.5	5.5	5.5	5.5	3.8	2.9
24.2	24.2	24.2	24.2	24.2	20.6	17.7
4.3	4.3	4.3	4.3	4.3	4.3	4.2
4.3	4.3	4.3	4.3	4.3	4.2	4.0
7.7	7.7	7.7	7.7	7.7	5.2	3.9
5.4	5.4	5.4	5.4	5.4	5.1	4.2
7.6	7.6	7.6	7.6	7.6	7.3	6.8
1.2	1.2	1.2	1.2	1.2	1.2	1.1
12.3	12.3	12.3	12.3	12.3	12.3	12.3
14.3	14.3	14.3	14.3	14.3	14.3	13.9
3.5	3.5	3.5	3.5	3.5	3.2	3.0
8.4	8.4	8.4	8.4	8.4	7.5	6.9
3.2	3.2	3.2	3.2	3.2	3.1	3.0
7.1	7.1	7.1	7.1	7.1	6.9	6.7
7.7	7.7	7.7	7.7	7.7	7.5	7.2
13.9	13.9	13.9	13.9	13.9	13.8	13.7
8.8	8.8	8.8	8.8	8.8	8.8	8.7
1.2	1.2	1.2	1.2	1.2	0.8	0.8
7.1	7.1	7.1	7.1	7.1	6.4	5.9
5.8	5.8	5.8	5.8	5.8	5.2	4.7
6.0	6.0	6.0	6.0	6.0	5.3	4.8
14.1	14.1	14.1	14.1	14.1	13.1	12.3
3.1	3.1	3.1	3.1	3.1	2.6	2.4

TABLE 12.13 Average Applied Tariffs for All Goods by Country/Region, for 2001 and 2015 Baselines, and for Doha Scenarios by 2015 (percent) (*Continued*)

d. All merchandise trade tariffs

Country/region	Baseline 2001	Baseline 2015	Scen. 1 2015
Australia and New Zealand	4.8	4.8	4.7
EU25 and EFTA	3.2	3.1	2.5
United States	1.8	1.8	1.7
Canada	1.4	1.4	1.1
Japan	5.2	5.1	3.2
Korea, Rep. of, and Taiwan (China)	7.6	7.3	5.6
Hong Kong (China) and Singapore	0.0	0.0	0.0
Argentina	10.0	10.0	10.0
Bangladesh	18.4	18.4	18.4
Brazil	9.5	9.5	9.5
China	13.6	6.2	6.0
India	28.1	26.8	26.4
Indonesia	4.8	4.7	4.6
Mexico	5.1	5.0	4.8
Russian Federation	9.7	9.7	8.8
South Africa	6.6	6.6	6.5
Thailand	10.2	8.6	8.4
Turkey	2.5	2.4	2.2
Vietnam	16.7	16.7	16.7
Rest of South Asia	14.6	14.5	14.4
Rest of East Asia and the Pacific	4.6	4.5	4.4
Rest of Latin America and the Caribbean	9.1	9.1	9.0
Rest of Europe and Central Asia	5.0	4.9	4.8
Middle East and North Africa	9.8	9.3	9.1
Selected Sub-Saharan Africa	8.7	8.7	8.6
Rest of Sub-Saharan Africa	16.2	16.1	15.8
Rest of world	9.1	8.9	8.8
High-income countries	2.9	2.9	2.3
Developing countries	9.9	8.4	8.2
Developing countries (WTO definition)	8.5	7.3	6.9
Middle-income countries	8.9	7.2	7.0
Low-income countries	15.9	15.5	15.3
World total	5.2	4.7	4.2

TABLE 12.13 (*Continued*)

Scen. 2	Scen. 3	Scen. 4	Scen. 5	Scen. 6	Scen. 7	Scen. 8
\multicolumn{7}{c}{2015}							
4.7	4.8	4.7	4.7	4.7	4.0	4.0
2.9	3.0	2.5	2.9	2.9	1.7	1.7
1.7	1.8	1.7	1.7	1.7	0.9	0.9
1.3	1.4	1.2	1.3	1.3	0.8	0.8
4.6	4.8	3.4	4.6	4.1	2.7	2.7
6.8	6.8	5.9	6.7	5.7	5.0	3.9
0.0	0.0	0.0	0.0	0.0	0.0	0.0
10.0	10.0	10.0	10.0	10.0	9.9	9.2
18.4	18.4	18.4	18.4	18.4	18.4	18.3
9.5	9.5	9.5	9.5	9.5	9.2	8.5
6.1	6.1	6.0	6.1	6.1	4.3	3.3
26.6	26.6	26.3	26.6	26.6	23.1	19.6
4.7	4.7	4.6	4.7	4.7	4.6	4.5
4.9	4.9	4.8	4.9	4.9	4.7	4.3
9.2	9.3	8.6	9.1	9.2	6.5	4.8
6.6	6.6	6.5	6.5	6.6	6.0	4.9
8.5	8.5	8.3	8.4	8.5	8.0	7.3
2.4	2.4	2.2	2.4	2.4	2.2	2.0
16.7	16.7	16.7	16.7	16.7	16.7	16.7
14.5	14.5	14.4	14.5	14.5	14.4	13.3
4.5	4.5	4.4	4.5	4.2	4.1	3.7
9.0	9.1	9.0	9.0	9.0	8.3	7.7
4.9	4.9	4.8	4.8	4.9	4.7	4.4
9.3	9.3	9.1	9.3	9.3	8.8	8.3
8.6	8.6	8.6	8.6	8.6	8.5	8.2
16.0	16.0	15.8	16.0	16.0	15.7	15.0
8.9	8.9	8.8	8.9	8.8	8.8	8.3
2.7	2.7	2.4	2.7	2.5	1.6	1.6
8.3	8.3	8.2	8.3	8.3	7.5	6.8
7.2	7.2	7.0	7.2	7.0	6.3	5.6
7.1	7.1	7.0	7.1	7.1	6.3	5.6
15.5	15.5	15.3	15.5	15.4	14.6	13.4
4.5	4.5	4.2	4.5	4.4	3.5	3.2

Source: World Bank LINKAGE model aggregations of HS6 tariff changes provided by CEPII.

TABLE 12.14 Change from Baseline in Real Income under Alternative Doha Scenarios, 2015

a. Dollar change (in 2001 US$ billions)

Country/region	Scen. 1	Scen. 2
Australia and New Zealand	2.0	1.1
EU25 and EFTA	29.5	10.7
United States	3.0	2.3
Canada	1.4	0.5
Japan	18.9	1.8
Korea, Rep. of, and Taiwan (China)	10.9	1.7
Hong Kong (China) and Singapore	−0.1	−0.1
Argentina	1.3	1.0
Bangladesh	0.0	0.0
Brazil	3.3	1.1
China	−0.5	−1.5
India	0.2	0.2
Indonesia	0.1	0.2
Mexico	−0.2	−0.3
Russian Federation	−0.3	−0.7
South Africa	0.1	0.3
Thailand	0.9	0.6
Turkey	0.6	0.0
Vietnam	−0.1	0.0
Rest of South Asia	0.2	0.1
Rest of East Asia and the Pacific	0.1	0.0
Rest of Latin America and the Caribbean	3.7	0.5
Rest of Europe and Central Asia	−0.2	−0.3
Middle East and North Africa	−0.8	−1.2
Selected Sub-Saharan Africa	0.1	0.0
Rest of Sub-Saharan Africa	0.0	−0.3
Rest of world	0.4	0.0
High-income countries	65.6	18.1
Developing countries (WTO definition)	19.7	1.2
Developing countries	9.0	−0.4
Middle-income	8.0	−0.5
Low-income countries	1.0	0.1
East Asia and the Pacific	0.5	−0.8
South Asia	0.4	0.3
Europe and Central Asia	0.1	−0.9
Middle East and North Africa	−0.8	−1.2
Sub-Saharan Africa	0.3	0.0
Latin America and the Caribbean	8.1	2.3
World total	74.5	17.7

TABLE 12.14 (Continued)

Scen. 3	Scen. 4	Scen. 5	Scen. 6	Scen. 7	Scen. 8
1.1	2.2	1.2	1.2	2.4	2.8
9.1	28.2	10.7	10.9	31.4	35.7
2.0	3.4	2.5	2.1	4.9	6.6
0.3	1.2	0.4	0.4	0.9	1.0
1.3	15.1	1.4	12.9	23.7	25.4
1.6	7.3	1.7	15.9	15.0	22.6
−0.1	−0.1	−0.2	−0.2	1.5	2.2
1.0	1.4	1.1	1.0	1.3	1.6
0.0	0.0	0.0	0.0	−0.1	−0.1
0.9	3.2	1.1	1.1	3.6	3.9
−1.6	−0.4	−1.4	−1.1	1.7	1.6
0.2	0.1	0.2	0.2	2.2	3.5
0.2	0.2	0.2	0.0	1.0	1.2
−0.3	−0.2	−0.3	−0.3	−0.9	−0.2
−0.8	−0.1	−0.7	−0.7	0.8	1.5
0.1	0.1	0.2	0.3	0.4	0.7
0.3	1.0	0.8	0.8	2.0	2.7
0.0	0.5	0.1	0.0	0.7	1.4
0.0	−0.1	−0.1	−0.1	−0.5	−0.6
0.1	0.2	0.1	0.2	0.3	0.7
0.0	0.1	0.1	1.0	0.3	0.6
0.5	3.7	0.5	0.4	3.9	4.0
−0.3	−0.2	−0.2	−0.2	−0.6	−0.7
−1.5	−0.9	−1.2	−1.2	−0.6	0.1
0.0	0.1	0.0	0.0	0.1	0.2
−0.3	0.0	−0.3	−0.3	−0.1	0.3
0.0	0.3	0.0	0.0	0.6	0.6
15.2	57.2	17.8	43.2	79.2	96.4
−0.3	16.3	1.7	16.8	32.6	47.7
−1.7	9.1	0.1	1.1	16.1	22.9
−1.9	8.3	0.0	1.0	12.5	17.1
0.1	0.8	0.2	0.0	3.6	5.9
−1.2	0.9	−0.4	0.6	4.5	5.5
0.3	0.3	0.3	0.4	2.5	4.2
−1.1	0.2	−0.9	−0.9	0.8	2.1
−1.5	−0.9	−1.2	−1.2	−0.6	0.1
−0.2	0.3	−0.2	−0.1	0.4	1.2
2.0	8.0	2.5	2.1	7.9	9.2
13.4	66.3	17.9	44.3	96.1	119.3

TABLE 12.14 Change from Baseline in Real Income under Alternative Doha Scenarios, 2015 (*Continued*)

b. Percentage change

Country/region	Scen. 1	Scen. 2
Australia and New Zealand	0.35	0.20
EU25 and EFTA	0.29	0.11
United States	0.02	0.02
Canada	0.15	0.05
Japan	0.38	0.04
Korea, Rep. of, and Taiwan (China)	0.86	0.13
Hong Kong (China) and Singapore	−0.02	−0.03
Argentina	0.32	0.26
Bangladesh	−0.06	−0.03
Brazil	0.50	0.16
China	−0.02	−0.06
India	0.02	0.03
Indonesia	0.05	0.07
Mexico	−0.02	−0.04
Russian Federation	−0.06	−0.16
South Africa	0.06	0.17
Thailand	0.43	0.29
Turkey	0.25	0.02
Vietnam	−0.20	−0.09
Rest of South Asia	0.13	0.05
Rest of East Asia and the Pacific	0.02	0.01
Rest of Latin America and the Caribbean	0.44	0.06
Rest of Europe and Central Asia	−0.06	−0.09
Middle East and North Africa	−0.07	−0.10
Selected Sub-Saharan Africa	0.21	−0.02
Rest of Sub-Saharan Africa	0.02	−0.13
Rest of world	0.19	0.00
High-income countries	0.20	0.06
Developing countries (WTO definition)	0.17	0.01
Developing countries	0.09	0.00
Middle-income	0.10	−0.01
Low-income countries	0.05	0.01
East Asia and the Pacific	0.01	−0.02
South Asia	0.03	0.03
Europe and Central Asia	0.01	−0.09
Middle East and North Africa	−0.07	−0.10
Sub-Saharan Africa	0.06	−0.01
Latin America and the Caribbean	0.29	0.08
World total	0.18	0.04

TABLE 12.14 (Continued)

Scen. 3	Scen. 4	Scen. 5	Scen. 6	Scen. 7	Scen. 8
0.18	0.38	0.22	0.20	0.42	0.48
0.09	0.28	0.11	0.11	0.31	0.36
0.01	0.02	0.02	0.01	0.03	0.05
0.03	0.13	0.05	0.05	0.10	0.11
0.03	0.30	0.03	0.26	0.48	0.51
0.13	0.58	0.14	1.26	1.19	1.79
−0.03	−0.02	−0.04	−0.04	0.35	0.52
0.25	0.34	0.27	0.26	0.34	0.39
−0.02	−0.06	−0.03	−0.04	−0.10	−0.09
0.13	0.49	0.17	0.17	0.55	0.59
−0.06	−0.01	−0.05	−0.04	0.07	0.06
0.02	0.02	0.03	0.02	0.25	0.40
0.07	0.08	0.09	0.01	0.37	0.44
−0.04	−0.02	−0.04	−0.04	−0.11	−0.02
−0.17	−0.03	−0.15	−0.15	0.16	0.31
0.05	0.09	0.11	0.17	0.25	0.49
0.15	0.49	0.38	0.38	0.99	1.33
−0.01	0.22	0.02	0.02	0.26	0.55
−0.06	−0.22	−0.11	−0.16	−0.83	−0.97
0.05	0.11	0.06	0.14	0.17	0.39
0.01	0.05	0.04	0.36	0.09	0.22
0.06	0.43	0.06	0.04	0.46	0.47
−0.09	−0.06	−0.09	−0.08	−0.22	−0.26
−0.13	−0.07	−0.10	−0.10	−0.05	0.01
0.00	0.19	−0.03	−0.05	0.19	0.26
−0.13	0.01	−0.14	−0.14	−0.02	0.13
0.00	0.14	0.00	0.02	0.26	0.28
0.05	0.18	0.05	0.13	0.25	0.30
0.00	0.14	0.01	0.14	0.27	0.40
−0.02	0.09	0.00	0.01	0.16	0.22
−0.02	0.10	0.00	0.01	0.15	0.21
0.01	0.04	0.01	0.00	0.18	0.30
−0.03	0.03	−0.01	0.02	0.13	0.16
0.02	0.02	0.03	0.03	0.21	0.36
−0.11	0.02	−0.09	−0.09	0.08	0.21
−0.13	−0.07	−0.10	−0.10	−0.05	0.01
−0.05	0.06	−0.04	−0.02	0.10	0.27
0.07	0.29	0.09	0.08	0.29	0.33
0.03	0.16	0.04	0.10	0.23	0.28

Source: Authors' World Bank LINKAGE model simulations.

TABLE 12.15 Welfare Effect of Retaining Agricultural Export and Domestic Subsidies, 2015

Country/region	(US$ billions)	
	Scenario 7	Scenario 7 (MD)
Australia and New Zealand	2.4	1.8
EU25 and EFTA	31.4	25.1
United States	4.9	5.3
Canada	0.9	1.0
Japan	23.7	24.8
Korea, Rep. of and Taiwan (China)	15.0	15.2
Hong Kong (China) and Singapore	1.5	1.7
Argentina	1.3	1.2
Bangladesh	−0.1	−0.1
Brazil	3.6	3.5
China	1.7	2.6
India	2.2	2.2
Indonesia	1.0	0.9
Mexico	−0.9	−0.8
Russian Federation	0.8	2.0
South Africa	0.4	0.3
Thailand	2.0	2.0
Turkey	0.7	0.7
Vietnam	−0.5	−0.5
Rest of South Asia	0.3	0.3
Rest of East Asia and the Pacific	0.3	0.4
Rest of Latin America and the Caribbean	3.9	4.2
Rest of Europe and Central Asia	−0.6	−0.3
Middle East and North Africa	−0.6	1.0
Selected Sub-Saharan Africa	0.1	0.2
Rest of Sub-Saharan Africa	−0.1	0.5
Rest of world	0.6	0.6
High-income countries	79.9	74.9
Developing countries (WTO definition)	32.6	38.0
Developing countries	16.1	21.1
Middle-income countries	12.5	16.9
Low-income countries	3.6	4.2
East Asia and the Pacific	4.5	5.5
South Asia	2.5	2.4
Europe and Central Asia	0.8	2.5
Middle East and North Africa	−0.6	1.0
Sub-Saharan Africa	0.4	1.0
Latin America and the Caribbean	7.9	8.1
World total	96.1	96.0

TABLE 12.15 (Continued)

		Percent		
Scenario 7 (M)	Scenario 7	Scenario 7 (MD)	Scenario 7 (M)
1.6	0.42	0.32	0.27
25.5	0.31	0.25	0.25
3.3	0.03	0.04	0.02
0.8	0.10	0.11	0.09
25.5	0.48	0.50	0.51
15.6	1.19	1.20	1.23
1.9	0.35	0.39	0.43
0.4	0.34	0.30	0.11
−0.1	−0.10	−0.09	−0.09
3.0	0.55	0.54	0.46
4.5	0.07	0.10	0.17
2.1	0.25	0.25	0.23
0.9	0.37	0.35	0.34
−0.5	−0.11	−0.09	−0.06
2.1	0.16	0.42	0.44
0.3	0.25	0.22	0.23
1.9	0.99	0.99	0.96
0.8	0.26	0.30	0.32
−0.5	−0.83	−0.81	−0.88
0.2	0.17	0.18	0.12
0.5	0.09	0.15	0.17
3.9	0.46	0.50	0.46
−0.3	−0.22	−0.09	−0.10
1.3	−0.05	0.08	0.10
0.1	0.19	0.28	0.19
0.3	−0.02	0.22	0.14
0.6	0.26	0.28	0.27
74.1	0.25	0.23	0.23
39.0	0.27	0.32	0.33
21.6	0.16	0.21	0.21
18.0	0.15	0.21	0.22
3.6	0.18	0.21	0.18
7.3	0.13	0.16	0.21
2.2	0.21	0.21	0.19
2.6	0.08	0.25	0.26
1.3	−0.05	0.08	0.10
0.8	0.10	0.23	0.18
6.8	0.29	0.29	0.25
95.7	0.23	0.23	0.22

Source: Authors' World Bank LINKAGE model simulations.
Note: Scenario 7 (MD) is the same as scenario 7 except export subsidies are not eliminated. Scenario 7 (M) is the same as 7 (MD) except domestic support is not cut. In other words, scenario 7 (M) includes only cuts in import tariffs. See table 12.12 for description of scenario 7.

if export subsidies are not cut and then if domestic subsidies also remain uncut. Not surprisingly, continuation of export subsidies reduces the welfare gain most for the European Union, while for the United States it is the continuation of domestic support programs. Recall that changes in a country's welfare effects result not only from efficiency of resource use but also from changes in its terms of trade, which are affected by reforms in other countries as well as the county itself. Unprotected Latin America, and Australia and New Zealand gain most from the progressive addition of subsidy cuts to the scenario (apart from the subsidy-cutting countries themselves).

Trade negotiators often think more in terms of the boost to the value of trade than to the increase in economic welfare. Would freeing global merchandise trade lead to greater trade gain for developing countries than for high-income countries, given the latter's high protection rates in agriculture and textiles? Table 12.16 suggests any imbalance of that sort is not likely to be a major problem, even with complete trade liberalization. Certainly in those two protected sectors, exports would increase more for developing than for high-income countries, but for other manufactures the trade growth for the two regions would have the opposite bias. Also, much of the developing countries' trade growth is with other developing countries. Hence for merchandise trade as a whole, developing countries would sell an additional $318 billion to high-income countries under free trade whereas high-income countries would sell an additional $290 billion to developing countries. A small amount of services trade liberalization by developing countries would be sufficient to close that gap, if full reciprocity was sought.

The trade consequences of scenario 7 also are summarized in table 12.16. The fourth column shows that by 2015, annual exports from developing countries would increase by $41 billion for agricultural products, $25 billion for textiles and clothing, and $12 billion for other manufactures. The total increase of $78 billion is somewhat smaller than that for high-income countries ($135 billion), but that difference is less when expressed in percentage terms (2.6 percent, compared with 3.1 percent for high-income countries). This takes the world economy one-fifth of the way toward where it would be if the world moved to completely free trade in merchandise (compare the first and fourth columns of table 12.16). Of more interest to trade negotiators are the changes in *bilateral* trade: they want to see how balanced any exchange of market access would be. Not surprisingly, developing countries expand their exports of agricultural and textile products to high-income countries more than they expand their imports of those products from high-income countries. But the opposite is true of other manufactures, so for merchandise trade in total the difference is not great: developing countries in 2015 would sell $62 billion more to high-income countries and would buy $55 billion in return under scenario 7 (see fifth and sixth columns of table 12.16). This small gap might be tolerated by high-income countries as a concession to development,

TABLE 12.16 Changes from Baseline in Bilateral Trade Flows from Full Global Liberalization and from Doha Scenario 7, 2015 (US$ billions)

Exporter	Importer, full liberalization			Importer, Doha Scenario 7		
	World	High-income countries	Developing countries	World	High income countries	Developing countries
Agriculture and food						
World	314	186	128	56	46	9
High-income	104	54	50	15	15	–0
Developing	210	133	77	41	31	10
Textiles and clothing						
World	164	79	85	41	28	12
High-income	47	8	40	16	5	11
Developing	117	71	46	25	23	2
Other manufacturing						
World	595	227	368	117	68	49
High-income	312	112	200	105	60	44
Developing	284	114	168	12	8	5
All merchandise trade						
World	1,073	492	581	213	142	71
High-income	463	174	290	135	80	55
Developing	610	318	291	78	62	16

Source: Authors' World Bank LINKAGE model simulations.
Note: Aggregations exclude intra-EU trade.

but otherwise it could be narrowed if developing countries demanded less special and differential treatment or gave more than they got from high-income countries in terms of opening up services trade.

How big would be the consequences of reform for farm output and employment growth over the implementation period post-2004? Table 12.17 shows what that annual growth would be in the baseline (no policy changes after 2004), what it would be if all distortions to merchandise trade were removed, and what it would be under scenario 7. If trade was completely freed, farm output would decline (instead of growing slightly) only in the EU and Japan while growing slower in a few other highly protective countries. But for most of the world, farming activities

TABLE 12.17 Average Annual Agricultural Output and Employment Growth under Alternative Scenarios, 2005–15 (percent)

Country/region	Output growth			Employment growth		
	Baseline	Full liberalization	Scen. 7	Baseline	Full liberalization	Scen. 7
Australia and New Zealand	3.5	5.2	4.3	0.4	1.9	1.0
EU25 and EFTA	1.0	−1.5	−0.3	−1.8	−3.9	−2.8
United States	2.2	1.3	1.9	−0.8	−2.1	−1.2
Canada	3.5	5.2	4.0	0.2	1.9	0.6
Japan	0.5	−4.3	−1.4	−2.7	−6.5	−4.1
Korea, Rep. of, and Taiwan (China)	2.2	0.1	1.5	−1.3	−3.9	−2.1
Hong Kong (China) and Singapore	2.8	3.3	2.9	0.0	0.2	0.0
Argentina	2.9	5.1	3.5	0.9	3.3	1.5
Bangladesh	4.2	4.4	4.2	1.1	1.2	1.2
Brazil	3.3	6.1	4.4	1.1	4.0	2.2
China	4.3	4.3	4.3	0.8	0.7	0.8
India	4.3	4.1	4.4	1.0	0.6	1.0
Indonesia	3.0	2.9	3.0	−0.7	−0.7	−0.6
Mexico	3.9	4.1	4.0	2.0	2.3	2.3
Russian Federation	1.5	1.0	1.4	−2.3	−2.7	−2.4
South Africa	2.5	3.3	2.6	0.0	0.8	0.1
Thailand	−0.1	1.3	0.4	−4.6	−3.7	−4.3
Turkey	3.0	2.6	3.0	−0.5	−1.2	−0.5
Vietnam	5.8	6.1	5.9	3.9	3.5	4.0
Rest of South Asia	4.8	4.8	4.9	2.0	1.9	2.1
Rest of East Asia and the Pacific	3.7	3.5	3.8	0.2	−0.1	0.3
Rest of Latin America and the Caribbean	4.4	6.6	5.3	1.9	3.8	2.6
Rest of Europe and Central Asia	3.3	3.3	3.3	0.0	−0.1	0.0
Middle East and North Africa	4.0	4.0	4.0	1.5	1.4	1.5
Selected Sub-Saharan Africa	5.3	5.7	5.4	3.0	3.3	3.0
Rest of Sub-Saharan Africa	4.6	4.8	4.8	2.2	2.5	2.3
Rest of world	5.0	6.4	5.5	2.4	3.5	2.7

TABLE 12.17 (Continued)

Country/region	Output growth			Employment growth		
	Baseline	Full liberalization	Scen. 7	Baseline	Full liberalization	Scen. 7
High-income countries	1.6	−0.1	0.8	−1.5	−3.1	−2.2
Developing countries	3.9	4.2	4.1	1.0	1.2	1.1
Middle-income countries	3.7	4.1	3.9	0.4	0.3	0.4
Low-income countries	4.4	4.5	4.5	1.2	0.9	1.2
East Asia and the Pacific	4.0	4.0	4.0	−0.5	−0.8	−0.5
South Asia	4.4	4.2	4.4	1.5	1.4	1.5
Europe and Central Asia	3.0	2.9	3.1	2.3	2.6	2.4
Middle East and North Africa	4.0	4.0	4.0	1.7	3.4	2.4
Sub-Saharan Africa	4.5	4.9	4.7	0.2	0.0	0.2
Latin America and the Caribbean	3.8	5.8	4.6	0.4	1.9	1.0
World total	3.2	2.9	3.0	−1.8	−3.9	−2.8

Source: Authors' World Bank LINKAGE model simulations.

would expand. Scenario 7 would involve much less reform than a move to free trade, and so would involve a much slower loss of farm output for the EU and Japan and less output growth for the vast majority of countries that would gain. A comparison of the first and third columns of table 12.17 reveals that for most of the protective economies, scenario 7 would simply slow the growth of farm output a little over the coming decade. This contrasts with the rhetoric suggesting that cuts in farm protection would cause a major collapse of protected sectors.

The farm employment picture is somewhat different. Typically, economic growth leads to declines not only in the relative importance of agriculture (for reasons explained in Anderson 1987 and Martin and Warr 1993) but also in absolute numbers employed in farming once a country reaches middle-income status. Thus it is not surprising that numerous middle- and high-income countries are projected to lose farm jobs over the next decade, as the baseline scenario of table 12.17 shows. For the most protected farm sectors, that rate of farm employment decline would more than double if the world were to move to completely free trade; but it would decline only slightly under scenario 7. For other economies,

TABLE 12.18 Share of Agricultural and Food Production Exported, by Country or Region under Alternative Scenarios, 2001 and 2015 (percent)

Country/region	2001 baseline	2015 baseline	Full global liberalization	Scen. 7
Australia and New Zealand	33.3	37.2	42.7	39.5
EU25 and EFTA	16.7	17.3	17.6	16.6
EU25 and EFTA (excluding intra-EU25)	4.0	5.1	7.7	5.0
United States	6.3	7.9	9.2	8.1
Canada	24.5	29.5	40.0	32.5
Japan	0.9	1.2	2.3	1.5
Korea, Rep. of, and Taiwan (China)	4.4	4.8	26.5	8.6
Hong Kong (China) and Singapore	26.0	30.0	47.8	30.8
Argentina	21.6	25.2	32.5	26.9
Bangladesh	1.7	3.6	5.7	3.5
Brazil	15.3	17.3	28.9	21.7
China	3.3	0.9	2.2	1.0
India	3.5	3.0	4.7	3.3
Indonesia	11.9	10.0	12.9	9.9
Mexico	5.6	7.8	13.2	8.5
Russian Federation	6.1	5.5	6.7	6.0
South Africa	16.0	12.7	18.8	13.5
Thailand	30.2	28.2	34.6	30.1
Turkey	9.6	6.0	12.4	7.0
Vietnam	23.9	26.9	35.3	26.7
Rest of South Asia	6.0	6.2	9.9	6.6
Rest of East Asia and the Pacific	16.1	14.6	22.1	14.9
Rest of Latin America and the Caribbean	13.9	18.1	27.1	20.7
Rest of Europe and Central Asia	2.4	1.7	3.7	1.9
Middle East and North Africa	5.2	6.7	11.2	7.2
Selected Sub-Saharan Africa	13.2	18.1	25.4	19.2
Rest of Sub-Saharan Africa	11.2	15.8	23.3	16.5
Rest of world	6.6	7.0	17.7	8.7

TABLE 12.18 (Continued)

Country/region	2001 Baseline	2015 Baseline	Full global liberalization	Scen. 7
High-income countries	5.8	7.5	11.6	8.2
Developing countries	7.5	6.9	11.6	7.8
Middle-income countries	7.6	6.6	11.4	7.6
Low-income countries	7.3	7.9	12.4	8.4
East Asia and the Pacific	7.2	4.1	6.5	4.3
South Asia	3.8	3.6	5.7	3.9
Europe and Central Asia	3.7	2.7	5.0	3.0
Middle East and North Africa	5.2	6.7	11.2	7.2
Sub-Saharan Africa	12.5	15.8	23.1	16.6
Latin America and the Caribbean	12.7	15.9	24.8	18.5
World total	9.5	9.5	13.2	10.0
World total (excl. intra-EU25)	6.6	7.2	11.6	8.0

Source: Authors' World Bank LINKAGE model simulations.

though, farm employment would grow a little faster under that scenario, allowing developing countries to absorb more workers on their farms.[12]

Scenario 7 also raises the share of agricultural and food production that is exported globally, from 9.5 to 10.0 percent, which is one-seventh the 13.2 percent share farm and food exports hold under the free merchandise trade scenario. Table 12.18 shows that even in the protected countries this ratio rises a little or, in the case of Europe, falls only very slightly. That change is small because farm resources would move within the sector from import-competing to more-competitive farming activities.

What about poverty alleviation? In a separate paper (Anderson, Martin, and van der Mensbrugghe 2006), we estimate that under the full merchandise trade liberalization scenario, the number of people in extreme poverty in developing countries (those earning no more than $1 a day) would drop by 32 million in 2015 relative to the baseline level of 622 million, a reduction of 5 percent. By 2015 a majority of the poor are projected to be in Sub-Saharan Africa, where the reduction would be 6 percent.[13] Under the Doha scenarios shown in table 12.19, the poverty impacts are far more modest. The number of poor living on $1 a day or less is estimated to fall by 2.5 million under scenario 7, (of which 0.5 million are in Sub-Saharan Africa) and by 6.3 million under scenario 8 (of which 2.2 million are in Sub-Saharan Africa). These estimates correspond to the relatively modest ambitions of the merchandise trade reforms as captured in these two scenarios. If only

TABLE 12.19 Changes in Poverty under Alternative Scenarios, 2015 (millions)

Region	Baseline	Full liberalization	Doha alternatives		
			Doha Scenario 1	Doha Scenario 7	Doha Scenario 8
a. 2015 headcount (%)					
East Asia and the Pacific	0.9	0.8	0.9	0.9	0.9
Latin America and the Caribbean	6.9	6.6	6.9	6.9	6.8
South Asia	12.8	12.5	12.8	12.7	12.6
Sub-Saharan Africa	38.4	36.0	38.4	38.3	38.1
All developing countries	10.2	9.7	10.2	10.2	10.1

	2015 level	Decrease from baseline	Decrease from baseline		
b. 2015 headcount					
East Asia and the Pacific	19	2.2	0.1	0.3	0.5
Latin America and the Caribbean	43	2.1	0.3	0.4	0.5
South Asia	216	5.6	0.2	1.4	3.0
Sub-Saharan Africa	340	21.1	−0.1	0.5	2.2
All developing countries	622	31.9	0.5	2.5	6.3

Source: Authors' World Bank LINKAGE model simulations as reported in Anderson, Martin, and van der Mensbrugghe (2006).
Note: Poverty is defined as earnings of $1 a day or less. Hong Kong (China), Republic of Korea, Singapore, and Taiwan (China) are not included in these estimates.

agriculture was reformed (scenario 1), there would be much less poverty alleviation globally and none at all in Sub-Saharan Africa. That result underscores the importance for poverty of including manufactured products in the Doha negotiations.

Caveats

Results such as those presented here are always dependent on the assumptions, data, and parameters underlying them and so are subject to numerous qualifications. A particularly important caveat has to do with the way preferences are treated in the

GTAP Version 6.05 database. In previous versions of that database, only key *reciprocal* preferences were included (notably between members within the EU, NAFTA, ASEAN, and Australia-New Zealand Closer Economic Relationship), whereas the new version added *nonreciprocal* tariff preferences provided by developed countries for their imports from developing countries under numerous arrangements such as the Generalized System of Preferences, the EU's provisions for former colonies under the Africa, Caribbean, and Pacific program and more recently for least developed countries under the Everything But Arms agreement, and the U.S. Africa Growth and Opportunity Act and the Caribbean Basin Initiative. We assume that there are no rules of origin or similar restrictions that discourage developing countries from taking full advantage of those preferences (even though we know rules of origin often lead to underutilization). We further assume perfect competition between traders in the two sets of countries, which determines how rents from those preferences are shared between the exporting and importing countries (even though we know the developed-country importers often have more market power than the developing-country exporters of standard commodities so that the latter receives a smaller share of the rents than our analysis generates).[14] We therefore overstate the extent of preference erosion that would occur, especially for least developed countries, and so understate their gains from trade reform. If instead those nonreciprocal preferences were excluded from the database, we would overestimate the preference-receiving countries' gains from developed-country trade reform. So until we have a better way to incorporate these real-world aspects of preference schemes, the reader should simply be aware that the welfare gains would be higher (or losses less) for least developed countries than indicated above.[15] The difference would not be great for Rest of Sub-Saharan Africa, however, according to the results presented in Bouët, Fontagné, and Jean (2006, table 6.9).

Imports of agricultural products subject to tariff rate quotas are handled less than perfectly in the World Bank's LINKAGE model and the GTAP database, in two respects. First, in the GTAP Version 6.05 database, the treatment of tariffs applied on TRQ commodities depends on the extent to which the quota is filled: if the quota is less than 90 percent filled, the in-quota tariff is assumed to apply on these commodities; if the quota is between 90 and 99 percent filled, the effective tariff is assumed to be the average of the in- and the out-of-quota tariffs; and if the quota is more than 99 percent filled, then the out-of-quota tariff is applied. Second, where TRQs are nonbinding and hence the in-quota tariff is used, and preferences are provided to developing countries, such a preference may well be illusory. If imports increased, for example, the out-of-quota tariff might kick in. Furthermore, de Gorter and Kliauga (2006) identify cases where the out-of-quota tariff has been applied at the margin even though the quota was not filled. This provides additional reasons to expect that we have overstated the benefits of preferences or the costs of preference erosion.

TABLE 12.20 Impacts on Real Income from Full Liberalization of Global Merchandise Trade with and without Endogenous Productivity Growth, 2015

Region	Productivity fixed		Endogenous productivity	
	US$ billions	Percent	US$ billions	Percent
High-income countries	202	0.6	261	0.8
Developing countries	86	0.8	200	1.4
Middle income	70	0.8	145	1.2
Low income	16	0.8	55	2.1
World total	287	0.7	461	0.9

Source: Authors' World Bank LINKAGE model simulations, as reported in more detail in Anderson, Martin, and van der Mensbrugghe (2006).
Note: Effects are given relative to the 2015 baseline.

Another important caveat is that our results do not incorporate the fact that trade reform typically boosts factor productivity.[16] If instead we were to assume productivity is positively related to changes in sectoral openness, as specified in World Bank (2002) and Anderson, Martin, and van der Mensbrugghe (2005a), then the estimated global gains from freeing merchandise trade increase by 60 percent.[17] More important, they increase by 130 percent for developing countries, because the initial protection rates are so much higher there (table 12.20). For this reason even more than because of our treatment of preferences, the welfare effects presented in this paper should be taken as very much lower-bound estimates.

The above analysis does not include costs of adjustment to reform, but these are typically far less than is commonly assumed.[18] Indeed, the structural changes that take place over time in the normal course of economic growth are shown above to be typically very much larger than the small changes that would accompany gradual and partial trade liberalization. Furthermore, adjustment assistance schemes (financed by foreign aid in the case of low-income countries) are a way to help fund adjustment to tariff and subsidy cuts, and they are just one-time payments, whereas the benefits of reform continue into the future.

Lessons and Implications

In summary, we provide the following as the key messages that emerge from our analysis:

- The potential gains from further global trade reform are large
- Developing countries could gain disproportionately from further global trade reform

- Benefits could be as much from South-South as from South-North trade reform
- Agriculture is where reform is needed most
- Large cuts in both agricultural tariffs and domestic support commitments are needed to erase binding overhang
- A complex, tiered formula may offer only a slightly greater gain than a proportional cut with a cap on farm tariffs
- Even large cuts in agricultural tariffs do little if exceptions are made for sensitive products, again unless a cap applies
- Cuts in cotton subsidies would help cotton-exporting developing countries
- Expanding nonagricultural market access would add substantially to the gains from agricultural reform and help balance the exchange of concessions
- Some poor countries may lose slightly, although that is less likely the more they reform themselves
- Farm output and employment would not decline in developing countries under Doha

The good news is that a great deal can be gained from liberalizing merchandise—especially agricultural—trade under Doha, with a disproportionately high share of that potential gain available for developing countries (relative to their share of the global economy). Moreover, it is the poorest people, namely, farmers and unskilled nonfarm laborers, who appear to be most likely to gain from global trade liberalization in developing countries. To realize that potential gain, it is in agriculture that by far the greatest cuts in bound tariffs and subsidies are required. However, the political sensitivity of farm support programs, coupled with the complexities of the measures introduced in the Uruguay Round Agreement on Agriculture and of the modalities set out in the Doha framework agreement of July 2004, ensure that the devil will be in the details of the final Doha agreement. It is for that reason that ex ante empirical analysis of the sort provided here is a prerequisite for countries engaged in the Doha round of negotiations.

Among the numerous policy implications that can be drawn from our analysis, several are worth highlighting. First, with gains on the order of $300 billion a year at stake from implementing the July Framework Agreement, even if no reforms are forthcoming in services, and even if the counterfactual would be the status quo rather than protectionist backsliding, the political will needs to be found to bring the round to a successful conclusion, and the sooner the better. Multilateral cuts in MFN bindings are also helpful because they can lock in previous unilateral trade liberalizations that otherwise would remain unbound and hence vulnerable to backsliding; they can also be used as an opportunity to multilateralize previously agreed preferential trade agreements and thereby reduce the risk of trade diversion from those bilateral or regional arrangements.

Second, agricultural reforms need to be significant if the Doha agreement is to be pro-development and pro-poor. Outlawing agricultural export subsidies is the obvious first step. That will bring agriculture into line with the basic GATT rule against such measures, and in the process help to limit the extent to which governments encourage agricultural production by other means (since the cost of surplus disposal will be higher without access to export subsidies). Concurrently, domestic support bindings must be cut very substantially to reduce binding overhang. In so doing, the highest-subsidizing countries, namely the European Union, Norway, and the United States, need to reduce their support, not just for the sake of their own economies but also to encourage developing countries to reciprocate by opening their markets as a quid pro quo. An initial installment of a 20 percent cut is nothing more than a start toward getting rid of that overhang. Even more important, agricultural tariff bindings must be cut deeply so that some genuine market opening can occur. Exempting even just a few sensitive and special farm products is undesirable because such exemptions would drastically reduce the gains from reform. If such exemptions prove politically impossible to avoid, then a cap should be imposed so that no bound tariff for any product could exceed, say, 200 percent. Should it prove to be too difficult or time-consuming to negotiate a complex, tiered formula for cutting farm tariffs, our results suggest a proportional cut of the same average magnitude plus a cap to bring down the very highest bound tariffs could be nearly as effective in raising welfare.

Third, expanding nonagricultural market access at the same time as reforming agricultural trade is essential. A balanced exchange of concessions is impossible without adding other sectors, and the sectors cannot be limited to textiles and clothing (which also benefit developing countries disproportionately) even though they make up the other highly distorted sector. With other merchandise included, the trade expansion would be many times greater for both rich and poor countries.

Fourth, South-South concessions also are needed, which means reconsidering the extent to which developing countries liberalize. Because developing countries are trading so much more with each other now, they are the major beneficiaries of reforms within their own regions. Even least developed countries should consider reducing their tariff binding overhang, since doing so in the context of Doha gives them more scope to demand concessions (or compensation for preference erosion or other contributors to terms-of-trade deterioration) from richer countries than if they hang on to their opportunity not to engage in reform.

What emerges from our analysis is that developing countries would not *have* to reform very much under Doha because of the large gaps between their tariff bindings and applied rates. But to realize more of their potential gains from trade, they would need to forgo some of the special and differential treatment they have previously demanded, and perhaps also commit to additional unilateral trade (and complementary domestic) reforms, and to invest more in trade facilitation. High-income countries could encourage them to do so by being willing to open up their own markets more to developing-country exports and by providing more targeted aid. To that end, a new proposal has been put forward to reward developing-country commitments to greater trade reform with an expansion of trade-facilitating aid, to be provided by a major expansion of the current Integrated Framework, which is operated by a consortium of international agencies for least developed countries (Hoekman and Prowse 2005). This proposal may well provide an attractive path for developing countries seeking to trade their way out of poverty, not least because it would help offset the tendency for an expanded aid flow to cause a real exchange rate appreciation (Commission for Africa 2005, 296–97). As well, it is potentially a far more efficient way for developed countries to assist people in low-income countries than is the current system of tariff preferences.

In conclusion, the July Framework Agreement does not guarantee major gains from the Doha Development Agenda. On the one hand, even if an agreement is ultimately reached, it may be very modest. How modest depends on, among other things, the nature of the agricultural tariff-cutting formula, the size of the cuts, the extent to which exceptions for sensitive and special farm products are allowed, whether a tariff cap is introduced, and the extent to which developing countries commit to participating in market access reforms. What is equally clear, on the other hand, is that major gains are possible, but only if the political will to reform protectionist policies—especially in agriculture—can be mustered.

Appendix 12A: Comparison of Versions 5 and 6.05 of the GTAP Protection Database and of LINKAGE Model Results with Those from the GTAP-AGR Model

The newest version of the LINKAGE model, Version 6.0, is based on the latest release of the GTAP database, Release 6.05.[19] That version has a 2001 base year, updated national and trade data, and, importantly, a new source for the protection data. (The base year in the previous release, Version 5, was 1997.) The new protection data set provides a tariff level detailed database on bilateral protection that integrates trade preferences, specific tariffs, and a partial evaluation of nontariff barriers such as tariff rate quotas.[20] The tariffs are lower in GTAP Version 6.05 than they were in the previous database because of the inclusion of bilateral trade preferences and of major reforms between 1997 and 2001 (table A12.1). These reforms included the continued implementation of the Uruguay Round Agreement,

TABLE 12A.1 Applied Tariffs by Sector for Selected Importing Regions, GTAP 6.05 (2001) Compared with GTAP5 (1997) (percent)

Trading sector	China GTAP6	China GTAP5	India GTAP6	India GTAP5
Merchandise trade	13.6	15.6	28.1	22.0
Agriculture and food	37.6	38.8	50.3	25.9
Agriculture	49.1	42.6	25.7	18.9
Rice	1.0	109.0	0.0	0.0
Wheat	1.0	113.5	0.0	0.0
Other grains	88.6	91.1	0.0	0.0
Oilseeds	101.2	110.4	35.0	0.0
Sugar	18.8	29.8	52.3	20.0
Other crops	17.8	10.8	28.1	25.4
Livestock	5.9	12.3	14.3	19.0
Processed foods	18.7	36.1	76.6	35.1
Processed meats	14.7	17.2	59.3	18.2
Dairy products	20.4	16.9	37.0	27.1
Other foods	19.8	40.3	78.7	35.2
Fossil fuels	4.3	4.5	17.3	15.0
Other natural resources	0.6	1.0	12.4	4.0
Manufacturing excluding food	12.8	14.5	28.4	22.1
Textiles	20.3	25.1	26.2	33.0
Wearing apparel	22.4	31.7	32.9	30.8
Leather	10.0	12.1	26.6	8.9
Chemicals, rubber, plastics	13.4	13.4	30.9	25.9
Iron, steel	7.0	9.7	34.6	28.3
Motor vehicles, parts	38.2	34.4	40.4	35.0
Capital goods	11.1	12.5	21.6	20.7
Other manufacturing	10.2	12.8	32.4	24.2

especially the elimination of quotas on textile and clothing trade, and China's reforms leading up to accession to the World Trade Organization. The version of the LINKAGE model used for this study is made up of a 27-region, 25-sector aggregation of the GTAP data set.

Using the GTAP Version 6.05 database for 2001 and the newest LINKAGE model, our analysis finds considerably larger welfare gains from full trade liberalization than the gains generated by Hertel and Keeney (2006) using a variant on

TABLE 12A.1 (Continued)

Brazil		Middle East and North Africa		Sub-Saharan Africa	
GTAP6	GTAP5	GTAP6	GTAP5	GTAP6	GTAP5
9.5	14.3	9.8	18.2	12.6	14.7
5.0	12.0	14.1	61.0	18.2	27.5
2.4	8.3	9.9	40.4	15.2	18.1
0.1	14.1	2.6	8.7	24.3	8.6
0.1	6.5	9.4	47.3	10.8	14.0
0.5	6.6	16.5	29.8	8.7	24.3
0.0	5.9	6.1	42.9	4.5	18.2
15.2	18.5	9.9	16.3	16.8	27.4
6.0	9.0	11.0	66.8	10.3	18.5
4.5	7.5	5.0	58.8	7.8	5.5
9.0	16.6	18.6	81.9	20.5	33.7
4.2	12.2	9.5	105.0	17.8	38.3
5.8	19.5	10.7	102.3	14.1	25.7
10.0	16.5	22.9	71.8	21.9	34.3
0.1	4.9	2.9	5.3	7.8	6.5
3.0	2.0	5.8	6.0	3.7	11.4
11.3	15.7	9.6	11.3	12.0	13.7
14.7	15.8	17.3	19.4	20.7	19.1
20.1	20.0	55.1	21.8	33.0	30.9
10.8	23.2	13.7	20.4	26.6	32.8
8.5	9.2	6.8	8.9	9.4	10.4
11.6	12.4	6.6	9.6	12.7	13.3
20.1	38.6	11.9	15.2	17.5	22.2
10.8	14.0	6.7	9.5	8.8	9.6
11.8	12.1	7.7	10.9	12.8	17.5

Source: GTAP (www.gtap.org); van der Mensbrugghe (2004a).

the standard GTAP model called GTAP-AGR. To understand the reasons behind this difference, we altered the LINKAGE model for this appendix exercise so that it mimics the comparative static GTAP-AGR model as of 2001, and we also altered assumptions about elasticities (see the differences in table A12.2) and factor mobility to make them similar to those used by Hertel and Keeney.

Obtaining a comparative static version of the LINKAGE model involves only a few modifications to the recursive dynamic version used in our Doha scenarios.

TABLE 12A.1 Applied Tariffs by Sector for Selected Importing Regions, GTAP 6.05 (2001) Compared with GTAP5 (1997) (percent) (*Continued*)

Trading sector	European GTAP6	European GTAP5	Japan GTAP6	Japan GTAP5
Merchandise trade	3.2	6.0	5.2	9.2
Agriculture and food	13.9	22.4	29.4	50.3
Agriculture	13.2	14.2	48.0	65.6
Rice	92.6	76.0	862.4	409.0
Wheat	10.3	68.2	184.6	249.2
Other grains	21.3	43.1	39.0	20.2
Oilseeds	1.8	2.6	0.2	76.4
Sugar	112.9	77.5	246.5	115.0
Other crops	9.3	9.3	6.2	29.5
Livestock	1.9	10.7	4.3	27.7
Processed foods	14.7	33.4	20.9	43.0
Processed meats	39.9	76.2	47.4	48.8
Dairy products	42.1	89.7	53.7	287.0
Other foods	9.0	23.4	9.8	30.0
Fossil fuels	0.3	0.7	0.3	−0.9
Other natural resources	0.0	0.2	0.1	0.1
Manufacturing excluding food	2.5	4.8	1.7	2.4
Textiles	4.6	9.5	7.1	8.5
Wearing apparel	5.5	11.9	10.2	12.5
Leather	5.7	8.1	12.6	15.3
Chemicals, rubber, plastics	2.2	4.8	1.0	2.0
Iron, steel	3.6	3.1	1.0	2.5
Motor vehicles, parts	6.1	7.7	0.0	0.0
Capital goods	1.1	3.5	0.0	0.1
Other manufacturing	2.9	2.8	0.9	1.5

Specifically, the "new" elasticities of substitution in production are imposed to mimic the long-term properties of the dynamic model, capital is assumed to be perfectly mobile, and adjustment costs are ignored. But the big difference between the comparative static and dynamic version results is the change in the structure of the global economy by 2015. This change is attributable to growth in factor

TABLE 12A.1 (Continued)

United States		Korea, Rep. of and Taiwan (China)		Canada, Australia, New Zealand	
GTAP6	GTAP5	GTAP6	GTAP5	GTAP6	GTAP5
1.8	2.9	7.6	8.8	2.3	3.0
2.4	10.8	55.0	49.4	7.4	15.9
2.3	13.8	88.3	64.9	1.1	3.4
4.4	5.3	874.8	4.4	0.0	0.7
0.2	2.6	3.4	3.8	0.4	43.1
0.0	0.6	258.0	180.3	0.0	8.7
3.4	17.7	223.1	66.3	0.0	0.2
25.5	53.1	30.5	7.4	0.5	4.4
1.4	13.9	21.4	36.6	0.3	2.0
0.1	0.8	3.6	6.5	7.1	10.9
2.5	8.9	22.7	33.5	11.0	22.1
2.1	4.6	31.8	22.5	23.3	38.8
18.3	42.5	23.0	39.2	64.3	107.1
2.0	7.9	20.6	35.1	6.1	16.1
0.1	0.4	4.7	4.7	1.4	0.4
0.1	0.3	1.1	1.3	0.0	0.0
1.9	2.6	4.0	5.9	2.0	2.3
7.9	8.9	8.7	7.5	7.1	9.2
9.9	11.6	12.2	9.4	16.4	20.5
12.2	13.0	6.2	5.7	9.3	12.7
1.7	2.7	5.2	5.5	1.2	1.8
0.9	2.5	3.2	5.6	0.9	2.2
1.3	1.3	20.4	16.7	3.2	2.1
0.6	1.4	2.4	5.6	0.8	1.4
1.1	1.6	4.9	4.7	1.3	1.7

Source: GTAP (www.gtap.org); van der Mensbrugghe (2004a).

stocks and to changes in the relative weights of countries and sectors in the global economy over those 14 years.

Table A12.3 reports the results from the LINKAGE model on the welfare cost of global trade barriers and agricultural subsidies in 2001 under various assumptions, compared with their cost in 2015. First, we scale the 2015 dynamic results back to

TABLE 12A.2 Global Average Top-Level Armington Elasticities in the GTAP-AGR and LINKAGE Models, by Product

Product	GTAP elasticities	LINKAGE elasticities	Percent difference
	(1)	(2)	([2] − [1])/(1)
Rice	3.20	4.45	39
Wheat	4.45	5.85	31
Other grains	1.30	4.93	279
Oilseeds	2.45	4.75	94
Sugar	2.70	5.91	119
Plant-based fibers	2.50	3.94	58
Vegetables and fruits	1.85	3.94	113
Other crops	3.25	3.94	21
Livestock	2.09	3.94	89
Other natural resources	1.21	2.80	131
Fossil fuels	5.70	4.93	−14
Processed meats	4.17	3.94	−6
Vegetable oils and fats	3.30	3.94	19
Dairy products	3.65	3.94	8
Other food, beverages, and tobacco	1.74	3.94	126
Textiles	3.75	3.94	5
Wearing apparel	3.70	3.94	6
Leather	4.05	4.93	22
Chemicals, rubber, and plastics	3.30	3.94	19
Iron and steel	2.95	3.94	34
Motor vehicles and parts	2.80	4.93	76
Capital goods	4.21	3.94	−6
Other manufacturing	3.52	3.94	12
Construction	1.90	1.50	−21
Utilities and services	1.92	2.09	9
Agriculture	2.64	4.63	75
Processed foods	3.22	3.94	23
Textile and wearing apparel	3.83	4.27	11
Other manufacturing	3.38	4.06	20
Merchandise trade	3.12	4.29	37
Total	3.03	4.09	35

Source: van der Mensbrugghe (2004b); Keeney and Hertel (2005).
Note: For convergence, the Armington elasticity for rice in Japan has been set at 2 in all simulations.

TABLE 12A.3 Comparison of Base Case in 2015 Versus Comparative Static Cases in 2001 for the Effects on Real Incomes of Full Liberalization of Global Merchandise Trade, by Country or Region (2001 US$ billions)

Country/region	2015		2001		
	Base case	Scaled dynamics	Comparative static	GTAP elasticities	GTAP elasticities plus fixed land
Australia and New Zealand	6.1	3.5	2.2	1.8	1.7
EU25 and EFTA	65.2	45.3	44.0	32.9	30.2
United States	16.2	9.8	4.1	4.5	5.2
Canada	3.8	2.5	2.1	1.0	0.8
Japan	54.6	28.0	30.8	25.1	25.3
Korea, Rep. of, and Taiwan (China)	44.6	14.3	16.1	8.9	9.1
Hong Kong (China) and Singapore	11.2	5.6	4.3	3.7	3.6
Argentina	4.9	2.9	1.7	1.1	0.8
Bangladesh	0.1	0.1	−0.2	−0.3	−0.4
Brazil	9.9	6.1	4.7	5.0	2.2
China	5.6	1.9	0.6	−0.5	−2.5
India	3.4	1.7	−0.8	−1.5	−0.8
Indonesia	1.9	1.0	0.2	0.1	−0.1
Thailand	7.7	3.7	2.1	1.4	0.9
Vietnam	3.0	1.6	1.1	0.7	0.7
Russian Federation	2.7	1.4	2.0	1.6	1.4
Mexico	3.6	2.3	−0.4	−1.5	−1.5
South Africa	1.3	0.8	0.7	0.5	0.4
Turkey	3.3	1.7	1.3	0.9	0.9
Rest of South Asia	1.0	0.5	−0.2	−0.3	−0.3
Rest of East Asia and the Pacific	5.3	2.7	2.9	2.0	1.7
Rest of Latin America and the Caribbean	10.3	6.6	2.0	−0.6	−2.1
Rest of Europe and Central Asia	1.0	0.3	0.6	−0.2	−0.4

TABLE 12A.3 (*Continued*)

Country/region	2015 Base case	2001 Scaled dynamics	2001 Comparative static	2001 GTAP elasticities	2001 GTAP elasticities plus fixed land
Middle East and North Africa	14.0	8.1	3.8	2.2	1.6
Selected Sub-Saharan Africa	1.0	0.6	0.3	0.4	0.3
Rest of Sub-Saharan Africa	2.5	1.4	−0.2	−0.6	−0.8
Rest of world	3.4	1.6	1.4	0.4	0.0
High-income countries	201.6	109.8	103.7	77.9	75.8
Developing countries	85.7	43.9	23.7	10.6	2.0
East Asia and the Pacific	23.5	9.4	6.9	3.7	0.6
South Asia	4.5	2.2	−1.2	−2.1	−1.5
Europe and Central Asia	7.0	3.5	3.9	2.3	1.9
Middle East and North Africa	14.0	8.1	3.8	2.2	1.6
Sub-Saharan Africa	4.8	2.8	0.7	0.2	−0.1
Latin America and the Caribbean	28.7	17.9	8.1	4.0	−0.5
World total	287.3	156.4	127.4	88.5	77.8

Source: Authors' World Bank LINKAGE model simulations.

Note: The scaled dynamic results refer to the impact of global merchandise trade reform with limited reductions in some key agricultural sectors in Japan (rice and sugar) and Republic of Korea and Taiwan (China) (rice, oilseeds and other grains). The percentage change in real income in each region in 2015 resulting from the dynamic simulation is scaled to the 2001 level of income for that region. Hong Kong (China), Korea, Singapore, and Taiwan (China) are considered high-income countries in this table and not developing countries.

2001 by assuming the percentage effect on income in each region is the same in 2001 as in 2015. This exercise reduces the real global cost from $287 billion to $156 billion simply because each regional economy is smaller. Second, when the dynamic effects themselves are removed, the global comparative static cost shrinks to $127 billion. Third, if the long-run Armington elasticities[21] used in the LINKAGE model (which we believe are more appropriate for the long-run analysis being undertaken in the current study) are replaced by the medium-term ones used in Hertel and Keeney's GTAP-AGR model,[22] the real global cost shrinks further to $89 billion. One other difference between the LINKAGE and GTAP models has to do with agricultural land: GTAP assumes a fixed supply of farm land and limited land mobility between farm sectors, whereas the LINKAGE model assumes farm land supply in the long run is somewhat responsive to farm product prices and that land is completely mobile among farming enterprises in the long run.[23] The final column of table A12.3 shows that replacing those two assumptions with the ones adopted in the GTAP-AGR model further reduces the global cost of trade-distorting policies to $78 billion. In short, these differences between the two models fully explain the different aggregate results, since $78 billion is very close to Hertel and Keeney's $84 billion comparative static estimate of the gains from freeing merchandise trade globally.

Notes

1. Centre d' Etudes Prospectives et d'Informations Internationales, at www.cepii.org.

2. This approach provides cuts in average tariffs without the discontinuities created by the proportional cuts involved in the Harbinson formula –but that are more or less comparable with those generated by Harbinson's proportional reductions of 25, 30, and 60 percent, because the larger cuts on higher tariffs apply only on the portion of the tariff above 15 or 90 percent, respectively.

3. The least developed countries are a special classification of 50 developing countries defined by the U.N. (http://www.unctad.org/Templates/WebFlyer.asp?intItemID=2161&lang=1).

4. See Finger (1974, 1976) for results from the Dillon and Kennedy Rounds, and Finger and Schuknecht (2001) for Uruguay Round results.

5. In the appendix to this chapter the results are compared with those from a comparative static version similar to the GTAP model, to show how key model specifications can affect the results.

6. For the sake of simplicity, government fiscal balances are fixed in US$ at their base-year level, minimizing potential sustainability problems, but this approach implies they decrease as a percentage of GDP (gross domestic product) for expanding economies.

7. These are the key internationally agreed and bound policy changes. We do not include unilateral and unbound policy changes such as recent reforms in EU and U.S. farm programs.

8. To get a sense of the effect of preferences on developing country and global welfare, we reran the model for 2001, prior to the presimulation experiment, without those preferences in place. The estimated global welfare gains from reform are then $382 billion instead of $341 billion, and the developing country gains are $150 billion instead of $113 billion. That is, the inclusion of preferences in the database reduces the estimated gains to global, developing country, and high-income country welfare by 11, 25, and 2 percent, respectively. Much of the difference is attributable to Sub-Saharan Africa, whose estimated gains from further reform are cut almost in half when preferences are included. The reductions for developing countries are overstated for two reasons, however. One is that we assume there are no rules of origin or other impediments that prevent developing countries from fully using their preferences. The second is that we also assume importers in the preference-providing rich countries do not use their power to gain a disproportionate share of the rent from that preferential access. In practice, neither of these assumptions holds, according to recent case studies (for example, Olarreaga and Özden 2005; Özden and Sharma 2004).

9. The technique for doing this using Gempack software was developed by Harrison, Horridge, and Pearson (2000).

10. As described in Jean, Laborde, and Martin (2006), each country presumably chooses its sensitive farm products by taking into account the importance of the product, the height of its existing tariff, and the gap between its bound and applied tariffs in that country.

11. In this and subsequent tables, Hong Kong (China), the Republic of Korea, Singapore, and Taiwan (China) are included in the high-income country category even though they are self-categorized in the WTO as developing countries (and so are assumed to cut their tariffs only to the same extent as other developing countries). In the tables where the WTO-define developing country group is also shown, the high-income country group results still include those four economies.

12. This finding of only small intersectoral labor movements in response to partial trade reform is consistent with econometric evidence of adjustments to past trade reforms (see, for example, Wacziarg and Wallack 2004).

13. The approach here has been to take the change in the average per capita consumption of the poor, apply an estimated income-to-poverty elasticity, and assess the impacts on the poverty headcount index. We have done this by calculating the change in the wage of unskilled workers, and deflating it by the food and clothing consumer price index change, which is more relevant for the poor than the total price index. That real wage grows, over all developing countries, by 3.6 percent, or more than four times the overall average income increase. We are assuming that the change in unskilled wages is fully passed through to households. Also, while the model closure has the loss in tariff revenues replaced by a change in direct household taxation, the poverty calculation assumes—realistically for many developing countries—that these tax increases only affect skilled workers and high-income households. While these simple calculations are not a substitute for more detailed individual country case study analysis using detailed household surveys as in, for example, Hertel and Winters (2006), they are able to give a broad regionwide indication of the poverty impact.

14. Evidence that the preference margin is often eroded by complex rules of origin, and that the rent is shared between importing and exporting countries with the latter getting less the more trade is concentrated on standard commodities, can be found in Olarreaga and Özden (2005) and Özden and Sharma (2004). A recent partial equilibrium study found that in practice export revenue losses from preference erosion are likely to be limited to a small subset of countries, primarily small island economies dependent on exports of sugar, bananas and, to a far lesser extent, textiles (Alexandraki and Lankes 2004).

15. A further complication is that the Africa, Caribbean, Pacific nonreciprocal preference scheme is to be replaced in 2008 with reciprocal Economic Partnership Agreements between the least developed countries in those regions and the EU.

16. For recent reviews of the literature on the links between trade liberalization, economic growth, and poverty alleviation, see, for example, Winters (2002, 2004), Winters, McCulloch and McKay (2004), and Dollar and Kraay (2004).

17. The trade-related productivity increase is limited to the manufacturing sectors in this simulation, unlike World Bank (2002) where agricultural productivity was also allowed to respond to changes in openness.

18. For a review of the empirical literature supporting this view, see Anderson (2004, 560–62).

19. The Global Trade Analysis Project, known as GTAP, is an international consortium of trade researchers from universities, research institutions, and national and international agencies. It is based at Purdue University. The GTAP Center provides four key resources to the trade community. First and foremost is an integrated and consistent international database for trade policy analysis. The current version is composed of 87 country and regional groupings and 57 economic sectors. The second resource is a publicly available global trade model, also known as the GTAP model. (The LINKAGE model is distinct from the GTAP model although it uses the same underlying database.) The third resource is an annual course in applied trade modeling. And finally, GTAP organizes and cohosts an annual Conference on Global Economic Analysis. More information on the GTAP Center and project can be found at http://www.gtap.agecon.purdue.edu.

20. More information on the MAcMaps database is available in Bouët and others (2004) and at http://www.cepii.fr/anglaisgraph/bdd/macmap.htm.

21. These elasticities represent the top-level Armington elasticity, that is, the elasticity between domestic demand and aggregate import demand. The second-level Armington elasticity, that is, across trading partners, is set at twice the top-level elasticity.

22. The new GTAP elasticities are the outcome of significant econometric work and are higher than the standard Armington elasticities used in previous releases of GTAP. While we recognize the extensive work behind the new elasticities, we also note that the controversy underlying these key parameters continues. The new GTAP elasticities reflect a move toward mid-range Armington elasticities, but are still much lower than those used by some, notably Tarr and Rutherford and their associates. The LINKAGE model elasticities are above those in GTAP but still in the mid-range; they are the outcome of literature surveys, best guesses, and adjustments that have been undertaken over a 15-year period since the inception of the LINKAGE model and its predecessors. The difference between the LINKAGE and the GTAP elasticities averages about one-third (table 12A.2).

23. In the standard LINKAGE model, an upward-sloping supply function is implemented for land, with supply elasticities higher for land-abundant countries than for land-scarce countries. There is also perfect land mobility across farm enterprises. In the final simulation the supply elasticity is set to 0, and the land transformation elasticity is set to 1.

References

Alexandraki, K., and H. P. Lankes 2004. "The Impact of Preference Erosion on Middle-Income Countries." IMF Working Paper 04/169, International Monetary Fund, Washington, DC, September.

Anderson, K. 1987. "On Why Agriculture Declines with Economic Growth." *Agricultural Economics* 1 (3, June): 195–207.

———. 2004. "Subsidies and Trade Barriers." In *Global Crises, Global Solutions*, ed. B. Lomborg. New York: Cambridge University Press.

Anderson, K., W. Martin and D. van der Mensbrugghe. 2005. "Distortions to World Trade: Impacts on Agricultural Markets and Farm Incomes." Policy Research Working Paper 3736, World Bank, Washington, DC.

———. 2006. "Long-Run Global Impacts of Doha Reform on Poverty." In *Poverty and the WTO: Impacts of the Doha Development Agenda*, ed. T. Hertel and L. A. Winters. Basingstoke, U.K.: Palgrave Macmillan; Washington, DC: World Bank.

Baffes, J. 2005. "The 'Cotton Problem.'" *World Bank Research Observer* 20 (1, Spring): 109–43.

Bouët, A., Y. Decreux, L. Fontagné, S. Jean, and D. Laborde. 2004. "A Consistent, *ad Valorem* Equivalent Measure of Applied Protection across the World: The MAcMap-HS6 Database." Centre d'Etudes Prospectives et d'Informations Internationales, Paris, December 20.

Bouët, A., L. Fontagné, and S. Jean. 2006. "Is Erosion of Preferences a Serious Concern?" In *Agricultural Trade Reform and the Doha Development Agenda*, ed. K. Anderson and W. Martin. Basingstoke, U.K.: Palgrave Macmillan; Washington, DC: World Bank.

Commission for Africa. 2005. *Our Common Interest*. London: UK Department for International Development.

de Gorter, H., and E. Kliauga. 2006. "Consequences of TRQ Expansions and In-Quota Tariff Reductions." In *Agricultural Trade Reform and the Doha Development Agenda*, ed. K. Anderson and W. Martin. Basingstoke, U.K.: Palgrave Macmillan; Washington, DC: World Bank.

Dollar, D., and A. Kraay. 2004. "Trade, Growth, and Poverty." *Economic Journal* 114 (February): F22–F49.

Finger, J. M. 1974. "GATT Tariff Concessions and the Exports of Developing Countries: United States Concessions at the Dillon Round." *Economic Journal* 84 (335, September): 566–75.

———. 1976. "Effects of Kennedy Round Tariff Concessions on the Exports of Developing Countries." *Economic Journal* 86 (341, March): 87–95.

Finger, J. M., and L. Schuknecht. 2001. "Market Access Advances and Retreats: The Uruguay Round and Beyond." In *Developing Countries and the WTO: A Pro-Active Agenda*, ed. B. Hoekman and W. Martin. Oxford: Blackwell Publishers.

Harrison, W. J., J. M. Horridge, and K. R. Pearson. 2000. "Decomposing Simulation Results with Respect to Exogenous Shocks." *Computational Economics* 15: 227–49.

Hart, C. E., and J. C. Beghin. 2006. "Rethinking Agricultural Domestic Support under the World Trade Organization." In *Agricultural Trade Reform and the Doha Development Agenda*, ed. K. Anderson and W. Martin. Basingstoke, U.K.: Palgrave Macmillan; Washington, DC: World Bank.

Hertel, T. W., and R. Keeney. 2006. "What Is at Stake: The Relative Importance of Import Barriers, Export Subsidies, and Domestic Support." In *Agricultural Trade Reform and the Doha Development Agenda*, ed. K. Anderson and W. Martin. Washington, DC: World Bank.

Hertel, T. W., and L. A. Winters, eds. 2006. *Poverty and the WTO: Impacts of the Doha Development Agenda*, Basingstoke, U.K.: Palgrave Macmillan; Washington, DC: World Bank.

Hoekman, B., and P. Messerlin. 2006. "Removing the Exception of Agricultural Export Subsidies." In *Agricultural Trade Reform and the Doha Development Agenda*, ed. K. Anderson and W. Martin. Basingstoke, U.K.: Palgrave Macmillan; Washington, DC: World Bank.

Hoekman, B., F. Ng, and M. Olarreaga. 2004. "Agricultural Tariffs versus Subsidies: What's More Important for Developing Countries?" *World Bank Economic Review* 18(2): 175–204.

Hoekman, B., and C. Özden. 2005. "Trade Preferences and Differential Treatment of Developing Countries: A Selective Survey." Policy Research Working Paper 3566, World Bank, Washington, DC, June.

Hoekman, B., and S. Prowse. 2005. "Policy Responses to Preference Erosion: From Trade as Aid to Aid for Trade." Paper presented at the World Bank Conference on Preference Erosion: Impacts and Potential Policy Responses, June 13–14, Geneva.

Jean, S., D. Laborde, and W. Martin. 2006. "Consequences of Alternative Formulas for Agricultural Tariff Cuts." In *Agricultural Trade Reform and the Doha Development Agenda*, ed. K. Anderson and W. Martin. Basingstoke, U.K.: Palgrave Macmillan; Washington, DC: World Bank.

Jensen, H. G., and H. Zobbe. 2006. "Consequences of Reducing AMS Limits." In *Agricultural Trade Reform and the Doha Development Agenda*, ed. K. Anderson and W. Martin. Basingstoke, U.K.: Palgrave Macmillan; Washington, DC: World Bank.

Josling, T. 2006. "Special and Differential Treatment for Developing Countries." In *Agricultural Trade Reform and the Doha Development Agenda*, ed. K. Anderson and W. Martin. Basingstoke, U.K.: Palgrave Macmillan; Washington, DC: World Bank.

Keeney, R., and T. W. Hertel. 2005. "GTAP-AGR: A Framework for Assessing the Implications of Multilateral Changes in Agricultural Policies." GTAP Technical Paper 24, Center for Global Trade Analysis, Purdue University, West Lafayette, IN.

Martin, W., and P. G. Warr. 1993. "Explaining the Relative Decline of Agriculture: A Supply-Side Analysis for Indonesia." *World Bank Economic Review* 7 (3, September): 381–401.

Olarreaga, M., and C. Özden. 2005. "AGOA and Apparel: Who Captures the Tariff Rent in the Presence of Preferential Market Access?" *World Economy* 2 (1, January): 63–87.

Özden, C., and G. Sharma. 2004. "Price Effects of Preferential Market Access: The CBI and the Apparel Sector." Policy Research Working Paper 3244, World Bank, Washington, DC, March.

Sumner, D. A. 2006. "Reducing Cotton Subsidies: The DDA Cotton Initiative." In *Agricultural Trade Reform and the Doha Development Agenda*, ed. K. Anderson and W. Martin. Basingstoke, U.K.: Palgrave Macmillan; Washington, DC: World Bank.

van der Mensbrugghe, D. 2004a. "Comparison of GTAP Release 5.4 and GTAP Release 6.05." World Bank, Development Prospects Group, Washington, DC.

———. 2004b. "LINKAGE Technical Reference Document: Version 6.0." World Bank, Development Prospects Group, Washington, DC.

Wacziarg, R., and J. S. Wallack. 2004. "Trade Liberalization and Intersectoral Labor Movements." *Journal of International Economics* 64 (2, December): 411–39.

Winters, L.A. 2002. "Trade Liberalisation and Poverty: What Are the Links?" *World Economy* 25 (9, September): 1339–68.

———. 2004. "Trade Liberalization and Economic Performance: An Overview." *Economic Journal* 114 (February): F4–F21.

Winters, L. A., N. McCulloch, and A. McKay. 2004. "Trade Liberalization and Poverty: The Empirical Evidence." *Journal of Economic Literature* 62 (1, March): 72–115.

Winters, L. A., T. Walmsley, Z. K. Wang, and R. Grynberg. 2003. "Liberalizing Temporary Movement of Natural Persons: An Agenda for the Development Round." *World Economy* 26 (8, August): 1137–61.

World Bank. 2002. *Global Economic Prospects and the Developing Countries 2002: Making Trade Work for the Poor.* Washington, DC: World Bank.

———. 2004. *Global Economic Prospects 2005: Realizing the Development Promise of the Doha Agenda.* Washington, DC: World Bank.

WTO (World Trade Organization). 2003a. "Negotiating Group on Market Access: Report by the Chairman." TN/MA/12 (Girard Text), WTO, Geneva, September 1.

———. 2003b. "Negotiations on Agriculture: First Draft of Modalities for the Further Commitments." TN/AG/W/1/Rev.1 (Harbinson Draft), WTO, Geneva, March 19.

———. 2004. "Decision Adopted by the General Council on 1 August 2004." WT/L/579 (July Framework Agreement), WTO, Geneva, August 2.

INDEX

ad valorem tariffs
  by country/region, 89t
Africa Growth and Opportunity Act (AGOA), 4, 164, 383
  preferences and textiles and apparel, 187
  ROOs, 185–186
Africa, Caribbean, and Pacific (ACP), 4
Agenda 2000, 258, 261
aggregate measure of support (AMS)
  Amber Box, 246
  bindings, 29
  calculations, 225–226, 230–231
  ceilings, 225
  current totals, 248t–249t
  de minimis, 224, 225
  definition, 224
  developing country reductions, 74
  difference from PSE, 226
  estimations, 231
  levels, 229
    average, 225
    by country (1999), 246
  market price, 29
  MPS, 234, 235, 338
    framework, 240
  product-specific, 229
  reductions, 230
  total, 226
  total bound, 13
  totals without payments, 250t
  URAA double coverage, 234–235

agriculture and food
  average import tariffs in developing countries, 45t
  bilateral trade flows from liberalization, 377t
  Doha scenarios, 362t–363t
  global losses, 12
  import-weighted average applied tariffs, 5t
  liberalization, 12t, 348
  liberalization impacts by country, 351t–352t
  merchandise trade liberalization, 58t
  production under Doha scenarios, 380t–381t
  removing all tariffs and agricultural subsidies, 46t
  volume changes from removal of tariffs and subsidies, 48t
  average applied tariffs by region, 43t
  average true preferential margin, 173t
  community development, 313
  decline in lending, 318, 319
  developing countries
    change in output under liberalization, 349t
    development role, 314–315
    distortionary protection, 324–325
    domestic support, 337–339
      disciplines, 29
      high-income countries, 42t
      tiered formula effects by country, 339t

401

agriculture (*continued*)
  duties
    by exporting country, 168t
    exports, 170
  economic development, 312–313
  employment, 32n
    Doha scenarios, 378t–379t, 379, 381
  exports
    average duties, 170
    preference simulation, 182t
    subsidies, 28, 339
      eliminating, 20
      welfare effect by country, 374t–375t
    tariffs, 104–105
  financial sector reforms, 319
  functions to support industry, 312–313
  global economy, 3
  historical trade policies, 311–312
  import-weighted average applied tariffs
    by sector/country, 343t, 345t
  imports
    GTAP and LINKAGE, 383
    tariffs, 6t, 44
  liberalization
    gains, 349t, 385
    merchandise liberalization, 56t
    policy instruments, 296
    regional losses, 50
    welfare effects by region, 49t
  market access, 106t–107t, 335–336
    binding overhang, 386
    gains, 60
    impact of barriers, 348
  negotiations, 112
  output
    Doha scenarios by country, 378t–379t
  policies
    developed countries, 297–311
    developing countries, 311–325
    evolution, 312
    nondistortionary approach, 324–325
  price collapse, 295, 316
  price incentives, 316
  producer subsidy, 38
  producer support, 7f, 8f
  producers, 7
  products
    impact of liberalization on self-sufficiency, 354t
  protection, 90
    by reform scenarios, 110t–111t
    levels, 7–8
    rates, 336
    three pillars of, 47, 49
  reform
    and food output, 350
    and nonagricultural tariff cuts
      Doha scenarios, 361
    farm subsidy cuts, 334
    global, 50
    market access gains, 60
    scenarios, 94–115
      alcohol and tobacco, 104
      bound duties, 96t–97t
      descriptions, 93
      market access, 106t–107t
  subsidies
    avoiding, 324–325
    cuts, 12
    elimination of, 11
      impact on developing countries, 46t, 48t
      welfare effects, 49t
  support
    pillars, 221
    policies, 195, 201
    programs, 28
    surpluses, 319
  tariff bindings, 20
  tariff protection, 318
  tariff protection by economy/region, 320t–321t
  tariff-cutting scenarios
    simulated impact on prices, 183t
  tariffs
    applied by country/region, 89t
    key features, 88
    welfare effects from removal, 49t
  trade liberalization, 37–38
  trade policies
    defensive and offensive approaches, 321–323
  trade reform
    assessing effects, 341–342
  value added
    liberalization impacts by country, 358t–359t
alcohol and tobacco
  agricultural reform scenarios
    trade volume, 104
  sensitive products, 94, 109
  tariffs, 95
Amber Box, 224, 227t, 228t, 245
AMS, 246
Brazil, 228t

CAP, 260
  definitions, 222
  EU, 227
  low support, 262
  policies, 224
  U.S. expansion, 227
  U.S. totals, 226t
AMS. *See* aggregate measure of support
analysis
  role in negotiations, 83
applied and bound agricultural tariff rates
  by country/region, 91t
applied duties, 101
applied rates
  reduction, 338
applied tariffs
  actual, by region, 6
  additional regulations, 157
  administration changes, 153t–154t
  administration method and additional regulations, 142t–143t
  average
    for all goods by country, 362t–369t
    import-weighted by sector/region, 343t
    total TRQ value, 157
  base tariff reductions by reform scenario, 98t–99t
  bound tariff relationship, 90
  GTAP 6.05 *vs.* 5
  by sector, 388t–391t
  import-weighted average, 345t
  imports by sector/region, 43t
  in-quota tariff binding, 140
  in-quota trade and fill rates, 138t–139t
  key features by country/region, 89t
  protection rates
    world average, 171t
  quota administration, 136
  quota regime, 129t
  quota restrictions, 147
Argentina, 238, 267t
Armington elasticities, 341, 397n
  global average in GTAP-AGR and LINKAGE by product, 392t
Asian tiger economies, 32n
asymmetric preferences. *See* nonreciprocal preferences
auctions, 143t
  in-quota trade and fill rates 138t–139t
  quota administration, 137
Australia, 265t, 391t
average-cut approach, 81, 84

base case
  incomes and trade liberalization by country, 393t–394t
baseline
  trade distortions, 40
basic-needs approach, 327n
  to poverty, 315
Benin
  Cotton Initiative, 272
bilateral agreements, 164
bilateral differences
  import-weighted average agricultural tariff, 343t
bilateral trade flows
  baseline changes from liberalization
    Doha scenario, 377t
  nonagricultural tariff cuts and agricultural reform, 16t
binding overhang, 13, 91, 158n
  after the Uruguay Round, 90
  developing countries, 15, 103
  in-quota and out-of-quota tariffs, 136
  reduction, 31, 386
  tariff reform, 83
bioenergy crops, 311, 327n
Blue Box, 245
  Brazil, 228t
  cap, 240, 241n
  definition, 222, 337
  direct payment schemes, 229
  Doha outcome, 308
  European Union, 227, 227t, 261
  exemptions, 246
  Japan, 228t
  July Framework Agreement, 229
  policies, 222
  reductions, 241
  separate rules, 225
  support limits, 247
  United States, 226t, 227, 298
bond schemes, 306–307
border barriers, 342
borrowing
  importers, 216
bound and applied agricultural tariff rates by country/region, 91t
bound duties
  base level and reductions by reform scenario, 96t–97t
  cap, 102
  freeing of, 101
  world average, 95

bound tariffs
  applied tariffs and market access, 90
  by region, 6t
  cuts, 12
Brazil
  agricultural credit, 327
  agricultural development, 239
  applied tariffs, 389t
  domestic support programs, 228t
  MPS, 231t
  transportation improvements, 239
Brazil-U.S. cotton dispute, 287–288
  agricultural support via litigation, 237
  Green Box inclusion, 230
  URAA framing, 234
Burkina Faso
  Cotton Initiative, 272, 274
buyout, 299, 299t
  Australia, 326n
  bond schemes, 306–307
  conducive conditions, 305
  large-sized, 306–310
  steps for adherence, 309
  tobacco, 301–302, 302, 305, 326n
  U.S. farm subsidy payments, 309
  U.S. farm support programs, 307–310, 308t
  U.S. peanut and tobacco, 303t
  U.S. peanut reform, 299–301

Cairns Group
  agricultural trade policies, 322
  members, 218n
Canada, 265t, 391t
Cancun Ministerial (September 2003)
  Derbez text, 73
  failure of, 274, 335
CAP. See Common Agricultural Policy
cap. See tariff cap
capital user cost, 356t
Caribbean Basin Initiative (CBI), 4, 164, 383
cash-out
  alternatives, 298–299, 299t
  sugar producers, 304
  U.S. farm policy, 297
  U.S. peanut reform, 300
CBI. See Caribbean Basin Initiative
ceilings
  AMS, 225
  bindings, 6, 90
Centre d'Etudes Prospectives et d'Informations
  Internationales (CEPII), 43

GTAP software, 88
MAcMAP, 162
cereals. See commodities
CGE. See computable general equilibrium
CGIAR. See Consultative Group on
  International Agricultural Research
Chad, 272
China
  applied tariffs, 388t
  cotton subsidies, 276–277
  tiered formula, 26
cigarettes. See tobacco
commitments. See WTO commitments
Committee on Agriculture
  Special Session
    cotton, 275
commodities, 110t–111t
  AMS totals without payments by country, 250t
  average true preferential margins 173t
  barriers, 90
  Cotton Initiative stimulating reform, 290
  differing tariff rates, 109
  EAGGF subsidies, 210t–211t, 213t
  EU subsidization rates, 214t–215t
  export credits, 217
  export subsidy rates, 206t
  protection, 109–110
  reform scenarios, 110t–111t
  rents, 150
  subsidy cuts stimulated by cotton reform, 286
  total AMS by country, 248t–249t
  TRQ, 112, 143–144
    versus non-TRQ
      production value by OECD countries, 120t–121t
      trade value by OECD countries, 122t–123t
  volume changes, 47
  water in tariff estimates for TRQs, 132t–135t
commodity-specific compensatory payments, 227
Common Agricultural Policy (CAP), 227, 258, 260
  1992 MacSharry reform, 205
Common Market, 164
community development, 313
  criticisms, 327n
  Cotton Initiative, 274
competition, imperfect, 151
composition effects, 171, 172

agricultural duties, 168t–169t, 170
computable general equilibrium (CGE)
  preferences, 178–179, 187
concessions
  SDT, 70, 77
  tariff schedules, 71t
conservation reserve program (CRP)
  idled crop land, 310
  United States, 297
Consultative Group on International
    Agricultural Research (CGIAR), 314
consumer demand systems, 39
Cotonou Agreement, 164, 165, 186
  preference erosion, 188
  textiles and clothing, 187
cotton
  countercyclical program reform, 287
  domestic support, 277
  elasticities, 280–281
  exporters, 275
  import tariffs, 276
  prices, 280
  producers and production, 277, 284
  subsidies, 15
    China, 276–277
    coverage of studies, 279
    cuts, 338
    elimination, 30, 272
    EU, 277
    future price effects, 279
    global, 276–278
    lack of benefits for poor countries, 273
    loss from continuance, 283
    market effects, 279–282
    marketing loans, 287
    policy, 272
    price effects, 350
    programs
      determining degree of harm, 286
      reduction negotiations, 275
      reform negotiations, 286
      simulation models, 279
      U.S. programs, 278
      West African countries, 328n
    supply response, 281–282, 282
    textile manufacturing, 276
    trade background, 275
    United States, 282
  cotton dispute. See Brazil-U.S. cotton dispute
Cotton Initiative, 29–30, 273
  becoming a global issue, 273
  benefits to LDC producers, 282–289, 286, 289
  compensation, 275, 282–285, 288
    basis, calculations, and criteria, 283, 284
    investments in public goods, 285
    proposal, 274
  DDA, 272
  farm commodities
    reform stimulation, 290
  pressuring EU and United States, 289
  price and welfare impacts, 281
  trade benefits, 285–289
  West African countries, 272
countercyclical payment
  cotton, 278
  U.S. 2002 Farm Bill, 309–310
  U.S. farm support program buyout, 307–308
  United States, 298
credit conditions, 318–319
crop insurance program, 278
crop insurance subsidies, 287
cross-product coefficient
  MFN tariffs by reform scenario, 100t–101t
CRP. See conservation reserve program
current access quotas, 117, 122, 130
cutout, 299, 299t

dairy, U.S., 131
DDA. See Doha Development Agenda
de minimis
  AMS rules and values, 224, 225
  July Framework Agreement, 229, 337
  levels, 229
  notified data for support, 246
  total AMS without payments (1999) by country, 250t–251t
  U.S., 225
debt crisis (1980s), 316
deceptions, 83
Decision, The, 70
decoupled income support
  EU, 227
  Green Box, 240
  guidelines, 223
  Single Farm Payment, 238
decoupling, 326n–327n
  dirty, 296
defensive approach
  agricultural trade policies, 321–322
Derbez text, 73

developed countries
  agricultural policy reform, 297–311
  AMS (1999), 248t–249t
  AMS totals without payments (1999) by commodity, 250t
  average tariffs, 90
  reciprocal tariff concessions, 63
  URAA implementation, 2224
  WTO notifications, commitments, and base levels of support, 254t–255t
developing countries, 41t
  agricultural assistance, 54t
  agricultural export average tariff, 104–105
  agriculture employment, 32n
  agriculture policies, 311–325
  AMS totals (1999), 248t–249t
  AMS totals without payments (1999) by commodity, 250t
  AMS, lower reductions, 74
  bilateral trade flows from liberalization by sector, 377t
  binding overhang, 91, 103
  change in output under liberalization, 349t
  definition, 32n
  Doha Round, view of, 321
  export volume changes, 48t
  GATT and SDT, 63
  Green Box use, 322
  import-weighted average tariffs by sector, 345t
  liberalization gains by sector, 349t
  liberalization impact on self-sufficiency in food and agriculture, 354t–355t
  market access from agricultural liberalization, 53t
  nonagricultural tariffs, 54
  pattern of trade
    subsidies, 201
  poverty issues, 296
  preferences on welfare, effect of, 395
  raising standards, 67
  rapid liberalization risks, 76
  reform participation, 31
    cost of, 103
    Doha scenarios, 353
  safeguards and special rules, 66
  SDT, 324, 386–387
  self-designation, 67, 334
  tariff cap, 72
  tariff-cutting formulas, 71
  tariffs and agricultural subsidies, 46t
  tariffs, higher average, 90
  trade distortions, 40, 54t
  trade liberalization, 45
    impacts on real income, 384t
  trade reform gains, 11
  TRQ rents received, 177t
  URAA implementation, 224
  URAA SDT provisions, 69t
  welfare gains
    removal of tariffs and subsidies, 52t
    services trade liberalization, 55f
  WTO notifications, commitments, and base levels of support, 256t–259t
  WTO usage, 357
developing economies
  applied import tariffs, average, 43t
  bilateral trade flows, 16t
  trade liberalization, 56t, 57t
  welfare effects from removal of tariffs and subsidies, 49t
development
  export-oriented strategies, 316
  poverty alleviation, 315
  role of agriculture, 314–315
  SDT, 68
Development Box, 75, 328n
DFID. See United Kingdom's Department for International Development
Differential and More Favorable Treatment, Reciprocity, Fuller Participation of Developing Countries, 64, 165, 190n
differential treatment. See Special and Differential Treatment
direct payment program
  Blue Box, 229
  cotton, 278
dirty decoupling, 296
disaster relief, 223
discontinuities, 85
distortion
  degree of, 237
  domestic support pillar, 236
  elimination, 37
    welfare impact, 50
  July Framework Agreement, 229
  reduction scenarios, 247–253
  SDT, 76
  tariffs, 33n
distortionary protection, 324
diversification, 172
Doha Development Agenda (DDA), 3. See also Doha Round
  Cotton Initiative, 29–30, 272

pressuring EU and United States, 289
inclusion of SDT, 68
split between developed and developing
   countries, 271
tightening classification of subsidy programs,
   288
Doha reform scenarios, 14
   agricultural and food production
      exported, 380t–381t
   agricultural value added
      liberalization impacts, 358t–359t
   and consequences, 353–382, 384–384
   applied tariffs
      average for all goods, 362t–369t
   bilateral trade flows from liberalization, 377t
   change from baseline in real income
      by country/region, 370t–373t
   cuts in nonagricultural tariff bindings, 357
   developing countries' gain, 17
   farm output and employment growth, 377
   Harbinson, 357
   modifications from LINKAGE model,
      389–390
   poverty and poor reduction, 19t, 382t
   proportional cut, 357
   sensitive products, 357
   summary of partial liberalization, 360t
   tariff cap, 357
   trade consequences, 376
   welfare and trade effects, 359–361
Doha Round, 3. *See also* Doha Development
   Agenda
   agreement, 334, 335
   banning export subsidies, 195
   cotton negotiations, 277
   cotton subsidy reductions, 275
   developing country perspective, 321
   export competition pillar, 75
   export subsidy discussions, 212
   framework, 8
   future policy changes, 263–264
   impact analysis, 31–32
   market access commitments, 5
   negotiations, 221
      position of countries, 264
   nonagricultural bound tariff cuts, 340
   outcomes, 20, 295, 323
   participation, 31
   preferences, 161
   pro-poor, pro-development, 386
   purpose, 245
domestic policy price supports, 154

domestic purchase requirements, 152
domestic support, 74–75
   base levels, commitments, and notifications,
      254t–258t
   binding overhang, 20, 386
   cuts to reduce applied rates, 338
   developing countries, 24
   global impact, 13t
   guidelines
      improving, 240
      new, 221–222
   high-income countries, 42t
   levels, 246–247
   liberalization gains, 52t
   pillar, importance of, 236–239
   policy reforms, 253, 258, 261–264
   programs, 225
   reductions, 247–253
      for selected countries, 265t–268t
   reductions needed in the United States
      and EU, 260t
   SDT, 70
   types, 222
   United States, 226t
   WTO, 236
double coverage
   AMS, 234–235
dual economies, 314
Dutch agricultural economics institute (LEI),
   xiii
duty by exporting country, 168t–169t

EBA. *See* Everything But Arms
economic development
   impact on agriculture, 312–313
economic growth
   structural changes, 384
Economic Partnership Agreements (EPAs),
   165, 188
   access compared with EBA, 190n
economic viewpoint
   SDT, 75
economic welfare
   liberalization gains, 12t
economies, 41t
EFTA. *See* European Free Trade Agreement
elasticities
   cotton, 280–281
   trade, 39–40
employment growth, 17
   Doha compared with baseline by country, 18t
   Doha scenarios, 377, 378t–379t

Enabling Clause, 64, 190n
  preferences, 165
environmental program, 224
environmentalism, dirty, 310
EU. See European Union
Euromed Initiative
  preferences, 165
European Agriculture Guarantee and Guidance Fund (EAGGF)
  cereals and dairy, 218n
  EU farm subsidies, 206–207
  exports subsidies, 213t
  refunds, 208t, 216t
  subsidies by commodity, 210t–211t
  subsidies by product category, 208–209
European Commission, xiii
  sugar reform plan, 261
European Free Trade Agreement (EFTA), 165
European Generalized System of Preferences, 165
European Union (EU)
  Agenda 2000, 178
  agricultural support changes, 229
  AMS, total, 246
  applied tariffs, 390t
  CAP, 227
    bond schemes, 306
    reform, 235
  cash-out price support interventions, 298
  cash-out reforms, 306–307
  cotton policy (2005), 287
  cotton subsidies, 277
    budget outlays, 284
  cotton supply responses, 281
  domestic support, 227
    Blue, Green, and Amber Boxes, 227t
    reductions needed, 260t
  domestic support reduction, 252–253
  EAGGF refunds, 216
  export subsidies
    and OECD PSEs, 208t
    ratio to production, 209
    reductions, 298
  farm trade policy, 206–209
  joint U.S. framework (August 2003), 323
  MPS, 231t
  notifications by commodity, 252t
  official administrative prices, 269n
  subsidies, use of, 208
  subsidization of farm production, 209
  subsidization rates
    based on production, 209
    by commodity, 214t–215t

sugar program, 232–233, 261
trade policy, 165, 166f
utilization rates by category, 204t–205t
Everything But Arms (EBA), 4, 164, 165, 185–186, 190n, 383
  access compared with EPAs, 190n
  preferences and textiles and apparel, 187
exchange rate
  1960s–1980s, 318
  real, 327n
export competition pillar, 75
export credits, 43, 212
  cereals, 217
  cotton guarantees, 278, 287–288
  distortion, 218
  July 2004 Framework Agreement, 195
  poor countries, 216
  United States, 217
export subsidies
  agricultural, 28, 339
  agricultural liberalization gains, 52t
  by product, 203–206
  comparisons, 206
  Doha Agreement, phasing out, 70
  EAGGF, 210t–211t, 213t
  elimination of, 12, 13, 23, 75, 195, 208
  equivalent forms, 212
  EU farm trade policy, 206–209
  EU ratio to production, 209
  EU reductions, 298
  global impact, 13t
  magnitude, 196, 207
  middle-income country use, 200–201
  notification, 28
  policy recommendations, 218
  price gaps, 196
  product classification, 218
  rates by commodity, 206t
  restricting use of, 201
  share in PSE, 207
  subsidization component size, 212–213
  trend, 200
  users, 43
  welfare effect of elimination by region, 49t
  WTO member total commitments, 197
export volume changes, 47
export-oriented strategy, 315
  development, 316
exports. See agricultural exports

FAO. See Food and Agriculture Organization
farm export subsidies

elimination of, 50
farm output, 17
farm policy, 30, 31
farm support programs
  dirty decoupling, 296
fill rates, 137
  by administration method and additional regulations, 142t–143t
  impact of regulations, 138
  reduction causes, 147
  TRQ, 141
  TRQ trade by economy, 144t, 146t
financial sector reforms, 319
financing
  importers, 216
first-come, first-served, 149–150
  additional regulations, 139
  administration changes, 153t–154t
  by administration method, 143t
  in-quota trade and fill rates, 138t–139t
  quota administration, 136–137
  TRQ commodities, 150
food. *See also* agriculture and food
  aid, 212
  liberalization impact on self-sufficiency by region, 354t
  liberalization impacts on output by country/region, 351t–352t
  production exported under Doha scenarios, 381
    by country/region, 380t–381t
  role of, 39
  security, 87
Food and Agriculture Organization (FAO), 32n
  cotton compensation, 274–275
  cotton price review, 280
food security box, 328n
food, processed
  import-weighted average applied tariffs by sector/country, 345t
  output change under liberalization, 349t
free trade, 22

G-20, 323
General Agreement on Tariffs and Trade (GATT)
  Article XXIV, 164
  balance of payments and Article XII, 77n
  Enabling Clause, 190n
  nonreciprocity and Part IV, 64, 77n
  preferences, 163, 164
  rules, 32n

SDT, 63
  WTO negotiations comparison, 271
Generalized System of Preferences (GSP), 164
  European, 165
  nonreciprocal tariff preferences, 383
  textiles and clothing, 187
global impact
  agricultural tariff and subsidy removal, 13t
Global Trade Analysis Project (GTAP), 9, 341
  agricultural imports and TRQs, 383
  background, 396n
  comparison by sector, 388t–391t
  elasticities
    real incomes and liberalization, 393t–394t
  market access geography, 88
  Version 5 and 6.05 comparison, 387–395
  Version 6.05, 10
    preferences, 382–383
    PTAs, 162
Global Trade Analysis Project-Agriculture (GTAP), 38, 60n–61n
  Armington elasticities, 392t
global welfare gains, 16
Green Box, 75, 245
  areas of concern, 237–238
  Brazil, 228t
  countercyclical payments, 310
  definition, 222
  developing countries' use, 322
  distortion, 237
  EU, 227, 227t, 261
  guidelines, 223, 229
  Japan, 228t
  payment cuts, 241
  phaseout of Amber and Blue Boxes, 236–237
  policies, 222, 240
  U.S. cotton programs, 288
  U.S. totals, 226t
green payments, 310
Green Revolution, 314, 315, 316
  poverty effects, 327n

Harbinson, 81
  agricultural reform scenarios, 94
  Doha scenarios, 357
  formula, 395n
  proposal, 84, 85f, 336
Harmonized System
  agricultural market access, 335
high-income countries, 41t
  agricultural domestic support, 42t

high-income countries (*continued*)
  agricultural support policies, 195
  bilateral trade flows from liberalization by sector, 377t
  definition, 32n
  liberalization
    gains by sector, 349t
    impact on self-sufficiency in food and agriculture, 354t–355t
    impacts on real income, 384t
  trade distortions, 40
high-income economies
  agricultural assistance removal, 54
  average applied import tariffs, 43t
  bilateral trade flows, 16t
  import-weighted average applied tariffs by sector, 345t
  nonagricultural tariff removal, 54t
  textiles and apparel, 57t
  trade distortions removal, 54t
  trade liberalization, 56t
  welfare effects from removal of agricultural tariffs and subsidies, 49t
historical importers
  additional regulations, 139
  administration changes, 153t–154t
  by administration method and additional regulations, 142t–143t
  in-quota trade and fill rates, 138t–139t
  quota administration, 136–137

ICAC. *See* International Cotton Advisory Committee
Iceland, 266t
ILEAP. *See* International Lawyers and Economists Against Poverty
IMF. *See* International Monetary Fund
import market access, 13t
import quotas, 152
  fill rate, 151
  monopsony, 151
import substitution industrialization (ISI), 312, 313, 315
  reevaluation, 316
import tariffs, average
  developing countries, 45t
import-weighted average applied tariffs, 5t
  by sector/country, 345t
importer financing, 216
imports
  out-of-quota, 126f, 127f
  overquota, 118, 127f

rationing, 117
TRQ trade by economy, 144t–146t
under tariff quotas, 119
with quota fill or underfilled, 125f
in-quota imports
  by regime, 128t–129t
  TRQ trade by economy, 145t, 147t
  with and without quota fill, 124f
in-quota tariff, 27
  applied tariffs and auctions, 138
  bound average and TRQ value, 157
  regime, 119–120, 155
  trade value effects, 130t
  TRQ administration, 136–137
  TRQ trade by economy, 145t, 147t
in-quota trade and fill rates
  by TRQ additional regulation, 140t–141t
  by TRQ administration method, 138t
income
  global trade reform, 344
  liberalization impacts by country/region, 346t
income insurance programs, 223
income support, decoupled. *See* decoupled income support
income tax, 86
income transfers
  poverty alleviation, 320
India, 388t
industry
  average true preferential margin, 173t
  decomposition of duties by exporting country, 169t
infrastructure, 237, 238
insurance program
  cotton, 278
Integrated Framework
  expansion, 387
  market expansion rewards, 31–32
  trade reform awards, 189
Integrated Rural Development, 315, 317–318
  revision, 316
International Cotton Advisory Committee (ICAC), 274, 276
International Lawyers and Economists Against Poverty (ILEAP), 283
International Monetary Fund (IMF)
  financial reform in agricultural agencies, 319
  Trade Integration Mechanism payment shortfalls, 188
International Trade Commission (ITC), 162
ISI. *See* import substitution industrialization

Japan, 390t
  domestic support programs, 228, 228t
  MPS, 231t
  rice imports, 155
  STEs, domestic policy response, and rice tariff quota, 156t–157t
July Framework Agreement, 3, 9, 10, 32
  agricultural negotiations, 112
  agricultural reform, 335
  Blue Box, 238, 337
  Cotton Initiative, 274, 275
  de minimis provision, 337
  development and agriculture, 335
  domestic support, 74
    base of reductions, 337
  future agreements, 247
  gains, 19, 385, 387
  implementation, 229
  liberalization schedule, 195
  market access
    features, 84–88
    nonexport subsidies, 196
  MPS, 337
  objectives missing from DDA, 81
  policy changes, 229–230
  reduction scenario basis, 264
  SDT, 23, 26, 196
    and annex, 70
    and paragraph 1, 69
    categories, 71t
  sensitive products, 25
    designation, 87
  STEs, 78n
  three pillars, 221–222
  tiered reductions in AMS, 337
  trade distorting policy, 237
  trade reform possibilities, 240
  URAA and subsidies, 197

Korea, Republic of, 268t, 391t

labor mobility, 353
land idled, 310
land reform, 313–314
land user cost, 356t
least developed countries (LDCs)
  binding overhang, 92
  classification, 395n
  tariffs, 90
LEI. *See* Dutch Agricultural Economics Institute
lending
  decline in agricultural, 318

liberalization
  agricultural policy instruments, 296
  agriculture
    high-income countries' output, 348–349
  agriculture and food
    global gains, 348
  agriculture, food output, and trade, 351t–352t
  assessment, 123
  cotton, 350
  developing countries
    output, 349t
    versus industrial countries, 348
  Doha scenarios, 353–382
  full and partial impact on agricultural value added, 358t–359t
  gains by region/sector, 349t
  gains for the poor, 385
  global merchandise
    impact on self-sufficiency in food and agriculture, 354t
  licenses on demand, 147–150
  merchandise trade, 60, 344
    poverty alleviation under Doha, 381–382
    real factor price impacts, 356t
    real income impacts, 384t
  nonagricultural, 51
  nonagricultural tariffs, 50
  of agricultural tariffs, 47, 49
  of merchandise trade
    global gains, 384
    impacts on income, 346t
  poverty impacts
    Doha scenarios, 382t
  preferences, 174
  rapid, 76
  regional losses, 50
  rents, 178
  schedule
    July 2004 Framework Agreement, 195
  services trade
    developing country gains, 55f
  simulation experiments, 92
  trade indicators by country/region, 347t
  welfare effects from removal of all agricultural tariffs and subsidies, 49t
license allocation, 147
licenses on demand
  additional regulations, 139
  administration changes, 153t–154t
  by administration method and additional regulations, 143t

licenses on demand (*continued*)
  in-quota trade and fill rates, 138t–139t
  liberalization, 147–150
  quota administration, 136
LINKAGE, 31, 397n
  agricultural imports and TRQs, 383
  Armington elasticities by product, 392t
  closure rules, 341–342
  future trade reform effects, 341–342
  GTAP version comparison, 387–395
  projection of world economy, 344
  subsidization, 212
livestock, 39
loss assistance payments, 224

MAcMAP, 43, 44
  aggregating tariffs, 190n
  applied tariffs, 83
  market access geography, 88
  preferences, 167
  PTAs, 162
MacSharry Reform, 258, 260
  CAP, 205
  cash-out, 298
Mali, 272
manufactures
  import-weighted average applied tariffs, 5t
  welfare effects of liberalization, 56t
manufacturing
  bilateral trade flows from liberalization, 377t
  developing countries
    output change under liberalization, 349t
  import-weighted average applied tariffs by sector/country, 345t
margin. *See* true preferential margins
market access, 5
  agricultural, 335–336
    formulas, 24
    increases, 12–13
    liberalization, 53
    reform, 60
  analysis of approaches, 82
  barriers
    impacts on welfare, 348
    preferences, 186
  expansion, 31
  expansion through TRQ expansion, 88
  gains, 23, 26, 52t, 105
  geography, 88–92
  nonagricultural, 16, 31, 51, 339–340
    expansion, 386
    welfare impact, 50

preferential, 117
SDT, 70
tariff caps reducing barriers, 108
tariff-cutting formulas, 104–109
TRQs, 15, 26
WTO members, 163
market loss assistance payments, 263t
market price support (MPS)
  abolishment, 338
  AMS, 240
    calculations, 234
    percentage by selected countries, 231t
    trade-distorting support, 338
  July Framework Agreement, 337
  loopholes, 235
  programs, 225–226
    AMS calculations, 230–231
    double coverage, 234–235
    removal from AMS, 235
marketing loan program
  cotton, 278
marketing subsidies, 238
marketing support, 240
meat. *See* commodities
merchandise
  average import tariffs for developing countries, 45t
  bilateral trade flows from liberalization, 377t
  freeing, 11
  import-weighted average applied tariffs, 5t
  liberalization, 12t, 55, 60, 344
    developing countries, 45
    efficiency and terms of trade, 59t
    gains, 349t, 384, 385
    income effects by country/region, 346t
    poverty alleviation under Doha, 381–382
    real factor prices, 356t
    welfare effects, 376
  real income impacts from liberalization, 384t
  removal of all tariffs and agricultural subsidies, 46t
  removal of cotton subsidies, 350
  trade distortions, 13
  trade facilitation, 52–53
  trade reform, 51, 53
  volume changes, 48t
  welfare gains by region, 54t
merchandise tariffs
  Doha scenarios, 366t–369t
merchandise trade liberalization, 384t
Mercosur, 164
Middle East and North Africa, 389t

Midterm Review (MTR), 258, 261
Millennium Development Goals
   nonreciprocal preferential market access, 164
minimum access quotas, 117, 122, 130
   percentage of TRQ trade, 158
Ministerial Declaration
   SDT for developing countries, 68
Mirage-Ag model, 179
models
   agricultural support policy, 201
   cotton subsidies simulations, 279
monopsony, 151
most-favored-nation (MFN)
   average duty, 190n
   bindings, 19, 385
   by region, 6
   cross-product variabilities, 102
   preferences, 65, 162–163
   tariffs, 97
      bound, 15, 20
      bound and applied agricultural rates by country/region, 91t
      cross-product coefficient by reform scenario, 100t–101t
      protection rates, 171t
   TRQ expansion, 87–88
MTR. *See* Midterm Review
multilateral liberalization
   policy implications, 187–188

NAFTA. *See* North American Free Trade Agreement
New Zealand, 391t
newly industrialized economies (NIEs), 320t
nonagricultural market access, 21, 31, 339
   expanding, 386
nonagricultural merchandise
   trade liberalization, 51
nonagricultural tariff bindings
   Doha scenarios, 357
nonagricultural tariff cuts, 16
   Doha scenarios, 361
nonagricultural tariff liberalization, 50
nondiscrimination, 68
nondiscriminatory market access, 163
nonmonotonicity, 85
nonreciprocal preferences, 185, 383
   access to markets, 161
   U.S. regimes, 186
nonreciprocal trade agreements, 164
North American Free Trade Agreement (NAFTA), 164, 184

Norway, 266t
notifications. *See* WTO notifications

offensive approach
   agricultural trade policies, 323
Organisation for Economic Co-operation and Development (OECD), 39, 226
out-of-quota imports, 128t–129t
   TRQ trade by economy, 145t, 147t
   with and without quota fill, 126f
out-of-quota regime, 155
out-of-quota tariffs, 27
   applied and auctions, 138
   effects on freeing trade, 131
   TRQ trade by economy, 145t, 147t
outward-oriented development strategies
   agricultural role, 314–316
overfill. *See* quota overfill
overquota
   by regime, 128t–129t
   import regime, 155
   imports, 118, 127f

participation
   in Doha reforms, 17
   in Doha Round, 31
payment-in-kind (PIK) program, 304
Peace Clause, 75
peanuts, 325n
   buyouts, 303t
   production distribution, 325n–326n
   U.S. reform, 299–300
PIK. *See* payment-in-kind
pillars, 221
   agricultural protection, 47, 49
   agricultural support programs, 23
   Doha framework, 8
   domestic support, 236
   export competition, 75
policies. *See* agricultural policies
policy recommendations
   export subsidies, 218
politics
   influence on negotiations, 264
poor
   decrease under trade liberalization, 19t
   location of, 17
poverty
   alleviation, 296, 318–321
      abandonment of sectoral interventions, 317
      Doha scenarios, 381–382
      income transfers, 320

poverty (*continued*)
  armed conflicts, 319
  baseline, 382t
  definition, 17
  development strategy, 315
  Doha scenarios, 382t
  Green Revolution effects, 327n
  liberalization gains, 385
  reduction, 17
  trade reform, 353
preference erosion, 17, 92, 162–163, 174, 187
  developing countries, 27–28
  diversification, 172
  Doha scenarios, 383
  impacts, 178
  International Monetary Fund's Trade Integration Mechanism (TIM), 188
  multilateral liberalization, 174
  poor countries, 188
  ROOs, 396n
preference simulations
  geographical breakdown, 180t, 181t
preferences. *See also* tariff preferences
  CGE simulations, 178–179, 187
  compensation, 65
  competing, 186
  depreciating assets, 65
  GATT Article XXIV, 164
  GTAP Version 6.05 database, 382–383
  importance of, 179
  multilateral liberalization, 174, 179
  nonreciprocal, 383
  preserving, 73
  reciprocal agreements, 162
  ROOs, 182
  tariff-cutting scenarios simulations, 185t
  textiles and apparel, 187
  TRQs, 163
  utilization of, 181–187
  welfare effect, 395n
preferential agreements, 4
preferential schemes, 163–164
  compliance costs, 183
preferential trade agreements (PTAs), 161
prices
  agricultural collapse, 316
  AMS calculations, 234
  band systems, 74
  gap between world and domestic, 196, 200
  incentives against agriculture, 316
  support, 154
    EU cash-outs, 298
    peanut reform, 300
    U.S., 297
  tariff cut simulations, 183t
  volatility, 152, 154
producer decisions, 238
producer group
  administration changes, 153t–154t
producer retirement programs, 223
producer support estimate (PSE), 7
  difference from AMS, 226
  EU estimates, 208t
  export subsidies, 207
  high-income countries, 42t
product classification
  export subsidies, 218
production flexibility contracts
  U.S. 1996 Farm Bill, 309
productivity
  liberalization impacts, 384t
proportional cut, 113
  Doha scenarios, 357
  preferences and liberalization simulation by country, 175t
  reform scenarios, 93, 94, 107, 108
  versus tiered formula, 14, 102–104
  with cap, 21
protection policies
  identifying implications, 201
  welfare impact, 344
provision for entry, 139
PSE. *See* producer support estimate
Purdue University
  GTAP database, 9

Quad, 201
  export subsidy commitments, 203f
quota administration
  changes in methods, 152, 153t–154t
  inefficient methods, 137
  methods, 138t
  methods of and additional regulations, 136–141
  trade effects, 147–152
quota binding, 128t
  regime, 155
  trade value effects, 130t
quota expansion, 27
  licenses on demand, 149
  versus tariff reduction, 118, 119
quota fill, 124f, 138t–139t
  and underfill, 125f
quota fill rate
  import, 151

Index **415**

quota overfill, 119–120, 137
quota regimes, 120–121
　value of trade by, 128t–129t
quota rents
　by quota regime, 129t
　dissipation, 137
　quota administration, 138
quota underfill, 118, 125f, 137
　by regime, 128t–129t
　licenses on demand, 149
　total TRQ value, 157
　TRQ trade by economy, 144t–146t
quotas
　increases and impact on trade expansion, 128–129
　seasonal, 139

random-walk
　simulation experiments, 92
real factor prices
　of liberalization, 356t
real income
　Doha scenarios by country/region, 370t–373t
　liberalization, 384t
　liberalization by country/region, 393t–394t
reciprocal agreements, 162
reciprocal tariff concessions, 63
Redistribution with Growth, 315
reform
　farm policies, 30
　in the EU and United States, 258
　participation, 17
refunds
　export subsidies, 206–207
regime switches, 151
regions by economy, 41t
regulations
　quota administration, 156–157
　TRQ, 140t–141t
rent appropriation, 150
rent seeking, 151–152
rents. *See also* quota rents
　assessment, 176
　impact of multilateral liberalization, 178
　TRQ value erosion, 178
rents received
　TRQs by developing countries, 177t
resource retirement programs, 224
returns to land by region, 184t
rice markets, 154
rice tariff quota, 156t–157t

rules
　equal participation, 108
rules of origin (ROOs)
　export subsidies, 183
　NAFTA, 184
　preference erosion, 396n
　preferences, 182
　textiles and apparel, 187, 189
rural development
　loan cuts, 319
rural growth, 296

safeguards, 66
safety net programs, 223
scaled dynamics
　real incomes and liberalization by country, 393t–394t
SDT. *See* special and differential treatment
seasonal licenses, 152
sectorwide initiatives, 273
self-designation
　developing countries, 334
　SDT, 23, 67
sensitive and special products, 15. *See also* special and differential treatment
　agricultural reform scenarios, 103
　alcohol and tobacco inclusion, 104
　bound tariff rates, 15
　exception rationale, 108–109
　excessive use, 86–87
　exemptions, 21, 98, 179
　farm products
　　Doha scenarios, 357
　flexibility, 25
　increasing share, 100–101
　linked to commodities and food security, 72
　rents and liberalization, 178
　restrictions, 112
　selection of, 396n
　self-selected, 113
　tariff lines, 105–106, 357
　tariff modulation, 164–165
　trade value and number of tariff lines, 94
　trade volume, 104
services trade, 340
　liberalization, 52–53, 55
　reform, 16, 22
　welfare gains for developing countries, 55f
shadow tariff, 176
simulations, 92–95
　Doha scenarios, 353–382
　preferences

simulations (*continued*)
  geographical breakdown, 180t
  liberalization by country, 175t
  tariff-cutting scenarios, 182t
    impact on Sub-Saharan countries, 185t
Single Farm Payment, 229–230, 238, 310
South-North trade reform, 11
South-South
  concessions, 21, 386
  trade, 11, 20, 77
special and differential treatment (SDT), 23–24
  categories, 71t
  concessions
    and economic benefits, 77
    by developing countries, 386–387
  developed countries, 66
  developing countries, 67, 69t, 324
  distortion, 76
  Doha scenarios, 361
  domestic support, 70
  economic view, 75
  GATT, 63
  July Framework Agreement, 70, 196
  market access for developing countries, 114
  negotiations, 64
  preferences, 165
  self-designation, 67
  types, 65
special products. *See* sensitive and special products
special safeguard mechanism (SSM), 70, 71t, 73–74
squeeze-out, 299, 299t
state trading enterprises (STEs), 138, 139, 212
  administration changes, 153t–154t
  by administration method and additional regulations, 143t
  efficiency and fill rates, 150, 156
  in-quota trade and fill rates, 138t–139t
  July Framework Agreement, 78n, 195–196
  quota administration, 137
  rice tariff quota in Japan, 156t–157t
Step 2 program, 278, 287
Sub-Saharan Africa, 185t, 389t
subsidies. *See also* agriculture, subsidies; cotton subsidies; export subsidies
  agricultural producer, 38
  banning, 195
  cuts necessary for reform, 334
  EAGGF by commodity, 210t–211t
  elimination of, 11, 12, 13
    impact on exports, 48t
  import protection database, 342–343

marketing, transportation, and infrastructure, 238
reform impacts on developing countries, 53
subsidy payments
  U.S. buyout, 309
subsidy rates, 200
  by country, 199t
  EU by commodity, 214t–215t
sugar program
  cash-out, 304
  EU, 232–233
  U.S., 154
    AMS calculations, 232t, 233t
    commitments exceed consumption, 304
sugar reform
  1996 U.S. Farm Bill, 304
  Agenda 2000 CAP reform, 261tn
  European Commission, 261
  U.S., 303–305
supply management, 310–311, 326n–327n
support. *See* agricultural support
surpluses, 319
Swiss formula, 84
  commodities, 112
  effects, 103
  reform scenarios, 93, 94, 108
Switzerland, 267t
synthetics, 280–281

Taiwan, 391t
tariff rate quotas (TRQs), 26–27, 82
  administration, 136–137
  administration methods and trade effects, 147–152
  agricultural imports
    LINKAGE and GTAP, 383
  agricultural protection, 155
  by country/commodity, 143–144
  by country/region, 89t
  commodities, 112
    barriers, 90
    production value, 120t–121t
  definition, 117
  expansion, 15
    market access, 88
    minimum access quotas, 122
    WTO negotiations, 118
  fill rates, 137, 141
  importance of, 118–119
  minimum access quotas, 158
  preference erosion, 176
  preferential, 163

Index   **417**

regimes, 155
rents
   methodology, 176
   received by developing country, 177t
   value erosion, 178
   research required, 158
   total values, 157
   trade by economy, 144t–146t
   trade liberalization and value, 130t
   water estimates, 132t–135t
tariff-cutting formulas, 335
   developing countries, 71
   market access impact, 104–109
   preferences and liberalization, 174
   tiered, 21
tariff-cutting scenarios
   Sub-Saharan countries, 185t
tariffication, 6, 32n–33n
   dirty, 91
   Uruguay Round, 221
tariffs
   aggregating across products, exporters, and importers, 190n
   agricultural export average, 104–105
   alternative tariff-cutting formulas, 106t–107t
   applied, 147
   by country/region, 89t
   average applied by region, 43t
   average import
      developing countries, 45t
   base tariff reductions for average applied tariffs by reform scenario, 98t–99t
   binding overhang, 158n
   cap, 14
      developing countries, 72
      Doha scenarios, 357
      market access, 108
      reform scenarios, 111
      tiered formula, 102
   commodities, 109
   cuts
      consequences, 336
      preference erosion, 27–28
      scenarios
         simulated impact on prices, 183t
         simulated impact on trade and welfare, 182t
   distortion, 33n
   escalation problems, 73
   global agricultural features, 88
   inquota regime, 119
   liberalization of developing country exports, 48t
   lower reduction commitments, 7172
   modulation, 164
   non-ad-valorem, 82
   nonagricultural cuts, 16
   nonagricultural removal, 50
   preferences, 27, 82
   protection
      agriculture, 318
      averages by region/economy, 320t–321t
      manufacturing, 8
   reciprocal concessions, 63
   reductions *versus* quota expansion, 118, 119
   reform complications, 82–83
   restrictive, 82
   revenues
      by quota regime, 129t
      lost potential, 137
   schedules
      trade agreements, 164
   shadow, 176
   TRQ trade by economy, 144t–146t
   water estimates, 132t–135t
   welfare effects from elimination of, 49t, 52t
terms of trade, 37–38, 51
   incurring a shock, 218n
   liberalization, 58t
   preference simulation by region, 184t
textile manufacturing
   cotton, 276
textiles and apparel
   average applied tariffs, 43t
      Doha scenarios, 364t–365t
   average import tariffs
      developing countries, 45t
   average true preferential margin by country, 173t
   bilateral trade flows from liberalization, 377t
   export quotas, 40
   high average tariffs, 44
   import increases, 47
   import-weighted average applied tariffs, 5t
      by sector/country, 345t
   liberalization, 12t, 22, 349t
   output under liberalization, 349t
   preferences, 187
   removal of all tariffs and agricultural subsidies, 46t
   ROOs, 187, 189
   tariff protection by region/economy, 320t–321t

textiles and apparel (*continued*)
   trade liberalization, 59t
     by region, 57t
   true preferential margins, 172
   volume changes from removal of tariffs and subsidies, 48t
   welfare gains by region
     removal of tariffs, assistance, and distortions, 54t
Thailand, 268t
tiered formula, 25, 85f
   applied rates effect, 97
   cap, 102
   China, 26
   commodities, 109
   consequences, 95–104
   discontinuities, 86f, 112–113
   domestic support, 339t
   freeing of bound duties, 101
   July Framework Agreement, 84
   market access, 24, 26, 105
   reform scenarios, 93, 95
   tariff cuts, 71
   tariff reduction, 105
   versus proportional cut, 14, 102–104, 360–361
tobacco. *See also* alcohol and tobacco
   buyout, 305, 326n
     compensation level, 302
     U.S., 303t
   production increase, 302
   U.S. consumption, 301
   U.S. reform, 301–303
trade
   agreements, 164, 165
   bilateral flows, 377t
   costs, 54, 55
   distortion, 13
     patterns, 40–47
     reduction, 247–253
     removal, 37
   Doha scenarios, 359–361, 376
   elasticities, 39–40
   expansion, 128–129
   facilitation, 54, 55, 340–341
     welfare gains for developing countries, 55f
   indicators by country/region, 347t
   liberalization
     absence of gains in Sub-Saharan Africa, 54
     agricultural, 37–38
     assessment, 123

     developing country implications, 45
     global welfare gains, 16
     licenses on demand, 147–150
     merchandise
       efficiency and terms of trade, 58t–59t
       welfare effects, 56t
     nonagricultural, 51
     policy measures, 22
     quota regimes, 155
     reduction in poor, 19t
     trade value effects by quota regime, 130t
     TRQs, 119–131
   liberalization impacts by country/region, 351t–352t
   policy (1960s-1980s), 318
   preferences, 161
   reform
     assessing effects, 341
     awards for commitment, 189
     global gains, 11
     income gains, 344
     major (1997–2001), 342
   simulation of impacts from tariff cut scenarios, 182t
   TRQ administration methods and regulations effects, 147–152
   TRQ by economy, 144t–146t
   TRQ *versus* non-TRQ commodities in OECD countries, 122t–123t
   value by quota regime, 128t–129t, 130t
   volume
     agricultural reform scenarios, 104
     WTO regime, 165–166
trade-weighted fill rates, 142
transition economies, 41t
   average applied import tariffs, 43t
   market access from agricultural liberalization, 53t
   merchandise trade liberalization, 56t, 57t
   trade distortions, 40
   welfare effects from removal of agricultural tariffs and subsidies, 49t
transition period, 72
transportation support, 237, 238
   Green Box, 240
traps, 83
true preferential margin, 168t–169t, 170, 172
   average by sector/commodity, 173t
   MFN-applied, 171t
   source, 174
   truncated, 139t

UNCTAD. *See* United Nations Conference on Trade and Development
underfill. *See* quota underfill
United Kingdom's Department for International Development (DFID), xiii
United Nations Conference on Trade and Development (UNCTAD)
  preferences, 164, 190n
United States
  1985 Farm Bill, 297
  1996 Farm Bill, 262–263, 297–298
    fixed payments, 307, 309
    peanuts, 325n
    production flexibility contracts, 309
    sugar loan rates, 304
  2002 Farm Bill, 263, 298
    countercyclical payments, 308, 309–310
    peanut reform, 300
    preferences, 178
  agricultural support changes, 229–230
  Amber Box expansion, 227
  AMS notifications by commodity, 253t
  applied tariffs, 391t
  Blue Box elimination, 227, 262–263
  buyout
    farm support programs, 307–310, 308t
    peanut and tobacco, 303t
    tax legislation, 326n
  cash-out reform, 297
  cotton counterrcyclical program, 288
  cotton dispute, 287–288 (*See also* Brazil-U.S. cotton dispute)
  cotton program, 276, 287–288
    estimates, 282
  cotton subsidies
    budget outlays, 284
    programs, 278
  countercyclical payments, 288, 298
  dairy price, adjusted AMS, 263t
  dairy program, 235
  de minimis, 227
  domestic support, 226t
    farm legislation, 227
    reductions needed, 260t
  export credits, 217
  farm policy, 297
  Green Box cotton programs, 286–287
  Green, Blue, and Amber Box totals, 226t
  joint EU framework (August 2003), 323
  market loss assistance payments, 263t
  MPS, 231t, 252

peanuts, 303t
price support programs, 297
Step 2, 287–288
sugar
  commitments, 304
  program
    AMS calculations, 232t, 233t
    reform, 303–305
  tobacco, 303t
    reform, 301–303
  total AMS, 246
  trade policy, 166–167, 167f
Uruguay Round
  agricultural price collapse, 295
  CAP negotiations, 258
  pillars, 221
Uruguay Round Agreement on Agriculture (URAA), 6
  agricultural support framework, 245
  Amber and Green Box, 337
  Amber Box spending, 224
  AMS ceilings, 225
  boxes, 222–223, 245
  commitments, 197
  framing, 234
  SDT, 68, 69t
  use-it-or-lose-it, 139
  rent seeking, 151
utilization rates, 200
  by country, 199t
  EU by category, 204t–205t
Uzbekistan
  cotton support, 277

volume, trade, 104
  developing country exports, 48t
  welfare indicator, 47

wages, skilled and unskilled
  trade liberalization impacts, 356t
water estimates for selected TRQs, 132t–135t
water in tariffs, 131, 158n
weighted, 147t
  trade-weighted fill rate, 139t
welfare
  agricultural distortion removal, 50
  agricultural export and domestic subsidies retention by country, 374t–375t
  agricultural tariffs and subsidies, 13t, 49t
    developing countries, 52t
  agricultural trade reform, 47

welfare (*continued*)
  distribution of income effects
    removal of trade barriers, 344
  Doha reform scenarios, 14, 359–361, 361
  free trade gains, 22
  liberalization effects, 12t, 56t, 376
  market access barrier impacts, 348
  nonagricultural market access impact, 50–51
  preference effects, 395
  preference simulation by country, 184t
  protection policy impact, 344
  tariff-cut scenario impacts, 182t
  trade liberalization
    developing countries, 58t
World Bank
  agricultural loan cuts, 319
  cotton compensation, 274–275
  LINKAGE, 31
  World Development Report (1986), 317
World Trade Organization (WTO)
  agricultural trade, 6
  commitments, 254t–258t
    by country, 198t
    category definition, 203–204
    EU, 204t, 208t
    notifications and record keeping, 218
    URAA, 197
    utilization rates, 200
    violations, 234
  Committee on Trade and Development
    SDT, 69
  cotton dispute, 287–288
  developing country participation, 321
  domestic support, 225, 236
  multilateral trade regime, 165–166
  negotiations, 271
  noncompliant members, 283
  notifications, 197–198, 200, 254t–258t
    challenge mechanism, 286
    EU, 208t
    LDC commodities, 201
    member relationships, 202
    middle-income countries, 200–201
    notified export subsidies, 202f
    of the EU by categories, 204t–205t
    quota administration methods, 152
    used export subsidies by country, 199t
  record keeping
    export subsidies, 218
  SDT, 68